ORGANIZATIONAL BEHAVIOR

Understanding and Managing People at Work

SECOND EDITION

DONALD D. WHITE
University of Arkansas

DAVID A. BEDNAR
University of Arkansas

ALLYN AND BACON
Boston • London • Toronto • Sydney • Tokyo • Singapore

Series Editor   Jack Peters
Managing Editor   Henry Reece
Senior Editorial Assistant   Carol Alper
Editorial-Production Administrator   Elaine Ober
Editorial-Production Services   York Production Services
Cover Coordinator   Linda Dickinson
Cover Designer   Design Ad Cetera
Manufacturing Buyer   Louise Richardson

A Division of Simon & Schuster, Inc.
160 Gould Street
Needham Heights, MA 02194

Library of Congress Cataloging-in-Publication Data

White, Donald D.
    Organizational behavior : understanding and managing people at work /
  Donald D. White, David A. Bednar. — 2nd ed.
        p.   cm.
    Includes bibliographical references and index.
  ISBN 0-205-12851-3
        1. Organizational behavior.   I. Bednar, David A.   II. Title.
  HD58.7.W49   1991
  658.3—dc20   90-46898
                                                                   CIP

Printed in the United States of America
10 9 8 7 6 5 4 3 2 1   94 93 92 91 90

*This book is lovingly dedicated to the memory of
Donald D. White, Sr. and Lavinia Whitney Bednar*

CONTENTS

TO THE STUDENT   *xiii*

CHAPTER

1   THE MANAGERIAL REVOLUTION: 1
Organizational Behavior Comes of Age

A NEW ERA   **2**

AN EVOLVING MANAGEMENT PHILOSOPHY   **3**
Industrial Revolution   3 • Social Darwinism and the Protestant Work Ethic   4 • Scientific Management   4 • Administrative Era   5 • Human Relations   6 • In Summary   7

ORGANIZATIONAL BEHAVIOR COMES OF AGE   **8**
International Issues in Organizational Behavior   12 • Ethics and the Study of Organizational Behavior   12

DEFINING THE FIELD OF ORGANIZATIONAL BEHAVIOR   **14**
Study and Application   15 • Theories and Concepts   16 • Individuals and Groups   16

SYSTEMS THEORY AND ORGANIZATIONAL BEHAVIOR   **17**

THE MANAGERIAL REVOLUTION: CONCLUSIONS   **18**

QUESTIONS FOR REVIEW AND DISCUSSION   19
REFERENCES   19

*CASE 1.1   Aeroline Mechanical Products Company   **20***
*CASE 1.2   Sell-for-Less-Discount   **22***
*EXERCISE 1.1   Assumptions about People at Work   **24***
*EXERCISE 1.2   A "Philosophy" of Management   **26***

CHAPTER

2   INDIVIDUALITY IN THE WORKPLACE   **28**

UNDERSTANDING OUR INDIVIDUALITY   **31**
Personality   31 • Physical and Mental Abilities   38 • Values, Attitudes, and Beliefs   39 • Traits and Psychological Characteristics   46 • Personality in Perspective   47

LIFE CHANGES AND THE MEANING OF WORK   **48**
Does Personality Change over Time?   49 • Levinson's Theory of Adult Development   49 • Additional Considerations Concerning Adult Development   54

INDIVIDUALITY IN THE WORKPLACE: CONCLUSIONS   **55**

QUESTIONS FOR REVIEW AND DISCUSSION   56
REFERENCES   57

*CASE 2.1   Trump   **59***
*CASE 2.2   Growing Pains   **60***
*EXERCISE 2.1   F.I.R.O.—B Exercise   **65***
*EXERCISE 2.2   Determining Your Values   **67***

CHAPTER

3   PERCEPTION   70

THE NATURE OF THE PERCEPTUAL PROCESS   **73**
The Activities of Perception   74

PERCEPTUAL BARRIERS AND EFFECTS   **79**
Stereotyping   79 • Halo Effect   80 • Projection   82 • Implicit Personality Theories   82 • Selective Perception   82 • Primary and Recency Effects   83 • In Summary   83

INTERPRETING WHY OTHERS BEHAVE AS THEY
   DO   84

>   *Attribution Theory   84 • Common Attribution
>   Errors   86*

PERCEPTION: CONCLUSIONS   89

QUESTIONS FOR REVIEW AND DISCUSSION   90
REFERENCES   90

CASE 3.1   *The Invisible Colleague*   91
CASE 3.2   *National Brickworks*   95
EXERCISE 3.1   *He Works, She Works (But What Different
                Impressions They Make!)*   98
EXERCISE 3.2   *Johari Window: A Feedback and Disclosure
                Activity*   99

CHAPTER

4   LEARNING, REINFORCEMENT, AND
         BEHAVIOR ANALYSIS   102

LEARNING THEORIES: WHY WE BEHAVE AS WE
   DO   104

>   *Classical Learning Theory   105 • Operant
>   Learning Theory   106 • Social Cognitive
>   Theory   107 • Classical, Operant, and Social
>   Cognitive Theory: A Managerial Perspective   109*

PRINCIPLES OF LEARNING AND
   REINFORCEMENT   110

>   *Principles of Learning   110 • The Practice of
>   Reinforcing   112 • The Context of
>   Reinforcing   114 • Reinforcement Scheduling   116*

APPLYING LEARNING THEORY IN
   ORGANIZATIONS: INITIATING AND CHANGING
   WORK-RELATED BEHAVIORS   118

>   *Organizational Behavior Modification   119 •
>   Modeling and Shaping Behavior   127 • Behavioral
>   Self-Management   129 • Maintaining Changed
>   Behaviors   131*

LEARNING, REINFORCEMENT, AND BEHAVIOR
   ANALYSIS: CONCLUSIONS   131

QUESTIONS FOR REVIEW AND DISCUSSION   132
REFERENCES   133

CASE 4.1   *The Sociable Salesman*   134
CASE 4.2   *Ron Brown's Problem*   136
EXERCISE 4.1   *Behavioral Analysis: "From A to C"*   138
EXERCISE 4.2   *Designing a Training and Development
                Program: Applying Learning Theory on the
                Job*   139

CHAPTER

5   THE MOTIVATION TO WORK: 142
         Content Theories

WHY STUDY MOTIVATION?   144

INTRINSIC, EXTRINSIC, AND VICARIOUS
   MOTIVATION   145

>   *Intrinsic and Extrinsic Motivation   146 •
>   Vicarious Motivation   146*

CONTENT THEORIES OF MOTIVATION   147

>   *Needs and Need Hierarchies   147 • Two-Factor
>   Theory of Work Motivation   152 • Affiliation,
>   Achievement, and Power   154 • Applying Content
>   Theories in Managerial Situations   158*

THE MOTIVATION TO WORK: CONCLUSIONS   159

QUESTIONS FOR REVIEW AND DISCUSSION   161
REFERENCES   161

CASE 5.1   *Going Back Home*   162
CASE 5.2   *Whatever Happened to Professional Pride?*   164
EXERCISE 5.1   *Understanding Work Motivation*   166
EXERCISE 5.2   *Applying Content Theories*   167

CHAPTER

6   PROCESS, GOAL-SETTING, AND
         REINFORCEMENT THEORIES OF WORK
         MOTIVATION   170

PROCESS THEORIES OF MOTIVATION   172

>   *Expectancy Theory   172 • Equity Theory   178 •
>   In Summary   182*

GOAL-SETTING THEORY   183

>   *Setting Goals   184 • In Summary   186*

REINFORCEMENT THEORY   187

>   *Behavior and Reinforcement   187*

PROCESS, GOAL-SETTING, AND REINFORCEMENT
   THEORIES OF WORK MOTIVATION:
   CONCLUSIONS   190

QUESTIONS FOR REVIEW AND DISCUSSION   192
REFERENCES   192

CASE 6.1   *It's Not My Job*   194
CASE 6.2   *The Need to Listen*   196

EXERCISE 6.1   *Understanding the Expectancy Theory of Motivation* **197**

EXERCISE 6.2   *Applying Motivation Theories* **198**

CHAPTER

7   DECISION MAKING   **200**

THE MANAGERIAL ROLE AND DECISION MAKING   **203**

Managerial Decision Making and Problem Solving   204

MODELS OF THE DECISION-MAKING PROCESS   **207**

The Rational-Economic Model   207 • The Administrative Model   208

BARRIERS TO EFFECTIVE DECISION MAKING   **211**

Tunnel Vision   211 • Previous Commitments   212 • Implicit Favorites   212 • Lack of Creativity   213

INDIVIDUAL VERSUS GROUP DECISION MAKING   **214**

Advantages of Group Decision Making   214 • Disadvantages of Group Decision Making   215

PARTICIPATION IN DECISION MAKING   **217**

Participation versus Delegation   218 • Putting Participation to Work   218

DECISION MAKING: CONCLUSIONS   **224**

QUESTIONS FOR REVIEW AND DISCUSSION   225
REFERENCES   225

CASE 7.1   *Changing the Shuttle Launch Decision Process* **226**

CASE 7.2   *Dilemma of a Young Manager* **228**

EXERCISE 7.1   *NASA Exercise* **232**

EXERCISE 7.2   *Creative Thinking* **234**

CHAPTER

8   UNDERSTANDING GROUP BEHAVIOR: Origins and Dynamics

GROUPS DEFINED   **240**

TYPES OF GROUPS   **243**

Task Groups   244 • Project Groups   244 • Informal Groups   245

STAGES OF GROUP DEVELOPMENT   **245**

Forming   246 • Storming   246 • Norming   247 • Performing   247 • Adjourning   247 • Timing and Environmental Influences on Group Development   249

SOCIALIZATION: THE PROCESS OF FITTING IN   **249**

Three Phases of Socialization   249 • Managing the Socialization Process   250 • Socialization in Perspective   252

FACTORS INFLUENCING GROUP EFFECTIVENESS   **252**

Individuality   253 • Leadership   253 • Group Norms   254 • Group Cohesiveness   257 • Task   257 • External Factors   259

UNDERSTANDING GROUP BEHAVIOR: CONCLUSIONS   **259**

QUESTIONS FOR REVIEW AND DISCUSSION   260
REFERENCES   260

CASE 8.1   *Executive Retreat: A Case of Group Failure* **262**

CASE 8.2   *Division E* **267**

EXERCISE 8.1   *Two-Four-Eight: Building Teams* **270**

EXERCISE 8.2   *Group Member Roles* **271**

CHAPTER

9   PUTTING GROUPS TO WORK   **274**

TECHNIQUES FOR MANAGING GROUP DECISION MAKING   **276**

Committees and Interacting Groups   276 • Brainstorming   278 • Nominal Group Technique   278 • Synectics   280 • Delphi Technique   281

EXPANDING THE ROLE OF GROUPS IN ORGANIZATIONS   **283**

Quality Groups   283 • Self-Managed Work Groups   289 • Interorganizational Groups   291

MANAGING INTERGROUP COMPETITION **293**

    *Group Activities During Competition 295 •
Consequences of Competition 295 • Insights into
Managing Competition 296*

PUTTING GROUPS TO WORK: CONCLUSIONS **296**

**QUESTIONS FOR REVIEW AND DISCUSSION 297
REFERENCES 298**

CASE 9.1 *The Case of Q.C.5* **299**
CASE 9.2 *Consumer Airlines: A Study in Autonomous
        Work Groups* **301**
EXERCISE 9.1 *The Bomb Shelter* **303**
EXERCISE 9.2 *Using the Nominal Group Technique* **305**

CHAPTER

10 COMMUNICATION 306

THE NATURE OF THE COMMUNICATION
  PROCESS **308**

    *What Communication Is and Is Not 308 • Verbal
and Nonverbal Communication 310 •
Communication Channels and Media 311*

BARRIERS TO EFFECTIVE COMMUNICATION **3II**

    *Perceptual Differences 312 • Language and
Meaning 314 • Noise 314*

OVERCOMING BARRIERS TO EFFECTIVE
  COMMUNICATION **316**

    *Listening 316 • Soliciting and Giving
Feedback 319*

ORGANIZATIONAL COMMUNICATION **321**

    *Networks 321 • Barriers to Effective
Organizational Communication 326 • Auditing
Organizational Communication 329*

COMMUNICATION: CONCLUSIONS **329**

**QUESTIONS FOR REVIEW AND DISCUSSION 332
REFERENCES 332**

CASE 10.1 *The Chief* **333**
CASE 10.2 *The J. R. Reston Company, Inc.* **337**
EXERCISE 10.1 *One-Way Versus Two-Way
           Communication* **341**
EXERCISE 10.2 *Serial Communication* **342**

CHAPTER

11 POWER AND CONFLICT 344

DISTINCTIONS AMONG INFLUENCE, POWER, AND
  AUTHORITY **347**

    Determinants of Power 348

INDIVIDUAL BASES OF POWER **348**

HOW POWER IS OBTAINED **351**

    *Doing the Right Things and Knowing the Right
People 351 • Coalescing 351 • Co-opting 352*

AN ALTERNATIVE PERSPECTIVE ON BEHAVIOR IN
  ORGANIZATIONS: ORGANIZATIONAL
  POLITICS **352**

    *A Strategic Contingencies Approach to
Intraorganizational Power 354*

EMPOWERMENT AND THE MANAGERIAL
  REVOLUTION **355**

UNDERSTANDING AND MANAGING
  CONFLICT **359**

CONFLICT AS A PROCESS **359**

    *Frustration 361 • Conceptualization 362 •
Behavior 362 • Outcome 363*

THE FUNCTIONAL AND DYSFUNCTIONAL
  CONSEQUENCES OF CONFLICT **363**

STRATEGIES FOR MANAGING CONFLICT **364**

    *Negotiations 364 • Establishing Superordinate
Goals 368 • Using a Third-Party
Intervention 368 • Removing Personnel and
Restructuring the Organization 369*

POWER AND CONFLICT: CONCLUSIONS **370**

**QUESTIONS FOR REVIEW AND DISCUSSION 371
REFERENCES 371**

CASE 11.1 *Just Who Runs This Show?* **372**
CASE 11.2 *Dissension at RANDEB* **375**
EXERCISE 11.1 *Win as Much as You Can* **377**
EXERCISE 11.2 *Disarmament Exercise* **377**

CHAPTER

12 EFFECTIVE LEADER BEHAVIOR   382

EARLY APPROACHES TO LEADERSHIP   385

The Great Man Approach   386 • The Trait Approach   386 • Early Approaches in Perspective   387

BEHAVIORAL THEORIES OF LEADERSHIP   388

Iowa Studies   388 • Michigan Studies   388 • Ohio State Studies   389 • The Managerial Grid   390 • Behavioral Theories in Perspective   391

SITUATIONAL THEORIES OF LEADERSHIP   392

Contingency Theory   392 • Path-Goal Theory   396 • Situational Leadership Theory   398 • Normative Model   402 • Situational Theories in Perspective   405

TRANSFORMATIONAL LEADERSHIP   407

Transformational Behaviors   409 • The Transformational Process   410 • Transformational Leadership in Perspective   413

OTHER PERSPECTIVES ON LEADERSHIP   414

Substitutes for Leadership   414 • Attribution Influences on Leadership   415

EFFECTIVE LEADER BEHAVIOR: CONCLUSIONS   416

QUESTIONS FOR REVIEW AND DISCUSSION   417
REFERENCES   418

CASE 12.1   *What It Takes to Be Number One: Lessons from Wal-Mart's Sam Walton*   420
CASE 12.2   *Dogfight at Texas Air: Leadership the Lorenzo Way*   421
EXERCISE 12.1   *Selecting the Right Leadership Style*   423
EXERCISE 12.2   *Leadership Questionnaire*   425

CHAPTER

13 FORMAL ORGANIZATION: 428
The Context of Organizational Behavior

FORMAL ORGANIZATION: FUNDAMENTAL ELEMENTS   431

Organizational Objectives   432 • Division of Labor   434 • Coordination   434 • Differentiation and Integration   436

ORGANIZATIONAL STRUCTURE: TRADITIONAL CONCEPTS   438

Bureaucracy   438 • Centralization and Decentralization   441 • Span of Management   443 • Line and Staff Organization   445 • Recent Changes in Traditional Organizations   446

CONTEMPORARY ORGANIZATION STRUCTURES   447

Project Organization   448 • Matrix Organization   451 • Organic Organization   454 • Network Organization   456 • Contemporary Structures in Perspective   457

FORMAL ORGANIZATION: CONCLUSIONS   457

QUESTIONS FOR REVIEW AND DISCUSSION   458
REFERENCES   458

CASE 13.1   *Organizations in Transition: From Taller to Flatter Structures*   459
CASE 13.2   *The Case of Two Masters*   461
EXERCISE 13.1   *Division of Work*   462
EXERCISE 13.2   *Organizing*   464

CHAPTER

14 WORK DESIGN   466

THE IMPORTANCE OF WORK DESIGN   468

EARLY APPROACHES TO WORK DESIGN   469

Scientific Management   469 • Job Enlargement   470 • Job Rotation   471

CONTEMPORARY APPROACHES TO WORK DESIGN   471

Job Enrichment   471 • Job Characteristics   473 • Sociotechnical Design   479

QUALITY OF WORK LIFE   482

Concern About the Quality of Work Life   482 • Applying the Quality of Work Life Concept in Modern Organizations   484

WORK DESIGN: CONCLUSIONS   488

QUESTIONS FOR REVIEW AND DISCUSSION   491
REFERENCES   491

CASE 14.1   Teamwork at General Motors: Progress and
             Problems   492
CASE 14.2   The Workplace Revolution   493
EXERCISE 14.1   Productivity/Quality Task Force
             Project   497
EXERCISE 14.2   Improving Organizational
             Effectiveness   499

CHAPTER

15 ORGANIZATIONAL CHANGE AND DEVELOPMENT   500

THE NATURE OF CHANGE IN MODERN ORGANIZATIONS   503

A Model of Change: Force Field Analysis   504

RESISTANCE TO CHANGE   509

Sources of Resistance   509 • Overcoming
Resistance to Change   510

ORGANIZATIONAL DEVELOPMENT: THE THEORY AND TECHNOLOGY OF CHANGE   512

A Definition of Organizational Development   512 •
Change Agent   513 • Intervention Strategies and
Technologies   514 • Do OD Interventions Really
Work?   522

ORGANIZATIONAL CHANGE AND DEVELOPMENT: CONCLUSIONS   523

QUESTIONS FOR REVIEW AND DISCUSSION   525
REFERENCES   525

CASE 15.1   A Time for Change   526
CASE 15.2   The Shipping Department   529
EXERCISE 15.1   Diagnosis, Change, and
             Implementation   531
EXERCISE 15.2   Using Force Field Analysis as a Diagnostic
             Tool   533

CHAPTER

16 STRESS IN ORGANIZATIONS   534

UNDERSTANDING THE NATURE OF STRESS   537

The Elements of Stress   538 • The Physiology of
Stress   540

SOURCES OF WORK-RELATED STRESS   543

Role Conflict   543 • Role Ambiguity   544 •
Overload and Underload   545 •
Responsibility   546 • Career Development   546 •
High-Stress Situations in Today's Workplace   546 •
Work-Related Stress in Perspective   549

EFFECTIVELY MANAGING STRESS   550

Individual Responses to Stress   550 •
Organizational Responses to Stress   553

STRESS IN ORGANIZATIONS: CONCLUSIONS   556

QUESTIONS FOR REVIEW AND DISCUSSION   557
REFERENCES   557

CASE 16.1   Happiness Is Success!?   559
CASE 16.2   Decision at Sea   561
EXERCISE 16.1   Behavior Activity Profile   564
EXERCISE 16.2   Are You Stress-Prone at Work?   568

CHAPTER

17 CAREERS AND CAREER DEVELOPMENT   570

MANAGING CAREER DEVELOPMENT   572

Career as Part of a Life System   573 • Self-
Assessment   575 • Managing Your Career over
Time   576 • Career Anchors   580

SPECIAL CONSIDERATIONS IN CAREER DEVELOPMENT   581

Women and Career Development   581 • Dual-
Career Couples   584 • Specialized Organizational
Responses   588

ORGANIZATIONAL APPROACHES TO CAREER DEVELOPMENT   589

Which Way to the Top?   589 • Organizationally
Developed Career Paths   592

CAREERS AND CAREER DEVELOPMENT: CONCLUSIONS   598

QUESTIONS FOR REVIEW AND DISCUSSION   600
REFERENCES   600

CASE 17.1   Latino Glass, S.A. (Latino, South
             America)   602
CASE 17.2   Predicting the Future   604
EXERCISE 17.1   Life and Career Planning   606
EXERCISE 17.2   Your Perception of Career Advancement
             Practices   607

INTEGRATIVE CASES 609

INTEGRATIVE CASE I: BRUISED APPLE 611

INTEGRATIVE CASE II: A SIMPLE PROBLEM OF COMMUNICATION 615

INTEGRATIVE CASE III: THE SKIL CIRCULAR SAWS PLANT 618

INTEGRATIVE CASE IV: DAVIS REGIONAL MEDICAL CENTER 624

INTEGRATIVE CASE V: ELECTRO-TEC, INC. 631

MANAGER'S DICTIONARY 635

INDEX 647

TO THE STUDENT

The decade of the 1990s is an exciting time to be a manager or a student of management. The economics and technology of work, the composition of the labor force, and the traditional roles of labor and management are changing in significant ways. Consequently, many long-held assumptions and beliefs about the practice of managing people in organizations are currently being challenged.

Business leaders, government officials, and scholars are searching for ways to remain competitive in the rapidly changing marketplace of the 1990s. Answers to the questions facing these men and women lie in many areas. However, modern managers, now more than ever before, are looking to their organization's human resources as a source of answers. Productivity, motivation, leadership, individual and group decision making, quality of work life, and work design are receiving increased attention on the job and in the classroom. In all types of organizations today, major emphasis is placed on developing and more effectively using human resources to meet the challenges of the future. People, not computers or technology, are seen as the key to organizational performance. Therein lies the challenge of understanding and managing people at work. Our goal has been to capture the excitement of this challenge.

The second edition of *Organizational Behavior: Understanding and Managing People at Work* has retained the readability and student orientation that made the first edition such a success. Each chapter of the second edition has been revised, expanded, and updated. The second edition includes expanded coverage of the move from a control-oriented to a commitment-oriented philosophy of management (Chapter 1), job satisfaction (Chapter 2), motivation (Chapters 5 and 6), interorganizational and quality groups (Chapters 8 and 9), negotiation (Chapter 10), empowerment (Chapter 11), the transformational approach to leadership (Chapter 12), network organizations (Chapter 13), and stress (Chapter 16). Extended examples from contemporary organizations such as Toyota, International Business Machines, General Motors, Springfield Remanufacturing Corporation, 3M, Xerox, Nucor, and Volvo are used in every chapter to illustrate the concepts and principles presented in the text.

Several new features have been added to the book as well; each feature is described briefly below.

Ethical Dilemmas

The importance of ethics in the study of organizational behavior is discussed in Chapter 1. In addition, every chapter contains a boxed insert entitled "Ethical Dilemma," each presenting a real situation related to the chapter content for review and discussion. There is no correct answer for these dilemmas; rather, their purpose is to stimulate your thinking about ethical issues and controversies.

International Dimensions

The internationalization of business also is highlighted in Chapter 1, and every chapter contains a boxed insert entitled "International Dimension." Each International Dimension focuses on an aspect of international business (e.g., the impact of EC 1992, work processes and decision-making styles in countries outside the U.S.). This feature is designed to enhance your awareness of business conditions and practices throughout the world as they relate to the management of people at work.

Extended Examples

Each chapter contains a number of extended examples. These examples are integrated into the text and highlight current business practices and procedures. Organizations such as International Business Machines, Ford, Apple, Volvo, Xerox, Scandinavian Airlines, General Motors, and 3M are used to illustrate principles presented in the text.

Manager's Dictionary

Key concepts and terms are presented in each chapter. The Manager's Dictionary, located at the end of the text, alphabetically lists and defines all key terms. This feature provides you with a quick and easy-to-use study aid which facilitates the integration of important concepts across the chapters.

Learning Objectives and Key Terms

Special learning aids are located at the beginning of each chapter. Learning objectives and key terms highlight important themes and concepts to which you should attend while reading the chapter.

Study Guide

A comprehensive student *Study Guide* has been prepared to facilitate study and understanding of the material covered in the text. Each chapter contains a content summary, exercises to reinforce learning of key concepts, practice tests, and challenging activities. The *Study Guide* was prepared by Professor William Keaton of the University of Wisconsin, Whitewater.

Readings in Organizational Behavior

A book of readings has been prepared to accompany the textbook. The readings book contains two very recent articles for every textbook chapter. The readings expand upon and provide additional examples of important concepts. The readings were prepared by Professor Ronald Sims of the College of William and Mary and Professors Donald D. White and David A. Bednar of the University of Arkansas.

ACKNOWLEDGMENTS

A project of this magnitude could not have been completed without the assistance of many individuals. We acknowledge the support and cooperation of Stanley S. Smith, Dean of the College of Business Administration, University of Arkansas; Professors Douglas Jenkins, Nina Gupta, Lew Taylor, Fred Luthans, Richard Hodgetts, Barry Wisdom, Calvin Kellogg, Mary Coulter, Tim Schweitzer, Mark Hearn, Kin Thompson, and Christine Clements. We particularly appreciate the tireless effort and assistance of Raghav Singh in the preparation of the manuscript. Eric and Michael Bednar also provided valuable research assistance. Other individuals who contributed their time and energy to this project are Jean Corn, Janet Hill, Cathy Knight, and Cindy Williams.

Several of our colleagues reviewed the manuscript and made insightful comments. Our sincere thanks to George Lyne, Appalachian State University; Marcia Ann Pulich, University of Wisconsin-Whitewater; Eugene Owens, Western Washington University; Marc Siegall, California State University-Chico; Dorothy Perrin Moore, The Citadel; Robert Taylor, Memphis State University; Mary Kernan, University of Delaware; Dennis Dossett, University of Missouri-St. Louis; Ronald Sims, College of William and Mary; Kevin W. Mossholder, Auburn University; Thomas Cawsey, Wilfred Laurier University; Jay Liebowitz, Duquesne University; E. Levanoni, Brock University; Nancy Langton, The University of British Columbia; and Paul N. Keaton, University of Wisconsin LaCrosse.

We would also like to thank our editor, Jack Peters, for his encouragement, assistance, and direction. He, Elaine Ober, Judy Fifer, Carol Alper, and Robin Tiano, together with Leslie Brunetta, helped make *Organizational Behavior: Understanding and Managing People at Work* a reality.

Most of all, our families deserve our thanks for making this book possible. They have supported, prodded, encouraged, and helped us keep our priorities balanced during the writing of this book. To Joyce, Chris, and Greg White, and to Susan, Eric, Mike, and Jeff Bednar we express our deepest love and appreciation.

ANCILLARY MATERIALS AVAILABLE FOR THE INSTRUCTOR

Test Bank
Computerized Test Bank
Transparencies
Computer Simulation: I/O Enterprises
CNN Video
Ethics Video

CHAPTER 1

THE MANAGERIAL REVOLUTION: ORGANIZATIONAL BEHAVIOR COMES OF AGE

LEARNING OBJECTIVES

1. To acquire a definition of organizational behavior.
2. To discover factors that have influenced today's dominant management philosophy.
3. To understand the difference between espoused theories of management and theories-in-use.
4. To learn why organizational behavior has come of age in the 1990s.

CHAPTER OUTLINE

A New Era

An Evolving Management Philosophy
Industrial Revolution
Social Darwinism and the Protestant Work Ethic
Scientific Management
Administrative Era
Human Relations
In Summary

Organizational Behavior Comes of Age
International Issues in Organizational Behavior
Ethics and the Study of Organizational Behavior

Defining the Field of Organizational Behavior
Study and Application
Theories and Concepts
Individuals and Groups

Systems Theory and Organizational Behavior

The Managerial Revolution: Conclusions

Questions for Review and Discussion

References

**Cases: 1.1. Aeroline Mechanical Products Company
1.2. Sell-For-Less Discount**

**Exercises: 1.1. Assumptions about People at Work
1.2. A "Philosophy" of Management**

KEY TERMS

Organizational behavior

Managerial philosophy

Industrial revolution

Social Darwinism

Protestant work ethic

Scientific management

Administrative era

Human relations

Theory X/Theory Y

Espoused theory

Theory-in-use

Control-oriented philosophy of management

Commitment-oriented philosophy of management

Ethics

System

Closed system

Open system

Equifinality

Feedback

Synergy

A NEW ERA

Today, major changes are taking place in management philosophy and practice. Some managers refer to these changes as a new era, others as a revolution. Whatever the label, people in organizations are currently being challenged as never before to examine their basic assumptions about the nature and meaning of work as well as their day-to-day management styles and work habits. The 1990s are an exciting time to be a manager or a student of management, and nowhere can these challenges and changes be appreciated more than in the field of organizational behavior.

Organizational behavior (OB) is the study of human behavior in organizations. By organizations, we mean all enterprises—business firms, government agencies, schools, hospitals, and even families and the clubs to which people belong. As a matter of fact, the increased attention to OB in nonbusiness areas is one of today's most exciting changes in organizational life.

Why is organizational behavior so important to understanding the current management revolution? The answer lies in the nature of the changes occurring in modern organizations. During the past one hundred years, managers have emphasized every aspect of business from finding the most efficient means for producing goods and delivering services to manipulating paper profits in order to increase the attractiveness of the enterprise to stockholders or taxpayers.[1] Only recently have managers begun to understand and appreciate the extent to which an organization's success depends on the contributions of its human resources. Human resources, in fact, may be the most important resource available to modern managers.

The heart of the change lies in a new approach to managing that is sweeping through organizations in every economic sector. Best-selling books, such as *In Search of Excellence*,[2] *A Passion for Excellence*,[3] *The Renewal Factor*,[4] *Thriving on Chaos*,[5] and *When Giants Learn to Dance*,[6] have emphasized that managers can no longer treat employees as mere factors of production. Instead, managers increasingly are aware that managing human resources effectively means understanding and accommodating the total person—individual needs, goals, values, and belief systems. Managers are focusing their attention on the people they manage and on how they manage them. Such topics as efficiency and quality continue to be important in the workplace. Increasingly, however, human beings, not computers and machinery, are being seen as the key to organizational performance.

Such phrases as *organizational health*, *quality of work life*, *participative management*, and *work redesign* have become common from the factory floor to the corporate board room. Important decisions once made by executives and middle managers are being made with increasing frequency at lower levels of the enterprise, and such leading corporations as Ford, Kodak, Chrysler, General Motors, Firestone, Motorola, and Westinghouse have indicated publicly that this basic change in philosophy has become the corporate policy of the 1990s.

KODAK

For example, Kodak, historically a dominant force throughout the world in the photographic supplies and photo-finishing industry, encountered serious financial setbacks in the early 1980s. Kodak had been slow to respond to the challenge of international competitors, such as Nikon, Canon, Fuji, and Konica. The result: Return on equity slipped from 20.9 percent in 1973 to 7.5 percent in 1983, and Kodak dropped from fourth to seventeenth place in *Fortune Magazine*'s annual rating of the most-admired United States corporations.

Kodak's top management reevaluated its policies and procedures and formulated a strategy to restore the company's competitiveness. Management restructured the organization, changed the compensation system, and emphasized quality in all aspects of the work process—all traditional methods of increasing productivity. However, a central feature of its revitalization strategy was to push decision-making authority to lower levels in the organization. Line managers throughout the company were given greater autonomy and responsibility in an attempt to stimulate innovation and increase accountability. The effort to change the corporate culture at Kodak revolved around a key assumption: employees represented an important, and undervalued, resource that could help the corporation become more agile and responsive to market conditions.

To be sure, other movements are afoot in the organizational world. Increased attention to quality, greater product knowledge, and an attempt to create relationships among employees at all levels and the organization's ultimate client[7] are themes on which executive energies are being focused. Yet, the common threads running through all of these movements are the development and more effective use of human resources to meet the challenges of the future.

AN EVOLVING MANAGEMENT PHILOSOPHY

Neither the practice of management nor attention to the human side of an enterprise is new. The history of management thought provides evidence that both have long received attention from management practitioners. However, political, social, and economic circumstances and changes in technology have contributed to the evolution of a pervasive managerial philosophy in the Western world.

The following section briefly examines conditions surrounding the emergence of large, complex organizations and a dominant managerial philosophy based on *control*. We are particularly interested in management patterns of thinking and acting as they have evolved since the early 1800s.

Industrial Revolution

The **industrial revolution** represented a culmination of events, the central themes of which were widespread mechanization of work and the growth of large centralized centers of output known as factories. The simple but profound concept of division of labor first described by Adam Smith in *The Wealth of Nations*[8] was applied widely during this period and radically changed the definition and nature of work. With the development and widespread use of machines and mechanized methods of production, workers no longer were hired to produce a total product. Instead, they made narrow and specialized contributions to the fabrication or assembly of a final good. Furthermore, it was generally believed that the smaller the contribution each worker made, the more efficiently that worker would perform and the less expensively the final product could be produced.

The desire for a high level of specialization lead to both the standardization and the simplification of work. Moreover, a general lack of education among the work force and the emergence of large, complex organizations resulted in the replacement of management through mutual adjustment (informal communication) with a more prominent form of direct supervision. Organizations thus began to embrace management approaches needed to cope with increasing size and complexity.

Social Darwinism and the Protestant Work Ethic

Important social values and doctrines of the nineteenth century also influenced management practices of the time and the evolving managerial philosophy.[9] One doctrine, **Social Darwinism,** was named for its similarity to Charles Darwin's theory of evolution. Darwin attributed the existence of various animal species to their superior ability to adapt and survive in a changing environment. The basic premise of Social Darwinism was that people who rose to the top of social and economic ladders did so because they were the "fittest to survive." Success, riches, and status were regarded as signs of progress and the just reward for those who had proved themselves in the struggle for economic survival. In essence, success entitled an individual to command and control; failure indicated a lack of the necessary personal qualities and effort. And in the struggle for survival, success was only for the few.

Another important social doctrine, the **Protestant Work Ethic,** provided additional support for the belief that persons of prominence and authority (often business leaders) had attained their positions by more than mere coincidence. The ethic was characterized by a strong desire for job-related achievement, a belief in the intrinsic value of hard work, and a striving to attain a responsible position. People successful in life were seen as being rewarded by God for their diligence and hard work. This philosophy is illustrated by a statement attributed to railroad executive George F. Baer in 1903:

> The rights and interests of the laboring man will be protected and cared for . . . by the Christian men to whom God in His infinite wisdom has given control of the property interests of the country.[10]

These social doctrines, along with rapid industrialization and technological changes in the nature of work introduced during the industrial revolution, had a substantial impact on the developing managerial philosophy. By the end of the nineteenth century, the distinction between the roles of **manager** and **worker** was clear. The manager's role was to direct and control; the worker's role was to comply dutifully.

Scientific Management

The United States industrialized rapidly between the late 1800s and the early 1900s. This rise to industrial prominence has been attributed in part to the scientific management movement founded by Frederick W. Taylor. **Scientific management** represented an effort to bring greater efficiency to the work place through the systematic analysis and design of work. Briefly, the goal of scientific management was to analyze jobs carefully and systematically, to assess the capabilities of workers, and then to match jobs and workers appropriately to achieve maximum efficiency. Tasks should be designed to make optimal use of human abilities; people, on the other hand, should be trained to perform work according to specific job procedures. Significantly, Taylor also believed that scientific management would bring about greater harmony and cooperation between management and labor.[11]

He believed that increased efficiency in production would mean greater profits to business and higher wages for labor. Consequently, fewer disputes would occur about how revenues would be divided. People would no longer argue about who would receive the larger piece of the pie. Instead, there would now be a larger pie for everyone to divide.

Taylor wrote that scientific management would require a "mental revolution" for employers, requiring them to reexamine their duties toward their employees. He concluded that the manager " . . . must do something more *for* his men than other employers are doing under similar circumstances . . . [so that] each side can get more than ever before."

Taylor was convinced that laborers would support his moves to increase labor efficiency since he believed that all workers were wage-maximizing individuals. A special compensation system, the differential piece rate, was created to reward workers for producing more. His efforts gave rise to careful job design and employee training as well as to a supervision style intended to insure that work was performed as planned. Taylor emphasized the importance of individual contributions to organizational success and suggested that social activities of the work force (small group and union activity) generally inhibited rather than positively affected worker productivity.

Taylor's efforts were not without opposition. Labor unions feared that increased efficiency in production would lead to unemployment. Some managers also resisted scientific management, anticipating it would put too much control in the hands of specialists.

The scientific management movement had two important impacts on management philosophy and behavior. On one hand, many writers and practitioners focused attention on the technical contributions Taylor made to industrial production. Most managers saw the technical orientation as the true meaning of scientific management, and it became the dominant line of thinking associated with the movement. Human concerns tended to be placed below concerns for efficiency and the maximization of output, and the training necessary to perform managerial duties clearly differentiated between managers and workers. Managers might be able to perform general labor, but laborers could not become involved in management.

The second group followed Taylor's advice about humanizing management-employee relations. These men and women were among the forerunners of a later era in management thinking known as **human relations.**

Administrative Era

The administrative era was somewhat similar to the scientific management era. Taylor's followers were occupied with finding the best way to do a job in the factory; managers during the administrative era were concerned with finding the best way to manage the entire organization. They also sought a better understanding of the nature of management. The era resulted in two significant developments in managerial thinking. First, universal prescriptions for organizing and managing were formulated. These principles of management emphasized tight control and were thought by many managers to represent the ultimate rules by which organizations should be administered.

Second, management came to be defined in terms of a unique set of functions. These functions consisted of such activities as planning, organizing (specifying how, where, and by whom work would be performed), directing (supervising), and controlling (evaluating performance and output). This definition of the manager's role focused additional attention on the importance of managing people (directing). It was also significant in light of earlier distinctions between managers and nonmanagers. Specifically, the definition clarified the types of activities in which nonmanagers should not be involved. This delineation of duties and responsibilities became an important element in the pervasive management philosophy and has remained until today. Only now are such assumptions beginning to be reexamined.

Human Relations

The need for managers to pay more attention to their workers received limited emphasis during both the scientific management and administrative eras. However, the genesis of the **human relations** movement is generally credited to a series of research studies conducted at the Hawthorne Electric Plant in Cicero, Illinois.

The Hawthorne Studies received considerable criticism for the manner in which they were planned and carried out.[12] However, it is now generally acknowledged that they opened the door to widespread research on human behavior in organizations. This research during nearly a decade in the 1920s and 1930s raised many questions about such subjects as motivation, leadership style, and the impact of group behavior in organizations. As interest grew in the conclusions of these studies, the scope of research on behavioral topics also increased. These efforts were not without problems. Even though careful attention to research design sometimes was lacking, there was no scarcity of believers or enthusiasts. It became fashionable in some management circles to advocate "caring for the needs of workers" and bringing democracy to the work floor. The movement's most quoted postulate was "high morale leads to high productivity." However, this basic human relations tenet has been questioned, and some evidence suggests that the relationship may even be reversed; that is, high productivity leads to satisfaction and high morale.[13]

Despite the shortcomings of the human relations movement, its contribution to the practice of management has been substantial. Managers and organizational researchers gave prominence to the role of people in the success of organizational ventures. Though still limited, knowledge of worker behavior also increased. Most important, many questions raised through research and application created a greater desire to learn more about human behavior in organizations.

This discussion of the evolution of managerial philosophy suggests that at least two distinct styles of management have evolved. One style appears to have evolved from the perception that managers are individuals with distinct and superior abilities. These men and women believe that most employees work primarily for wages and are motivated by little else. When financial incentives are unavailable, managers are justified in using manipulation or force. One famous management writer, Douglas McGregor, referred to this style as Theory X.[14]

A second management style seems more closely linked to the human relations movement. These managers view workers in a more favorable light and advocate a considerate approach with employees, believing that "workers are people, too." They are more likely than their Theory X counterparts to encourage open, friendly relations on the job and to spend time talking with and listening to employees. This approach appears to place a high priority on the employees' well-being. However, some managers have been accused of using this so-called Theory Y style to placate subordinates. They are viewed as being just as controlling and manipulative as other managers but less open about their intentions. Undoubtedly, many managers have been guilty of that deception.

Both Theory X and Theory Y are oversimplifications, and neither represents how a manager may always view employees. On the other hand, the terms are widely known and used by people in business and industry to describe management styles. The complete assumptions of Theory X and Theory Y are shown in Exhibit 1.1.

In Summary

What philosophy is most prevalent in management circles today? According to one prominent authority, managers generally endorse the use of a participative style, although they doubt whether their subordinates are creative or can exercise self-direction or self-control.[15] Their decisions to use participation, he concludes, are based on a desire to improve morale and satisfaction. (As mentioned, research has not substantiated the widely held belief that high morale and satisfaction will lead to greater productivity.)

A second important question is, what management style actually is in use? The implication here is apparent. What managers claim to believe and what they do may differ. A noted writer in the field of management concluded:

> When someone is asked how he would behave under certain circumstances, the answer he usually gives is his espoused theory of action for that situation. . . . However, the theory that actually governs his actions is his theory-in-use, which may or may not be compatible with his espoused theory; furthermore, the individual may or may not be aware of the incompatibility of the two.[16]

EXHIBIT I.I   THE ASSUMPTIONS OF THEORY X AND THEORY Y

THEORY X	THEORY Y
1. The average human being has an inherent dislike of work and will avoid it if possible.	1. The expenditure of physical and mental effort in work is as natural as play or rest.
2. Because of this human characteristic of dislike of work, most people must be coerced, controlled, directed, and/or threatened with punishment to get them to put forth adequate effort toward the achievement of organizational objectives.	2. External control and the threat of punishment are not the only means of bringing about effort toward organizational objectives. People will exercise self-direction and self-control in the service of objectives to which they are committed.
3. The average human being prefers to be directed, wishes to avoid responsibility, has relatively little ambition, wants security above all.	3. Commitment to objectives is a function of the rewards associated with their achievement.
	4. The average human being learns, under proper conditions, not only to accept but also to seek responsibility.
	5. The capacity to exercise a relatively high degree of imagination, ingenuity, and creativity in the solution of organizational problems is widely, not narrowly, distributed in the population.
	6. Under the conditions of modern industrial life, the intellectual potentialities of the average human being are only partially utilized.

Adapted from: Douglas McGregor, *The Human Side of Enterprise* (New York: McGraw-Hill, 1960), 33–57.

Managerial actions, for the most part, are tied closely to the dominant managerial philosophy that has evolved during the last two centuries. The traditional—or **control-oriented**—approach to work-force management took shape during the early part of this century in response to the division of work into small, clearly defined jobs for which individuals could be held accountable. The actual definitions of jobs, as well as of acceptable standards of performance, rested on "lowest common denominator" assumptions about workers' skills and motivations. In order to monitor and control workers who were assumed to have an inherent dislike of work, management responsibilities were organized into a hierarchy of specialized roles which reinforced a top-down allocation of authority.

At the heart of this traditional model is an attempt to establish order, exercise, control, and achieve efficiency. This managerial philosophy of control is also characterized by these beliefs:

1. A clear difference exists between the duties and responsibilities of managers and nonmanagers.
2. Management duties and responsibilities include making decisions about planning, organizing, and controlling work.
3. Managers are better able to perform these duties than are nonmanagers and may even have come by this ability naturally ("it is the natural order").
4. Past influences on modern managerial beliefs and actions are so subtle that today's managers may have acquired their theory-in-use without recognizing its origins.

ORGANIZATIONAL BEHAVIOR COMES OF AGE

The first part of this chapter suggested that a revolution in management thinking is currently taking place. Changing expectations among workers have recently prompted growing disillusionment with the traditional, control-oriented approach to managing. At the same time, intensified international competition has focused attention on the disadvantages of the control model. A model that assumes low employee commitment and that places emphasis on reliable rather than outstanding performance is simply not designed to match the standards of excellence set by world-class competitors. Market success in the 1990s depends on a superior level of performance which many authorities today believe requires the commitment (not merely the obedience) of workers.

NORDSTROM

Nordstrom Department Stores provide an example of how employee commitment can foster superior performance. Nordstrom is a unique organization that competitors admit leads the industry in customer service. Nordstrom may well lead the industry in something even more basic—employee commitment.

"Nordies," as Nordstrom employees are known, are recognized for their dedication and willingness to do whatever it takes to make a customer happy. Nordies are described as upbeat, ambitious, and selfless. A customer unable to locate a desired product at Nordstrom's is likely to find that a Nordie is willing to shop at another store to obtain the desired product for the customer. If a customer needs an item on short notice, salespeople will often deliver the item personally, even on their own time. These little extras are known by Nordies as "heroics" and involve everything from personally altering clothing for customers to changing flat tires in the parking lot.

The company is run by four brothers who believe in a simple formula: "The system is to have self-empowered people who have an entrepreneurial spirit, feel that they are in this to better themselves, feel good about themselves, make more money, and are successful." Not everyone who works for Nordstrom is equally committed to his or her job or the company. However, the commitment displayed by most Nordstrom employees is anything *but* ordinary or average.[17]

In a *commitment-based* approach to work-force management, jobs are designed to be broader in scope than before, to combine planning and implementation, and to include efforts to upgrade operations, not just to maintain them. Individual responsibilities are expected to change as conditions change, and teams, not individuals, are often held accountable for performance. Management hierarchies are smaller and differences in status minimized. Control and coordination therefore depend on shared goals, and expertise rather than formal position determines influence.

This revolution is significant in that it poses a fundamental challenge to the control-oriented philosophy of management that has evolved during the last century. Although interest in human resources has existed in organizations for some time, only recently has that interest taken the form of a theory-in-use in American business. What was once an occasional topic of conversation has become the most talked- and written-about subject at business meetings and in business publications. This challenge has been brought about by four major factors:

1. Increased foreign competition, especially from the Japanese.
2. A steady and prolonged decline in the rate of productivity in the United States.
3. Rapid technological development.
4. The changing composition of the labor force in the United States.

We will now discuss how each of these factors has affected this dominant managerial culture.

Since World War II, the United States had been recognized as the world's leading industrial power. In recent years, however, other industrial nations have been willing and able to compete with American business in both the world marketplace and the United States. Japan, West Germany, Korea, and Taiwan have emerged as industry leaders in steel, textiles, rubber, electronics, and computers. Even the one-time bastion of American technology and expertise, the automobile industry, has been shaken by competition from abroad.

In the 1960s, United States companies dominated the world's markets for manufactured goods. The United States supplied over three-quarters of the television sets, half of the automobiles, and a quarter of the steel used around the world. Yet, by the 1980s, Japan, Korea, and Taiwan had become the major suppliers of such products.

The decline of the United States' industrial power has had a significant impact upon its citizens and business organizations. For example, United States citizens have seen their share of world trade fall from 21 percent in 1960 to 14 percent in 1987. Their trade balance has changed from a surplus of $5 billion in 1960 to a deficit of $110 billion in 1989. Their trade balance in manufactured goods has slipped from a healthy surplus of $11 billion in 1981 to a deficit of $141 billion in 1987. Their volume of manufacturing exports tumbled 32 percent between 1980 and 1985—with every $1 billion of exports lost costing an estimated twenty-five thousand United States jobs.

This chipping away of United States industrial dominance has occurred concurrently with the rate of productivity in the United States leveling off and even declining. These two factors, increased competition from abroad and a decline in United States productivity, have caused leaders in business and industry to question existing management philosophies and practices. These factors also have promoted comparisons between management approaches in the United States and those of successful competitors, especially the Japanese.

Japan's impressive rise in the marketplace has been noted throughout the world. At first, such successes were met with skepticism and some antagonism. However, these reactions were soon replaced by an interest in the factors contributing to Japanese business prosperity.

Many reasons have been offered to explain this prosperity, and a detailed discussion of them is beyond the scope of this book. However, one explanation, the predominant Japanese management style, has received particular attention from Western managers.[18] Popularized in such books as *The Art of Japanese Management* by Richard Pascale and Anthony Athos[19] and *Theory Z* by William Ouchi,[20] this style focuses attention on forming and maintaining manager-employee relationships. Ouchi, for example, contrasted the characteristics of American and Japanese organizations and recommended that United States and Canadian organizations adopt such Japanese management practices as bringing about a richer, long-term relationship with employees, making greater use of employee involvement and of decision making by consensus, relying more heavily on informal control, and encouraging a sense of family or community within the organization. Although few experts would advocate transplanting all Japanese management techniques into Western organizations, most agree that a careful reevaluation of our present practices, in light of these techniques, is called for.

GENERAL MOTORS

In 1982, for example, General Motors' auto assembly plant in Fremont, California, was a model of the United States in decline. Absenteeism hovered at 25 percent, and outstanding grievances numbered about one thousand. Wildcat strikes interrupted production, and labor and management were continually in conflict. In 1982, GM shut Fremont's doors and later turned the plant over to Toyota Motor Corporation as part of a joint venture called New United Motor Manufacturing, Inc. (NUMMI). GM and Toyota each held a 50 percent interest in the joint venture.

Adding little new technology, NUMMI's Japanese bosses set up a typical Toyota production system with just-in-time delivery and a flexible assembly line run by teams of workers in charge of their own jobs. The 2,500 employees today can assemble 250,000 cars per year; this number of cars is roughly equal to what was produced by GM's 5,000 employees. By February of 1989, there were only fifteen outstanding grievances, and absenteeism, including scheduled time off, amounted to about 3 percent.[21]

A key element in the successful transfer of Japanese manufacturing and labor practices has been the skillful managing of United States workers. The Japanese approach to production, emphasizing flexibility and attention to quality, demands extremely high employee loyalty; this represents a sharp departure from the traditional adversary relationship in most United States and Canadian factories. "The Japanese philosophy is to make people an important item, as opposed to the typical U.S. philosophy that workers are just an extension of machines," says D. William Childs, NUMMI's general manager of human resources.[22]

Other factors also have focused attention on the assumptions and practices of the control model of managing in the United States. Technological innovations are again redefining the nature of work. Just as the introduction of mechanization during the industrial revolution altered the meaning of work, so the arrival of the information revolution has required adjustments in management thinking. Technological changes have rapidly altered work practices and customs in the traditional heavy industries, as well as in such areas as insurance, banking, and government. Methods and practices established over decades have been challenged and revised almost daily to keep abreast of these changes.

Computers, for example, often do a better, faster job of collecting and analyzing information now handled by foremen and other managers. Placing terminals that display easily understood reports on the factory floor enable workers to exercise direct control of production without oversight approval from foremen. The Pontiac Motor Division of General Motors now operates an engine-assembly plant with roughly one hundred workers and only two salaried "coordinators." Before it was automated, the line needed about twice as many workers—plus a dozen foremen—and about one in every nine hundred engines was rejected. Today the reject rate has plummeted to one in nine thousand.

Finally, the composition and nature of the labor force in the United States have changed dramatically over the last five decades. During the 1940s, 1950s, and 1960s, the United States labor market was relatively homogeneous and dominated by white males. The decline in birth rates after 1960, however, reduced the supply of young people available for employment. The continuing demand for workers has been met, in part, by increasing numbers of women and minorities moving into the labor force. Consequently, the work force of the 1990s is much more diverse in terms of sex, race, and age than the work force of the mid-1900s. Managing this diversified labor force requires managers to address issues such as literacy and family responsibility (e.g., child and elderly care), and affects the methods managers use to perform their jobs (i.e., participative versus autocratic decision making).[23]

Workers' increasing expectations, a result of their higher overall level of education, have also altered the nature of managing. People looking for responsibility, autonomy, and challenge in their work have become frustrated by management practices that grew out of nineteenth-century factories as well as by manipulative participative management schemes.

None of these explanations, alone, is sufficient to explain the new wave of thinking currently occurring in management circles. Each, however, provides additional insight as to why managers are anxiously pursuing new avenues to greater productivity and why those avenues are leading to human solutions to organizational problems.

It is within the context of this shift from control-oriented to commitment-oriented approaches to managing that the field of organizational behavior has come of age. The theories, concepts, and research results presented in this book provide managers with tools they can use as they attempt to obtain employee commitment.

As indicated in our discussion thus far, factors such as technology, productivity, and international competitiveness have significantly affected management philosophy and practices in recent years. Two specific issues that will continue to have a major impact on our study and understanding of organizational behavior are (1) the increasing internationalization of business, and (2) ethics in businesses and other types of organizations.

International Issues in Organizational Behavior

Most of the theories and research findings presented in this book originated in the United States, Canada, and Europe. The increasing internationalization of business, however, has stimulated important questions that should be considered by all students of organizational behavior: Can these theories and research results be applied in all countries in the same way? Must a manager use different motivational approaches with people from Mexico, Sweden, or Taiwan? Do principles of effective leadership vary from country to country? Do managers from different cultures share similar expectations about career advancement? Are management practices that are successful in one part of the world equally successful elsewhere?

In every culture, cognitive and behavioral patterns (ways of thinking and acting) are handed down from one generation to another. The result is a set of implicit values that, in many cases, influence management decisions and behavior. For example, Japanese managers are likely to use group approaches to decision making while United States managers may rely more frequently on unilateral decision-making processes. Similarly, Swedish companies such as Volvo incorporated work teams into their production processes while most Canadian and United States manufacturers were designing and building assembly lines that isolated workers from one another. Are such differences culturally based?

In an attempt to address these important international issues, we will present examples of organizational behavior in different parts of the world. In addition, look for special exhibits entitled "International Dimensions" in which actual management practices in countries other than the United States and Canada will be described in greater detail.

Ethics and the Study of Organizational Behavior

When a person is involved in managing individuals, groups, or large organizations, the decisions she makes can affect the professional and personal lives of employees and, ultimately, customers. Associated with all such decisions are important ethical responsibilities. Unfortunately, the unique situations that we face each day do not always lead to clear-cut ethical conclusions. Consider the following situations:

Kathy discovers a possible error while reviewing research data and findings on the safety features of a new product. She knows her boss is the key advocate for the product and is anxious for the project to succeed. Should she draw attention to the possible error or avoid making waves (and perhaps thereby increase her chances for a favorable performance evaluation)?

John is evaluating the performance of two work associates. Both have performed well during the last quarter, and their evaluations are basically equal. However, John is aware that one of the associates has an ill child at home and is having financial difficulties. Should he recommend a larger pay increase for the associate with the ill child?

INTERNATIONAL DIMENSION
The Search for the Global Manager

Jan Prising is a Swede who runs a United States-owned company from an office overlooking Lake Varese in Italy. He speaks five languages (but not Italian) and conducts most of his business in English. Is Prising unique? Not anymore: Prising, aged fifty-one, is part of a growing group of executives having the skills and experience to manage across international borders. Nor is the way he got his job so unusual, though it would have been a scandal only a few years ago. A headhunter lured Prising, a twenty-one-year veteran of Sweden's Electrolux, to his present position by offering salary and bonuses of approximately $500,000 per year.

The hunt for the global manager is on, and many companies are now turning to executive search firms for help in locating these rare individuals. From Antwerp to Toronto to Hong Kong, recruiters are looking for a new breed of multilingual, multifaceted executives who can formulate business strategies and make decisions in the international marketplace. The demand for such executives is especially heavy in Europe in anticipation of sweeping economic changes in 1992. According to Lester B. Korn, chairman of the world's largest executive search firm, "Europe will be the world's fastest growing market of the 1990s, outperforming even the Pacific Rim."

As new markets for goods and services are opened in Eastern Europe, the USSR, and other parts of the world during the 1990s, the need for "global" managers will continue to increase.

Questions
What characteristics and skills do you think a good "global" manager must have?
What can students do to increase their awareness and understanding of the international aspects of business?

SOURCE: Shawn Tully, "The Hunt for the Global Manager," Fortune, 21 May 1990, 140–141.

An employer's profits during the last two years have been less than anticipated. Consequently, Janet's raises have been smaller than in previous years. She takes office supplies and materials home for personal use and rationalizes her behavior with the thought, "They owe it to me." Is Janet's behavior ethical?

Ethics is the set of standards that defines what is right, wrong, and just in human actions. Typically, ethical judgments are based on personal values that have been learned over a lifetime. Recent controversies on Wall Street, in the White House, and in political capitols around the world have drawn attention to the importance of ethics. Decisions involving the use of power and authority, the distribution of rewards, and the exercise of control raise a variety of complex ethical questions with which managers must wrestle.[24] We will pose such ethical questions throughout this book. Watch for special sections entitled "Ethical Dilemma" and ask yourself how you would respond in the same situation. Keep in mind that absolute answers may not always exist when ethical dilemmas arise. Answers, therefore, will reflect personal values and the values of the organization and society in which an individual works and lives.

ETHICAL DILEMMA
Whose Shoes Is He Wearing?

Mike Schmidt, the brilliant third baseman of the Philadelphia Phillies, received the coveted Most Valuable Player award in the National League three times during his career. One year Schmidt was paid $5,000 for wearing shoes made by Nike Incorporated of Beaverton, Oregon, and given the use of a $100,000 Rolls-Royce for a year. Finding the Nike shoes uncomfortable on artificial turf, Schmidt used shoes made by the Brooks Company and painted the Nike symbol on them.

Suppose that a Nike company official learned of Schmidt's shoe replacement, was asked by a sportswriter whether it was true, and answered: "We paid a small endorsement fee to Schmidt and, so far as we're concerned, he is wearing shoes showing the great Nike symbol."

Questions
Did the company official lie? Was he ethical? Did Schmidt lie? Was he ethical?

SOURCE: J.A. Livingston, *Philadelphia Inquirer,* 18 March 1984, p. 16D.

DEFINING THE FIELD OF ORGANIZATIONAL BEHAVIOR

The study of organizational behavior has historically used three basic units of analysis: the individual, the group, and the organization. A micro approach to organizational behavior focuses primarily on the first two units of analysis—the behavior of individuals and groups within organizations. The underlying premise of this perspective is that people, not organizations, behave.[25] Such topics as personality, perception, learning, motivation, and group formation and processes fall within this micro approach.

The macro approach, on the other hand, emphasizes the organization as the primary unit of analysis. People viewing organizational behavior from this perspective contend that organizations can be understood as entities unto themselves and that it is unnecessary (perhaps even undesirable) to try to explain activities unique to an organization in terms of individual behavior.[26] People approaching organizational behavior from a macro perspective are concerned with such subjects as organizational environment, organizational effectiveness, climate, culture, and structure.

Both micro and macro topics have their roots in the behavioral and social sciences of psychology, sociology, political science, economics, anthropology, and social psychology. Exhibit 1.2 presents each behavioral science and summarizes its contributions to the field of OB.

This book defines organizational behavior in the following way:

> **Organizational behavior** includes the study and application in everyday organizational life of theories and concepts about human behavior. OB relies on careful, systematic inquiry into phenomena associated with

EXHIBIT 1.2   CONTRIBUTIONS OF BEHAVIORAL AND SOCIAL SCIENCES TO ORGANIZATIONAL BEHAVIOR

DISCIPLINE	NATURE OF THE FIELD	CONTRIBUTION TO OB
Psychology	Individual behavior	Provides insights into personality, perception, learning, motivation, and decision making
Sociology	Groups and complex organizations	Focuses on the development and functioning of small groups, the nature of formal organization, and various social processes
Social Psychology	Individual behavior in relation to the social environment	Concentrates on attitude formation and change, interpersonal communication, problem solving, social influence, and leadership
Anthropology	Origins and history of human culture (ways of thinking and behaving)	Contributes to an understanding of factors in the cultural environment that influence behavior. Can include societal patterns in general as well as patterns that evolve within an organization
Economics	Allocation of scarce resources to competing ends as choices are influenced by the self-interest of the individual decision maker	Provides perspectives on how and why individuals rationally choose certain behaviors to achieve personal goals or ends
Political Science	Organization and government of political entities	Increases understanding of power, conflict, coalitions, and bargaining

individual and group behavior in organizations. The ultimate purpose of the field is to provide managers with knowledge, analytic tools, and the ability to influence human and organizational performance.

In the following section, we briefly examine some important parts of this definition.

Study and Application

Organizational behavior is a field of inquiry intended to provide meaningful information about human behavior in organizations as well as ways to apply that information. Study and application are both important in OB. The field provides ways of approaching and systematically thinking about situations that arise in organizations. In the following chapters, you will discover answers to certain questions about human behavior in organizations. You will also learn what questions a good manager must ask, where to obtain necessary information, and how to derive answers from that information.

Organizational behavior is concerned with identifying and refining tools that can be used to manage human relationships on a day-to-day basis. After all, the ultimate purpose of your studies is to be able to apply what you have learned in your own organizational relationships.

Theories and Concepts

Organizational behavior makes extensive use of theories to explain human behavior. A **theory** is a tentative explanation about how and why something occurs. More precisely, a theory is a set of interrelated concepts, definitions, and statements used to explain and predict a particular phenomenon or set of phenomena. Theories serve several basic and important functions.

The principal functions of a theory are explanation and prediction. A theory explains a phenomenon by specifying and defining important variables and the relationships among those variables. Such an explanatory framework, if it is complete and adequate, can also result in reasonably accurate predictions of future events. A theory of motivation, for example, should enable you to predict the level of effort an employee will put forth on the job. The ultimate purpose, then, of any theory is increased *understanding* of a phenomenon through the explanation and prediction of that phenomenon.

Theories also are useful in organizing and summarizing large amounts of factual information. A theory provides a framework for observing and thinking, a tool for identifying patterns and relationships in facts or observed events. In this sense, a theory is like a rule that provides a shorthand method for dealing with similar situations. It is much easier, for example, to remember the multiplicative identity rule ($1 \times P = P$) than to perform the calculation every time such a problem is encountered.

Theories also serve to guide research and aid in the interpretation of research results. Because theories are tentative, they must be tested empirically to determine if the specified relationships and predictions are valid. Every theory focuses attention on certain concepts or relationships that need this empirical scrutiny. A theory also provides the backdrop for interpreting research results as either supporting or refuting the original predictions.

A basic understanding of theory and the functions it serves is essential to your study of human behavior in organizations. You will encounter theories attempting to explain and predict motivation, leadership, organizational change, decision making, and so on. Each theory must be analyzed in terms of its ability to explain and predict adequately and in light of the accumulated research evidence pertaining to that theory.

Individuals and Groups

As explained, organizational behavior can be approached from either a micro or a macro perspective. This book examines behavior occurring within organizations (micro) rather than the behavior of organizations themselves (macro). The primary focus is on individuals and the relationships among individuals in organizations. At the same time, we cannot completely ignore the context or environment in which these behaviors take place. Such things as the formal organization structure, the management system, and the nature of the work being performed must all be considered if we are to manage human relationships effectively.

SYSTEMS THEORY AND ORGANIZATIONAL BEHAVIOR

Viewing an organization as a **system** greatly enhances our understanding of human behavior in organizations. A system is a collection of interdependent parts that function as a single entity. Systems thus have three essential characteristics: (1) they are entities; (2) they consist of parts; and (3) their parts interact and are interdependent with one another. Systems also exist in and interact with an environment. Things outside the system are not (at least for the time being) part of the system. Systems, then, can be identified by their parts (e.g., the positions on a baseball team—pitcher, catcher, etc.), as an entity (the Dodgers), and in some cases, by their environments ("If you're not on the bus, you're not on the team").

A system requires **inputs** from the environment in order to operate. Organizational inputs include money, machines, people, and ideas. These inputs are transformed in the **throughput** process into a variety of **outputs** that are returned to the environment. For example, an automobile manufacturer takes tires, transmissions, machinery, and workers (inputs) and transforms them into finished cars (outputs). Thus, the system is viewed as continually interacting with its environment in an ongoing series of exchange relationships intended to further the well-being of the organization and its members. Exhibit 1.3 portrays a system as a repeating cycle of input-throughput-output.

Applying systems theory can help us understand the behavior of individuals as well as the activities of organizations. Systems theory encompasses many concepts but this discussion is limited to a few of the more useful concepts that can add to our understanding of organizational behavior.

Subsystems

Systems are composed of interrelated and interdependent parts, some of which may be smaller systems. For example, every person is a system comprised of values, motives, attitudes, and learned behaviors. Similarly, each department in an enterprise (marketing, production, finance, etc.) is a system and therefore a **subsystem** of the enterprise (system).

Suprasystem

Systems exist in an environment. To the extent that the environment may itself be identified as a system, it becomes a **suprasystem.** An organization such as a college

EXHIBIT I.3   THE INPUT-THROUGHPUT-OUTPUT CYCLE

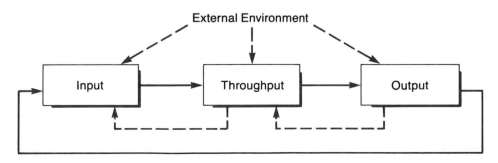

of business administration operates within the framework of a larger system, the university (the suprasystem).

Open versus closed systems

Open systems exchange information and energy (interact) with their environments. **Closed systems,** on the other hand, are self-contained (i.e., they are not dependent on the environment as a source of inputs or as a receiver of outputs). It is difficult to envision a system as being totally closed. Instead, "we prefer to think of open–closed as a dimension; that is, systems are relatively open or relatively closed."[27] Organizational behavior recognizes the importance of events in the environment and their subsequent impact on behavior in the system. At the same time, however, solutions to problems may arise completely from within the system and not be influenced substantially by the environment e.g., a student may be shown how to study more efficiently rather than taking time off work to prepare for an examination.

Equifinality

Equifinality suggests that open systems can achieve their purposes using diverse sets of inputs and different arrangements of system components. That is, more than one set of resources, methods, or management styles can produce a desired output. Outputs can be attained by transforming different inputs in different ways. For example, a supervisor may judge an employee's performance to be unacceptable. The supervisor knows that performance can be improved through technical training. However, changing what is expected of the worker or offering a bonus also may bring about the desired level of productivity.

Feedback

A system must receive information about its outputs in order to maintain itself. Returning information to a system (or subsystem) for evaluation is referred to as **feedback.** An archer who is not permitted to see where the arrow strikes the target cannot adjust subsequent shots to compensate for errors. Feedback in organizations may take the form of formal reports, employee grievances or customer complaints, or informal conversations. In some cases, important feedback includes nonverbal expressions or gestures.

Synergy

Synergy refers to the unique system quality sometimes expressed in the phrase, "the whole is greater than the sum of its parts." A system is synergistic when its inputs combine in unique ways to create something more than the sum of inputs alone. Even though a basketball team has outstanding individual stars, it may only have the magic needed to win when the members play together.

A systems view of organizational behavior (1) provides a way of analyzing and communicating about the complexity of organizational processes, and (2) emphasizes the key interdependencies that exist in all organizations. We will highlight these important characteristics throughout this book.

THE MANAGERIAL REVOLUTION: CONCLUSIONS

Every manager has seen signs of change in organizational life over the past few years. Foreign competition, decreased productivity, rapid technological innovation, and changes in the composition of the labor force have ushered in a new era of managerial thinking. To survive and compete in today's world, the manager must more effectively use an underused resource—people!

Most managers have been aware that human resources influence organizational performance. Some managers have tried to manage around people to minimize their disruptive influence. Others have adopted styles they believed would allow them to understand and manage workers better. Today, many managers are not aware of either their management styles or the impact of those styles. Their ways of thinking and behaving have been influenced, perhaps without their realizing it, by a pervasive managerial philosophy that has evolved over many decades. Managers should carefully examine their assumptions about people and assess the potential impact of those assumptions on the process of managing work behavior.

The managerial revolution discussed in this chapter has increased the use of commitment-oriented (as opposed to control-oriented) approaches to managing people in organizations. This revolution is the context within which the field of organizational behavior has come of age. Studying organizational behavior will increase your understanding of people as they perform vital roles in enterprises of all types. You can draw on your existing knowledge of human behavior—knowledge gained from studying various behavioral sciences—as well as on the information in this book to help you develop an approach to management that fully uses human resources.

QUESTIONS FOR REVIEW AND DISCUSSION

1. Define organizational behavior.
2. How did the definition and nature of work change during the 1800s?
3. What is Social Darwinism? What impact did this social doctrine have on the evolving managerial culture?
4. What functions and activities defined the manager's role during the administrative era?
5. Describe how the human relations movement differed from previous approaches to management.
6. Why are major changes in management philosophy and practice occurring today?
7. Why must a manager be concerned with the international aspects of business?
8. Define ethics.
9. What is the difference between micro and macro approaches to the study of organizational behavior?
10. What are the characteristics of a system?

REFERENCES

1. R. B. Reich, "The Next American Frontier," *The Atlantic Monthly* (March 1983): 50.
2. Thomas J. Peters and Robert H. Waterman, *In Search of Excellence: Lessons from America's Best Run Companies* (New York: Harper and Row, 1982).
3. Thomas J. Peters and Nancy K. Austin, *A Passion for Excellence* (New York: Random House, 1985).
4. Robert H. Waterman, *The Renewal Factor* (New York: Bantam Books, 1987).
5. Thomas J. Peters, *Thriving on Chaos* (New York: Alfred Knopf, 1987).
6. Rosabeth M. Kanter, *When Giants Learn to Dance* (New York: Simon and Schuster, 1989).
7. Frederick Herzberg, "Up the Staircase to Productivity Burnout," *Industry Week* 10 January 1983, 65, 68, 70.
8. Adam Smith, *The Wealth of Nations* (New York: The Modern Library, 1937), 5.
9. C. Perrow, *Complex Organizations* (Glenview, Ill.: Scott Foresman, 1972), 61–65.
10. H. Harris, *American Labor* (New Haven: Yale University Press, 1938), 127.
11. Frederick W. Taylor, "The Principles of Scientific Management," *Bulletin of the Taylor Society* (December 1916).
12. Perrow, op.cit., 101–106.
13. C. N. Greene, "The Satisfaction-Performance Controversy," *Business Horizons*, Vol. 15, No. 5 (1972): 31–41.
14. Douglas M. McGregor, "The Human Side of Enterprise," *Management Review*, Vol. 46, No. 11 (1957): 22–28, 88–92.

15. R.E. Miles, *Theories of Management: Implications for Organizational Behavior and Development* (New York: McGraw-Hill, 1975), 46–47.

16. C. Argyris and D. A. Schon, *Theory in Practice: Increasing Professional Effectiveness* (San Francisco: Jossey-Bass, 1974), 6–7.

17. "60 Minutes," CBS, 6 May 1990.

18. Some authorities contend that the term "Japanese Management Style" is too broad and cannot be applied to all management in Japan.

19. Richard T. Pascale and Anthony G. Athos, *The Art of Japanese Management* (New York: Simon and Schuster, 1981).

20. William Ouchi, *Theory Z* (Reading, Mass.: Addison-Wesley, 1981).

21. Powell Niland, "U.S.-Japanese Joint Venture: New United Motor Manufacturing, Inc. (NUMMI), *Plan-ning Review*, Vol. 17, No. 1 (January-February 1989): 40–45.

22. "The Difference Japanese Management Makes," *Business Week*, 14 July 1986, 47–50.

23. "The Skills Crisis," *Inc.*, January 1990, 28.

24. Richard P. Nielsen, "Changing Unethical Organizational Behavior," *The Academy of Management Executives*, Vol. III, No. 2 (May 1989): 123–130.

25. K. E. Weick, *The Social Psychology of Organizing* (Reading, Mass.: Addison-Wesley, 1969).

26. J. Pfeffer, *Organizations and Organization Theory* (Boston: Pitman Publishing, 1982), 20–22.

27. F. E. Kast and J.E. Rosenzweig, "General Systems Theory: Applications for Organizations and Management," *Academy of Management Journal*, 15 (December 1972): 448.

CASE 1.1 *Aeroline mechanical products company*

ROBERT E. COX   *Bendix Corporation*

Roger Smith enjoyed his job as director of employee relations for Aeroline Mechanical Products Company. It was a progressive company, Roger believed, one that managed to expand over the years from a mere handful of employees to over five thousand employees. AMP, in the beginning, fabricated only small mechanical parts for aircraft door closures, but had broadened the product mix to include a variety of mechanical, electro-mechanical and, to an increasing degree, electrical and electronic products. The company had been in existence since the early days of World War II, with many of the employees now having over twenty years service. The average age of the bargaining unit employees was 48 years and the average service 18.3 years. Approximately thirty-two hundred employees were covered by a single collective bargaining agreement, which was to expire within the next ninety days.

The upcoming negotiation was on his mind as Roger looked out over the company parking lot, viewing early morning arrivals. Today was the day he was to brief the general manager on his plans for union negotiations, and he had not decided just what his negotiating priorities would be. Roger had been dis-tracted by several matters which had recently come to his attention.

First, there was the visit from Susan Black, the manufacturing manager, in which Black complained about the union committee members, "who," she said, "do little else but stir up problems in the shop." This was not a new complaint nor was it without some merit. Black's idea was to give the union a small office in an out-of-the-way place in the plant. "Either get them out of my production departments, or I'll put them all to work!" exclaimed Black. Roger had doubts about his ability to do anything about the problem, but he was scheduled to meet with Black again this morning.

The company and the union had agreed in the past negotiation to a ratio of one steward to every fifty production employees, and to a total of twelve full-time paid committee members who served on the grievance committee, which met regularly each week. The stewards were granted up to eight hours paid union time each week, which the records reflected was about 90 percent used by the stewards.

Roger was also concerned about the grievance meeting scheduled for that day in which a number of discipline matters were to be discussed. One such grievance related to written workmanship warnings given to about ten of the twenty employees in the special assembly department. Pete Rose, Roger's assistant, had commented that he had been getting conflicting stories on the problem in that area.

"The union steward tells me," Pete said, "that they were not given process sheets for the new TXP timer that they have started in production, and there is some confusion on the operational sequence. Also," Pete continued, "there has been some longstanding feeling that people don't know where they stand in that department . . . no feedback on production schedules and performance.

"On the other hand," Pete continued, "the supervisors tell me that the TXP is enough like the old Mod 3 that no one should have had a problem with it. And as for feedback, those operators are smart people and should recognize that no news is good news."

Roger thought to himself, "I'll go out to see for myself just what is going on in that area."

With that, Roger left his office and headed for the factory floor. As he passed through the main door leading into the factory, he was struck by the physical differences between the office and manufacturing area. The offices had recently been redone, with new, attractive modular furniture and carpeting. The factory, on the other hand, looked about like it did in the early 1940s, except for being a bit worse for the wear.

As Roger made his way through the tool room, he was pleased to see so many familiar faces. He had long ago forgotten the names that went with them, but as he always said, "I never forget a face." He even took a few minutes to stop and visit with a number of people at the coffee machine where they were enjoying that first cup of the day.

Roger entered the special assembly area, looking for one of the department supervisors. But none were in view.

"Can I help you," asked a young woman, looking up from her microscope.

"Yes," replied Roger. "I'm looking for one of the supervisors."

"Oh, I think they are both over in receiving inspection, trying to get the 626059 grommet released to the line. You know, that part has us shut down."

"No, I didn't know that," Roger replied. "Thanks, just the same." Roger returned to his office without having found the supervisors.

Roger's reflections on the futility of his visit to the factory were interrupted by Pete Rose's arrival.

"Good morning, Pete. Tell me, are you ready for the grievance meeting today?"

Pete responded with a knowing smile, "About as ready as I'll ever be, considering some of the issues we have to discuss."

"I know what you mean," Roger replied. "Tell me where you expect to end up with the discipline dispute in maintenance?"

"Oh, you mean the early quitting?"

"Yes, that and lining up at the clock."

"No problem," said Pete. "Discipline stands. Clear cut case of violating rule number 32."

"Have we uniformly enforced the not quitting early rule?" Roger asked.

"Hmmm! I guess so," responded Pete. "You know it's hard to keep track of things like that now since the work force has grown so much. It sure isn't like the old days when I knew everyone by their first name."

"Do you think that everyone is aware of our shop rules?" asked Roger.

"You mean all 67 of them?"

"Yes."

"Beats me," replied Pete. "You know they have kind of multiplied over the years. I'm not sure that all the postings are up to date. It seems like all I can get done any more is keep up with the paper work. I'm just not able to get out to the shop as much as I'd like."

"Pete, I look for the union to come on pretty strong on some of these issues."

"You bet, Rog, but you can be sure that I'll take the hard line and protect the crown jewels."

"Good man, that's the spirit."

At that moment, the conversation was interrupted by the shrill ring of Roger's phone.

"Hello."

"Yes, this is Ralph Stevens down in department 122. I've got the same problem I spoke to you about last week. Old Bill Smith, my lead man, is back pestering me about a better way to process the "Z" project. I've told him a hundred times that he should keep his nose out of that part of the business. Leave that to engineering. What am I going to do with Smith? He is getting to be a real pain. I think he is affecting others in the department because I've gotten several questions on how the job could be done better. I just can't cope with this."

"You say you just can't cope with those suggestions?" asked Roger.

"You're damn right," replied Stevens. "I've got a quota to get out. I can't spend all day listening to guys like Smith. What do they know about processing a job? That's engineering's job."

"I guess you're right," replied Roger. "But what do you want me to do about it?"

"Well, I wanted you to know. Maybe you could call Smith down to the front end and talk some sense into him."

"Perhaps, but not right now. Let me think on it. I'll get back to you."

"O.K. I'll wait to hear from you."

"What next?" thought Roger as he hung up the phone. "I guess it's just the sign of the times."

At that moment, Susan Black entered Roger's office with a deep scowl on her face.

"What's going on?" queried Roger.

"I'll tell you what's going on, chum. I've got committee members coming out my ears. All they are doing is causing problems in the departments. You have got to do something about them."

"Let me ask you a question, Susan. Are your supervisors using the check-in, check-out pass system for people on union business?"

"Hell, I don't know. What difference does it make, anyway? They are on me like fleas on a blue tick hound. How do I get 'em off?"

"I'm not sure what the problem is, Susan. Are all the committee members causing disruptions, or are there some specific ones?"

"Well, you know how it is. Some are worse than others. It's just a general thing."

"O.K., Susan, we will look at that, but there is something else that the boss asked me about the other day that I need to speak with you on."

"What's that?"

"Lost time, tardies, and absence."

"Yes, that is becoming a problem. We apparently need to tighten up, but I'm not sure where to begin."

"Well, Susan, maybe the first step is to determine just how big a problem we have, and then move from that point."

"Good idea, Roger. I'll start looking at it."

"By the way, Susan, we have a number of grievances for this week's meeting dealing with discipline issued by some of your supervisors. It seems to me that maintenance might be cracking down pretty hard. How about that?"

"Well, they have real problems," replied Black.

"But, I have the feeling that people in other departments are being permitted to do those things for which maintenance is issuing discipline."

"Roger, that might be true, but the problem is much more severe in maintenance. We'll crack down elsewhere when it becomes necessary. You know we always step up to our problems. Besides that, we have a number of new supervisors and some are not all that familiar with the agreement. They'll have to get up to speed on that and try their wings."

Roger looked up just in time to see the general manager walk by his door. "Oh my," he thought. "There seem to be so many problems to deal with, and now we have our labor negotiations to prepare for. This could be a 'hot' one this year. In fact, I'm not sure the answer to all our problems lie in negotiations alone!"

CASE 1.2   *Sell-for-less discount*

DONALD D. WHITE   *University of Arkansas*

BACKGROUND

Sell-For-Less Discount was founded in 1974 by Harold Anderson. Anderson, an employee-oriented leader, opened his first store in suburban Dallas and watched his company expand throughout the southwestern and southeastern United States. Today, there are six hundred stores in the chain. Sell-For-Less's marketing strategy has been highly successful, and the company has shown dramatic growth over the last five years.

According to Anderson, "Our success is part luck, part good business sense, and a lot of cooperation from loyal, hardworking people."

During the last two years, management of the chain has been complicated by labor unrest in a growing number of stores. Most company stores had been unionized for years. But a new union successfully challenged the existing union and established itself as the new collective bargaining agent; now, in some areas, a high level of hostility exists between management and the new union.

Union and financial problems as well as his failing health finally resulted in Harold Anderson stepping down from his position as president. He turned the reins of the company over to his oldest son, Randall, who had recently come back from school in the Northeast. Randall believed that the company's problems were due largely to the union, and let his dislike for its representatives be known throughout the company. In a power play which threatened the loss of many jobs, young Anderson quieted union malcontents and ran the company with a firm hand. It was rumored that he was prepared to close a number of outlets if union activity in any way adversely affected the stores' profitability.

Although retailing technology has progressed in recent years, Sell-For-Less's rapid growth, much of which has resulted from acquisitions, had caused it to put off updating store equipment. Randall Anderson recently decided to upgrade all point-of-purchase technology in Sell-For-Less stores. The first step was to purchase state-of-the-art UPC scanners for twenty-five stores. The scanners purchased represented the latest in holographic technology. In fact, Sell-For-Less was able to acquire all units from the vendor at a discounted price because the scanners had not yet been widely field-tested.

THE NEW ACQUISITION

Sell-For-Less's growth strategy was recently augmented by the acquisition of thirty-five stores in Alabama and Georgia. To manage the transition, Randall Anderson assembled a management team consisting primarily of former college friends, most of whom were brought in from the Northeast.

Randall gave the new management team three primary objectives. First, the team was to change all purchasing and financial systems to the Sell-For-Less model. Second, the team was told to eliminate or minimize any union interference in the new stores. Third, the team was asked to identify twenty-five stores in which to test the new UPC scanners. Team members were instructed to inform employees in the stores that everyone would be evaluated carefully over the next month and that those who were able to make the transition successfully would be retained. About one month ago, a small group of employees approached the team leader, Terry O'Leary, with suggestions for changing the ventilation systems in a number of the newly acquired stores. Terry looked over the plans with an engineer, the controller, and the new district manager. The group believed that, so soon after the acquisition, the expense of making the changes was prohibitive. Following the meeting, O'Leary sent the following notice to each of the thirty-five stores:

> Working conditions in this store presently meet OSHA standards. Expenses necessary to alter the ventilation system cannot be justified at this time, considering the low profitability of the store. The cost for changing the ventilation system is further complicated by our expenditures for the new UPC scanners recently installed in your store. All doors and windows will be left open to improve ventilation. You may want to wear warmer clothes if it gets too cold in your work area.

PROBLEMS WITH THE NEW SCANNERS

Shortly after this incident, the first UPC units were delivered. Systems personnel began installing the new equipment in five stores. O'Leary was confident the scanners would greatly improve the productivity and morale of store personnel. The equipment was highly sophisticated and could read product codes with less difficulty than other brands on the market. In fact, the scanners were so sensitive that operators were required to scan items without touching the equipment itself. One of the systems engineers questioned whether, given its newness on the market, purchasing the equipment was premature. But all indications from the manufacturer and two other experts whom management personnel had visited suggested that the equipment could successfully increase productivity.

Many employees expressed concerns about the new equipment, but systems personnel told them not to worry. As one installer put it, "this won't be the last new piece of modern equipment you see in this store, so don't let it bother you. Anyway, if you pay attention you will learn all there is to know about this thing and you'll be able to get it to do anything you want it to."

The equipment appeared to work well for the first few days, but it soon began to experience considerable problems. Some readers and systems responsible for automatically recording changes in inventory levels began malfunctioning at a much higher rate than had been expected. Employees working with the equipment were told to keep a close eye on it. Frustration among the management team prompted Tony Balboa, the company treasurer, to tell one group of operators, "This is as fine a piece of equipment as you're ever likely to see in this store. Three of these units can do the work of five checkers, but they need to be cared for. I'll be damned if we're going to put this kind of money into a piece of equipment and have it let us down."

Katy Allen, a long-time employee, asked Balboa what he thought the problem was. The treasurer responded, "Who knows? It's impossible to find people anywhere these days who can do a quality job, and I guess the ones building these scanners are no different from all the rest. All I know is that somebody around

here had better get this thing straightened out before it costs us any more money."

In a meeting with O'Leary, Balboa, and a group of store managers, one of the systems engineers suggested that the employees might be "messing this thing up themselves." A store manager added that there had been "a lot of grumbling among the union people." Everyone at the meeting agreed to keep an eye on those working with and around the equipment. However, O'Leary stated that he believed nothing should be said directly to them because "they already are too paranoid about the new scanners."

Engineers working with the scanners continued to be unable to find any major technical problems with the equipment. Control calibration appeared to be at the heart of the matter, but no one was sure why the units appeared to malfunction from time to time. A recent visit from a manufacturer's representative failed to shed additional light on the situation. At one point, the representative mumbled, "Someone must be messing with these babies!"

No one has the answers yet, but tension at Sell-For-Less is rising as the management team becomes increasingly aware that ever-poorer performance figures are being sent back to the home office.

EXERCISE 1.1
ASSUMPTIONS ABOUT PEOPLE AT WORK

INSTRUCTIONS

The purpose of this exercise is to help you better understand the assumptions you make about people and their work behaviors. On the following questionnaire you will find ten sets of questions. Assign a weight from zero to ten to each item in each pair. (Zero indicates that you completely disagree with the statement and ten means that you completely agree with the statement.) Answer each question as honestly as you can. There are *no correct answers*, so don't respond to a question because it will sound good to others or because you think that this is the way you are supposed to answer it.

QUESTIONS

1. It's only human nature for people to do as little work as they can get away with.   _____ (a)

SOURCE: M. Scott Meyers, "Assumptions about People at Work" *Every Employee A Manager.* Used with permission of the publisher. (New York: McGraw-Hill, 1970).

2. When people avoid work, it's usually because their work has been deprived of its meaning. _____ (b)

3. If employees have access to any information they want, they tend to have better attitudes and behave more responsibly. _____ (c)

4. If employees have access to more information than they need to do their immediate tasks, they will usually misuse it. _____ (d)

5. One problem in asking for the ideas of employees is that their perspective is too limited for their suggestions to be of much practical value. _____ (e)

6. Asking employees for their ideas broadens their perspective and results in the development of useful suggestions. _____ (f)

7. If people don't use much imagination and ingenuity on the job, it's probably because relatively few people have much of either. _____ (g)

8. Most people are imaginative and creative but may not show it because of limitations imposed by supervision and the job. _____ (h)

9. People tend to raise their standards if they are accountable for their own behavior and for correcting their own mistakes. _____ (i)

10. People tend to lower their standards if they are not punished for their misbehavior and mistakes. _____ (j)

11. It's better to give people both good and bad news because most employees want the whole story, no matter how painful. _____ (k)

12. It's better to withhold unfavorable news about business because most employees really want to hear only the good news. _____ (l)

13. Because a supervisor is entitled to more respect than those below him in the organization, it weakens his prestige to admit that a subordinate was right and he was wrong. _____ (m)

14. Because people at all levels are entitled to equal respect, a supervisor's prestige is increased when he supports this principle by admitting that a subordinate was right and he was wrong. _____ (n)

15. If you give people enough money, they are less likely to be concerned with such intangibles as responsibility and recognition. _____ (o)

16. If you give people interesting and challenging work, they are less likely to complain about such things as pay and supplemental benefits. _____ (p)

17. If people are allowed to set their own goals and standards of performance, they tend to set them higher than the boss would. _____ (q)

18. If people are allowed to set their own goals and standards of performance, they tend to set them lower than the boss would. _____ (r)

19. The more knowledge and freedom people have regarding their jobs, the more controls are needed to keep them in line. _____ (s)

20. The more knowledge and freedom people have regarding their jobs, the fewer controls are needed to insure satisfactory job performance. _____ (t)

AFTER COMPLETING THE QUESTIONNAIRE

When you have completed all the questions, you may score the questionnaire in the following manner. Add together the scores of items: (a), (d), (e), (g), (j), (l), (m), (o), (r), and (s). The sum of these scores will provide you with your "Theory X" score. Then, add together the remaining scores: (b), (c), (f), (h), (i), (k), (n), (p), (q), and (t). The sum of these scores will give you your "Theory Y" score.

In a group, discuss the relative strength of each of your scores. Is there a significant difference in the two scores? What might this mean? How do you believe your assumptions might affect your actions as a manager? Do your past experiences support the self-profile that has emerged from your discussion? Discuss with other members of your group how your scores may be related to the concepts of "espoused theory" and "theory-in-use."

EXERCISE 1.2
A "PHILOSOPHY" OF MANAGEMENT

PART I A STATEMENT OF PHILOSOPHY

Introduction

Every manager probably behaves in accordance with certain basic assumptions; when taken together as a cluster of beliefs or convictions, they can be called a philosophy.

As a person occupying a position in which you supervise the work of others, you are being asked to respond to the paragraph below in terms of the degree to which you agree with it, or disagree with it, *as a whole*. Read the paragraph one or more times, then indicate with a check mark in the most appropriate blank the degree to which you accept or reject the point of view expressed in the paragraph.

> In American culture, people share a common set of needs: to belong, to be liked, to be respected. They normally desire individual recognition; but, more than this, they want to feel a useful part of the company (or organization in which they are employed), and of their own work group or department. They will tend to cooperate and to comply with organizational goals if these important needs are fulfilled. Hence, one of the manager's basic tasks is to make each worker believe that he or she is a useful and important part of the department (or company) "team." Managers should be willing at all times to explain their decisions and to discuss with their subordinates any objections they may raise to their plans. On the more routine or less complex matters, managers should actively encourage their subordinates to participate in planning and choosing among alternative solutions to problems. And within limits, the work group or individual subordinates should be urged to exercise self-direction and self-control in carrying out organizational plans. Sharing information with subordinates and involving them in departmental decision making will help satisfy their basic needs for belonging and for individual recognition. Satisfying these needs will, in turn, improve

subordinates' morale, help to reduce friction between subordinates and their superiors, and possibly lead to improved job performance.

Check only *one* of the blanks below:

A. _____ On the whole, I find this paragraph highly acceptable.
B. _____ I find the paragraph basically acceptable, with a few reservations.
C. _____ I find the paragraph about half-acceptable and half-unacceptable.
D. _____ Although it contains a few good ideas, I find the paragraph basically unacceptable.
E. _____ I find this paragraph, on the whole, unacceptable.

When you have completed Part 1, meet with a small group of your classmates and discuss the following questions.

1. Why did you agree or disagree with the statement as a whole?
2. Were there certain parts of the statement with which you felt more or less comfortable?
3. Do all members of your group have similar perceptions concerning the paragraph you just read? What is the basis for general agreement or disagreement within the group?

PART 2 IDENTIFYING YOUR OWN MANAGEMENT PHILOSOPHY

The paragraph you read in Part 1 of this exercise was intended to prompt you to think about management philosophy in general. Now you are asked to write a series of short statements about your own philosophy of management.

First, look over the outline to this book in the table of contents. Then, write a brief statement (two or three sentences is adequate) expressing your beliefs about each of six topics that you believe should be particularly important to a manager. For example, you may wish to write a statement about the importance of individuals in the work place, what you believe about employee motivation, how groups of employees should be managed, or how a manager should best approach a leadership role. When you have completed your philosophy statements, share them with a small group of your classmates. Discuss your philosophies in the group and contrast them with those of other group members.

Questions that might guide your group discussions include:

1. How do your philosophies differ from one another?
2. Does your choice of subjects on which to write statements imply anything about your own philosophy?

Hold on to your philosophy statements throughout the semester. It will be interesting for you to compare your perceptions today with those you develop as you study each chapter in this book. (You may write as many separate philosophy statements as you wish.)

CHAPTER 2

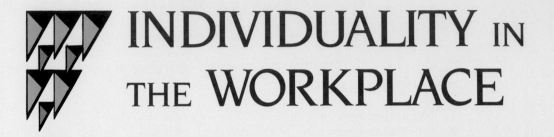

INDIVIDUALITY IN THE WORKPLACE

LEARNING OBJECTIVES

1. To understand the importance of individuality in the workplace.
2. To understand the influence of values, attitudes, and beliefs on organizational activity.
3. To recognize the nature of individuality and how it is related to behavior.
4. To examine how individuals change during their working years and the implications of those changes for organizational behavior.

CHAPTER OUTLINE

Understanding Our Individuality
    Personality
    Physical and Mental Abilities
    Values, Attitudes, and Beliefs
    Traits and Psychological Characteristics
    Personality in Perspective

Life Changes and the Meaning of Work
    Does Personality Change Over Time?
    Levinson's Theory of Adult Development
    Additional Considerations Concerning Adult Development

Individuality in the Workplace: Conclusion

Questions for Review and Discussion

References

Cases: 2.1 Trump
        2.2 Growing Pains

Exercises: 2.1 F.I.R.O.—B Exercise
           2.2 Determining Your Values

KEY TERMS

Individuality

Personality

Trait theories

Self theories

Values

Value system

Attitudes

Job satisfaction

Beliefs

External locus of control

Internal locus of control

Authoritarianism

Risk-taking propensity

Cognitive complexity

Developmental stages

Levinson's theory of adult development

Getting into the adult world

Age thirty transition

Becoming one's own person

Mid-life transition

Michael Milken, the junk-bond king, stood up, lawyers on both sides. Behind him, in eerie silence, waited hundreds of onlookers who had squeezed their way into Room 110 of the Manhattan federal courthouse. Outside, it was a beautiful April morning, perfect for playing hooky. Then, U.S. District Court Judge Kimba M. Wood looked down from the bench and started asking questions. "Is your mind clear today?" she asked. "Yes," replied Milken.

Moments later, the most powerful financier since J.P. Morgan was sobbing about how "extremely painful" his ordeal had been for family and friends, some of whom had traveled from far parts of the country to join him in court. No mention of the clients or anonymous investors he had victimized. Judge Wood pressed ahead: "Mr. Milken, how do you plead to the charges set forth?" Voice cracking, the defendant replied: "Guilty, your honor."[1]

Up until now, taking charge and wielding influence had almost been a way of life for Mike Milken. At Birmingham High School in Van Nuys, a prosperous Los Angeles suburb, he had dominated several of the organizations he had joined. He had been the head cheerleader in 1964 and king of the senior prom. As a business major at the University of California at Berkeley, Milken had been elected head of his pledge group and then, in his senior year, president of his fraternity. Jeff Unickel, Milken's fraternity brother at Berkeley and close personal friend, observed that Milken "was as driven to succeed as anybody."[2] Virtually a straight-A student, Milken had been elected to Phi Beta Kappa.

After graduating from Berkeley in 1968, Milken had married Lori Hackel, his girlfriend since high school. He had then headed east to Pennsylvania's Wharton School for an M.B.A. He had attended school part-time while working in Philadelphia at Drexel Firestone, one of the forerunners of Drexel, Burnham, Lambert. It was while working at Drexel that he had begun in earnest his rise to a position of prominence and power in the financial world.

During the 1980s, Mike Milken had used his boundless energy, ambition, intelligence, and creativity to become the ultimate charismatic salesman of junk bonds. He had transformed a mediocre investment bank into a Wall Street giant and helped to create a market for the bonds of poorly performing companies that eventually surpassed $200 billion in size. From his Beverly Hills office, Milken had found funding for a new class of entrepreneurs and financial engineers, spurring a wave of takeovers that restructured corporate America.

Mike Milken now stood pleading guilty to charges of manipulating securities markets, evading net capital rules, and cheating the government of taxes. His punishment included payment of over $200 million in fines, payment of an additional $400 million to settle a Securities and Exchange Commission civil suit, and the possibility of serving up to twenty-eight years in prison.

What had driven Milken and brought him to this point? Was it ambition, greed, ego, a desire for power, or some combination of these factors that had contributed to his downfall? Are there characteristics or attributes unique to Mike Milken that account for his behavior?

UNDERSTANDING OUR INDIVIDUALITY

In this chapter, we will explore the nature of **individuality.** We will discuss the factors that influence individuality and how the unique characteristics of each person contribute to organizational behavior. We will begin by examining the concept of personality, what it is, how it is influenced, and how it relates to actual behavior. Next, we will look at individuality in terms of physical and mental abilities, of values, attitudes, and beliefs, and of other traits and characteristics that contribute to individual differences. Finally, we will consider the life changes experienced by adults and how those changes affect personal and work-related behavior.

Personality

The term most often used to describe individuals and explain the source of their behaviors is **personality.** Unfortunately, it is also a term that is often misused. Let us look more closely at what this term actually means. Personality is a *distinctive set of characteristics that tend to remain the same across similar situations and are relatively stable over time.* The concept of personality is characterized by three key themes: uniqueness, situational consistency, and stability.

Uniqueness

Unique combinations of characteristics result in variations in thought and behavior that differentiate one person from another. Difficulties inherent in trying to understand uniqueness have led to an emphasis on measurable characteristics such as intelligence, authoritarianism, and sociability. Questionnaires and other instruments developed and validated by psychologists have been used by managers in an attempt to measure personality and the information obtained is sometimes employed for purposes of recruitment, selection, and placement. (The use of such tests should be supervised by persons trained in their administration and evaluation.)

In some cases, a second party (e.g., a supervisor or co-worker) may be asked to complete an evaluation instrument that includes an assessment of an individual's personality. Serious questions have been raised concerning both the validity and reliability of such observational techniques, however. Attempts to summarize many individual characteristics into a single measure of personality can also be misleading.

For example, a job reference form used by a leading computer company requested that the evaluator rate an applicant's personality on a scale of one to ten, with one being "very undesirable" and ten being "very desirable." In this case, the word *personality* was used inappropriately because it reflected the evaluator's subjective assessment of the individual and did not focus on measurable characteristics.

Situational consistency

There has been much debate concerning the consistency or variability of individual characteristics in differing situations. Some psychologists believe that personality characteristics carry over in a variety of situations. For example, we may assume that a woman who is assertive on the job or in a political caucus will be equally assertive in a church board meeting, although the manner in which she asserts herself in the latter case may be somewhat different. Similarly, a young man who is shy in the classroom is also likely to be shy at the class party. On the surface, then, it may appear that personality characteristics are consistent across all situations.

An alternative explanation, however, suggests that individual characteristics will be similar in different situations only if (1) the situations are similar, or (2) the characteristics have produced similar outcomes in these situations in the past.[3] In the example above, the woman is likely to be assertive in both situations to the extent that the situations are similar and she has previously achieved positive outcomes in both situations after being assertive.

Stability

Although personality characteristics may not be consistent across *all* situations, they do appear to be relatively stable over time.[4] We can view an individual's personality as being similar to a mountain. The mountain is made up of certain elements and minerals; its geology is stable and unchanging. The face of the mountain may take on a different appearance due to weather or other disruptions; however the fundamental elements themselves remain unchanged. The underlying characteristics of our personalities are also relatively enduring. Preferences for foods, clothing, and companions may change from day to day (surface features), but our deeply rooted characteristics remain the same. For example, the traits of perseverance and desire to succeed possessed by Mike Milken (see opening vignette), appeared to remain relatively stable from his adolescence through his later work life. Some experts believe that we do change over time, and their ideas will be examined later in this chapter. For now, however, we will accept the premise that personality is relatively stable and unlikely to undergo significant variation over time.

JAMES MORGAN, APPLIED MATERIALS, INC.

James Morgan recalls that the first time he "took charge" was when he was thirteen years old and supervising field hands who picked vegetables for the family cannery. By the age of sixteen, he had become a foreman in the cannery and wielded power over 350 workers. According to Morgan, that is when he first knew that "I wanted to run something." Today, he is CEO of a $500 million semiconductor-equipment company in Santa Clara, California. Morgan was given an opportunity to head up the family cannery at the age of twenty-one, but concluded that his future was with something much bigger, and his shepherding of industry-leader Applied seems to confirm his early suspicions.

James Morgan is blessed with more than an ample amount of self confidence. That and his drive to achieve goals and make things happen have contributed much to his success. Whether supervising farm workers at thirteen, running two divisions of his Army company while fulfilling a college ROTC commitment, or competing head to head with the Japanese on the Japanese mainland, he has always coupled desire and commitment with the need to make big things happen. What is it about men and women like James Morgan that causes them to behave in the way they do? Are such characteristics inborn or do they develop throughout one's life? Whatever the answer, James Morgan appears to those who have known him throughout his life to have changed little in his fifty-three years.[5]

Influences on personality

Personality characteristics tend to be relatively stable over time. Knowing the factors that influence the origin and development of such characteristics can therefore enable us to understand human behavior more completely.

Personality is the result of a complex interaction of genetic and environmental factors. A classic treatise on the nature of personality concluded that every person is in certain respects like (1) all other persons; (2) some other persons; and (3) no other person.[6] In other words, each person has some attributes in common with all other human beings, some attributes similar to the characteristics of select groups of people, and other qualities that are unique to him or her alone. The logic of these observations hinges on factors that influence personality development.

Let us examine each of the three major influences on personality development. First, we share certain characteristics with all other human beings as a result of our common biological makeup. In addition, certain physical traits affect the way that we adapt to our environment. For example, human beings respond in similar ways when they encounter stress.[7] Each person experiences a series of stages (alarm, adaptation, and exhaustion), also known as the general adaptation syndrome or GAS, during which our bodies undergo either neural or chemical changes depending on the nature of the stressor. There are significant variations in the degree of response and in the after-affects among individuals; however, the basic pattern is the same for all people.

A second important factor in personality development is culture and the groups and institutions through which that culture is transmitted. Some of what characterizes us as individuals is learned from those around us. Our families, friends, and associates are important reference groups that influence our distinctive personality characteristics. These social units share certain pervasive values, beliefs, and attitudes, many of which are adopted by us over time. Social institutions such as churches and schools also affect how we think and act. These groups and organizations all act as conduits for the more encompassing culture in which we live. Norms (accepted ways of behaving) and values related to work and interpersonal relationships can become deeply ingrained in our culture and exert a strong influence on individuality.

Sociability, the inclination to associate with others, for example, is a characteristic that is influenced by culture. Walk down a busy street in Manhattan and you

EXHIBIT 2.I   THREE INFLUENCES ON PERSONALITY

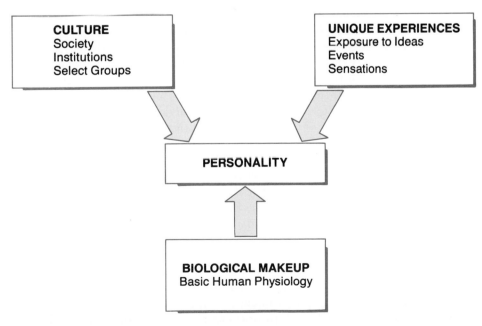

will find it difficult to catch the eye of a passerby let alone to exchange greetings. However, a stroll down the street of a small midwestern community will produce a very different pattern of social interaction where eye contact and verbal greetings between strangers are commonplace.

Recent emphasis on the internationalization of business has focused new interest on culture-related personality characteristics. This is especially true for transactions involving representatives from Pacific Basin countries. The primary source of cultural influence on most of the United States and Canada has traditionally been Europe. Now that we are heavily involved in joint undertakings and other forms of trade with countries such as Japan, Korea, and Taiwan, we are experiencing significantly different ways of doing business and interacting. The International Dimensions box on page 37 illustrates differences between individuals in two different cultures.

The third influence on personality, unique experiences, adds individuality. From birth until death, every individual experiences events and sensations which, due to his or her unique physical and psychological makeup, are unlike those experienced by anyone else. Furthermore, we do not simply experience life events in a vacuum. We are strongly influenced by approval or disapproval from others that accompany those events. A small child who "takes charge" of his playmates during a game may be scolded for being too "bossy" ("Don't always try to be the big shot!") or rewarded for showing leadership ("I'm glad you showed everyone what to do; that was good"). If a consistent pattern of behavior and reinforcement (reward or punishment) is established, certain personality characteristics may develop.

Some experts believe that differences in personality can be explained primarily, if not completely, by how individuals acquire their behavior patterns. These learning theorists (or behaviorists) tend to view personality as consisting only of observable behaviors. In Chapter 4, we will look more closely at learning theory and its implications for organizational behavior. For now, however, we will view experience as an important factor that differentiates individuals from one another and supports the conclusion that every person "is like no other person."

The relationship of personality to behavior

Among the most fundamental concepts in the study of human behavior is the belief that behavior is a function of both the personality and the environment.[8] However, theories of personality tend to focus on the individual as the primary source of behavior. To many, the individual represents the unknown in the behavior equation. Although some authorities (behaviorists) are concerned with environmental influences on behavior, most personality theories attribute much of what we see as overt behavior to personality factors existing within an individual.

Sigmund Freud, the father of **psychoanalytic theory,** for example, explained behavior as the result of the subconscious interplay of the Id (unrestrained drive), Ego (rational mediator), and Superego (conscience). The Id was viewed as the basic force driving behavior, but it was also seen as completely submerged in the human unconscious.[9] In fact, most experts agree that a large part of individual personality lies below our level of consciousness (see Exhibit 2.2). Recognition of the importance of the unconscious is perhaps Freud's major contribution to our understanding of personality and human behavior.

Trait theories of personality also look beneath the surface for explanations of the relationship between personality and behavior. Two prominent psychologists, Gordon Allport and R.B. Cattell, for example, suggested that individual traits (e.g., extroversion, agreeableness, conscientiousness, and emotional stability) were the source of behavior.[10] Although trait theories provide a convenient vehicle for describ-

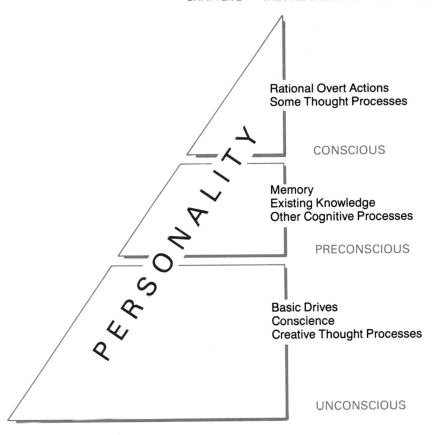

Rational Overt Actions
Some Thought Processes

CONSCIOUS

Memory
Existing Knowledge
Other Cognitive Processes

PRECONSCIOUS

Basic Drives
Conscience
Creative Thought Processes

UNCONSCIOUS

EXHIBIT 2.2   A VIEW OF THE PERSONALITY

ing certain characteristics (and certain types of behaviors), they are less useful in explaining how or why those behaviors occur.

Finally, theories of personality known as **self theories,** which have received attention from managers, also attempt to explain personality-related behavior.[11] Self theories view personality in terms of its "gestalt" (or integrated whole). In essence, personality is seen as the relationship of the person (or *self*) to the external world. The nature of this concept of self is determined by the person's perceived relationship to others and various aspects of the environment. According to self theory, then, the self's perceptions of the environment determine behavior. How one sees and interprets events affects how one behaves in response to them. Individual perceptions, experiences, and desired outcomes provide unique explanations for every person's behaviors. Exhibit 2.3 reflects three views of the personality-behavior relationship.

This brief overview of these three personality theories is intended to help you understand the relationship between personality and behavior. Of course, other theories exist, and it is impossible to say which model explains the relationship most accurately. However, we can conclude that much of what is referred to as personality is found within the individual and that its relationship to behavior is a function of each person's ongoing development.

Using the concept of personality

Personality is a useful concept because it helps us to attach meaning to the total person and provides us with a frame of reference that can be used to understand and predict individual behavior. If the validity of such predictions can be assumed, organizations can attempt to attract employees who fit their own "personality pro-

Ego-States   **Traits**   **Behaviors**   **Self-Concept**

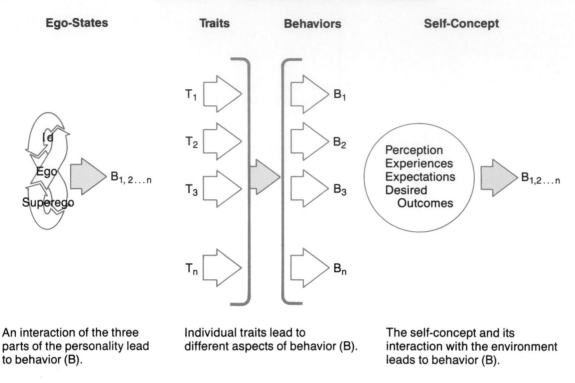

An interaction of the three parts of the personality lead to behavior (B).	Individual traits lead to different aspects of behavior (B).	The self-concept and its interaction with the environment leads to behavior (B).

EXHIBIT 2.3   THREE VIEWS OF THE PERSONALITY-BEHAVIOR RELATIONSHIP

files." Apple Computer CEO John Skulley, for example, observed that PepsiCo (his former employer) attracted ambitious achievers who shared a common value, "winning." Skulley found that Apple Computer, on the other hand, attracted people looking for personal growth and wanting to make an important contribution to society.[12]

HELEN SOLOMONS

When recruiting managers, Helen Solomons, general manager for human resources at Systems & Computer Technology Corporation, is particularly interested in how candidates talk about managing people. She believes that managers need to use a range of behaviors "because the people being managed are different, and even the same individual can be different at different times." Solomons has also found that her knowledge of personality and individual differences has been valuable in designing compensation and benefit plans, management training programs, and performance systems, and in resolving specific human resource issues with executives and other managers. Solomons concludes:

> One of the most important contributions I make to the organization in which I work is to help managers bridge the gap between what we all agree to be true—"people are different"—and using this knowledge in a world in which there is work to be done, goals to be reached, deadlines to be met, and profits to be made.[13]

INTERNATIONAL DIMENSION
Make Haste Slowly

"Haste" is defined by Webster's as "to move or act swiftly." It comes as a surprise to many Western businesspeople that "fast talk" and hasty action may cause their Japanese counterparts to hesitate or even withdraw from negotiations or other business activities. The reason lies in the Japanese belief that those who have too much to say or say it too quickly are probably not listening very closely to those with whom they are talking. In addition, the Japanese are likely to question how trustworthy such people are. Characteristics such as dominance, aggressiveness, and individualism may be valued highly in the American business community, but they are not necessarily valued throughout the rest of the world. Such cultural differences clearly exist between Japan and the United States. American managers in Japan may therefore do well to "make haste slowly!"

Questions

Should non-Japanese businesspeople adjust their "styles" or simply be themselves when conducting business with the Japanese?

What cultural differences might influence our dealings with persons from nations other than Japan?

SOURCE: H. Eason, "In Japan, Make Haste Slowly," *Nation's Business*, May 1986, 48.

CYPRESS

The case of John Sculley and Steve Jobs of Apple Computer is widely known in business circles; differences in individual characteristics ultimately led to a breakup of their business relationship. However, not all "personality differences" necessarily lead to a split between parties. Thurman Rodgers, CEO, and Lowell Turriff, vice-president of marketing and sales, have worked together to build and operate the thriving Cypress Semiconductor Corporation of San Jose, California, despite considerable individual differences. Rodgers is an aggressive, high-fashion type and a "no punches barred" executive. Turriff, on the other hand, is described by colleagues as formal and mannerly in an almost old-world way. Unlike Rodgers, who is outspoken and impatient, Turriff goes about his business in a calm and orderly manner. One Cypress executive refers to the two men as the classic "left-brain, right-brain separation."

In fact, Rodgers chose Turriff because he believed his diplomatic style would counterbalance his own flamboyance. To be sure, Rodgers and Turriff have had their differences. But both men believe that bringing their two styles together has nurtured creativity and cultivated new opportunities for Cypress.[14]

Personality raises questions important to the long-term success of an organization. For example, might individuals with certain characteristics be more effective in one type of job than another? Are certain jobs more satisfying to some workers than to others? Do adults experience personality changes, and how might these changes be related to organizational behavior? We will address these and other questions throughout the remainder of this chapter.

Physical and Mental Abilities

People are generally hired to perform certain physical and mental tasks in organizations. It is therefore natural that we observe and evaluate physical and mental abilities as they relate to the workplace. In this section, we will examine both physical and mental abilities and how they influence individuality.

Physical ability

Physical ability refers to a person's capacity to perform those tasks that normally require motor skills. We are most likely to identify differences in individuals by observing the things that they do. You may have noticed, for example, that some individuals speak more clearly or write more legibly than others. You may have observed that a particular athlete is stronger, faster, or more agile than others with whom he or she competes. These characteristics (speech clarity, strength, speed, etc.) are examples of physical abilities.

Physical abilities tend to play a more important role in "unskilled" jobs, or those that rely primarily on the performance of simple tasks. These types of jobs are characterized by a high degree of standardization, and such job positions can therefore be filled satisfactorily by matching employee skills and capabilities to particular job requirements. Physical abilities are relatively easy to measure. Examples of physical abilities that may influence job selection (and performance) are strength, quickness, dexterity, hand-eye coordination, and stamina.

Mental ability

Mental ability refers to a person's capacity to decipher, understand, and reason. Some individuals seem to be able to sort out information, work through problems, or comprehend instructions better than others and are credited with above-average mental ability. Jobs requiring higher levels of mental ability are typically found toward the top of an organization (executive and other upper-level management positions) or in certain positions requiring higher levels of education (e.g., engineering, systems analysis, nursing, and technical advising positions). Of course, merely having such a job is no guarantee that mental skills will be used.

Rapid changes in technology have increased the need for higher levels of mental ability throughout the organization. It is estimated that by the year 2000, fewer than one in four new employees will have the reading, writing, and mathematics skills required for available jobs and only 5 percent will have educations permitting them to function at management or professional levels.[15] In the immediate future, therefore, mental abilities will play an even more important role in organizational staffing than they already do today.

This phenomenon presents two major problems for employers. First, they must locate persons who have necessary mental abilities or must provide training programs that will increase mental-skills levels. Traditionally, employers have not provided such programs but have instead concentrated on training programs designed to improve physical skills. The second problem is even more fundamental. Instruments used to assess mental ability and other individual characteristics must be valid and reliable, yet many such tests have been found to discriminate against certain racial and ethnic groups.[16] Any use of these tests therefore raises important legal and ethical issues. The Ethical Dilemma posed on page 39 outlines one such problem faced by managers today.

ETHICAL DILEMMA
Personality Tests
Are Back

An increasing number of businesses and other organizations are returning to the once-shunned practice of using personality and other psychological tests to hire and place employees. The use of one instrument, the Myers-Briggs Type Indicator (MBTI), which identifies sixteen "personality types," doubled in less than three years. Companies such as Apple, AT&T, Exxon, General Electric, and 3M use the tests primarily as a management development tool. Others, like Compass Computer and Knight-Ridder's *Charlotte Observer*, have used test results to address morale problems and support more effective team building.

Still, not everyone is sold on the use of personality tests or the theories on which they are based. Legal and ethical questions about validity, job relevance, and fairness persist, and experts warn that those who rely on such instruments to make important personnel decisions should be sure that they are administered and evaluated carefully and fairly. Even those who use the tests are sometimes left wondering. One Compass Computer executive, referring to the company's use of the MBTI, concluded, "You can't measure the results, and the consequences are not predictable."

Questions
What ethical dilemmas are raised by the use of personality and other psychological tests in organizations?

Do these types of tests pose risks for (a) the organization, and (b) the individuals who take them?

What guidelines do you believe should be set forth for managers who intend to use such tests?

SOURCE: G. S. Taylor and T. W. Zimmerer, "Personality Tests for Potential Employees: More Harm than Good," *Personnel Journal*, January 1988, 60–64, T. Moore and W. Woods, "Personality Tests Are Back," *Fortune*, 30 March 1987 74–82; J. L. Kovach, "Psychological Testing Is Fair... True or False?" *Industry Week*, 20 January 1986, 44–47.

Values, Attitudes, and Beliefs

Individuality is influenced by a complex interaction of motives, values, attitudes, beliefs, traits, and abilities. This section specifically examines values, attitudes, and beliefs. Although they are often used interchangeably, important distinctions exist among all three concepts. Just as the bones of your skeleton determine the basic size and shape of your physical body, these internal factors constitute the basic psychological framework or skeleton of your personality.

Values

A **value** is an internalized standard of evaluation that denotes some desirable state.[17] Understanding values is important to our study of human behavior in organizations for several reasons. First, values exert a strong influence on cognitive processes and behavior; they influence *what* we perceive and *how* we act. Second, re-examination of established work values in society constitutes an important cornerstone of the managerial revolution currently taking place in countries throughout the world.

Values:

1. provide standards of competence and morality;
2. transcend specific objects, situations, or persons;
3. are relatively permanent and resistant to change; and
4. are central to that core of a person that we identify as the "self."[18]

Extensive research conducted over the last two decades has identified two basic types of values: (1) terminal, and (2) instrumental.[19] (See Exhibit 2.4.) A **terminal**

EXHIBIT 2.4   ROKEACH'S TERMINAL AND INSTRUMENTAL VALUES

TERMINAL VALUES	INSTRUMENTAL VALUES
A COMFORTABLE LIFE a prosperous life	AMBITIOUS hard-working, aspiring
AN EXCITING LIFE a stimluating, active life	BROADMINDED open-minded
A SENSE OF ACCOMPLISHMENT lasting contribution	CAPABLE competent, effective
A WORLD AT PEACE free of war and conflicts	CHEERFUL lighthearted, joyful
A WORLD OF BEAUTY beauty of nature and the arts	CLEAN neat, tidy
EQUALITY brotherhood, equal opportunity for all	COURAGEOUS standing up for your beliefs
FAMILY SECURITY taking care of loved ones	FORGIVING willing to pardon others
FREEDOM independence, free choice	HELPFUL working for the welfare of others
HAPPINESS contentedness	HONEST sincere, truthful
INNER HARMONY freedom from inner conflict	IMAGINATIVE daring, creative
MATURE LOVE sexual and spiritual intimacy	INDEPENDENT self-reliant, self-sufficient
NATIONAL SECURITY protection from attack	INTELLECTUAL intelligent, reflective
PLEASURE an enjoyable, leisurely life	LOGICAL consistent, rational
SALVATION saved, eternal life	LOVING affectionate, tender
SELF-RESPECT self-esteem	OBEDIENT dutiful, respectful
SOCIAL RECOGNITION respect, admiration	POLITE courteous, well-mannered
TRUE FRIENDSHIP close companionship	RESPONSIBLE dependable, reliable
WISDOM a mature understanding of life	SELF-CONTROLLED restrained, self-disciplined

value is an ultimate goal in life and represents a desired status or outcome. An **instrumental value,** on the other hand, is a "tool" or means for achieving a terminal value. For example, a person may desire and strive to achieve *happiness* (a terminal value) by being *ambitious, independent,* and *responsible* (instrumental values). An individual's terminal and instrumental values combine to create an enduring cluster of values known as a **value system.** Our values and value systems, then, are important determinants of "who" and "what" we are.

Values are learned and acquired primarily through experiences involving people and institutions. Parents, for example, usually have a substantial influence on their children's values. A parent's reaction to everyday events demonstrates what is good or bad, acceptable or unacceptable, and important or unimportant. Values are also taught and reinforced in schools, churches, and social groups. As we grow and develop, each of these sources of influence contributes to our definition of what is important in life.

Values are held individually, although considerable attention has been given in recent years to patterns of values that may dominate different cultures. A major study conducted by researchers at the Institute for Research on Intercultural Cooperation in The Netherlands explored work-related values in countries throughout the world. The study, using the Values Survey Module (VSM), focused on four values: power distance, individualism versus collectivism, masculinity versus femininity, and uncertainty avoidance.[20] (These four values are explained further in Exhibit 2.5.) The survey of over 116,000 managers found distinctly different value patterns throughout

EXHIBIT 2.5　HOFSTEDE'S WORK-RELATED VALUES

	DEFINITON	MANAGEMENT IMPLICATIONS
Power Distance (PDI)	The extent to which a less powerful person accepts inequality and considers it to be normal.	A low-PDI person is likely to favor shared decision making and less likely to differentiate among others on the basis of status, titles, etc.
Individualism (IDV)	The extent to which a person looks after his/her own interests (as opposed to Collectivism, the extent to which a person assumes that individuals belong to close in-groups and reciprocally gives and expects loyalty from them.)	A high-IDV person is likely to favor merit pay systems and other personnel actions that recognize individual achievement; a low-IDV person tends to value seniority, internal promotion, and similar personnel actions that reward loyalty.
Masculinity (MI)	The extent to which social roles are defined by biological sex differences. Men are expected to be assertive and competitive; women are expected to be concerned with quality of life and relationships.	A high-MI person tends to be less concerned with material outcomes and sees male/female roles as distinctly separate; a low-MI person may pursue either material or nonmaterial outcomes but generally accepts male values as dominant.
Uncertainty Avoidance (UAI)	The extent to which one is made nervous by unstructured, unclear, or unpredictable situations and in turn tries to avoid them.	A high-UAI person is likely to be aggressive, emotional, and more task oriented than a low-UAI person; he or she also tends to avoid high risk situations.

the world. Other studies using the VSM and List of Values (LOV) have examined value patterns across the United States and found different patterns to exist in different geographic regions.[21]

Although values are typically used to predict individual behavior, knowing national or other subcultural value patterns related to ethnic origin, language, etc., may also help us to better understand behavior in certain countries or geopolitical areas. This knowledge can in turn enable us to understand the possible strengths and weaknesses of various management practices when they are used in different cultural settings.

Attitudes

An **attitude** is a predisposition to act toward a specific object or person in a particular way. Attitudes and values are related and reciprocally influence each other, but we should not let their similarity obscure the important distinctions between the two concepts. Attitudes are learned and evaluative in nature, but differ from values in that they are linked to specific referents. A person can potentially have as many attitudes as there are objects or persons in his or her environment. For example, you have attitudes about the university or college you attend, the classes in which you are enrolled, and the community where you live. Values transcend particular situations or objects and are more resistant to change than attitudes. Both attitudes and values are inferred from observed behavior; we cannot see a person's values or attitudes, although we often assume that the actions and behaviors that we encounter are the consequences of another's values or attitudes.

An attitude has three major components: (1) affective, (2) cognitive, and (3) behavioral intention.[22] The **affective** part of an attitude includes feelings of like or dislike toward a person or object. The **cognitive** component is made up of information and beliefs an individual has about a particular person or object. The **behavioral intention** aspect of an attitude consists of intent or desire to behave toward a person or object in a particular way. An attitude is therefore the sum of many experiences with and judgments about a specific person or object.

The following example illustrates the three components of an attitude. Eric and Jeff were discussing the department to which they both had recently been assigned. "I sure don't look forward to working over there (affective)," remarked Eric. "Those jobs don't seem to have any relevance to what we're trying to accomplish around here, and I believe the division manager is really autocratic (cognitive). I'd transfer in a minute if I could find an opening somewhere else (behavioral)."

Jeff responded, "I agree that not many of those people seem to get promoted, but the work they do over there is pretty interesting (cognitive). I talked with him yesterday and he had some useful ideas about how we can get some of these concepts directly to the customer. He's new in the job and I think he'll get better in time (cognitive). I'm going to give it a try and see what happens (behavioral)."

Eric's attitude can be described as negative. He generally dislikes the assignment, and specifically believes (1) the jobs aren't relevant, and (2) the division manager is a jerk. He seems inclined to transfer out of the work area at the earliest opportunity. Jeff's attitude, although not overly positive, is considerably less negative than Eric's. He thinks he might enjoy the work more than Eric does, and believes the boss will improve in time. Jeff appears ready to stick with the new assignment. Eric's and Jeff's attitudes about the assignment result from complex interactions of beliefs, affective responses, and behavioral intentions and reflect a readiness or predisposition to act toward the new work assignment.

A specific attitude that has received a great deal of attention from managers, scholars, and researchers is **job satisfaction.** In fact, job satisfaction is currently one of the most widely studied subjects in the field of organizational behavior. Job satisfaction is "a pleasurable or positive emotional state resulting from the appraisal of one's job or job experience."[23] In other words, job satisfaction basically refers to how much employees like their jobs. Although job satisfaction and employee morale are often used interchangeably, an important distinction exists between the two concepts. Job satisfaction refers to the attitudes of a single individual towards her job situation, while morale is used to describe the overall feeling of a work group, department, or organization.

From an individual's perspective, job satisfaction is an important outcome of job behavior. It is a significant component of the overall quality of work life that an employee experiences and influences individual motivation, behavior, and other attitudes and beliefs. From an organizational perspective, job satisfaction is of interest because it affects work outcomes such as absenteeism, turnover, grievances, accident rates, physical and mental health, training readiness, and performance.

Overall job satisfaction is a function of several related attitudes. The following five dimensions are important characteristics of jobs about which people have affective responses:

▶ *Work itself.* The extent to which tasks performed by employees are interesting and provide opportunities for learning and for accepting responsibility.
▶ *Pay.* The amount of pay received, the perceived equity of the pay, and the method of payment.
▶ *Promotional opportunities.* The availability of realistic opportunities for advancement.
▶ *Supervision.* The technical and managerial abilities of supervisors, and the extent to which supervisors demonstrate consideration for and interest in employees.
▶ *Co-workers.* The extent to which co-workers are friendly, technically competent, and supportive.

Additional facets of job satisfaction have been identified (e.g., satisfaction with company policies and fringe benefits), but the five described above are used most often in examining work-related attitudes.

Understanding attitudes in general and job satisfaction in particular is important to the extent that attitudes are related to subsequent behavior and job-related outcomes. Research evidence has consistently shown that job satisfaction is related to employee turnover.[24] Although other factors obviously affect turnover, satisfaction is a clear, consistent, yet moderate influence. Research results also suggest a moderate inverse relationship between satisfaction and employee absenteeism.[25]

Job satisfaction is also related to physical and mental health. One study has shown a fairly strong relationship between the incidence of death from heart disease and job dissatisfaction caused by stress, conflict, and boredom.[26] In a longitudinal study of life expectancy, analysis of numerous attitudinal and physiological variables (e.g., physical condition and tobacco use) revealed that the single best predictor of longevity was work satisfaction. Those who felt their work was meaningful and useful outlived their less satisfied co-workers.[27] Furthermore, a study of blue-collar workers revealed consistent relationships between job satisfaction and mental health. In this study, the most important job attributes for good mental health were challenging work and opportunities to use abilities and skills.[28]

One of the most controversial consequences of job satisfaction is its relationship to job performance. The results of the Hawthorne studies led many managers to believe that satisfaction caused performance; in other words, satisfied workers were more productive workers. Research evidence, however, did not support this belief.

EXHIBIT 2.6   RELATIONSHIP BETWEEN SATISFACTION AND PERFORMANCE AS MODERATED BY REWARDS

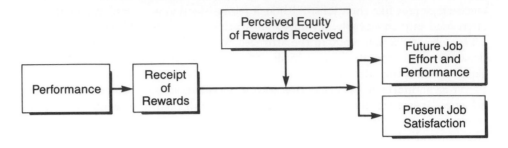

During the 1960s, it was argued that performance caused satisfaction. Further empirical research, however, suggested that neither satisfaction caused performance nor performance caused satisfaction.[29] Rather than causing each other, satisfaction and performance are both caused by the rewards employees receive and the methods used to administer those rewards. Exhibit 2.6 outlines the relationship between satisfaction and performance as it is moderated by rewards.

An employee's performance leads to the receipt of rewards such as pay, benefits, recognition, opportunities for advancement, and feelings of personal accomplishment. The individual is satisfied to the extent that he perceives these rewards to be equitable (fair when compared to effort expended and rewards received by other employees). The receipt of equitable rewards also tends to create strong performance-reward relationships in the mind of the employee, leading to future effort and performance. Performance, therefore, is *not* a consequence of satisfaction; the two variables by themselves have little or no relationship to each other. It is only when rewards and reward contingencies are considered with performance and satisfaction that a substantial relationship emerges.

Job satisfaction can lead to a variety of positive and negative consequences, from both individual and organizational perspectives. It influences how employees feel about themselves, their work, and their organizations and can significantly affect their contributions to goal attainment in the work environment.

Beliefs

A **belief** is an idea held to be true about an object or a person; in other words, a belief is an accepted piece of information. Beliefs, like attitudes, have specific referents. However, whereas a single attitude is linked to a particular object or person, an individual usually has many beliefs about a single referent. For example, do you *believe* that imported cars are better built than cars made in the United States? Do you believe an imported car is more reliable? Do you believe an imported car is easier to maintain? Do you believe an imported car gets better gas mileage? A person can have as many beliefs about a referent object as there are observable characteristics. In contrast, a person is likely to have a single attitude about an object. You are either positively or negatively predisposed to foreign automobiles.

Beliefs are acquired through personal experience with or observation of a referent object, or through inferences based on information from secondary sources. You may believe, for example, that foreign cars are better built because you own one (personal experience) or because a friend has one and raves about the low maintenance cost (inference based on information from a secondary source). Such beliefs may or may not be based on facts or objective evidence. The important point is that beliefs are accepted as true and considered factual by the individual who possesses them.

Let us look more closely at the relationship between beliefs and attitudes. First, beliefs precede and influence attitudes. Second, an attitude includes the affective response toward an object or person. Finally, a behavioral intention is the result or outcome of an attitude.[30] Beliefs, then, constitute the cognitive component of an attitude toward an object and establish the basis for feelings of "like" and "dislike" ("I sure do like those imported cars!") and behavioral intent ("I'd really like to buy one").

The conceptual distinction between beliefs and attitudes has practical implications in organizational behavior. Beliefs are more susceptible to change than attitudes because they are based on experiences with, observations of, or information about a referent object. As our experiences, observations, and information about a referent change, our beliefs are also likely to change and to influence our attitude toward that referent.

Consider the question posed in the advertisement slogan, "Have you *driven* a Ford lately?" The question is essentially a challenge to *experience and observe* the "quality" of a new model car. The manufacturer hopes you will actually sit in, drive, and be impressed with the car, thereby providing an experiential basis for new or changed beliefs about the car itself. Such changed beliefs could then result in a more positive attitude (affective response) toward Ford products and a behavioral intent to buy. Beliefs, therefore, would act as the primary means or vehicle for influencing or altering a person's attitudes.

ANITA RODDICK: THE BODY SHOP

Anita Roddick believes that her values and beliefs can be carried into the workworld. Roddick is the founder and chief executive officer of The Body Shop International, a London-based cosmetics and beauty aids company. Today, The Body Shop has estimated pretax profits of $23 million on $141 million in sales. But sales volume and profits are not the only things that are important to Anita Roddick.

Roddick firmly believes that a company has an obligation to be socially active. She embraces numerous causes including saving the Amazon rain forest, preventing animal testing for commercial purposes, and protecting a Brazilian Indian tribe. Roddick carries her personal values to her customers as well as to her employees. Displays opposing social injustices and supporting natural products can be found throughout her stores. Employees are well-informed about causes that are important to the company as well as product lines. Socially relevant slogans can be found boldly displayed on company trucks, and she and fellow employees have been known to picket and protest publicly on behalf of selected causes.

Values, attitudes, and beliefs clearly influence the way we conduct our personal lives. Anita Roddick would like her values and those shared by her employees to influence the business and public lives of others as well.[31]

The changing world of work

In Chapter 1, "The Managerial Revolution," we suggested that important changes are taking place in values, attitudes, and beliefs in and around the workplace. There appears to be a discernible shift away from materialism and back toward such basics as individual dignity, self-reliance, and the importance of personal relationships both in and away from the workplace. These changes take various forms from an increasing number of community action groups at the local level to nonsmoking lobbies that have dramatically altered federal and state laws limiting smoking on airlines, in restaurants, and at work.[32] In business and government organizations, these changes are being reflected in the increased use of participative management, autonomous, self-managed work teams, and flexible work schedules. If you are to be an effective manager, you must remain sensitive to the values, attitudes, and beliefs of those with whom you work. Exhibit 2.7 presents one observer's view of the changes Americans are experiencing.

Traits and Psychological Characteristics

Some managers explain behavior patterns on the basis of perceived values, attitudes, and beliefs. Others may attempt to use more sophisticated psychoanalytic models or focus on particular individual traits or characteristics that distinguish one person from another. Researchers have identified a number of individual characteristics that are linked to various behavior patterns. In this section, we will examine four such characteristics, locus of control, authoritarianism, risk-taking propensity, and cognitive complexity, and briefly discuss how they influence specific behaviors.

Locus of control

Locus of control refers to an individual's perception of the location or source of influence over his behavior. A person who has an *internal* locus of control believes the control of one's behavior lies primarily within the self (i.e., is determined by self-initiative or personal action). Such a person is likely to believe that individual effort and competence are the major factors leading to organizational reward and will therefore be inclined to work harder toward that end.

An individual whose locus of control is *external* believes that outside forces such as fate, luck, or chance, are the principal determinants of behavior. An *external* tends to view the world as unpredictable and believes destiny is determined by circumstances beyond direct personal control.[33] A salesperson with an external locus of control, for example, might blame her sales manager for a low pay check even if she were working on a commission basis.

A person's locus of control may also determine the level of stress experienced on the job. One study found that increased structure (measured by job specificity) resulted in higher levels of stress for internals but was negatively related to stress for externals.[34]

EXHIBIT 2.7   THE HOPE FOR THE 1990S

"The frontier, as reality and symbol, is what has shaped the American way of doing things and the American sense of what's worth doing.... More money, more tokens of success—there will always be people for whom there are adequate goals, but those people are no longer setting the tone for all of us. There is a new sort of *more* at hand: more appreciation of good things beyond the marketplace, more insistence on fairness, more attention to purpose, more determination truly to choose a life, and not a lifestyle, for oneself.

Dare we suggest that these new forms of *more* comprise a species of frontier?"

SOURCE: Laurence Shames, *The Hunger for More: Searching for Values in an Age of Greed* (New York: Times Books, 1989).

Authoritarianism

Individuals high in **authoritarianism** are more inclined than others to believe that lines of power and status should be clearly delineated.[35] These persons create and maintain such differences by actively using titles and symbols of their position and by conforming to rules. They are less likely to employ participative techniques that would result in subordinates being treated as equals, although authoritarianism itself does not preclude the use of certain types of participative management. Subordinates high in authoritarianism show particular deference to their superiors and are willing to abide by established rules.

Risk-taking propensity

Risk-taking propensity is concerned with an individual's willingness to take risks. Some individuals feel comfortable taking risks; others do not. Researchers have found that persons with a high propensity to take risks also tend to make decisions more quickly than those whose risk-taking propensity is low.[36] Thus, performance might be positively affected by high risk-taking propensity in jobs requiring immediate decisions, like those of police officers, fire fighters, or floor traders on a stock or commodity exchange. Of course, risk-taking propensity is only one of many characteristics that might be considered when selecting individuals to fill important decision-making roles.

Cognitive complexity

Cognitive complexity is the capacity to acquire and sort through information. Cognitive complexity, therefore, can influence the *quality* of an individual's decisions. A person with a high level of cognitive complexity can discern a large number of discrete information inputs in the environment and understand the relationships among those inputs. Such an individual tends to use more information on which to base decisions than someone with low cognitive complexity. People with low cognitive complexity, on the other hand, tend to make decisions more rapidly and are apt to apply their solutions more broadly (in more situations).[37] Research also indicates that individuals high in cognitive complexity are likely to be innovative,[38] have good listening comprehension,[39] and be less apprehensive about communicating with others.[40]

Personality in Perspective

Characteristics that contribute to individual differences are important sources of information about the behaviors of those with whom we work. Assessing such characteristics, whether through instruments that measure them precisely or by observing and interacting with individuals, can provide important information on which to predict future behaviors. Selection, placement, and day-to-day managing all require us to predict the behaviors of others with a reasonable degree of accuracy, although over-reliance on perceptions or unsubstantiated observations may lead to ethical as well as legal complications. Let us look at the case of Eileen.

Eileen had been employed at the medical center as a public relations representative for six years. She enjoyed her work but felt she was ready for a change of pace. Last week she applied for an opening as a records manager in the treasurer's office. During an interview for the job she told the office manager that she found out about the job through her many friends in the office. She explained, "I really like everyone in the office, and when I heard about the opening, I knew it was the right place for me." When asked about her training for the job, Eileen responded, "I know I can do the work. I always can find a way to get a job done when I'm motivated."

Eileen's personnel records indicate that she is friendly and outgoing and likes to be innovative on the job. The office manager noted that she had once been reprimanded for initiating a new public relations program without first clearing it with her superior. The reprimand, written by her supervisor, read, "Although I have come to expect Eileen to act on her own without first asking my permission, this incident created a serious conflict between patients and the nursing staff. I believe, therefore, that this formal reprimand should be entered in her permanent file." When asked about the reprimand, Eileen responded, "I guess I may have been out of line, but I think if you know a better way to do something, then you should do it."

In recommending Eileen for the job, the office manager explained to the treasurer, "I think almost anyone with a little training can do the job if they'll just follow the rules. As for the reprimand, that was the only negative remark in the file."

It is impossible to predict with complete accuracy either Eileen's performance level or her job satisfaction in the new position. However, knowledge of her individual characteristics (her internal locus of control and low authoritarianism) provides information that might be used by the office manager to make the job placement decision. Keep in mind that individual behavior is extremely complex and casual observations of those around us, no matter how well-intentioned, may lead to erroneous conclusions. Despite our desire to make the "right" decisions based on the evidence at hand, we should recognize the limits of our training and knowledge when it comes to applying the theories and concepts thus far discussed.

Some individuals may appear to reveal their traits and characteristics more definitively than others. It might appear, for example, that billionaire real estate developer Donald Trump, who claims, "No one has done more . . . than me,"[41] or successful businesspeople like Ross Perot and Sam Walton are driven by a belief that they can accomplish whatever *they* set out to do (high locus of control). It is less clear, however, if they are capable of making complex decisions or if they simply employ others to make such decisions for them. Thus, while personal observations may significantly influence our assessment of individuals, it would be naive to assume that those observations are always accurate or complete.

LIFE CHANGES AND THE MEANING OF WORK

To this point, we have focused our discussion on the *relatively stable* factors that contribute to our individuality. Now, we will turn our attention to the *dynamic* nature of our individuality.

For many years, students of human behavior have explored the question of whether personality is firmly established in early childhood or continues to change throughout our adult lives. Some characteristics, such as expressiveness and introversion-extroversion, appear to remain constant throughout the span of one's life;[42] however, others, such as self-esteem, sense of self-control, and some values, may undergo important changes over time.[43]

Evidence exists to suggest that, "humans have a capacity for change across the entire life span."[44] We will now examine the nature of these changes and their significance to organizational behavior.

Does Personality Change Over Time?

Authorities generally agree that specific experiences and situations influence our personalities. A particularly positive or negative experience at a critical juncture in life can have a lasting impact on an individual. Some experts suggest that certain "stages" of development are more critical than others. Sigmund Freud, for example, believed that the ease or difficulty with which a child adjusted during certain psychosexual stages was largely responsible for his or her adult personality.

While other experts also emphasize the early stages of development, some have focused on stages that extend throughout adulthood. Erik Erikson, for example, concluded that psychosocial stages roughly equivalent to those theorized by Freud did exist. However, he believed that three additional stages, young adulthood, middle adulthood, and mature adulthood, also influenced the development of important personality characteristics. In particular, he hypothesized that characteristics such as intimacy and isolation, generativity (concern for others beyond one's immediate family) and self-absorption, and integrity and despair, all developed during the *adult* years.[45] Thus, as one leading psychologist observed, "as the adult lives out his existence, his behavior reflects (a) old elements of personality—derivatives of childhood and adolescence; and (b) new elements—new motives, additives, interests— that he acquires in the course of his adult years."[46] Exhibit 2.8 shows the relationship of the developmental stages set forth by Freud and Erikson.

The relevance of such observations to organizational behavior is clear. Changes in personality can occur during adulthood and, therefore, can affect job-related behaviors. Moreover, studies indicate that an individual's job may have a significant impact on his personality.[47] We can thus conclude that our personalities are *shaped* in our early years but continue to evolve as we age and encounter new life experiences.

Levinson's Theory of Adult Development

In recent years, a number of researchers have sought to understand and shed more light on questions surrounding adult development. Daniel Levinson, for instance, concentrated his studies on male development during early and middle adulthood.[48] His findings and subsequent theory of "individual life structure" have direct implications for the relationship of adult development (especially of career-oriented males and females) and organizational behavior.

EXHIBIT 2.8 A CHRONOLOGY OF DEVELOPMENTAL STAGES: FREUD VERSUS ERIKSON

FREUD'S STAGES	AGES	ERIKSON'S STAGES
Oral	0 to 1 year	Oral-Sensory
Anal	1 to 3 years	Muscular-Anal
Phallic	4 to 5 years	Locomotor-Genital
Latency	6 to 12 years	Latency
Genital	13 to 18 years	Puberty and Adolesence
	19 to 25 years	Young Adulthood
	26 to 40 years	Adulthood
	41 and beyond	Maturity

According to Levinson, an individual's life consists of four broad eras or "seasons," preadulthood, early adulthood, middle adulthood, and late adulthood. The three adult eras build on the foundation laid during the formative years of childhood and adolescence. Central to Levinson's theory is the concept of life structure. *Life structure* is the pattern of a person's life at a given point in time. It results from the interaction of three components:

1. the sociocultural environment;
2. one's participation in that environment through relationships and multiple roles; and
3. aspects of the self that are either lived out or inhibited within the structure.

EXHIBIT 2.9   DEVELOPMENTAL PERIODS FROM PREADULTHOOD THROUGH LATE ADULTHOOD

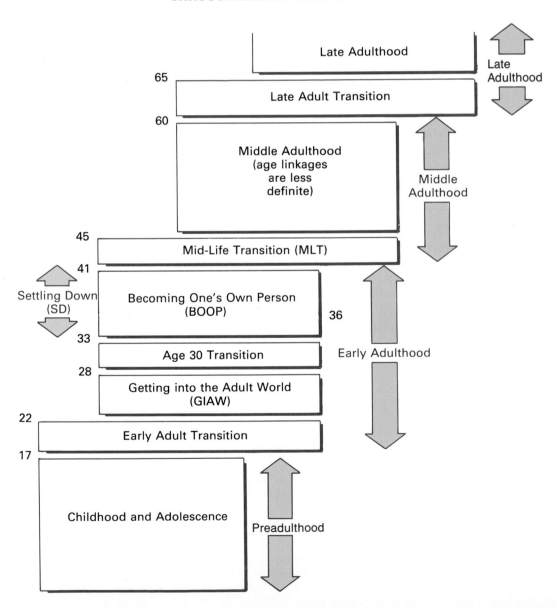

The life structure evolves through a series of intermittent *structure-building* and *structure-changing* (transition) periods. The four broad eras and more specific periods of adult development are shown in Exhibit 2.9.

Early adult transition

Preadulthood is followed by the first of three important adult transitions. During the **early adult transition,** a young person begins to grow out of adolescence and to encounter various aspects of early adulthood. From about age seventeen to twenty-two, the "young adult" is faced with greater financial and social independence and is apt to experience the joys and pains of both more independently than in the past.

Life transitions can be likened to a student who moves (physically and mentally) from one classroom to another. The relative order of the first setting is left and replaced by the turmoil and noise of the hallway between classes. The motivation, of course, is to reach the second classroom and settle into the new environment or structure. During the early adult transition, young people may find that they are not yet fully part of the adult world; yet, it becomes increasingly difficult to return to the relatively more protected world of the adolescent.

Getting into the adult world

The period known as **getting into the adult world (GIAW)** lasts from the early twenties through the late twenties. Critical events such as establishing an occupation, finding a mate, and raising a family are made by career-oriented men and women at this time. GIAW is also a period of exploration. The young adult more fully develops interpretations of roles, memberships, and long-term goals. The period is characterized by searching, making initial choices, and increasing commitments.

Age thirty transition

GIAW culminates with a self-reexamination known as the **age thirty transition.** Initial occupational choices and other decisions are reevaluated during this period. The individual faces a central question: "Should a deeper commitment be made to my earlier choices (job, family, belief systems, etc.) or should changes be made?" Since the investment in the young adult's work is not yet great, the decision may not exact a high emotional toll. However, the transition is more difficult for some than for others, and reexamining some earlier choices can cause considerable anxiety.

Women who work outside the home are likely to encounter choices similar to their male counterparts. Women who, due to child-rearing responsibilities, have not yet entered the job market may desire greater independence and seek their own career opportunities.

Settling down

During the next period, **settling down,** commitments are deepened and elements of the new life structure evolving out of the age-thirty transition begin to take shape. Stability, security, and control become more important during this phase of life. Choices made during the age-thirty transition are affirmed, and activities such as work become vehicles for settling in. Settling down may also be accompanied by the desire to set and obtain major goals. Activities both on and off the job often become a means for achieving personal security and self-worth, and individuals tend to become more involved in efforts to achieve those goals.

Becoming one's own person

Settling down involves a second phase known as **becoming one's own person.** This phase usually occurs in the late thirties and is characterized by a feeling that no matter what has been accomplished, one has still to become one's own person. Such feelings may be accompanied by the need to get out from under the control of an immediate superior or to break away from a mentor who has guided and nurtured earlier development. In essence, the individual senses it is time to accomplish something meaningful without the direct assistance of others.

Becoming one's own person, then, is characterized by the desire to attain some life- or work-related goal (e.g., a new position or job, writing a book, or attaining some elected office) on one's own and working to achieve that goal. Of course, neither our achievements nor our efforts are necessarily viewed as satisfactory. Personal and occupational barriers and the frustrations they produce lead in turn to yet another period, the mid-life transition.

Mid-life transition

The **mid-life transition (MLT)** is a period in which major life decisions and commitments are reexamined; it is generally considered to be the most tumultuous of the adult transitions. MLT is characterized by concerns about whether the previous decade's chosen life structure is really the structure that one wishes to live with indefinitely. Repressed and latent feelings and a desire to reconcile them with the present life structure are often paramount.

Some individuals pass through MLT with little difficulty. They either do not question their life structure or are able to manage the transition without a major crisis. Many others, however, experience inner turmoil and struggle. Negative outcomes often associated with the mid-life transition include dissatisfaction with (and possibly quitting) one's job, divorce, and leaving a family. For the less adventuresome, a "change of scenery" alone may be enough of a new beginning. The results of one study concluded that midlife reactions are the result of a complex interaction between individual psychological factors, cultural influences, and family influences that may lead to any of four distinct developmental paths, each having its own set of behaviors and outcomes. Among the most common characteristics were movement toward self-insulation and a heightened sense of vulnerability.[49] Exhibit 2.10 describes each of the four paths, their related behaviors, and their outcomes.

For most people, MLT is a period when they may question many aspects of their lives and when rational and staid processes of the past may give way to seeming irrationality. However, this lack of structure (irrationality) may be necessary for a person to become free from her existing life structure. Unfortunately, many people are not able to approach MLT in a calm, self-controlled manner; rather, they experience emotional turmoil and personal upheaval. This can lead to feelings of being abandoned or misunderstood by family, colleagues, and other acquaintances.

Mid-life transition not only results in a reexamination of life's central issues, but also provides us with a glimpse of things to come. For example, the aging process characterized by weight gain and redistribution, loss of muscle tone, etc., focuses attention on our physical limitations. Noting physical and career declines of those around us results in a closer monitoring of our own bodies and occupational progress.

Middle and late adulthood

Age linkages and life cycles become less definite as we approach old age. This may be due to varied rates of physical degeneration experienced by individuals, unique

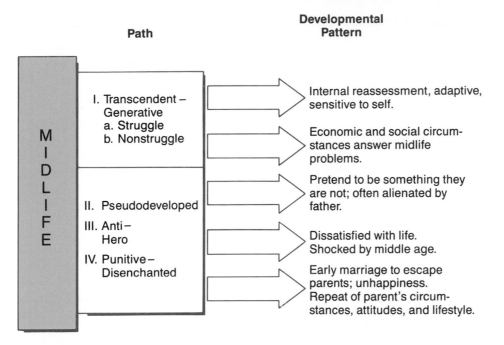

EXHIBIT 2.10   FOUR DEVELOPMENTAL PATHS AT MIDLIFE

work and social environments, and a divergence of post-work alternatives available to members of our own society and of different cultures.

Researchers examining middle and old age generally observe a "restabilization" of life structure. Middle-aged adults become more self-aware and selective, and they experience an increasing desire to regain control of their environment. Thus, the later years of middle adulthood are characterized by cognitive, social, and emotional maturation.[50] Researchers have observed changes:

1. from valuing physical powers to valuing wisdom;
2. from sexualizing to socializing human relationships;
3. from emotional impoverishment to emotional flexibility (the capacity and necessity to shift emotional investments from one person or activity to another); and
4. from mental rigidity to mental flexibility.[51]

Evidence suggests that older employees are potentially among the most loyal, dependable, and committed persons in the work-force. Social and emotional maturity combined with a supportive work environment can pay dividends to employers. Although failing to stay abreast of new technologies or techniques may hinder productivity for some older workers, organizationally sponsored training, off-site seminars, and sabbatical leaves can facilitate learning and in turn contribute to improved job performance.

A number of companies, including McDonald's, Andy Frain Services, and some day-care organizations, have begun to reemploy retirees. Travelers Insurance has had particular success bringing retirees back into the workforce and has created a retiree job bank to facilitate the practice.[52] The company has found the practice to be more cost-effective than hiring temporary employees. Jobs filled by retirees need not be menial or routine. General Alum & Chemical Corporation had so much success when it hired a "retired" marketing executive that it employed other retired businesspeople as advisers and mentors to less-experienced, younger managers.[53]

Late adult transition

The **late adult transition** essentially involves a shift from a work-related to a nonwork-related behavior setting. For most older adults, these changes begin during the last few years of employment and may be related to the adjustment patterns discussed above. In some cases, older adults may become apprehensive about their futures. Concerns range from those about physical limitations to those about financial security and personal influence with colleagues and others.

Those who have held positions of authority, for example, may suddenly have to readjust their concepts of themselves and the world in which they have worked and lived. A retired executive of a major oil company shared with us a story about his own retirement. He cleaned out his desk on his final day of work and was somewhat put off when he was asked to return all building keys before leaving the premises. The following morning, he returned to the office to pick up a few papers he had left the day before. Not only would the security guard, whom he had known for nearly two decades, not permit him to go to his office, but another executive had to come to the lobby and authorize the "visitor" to enter the premises.

Researchers have identified three important adjustments made during this transition. First, the older adult becomes less preoccupied with work and more concerned about a broader range of nonwork-role activities. These activities result in more diverse sources of satisfaction and identity and can permit a definition of self-worth that goes beyond the work role alone. The second and third transitions include the acceptance of the physical aging process and the recognition of and dealing with our own mortality.[54]

Additional Considerations Concerning Adult Development

Many factors affect individuality during the adult years. Patterns of male development have been better researched and appear to be better understood than female development patterns. In addition, debate continues over the question of whether our personalities remain relatively stable or are subject to change. Each of these topics is addressed briefly below.

Unique aspects of adult development among women

There appear to be similarities between the development of adult males and females, although unique patterns have been observed for some females. In particular, development appears to be different for women who choose to remain at home and care for their families than for those who begin careers in their early twenties. A woman in the former category may question her identify (increasingly considering it as separate from that of her husband) and enter the job market later in life. Career women are more likely than their male counterparts to face difficult decisions concerning marriage and childbearing during their early and mid-thirties. One study found that some women experienced difficult transitions at certain times in their lives such as family creation, launching a new generation, and postparental years.

However, most women did not experience the difficulty; and those that did responded in relatively unique ways rather than according to set patterns.[55]

Personality stability versus personality change

Does adult development bring about permanent changes in our personalities or simply result in temporary changes in behavior patterns? Recent longitudinal studies have found no evidence of systematic, long-term changes in adult personality. In one study, researchers concluded that such changes are possible, although they typically do not take place.[56] Other studies have concluded that changes, when they do occur, may be linked to specific educational or cultural factors or certain antecedent personality types.[57] In other words, some individuals may be more likely to change over time than others.

For some executives and managers, adjusting their own values to the changing values of their organizations poses a significant challenge. Roger Smith, chairman of General Motors, for example, has faced such a challenge. Concluding that, "when you're at the top, it's always a hell of a lot easier to be autocratic than team-oriented," Smith has made major adjustments in his personal style since taking over the corporate reigns, although few GM managers believe that those changes represent deeper changes in his personality.[58]

Apple CEO John Sculley, on the other hand, seems to many to have experienced a genuine change in his work-related beliefs, attitudes, and values. Once a self-described arrogant, impatient perfectionist for whom winning was an obsession, Sculley now thrives on dissent and has learned to listen rather than command in order to facilitate change.[59] Are such changes really permanent or do they merely represent a temporary departure from Sculley's day-to-day behavior patterns? Only time will provide the answer to that question.

A more detailed discussion of life stages plus additional observations about women's career choices appear in Chapter 17, "Careers and Career Development."

INDIVIDUALITY IN THE WORKPLACE: CONCLUSIONS

The very term *individuality* suggests that characteristics exist which distinguish one person from another. This uniqueness does not mean that those in organizations have nothing in common with one another, but rather that you as a manager should try to understand every person with whom you work in terms of their unique attributes. Understanding individuality means looking closely at (perhaps even measuring when possible) a person's characteristics in order to acquire an accurate picture of "who" he or she is. This knowledge can help you to employ the talents of individuals effectively while helping each employee achieve greater satisfaction with his or her work.

A manager can only see an employee's overt behavior or the consequences of that behavior. However, behaviors are influenced by underlying values, attitudes, and beliefs that develop throughout our lives. Understanding these and other personality characteristics may contribute to your ability to manage human behavior in organizations effectively. You should take time to learn about the personal characteristics and distinctive behavior patterns of those with whom you work. It is also important to pay attention to subtle changes that you and those around you experience. Evidence continues to support the hypothesis that individuals may change, if only temporarily, at certain times in their lives. Therefore, it is useful to understand and recognize patterns of adult development especially as they pertain to work-related situations.

Research continues to provide insight into the important transitions through which many working-age adults pass. Failure to make transitions smoothly from one life stage to another can cause personal and professional anxiety. An individual's ability to make healthy transitions from one stage of life to another depends on (1) the way earlier life crises have been managed; (2) the support of family, friends, and co-workers; and (3) whether a person is prepared to meet those transitions. Although parents and siblings have traditionally provided assistance to those experiencing life transitions, increasing mobility of the general population has separated many individuals from these important support groups.

Direct commitment of a company's resources to ease difficult transitions may be called for when organizational performance is threatened. These resources can take the form of special positions or departments (e.g., organizational psychologists and employee counseling groups) or specialized programs like one at Lockheed Aircraft that is designed to meet specific employee adjustment needs. Whatever the life stage, awareness and preparation can ease the adjustment, and organizational investments to facilitate such adjustments can benefit both individuals and organizations.

Today, we know far more about individuality than at any time in the past. Nevertheless, managers must use available information carefully and ethically. Personal observations and even information gathered through measurement tools provide less-than-perfect insights into why people behave as they do or how they are likely to behave in the future. The validity of measurement instruments should be known and taken into consideration when human-resource decisions are made. In addition, such information is generally protected under federal and state privacy laws and should be kept confidential.

Much remains to be learned about individuality and its impact on organizational behavior. There is evidence, for example, that an individual's job satisfaction is influenced by his personality, although questions still persist as to the extent to which personality influences performance itself.[60] Nevertheless, the information presented in this chapter can assist you in understanding the nature of those with whom you work and provide a frame of reference for understanding the importance of individuals in organizations. Above all, however, keep in mind that no two people are exactly alike. Each has his or her own **individuality**!

QUESTIONS FOR REVIEW AND DISCUSSION

1. Explain how the terms uniqueness, situational consistency, and stability relate to the concept of personality.
2. Name and explain the three major influences on personality development.
3. What is the difference between terminal and instrumental values? Give an example of each.
4. How can knowledge about and an understanding of values benefit a manager who conducts business in different cultures?
5. How do attitudes differ from values?

6. What is job satisfaction? How does job satisfaction relate to turnover, absenteeism, and performance?
7. Individual differences are sometimes reflected in certain characteristics. Name and describe two such characteristics. How may each characteristic affect a person's work behavior?
8. Of what relevance to organizational behavior are Erikson's and Freud's views on personality development?
9. How might knowledge of Levinson's adult development theory be of value to you as a manager?

REFERENCES

1. Michelle Galen, Dean Foust, and Eric Schine, "Guilty, Your Honor," *Business Week,* 7 May 1990, 33–34.

2. Brian O'Reilly and Myron Magnet, "Mike's Midas Touch," *Fortune,* 10 October 1988, 61–62.

3. Walter Mischel, *Introduction to Personality,* 2d ed. (New York: Holt, Rhinehart and Winston, 1976), 502–504.

4. Walter Mischel and Philip K. Peake, *Psychological Review,* Vol. 89 (November 1982): 730–755; Mischel and Peake, "Analyzing the Construction of Consistency in Personality," *Nebraska Symposium on Motivation* (Lincoln: Univ. of Nebraska Press, 1982): 233–260.

5. John Sedgwick, "The Life and Times of a Fast Growing CEO," *Business Month,* May 1990, 32–35, 38–39.

6. Clyde K. Kluckhohn and Henry A. Murry, *Personality in Nature, Society, and Culture* (New York: Alfred A. Knopf, 1953), 53.

7. J. W. Greenwood III, and J. W. Greenwood, Jr., *Managing Executive Stress: A Systems Approach* (New York: John Wiley & Sons, 1979), 41.

8. K. Lewin, *Field Theory in Social Science* (New York: Harper, 1951), 62.

9. Sigmund Freud, *New Introductory Lectures on Psychoanalysis* (New York: W.W. Norton & Co., 1933).

10. Gordon W. Allport, *Pattern and Growth in Personality* (New York: Holt Rinehart & Winston, 1961); R. B. Cattell, *The Scientific Analysis of Personality* (Baltimore: Penguin Books, 1965).

11. C. R. Rogers, "A Theory of Therapy, Personality, and Interpersonal Relationships, As Developed in the Client Centered Framework," in S. Koch, ed., *Psychology: A Study of Science,* Vol. 3 (New York: McGraw-Hill, 1959).

12. J. Sculley and J. A. Byrne, *Odyssey* (New York: Harper & Row, 1988).

13. Helen Solomons, "Executive Perspective," in D. D. White and D.A. Bednar, *Organizational Behavior* (Boston: Allyn & Bacon, 1986), 140–141.

14. Michael Rogers, "The Boss's Best Friend is a Mean Alter Ego," *Business Month,* April 1990, 16–19.

15. Ken Kerbs, "Where the Jobs Are Is Where the Skills Aren't," *Business Week,* 19 September 1988, 104–105, 108.

16. L. Sinai and L. Mazzuca, "Written Tests Not Always Valid," *Business Insurance,* Vol. 22 (19 September 1988): 19–22; J.L. Kovach, "Personality Testing Is Fair . . . True or False?" *Industry Week,* 20 January 1986, 44–47.

17. Clyde K. Kluckhohn, "Values and Value Orientations in the Theory of Action," in T. Parsons and E. A. Sills, eds., *Toward a General Theory Action* (Cambridge: Harvard University Press, 1951).

18. R.M. Williams, "Values," in E. Sills, ed., *International Encyclopedia of the Social Sciences* (New York: MacMillan, 1968); R.M. Williams, "Change and Stability in Values and Value Systems: A Sociological Perspective," in M. Rokeach, ed., *Understanding Human Values: Individual and Societal* (New York: Free Press, 1977).

19. M. Rokeach, "Value Theory and Communication Research: Review and Commentary," in D. Nimmo, ed., *Communication Yearbook 3* (New Brunswick: Transaction Books, 1979), 7–28.

20. G. Hofstede, *Culture's Consequences* (Beverly Hills: Sage Publications, 1980); Hofstede, "The Cultural Relativity of the Quality of Life Concept," *Academy of Management Review,* Vol. 9 (1984): 389–398.

21. D. D. White and T. D. Jensen, "Redefining Cross National Comparison: The Case for Subcultural Analysis," paper presented at Academy of Management Annual Meeting, New Orleans, August 1987; L. Kahle and J. Russell, "A Value Basis for Regional Subcultures in the United States," paper presented at Academy of Management Annual Meeting, New Orleans, August 1987.

22. G. W. Allport, "Attitudes," in C. Murchison, ed., *Handbook of Social Psychology* (Worcester, Mass.: Clark University Press, 1935), 810; H. C. Triandis, *Attitude and Attitude Change* (New York: John Wiley and Sons, 1971).

23. Edwin A. Locke, "Nature and Causes of Job Satisfaction," in M. Dunnette, ed., *The Handbook of Industrial and Organizational Psychology* (Chicago: Rand McNally, 1976), 1300.

24. L. W. Porter and R. M. Steers, "Organizational, Work, and Personal Factors in Employee Turnover and Absenteeism," *Psychological Bulletin,* Vol. 80 (1973): 151–176.

25. P. Muchinsky, "Employee Absenteeism: A Review of the Literature." *Journal of Vocational Behavior,* Vol. 10 (1977): 316–340.

26. M. J. Cavanaugh, M. W. Hurst, and R. Rose, "The Relationship Between Job Satisfaction and Psychiatric Health Symptoms for Air Traffic Controllers," *Personnel Psychology,* Vol. 34 (1981): 691–707.

27. E. Palmore, "Predicting Longevity: A Follow-up Controlling for Age," *The Gerontologist,* Vol. 9 (1969): 247–250.

28. M. Jamal and V. F. Mitchell, "Work, Non-Work, and Mental Health: A Model and a Test," *Industrial Relations,* Vol. 19 (1980): 88–93.

29. D. J. Cherrington, H. J. Reitz, and W. E. Scott, Jr., "Effects of Contingent and Non-Contingent Reward on the Relationship Between Satisfaction and Task Performance," *Journal of Applied Psychology,* Vol. 55 (1971): 531–537; D. W. Organ, "A Reappraisal and Reinterpretation of the Satisfaction-Causes-Performance Hypothesis," *Academy of Management Journal,* Vol. 2, No. 1 (1977): 46–53.

30. M. Fishbein and I. Ajzen, *Belief, Attitude, Intention and Behavior: An Introduction to Theory and Research* (Reading, Mass.: Addison-Wesley, 1975).

31. Bo Burlingham, "This Woman Has Changed Business Forever," *Inc.*, June 1990, 34–38, 42–47.

32. "Leave the Butts Behind," *Time*, 30 October 1989, 59; "No Smoking Sweeps America," *Business Week*, 27 July 1987, 40–46.

33. J. B. Rotter, "Generalized Expectancies for Internal vs. External Control of Reinforcement," *Psychological Monographs*, Vol. 80 (1966): 1–28.

34. K. E. Marino and S. E. White, "Departmental Structure, Locus of Control, and Job Stress: The Effect of a Moderator," *Journal of Applied Psychology*, Vol. 70, No. 4 (November 1985): 782–784.

35. T. Adorno et al., *The Authoritarian Personality* (New York: Harper and Brothers, 1950).

36. R. Taylor and M. D. Dunnette, "Influence of Dogmatism, Risk-Taking Propensity and Intelligence on Decision-Making Strategies for a Sample of Industrial Managers," *Journal of Applied Psychology*, Vol. 59, (1974): 420–423.

37. R. J. Ebert and T. R. Mitchell, *Organizational Decision Processes: Concepts and Analysis* (New York: Crance, Russak, and Co., 1975), 81.

38. S. K. Payne and M. J. Beatty, "Innovativeness and Cognitive Complexity," *Psychological Reports*, Vol. 51 (1982): 85–86.

39. Beatty and Payne, "Listening Comprehension as a Function of Cognitive Complexity: A Research Note," *Communication Monographs*, Vol. 51 (1976): 85–89.

40. J. W. Neuliep and V. Hazleton, "Cognitive Complexity and Apprehension About Communication: A Preliminary Report," *Psychological Reports*, Vol. 57 (1985): 1224–1226.

41. O. Friederich and J. McDowell, "Flashy Symbol of an Inquisitive Age," *Time*, 16 January 1989, 48–54; "Welcome to the Nineties, Donald," *Business Week*, 14 May 1990, 118–124.

42. H. A. Moss and E. J. Susman, "Longitudinal Study of Personality Development," in O.G. Brim, Jr., and J. Kagan, *Constancy and Change in Human Development* (Cambridge: Harvard University Press, 1980), 591.

43. Z. Rubin, "Does Personality Really Change After 20?" *Psychology Today*, May 1981, 18–24.

44. Brim and Kagan, op. cit., 1.

45. Erik Erikson, *Childhood and Society* (New York: Norton Publishers, 1950).

46. I. Sarnoff, *Personality Dynamics in Development* (New York: John Wiley & Sons, 1962), 402–403.

47. M. L. Kohn and C. Schooler, "Occupational Experience and Psychological Functioning: An Assessment of Reciprocal Effects," *American Sociological Review*, Vol. 38 (1973): 14–117.

48. Daniel J. Levinson, "A Conception of Adult Development," *American Psychologist*, Vol. 41 (January 1986): 3–13; Levinson et. al., "Periods in the Adult Development of Men: Ages 18 to 45," *The Counseling Psychologist*, Vol. 6 (January 1976): 121–25; Levinson, "The Mid-Life Transition: A Period in Adult Psychological Development," *Psychiatry*, Vol. 40 (May 1970): 108; Anne Rosenfeld and Elizabeth Stark, "The Prime of Our Lives," *Psychology Today*, May 1987, 62–64ff.

49. M. P. Farrell and S. D. Rosenberg, *Men at Midlife* (Boston: Auburn House Publishing Co., 1981).

50. B. L. Neugarten, "Adult Personality: Toward a Psychology of the Life Cycle," in W. C. Sze, *Human Life Cycles* (New York: Jason Aronson, Inc., 1975), 383.

51. R. Peck, "Psychological Developments in the Second Half of Life," in W. C. Sze, *Human Life Cycles*, 610–618.

52. M. Zetlin, "Help Wanted: Life Experience Preferred," *Management Review*, Vol. 78 (January 1989): 51–55; H. E. Johnson, "Older Workers Help Meet Employment Needs," *Personnel Journal*, Vol. 67 (May 1988): 100–105; D.V. Lewis, "Make Way for the Older Worker," *HRMagazine*, Vol. 36 (May 1990): 75–77.

53. L. R. Sheeran and D. Fenn, "Management: The Mentor System," *Inc.*, June 1987, 138–142.

54. Peck, op. cit.

55. B. J. Reinke et al., "Timing of Psychosocial Changes in Women's Lives," *Human Development*, Vol. 28 (1985): 259–280.

56. P. T. Costa, Jr., and R. R. McRae, "Still Stable After All These Years: Personality as a Key to Some Issues in Adulthood and Old Age," *Life-Span Development and Behavior*, Vol. 3 (1980): 65–102; McCrae and Costa, *Emerging Lives, Enduring Dispositions: Personality in Adulthood* (Boston: Little, Brown, 1984).

57. N. Datan, D. Rodeheaver, and F. Hughes, "Adult Development and Aging," *Annual Review of Psychology*, Vol. 38 (1987): 153–180.

58. John Simmons, "The Painful Reeducation of a Company Man," *Business Month*, October 1989, 78–80; Roger Smith, "The U.S. Must Do As GM Has Done," *Fortune*, 13 February 1989, 70–73.

59. Sculley and Byrne, op. cit.

60. R. W. Goddard, "Inside the Psychological Employee," *Management World*, Vol. 17 (March/April 1988): 24–26; D. V. Day and S. B. Silverman, "Personality and Job Performance: Evidence of Incremental Validity," *Personnel Psychology*, Vol. 42 (Spring 1989): 25–36.

CASE 2.1 *Trump*

DONALD D. WHITE and RAGHA SINGH *University of Arkansas*

They call him "Trump!" To some he's a "visionary," to others a "flamboyant child of Mammon," but to most, he is known simply as Trump. Donald J. Trump is a six-foot-two-inch forty-two-year-old billionaire real estate tycoon whose name can be found on everything from his private helicopter (according to Trump, "It's the best in New York!") to buildings and commercial airplanes. Rarely humble, "Trumpisms," as his quotes have become known, reveal a great deal about Donald Trump. Consider the following:

"Who has done as much I have? No one has done more in New York than me."

"I love to have enemies. . . . I like beating my enemies to the ground."

"I like thinking big. If you're going to be thinking anyway, you might as well think big."

"A little more moderation would be good. Of course, my life hasn't exactly been one of moderation."

There are few topics on which Donald Trump does not have an opinion. On President George Bush: "I like George Bush, but this kinder, gentler crap is killing us." On former New York mayor Edward Koch: "He's got no credibility anymore. He said, 'I don't believe in hate.' Ask him what he thinks of Donald Trump." On the Japanese: "They're taking this country for one of the great rides in history . . . why doesn't somebody say to Japan, 'you're ripping us off'?"

SOURCE: Donald Trump and T. Schwartz, *Trump: the Art of the Deal* (New York: Random House, 1987); O. Friedrich and J. McDowell, "Flashy Symbol of an Acquisitive Age," *Time*, 16 January 1989, 48–54; S. Elliot, "Trump, True to Form, Speaks His Mind," Gannett News Service; C. Welles, "Welcome to the Nineties, Donald," *Business Week*, 14 May 1990, 118–121, 124; N. Barsky, "Trump's Growing Appetite for Cash," *Wall Street Journal*, 27 April 1990; N. Barsky, "Trump Could Face Big Personal Liability if Empire Collapses," *Wall Street Journal*, 18 June 1990, pp. A1, A7.

Where did Trump get his brash confidence, and why does he drive himself so relentlessly?

Donald Trump did not exactly fight his way up from the bottom. His father, orphaned at eleven, became a prosperous businessman who built over 24,000 apartments in Brooklyn, Queens, and Staten Island. He and his wife raised five children in a twenty-three-room home. By the age of five, young Donald was traveling with his father to inspect building sites and at thirteen was driving a bulldozer. As Trump himself says, "I learned about toughness in a very tough business." His older brother wanted nothing to do with the family business; he became an airline pilot, but died of alcoholism at the age of forty-three. Donald loved his brother and had a difficult time dealing with his death.

Trump spent his early years at New York Military Academy where he became captain of cadets. He received his degree from the Wharton School before launching a career in real estate. By the age of twenty-nine he had made his first major deal: he bought the run-down Commodore Hotel for $10 million from the bankrupt Penn Central Railroad. Four years later, the renovated structure was reopened as the Grand-Hyatt Hotel, which now nets a profit of $30 million annually. Deal making is Trump's business, and he lives it: "My style of deal making is quite simple and straightforward. I just keep pushing and pushing and pushing to get what I'm after."

Employees like working for Trump but they and those with whom he does business know he's not afraid to use his clout. Litigation is a way of life for Trump. Currently, ten different legal firms, many of whom are involved in litigation on his behalf, are on his payroll. He once even sued two brothers in South Africa who had operated a small corporation for over twenty years and whose last name was Trump. According to Donald, they were trying to use the Trump name.

Donald Trump doesn't always get what he wants, but he is rarely disappointed. Although he had first reserved a $10 million triplex penthouse for himself in the luxurious Trump Tower, he doubled the size of his own residence after seeing a larger apartment owned by Adnan Khashoggi. When he could not add ten additional floors to the Tower because of zoning rules, he simply changed the floor numbers, explaining that residents would feel more important living on "higher" floors.

How well does Donald Trump know himself? He claims not to want to look too closely. "When you start studying yourself too deeply, you start seeing things that maybe you don't want to see." To others, however, he looks like a brilliant, driving force in business and the world of high finance. Says Trump, "We're here for a short time. When we're gone, most people don't care, and in some cases they're quite happy about it."

EPILOGUE

1990 proved to be a difficult year for Donald Trump. His personal problems with his wife, Ivana, and reports

of an extramarital affair livened up tabloid headlines and observers in the financial community increasingly questioned the viability of Trump's financial empire. Trump retained Merrill Lynch & Co. to negotiate the sale of the Trump shuttle, and the possible sale of many of Trump's prime properties, including Trump Tower and Trump's Castle Casino, was reported widely in the business press. Many speculated that Donald Trump suffered from a serious cash flow problem due primarily to the heavy debt load he took on in the purchase and development of many of his high-profile properties.

Trump himself angrily denied that he had a problem. When questioned about his cash position, he replied, "There's nobody that has the cash flow that I have." And when asked by another reporter how much cash he had, he responded simply, "A lot!" Nevertheless, Trump was publicly sensitive about his situation and the questions raised by reporters. In true Trump style, he threatened reporters and brokerage firms with libel suits for even suggesting there was a problem in the Trump empire.

CASE 2.2   *Growing pains*

CHARLES W. HUBBARD   *Southwest Texas State University*
DONALD D. WHITE   *University of Arkansas*

John Withrow sat in his dimly lit office surrounded by a week's paper work. He leafed through the stacks of files, occasionally glancing at the pictures of his wife and children that sat on the desk before him. Although he often worked late, this evening was different from the rest. He had left the ball park after his sons had completed their game (he rarely ever missed an opportunity to see them compete) and returned to the office to do some serious thinking.

A great deal had happened to John in the last few years. Summers were always the busiest seasons for him in the moving and storage business, and this had been no exception. In fact, the summer months had been so complicated by skyrocketing costs, frustrations over state rate control, and problems with hiring and

holding a reliable work force that John was convinced he was at a major crossroads in his life.

Earlier that year, he had seriously considered selling his business and entering a different line of work. In fact, such a sale might well have taken place had a prospective buyer not backed out at the last minute. The frustration of working well into the evening and then carrying business problems home with him at night had also led to uneasiness in his home life. Although he had always been a family man, the increasing tensions surrounding his work had become evident to his wife and close friends. John was a regular Jekyll and Hyde during his busy season. On more than one occasion, his wife confided to friends her deep concern for his physical and emotional well-being. And, although he did not show any signs of instability, his moodiness and openly expressed dissatisfaction with the course of his own life had set the stage for this evening.

THE EARLY YEARS

John was the product of what could best be described as a very typical public education. He attended elementary and secondary schools with children from a variety of cultural and socioeconomic backgrounds. However, most came from lower-middle to middle-class families. He did not realize it at the time, but John's early education had exposed him to people from widely varying backgrounds.

From an early age, John tried to make the best grades he possibly could. Good grades served a dual purpose: they were a source of personal satisfaction, and they gave him the reputation of being a good student. He enjoyed this reputation, and it further strengthened his self-concept. Additionally, his good marks in school were a constant source of pride for his parents. From an early age, they encouraged him to do a good job. After awhile, however, the encouragement turned into expectation. Parents and friends and John himself expected him to be one of the top students in the class.

John tended to view himself as a likeable person with an extroverted personality. He related well to most of his peers, but he did have a reputation for being "straight." In junior and senior high school he didn't drink, smoke, or run with the "wrong crowd." He dated only "nice" girls and he didn't attend social gatherings in which "questionable" activities were taking place. The majority of his social life was associated with school athletic programs, the Boy Scouts, and church.

The Boy Scout movement, in particular, exerted a strong and positive influence on John's formative years. He was a very active participant, and, as in school, he strove to be the best in the group. By age fifteen, he had achieved Scouting's two highest awards. The organization to which he belonged was one of the finest in its region, and its members and leaders were instrumental in the development of his character, self-discipline, and self-reliance.

John's working-class family simply could not provide him with *all* the material possessions he wanted. While his basic needs were always provided for, John had an unusually strong desire for money and nonessential possessions—a need which simply could not be met with the financial resources available to the family.

Holding firmly to the Protestant work ethic, the family encouraged and aided John at an early age to perform small tasks and to accept odd jobs in order to "learn the value of a dollar." Indeed, throughout his formative years, the work ethic was strongly encouraged in John. The family found it both desirable and necessary for him to contribute part of his own support. As time passed, he became more financially independent, looking to the family only for basic food, shelter, and medical attention; he provided increasingly more of his own clothes, transportation, entertainment, and the other extras desired by this growing, active young man.

In reflecting on his boyhood, John could not overlook relations with his father and mother and the impact they had exerted on his development. Mr. Withrow was forty years old when John was born. This large age difference between John and his father had made it difficult to establish a relationship that could be described as warm and supportive. Mr. Withrow found it difficult to accept the value system of John's generation. However, he did subtly implant the Protestant work ethic into John's character.

John's mother was sixteen years younger than his father, and John felt better able to identify with her. Her ideas and views seemed to him to be more modern and more closely aligned with his own. She, too, was strongly imbued with the Protestant work ethic.

Due to their age differences, it seemed that his parents' personal relationship left something to be desired. As John grew older, Mrs. Withrow increasingly relied on John to perform duties normally thought to be the husband's. Neither John nor his mother realized this gradual evolution in their relationship at the time. However, his mother's increased reliance on him tended to have a maturing effect on John. In many ways it seemed to cut short his adolescence and to launch him into manhood well before his time.

LOOKING FOR A LIFE-STYLE

Even before entering high school, John made the decision to attend the large metropolitan university in his home town. There was really never any question about his attending college. His parents had not been able to go and from his early years they had preached to him the virtues of education and their expectations that he would attend college.

Money for college was short, but jobs in the city were plentiful, so it made good sense to live at home and work and go to school in his home town. Moreover, remaining in the area allowed him to pursue marriage plans with Dina, his high school sweetheart.

John completed his four-year undergraduate program with a B+ average, majoring in business administration. He and Dina were married at the beginning of his junior year. During the final two years of college, both he and Dina were kept busy working, attending school, and maintaining an active social life. At the same time, they gave serious thought to the future. And from John's viewpoint, the future meant more money and more education.

Immediately upon graduation, John was hired by a large, nationally known food processing firm. His initial job responsibility was sales to retail food stores and supermarkets. Saleswork seemed to fit his personality and to provide him with the competition and the challenges he enjoyed.

At the same time, John recognized that a master's degree would be helpful to his career. With that in mind, he enrolled in the evening M.B.A. curriculum at his alma mater. Once again, John settled into what had by now become a well established life-style for him: working and going to school.

Not long after his new full-time work/graduate school career began, John received his military notice. Fearful of the draft and a lengthy interruption of his career, John scurried to find a way to minimize the interruption. He enlisted in a program of six-months' active duty and six-years' reserve obligation with week-end active duty. While the six months seemed never to end, John was soon back home attending night M.B.A. classes and selling his company's products with renewed vigor. However, his enthusiasm for his job seemed to diminish rapidly, and he found instead a growing interest in pursuing his M.B.A.

There seemed to be but one course to follow that would bring John the satisfaction and fulfillment he longed for. This course would require certain fundamental decisions, decisions that would have a far-reaching impact on the Withrow's lives, although they did not realize it at the time. He and Dina concluded that he would quit his job, they would sell their recently purchased home, and once again he would become an apartment-dwelling full-time student supported by a working wife. John was able to complete his M.B.A. in one semester, during which he was given an opportunity to teach his first college course.

He was captivated by the teaching experience. He liked the feeling of being at the head of the class, of being the leader—the authority on the subject. He became so fascinated with teaching that new career thoughts began to enter his head—perhaps teaching on a permanent basis. He realized, of course, that full-time college teachers had more education than he; it would be necessary to earn a Ph.D. Simultaneously, he experienced feelings of excitement and uncertainty. Was he Ph.D. material? Were the time and financial commitments really worth it? Was teaching *really* the career for him? He felt two things were certain: he had never before walked away from a challenge, and he did not have a lot to lose. With these thoughts in mind, and with the assurance of continued support and cooperation from his wife, John was accepted into the doctoral program at a distant university.

The decision to pursue a Ph.D. proved to be the prelude to a series of significant events that developed during his years on campus. These events would have a lasting impact on his life and on his family. John enthusiastically entered his graduate studies. He taught part-time in order to make ends meet, since his wife had also returned to the classroom as a full-time student in pursuit of her bachelor's degree.

Three years on the new campus were highly productive. Dina completed her B.A., graduating as class valedictorian, and John finished his Ph.D. coursework requirements. The most important event to both John and Dina was the birth of twin boys. However, the new additions, along with long hours of work on his dissertation, created additional financial and time pressures for him and Dina.

Upon nearing the completion of his formal studies, John received an appointment as an assistant professor of a recognized university in a city far from the region where he had spent his first twenty-six years. Shortly after moving to his new position, John and his wife began to experience sharp pangs of homesickness. They did not long for their big city hometown; they sought to return to the small town where he had attended graduate school. The longing for that small town not only lingered, but grew. In fact, the feeling became an almost compulsive drive. John and his wife became convinced that their ultimate happiness lay in permanently residing in this one locale.

Although he thought often about returning "home," John was highly motivated in his new job. He became involved in consulting activities and, with a colleague, published a book in his field. His efforts gained him recognition, and after two years he was offered a new position at a major state university. The new position was a step up for John and was somewhat closer to the community to which he and his wife wished to return.

Again he poured himself into his work, developing an innovative program in minority business and continuing to write. However, after two years John and his family were given the opportunity to return to the community where they had for so long wanted to live. He was not to do so as a terminally qualified college professor, but rather as the owner of a small transfer and storage business. John and his wife opted to forego the secure and comfortable world of academia for the uncertainties of entrepreneurship. Some of his friends and colleagues were surprised by his decision, but John explained, "the money was never really good, and the reward systems that I worked under never gave you a fair shake. No matter how hard I worked, I never could get ahead."

RETURNING HOME

Once back home, John rapidly set about establishing himself as a reputable, dependable, and progressive businessman. He saw his operation as a perfect laboratory in which to experiment with the theories, ideas, and concepts he had so long worked with in the classroom. Dina worked by his side as office manager and head bookkeeper. Together, they quickly became immersed in the business and its challenges. John was thirty-one years old and full of energy and enthusiasm. His persevering nature, his supportive wife, and "lady luck" all combined to create success. The business's facilities and fleet grew in size and quality. The Withrows lived comfortably, and the company was making money.

Yet John again became restless. He believed that it was time to undertake a major business expansion. He obtained a second freight office in a larger community sixty miles from the original operation. Although the new venture was not yet profitable after eighteen months of operation, he planned to add a third outlet in another nearby community and buy yet another major freight office in the state capitol some two hundred miles away. He envisioned his role as that of a corporate executive, rather than as simply the general manager of a local operation as he now was. His business and his plans were growing rapidly.

Unfortunately, John's problems grew, too. Shortages of qualified labor, increased government regulation, and the growing pressures on profits caused by rapidly rising costs were but a few of the problems he encountered. As margins began to slip, so did John's ability to afford additional administrative personnel who could help share the managerial responsibilities and headaches. The second office continued to lose money, and he discarded what was once a priority plan for expansion. In addition to mounting frustration, he had self-doubt that he had never before experienced.

As time passed, John found the pressures of the business becoming more burdensome and his enthusiasm waning. It became more and more difficult for him to get himself and his employees "fired up" about what they were doing. Increasingly, it appeared to John that he should now, at age thirty-nine, seriously reassess his life and career goals.

FACING THE FUTURE

Once he made the basic decision to reevaluate his career path, John began to discuss thoroughly with Dina, friends, and business associates the options which were open to him.

He asked those around him to give him direct, objective answers to questions about himself and his future. The questions were asked over a period of several months—months that seemed agonizingly long as John searched for the right path to take during the coming years. He felt a sense of urgency in making a decision for, after all, he "wasn't getting any younger." He had to decide how to use the maturity and experience he had gained in the last eight years.

While they seemed to come at a snail's pace, the answers he sought finally began to emerge. Close friends seemed to say he would be wise to consider another occupation. Almost simultaneously, possibilities seemed to begin appearing. One such possible opportunity developed in the life insurance industry.

Due in part to his interest and to his "desired personality traits" for the business, one close friend urged John to consider a new career in life insurance sales work. John believed he could handle the job and was curious about an industry test battery that was available. Therefore, he agreed to subject himself to a lengthy and intensive set of "career profile examinations" administered by a large, nationally recognized life insurance company. Not surprisingly to his family, close friends, or himself, the tests were returned with very favorable results. While obviously pleased and flattered, John could not firmly convince himself that this was the new direction he wanted to take. A number of obstacles to a new career in life insurance sales lingered in the back of his mind and made him hesitate and ultimately reject insurance as a serious career change possibility.

At the same time that John pondered his decision, Dina concluded that she, too, had grown tired of the demands and the problems associated with running and owning a family business. She freely voiced her disenchantment to her friends and to John. John, in response, had encouraged her to reduce drastically her workload in the company office and to stand ready to accept another opportunity should one be offered.

Having at least considered one new position, even though he had rejected it, John found that the process of thinking about selling his business and changing careers was becoming easier. In fact, he actually enjoyed daydreaming about doing something different. He longed to move into an occupation that was more "professional," something that would let him better use the graduate education and work experiences he had acquired, some of which had lain dormant for nearly eight years. He had thought about how refreshingly different it would be to return to the college classroom; he could surely be more effective now than before thanks to his "real world" experience.

These thoughts were running through his head one afternoon when he received a call from his close friend, Jim Scott. Jim was a faculty member at the university and had been one of John's closest confidantes during his "rough days." Jim knew that John had an interest in returning to the academic community in some capacity, and an opportunity to do so appeared to be on the horizon. Jim told John that it made good sense to have university officials at least contact him. Perhaps both their needs and his could be simultaneously satisfied.

Within a few days, Jim had given John's name to one of the officials, and agreement had tentatively been made for him to occupy a temporary teaching position. The teaching job meant rearranging busy business days and delegating additional duties to employees, and it was understood that his assignment was only temporary, due to university hiring policies. Still, John was excited about the opportunity.

John's life seemed to improve markedly in the following weeks. While he was working hard and logging many hours in his dual role as businessman and professor, he seemed to thrive on the work. Jim frequently commented to John that he seemed like a different person. John actually both looked and felt better. His attitude improved, and it seemed easier for him to cope with problems at his company office. John was thoroughly enjoying his experiences at the university. Sometimes he reluctantly looked at the calendar, noting the last day of the semester approaching.

He was reminded that this pleasant experience would soon end and the diversion from his business would soon be over. He tried not to think about returning full-time to the business; however, his thoughts haunted him. "Perhaps this [the university] really is the life for me."

THE DECISION

Shortly before fall semester ended, Jim came to John with news that would complicate John's already confusing and frustrating situation. The associate deanship of the College of Business was soon to be vacated. Jim suggested that John consider submitting his credentials. It appeared the position would require an academic background, administrative skills, and a degree of maturity. On the surface, it seemed that John could qualify. There was no way of knowing just what his chances were of receiving the appointment, but one thing was clear—he must make the decision to submit his credentials soon if he wanted to be considered for the job.

John's wife encouraged him to weigh the various options open to him carefully, and, as he sat alone in his office he was determined to do just that. As he examined the situation, he viewed his first option as completely abandoning a career change and firmly recommitting himself to his moving and storage business. The business did offer the challenges he felt were needed in his life, and he knew it potentially offered him the financial rewards he had always sought. Business conditions had improved slightly, and industry associates had suggested improvements in his operations. If he sharpened his management skills, he was sure the business would produce sufficient profits and income to allow his family to live well.

A second option was to apply for the associate deanship. He felt this position would present new and challenging work and would pay a comfortable salary with limited burdens and headaches. Moreover, the job might provide him with an avenue to a permanent teaching position at the university in future years. On the negative side, John wondered if he would enjoy this new type of work. After all, he had never had a position exactly like this before and really didn't know what to anticipate. Additionally, he knew from past experience that salary increases would be limited. Taking the position would mean losing a certain amount of control over his financial future. Finally, he was aware that leaving the business entirely would mean leaving the day-to-day operation in the hands of unprepared subordinates until a buyer could be found.

As he saw it, his third possibility was to make no firm decision at the present time. With respect to an immediate career change, he could simply, for now, keep an open mind and an ear to the ground. The strength of this position, he believed, was that once it became common knowledge that he was considering a career change, more employment possibilities might soon appear, and he might be able to accept a more attractive offer. However, if he really did feel that the academic environment was where he should be, John had to make a commitment now. In all probability, there would never be another opportunity like this one.

He thought about the need to be rational about this important decision, but he seriously questioned his rationality after "bouncing" from career to career. He confessed to himself that the entire experience was embarrassing yet he knew he *had* to do something.

EXERCISE 2.1
F.I.R.O.—B EXERCISE

INTRODUCTION

How do you interact with others? That is the question this exercise is intended to answer. Each individual has his or her unique way of establishing and maintaining relationships. This exercise, developed by Dr. William Schutz, will measure your inclusion, control, and affection. You may be tempted to answer these questions in the "right" way. However, there are no right or wrong answers. Therefore, answer each question in a manner that will accurately reflect your own behavior. Simply place the number of the answer that best applies to you on the line to the left of the question. (Questions begin at the top of page 66.)

UPON COMPLETION

After you have completed the questionnaire you may score this exercise based on instructions given to you by your professor. After you have tallied your score, meet in a small group of three to five members and discuss the following questions:

1. What differences exist in the need patterns of group participants?
2. How might these differences affect interpersonal relationships in this group (a) on a social level; (b) in a work-group situation?
3. How might the knowledge you have gained about yourself and others be used by you?

For each statement below, decide which of the following answers best applies to you. Place the number of the answer at the left of the statement.

1. usually   2. often   3. sometimes   4. occasionally   5. rarely   6. never

_____   **1.** I try to be with people.
_____   **2.** I let other people decide what to do.
_____   **3.** I join social groups.
_____   **4.** I try to have close relationships with people.
_____   **5.** I tend to join social organizations when I have an opportunity.
_____   **6.** I let other people strongly influence my actions.
_____   **7.** I try to be included in informal social activities.
_____   **8.** I try to have close, personal relationships with people.
_____   **9.** I try to include other people in my plans.
_____   **10.** I let other people control my actions.
_____   **11.** I try to have people around me.
_____   **12.** I try to get close and personal with people.
_____   **13.** When people are doing things together I tend to join them.
_____   **14.** I am easily led by people.
_____   **15.** I try to avoid being alone.
_____   **16.** I try to participate in group activities.

For each of the next group of statements, choose one of the following answers:

1. most   2. many   3. some   4. a few   5. one or   6. nobody
   people   people   people   people   two people

_____   **17.** I try to be friendly to people.
_____   **18.** I let other people decide what to do.
_____   **19.** My personal relations with people are cool and distant.
_____   **20.** I let other people take charge of things.
_____   **21.** I try to have close relationships with people.
_____   **22.** I let other people strongly influence my actions.
_____   **23.** I try to get close and personal with people.
_____   **24.** I let other people control my actions.
_____   **25.** I act cool and distant with people.
_____   **26.** I am easily led by people.
_____   **27.** I try to have close, personal relationships with people.

For each of the next group of statements, choose one of the following answers:

1. most   2. many   3. some   4. a few   5. one or   6. nobody
   people   people   people   people   two people

_____   **28.** I like people to invite me to things.
_____   **29.** I like people to act close and personal with me.
_____   **30.** I try to influence strongly other people's actions.
_____   **31.** I like people to invite me to join in their activities.
_____   **32.** I like people to act close toward me.
_____   **33.** I try to take charge of things when I am with people.
_____   **34.** I like people to include me in their activities.
_____   **35.** I like people to act cool and distant toward me.

_____ **36.** I try to have other people do things the way I want them done.
_____ **37.** I like people to ask me to participate in their discussions.
_____ **38.** I like people to act friendly toward me.
_____ **39.** I like people to invite me to participate in their activities.
_____ **40.** I like people to act distant toward me.

For each of the next group of statements, choose one of the following answers:

1. usually   2. often   3. sometimes   4. occasionally   5. rarely   6. never

_____ **41.** I try to be the dominant person when I am with people.
_____ **42.** I like people to invite me to things.
_____ **43.** I like people to act close toward me.
_____ **44.** I try to have other people do things I want done.
_____ **45.** I like people to invite me to join in their activities.
_____ **46.** I like people to act cool and distant toward me.
_____ **47.** I try to influence strongly other people's actions.
_____ **48.** I like people to include me in their activities.
_____ **49.** I like people to act close and personal with me.
_____ **50.** I try to take charge of things when I'm with people.
_____ **51.** I like people to invite me to participate in their activities.
_____ **52.** I like people to act distant with me.
_____ **53.** I try to have other people do things the way I want them done.
_____ **54.** I take charge of things when I'm with people.

FIRO-B SCORING WORKSHEET (to be used later)

$e^i =$	$e^c =$	$e^a =$	$w^i =$	$w^c =$	$w^a =$

EXERCISE 2.2
DETERMINING YOUR VALUES

INTRODUCTION

In the preceding chapter, you were introduced to the concepts of terminal values and instrumental values developed by Milton Rokeach. Following these instructions, you will find a list of each of these sets of values.

First, carefully examine the list of terminal values and arrange them in their order of importance to you. When you have completed this ranking process, turn to the list of instrumental values. Carefully read over this second list of values and array them from most important to least important as they apply to you. In completing this exercise, we have found that it may be easier for you to identify your most important value (Rank #1) first, your least important (Rank #18) second, your second most important value (Rank #17), etc. This procedure should simplify the ranking process. When you have completed both lists of values, bring them to class to complete the exercise.

IN-CLASS ACTIVITY

Your professor will provide you with a list of value rankings obtained from national samples. Compare your ranking to those of the appropriate national samples. You may also wish to calculate averages for your class. Remember, however, that the small sample size may bias your conclusions. After assembling and reviewing all of the information made available to you, discuss in a small group the following questions:

1. How and why do the rankings of each individual differ from those of respective (and appropriate) samples?
2. Do your day-to-day observations support the highly ranked and lowly ranked values identified in this exercise?
3. Do you believe that management should conduct a values analysis of all employees in the organization? How might such an analysis be used? What limitations should be placed on its use?

TERMINAL VALUES		INSTRUMENTAL VALUES	
1. A COMFORTABLE LIFE a prosperous life	_____	1. AMBITIOUS hard-working, aspiring	_____
2. AN EXCITING LIFE a stimluating, active life	_____	2. BROADMINDED open-minded	_____
3. A SENSE OF ACCOMPLISHMENT lasting contribution	_____	3. CAPABLE competent, effective	_____
4. A WORLD AT PEACE free of war and conflicts	_____	4. CHEERFUL lighthearted, joyful	_____
5. A WORLD OF BEAUTY beauty of nature and the arts	_____	5. CLEAN neat, tidy	_____
6. EQUALITY brotherhood, equal opportunity for all	_____	6. COURAGEOUS standing up for your beliefs	_____
7. FAMILY SECURITY taking care of loved ones	_____	7. FORGIVING willing to pardon others	_____
8. FREEDOM independence, free choice	_____	8. HELPFUL working for the welfare of others	_____
9. HAPPINESS contentedness	_____	9. HONEST sincere, truthful	_____
10. INNER HARMONY freedom from inner conflict	_____	10. IMAGINATIVE daring, creative	_____
11. MATURE LOVE sexual and spiritual intimacy	_____	11. INDEPENDENT self-reliant, self-sufficient	_____
12. NATIONAL SECURITY protection from attack	_____	12. INTELLECTUAL intelligent, reflective	_____

CHAPTER 3

 PERCEPTION

LEARNING OBJECTIVES

1. To understand the nature of the perceptual process.
2. To know the activities of perception.
3. To understand perceptual barriers and effects.
4. To learn how we interpret the behavior of others.

13. PLEASURE
     an enjoyable, leisurely life   _____

14. SALVATION
     saved, eternal life   _____

15. SELF-RESPECT
     self-esteem   _____

16. SOCIAL RECOGNITION
     respect, admiration   _____

17. TRUE FRIENDSHIP
     close companionship   _____

18. WISDOM
     a mature understanding of life   _____

13. LOGICAL
     consistent, rational   _____

14. LOVING
     affectionate, tender   _____

15. OBEDIENT
     dutiful, respectful   _____

16. POLITE
     courteous, well-mannered   _____

17. RESPONSIBLE
     dependable, reliable   _____

18. SELF-CONTROLLED
     restrained, self-disciplined   _____

SOURCE: Milton Rokeach. Research and theory dealing with these values can be found in Milton Rokeach, *The Nature of Human Values,* (New York: Free Press, 1973).

CHAPTER OUTLINE

The Nature of the Perceptual Process
  The Activities of Perception

Perceptual Barriers and Effects
  Stereotyping
  Halo Effect
  Projection
  Implicit Personality Theories
  Selective Perception
  Primacy and Recency Effects
  In Summary

Interpreting Why Others Behave As They Do
  Attribution Theory
  Common Attribution Errors

Perception: Conclusions

Questions for Review and Discussion

References

Cases: 3.1. The Invisible Colleague
          3.2. National Brickworks

**Exercises: 3.1. He Works, She Works (But What Different
              Impressions They Make!)
              3.2. Johari Window: A Feedback and Disclosure
              Activity**

KEY TERMS

Sensation   **Implicit personality theory**

Perception   **Selective perception**

Figure/ground   **Primacy effect**

Closure   **Recency effect**

Proximity   **Attribution**

Resemblance   **Actor-observer effect**

Stereotyping   **Self-serving bias**

Halo effect   **Negative bias**

Projection   **False consensus bias**

As Michael walked out of Mr. Vincent's office, he was visibly upset. "That guy wouldn't recognize talent if it walked up and bit him," he muttered. "After all the good things I've done for this company, he's trying to blame me for the problems with the Gooding account. Can I help it if the Gooding Company doesn't order as much plastic pipe during bad economic periods?"

Michael had just finished his yearly performance interview with Mr. Vincent, vice-president for marketing at Amet, Inc. Much of the discussion had focused on Michael's handling of an account with the Gooding Company, one of Amet's largest customers. Amet's orders had decreased over the last six months, and Mr. Vincent believed Michael's mishandling of two key situations had caused Gooding's buyers to look for other suppliers of plastic pipe products. Michael, on the other hand, attributed the decreased orders to a downturn in the regional construction market. Increasing interest rates and uncertainty about a recession, he believed, were causing Gooding to keep inventory low and proceed cautiously on new projects.

As Michael walked back to his office, he wondered how Mr. Vincent could come to such a conclusion about his performance. "Vincent's just not in touch anymore," Michael thought. "He's been in that office and away from the field for too long. He either doesn't understand the difficulties in today's market or can't remember what it's like out on the front lines."

Perhaps you have had an experience similar to Michael's (or one like Charlie Brown's—see Exhibit 3.1). Is it in fact possible that two people can see an object or event but not really "see" the same thing? If an automobile accident were witnessed by a medical doctor, an attorney, and an insurance agent, would they observe the same accident? Does a manager with an accounting background interpret organizational problems in the same way as a manager with extensive training in marketing?

EXHIBIT 3.1   PERCEPTION: ORGANIZING AND INTERPRETING THE WORLD AROUND US

The answers to these questions emerge from an understanding of the process through which we come to know and interpret the world around us—the process of perception. Most of the concepts and much of the research that help us to understand the perceptual process come from the field of psychology. In this chapter, we focus on how a manager can use these concepts and research findings to better understand and manage people at work.

THE NATURE OF THE PERCEPTUAL PROCESS

Every second, we are bombarded with countless stimuli from the environment around us. Our sense organs respond continuously to stimulation by light, sound, pressure, taste, and smell. Through these stimulations, for example, we become aware of color brightness, vocal pitch and loudness, warmth, pungency, and so on. **Sensation,** then, is the physiological process by which we take in stimuli from and interface with the environment.

Perception on the other hand, is the psychological process of selecting, organizing, and interpreting stimuli from the environment. Through the perceptual process, a person focuses on and attends to certain stimuli (to the exclusion of other stimuli), organizes them into recognizable patterns, and interprets and assigns meaning to them. Perception is the process by which the environment becomes real to an individual and through which meaning is given to sensory experiences. As shown in Exhibit 3.2, perception is the interface or link between an individual and the environment.

We often assume a person perceives in much the same way as a camera takes a picture—recording an image of an event or place as it really is. According to this point of view, the environment is an objective reality that all people experience in basically the same way. The process of perception, however, is not objective; it is *subjective*. Every person perceives the world through a unique frame of reference influenced by physiological and psychological factors and past experiences. Each of us subjectively creates our own view of the world, and personal biases, prejudices, motives, and physical conditions influence what and how we perceive.

Perception is also *active* in nature. People are not passive receivers of stimuli and information from the environment. Our senses do not transmit impartial photos or copies of the external world to our brain. Our perception is an active and creative mixture of what is out there and what is in us. Consequently, a marketing or project manager not only senses and perceives "what's out there" but also actively creates an interpretation of events based upon personal background, education, and previous work experiences.

EXHIBIT 3.2   PERCEPTION IS THE PROCESS THAT LINKS THE INDIVIDUAL (ORGANISM) WITH THE ENVIRONMENT

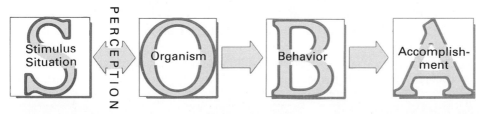

SHELDON WEINIG: MATERIALS RESEARCH CORPORATION

Perhaps nowhere are the subjective and active aspects of perception more graphically illustrated than in investment decisions currently being made by Japanese and United States business persons. Sheldon Weinig, founder and chief executive officer of Materials Research Corporation (MRC), discovered just how differently Japanese and Americans view investment opportunities when he sought capital to expand MRC's operations. As Weinig explains, "Our banks . . . were not willing to sustain the long periods of time required for technology companies to mature through new product cycles." Instead of obtaining funding within the United States, Weinig was forced to turn to the Japan-based Sony Corporation for support. Weinig points out that Americans have all but given up on the semiconductor industry and have allowed isolationism to affect their thinking and global business strategies. Perceptual differences between the Japanese and United States business executives, and the resulting decisions and business practices that stem from those differences, may explain in part the willingness of Japanese businesses to invest in longer-term business ventures.[1]

The Activities of Perception

As defined, perception is the process of selecting, organizing, and interpreting sensory stimuli. Each of these perceptual activities has a significant impact on how we experience the world.

Selecting

We select and attend to only a limited number of stimuli from the environment. For physiological and psychological reasons, a person cannot sense and perceive all available stimuli. In fact, at any given moment we are aware of relatively little of what is going on around us. (Consider the times when you did not hear someone speak to you because you were busy thinking about other things!)

What we perceive in the world around us is largely determined by the limitations of the five sense organs. For example, there are many sounds our ears cannot hear (such as a dog whistle) and sights we cannot see (ultraviolet and infrared rays). The sense of touch generally provides little information about an object unless accompanied by the ability to see what we are touching. Exhibit 3.3, which shows the old fable of the blind men and the elephant, illustrates this point. The limitation of our senses simply do not permit us to take in all of the stimuli in the environment. In fact, our sense organs literally select certain stimuli for us.

Psychological factors also cause us to perceive selectively. Our past experiences, values, attitudes, and beliefs act as screens or filters through which we receive stimuli from the environment. We tend to perceive what our psychological filters allow us to perceive and to ignore or avoid things inconsistent with our predispositions. A young management trainee in a large oil company, for example, might view a decline in oil and gas prices (and the possible loss of her job) as bad news. To a salesperson who must travel long distances via car, however, such a decline would be pleasant news. Similarly, the specialized training and experiences of an engineer, a marketing specialist, and an information systems professional direct their attention to different aspects of an organizational problem and influence the nature of their solutions. No two people have exactly the same attitudes, values, or past experiences. Thus, every

EXHIBIT 3.3   THE PARABLE OF THE BLIND MEN AND THE ELEPHANT
By John Godfrey Saxe

It was six men of Indostan
  To learning much inclined.
Who went to see the Elephant
  (Though all of them were blind),
That each by observation
  Might satisfy his mind.

The First approached the Elephant,
  And happening to fall
Against his broad and sturdy side,
  At once began to bawl:
"God bless me! but the Elephant
  Is very like a wall!"

The Second, feeling of the tusk
  Cried, "Ho! what have we here
So very round and smooth and sharp?
  To me 'tis very clear
This wonder of an Elephant
  Is very like a spear!"

The Third approached the animal
  And, happening to take
The squirming trunk within his hands
  Thus boldly up he spake:
"I see," quoth he, "the Elephant
  Is very like a snake!"

The Fourth reached out an eager hand,
  And felt about the knee:
"What most this wondrous beast is like
  Is very plain," quoth he.
"'Tis clear enough the Elephant
  Is very like a tree!"

The Fifth, who chanced to touch the ear,
  Said: "E'en the blindest man
Can tell what this resembles most;
  Deny the fact who can
This marvel of an Elephant
  Is very like a fan!"

The Sixth no sooner had begun
  About the beast to grope
Than, seizing on the swinging tail
  That fell within his scope.
"I see," quoth he, "the Elephant
  Is very like a rope!"

And so these men of Indostan
  Disputed loud and long,
Each in his own opinion
  Exceeding stiff and strong.
Though each was partly in the right,
  They all were in the the wrong!

SOURCE: Center for Creative Leadership, *Issues & Observations*, Vol. 7, No. 2 (spring 1987): 8.

individual has a unique psychological filter through which stimuli from the environment are screened.

Organizing

Perceptual organization follows selection. Organizing stimuli does not occur in a random or haphazard way. Rather, we tend to organize stimuli according to basic

EXHIBIT 3.4   FIGURE/GROUND: A DEMONSTRATION

rules or principles. Three common principles guide the organizing activity of perception: (1) figure/ground relationships, (2) closure, and (3) proximity and resemblance.

Look at Exhibit 3.4. What do you see? At first, you may perceive only an ambiguous arrangement of gray shapes on a white background. If so, then you have organized the picture with the gray objects as the figure and the white area as the ground. Now try to organize the picture with the white area as the figure and the gray objects as the ground. Do you see anything different? You should now be able to see the word HOGS spelled with block letters.

In any attempt to organize stimuli, the **figure** is the focal point. The setting in which the figure is located or embedded is the **ground** (background). Organizing is thus an attempt to sort out and distinguish which stimuli belong in the foreground and which belong in the background. A new employee in the marketing department, for example, may initially have trouble recognizing the figure/ground relationships among his colleagues. Gradually, he may learn that Don Jackson (an employee with sixteen years of experience), Becky Schmidt (the departmental secretary), and Sheila Jones (the department head) are important figures for him as a new employee in the ground of the marketing department. As time passes, the marketing department may emerge as the figure for the new employee against the ground of the entire company. Exhibit 3.5 provides additional examples of figure/ground relationships.

Closure is another common principle guiding the perceptual activity of organizing. People tend to fill in the gaps and organize stimuli into whole figures. In Exhibit 3.6, for example, you probably perceive the object on the left as a square

**EXHIBIT 3.5   EXAMPLES OF REVERSIBLE FIGURE/GROUND
                RELATIONSHIPS**

In the figure, you can see either a vase or two faces in profile. If you continue to gaze at the figure for a while, the figure/ground relation will spontaneously change back and forth.

Can you recognize the figure/ground relationship in this example?

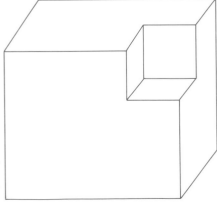

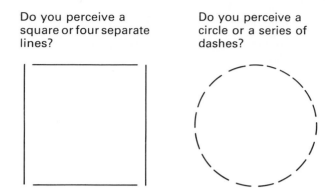

Do you perceive a square or four separate lines?

Do you perceive a circle or a series of dashes?

EXHIBIT 3.6 **EXAMPLES OF PERCEPTUAL CLOSURE**

instead of as four separate lines. Similarly, the object on the right usually is organized as a circle instead of as a series of curved dashes. This tendency to close can often lead to inaccurate perceptions as someone fills in the parts of an object or person that she does not actually observe. For example, Bill's refusals to have lunch with his co-workers over the last two weeks may cause them to conclude that he is becoming socially distant and aloof. In actuality, however, Bill may need the time to work on an important report that must be completed by the end of the month.

Proximity and **resemblance** are the final principles affecting perceptual organization. Stimuli or objects located together or close to one another tend to be grouped together. Proximity is the reason for the obvious and compelling organization in Exhibit 3.7. Within business organizations, people physically situated in a particular department or location (e.g., accounting or the West Coast facility) frequently are seen as similar because of their proximity.

Objects also tend to be organized by similarity or resemblance. The repetitive patterns you see in Exhibit 3.8 are organized into groups of figures based on similarity.

EXHIBIT 3.7 **PERCEPTUAL GROUPING BY PROXIMITY**

In the first set of figures, simple proximity produces a grouping. In the second set, the direction of the added lines reverse the pattern of grouping.

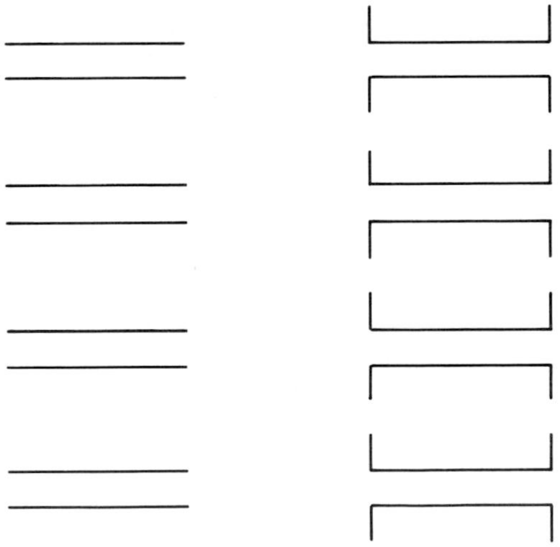

The filled circles group themselves to form a figure (the ×). The grouping occurs even though the closed circles are separated by open figures.

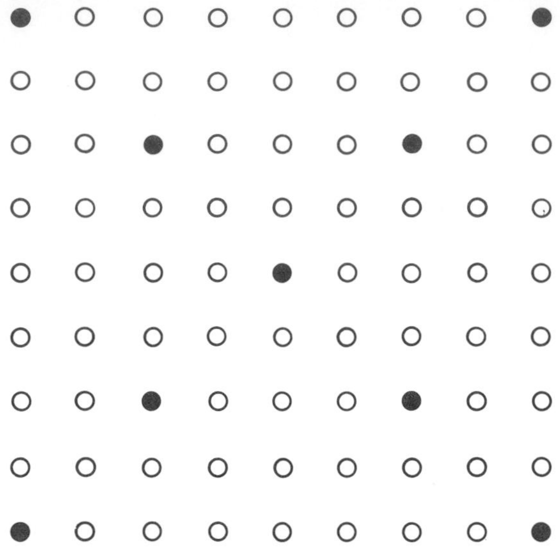

EXHIBIT 3.8   PERCEPTUAL ORGANIZATION BY SIMILARITY

The X in the figure is made perceptible by the contrast between the solid-colored dots and the uncolored dots. Even when uncolored dots intervene between solid dots, as they do in Exhibit 3.8, the solid dots are unified into a pattern. We similarly group people within organizations on the basis of sex, skin color, professional training and degrees, and experience.

Interpreting

Perceptual interpretation involves formulating judgments or inferences about the stimuli we select and organize. The subjective nature of perception is most evident in the activity of interpretation. A simple experiment helps demonstrate this point.

To perform this experiment, you need three similar containers and two volunteers. Fill the three containers with water as follows: one container with hot water, one container with cold water, and one container with lukewarm or room-temperature water. Ask one volunteer to soak his or her hands in the container filled with hot water and the other volunteer to soak his or her hands in the container filled with cold water. The volunteers should leave their hands in the respective containers for approximately one minute. Then instruct the volunteers simultaneously to place their hands in the container filled with the room-temperature water and ask them to describe the water temperature. The result is interesting! The volunteer with hands in the hot water will describe the water as cool, and the volunteer with hands in the cold water will describe it as warm. Their interpretations and descriptions of the sensory stimulation differ even though the two people have their hands in the same container of water!

As this experiment shows, the interpretation of sensory stimuli is influenced significantly by a person's past experiences and frame of reference. The interpretation or meaning of a situation is, to some extent, in the eyes, ears, and other senses of the beholder. However, it is more a function of an individual's previous experiences, knowledge, values, and beliefs. Several people can thus interpret the same event or action differently because no two individuals have exactly the same physiological and psychological characteristics or past experiences. In fact, two people can select and focus on the same stimuli, organize and interpret them differently, and both be right!

The discussion so far may create the impression that perceptual selection, organization, and interpretation are separate and discrete phases of the total perceptual process. In reality, these activities occur almost simultaneously. We do not sense and perceive in segmented steps. Rather, we instantaneously and continuously sense and attach meaning to our environment.

STEELCASE

In many organizations today, discussions about productivity generally focus on topics such as input-output ratios, "doing it right the first time," and the number of worker-hours it takes to assemble a specific product. A study commissioned by Steelcase, Inc., however, addresses the issue of productivity in a different way and provides an example of how people or groups of people can perceive and interpret a situation quite differently.[2]

Steelcase, a Michigan manufacturer of office furniture, asked one thousand office workers nationwide how things were going on the job. It then put the same question to executives. While it is not surprising that the two groups did not always see eye-to-eye, the differences on the question of productivity were startling.

Some 46 percent of the employees said they "certainly do as much as they can" at work. Only 28 percent conceded they "could probably do more." And what did the bosses think about this? Only 16 percent reported their employees were working at capacity.

PERCEPTUAL BARRIERS AND EFFECTS

Have you ever said to another person or had someone say to you, "Can't you see that this is what needs to be done?" By now, you should realize that the other person perhaps could not "see" (organize and interpret) the situation exactly as you did because perception is a subjective, active, and complex process.

The process of perceiving the world around us is complicated by barriers, biases, and such effects as stereotyping, halo effect, projection, implicit personality theories, selective perception, and primacy-recency effects. An awareness of these barriers and effects enhances our overall understanding of the perceptual process.

Stereotyping[3]

A **stereotype** is a belief about the characteristics of a special social group; it is also defined as a mental picture of a group or category of people, objects, or things. The picture or image includes characteristics many people tend to associate with any member of that particular group or category. For example, accountants (as a group) often are considered detail- and bottom-line oriented. We automatically tend to attribute these characteristics, regardless of their accuracy or appropriateness, to any person labeled accountant. We may also have such pictures for other groups, including women, men, minorities, professors, union leaders, engineers, politicians, used-car salespeople, liberals, conservatives, and so on.

Stereotypes are an inevitable consequence of our need as perceivers to make sense of the world around us. In our fast-paced and inherently complicated social environment, people look for ways to interpret events simply, predictably, and coherently, and stereotyping provides a shorthand method for accomplishing the perceptual activities of organizing and interpreting. It is important, however, to recognize stereotypes for what they are: overgeneralizations that can frequently lead us to overlook individual characteristics and differences. Thus, a male manager who accepts the stereotype that women are emotional may be reluctant to criticize a female employee's job performance for fear of upsetting her. In fact, she may want the information and would be able to handle the feedback.

Two of the distinguishing characteristics of stereotypes are their persistence over time and resistance to change, even when the holders of stereotypes receive information that does not confirm them.[4] It is not surprising, for example, that different traits are ascribed to females and males in our society.[5] Men tend to be described as more assertive, active, objective, rational, and competent than women; women are described as more passive, emotional, submissive, compassionate, and socially sensitive. Research has by and large proved these stereotypic beliefs about gender differences to be false.[6] These findings, however, do not prevent stereotypes of men and women from affecting social perception. (Exercise 3.2 at the end of this chapter provides an opportunity for you to increase your awareness of common gender stereotypes that many individuals still hold today.) Stereotypes regarding age, race, and occupation can also have a significant effect on the interpretation and processing of social information.

Halo Effect[7]

A **halo effect** is the tendency to let one characteristic or trait of an individual influence the evaluation of that individual's other characteristics. For example, if a candidate for a sales position has a high grade-point average (GPA), the recruiter may be influenced positively by this characteristic in evaluating other job-related qualifications (e.g., communication skills, work habits, conscientiousness). The positive evaluation of one characteristic can carry over to other characteristics, even when objective evidence may not justify such an evaluation. In this example, GPA may have no relationship to other job-related characteristics for the individual being interviewed.

A halo effect can be positive or negative and, like other perceptual phenomena, can have serious social consequences. For example, one study concluded that jurors in rape cases may be less likely to convict a rape suspect if he is perceived to be "attractive." Eighty-two percent of student jurors in a mock trial found "unattractive" suspects guilty; only fifty-seven percent found "attractive" suspects guilty. The jurors also tended to have more sympathy for "attractive" (as opposed to "unattractive") victims.[8]

Halo effect in performance evaluations is one of the longest recognized and most pervasive forms of rating error.[9] To minimize halo effect in performance evaluations, numerous rating methods, instrument formats, and rater-training techniques have

INTERNATIONAL DIMENSION
Learning How to Conduct Business in China

Tomei, Inc., a Hong Kong-based producer of small electronic goods for retailers in the United States and Japan, has been unusually successful in establishing a major manufacturing base in the southern Chinese city of Zhongshan. After trying and failing to set up profitable manufacturing facilities in several Chinese cities, Tomei decided in 1984 to focus its attention and resources on the Zhongshan factory. By the end of 1988, the plant was producing 18 percent of the world's portable cassette players and 25 percent of its intermediate-frequency radio tuners.

Unlike most production facilities in China, the Zhongshan plant turns out a respectable percentage of products that meet the high quality standards demanded by companies selling under foreign brand names— names such as Aiwa, Sony, Emerson, Panasonic, and Toshiba. Obviously, for Tomei, the romance with China has blossomed into a successful marriage.

Tomei's success has come at a time when and in a place where many other firms have failed. Foreign corporations seeking to take advantage of China's inexpensive labor have often moved into the country confident that "people are people everywhere," and that doing business in China will be essentially the same as in Austria or California. Such companies have frequently found themselves confounded by the complicated and often baffling differences between their own managerial practices and the cultural world of the Chinese. The most striking aspect of Tomei's success in Zhongshan has been its ability to understand and overcome cultural barriers that can inhibit effective business relationships.

One barrier encountered by foreign firms is the large and politically based Chinese bureaucracy. The Chinese prefer to negotiate the bureaucracy's complexity through interpersonal connections (*guanxi*) rather than through official channels. Non-Chinese find it difficult enough to figure out the stated bureaucratic procedures; when it comes to the intricacies of *guanxi*, they are likely to become hopelessly lost. Without fluency in either the Chinese language or the nuances of interpersonal relationships in China, foreigners trying to forge a link between China and the home market are likely to become bewildered and frustrated by the Chinese bureaucracy.

Many foreign firms also fail to appreciate and understand how different China's experience has been from that of most other nations. Until 1911, when the last of China's imperial dynasties was overthrown, the country deliberately limited its contact with foreign traders. From 1911 until the "open door" policies of the 1970s, China has been either closed to Western cultural and economic practices or afflicted by severe internal disorder. This history accounts for part of the distance between Chinese business practices and those of the developed world.

Tomei's awareness of and sensitivity to these cultural barriers have paid tremendous dividends, enabling the firm to establish a strong link between its manufacturer and its markets. Tomei's experience also highlights the need for foreign firms to understand cultural differences that can affect business practices and profitability.

Questions
What perceptual factors may influence managers to believe that "people are people everywhere"?

What specific actions can a manager take to overcome perceptual and cultural barriers?

SOURCE: John C. Beck, Martha Nibley Beck, J. Bonner Ritchie, and Fannie Tsui, "Mainland Manufacturing: Bridging the Cultural Gap," *Exchange*, Spring 1990, 3–7.

been developed. Familiarity with such techniques can help a manager to be aware of and to reduce the negative effects of the halo effect errors when making judgments about subordinates' performance.

Projection[10]

Projection is the tendency for people to see in others traits or characteristics they themselves have. Individuals project their own feelings, emotions, anxieties, and motives into their judgments of other people. This perceptual effect often occurs with the negative or undesirable characteristics an individual possesses but fails to recognize. Consequently, perceptions may be distorted by emotions an individual is experiencing or traits the individual possesses. For example, a domineering supervisor may complain about workers who " . . . are too pushy and always trying to run the show around here!" An executive may think people in the financial department are unwilling to take appropriate risks when in fact the executive tends to be a conservative decision maker.

Projection also occurs when people assume that others are like themselves. Thus, a hard-working manager may believe that all employees are equally industrious, or a cautious accountant may expect that associates also will be strict in interpreting tax laws.

Implicit Personality Theories[11]

We are all amateur social scientists who observe other people and formulate explanations for their behavior and personal characteristics. Based primarily on observation and personal experience, we each develop over time an individual theory about people and human traits that incorporates our particular biases and opinions. Such a personal theory can significantly influence our judgments of others. You may believe, for example, that diligent, hard-working individuals also have integrity or that assertive and forceful people are unfriendly. This relatively stable collection of associations among human traits is an **implicit personality theory.**

To the extent that such a personal theory is incomplete or inaccurate, it can contribute to perceptual distortion and misunderstanding. For example, Jeff's office is cluttered, messy, and seemingly unorganized. Since Jeff's boss believes that neatness and efficiency are related (according to his implicit personality theory), he assumes Jeff is not an efficient worker. In fact, however, Jeff may be efficient when performing his job. As in stereotyping, individual differences can be distorted, overlooked, and obscured if we rely too heavily on an implicit personality theory when attempting to interpret and understand the behavior of other people.

Selective Perception[12]

Selective perception is the process by which a person systematically screens out or focuses on particular cues and information. For example, at the beginning of this chapter, we asked if a medical doctor, an attorney, and an insurance agent all witnessing an automobile accident would really "see" the same accident. We also asked if a manager with an accounting background would interpret organizational problems in a manner similar to that of a manager with extensive training in marketing. In each instance, the training and past experiences of these professionals direct the perceptual process to selected cues and information. The medical doctor probably will notice the nature and severity of physical injuries requiring treatment; the lawyer or insurance agent may be concerned with who caused the accident. Similarly, the manager with a marketing background may view increased sales as the most appropriate solution to an organizational problem; his counterpart in accounting may suggest greater cost control as the best method for correcting the situation.

Physiological limitations and psychological filters make it impossible to perceive everything going on around us. An individual's unique frame of reference thus greatly influences what cues and information are selected and interpreted.

Primacy and Recency Effects[13]

Both primacy and recency effects are concerned with the ordering of stimuli. A **primacy effect** occurs when initial cues and information about another person or object have the greatest influence in shaping an overall impression. In the judicial system of the United States, for example, the prosecuting attorney presents his or her case first. Prosecutors usually are thus quite skilled in presenting evidence and arguments to create a positive and lasting first impression in the minds of the jury. Similarly, a new employee who successfully impresses the boss during the first week of work may benefit from a primacy effect in later performance evaluations.

A **recency effect** occurs when the last or most recent cues and information about another person or object exerts the greatest influence on an overall impression. In the judicial system, a defense attorney follows the prosecution in presenting his or her case to the jury. The objective is to refute the prosecution's arguments and create a strong recency effect the jurors will retain as they deliberate. A political candidate who wants to be the concluding speaker in a debate in order to have the last say tries to establish a favorable impression in the minds of potential voters.

Within organizations, primacy and recency effects can influence the accuracy of employee performance evaluations when a manager recalls only the first or most recent activities of the person being evaluated rather than the employee's performance during the entire evaluation period. To avoid such a potential source of rating error, many personnel experts suggest that instances of both positive and negative work activities ("critical incidents") be recorded throughout the evaluation period. Such a record provides a more complete and accurate picture of the employee's actual performance and reduces the likelihood that a primacy or recency effect will occur.

In Summary

By this point, you should have increased your understanding of the nature, activities, and complexity of the perceptual process. Each barrier and effect discussed can significantly influence how we experience and interpret the world around us. We may not be able to "see" things exactly as other people do, but we can become more aware of and sensitive to the causes of perceptual differences. (The Ethical Dilemma on page 84 provides examples of current advertisements that can yield *very* different interpretations.) Such awareness of and sensitivity to others, as well as ourselves, are crucial elements in the formula for effective management of human resources in organizations.

ETHICAL DILEMMA
Can Your Morning Cereal Stop a Heart Attack?

The United States is entering a new era of superfoods. Marketers, acting without government guidance or regulation, can now claim that their food products help improve consumers' health as well as offer good taste or convenience. And research is yielding new ingredients and new uses for potentially potent foods.

Fully 30 percent of the $3.6 billion in annual United States food advertising now includes some type of health message. Today, supermarket food aisles look like a modern medicine show with a vast assortment of health-related products. These new products are the focal point for a labeling and claims controversy that affects millions of consumers.

Consider the ethical implications of using the healthy, dietetic-sounding word "light" in the following marketing tactics:

1. Two major marketers of olive oil have developed "light" products. However, these oils are lighter only in color and taste, not in calories or fat. The companies say the products are intended only to address many consumers' dislike of strong-tasting olive oil.

2. The CEO of a major food company insisted that his company was not attempting to mislead consumers with its "light" dessert products (which were eventually renamed to avoid a legal fight with a group of state attorneys general). He stated that the word "light" referred to the light, airy texture of the products, not to their caloric content.

Today, marketers of food products must operate in a vacuum of federal regulation concerning health claims; the word "light" has little legal or regulatory meaning.

Questions
Do you think the term "light" affects consumers' perceptions of products?
Is use of the word "light" ethical in the examples described above?
What perceptual effects do you think influence the interpretation of these messages?

SOURCE: "Healthy Food Pace Quickens: Leaving Regulatory Forces Behind," *Advertising Age*, 25 September 1989, 3–12; "The Great American Health Pitch," *Business Week*, 9 October 1989, 114–123; "How I Made $812 in the Oat Bran Craze," *Fortune*, 9 October 1989, 125–130.

INTERPRETING WHY OTHERS BEHAVE AS THEY DO

Attribution Theory

Consider the following examples of behavior you might see in everyday life:

A man volunteers to give blood at the local Red Cross office and receives twenty-five dollars for each pint. Is he a person committed to helping others? Or is he an expedient person who would do anything for money?

A colleague receives a promotion and a substantial increase in pay. Is she just lucky? Was she promoted because she knows the right people? Or is she a competent and conscientious worker who deserves the promotion?

A salesperson greets you cordially as you enter the store and speaks highly of his product. Does he really like you or is he playing up to you to make a sale? Is the product really that good or does he talk glowingly only to make a sale?

In these and similar situations, we usually try to understand why a person behaves in a particular way. Using what psychologists term the **attribution process,** we attribute to others motives or possible causes for their behavior.[14] The process of making such attributions helps us understand their behavior and enables us to make predictions about how they may behave in the future.

The attribution process basically involves reasoning backward from the observation of an event or behavior to a judgment about its cause. In this respect, the attribution process fundamentally differs from the more common problem of prediction in organizations. In prediction, we attempt to infer what will happen in the future (e.g., level of satisfaction, motivation, or performance) based on facts known to us at the time. The attribution process, on the other hand, attempts to provide an explanation for an event that has already occurred.

A person's behavior is influenced by (1) internal states and personal dispositions (attitudes, values, beliefs, traits, etc.), and (2) certain external factors. The basic attribution task we encounter when observing another individual is to determine if certain behaviors reveal something specific about that person or the situation. For example, can we infer from a co-worker's promotion and pay raise that she is lucky, or do we conclude that she is a conscientious and competent employee who deserves the reward? If we conclude that something about the person is responsible for the behavior, we have made a **dispositional attribution.** If we decide some external factor is responsible for the behavior (e.g., money, knowing the right people, social pressure, threats), we have made a **situational attribution.** Thus, our observation and analysis of other people usually lead us to conclude that their behavior is caused either by themselves or by something in the environment.

Three basic criteria are used to process information about the behavior of other people: (1) consistency (the extent to which a person behaves in the same way on other, similar occasions); (2) consensus (the extent to which other people behave in the same way as the individual being observed); and (3) distinctiveness (the extent to which a person behaves in the same way in other situations).[15] Exhibit 3.9 presents information and examples about the process of formulating dispositional and situational attributions.

Imagine, for example, that a co-worker is in dispute with a supervisor over a work procedure. As you observe and analyze the incident, you recall that this co-worker (1) has had disputes with this particular supervisor about work procedures on other occasions (consistency is high), and (2) other employees frequently have had disputes with this supervisor about work procedures (consensus is high). Also, the co-worker has not had similar disagreements with other supervisors or employees about work procedures (distinctiveness is high). Given this information, you probably would attribute the cause of your colleague's behavior to situational or external factors. In other words, the dispute probably was caused by conditions your co-worker could not control (the supervisor's interpretation of work procedures) rather than by dispositional factors or characteristics (a contentious and/or disagreeable temperament).

EXHIBIT 3.9   FACTORS INFLUENCING THE ATTRIBUTIONS WE MAKE

We are inclined to attribute a person's behavior to situational (external) factors when there is

1. *High Consistency*: The person behaves in the same manner in this situation on other occasions.
2. *High Consensus*: Many other people behave in the same manner in this situation on other occasions.
    3. *High Distinctiveness*: The person behaves differently in other situations.

Grant Smith expresses dissatisfaction every time he is assigned the task of cleaning up the work area (High-Consistency). Other employees also express dissatisfaction when asked to clean up (High-Consensus). Grant is not dissatisfied with other tasks to which he is assigned (High-Distinctiveness).

Perceived Cause: The most likely cause of Grant's dissatisfaction is something to do with the task itself (e.g., cleaning up is messy and boring).

On the other hand, we are inclined to attribute a person's behavior to dispositional (internal) factors when there is:

1. *High Consistency*: The person behaves in the same manner in this situation on other occasions.
2. *Low Consensus*: Few people behave in the same manner as this person.
3. *Low Distinctiveness*: The person behaves in the same manner in other situations.

Grant Smith expresses dissatisfaction every time he is assigned the task of cleaning up (High-Consistency). Other employees are not dissatisfied when asked to clean up (Low-Consensus). Grant expresses dissatisfaction with just about every task he is assigned (Low-Distinctiveness).

Perceived Cause: The most likely cause of Grant's dissatisfaction is something to do with his personal characteristics (e.g., he complains about everything).

Consider another dispute over work procedures involving a different co-worker and supervisor. In this situation, you observe that your co-worker (1) has had similar arguments with other supervisors and employees about work procedures (distinctiveness is low) and (2) has disputed with this particular supervisor about work procedures on other occasions (consistency is high). In addition, (3) other employees have not argued with this supervisor about work procedures (consensus is low). You would probably make a dispositional rather than a situational attribution (the behavior is caused by the co-worker's quarrelsome nature rather than by the supervisor's interpretation of work rules).

Common Attribution Errors

Understanding the attribution process is particularly relevant to the study of organizational behavior. We constantly observe people and formulate explanations for their behavior. These attributions affect our judgments and attitudes about the people we observe and also influence our expectations about their future behavior. Sometimes, however, we make mistakes in interpreting our own or another person's behavior. Such errors are particularly critical in such situations as employment interviews and performance evaluations. This section discusses several sources of error and bias in the attribution process.

The actor-observer effect

Generally, we tend to attribute the causes of other people's behaviors to their personal characteristics. When it comes to our own behavior, however, we tend to be more aware of the environmental constraints we face, and so emphasize these factors more than personal characteristics. In other words, we usually explain someone else's behavior as internally caused and our own behavior as externally caused. This type of attribution error is referred to as an **actor-observer effect.** If, for example, Brian did not receive an important promotion, his co-worker Scott might attribute this action to Brian's poor work habits and mediocre job performance during the last eighteen months. If Scott were the one passed over for the promotion, however, he would probably attribute the decision to situational causes (e.g., "I was ill during most of the peak season for our business," or "the boss never liked me").

The vignette at the beginning of this chapter provides another example of the actor-observer effect. Mr. Vincent attributed the decrease in Amet's orders to Michael's mishandling of the account. Michael, on the other hand, thought increasing interest rates and uncertainty about a recession were causing Gooding to reduce its inventory and proceed cautiously on new projects. Mr. Vincent believed Michael himself was the cause of the problem; Michael believed external factors had caused the reduction in orders for pipe products.

Two possible explanations for the tendency to attribute our own behavior to external causes and the behavior of other individuals to internal causes have been offered.[16] First, we focus our attention on the external factors surrounding us because we cannot observe our own behavior directly. Consequently, we tend to (1) see these factors as the major causes of our behavior and (2) overlook consistent patterns in our own behavior. A worker who constantly argues with the department head, for example, will probably perceive external causes for the repeated conflicts (e.g., "That manager is always on my back," or "Wouldn't you know he'd come around right when my equipment broke down"). The real causes of the problem, however, may be the worker's abrasive personality or sarcastic style of communication.

Second, we cannot know for certain what external factors are causing another person's behavior. We are, therefore, more likely to (1) attribute the causes of that person's behavior to personal dispositions, and (2) overestimate the stability of others' behavior. For example, John Billingsley, president of Acme Tool, expects all managerial and supervisory employees to complete their work assignments punctually. According to Billingsley, "There are no excuses for being late." Consequently, Mr. Billingsley may attribute Mary's tardiness in turning in a report to her lack of organization and poor time-management skills. In fact, however, the report may have been late because of problems beyond her control, such as broken equipment or inaccurate information about the deadline.

JAPAN

Another example of the actor-observer effect is found in the results of a recent poll conducted by Louis Harris and Associates concerning Japanese perceptions of the United States and its people.[17] A majority of the one thousand Japanese adults who participated in the survey believed that (1) the United States itself is to blame for the limited success of its exports to Japan; (2) United States companies should work harder to increase sales in Japan; (3) the United States is growing more dependent upon Japanese technology; and (4) Japan should rely less on the United States for defense. In addition, a plurality of the respondents expected Japan eventually to replace America as the world's leading economic and political power.

The Japanese perception was not completely one-sided, however. A majority of the respondents also believed that Japan is imposing unfair barriers on some American imports and should be more flexible on trade. Sixty-four percent of the respondents indicated that Japan's cumbersome distribution system should be reformed, and forty-five percent would require that a certain amount of United States products be allowed into Japan. Only twenty-one percent of the respondents believed that the United States had begun a process of irreversible decline.

The Japanese perceptions described above may result in part from the actor-observer effect. The Japanese attribute the limited success of United States exports to the United States itself (internal cause); they further believe that working harder (internal cause) will lead to increased United States sales. On the other hand, United States politicians and businesspeople frequently point to trade barriers and restrictions (external cause) as the reasons for failure to penetrate Japanese markets.

Self-serving bias

People frequently view themselves as the cause of positive outcomes and deny responsibility for negative outcomes. We tend to perceive internal causes for our successes (our own ability and effort) and external causes for our failures (bad luck, situation, task difficulty). This type of attribution error is referred to as a **self-serving bias.**[18]

For example, high-performing employees may be more likely to believe their success is due to skill and ability while low-performing employees may blame their failure on the lack of proper tools, poor supervision, or a host of other factors. Note that the tendency of poor performers to blame environmental factors for their failure would also be predicted by the actor-observer effect, although the tendency of people to claim personal credit for their successes would not.

Janet Hill received an assignment to develop an orientation and basic training program for new employees in the finance department. She worked diligently for three weeks preparing her presentation and supporting materials. The completed program was reviewed by her immediate supervisor and revised slightly before the initial presentation. Participants in and observers of the first orientation program were pleased with Janet's work and positive in their evaluations. In fact, the head of the finance department, Mr. Hudson, told Janet that her program "was the best I've ever attended." If you were Janet, what would you perceive as the cause of the successful program? More than likely, you would view your own effort and ability as the causes of the program's success (dispositional attribution). If the program had been a flop, though, you might attribute the failure to the unresponsive audience or to the supervisor who revised your original presentation (situational attribution).

The self-serving bias can affect managerial decision making, planning, and policy formulation. In one research study, for example, the presidents of forty-eight manufacturing firms were interviewed to find out how accurately they could predict the future performance of their firms. Fifty-six percent of the executives predicted they would perform better than they actually did; only eight percent estimated they would do worse. In other words, there was a strong tendency to overpredict performance. Thirty-five percent of the presidents accurately predicted their performance. The researchers concluded that managers often perceive themselves to be more capable than they really are, and this bias affected their ability to predict organizational performance accurately.[19] This bias can also influence other aspects of a manager's job such as evaluating subordinates' performance and making personnel decisions (hiring, firing, and promotion).

Negative bias

Another attribution error is the tendency to be unduly influenced by the negative information we have about a person. Even when we are knowledgeable about both the positive and negative aspects of another person's behavior, we are likely to be more influenced by that individual's negative than positive qualities. Although the exact nature of this **negative bias** is not yet fully understood, it may serve a defensive function by protecting a person from unfavorable comparisons with others.[20]

Research studies suggest that this negative bias can affect a wide range of organizational decisions. For example, one study determined that this type of attribution error is especially applicable when people are interviewing for a job.[21] Negative information was more highly related to decisions to hire or not hire than was positive information. Particularly if received early in the interview, negative information was likely to lead to a candidate's rejection even when the total amount of information was overwhelmingly positive. Managers, then, must be aware of and sensitive to this type of attribution error and the possible impact it can have on their judgments and decisions.

False consensus bias

People frequently believe that the attitudes they hold are appropriate for a particular situation and thus must be widely shared by others. For example, a person who is satisfied and motivated to do her work well may assume that co-workers feel the same way. This attribution error is known as the **false consensus bias.**

Attributions we make about another person's behavior may be influenced by our assumptions concerning that person's attitudes. For example, one investigator found that employees who are highly committed to an organization are less likely to believe that others quit their jobs because they are dissatisfied.[22] It appears that committed employees projected their own attitudes onto co-workers and then explained that co-workers quit for reasons consistent with their own attitudes.

PERCEPTION: CONCLUSIONS

The most practical lesson you can take from this chapter is an awareness that perception is not an objective process leading to correct or incorrect views of the world. The process of perception is subjective and can often result in different interpretations of the same stimuli. An individual's attitudes, biases, values, and past experiences greatly influence what and how stimuli are selected, organized, and interpreted. Thus, a union official can interpret a contract proposal as "insulting and unfair" when a management representative considers it "reasonable." Two people can perceive the same stimuli, organize and interpret those stimuli differently, and both be right.

An awareness that perception is subjective in nature, however, is only a first step toward the more effective management of work behavior. Specific perceptual problems such as primacy and recency effects, projection, halo effect, and stereotyping can occur because of this subjectivity. A manager who understands and is sensitive to the complexity of the perceptual process can anticipate and minimize such problems. For example, knowing that we perceive selectively may prompt a manager to collect more detailed information before making a final decision, or to listen to both sides of an issue or problem before formulating a proposal. Similarly, the tendency to stereotype can be overcome by paying more attention to the characteristics and abilities that make a person unique.

As we work with other people, we attempt to explain and interpret their behavior. Attribution theory provides a useful framework for understanding this process by which we assign motives and causes to the behavior of others. A manager's attribution processes play an obvious role in the diagnosis of organizational problems. For example, a manager who recognizes that an absenteeism problem exists should first ask why employees are not reporting to work. Causal beliefs play a crucial role at this initial stage of the problem-solving process. Biases associated with the attribution process can also affect a manager's judgments.

A substantial proportion of a manager's work involves evaluating employee performance. Conflict in the performance-appraisal process may result from the different perceptions held by a manager and an employee about the reasons behind the employee's performance, particularly when it is poor.

The dispositional or situational attributions a manager makes also can have a significant impact on (1) rewarding and punishing the employee's performance; (2) closeness of supervision; (3) expectancies about the employee's future work performance; and (4) aspirations or goals the manager might have for the employee.[23] Knowing about the attribution process and common attribution errors thus can help a manager reduce distortion and bias in making these important personnel decisions.

QUESTIONS FOR REVIEW AND DISCUSSION

1. Discuss the relationship between sensation and perception.
2. What are the activities of perception? Describe the nature of each perceptual activity.
3. Explain how two people can interpret the same facts or events differently.
4. What is the difference between a stereotype and an implicit personality theory? Give an example of each.
5. What can a manager do to reduce perceptual barriers and biases?

6. What is the difference between situational and dispositional attributions?
7. Describe the factors that influence the kinds of attributions we make.
8. What is the actor-observer effect?
9. What are the implications of the attribution process for managers (1) evaluating subordinate performance, (2) determining rewards and punishments, and (3) interviewing job candidates?

REFERENCES

1. "Inside Business," Cable News Network, 11 February 1990.
2. Paul B. Brown, "Are You Really Running As Fast As You Can?," *Inc.*, October 1987, 10.
3. S. S. Zalkind and T. W. Costello, "Perception: Some Recent Research and Implications for Administration," *Administrative Science Quarterly*, 9 (1962) 219–235.

4. J. C. Brigham, "Ethnic Stereotypes," *Psychological Bulletin*, 76 (1971): 15–38; Galen V. Bodenhause and Robert S. Wyer, Jr., "Effects of Stereotypes on Decision Making and Information Processing Strategies," *Journal of Personality and Social Psychology*, Vol. 48, No. 2 (1985): 267–282; Loren Falkenberg, "Improving the Accuracy of Stereotypes Within the Workplace," *Jour-*

nal of Management, Vol. 16, No. 1 (1990): 107–118; Harvey J. Brightman, "Crisis! Managerial Lessons from Pearl Harbor," *Business*, January-March 1989, 3–11.

5. Kay Deaux and Laurie L. Lewis, "Structure of Gender Stereotypes: Interrelationships Among Components and Gender Label," *Journal of Personality and Social Psychology*, Vol. 46, No. 5 (1984): 991–1004; A. Locksley, E. Borgide, N. Brekke, and C. Hepburn, "Sex Stereotypes and Social Judgment," *Journal of Personality and Social Psychology*, Vol. 39, No. 5. (1980): 821–831; J. P. McKee and A. C. Sherriffs, "The Differential Evaluation of Males and Females," *Journal of Personality*, 25 (1957): 256–271.

6. J. E. Parson, T. Adler, and J. L. Meese, "Sex Differences in Achievement: A Test of Alternative Theories," *Journal of Personality and Social Psychology*, 46 (1984): 26–43.

7. Zalkind and Costello.

8. M. B. Jacobson, "Effects of Victim's and Defendant's Physical Attractiveness on Subjects' Judgments in a Rape Case," *Sex Roles*, Vol. 7, No. 3 (March 1981): 247–255.

9. R. Jacobs and S. W. J. Kozlowski, "A Closer Look at Halo Error in Performance Ratings," *Academy of Management Journal*, Vol. 28, No. 1 (1985): 201–212.

10. Zalkind and Costello.

11. J. S. Bruner and R. Tagiuri, "The Perception of People," in G. Lindzey, ed., *Handbook of Social Psychology* (Reading, Mass.: Addison-Wesley, 1954), 601–633.

12. D. C. Dearborn and H. A. Simon, "Selective Perception: A Note on the Department Identification of Executives," *Sociometry*, 21 (1958): 140–144; James P. Walsh, "Selectivity and Selective Perception: An Investigation of Managers' Belief Structures and Information Processing," *Academy of Management Journal*, Vol. 31, No. 4 (1988): 873–896.

13. E. E. Jones and G. R. Goethals, "Order Effects in Impression Formation: Attribution Context and the Nature of the Entity," in E. E. Jones, D. E. Kanouse, H. H. Kelley, R. E. Nisbett, S. Valins, and B. Weiner, eds., *Attribution: Perceiving the Causes of Behavior* (Morristown, N.J.: General Learning Press, 1972).

14. F. Heider, *The Psychology of Interpersonal Relations* (New York: Wiley, 1958).

15. H. H. Kelley, "Attribution Theory in Social Psychology," in D. Levine ed., *Nebraska Symposium of Motivation* (Lincoln, Neb.: University of Nebraska, 1967).

16. E. E. Jones and R. E. Nisbett, "The Actor and Observer: Divergent Perceptions of the Causes of Behavior," in E. E. Jones, et al. *Attribution: Perceiving the Cause of Behavior.*

17. Robert Neff, "Japan's Hardening View of America," *Business Week*, 18 December 1989, 62–64.

18. C. S. Carver, E. DeGregario, and R. Gillis, "Ego-Defensive Bias in Attribution Among Two Categories of Observers," *Personality and Social Psychology Bulletin*, 6 (1980): 44–50.

19. Larwood L. W. Whittaker, "Managerial Myopia: Self-Serving Biases in Organizational Planning," *Journal of Applied Psychology*, 62 (1977): 187–201.

20. D. E. Knouse and L. R. Hanson, "Negativity in Evaluations," in E. E. Jones et al. *Attribution: Perceiving the Causes of Behavior.*

21. E. C. Webster, *Decision Making in the Employment Interview* (Montreal: Industrial Relations Center, McGill University, 1964).

22. R. Mowday, "Viewing Turnover from the Perspective of Those Who Remain: The Relationship of Job Attitudes to Attributions About the Causes of Turnover," *Journal of Applied Psychology*, 66 (1981): 120–123.

23. T. R. Mitchell, S. G. Green, and R. Wood, "An Attributional Model of Leadership and the Poor Performing Subordinate," in L. L. Cummings and B. Staw, eds., *Research in Organizational Behavior* (Greenwich, Conn.: JAI Press, 1981), 197–234.

CASE 3.1 *The invisible colleague*

ELLEN KIMMEL *University of South Florida*

PART A

Eight men and one woman were seated at a cloth-covered, rectangular table in a small meeting room of the kind typically provided by large downtown hotels.

They were participants in an invitational workshop exclusively for directors of privately funded educational reform grants.

The workshop was designed to help the grant directors produce well-written case reports illustrative of the problems they encountered in educational change that could be considered for inclusion in a yearbook published by a prestigious national institute on educational futures. The participants were assigned to five-person teams to critique case reports by members of several presentation teams. Midway through the workshop, the members of the critique teams were assigned to presentation teams while those who had already presented reconstituted the critique teams. Thus, by the end of three and one-half days of tightly scheduled meetings, all participants had read and reacted to many case reports as well as presented their individual reports and obtained rigorous feedback. Each participant received extensive encouragement to rewrite the case and submit it to the editor of the institute's yearbook.

It was now the morning of the last day, and Dr. Erica Howe along with the other three members of the presenting team were meeting the five-person critique team. Because of her scheduled afternoon departure, Howe had asked the critique team's chairman to schedule her presentation earlier rather than later in the morning session.

Howe was conscious of her peculiar status in the group both as the sole woman and as a person who, with a Ph.D. in experimental psychology, had little formal preparation in the fields of higher education, educational administration, and curriculum that comprised the backgrounds of most of her peers at the workshop. Despite her experience as a co-professor of a special master's degree course in educational administration, Howe remained somewhat skeptical about educational disciplines that lacked a rigorous experimental base. Howe, a full professor holding joint appointments in psychology and educational psychology, achieved her present position with no small effort and personal sacrifice. Howe, in concert with other feminist women on the campus, had engaged in a long and sometimes bitter fight to equalize promotion, salary, and other considerations for women. Howe felt her career had blossomed since her early involvement in the feminist movement on the campus. She published extensively in her disciplines, was a much sought-after consultant on sex-equity practices in both the public and private sectors, and was a recipient of state and federal grants. By any standard, Howe judged herself to be academically productive, a superachiever, and a "workaholic" who managed as well her roles as a mother of four daughters and wife of a distinguished scholar.

As one who attended a similar conference in the preceding year, Howe was aware that her case report was different in its emphases from the concerns and interests of most of the people at the workshop. She had been restless while listening to the critiques of others' cases. In many instances she had felt poorly informed about the "finer points" of interpretation in matters such as school law, budget management, and planning formats that had been presented to her critique team. Howe had not been comfortable in such a passive, silent role within the workshop meetings. To better inform herself about the views and special interests of fellow participants in the workshop, Howe had actively initiated discussions with them during the breaks and at meals.

Howe had found her new colleagues, 95 percent of whom were male, generally friendly and willing to talk with her. However, for the first time in her career, she had a gnawing feeling that their responses to her were more social than professional. Aware, too, of an intense sexual interest in a male participant at the workshop—this was the first time she had experienced such an interest in a professional setting—she had wondered whether her behavior around men had betrayed her interest.

Howe was greatly relieved that the person who so strongly appealed to her was not on her presentation team or on the critique team she faced today. Despite his absence, she experienced some difficulty attending to the discussions of the case reports, forcing her to renew her efforts at concentration. Howe's new sense of vulnerability reminded her of her belief that "sex in the office" or in this case "sex in the workshop" was largely a mythical problem, but one she now felt was potentially a problem for her. She rebuked herself angrily when she caught her thoughts wandering over the possibilities.

Now, on the last day, Howe, impatiently awaited the beginning of the morning's session and hoped that the chairman would put her report at the top of the schedule. Seated across from Jack Hammond, who was a bit long-winded but relatively friendly, and next to Mark Thane, she recalled her serious discussion with Mark about the problems of rearing his daughters so they could avoid becoming, in Mark's words, "soft as all the professional women he had ever met." It disturbed her then to think he might see her in the same light, but she didn't pursue the matter with him. She wondered now whether she could be taken seriously as a professional colleague in this group.

PART B

Looking at his watch and glancing around the table, Dr. Martin Muehl opened the meeting. "Well, it's time we got started and there remain a number of case reports to review before our day ends. Let's let the young lady go first this morning."

Without thinking, Howe retorted, "How about the 'old woman'—that's more accurate."

Muehl looked at her over his reading glasses and blithely amended. "Fine . . . the little lady then."

Now, standing outside herself, Howe wryly predicted that her comments would fall on deaf ears. She composed herself to begin with a description of the case's objectives and an overview of the concepts students would apply to its analysis. However, before she could begin, Jack Hammond launched into a story about how fortunate he had been to ride to work each day with a female colleague and to learn all about the "woman's issue." He had been sensitized through this experience, he assured the group.

"How can he so thoroughly delude himself?" Howe thought to herself. "Before I've had a chance to say a word, he has sidetracked the discussion to center on himself. It's hardly relevant even if he were sensitized! I've got to get my presentation going before my time runs out."

Referring to her notes, Howe began her presentation the moment Jack indicated the end of his story. "I think it is important to comment on the ways my case report differs from those you have been seeing," she began. "I have written this case to illustrate the application of behavioral principles that affect people's performance in formal . . . "

"Say, Erica," George Kennedy intruded, "where's my page three? I'm missing page three. Does anybody have an extra page?"

"I don't have one, but I have two page sevens in my report, George," Bill VerHove added.

Howe inwardly groaned. "God, what next! Will I ever get this report going? This scene, important men interrupting trivial women is a classic. I wish I could film this for my class. Is Mark catching the meaning of this diversion? Does he see how this fits with our discussion about the absence of real competition and criticism for women as part of the experience they need to develop fully as professionals?" She glanced covertly in his direction but couldn't read his expression.

"O.K.," Howe replied. "It looks like some of your reports were poorly assembled. I'll fill you in on the substance of the missing page because it is central to the purpose of my case. First, as I was indicating before George discovered the missing page, the case illustrates the way certain behavioral principles affect the actions of people in formal organizations. My work has been directed toward training undergraduates, more specifically, women undergraduates, in conflict resolution by sharpening their skills in assertiveness training."

"Erica, excuse me for interrupting," the normally silent Joseph Grang began, "but I'm troubled by the implicit value judgment you seem to make in your use of assertiveness training techniques for women."

"Hold on, Joe," Larry Raines blurted, "that's not the purpose of our review. It's really immaterial to the use of the case and will likely lead to a discussion that won't be too profitable."

Turning to Howe, Larry continued, 'You know, I had a hard time getting the sense of what motivated your Cynthia Sherrill, Professor Sherrill in the case. I couldn't quite figure her out, and I wondered if you could help me see her more clearly?"

Howe was simultaneously troubled and relieved. Troubled that her main character wasn't clearly portrayed, but relieved that Larry had raised the first serious concern, she replied warmly, "Larry, that's helpful to me. I might be able to clear her up if you could pick out a sentence or something that you find particularly confusing, and I could then tell you what I meant."

"Larry, I didn't have any trouble understanding what the character Sherrill is intended to accomplish." The speaker, George Kennedy, looked with open amazement at Larry.

Immediately several people began to speak at once, and Howe watched the discussion break down. Seemingly out of the blue, she heard Jack Hammond across from her say with a fatuous grin, "Well, it's nice to have something to look at in here after all. Usually we just have each other to look at."

Stunned, Howe replied with an edge in her voice, "I don't know. I would rather look at Gerry over there—he's a lot more handsome . . . " Her voice trailed off as she knew it served no purpose to continue the discussion.

Feeling a growing sense of helplessness, she said to no one in particular, "Could we go on? I think maybe you, Martin, as the chair of the reviewers, could give me your comments."

Martin, who up to then had said nothing, began, "Yes, I do have several points to make. First, on the cover page, I would suggest that. . . . " To herself, Howe thought, "At last, something concrete, straightforward and substantive. I don't know you, Martin, but you have my everlasting thanks! I feel you have invited me to join this group, even if it means having to hear some critical things about my case. After all, that's what I came for. Now, I must be careful not to act defensive or in any way discourage this sort of direct help."

Following Martin's list of questions and comments, several reviewers vied for the floor, but Jack, as usual prevailed. Undaunted by colleagues' subtle and not-so-subtle suggestions that he stop, he began a tangential story. At the end, he turned to Howe and said, "Here are the names and addresses of two girls in my department who would like to have copies of this case."

Howe looked at the addresses she had been handed and shook her head in disbelief that the two "girls" referred to were Ph.D. faculty members.

PART C

"Jack," Howe began in measured tones, "I want to make clear that you are in fact referring to two grown women who are your faculty colleagues?"

"Yes, that's right. One's an associate, the other one's an assistant professor," he answered blandly.

"And do you refer to your male colleagues in the department as 'boy?'" she countered.

"What do you mean? . . . I, uh, these females are girls. Well, one is getting past that now, I guess, since she's actually not so young. But women want to be called girls—that's what they are, really," he blustered and squirmed.

Howe recognized the usual incredulity, defensiveness, disbelief, and finally rejection so common when such a discussion of labels takes place. Unable to let go, she persisted as calmly as she could, "I am sure that you believe what you said, and no doubt there are many women who accept or even prefer to be called 'girls,' but I can only assure you that it is offensive to many adult females to be referred to by a term defined in Webster's as a 'female child, barmaid, or maidservant.'"

There was a heavy silence. All eyes were downcast or averted, and Jack, the target of Howe's lecture,

shuffled his papers. George noted that it was close to ten o'clock and probably time to wind up the review of Howe's report. However, Martin Muehl reviewed quickly the day's schedule and assured the team that ample time remained for Howe's report. Howe hastily assured George and the chairman that she had no wish to belabor the discussion of her work and would try to avoid future off-task exchanges.

Howe tried to put on a cheerful face and asked the review team for additional reactions. She felt as though she were pleading, and was angry at herself for engaging in the exchange with Jack that so muted the group.

Mark Thayne, essentially silent throughout the session, observed that he knew a woman activist "reformer" working in a different county in Howe's home state who would be a good subject for another case. She thanked him and said she would get the name from him after the session.

Howe looked around the review team with a growing feeling of despair. "Oh damn, now they are really afraid to deal with me except in this 'sweet' fashion. Maybe they think I need handling with kid gloves. O.K., one more try for feedback, and, if that fails, I'll not waste any more time," she thought.

"I thought you might be about to say something, Larry," Howe tried. "Do you have any further questions about what I've written here?"

"No, not really, I guess," Larry replied not looking directly at her. "I think Martin pretty much covered the other questions I had. I am not sure I will ever understand the application of the so-called behavioral principles, but that's my problem."

"Part of your reaction could be due to the way in which I have presented the material in the case. Others might be having difficulty with the same things that trouble you," Howe ventured, hoping Larry would explore more completely his reaction to her report.

"No, not really. I really don't have anything helpful that I can give you. Hey," he turned to the others, "take me off the hook!"

Howe wilted inside. "Now I've done it! He's cornered, threatened, and I'm the pushy bitch who can't leave well enough alone. I give up. It's a lost cause now."

"Thank you for your help. Your recommendations and observations will help me in the rewrite. I think we should turn to Mark's report now so we can finish at least part of it before the break," Howe concluded.

CASE 3.2   *National brickworks*

DONALD D. WHITE   *University of Arkansas*

National Brickworks was organized in 1866 and has developed into a leading producer of fire brick and high-temperature mortar. The company now has thirteen plants throughout the United States. The St. Louis plant, built in 1900, produces fire brick, high-temperature mortar, and brickram, a packing used to fill cracks in high-temperature kilns.

Employees under Frank Trouse, plant supervisor, work in one of six locations. All clerical and other administrative workers are located in the Main Office Building. Shipping and receiving of goods takes place in an area referred to as "the Docks." Production is housed in two separate plants, with brickram and high-temperature mortars being made in Plant #1 and fire brick being made in a second building—the Hill Plant. Quality-control personnel are located in

the Laboratory, and machinists' equipment is located in the Shop. The Shop and Laboratory are adjoining buildings (see Exhibit 3.10).

Most of the laborers employed at the St. Louis plant have been with National Brickworks for more than fifteen years, the oldest worker having forty-six years' seniority. Although many laborers were in their late thirties or early forties, the strenuous work involved kept them in excellent physical condition. The work of the plant employees ranged from unskilled to semiskilled in nature.

A problem arose in early 1988 when, despite the availability of work in the plant, the work force hit an all-time low. Turnover among new workers was particularly high, and the number of people applying for jobs as laborers was negligible. Plant supervisor

EXHIBIT 3.10   BRICKYARD LAYOUT

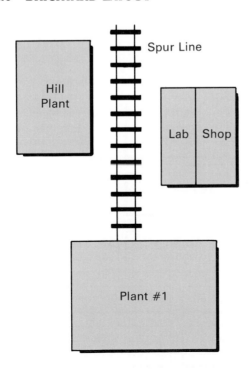

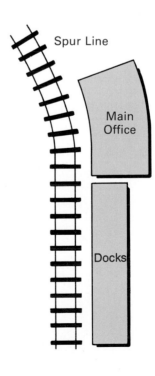

Trouse took note of the problem and decided it needed immediate attention. One Tuesday morning, he called his foremen together to present the problem to them and get their reactions (see Exhibit 3.11). When everyone was assembled, he walked to the head of the table and said:

> We have a problem on our hands. We've all seen its physical symptoms, but we mistakenly thought they would go away if we let time take its course. Well, time has revealed only one thing, and that is that the problem will have to be met head-on. Let's start by getting the physical symptoms of our problem down on paper.

Thus began a brainstorming session which lasted many hours. After they had exhausted their resources trying to pinpoint the symptoms of the problem, the following list was read:

1. A high rate of turnover exists in the two production plants, especially among the newly hired workers.
2. Turnover tends to remain low in the quality-control groups as well as among the dock workers (only four people actually worked full-time on the dock).
3. Safety violations in the two plants are becoming more numerous, and more hours are being lost to on-the-job injuries than ever before.
4. Conditions in the two plants, such as excessive heat and dust, are being complained about more frequently by both younger and older workers, yet these conditions have always existed to some extent and have actually been improved during the past two years.
5. Complaints about wages have increased recently. (Even though base rates were below average in the field, a piece-work program gave most of the workers a weekly wage that was far in excess of the average wage in the field.)
6. Talk of a possible strike is in the air, but no reasons are being mentioned by the workers.

EXHIBIT 3.11   ORGANIZATION CHART, NATIONAL BRICKWORKS

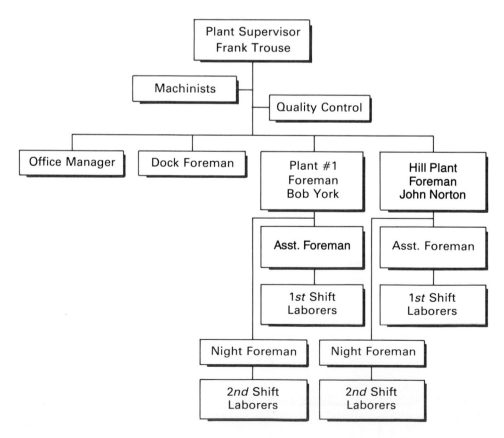

The list was studied by those attending the meeting. After lunch, a second phase of the meeting was begun. During the afternoon sessions, the foremen discussed specific occurrences and reasons particular problems arose more frequently in some work areas than in others.

The foreman of Plant #1, Bob York, was the first to bring out important factors. The symptoms listed had their origin in Plant #1 and the Hill Plant, although they were beginning to spill over into the quality-control group and some of the clerical staff. Both of these production plants had large work forces compared to the number of personnel in the other locations; those workers with the most seniority also worked in these two areas. York mentioned that his relations with the workers in his plant were, in his opinion, extremely good. Only two major and six minor grievances were turned in to him during his seven years as foreman, and all were effectively handled immediately. York said he believed that the older workers had recently tended to segregate themselves from the new personnel, yet neither group, young or old, associated themselves with the plant or the company.

At this time, John Norton, foreman of the Hill Plant, interrupted. He agreed that he found conditions in the Hill Plant to be similar to those in Plant #1, but said that he found a different atmosphere existing on the second shift. Workers on the second shift, he said, seemed to "work more harmoniously" and he considered them to be a "cohesive group." Although working conditions were similar for both the first and second shifts, the workers on the evening shift considered themselves to be a team and often referred to each other as the "Night Riders" or the "Late Oil Burners." Bob York agreed that Norton's observations were consistent with those of his own concerning the second (night) shift.

Foremen from other areas felt that the problems mentioned by York and Norton were not nearly as serious as in the two production plants but admitted that they felt the uneasiness in the air. The cohesiveness of the other work groups was beginning to break down. Not only were they losing their teamwork attitudes, but loyalty to the company also seemed to be losing meaning, as evidenced by the machinists and quality-control personnel who had stopped wearing their company shirts regularly and had recently been removing National "morale posters" from the area bulletin boards.

After this information had been accumulated, Trouse pointed out two factors he had discovered from personnel records kept during the previous twelve months. "These factors," said Trouse, "indicate possible underlying aggravation of the workers." He went on:

During the end of 1987, a rash of accidents occurred in the shop, on the dock, and in the Hill Plant. As you remember, it was at this time that we began to crack down on horseplay in all locations. A form letter went out to each department indicating that punitive action would be taken against any worker engaged in horseplay while on company property. The new rules were strictly enforced; some workers received docks in pay, and others were laid off work for up to one week.

As you remember, in mid-1987 we received notice from the home office that unnecessary costs were getting out of line in a number of the plants throughout the country. We were asked to cut back wherever we felt it would be feasible to do so. Our cutback was in the previously planned modernization of facilities. We hated to do it, especially after explaining our plans to the union, but we discarded our proposed program since it seemed to be the only answer. A union grievance was filed, but we knew the cost conditions and just let time heal the unrest.

At this time, Barbara Wulff, the head machinist, spoke up.

You know, this may not have seemed important at the time, but we made one other change when the memo on cost came through. The workers had quite a company softball team. They took second place in the Industrial League and often talked about how they were going to clobber Universal, the league champs, in the upcoming season. Unfortunately, there won't be an upcoming season for our ball club and the workers in the shop have recently been commenting about the fact.

The team members were occasionally let out of work early, with pay, to attend away games; this appeared to be an undue expense. It was also felt that afternoon practices might be tiring to the workers and could have an adverse effect on individual performance during working hours. All of the foremen agreed that they had heard comments about not having a team this year, and about how the workers would miss the big turnouts when each department would cheer for their fellow workers.

No other comments were made by the assembled group of foremen regarding the discussion topic, so Trouse once again took the floor.

I think that this meeting has brought many of the problems here at National to the surface. A summary of today's discussion will be printed and sent to you tomorrow. Look it over carefully. We'll meet back here at 9:30 Thursday morning. We'll decide on a course of action at that time.

That afternoon, as Bob York was planning to leave the plant, Henry Johnson, the union president approached him. Johnson asked Bob about the meeting.

Bob decided that most of what had been said should be kept confidential. However, he did say that termination of the company softball team had been discussed and that he, Bob, believed that there was a good chance the team would be active again in the spring.

The following morning Bob and the other foremen were called into Frank Trouse's office. Frank looked disturbed. His message was brief and to the point:

Henry Johnson just stopped in here and told me that the union met last night. They voted to give their officers the power to call a strike when the contract ends next Friday. That's the first time this has happened in fifteen years.

EXERCISE 3.1
HE WORKS, SHE WORKS (BUT WHAT DIFFERENT IMPRESSIONS THEY MAKE!)

OBJECTIVE

To increase your awareness of common stereotypes that exist in many organizations about male and female characteristics.

INSTRUCTIONS

1. Complete the "He Works, She Works" worksheet. In the appropriate spaces, write what you think the stereotyped responses would be. Do not spend too much time considering any one item. Rather, respond quickly and let your first impression or thought guide your answer.
2. Compare your individual responses with those on the "He Works, She Works" answer sheet provided by your instructor.

HE WORKS, SHE WORKS (WORKSHEET)

The family picture is on *his* desk: (e.g., *He's a solid, responsible family man*)

The family picture is on *her* desk: (e.g., *Her family will come before her career.*)

His desk is cluttered:

Her desk is cluttered:

He's talking with co-workers:

She's talking with co-workers:

He's not at his desk:	*She's* not at her desk:
He's not in the office:	*She's* not in the office:
He's having lunch with the boss:	*She's* having lunch with the boss:
The boss criticized *him*:	The boss criticized *her*:
He got an unfair deal:	*She* got an unfair deal:
He's getting married:	*She's* getting married:
He's going on a business trip:	*She's* going on a business trip:
He's leaving for a better job:	*She's* leaving for a better job:

3. Compare your individual responses with those of other class members or participants. It is interesting to identify and discuss the most frequently used stereotypes.

QUESTIONS

1. How pervasive do you think such stereotypes are in organizations today?
2. What impact can male and female stereotypes have (1) in employment interviews, and (2) on performance appraisals?
3. How can such stereotypes be overcome?

EXERCISE 3.2

JOHARI WINDOW: A FEEDBACK AND DISCLOSURE ACTIVITY

To a large extent, our attitudes and intentions are judged by others on the basis of our overt behavior. In the same way, we judge others by what they do. Sometimes, actual reasons for behavior are hidden from others. Events from our past and privately held beliefs may not be known to them. Consequently, their actions may not be based on complete information. On the other hand, we also might overlook certain characteristics of our own behavior while they are clearly observed by those with whom we come in contact. The net result is that the behavior of individuals toward one another is limited to what they think they see (or perceive) and thus may be inappropriate.

The purpose of the Johari Window is to develop a more complete and accurate awareness of ourselves and those with whom we interact. This exercise will allow you to discover your own assets and liabilities as you and others perceive them and to disclose to those individuals certain reasons for your behavior. Your relationships with those around you can become more meaningful and realistic as you acquire a more accurate perception of yourself and others.

This exercise can be carried out within a designated group (e.g., selected classmates or a work group) or completed outside of class by selecting certain persons with whom you desire to exchange information.

INSTRUCTIONS

1. Using a pencil or pen, divide a sheet of paper into four equal quadrants. Place the following headings over each of those areas: upper left area: My assets as I perceive them; upper right area: My assets as others perceive them; lower left area: My liabilities as I perceive them; lower right area: My liabilities as others perceive them.
2. Now, list as many of your assets and liabilities as you can think of in the proper areas of this work sheet (additional paper can be used if necessary).
3. Feedback and disclosure:
   A. Decide which assets and liabilities (self-perception) you wish to disclose to others. Place a check mark by those items if you believe others already are aware of them. Then, disclose the characteristics you wish to share. (You probably have not, nor will not, disclose all of the items on your original list.)
   B. Ask others with whom you wish to exchange information to provide you with feedback about yourself and record the feedback in the appropriate areas on your worksheet. This can be done on a face-to-face basis, or the information can be provided by a number of individuals in a manner that permits them to maintain anonymity.

EXHIBIT 3.12   JOHARI WINDOW

	Known to Self	Not Known to Self
Known to Others	I. Open	II. Blind
Not Known to Others	III. Hidden	IV. Unknown

4. Preparing the Johari Window:
   On another sheet of paper, reproduce the Johari Window diagram shown in Exhibit 3.12. The Johari Window will be used to facilitate the comparison of information already known to you with information you are now acquiring from others. As you can see from the diagram, the window consists of four quadrants. Each quadrant represents a different category in which information about you may be placed. For example, if either assets or liabilities originally written down by you also have been fed back by others, those items should be placed in the Open Quadrant. Characteristics observed by others but not by you will be placed in quadrant II, the Blind Quadrant. Information that you know about yourself but have chosen not to disclose to others will be listed in the quadrant labeled Hidden. Finally, you may possess characteristics that neither you nor others have yet recognized. Although this quadrant remains empty on your diagram, it is important that you are aware that other characteristics do exist and may surface in the future.

   When you have all of the information before you, compare the feedback you have received on your assets and liabilities (as perceived by others) to the characteristics you believe you possess.
5. You may wish to develop a Johari Window diagram as you now have come to know yourself and compare it to a comparable diagram which reflects your self-awareness before participating in this feedback and disclosure activity.

Note: Feedback and disclosure exercises generally require an exchange of information between two or more individuals. Therefore, each participant in the activity may wish to develop his or her own Johari Window. In addition, a group facilitator or some other third party may help to ease tensions that can be created by such an information exchange.

QUESTIONS FOR GROUP DISCUSSION

1. Were you surprised by any of the feedback you received?
2. Did you reveal information about yourself that others did not already know?
3. Does your Johari Window reflect conflicting information? If so, how do you explain this?
4. What have you learned from this exercise concerning (a) yourself; (b) others; (c) perceptions, in general?
5. In what ways have your feedback and disclosure experience affected (a) you, (b) others?

CHAPTER **4**

LEARNING, REINFORCEMENT, AND BEHAVIOR ANALYSIS

LEARNING OBJECTIVES

1. To appreciate the influence of classical, operant, and social cognitive theory on learning and work-related behavior.
2. To understand the role of positive reinforcement, negative reinforcement, and punishment and the importance of reinforcement scheduling.
3. To learn ways in which learning theory can be applied in organizational settings.
4. To gain insight into learning-based self-management.

CHAPTER OUTLINE

Learning Theories: Why We Behave as We Do
Classical Learning Theory / Operant Learning Theory / Social Cognitive Theory / Classical, Operant, and Social Cognitive Theory: A Managerial Perspective

Principles of Learning and Reinforcement
Principles of Learning / The Practice of Reinforcing / The Context of Reinforcing / Reinforcement Scheduling

Applying Learning Theory in Organizations: Initiating and Changing Work-Related Behaviors
Organizational Behavior Modification / Modeling and Shaping Behavior / Behavioral Self-management / Maintaining Changed Behaviors

Learning, Reinforcement, and Behavior Analysis: Conclusions

Questions for Review and Discussion

References

Cases: 4.1 The Sociable Salesman / 4.2 Ron Brown's Problem

Exercises: 4.1 Behavioral Analysis: "From A to C"
4.2 Designing a Training and Development Program

KEY TERMS

Learning
Classical learning theory
Operant learning theory
Social cognitive theory
Law of effect
Positive reinforcement
Negative reinforcement
Punishment/Extinction
Reinforcement schedule
Continuous reinforcement
Intermittent reinforcement

Ratio schedule
Interval schedule
Fixed schedule
Variable schedule
Organizational behavior modification
Baseline/Frequency counts
Modeling/Shaping/Chaining
Stimulus management
Consequence management

J ulie thought to herself, "I'll just never understand some people, especially not Tim." Tim Roberts had been a safety inspector with Julie's department for nearly eight months. He had impressed her with his drive and sincerity from the day he arrived, and she was always there with a compliment while he was learning the complex regulations and reporting procedures so critical to the performance of his job. Now, things were different. Neither Julie, nor the line supervisors who depended on Tim's decisions, could find him in when he was needed. As one department manager grumbled, "Sometimes it's like he's disappeared from the face of the earth."

For his part, Tim liked the people he worked with and had nothing against Julie. However, he felt increasingly uncomfortable in his job. It seemed no one appreciated the work he did. Julie was always quick to point out his errors, and although her criticisms had become fewer, it seemed to Tim that she rarely spoke to him unless it was to point out some aspect of his work that needed improvement. Plant foremen who were responsible for complying with his directives always seemed to grumble. Recently, he confided to a friend, "The foremen never realize that I'm probably saving them a lot of time and trouble later on. I'm paid well, but the job just doesn't seem to have any other rewards."

Julie faces a problem similar to that experienced by many other managers. She is perplexed by changes in Tim's work-related behaviors. From Julie's point of view, Tim had learned his job well and had once been a model employee. Now, she could find little evidence of that learning. Familiarity with the fundamental concepts of learning can help us to understand Tim's behaviors and the behaviors of others.

Learning theories and principles explain how behaviors are acquired, when and why they occur, and how they can be sustained or terminated. Some management authorities believe that it is primarily these overt behaviors, rather than internal states like attitudes or beliefs, that directly influence individual performance. A growing number of managers share that belief and have begun to systematically apply learning principles in the workplace.

In this chapter, we will examine the nature of learning. We will explore how and under what conditions learning takes place and how learned behaviors can be sustained over time. First, we will focus on why people behave as they do by discussing three learning theories and some selected principles of learning. Next, we will look at hands-on techniques such as organizational behavior modification, modeling and shaping behavior, and ways to manage our own behaviors more effectively (self-management). Understanding these learning concepts should help you to become a more effective manager.

LEARNING THEORIES: WHY WE BEHAVE AS WE DO

Sometimes, managers are perplexed by what they see (or don't see) their employees do. "Why does she continue to do it 'the old way'?" "Why doesn't he ever ask me first?" The answers to these and similar questions usually lie in the behaviors an employee has learned or not learned. Understanding how such behaviors are learned can best be accomplished by first examining three distinct **learning theories:** classical learning theory, operant learning theory, and social cognitive theory.

Classical learning theory and operant learning theory are the basic constructs on which most of our knowledge about human learning is based. Both theories include three essential components:

1. Learning involves a change in overt (or outward) behavior.
2. Learning represents a relatively permanent change in behavior and not a one-time occurrence or temporary behavior change.
3. Learning is the result of past experiences that have been reinforced.

Social cognitive theory (SCT), also known as social learning theory, is a relatively new approach to understanding human learning.* SCT differs from classical and operant learning in that it recognizes the influence of our cognitions (beliefs, perceptions, etc.) and our observations of others, as well as our firsthand experiences, on learning. Our definition of learning is based on all three of these theories. For our purposes, therefore, **learning** is defined as any relatively permanent change in behavior that occurs as the result of reinforced experiences or the observation of others' behaviors and their related consequences.

Before we look at how behaviors can actually be managed, we will examine each of these three approaches to learning more closely.

Classical Learning Theory

According to **classical learning theory,** learning occurs when a specific stimulus is paired with a specific behavioral response. Once the relationship is learned, the appearance of the stimulus will always produce the same behavior. The classical approach to learning was popularized by early students of learning such as Ivan Pavlov[1] and John Watson.[2]

Pavlov, in his famous study, conditioned a dog to respond by salivating (reflexive behavior) to the sound of a bell (stimulus). This was done by causing the dog to associate an unconditioned stimulus (food) with the conditioned (learned) stimulus (bell). The degree of association was measured by the dog's salivation. In essence, Pavlov caused the dog to learn, or associate, a specific response with a specific stimulus. Comparable examples of stimulus-response relationships in organizational life would be the learned behavior of a worker who associates ending a task (whether he is through or not) with the clock that indicates 5:00 (quitting time) and students who begin to gather up their books when they hear commotion in the hall before the end of a class period.

Watson broadened the range of study of stimulus–response learning situations and focused attention on behavioristic (learning theory-based) explanations of why we behave as we do. Perhaps even more important for managers, he encouraged those interested in human behavior to deal with observable, outward behavior rather than with unobservable activities of the mind.

Classical (or S→R) learning explains those behaviors in organizations that are *caused* by someone or something in an individual's environment. The sound of a

---

*The term *social cognitive theory* reflects the role and importance of thought processes in learning and has been used in place of an earlier expression, social learning theory. See Albert Bandura, *Social Foundations of Thought: A Social Cognitive Theory* (Englewood Cliffs, N.J.: Prentice-Hall, 1986).

EXHIBIT 4.1

SOURCE: *NorthWest Arkansas Times*, January 18, 1990, © 1990. Reprinted with special permission of King Features Syndicate.

voice, the presence of another person, or a specific command such as "Start!" or "Stop!" can initiate a learned response (behavior) to that stimulus. It appears that Dagwood in Exhibit 4.1 requires such a stimulus to behave as Mr. Dithers wants him to. Similarly, a pilot may be prompted to take a specific action (behavior) when, and only when, a particular warning light begins to flash (stimulus). A safety checklist used by an engineer in a nuclear plant actually represents a set of specific behavioral stimuli. Exhibit 4.2 illustrates how a stimulus might cause a specific behavior to occur.

Operant Learning Theory

Classically learned behaviors are seemingly involuntary actions *elicited* from an individual by a stimulus. Operantly learned responses, on the other hand, are *emitted* by an individual who wishes to influence the environment. Thus, in **operant learning,** a particular behavior is associated with a specific consequence in a given situation. The behavior, or response (e.g., a student raises his hand), precedes the learned consequence (e.g., professor recognizes the student). Exhibit 4.3 illustrates how a worker's behavior occurs in order to produce a desired consequence in a work situation.

Operant learning theory emphasizes that a person is instrumental in his or her own learning. Through personal trial-and-error, a person learns behaviors in relation to the immediate environment, which is a source of positive and aversive consequences. Behaviors are then emitted voluntarily to obtain desired consequences or to avoid punishment from the environment.[3]

The operant view of learning has contributed significantly to the application of learning theory in organizational settings. Employees theoretically emit behaviors based on the rewards (organizational, social, or others) they desire from given

EXHIBIT 4.2   CLASSICAL LEARNING

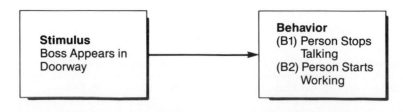

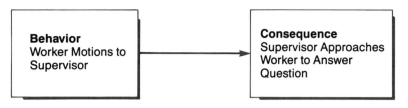

EXHIBIT 4.3   OPERANT LEARNING

situations. For example, Sandra enters her office (stimulus situation) each morning. She may influence the responses of her co-workers or her boss by varying her behavior. If Sandra arrives late, her boss may reprimand her. On the other hand, arriving late may attract more notice from her co-workers (possibly a desirable consequence). Sandra's promptness or tardiness (learned voluntary behavior) thus depends on the consequences she seeks and receives from her environment. Exhibit 4.4 briefly outlines the differences between classical and operant learning situations.

An important operant strategy for bringing about a desired behavior is known as shaping. Shaping allows a manager to systematically develop employee behaviors for which there are no precedents—in other words, to help an employee form a *new* behavior. Shaping and a related technique, chaining, will be discussed in greater detail in the "Applying Learning Theory in Organizations" section.

Social Cognitive Theory

Both classical and operant learning theory emphasize the importance of learning through immediate personal experiences. Learning is viewed as a slowly unfolding sequence of trials and errors rather than a carefully thought-out process. In recent years, however, increasing attention has been given to explanations of behavior that go beyond purely experience-based learning. **Social cognitive theory** [4] represents a radical departure from earlier approaches to learning in that it also considers the importance of human cognitions (perceptions, values, and reasoning).

The social cognitive theory model of learning (see Exhibit 4.5) has three basic elements (see Exhibit 4.5): (1) an individual's cognitive processes; (2) an individual's behaviors; and (3) environment. SCT explains learning in terms of a contin-

EXHIBIT 4.4   DIFFERENCES BETWEEN CLASSICAL AND
                        OPERANT LEARNING

CLASSICAL LEARNING	OPERANT LEARNING
1. Responses are elicited *from* a person (reactive).	1. Responses are emitted *by* a person (proactive).
2. Responses are fixed to a stimulus (no choice).	2. Responses are variable in type and degree (choice).
3. Learned stimulus is a sound, an object, a person, etc.	3. Learned stimulus is a situation such as an office, a social setting, a specific *set* of circumstances.
4. Reinforcement is not received by choice.	4. Person is instrumental in securing reinforcement by "operating" on the environment.

uous, reciprocal interaction among these three elements. As with classical and operant theory, the environment influences a person's behaviors. However, SCT also provides that behaviors alter the environment. For example, you may find that constant interruptions by a friend (environment) interfere with your ability to read an assignment. Asking the person to stop interrupting (behavior) may cause him or her to comply and thereby end future interference from the environment.

While the environment may influence the way we think about a situation, our cognitive processes influence the meanings we attach to the environment. For example, you may view a ten-dollar reward as a positive consequence of behavior until you discover that someone else received twenty-five dollars for the same deed. Your perception of the reward, rather than the actual reward, will influence your future behavior.

Social cognitive theory may help us to understand Wall Street's recent rash of insider trading scandals. According to SCT, we create our own environmental reality, and actions arising from what may actually be erroneous beliefs can create social effects that confirm those misbeliefs.[5] The news media have reported that many traders believe "everybody" is becoming involved in illegal trading. Such beliefs, in turn, can lead some traders into illegal practices whether their original assumption that "everybody's doing it" was correct or not. In effect, many of those caught up in insider trading activities (behaviors) no doubt have created (through cognitions) their own reality concerning the pervasiveness of the insider trading phenomenon (the environment). This reaction is illustrated in Exhibit 4.6.

Tom Peters, author of the bestselling books *In Search of Excellence* and *Thriving on Chaos,* found that customers at Walt Disney World also *created* their own environmental reality. Peters rated sixteen contacts between Disney World visitors and employees. He found that only four were favorable and three were actually unsatisfactory. Nevertheless, he, like so many other visitors, "felt good" about Disney World and its customer relations. Evaluating the situation, he concluded that Disney World customers forget those contacts that are inconsequential, rationalize away those that are unsatisfactory, and see those Disney workers who are helpful as "the real thing." Not only does Disney's positive image influence customers, but employees themselves

EXHIBIT 4.5   A MODEL OF SOCIAL COGNITIVE THEORY

According to SCT, learning results from the reciprocal interaction of cognitive processes, behaviors, and the environment.

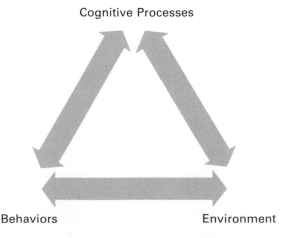

Cognitive Processes

Behaviors   Environment

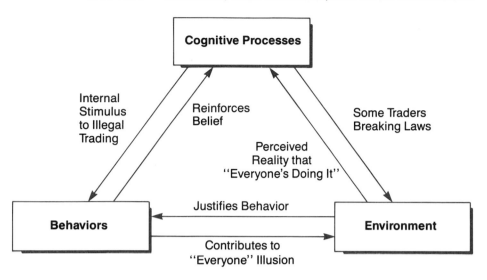

EXHIBIT 4.6

also perceive the Disney organization to be the finest in family entertainment. Thus, the *perceived* environment, not just how employees deliver services, influences Disney customer satisfaction.[6]

SCT also has implications for the exercise of self-control. According to both classical and operant approaches to learning, behavioral consequences come solely from the environment. SCT, however, states that each person has the capacity to reward or punish him- or herself. Both reward and punishment are "reinforcement" in SCT terminology. Self-reinforcement can be accomplished simply by feeling good or bad about one's own behavior ("It's great to have that paper done!") or by tangibly rewarding or punishing oneself ("Now that I'm done reading that chapter, I'm going to go to the game").

The notable difference between social cognitive theory and classical and operant learning theories lies in the role of cognitive processes (thinking, reasoning, interpreting, etc.) rather than firsthand experiences in the learning process. In fact, research indicates that people acquire and retain behavioral capabilities much better by generating and using cognitive aids than by reinforced repetitive performances.[7]

Classical, Operant, and Social Cognitive Theory: A Managerial Perspective

Managers often become frustrated when employees or others in the organization either do things that they should not (undesirable behaviors) or do not do those things that they should (desirable behaviors). Managers need to recognize, however, that virtually all work-related behaviors are learned. Thus, the presence or absence of specific behaviors can be traced to the environment in which work is performed.

Using learning theories to understand the framework of the learning process can enable you to manage people more effectively. Classical learning theory, for example, may help you understand how your own actions may prompt certain responses from others. Operant theory may help in the design and administration of organizational reward systems and can help predict employee behaviors in certain situations.

Learning, of course, is not always tied to an organization's formal programs or reward systems—learning informally from one's own experiences or from the experiences of others is equally important. According to A.M. Williams, former executive vice-president of the Campbell Soup Company, management by example is an essential part of developing an employee: "Employees need positive role models, and managers must demonstrate the styles of behavior they would like to encourage in their employees."[8]

JOE BAUM

Joe Baum has acquired a life's worth of personal experience in the business world and is now trying to teach others what he has learned. Baum has designed and managed over three hundred restaurants, including New York's Rainbow Room at the top of 30 Rockefeller Plaza and Windows on the World on the 107th floor of the World Trade Center. All are known for the quality of their cuisine and the magnificent dining experience they offer. At sixty-nine years of age, Joe Baum loves his work. He often speaks of the pleasure it brings him and the pride he feels when he walks into one of his many creations.

There are tangible rewards for his efforts, but it is the feeling of personal satisfaction that seems most important to Baum. Recognizing just how important that feeling is, Baum has tried to help those who work for him experience the deep pleasure he associates with doing a job right and delivering high-quality customer service. Baum learned his trade and his style from his parents, during his formal education at Cornell University's School of Hotel Administration, and through his own experiences on the job. Now, he is trying to pass on to others the keys to his own success by helping them find for themselves the many rewards a career in the restaurant industry has to offer.[9]

Through an understanding of the three theories of learning (classical, operant, and social cognitive theory) individuals in the workplace can be better understood and managed. In the following sections we will look more closely at the specific conditions that are necessary for learning to take place, the important role of reinforcement in the learning process, and specifically how learning theory-based approaches to management can be employed.

PRINCIPLES OF LEARNING AND REINFORCEMENT

Principles of Learning

Understanding a few important principles of learning will help you to use learning theory in organizations more effectively. These principles include conditions that must generally exist for learning to take place and a law of reinforcement known as Thorndike's law of effect.

Conditions for learning

Three conditions must exist for learning to take place:

1. arousal and motivation;
2. association; and
3. reinforcement.

Arousal and Motivation.   First, a person must be aware that a learning situation exists in order to learn a behavior; otherwise, he may overlook the behaviors that are to be acquired. In addition, learning is more likely if he is also motivated to learn. For example, a student in a beginning computer class may be told that he will be shown how to use a personal computer (PC). The instructor then turns on the equipment and proceeds to demonstrate how it is operated. If the student focuses on various operating procedures but does not pay attentiion when the PC is turned on (is not aroused), he will be unable to use it even though he has learned other important procedures. If the student is not motivated to learn how to use the PC ("I won't have any need for this"), the likelihood that he will acquire the necessary behaviors will also be reduced significantly.

Association.   Second, an individual relates learned behaviors in terms of time and place (situation). For example, a salesman learns that a particular sales pitch works best when the buyer shows some reluctance to complete the purchase and that another approach is more appropriate when the buyer has expressed previous interest in the product. A student raises her hand in class when she wishes to speak to the professor. However, the same student encountering the same professor at a local restaurant would no doubt speak directly without first asking permission. Not only do we associate events in learning, but we also associate a given stimulus with the appropriate response. This pairing of events or pairing of a stimulus and a behavior is known as *association*.

Reinforcement.   Finally, an individual must receive some form of reinforcement or perceive that others performing the behavior are reinforced if he is to learn such a pairing. The "principle of reinforcement" refers to an increase in a behavior's frequency resulting from its association with a specific consequence. In other words, any time the frequency of a behavior increases systematically, reinforcement has occurred. Reinforcement strengthens the learned association that has been formed whether its source is external (praise from another), internal (self-gratification), or vicarious (related to others' behaviors).

Law of effect

Central to almost all applications of learning theory is a proposition known as Thorndike's **law of effect:**

> Of several responses made to the same situation, those which are accompanied or closely followed by satisfaction . . . will be more likely to recur; those which are accompanied or closely followed by discomfort . . . will be less likely to occur.[10]

The law of effect suggests that several responses (or behaviors) can occur in a given situation. Not all behaviors, however, will be associated with that situation in the future. Only positively reinforced (rewarded) behaviors will be more likely to recur. Conversely, behaviors associated with punishment or some other aversive feedback will diminish. A careful reading of this proposition also suggests that behaviors not reinforced in any way are unlikely to recur. Thus, a supervisor who fails to compliment or otherwise positively reinforce an employee's desirable job-related behaviors should not expect those behaviors to occur in the future.

Consider the case of Jamie. Jamie has made a conscious effort to be the "perfect" employee. He arrives at the office long before his supervisor, is prompt and complete with his work, and is always neat in his appearance. These behaviors are somewhat new to Jamie. Through most of his college years, he tended to be his own person, doing things in his own time and in his own way. Now, however, he is a senior, and this job has given him a chance to turn over a new leaf.

Jamie's supervisor, Cheryl, attends management meetings each morning and rarely enters the work area early. She has noticed Jamie's good work and compliments him on it regularly. Although Cheryl has never commented on his appearance to Jamie, he has overheard others in the office comment on his "preppy" wardrobe. A supervisor in another department even told him that a particular shirt and tie he was wearing might be out of place.

According to the law of effect, we might expect to see some of Jamie's behaviors continue or increase in frequency, while others are likely to decrease in frequency. Can you identify which behaviors are likely to increase, which are likely to decrease, and explain why?

The Practice of Reinforcing

On the surface, influencing behavior through the use of reinforcement seems simple enough. However, intricacies do exist. For example, positive reinforcement is not necessarily synonymous with reward. Negative reinforcement and punishment also have two different meanings. Before discussing how learning theory can be applied in organizations, it will help to define some key terms often associated with reinforcing behavior.

Positive reinforcement

Technically, a *reinforcement* is anything that when associated with a behavior will lead to an increase in the frequency of that behavior. **Positive reinforcement** thus occurs when a behavior is paired with a favorable consequence (reinforcement) leading, in turn, to an increase in the behavior. Giving an employee a day off for doing a good job might be a form of positive reinforcement. Other positive reinforcement might include praise, a bonus, or special privileges.

Of course, not everybody agrees on just what *is* a positive reinforcement. Allan and Gail, for instance, worked long and hard to complete an important report. Their boss was particularly pleased with the product and decided to reward them by sending them to New York to present their findings to the board of directors. Allan was excited about the opportunity. The trip, however, meant that Gail would have to miss her son's all-star baseball game. Half jokingly, she commented to Allan, "If I had known that this report was going to put me in New York over the weekend, I might not have tried to do such a good job on it." This example suggests that *rewards* are determined by those who give them, while the value of a *reinforcement* depends upon the recipient.

Negative reinforcement

Negative reinforcement is one of the most confusing concepts in learning theory. Remember, *reinforcement* results in the increase of a behavior. Therefore, negative reinforcement, unlike punishment, should lead to more, not less, of a given behavior. **Negative reinforcement** is accomplished by contingently withholding an aversive consequence when a desirable behavior occurs. For example, as long as the book-keeper continues to make accurate entries, the supervisor will not peer over his shoulder and make snide remarks. Logically, the bookkeeper will do a better job to keep the supervisor off his back! The use of negative reinforcement is sometimes called avoidance learning since a behavior is increased to avoid the negative consequence of not performing the behavior.

Punishment

Punishment results in a decrease in the frequency of a behavior. It can take either of two forms.[11] Ordinarily, we think of punishment as the association of a behavior with an undesirable consequence (aversive stimulus). For example, an employee found drinking on the job (behavior) might be suspended for three days (punishment). Assuming the worker perceives the suspension negatively, the frequency of on-the-job drinking should decrease. A second form of punishment occurs when an undesirable behavior is accompanied by the withdrawal of something valued by the individual. A parent may punish a sixteen-year-old by taking away the car keys.

Punishment can be an effective means for altering behavior; it also has several limitations. Therefore, it should be used carefully and sparingly. Exhibit 4.7 presents reasons why punishment sometimes is used to change behavior along with reasons many experts believe it should be avoided.

Extinction

Extinction involves withholding a positive reinforcement that has prevously been associated with a behavior in order to terminate or reduce the frequency of the behavior. For example, an individual is likely to stop telling sexist jokes in the office if the employees around him withhold the laughter to which he has become accustomed. In the short case at the beginning of this chapter, the performance of a safety inspector, Tim Roberts, was being questioned by his supervisor and some of the plant foremen. Those working with Tim claimed that his performance had deteriorated. For his part, Tim was unhappy that those around him *no longer* seemed to appreciate the work he did. In essence, Tim's once-learned, high-performance behaviors dropped off (becoming extinct) because he no longer received the kind of reinforcement he had become used to.

An important distinction exists between punishment and extinction. In the case of punishment, the withheld reinforcement is desired by the individual behaving in a certain way but *has not been* previously associated with the behavior. But in extinction, the positive reinforcement *has been* previously associated with the behavior. Let's look at an example.

Karen and Arlene had worked together as sales clerks for nearly a year. Arlene had often criticized the store's management, and Karen, although not voicing her own opinions, had always been a good listener. Now, Karen has been promoted to

EXHIBIT 4.7   REASONS FOR USING AND NOT USING PUNISHMENT

WHY USE PUNISHMENT	WHY NOT USE PUNISHMENT
Temporarily Stops or Lessens Frequency of Behavior	May Damage Employee Emotionally
Quick and Easy to Use	May Lead to Negative Side Effects (e.g., Covert Undesirable Behaviors)
	Attention is *Not* Focused on Desired Behavior
	Inefficient: Relatively Rapid Extinction
	May Create Distress for the Punisher

supervisor and believes that Arlene's continued complaints are adversely affecting the morale of some of the new sales clerks.

Karen may adopt one of two strategies to eliminate Arlene's negative comments. She may choose not to provide a ready ear any longer and encourage others not to get involved in such discussions with Arlene. Karen would be adopting an extinction strategy, since a *previously associated reinforcement (listening) would be withheld*. A punishment strategy, on the other hand, would require that Karen present an aversive consequence (e.g., a reprimand) when Arlene complains or that she *withhold a previously unrelated positive consequence* from Arlene. For example, Karen may tell Arlene that her choice of work schedules cannot be granted as long as Arlene continues to complain. What advantages and disadvantages exist with each strategy?

Exhibit 4.8 shows the expected impact of positive reinforcement, negative reinforcement, punishment, and extinction on subsequent behavior.

The Context of Reinforcing

The context in which behavior and consequences take place influences subsequent behaviors. Context includes the (1) history of the situation; (2) perception of the consequence; and (3) source of the consequence (extrinsic or intrinsic). See Exhibit 4.9.

History of the situation

Gary has a habit of arriving late at his work station each morning. His foreman has decided to give him eight tokens (slips of papers) at the beginning of the month. Each token Gary still has at the end of the month can be cashed in for one-half hour off the job during the following month. The foreman will take a token each time

EXHIBIT 4.8   IMPACT OF REINFORCEMENT, PUNISHMENT, AND EXTINCTION ON BEHAVIOR

Action		Impact	
		Increase in Behavior	Decrease in Behavior
Positive Reinforcement	Apply Positive Consequence	X	
Negative Reinforcement	Withhold Negative Consequences	X	
Punishment	Apply Negative Consequence		X
Extinction	Withhold Expected Positive Consequence		X

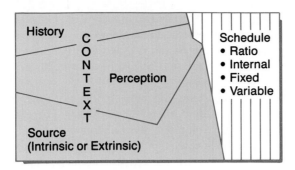

The effectiveness of reinforcement depends on its *context* (history of the situation, perception of the consequence, and the source of the consequence) and the *schedule* according to which the reinforcement is administered.

EXHIBIT 4.9   THE REINFORCEMENT PUZZLE

Gary arrives late. If Gary has all eight tokens left at the end of the month, he can take half a day off work. If he has no tokens left, he will receive no time off.

Is the foreman using a strategy of punishment or negative reinforcement? The answer lies in the history of the situation surrounding the arrangement between the two men. If Gary and his foreman agree beforehand on the reinforcement scheme, it is less likely that Gary will perceive the foreman's action (taking away a token) as a punishment. Gary will be more likely to focus on his own behavior than on the foreman's action. On the other hand, a superior's arbitrary removal of privileges might be viewed as a punishment. The key lies in the subordinate's expectations relative to the superior's actions.

Perception of the consequences

Ultimately, the individual being reinforced or punished determines whether consequences experienced are positive or negative. An employee praised publicly for exceptional work may be positively reinforced and continue to perform in an outstanding manner. Another employee receiving similar praise in front of co-workers may consider the special attention embarrassing and intentionally lower the work quality.

No matter what type of reinforcement or punishment managers use, one important premise must guide their thinking. The impact of any behavioral consequence depends on how that consequence is perceived by the individual experiencing it. The perception of the receiver, not the giver, determines the value of a reinforcement. Remember, the best indicator of whether a consequence is a reinforcement or a punishment is the measurable impact it has on behavior.

Extrinsic versus intrinsic reinforcement

Reinforcement (as well as punishment) can come from a second party (superior, acquaintance, etc.) or, according to social learning theory, from within the individual. Consequences controlled by other people are extrinsic reinforcement. Examples of extrinsic reinforcement include compliments from other people, a pay check, and classroom grades.

Intrinsic reinforcements come from within. They include such things as the satisfaction associated with successful completion of a job, feelings of self-worth, and feelings of security. Managers who attempt to influence the behavior of their employees generally rely on extrinsic reinforcement. However, individuals are capable of reinforcing themselves, and managers can take advantage of this fact. For example, a person can be trained to be more sensitive to his own behaviors and to reinforce himself.

Individuals who reinforce themselves tend to do so in a manner similar to the way in which they were originally reinforced by others.[12] Therefore, managers can influence employees directly by reinforcing certain behaviors, and indirectly by setting expectations of how those behaviors should be self-reinforced in the future. There is no doubt that intrinsic reinforcement is an effective means for influencing one's own behavior. Self-punishment, however, is more difficult to use. Self-punishment must be negative enough to suppress an undesirable behavior but not so negative that it won't be used.[13]

Managers can also influence intrinsic reinforcement through their control of the work environment. For example, an employee may enjoy certain types of tasks more than others and experience intrinsic reinforcement differently depending on which task she is performing. Her manager can therefore indirectly affect her feelings of intrinsic satisfaction by controlling her work assignments.

Extrinsic reinforcement usually depends on the presence of another person (e.g., a supervisor). Intrinsic reinforcements, on the other hand, are potentially present at all times, and can therefore be experienced directly and immediately. Earlier, we presented the example of restaurateur Joe Baum. Baum's early enchantment with the restaurant industry came from his father and mother, who reinforced what he learned (extrinsic reinforcement). Today, however, it is the feelings of personal satisfaction (intrinsic reinforcement) that Baum finds most rewarding about his job.[14]

No clear evidence exists as to whether intrinsic or extrinsic reinforcement is most effective. However, individuals reinforced extrinsically appear to experience less intrinsic interest in their tasks under certain conditions. This is likely to occur when (1) jobs require creativity; (2) individuals sense they are losing control of their immediate situation; or (3) feelings of self-determination are decreased.[15] Finally, rewards that control behavior ("You performed that task correctly!") seem to have a greater negative impact on intrinsic motivation than rewards that are informational ("You're doing much better.").[16]

Reinforcement Scheduling

An additional important factor influencing the effectiveness of reinforcement is the reinforcement schedule. A **reinforcement schedule** is the systematic pattern by which reinforcements are administered. Such schedules determine when and under what conditions reinforcement takes place.

Ratio and interval schedules

Ratio and interval schedules refer to whether a reinforcement is given based on the occurrence of the behavior or according to a designated time period. Thus, reinforcing an employee for each unit produced would be a **ratio schedule**, reinforcing an employee every hour on the hour after the first unit was produced would be an example of reinforcing according to an **interval schedule.** Determining the type of schedule to be used depends on the job and the immediate work environment. For example, jobs that can be performed and measured by each unit produced are easily adapted to ratio schedules. Administrative positions may be better suited to interval scheduling.[17]

Fixed and Variable Schedules.   The regularity with which behavior is reinforced influences the rate of learning as well as how rapidly extinction occurs when reinforcement stops. The simplest reinforcement schedule is one in which behavior is reinforced every time it occurs. This is known as **continuous reinforcement.** Rarely, however, is a manager in a position to administer reinforcement continuously.

**EXHIBIT 4.10   IMPACTS OF REINFORCEMENT SCHEDULING
                ON BEHAVIOR**

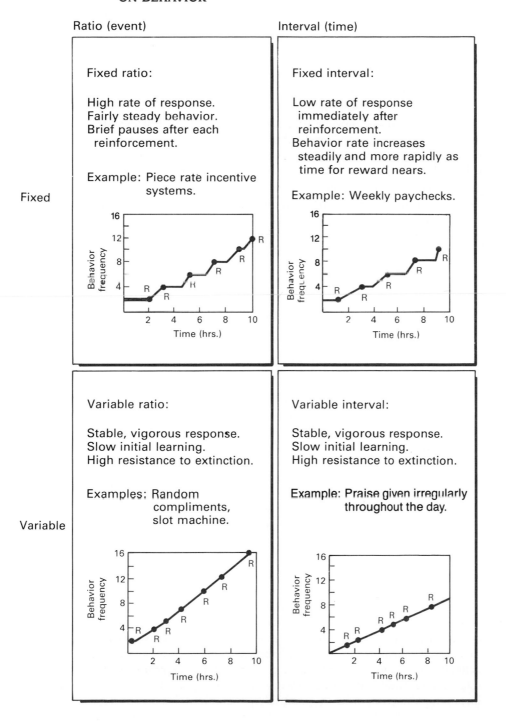

Ratio (event)   Interval (time)

Fixed

Fixed ratio:

High rate of response.
Fairly steady behavior.
Brief pauses after each
 reinforcement.

Example: Piece rate incentive
        systems.

Fixed interval:

Low rate of response
 immediately after
 reinforcement.
Behavior rate increases
 steadily and more rapidly as
 time for reward nears.

Example: Weekly paychecks.

Variable

Variable ratio:

Stable, vigorous response.
Slow initial learning.
High resistance to extinction.

Examples: Random
          compliments,
          slot machine.

Variable interval:

Stable, vigorous response.
Slow initial learning.
High resistance to extinction.

Example: Praise given irregularly
         throughout the day.

The alternative is to use some form of **intermittent reinforcement,** in which reinforcements occur after selected—but not all—behaviors. Practically all organizational situations call for the use of intermittent reinforcement. In a **fixed schedule,** reinforcement is administered on a regular basis. A supervisor who approaches an employee every thirty minutes and praises the work quality is using a fixed schedule (fixed interval). A fixed schedule also can be used based on the number of behaviors that occur (fixed ratio). For example, the employee might be praised every second (1:2) or every third (1:3) time he completes an assigned task. Fixed schedules, then, are predictable.

A variable schedule is irregular and not predictable. The reinforcement is administered on a random basis. Using the examples from above, the supervisor might praise the work at different times during the day without any pattern (variable interval) or might compliment the employee when units of work are completed but on a random basis (variable ratio).

Reinforcement scheduling is important in that it influences how quickly a behavior is learned and how resistant it is to extinction. For example, a behavior reinforced according to a fixed schedule will be learned more rapidly than one reinforced on a variable basis. (A 1:1 fixed schedule, known as a continuous schedule, will result in the most rapid learning experience.) On the other hand, fixed schedules can also lead to rapid halting of the behavior if the rewards are terminated (e.g., the supervisor leaves on vacation). Variable schedules result in a much slower rate of learning but behaviors reinforced on such a schedule are more resistant to extinction. Exhibit 4.10 reflects the different learning, performance, and retention patterns produced by various reinforcement schedules.

APPLYING LEARNING THEORY IN ORGANIZATIONS: INITIATING AND CHANGING WORK-RELATED BEHAVIORS

The application of learning theory in organizations is not new, although it has thus far been largely restricted to the area of employee training. Use of the principles discussed in this chapter is particularly evident in training materials known as "programmed learning aids."

Programmed learning is a form of instruction that permits students to progress at their own speed. Early programmed materials took the form of manuals and books. More recently, innovative and highly interactive computer programs have been used in such training. Some programmed materials that are particularly "user friendly" incorporate praise and other forms of positive reinforcement to reward learning progress. Exhibit 4.11 presents a segment containing learning statements and responses from one such programmed training manual.

In recent years, managers also have begun to use their knowledge of learning theory in day-to-day activities. General Motors' Positive Leadership and Wal-Mart's Positive Centered Leadership programs, for example, have become important focal points for those companies' management training programs and the basis for conducting interpersonal relations throughout both organizations. In addition, concepts such as self-management, behavior-based performance evaluation, and behaviorally defined work rules have also emerged as important management tools. These and related applications of learning theory in the workplace have resulted in improvements in productivity, quality, and safety,[18] and have been credited with reducing

EXHIBIT 4.11   LEARNING AT YOUR OWN PACE

The following questions and responses have been taken from a programmed learning manual designed to provide basic instruction in PERT* (Program Evaluation Review Technique).

Page 11:
   Would you consider "final assembly" a PERT event?
      No .... Turn to page 12
      I don't know if it is or not .... Turn to page 13
      Yes .... Turn to page 14

Page 12:
   You said that "final assembly" is not a PERT event.
   You are wrong!
   [Complete Explanation Provided]
   Return to page 11 and select the correct answer.

Page 13:
   Well, we appreciate an honest answer. Let's see if we can't clarify the matter.
   [Complete Explanation Provided]
   With these facts in mind, return to page 11 and select the correct answer.

From page 14:
   RIGHT YOU ARE!
   Go on to page 15.

---

*PERT is a time-based scheduling technique.

Adapted from: Federal Electric Corporation, A *Programmed Introducton to* PERT (New York: John Wiley and Sons, 1967, 11–15.

---

grievances and turnover. CAMECO, Inc., for example, found that clearly defining *safe behaviors* established a basis for understanding and learning safe behavior patterns that were more effective than merely encouraging workers to work "safer" in reducing accidents. Examples of behaviorally defined safety rules used by CAMECO are shown in Exhibit 4.12.

Applied learning theory is a powerful management tool, and companies such as retail giant Wal-Mart have integrated it into their training and their day-to-day management practices. Suzanne Allford, vice-president of Wal-Mart's people division, recognizes the impact of the company's Positive Centered Leadership program and knows the importance of consciously insuring that managers use positive reinforcement skills wisely and ethically. Allford addresses this issue in the "Ethical Dilemma" on page 122.

Organizational Behavior Modification

Theories and principles of learning provide us with a means for understanding and explaining how behaviors are acquired, strengthened, and weakened. Organizational behavior modification (OB Mod)[19] is a systematic approach for applying learning concepts in organizational settings. OB Mod involves identifying important performance-related behaviors, measuring and analyzing those behaviors, and developing and implementing behavior-change strategies.

A large number of companies, including General Electric, Emery Air Freight, Firestone, and Chase Manhattan Bank, have used OB Mod or similar approaches to train workers, decrease absenteeism, increase productivity, and improve quality.

EXHIBIT 4.12   BEHAVIORALLY DEFINED SAFETY RULES USED BY CAMECO, INC.

General Safety:
When driving pins or bolts, check to see that no one is on the opposite side where they may be struck by a flying pin or bolt.

General Protective Equipment:
Approved safety glasses or goggles shall be worn when working beneath equipment where the danger of falling particles exists.

Housekeeping:
If oil, grease, or other liquid substances are spilled, wipe them up using rags or floor-dri so you or other employees will not slip or fall.

Material Handling:
Before attempting to drill, grind, or ream small objects, clamp or secure the item first. Avoid holding the object with one hand while performing the operation with the other.

Tool & Equipment Use:
The use of buckets, chairs, forklifts, or other makeshift devices for work platforms is prohibited. Always stand on a ladder or scaffold when working more than 1 ft off the ground.

SOURCE: R. A. Reber and J. A. Wallin, "Validation of a Behavioral Measure of Occupational Safety," *Journal of Organizational Behavior Management*, 5 (Summer 1983): 73. Copyright © 1983. Reprinted courtesy of Haworth Press, 10 Alice St., Binghamton, N.Y.

Successful applications of OB Mod have also been reported in smaller organizations including hospitals and government agencies.[20]

Organizational behavior modification is based largely on the premise that performance, defined in terms of specific behaviors, can be altered by systematically applying various forms of reinforcement, punishment, and extinction. Thus, according to OB Mod, all parts of the organization's reward system (e.g., recognition, compensation, and special privileges) must be carefully managed to bring about desired organizational behavior.

Organizational behavior modification essentially consists of six steps (see Exhibit 4.13):

1. Identification of Performance-Related Behavioral Events.   Many activities and behaviors occur in the workplace. OB Mod, however, is concerned with only those specific behaviors that contribute to or detract from the accomplishment of an organization's goals. It thus is important to identify performance-related behaviors. Subsequent steps in the OB Mod process are designed to increase or decrease the frequency of such behaviors. For example, occasional conversations between employees that do not detract from job performance would be of no concern to the supervisor and would not be altered. On the other hand, if such conversations interfered with the performance of a task or accomplishment of an organizational goal, steps would be taken to decrease their frequency and increase the frequency of goal-directed behaviors.

Pinpointing specific behaviors is critical to the OB Mod process. First, the behaviors should be *observable*. Subsequent steps of the process require the manager to measure changes in the behavior; therefore, it is necessary that the behavior can be seen. Second, the behavior should be identified in the *situation* in which it is critical. Proofreading, an important behavior for most secretaries to learn, may only be considered critical when applied to a final draft (specific situation) as opposed to a preliminary draft (another situation) of an important report. Third, problems

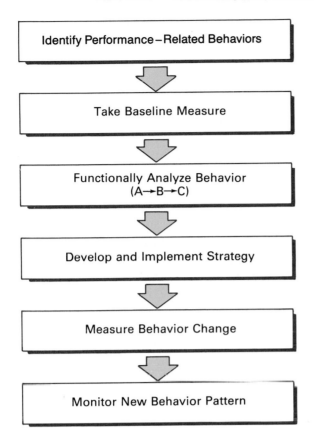

| Identify Performance-Related Behaviors |
| Take Baseline Measure |
| Functionally Analyze Behavior (A→B→C) |
| Develop and Implement Strategy |
| Measure Behavior Change |
| Monitor New Behavior Pattern |

**EXHIBIT 4.13   APPLYING LEARNING THEORY IN THE WORKPLACE:
USING OB MOD**

encountered should be *behaviorally defined*.[21] If our desire is to alter a behavior, then we must define the problem accordingly. Stating that you would like to "improve Larry's attitude" does not provide a clear definition of the behavior you would like changed. The specific behaviors reflecting Larry's attitude (e.g., comments negatively, slams doors, fails to greet co-workers in a friendly manner) should be specified. Remember, OB Mod is intended to alter behavior patterns, not how a person thinks or feels.

2. Measurement of Behavior.   OB Mod is a data-based technique. Once a performance-related behavior has been isolated, the frequency with which it occurs is recorded and graphed. This initial measurement is known as a **baseline.** Baseline data and corresponding graphs are used to (1) determine the extent to which a behavior is occurring, and (2) provide a benchmark against which changes in that behavior can be measured.

Measuring is accomplished primarily by counting how often a behavior occurs. Four techniques are typically used to measure behavior.[22] **Frequency counts** require the manager to count the number of times a behavior occurs. This technique is useful when the behavior occurs infrequently. **Fixed interval counts** are appropriate when the behavior lasts for longer periods of time. The measurement would be taken at predetermined regular intervals to determine if the behavior was occurring at that time. For example, an employer might observe a bookkeeper every thirty minutes to see if he is continuing to make entries. **Time-sample counts** are similar to fixed

ETHICAL DILEMMA
An Executive Observation from Suzanne Allford, Vice-President of the People Division, Wal-Mart Stores, Inc.

"Belief in the individual" has been the cornerstone of Wal-Mart's success. From the beginning, Chairman Sam Walton valued and encouraged individual contributions from our Associates. Reinforcement-based Positive Centered Leadership* fits our philosophy of individual contribution because it focuses on individual motivation and recognition. We teach our managers how to determine and evaluate the antecedents and consequences of an individual's performance both positive and negative.

Each organization has a responsibility to act in accordance with its belief system. At Wal-Mart we are careful to insure that Positive Centered Leadership does not become a means for manipulating people to do things they don't want to do. Rather, it provides us with a vehicle for helping our Associates and Wal-Mart alike achieve productive, satisfying end results. Wal-Mart long ago recognized the importance of dealing fairly and openly with each Associate, and Positive Centered Leadership has become an important means for achieving those ends. If applied unethically, reinforcement-based leadership could become little more than a manipulative technique. We intend to make sure that does not happen at Wal-Mart.

Questions
How could the effective use of reinforcement lead to unethical management practices?
What concrete steps can an organization take to insure that managers do not use the company reward system or other forms of reinforcement unethically?

*Positive Centered Leadership is a positive-reinforcement-based program that is part of the formal training of all Wal-Mart managers.

interval counts in that measurements are taken at regular intervals. However, measurements are taken only during selected (sampled) time spans. In the preceding example, the employer might record the behaviors from 9 to 11 A.M. and from 1 to 3 P.M. each day. The fourth technique, **rating measure,** results in a grade (good, average, poor) being applied to a behavior. Thus, the quality of the behavior can be evaluated either independently or in conjunction with one of the other three measuring techniques. OB Mod, as are all behavioral technologies, is concerned primarily with behavior frequency. However, some situations call for qualitative as well as quantitative evaluations of important performance-related behaviors. In such cases, a rating measure is used.

NUCOR

If you want improved performance, pay people for performance rather than for simply coming to work. NUCOR's CEO, Kenneth Iverson, believes in such an approach.[23] At NUCOR, a $60,000-salaried department manager can earn as much as $105,000 from performance-related incentives and bonuses. Other companies, such as General Motors, have also attempted to use a "variable pay" approach to compensation, in which better performance leads to better income. Such programs sometimes run into difficulties, however, due to problems in measuring actual performance—let alone measuring the actual behaviors that lead to performance.

At NUCOR, for example, it has been difficult to develop incentives for staff personnel. Such rewards are easier to measure for line employees and managers than they are for engineers and personnel specialists. Some companies, such as Boise Cascade, have attempted to attach hard measures to staff employees' performance by relating the performance of the departments and divisions they serve to their incentive bonuses. Another problem arises when firms attempt to tie rewards to long-term success: Rewards and reinforcements should be received when behaviors occur or as soon as possible after performance can be measured. The top five thousand officials at General Motors Corporation will now receive restricted stock grants rather than instant cash bonuses. These stock rights are executed months after they are awarded, thus giving managers an incentive to influence long-term rather than only short-term performance. Other long-term rewards may be tied to new product innovations or technology developments. Designing such systems is complex, and creative solutions will have to be sought if long-term performance is to be rewarded adequately in the future.

3. Functional Analysis of the Behavior.   Understanding the relationship of a behavior to its cause or consequence is critical to successful behavior change. Classical and operant learning theories hold that learned behaviors occur under one of two sets of conditions. According to classical theory, the appearance of an antecedent cue (or stimulus) will "cause" a behavior to take place if the stimulus-behavior relationship is (or has previously been) reinforced. Operant theory, on the other hand, holds that certain behaviors are contingent on the anticipated consequence of those behaviors rather than the appearance of an antecedent cue.

Let's return to the short case at the beginning of the chapter and see how functional analysis may be used to understand Tim's absence from the office. You may recall that Tim felt his supervisor, Julie, was too critical of his work and the people he was trying to help were unappreciative. Functional analysis suggests that one of two broad explanations exist for Tim's increasing absence from the work area.

Something (antecedent cue) may be causing Tim to leave the area. Perhaps seeing Julie prompts him to leave rather than to hear another complaint. This would be a *classical* explanation of his behavior. An *operant* explanation would be more concerned with the consequences (or lack of consequences) of certain behaviors. In this case, Tim does not feel appreciated (reinforced) by the foremen he is trying to assist. In other words, he has not learned (through reinforced behavior) to continue to provide the foremen with assistance. Exhibit 4.14 illustrates how functional analysis can be applied to Tim's situation.

The A→B→C analysis shown in Exhibit 4.14 does not address directly the role of social cognitive theory in explaining Tim's behavior.[24] Clearly, however, Tim's *perception* of his environment (Julie's actions and the reactions of the supervisors), influences Tim's actual behavior.

Functional analysis is the means by which a manager determines why a performance-related behavior is or is not currently taking place. In addition to explaining the existing situation, the easy-to-remember A→B→C formula is the foundation for developing and implementing an appropriate behavior-change or behavior-strengthening strategy.

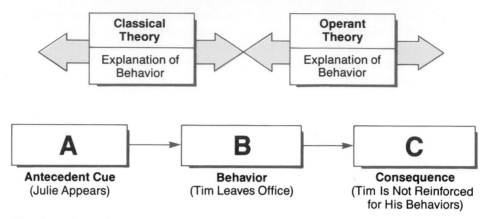

The A→B→C model explains the relationship of behavior to antecedent and consequences.

EXHIBIT 4.14   ABCs OF FUNCTIONAL ANALYSIS

4. Developing and Implementing an Appropriate Strategy.   The ultimate purpose of organizational behavior modification is to bring about, maintain, or increase the frequency of behaviors that will lead directly to attaining organizational goals. (OB Mod can also be used to decrease the frequency of behaviors that inhibit the attainment of goals.) Therefore, once a functional analysis of the critical behavior has been completed, a behavior change strategy based on that analysis should be developed.

Using OB Mod, behavior changes are brought about by systematically applying learning principles and reinforcement practices, including timely, positive reinforcement and the knowledgeable use of reinforcement schedules. In some cases, special approaches, such as modeling and shaping, also may be used (see page 127).

An effective behavior-change strategy can also be accomplished indirectly. Changes in work schedules, work assignments, or the composition of work groups can alter both the antecedent cues and the consequences of on-the-job behaviors. OB Mod merely encourages managers to understand the impact of such reinforcements and working conditions and to use this information *systematically* to manage organizational behavior more effectively.

The effectiveness of specific actions taken by managers may be influenced by the cultural settings in which they work. The rationale underlying OB Mod strategies, however, is understood and practiced in a variety of cultural settings. The use of specific work-rule interventions suggested by Toyota managers on the General Motors-Toyota NUMMI project illustrates this point and shows how a combination of direct and indirect strategies can influence worker behavior. The International Dimension on page 125 describes how NUMMI addressed potentially serious personnel problems when they opened their Fremont, California, facility.

Finally, whatever strategy is adopted must be analyzed in terms of its impact on the organization as a whole. Behavior-change strategies' impact on individuals or groups other than those directly affected should be taken into account. For example, reinforcing an employee with public praise or by providing special privileges may create negative feelings among others who are already performing their jobs in the desired manner. Similarly, reinforcements used should be consistent with company or work-area policies to insure that unintended precedents are not set.

In Tim's case, Julie may call Tim rather than approach him at this desk, or may attempt to alter Tim's perception of her recommendations through some form of

INTERNATIONAL DIMENSION
Score a Turnaround for Toyota

In 1982, executives at General Motors decided to throw in the towel at their Fremont, California, plant. GM had experienced high levels of labor unrest and an unsettling number of drug- and alcohol-related personnel problems. Relations between management and the union were no better than the plant's poor production record.

But all that was to change when Toyota Motor Corporation and General Motors agreed to enter the joint venture known as NUMMI (New United Motor Manufacturing, Inc.). NUMMI was the first joint venture of its type undertaken by the two automotive giants in the United States. Under their agreement, General Motors supplied the dealer network through which the new Chevrolet Nova would be distributed. (The Toyota FX, also produced by NUMMI, was distributed through existing Toyota dealers.) Toyota, in turn, provided much of the techology and the integrated sociotechnical work system to insure the plant's efficient operation.

A problem faced by the joint management team was to reduce absenteeism and prevent substance abuse among plant workers. (Many of the employees who had worked at the original GM plant had been rehired.) Although numerous causes existed for both problems, managers recognized that workers who left the plant during work or lunch breaks were more likely to return having used drugs or alcohol than those who remained on the premises. Furthermore, it was observed that some employees working under the earlier GM system would leave for lunch and simply not return.

The NUMMI solution was simple and clearly employed learning principles. First, a high-quality cafeteria was provided at the plant and workers who remained in the plant during lunch were paid for the half hour at their regular wage rate. Second, those choosing to leave the plant were required to sign out when they left and sign in when they returned to work. Although a few employees initially objected to the new procedures, the net effect was a reduction of both absenteeism and substance abuse in the reopened facility.

Questions
What principles of learning were applied by NUMMI to reduce absenteeism and substance abuse in the plant?

Do differences in corporate or national culture seem to have influenced the effectiveness of applying behavior-consequence strategies at NUMMI?

---

personal counseling. Conspicuously rewarding Tim might reinforce the wrong (existing) behaviors and raise questions or expectations among other office personnel.

5. Measuring the Impact of Behavior Change. The purpose of OB Mod is to encourage behaviors that will lead directly to improved performance. Initially, changes may be measured on the basis of the frequency of the desired behaviors by comparing postintervention performance against preintervention baseline measures. Failure to produce desired changes can be followed by reanalysis of functional relationships (step 3) and redesign of the intervention strategy (step 4).

Graphing behavior is an important part of the overall OB Mod process. Graphs can benefit a manager in two ways. First, physically recording behavior frequencies provides a means of evaluating the impact of the behavioral intervention. Second, such graphs tend to encourage employees who can now see evidence of their progress. The graph in Exhibit 4.15 shows a positive change in record keeping behaviors of hospital laboratory personnel at South Community Hospital in Oklahoma City, Oklahoma, before and after an OB Mod intervention.

Revenues produced by the department appeared inconsistent with the number of lab tests being conducted. The department head decided to chart the percentage of tests that were being run but for which no billing slip could be located. Billing behaviors were baselined for two weeks, and it was discovered that an average of 30 percent of the tests were not being billed to patient accounts. The chart was shown to employees at point A and they were instructed to try to do better. Billings improved briefly but returned to earlier levels. At point B, the department head again showed the graph to the employees. However, this time he initiated a positive reinforcement strategy. Employees were complimented on their attention to billing matters three times a day for the first week and once a week thereafter.

6. Monitoring Changed Behaviors. The final step in the OB Mod process is to monitor changed behaviors. Although learned behaviors are relatively permanent, there is a chance that changing conditions in the environment or other factors such as lack of continued reinforcement may later lead to extinction. It is necessary,

EXHIBIT 4.15   PERCENTAGE OF TESTS NOT RECORDED

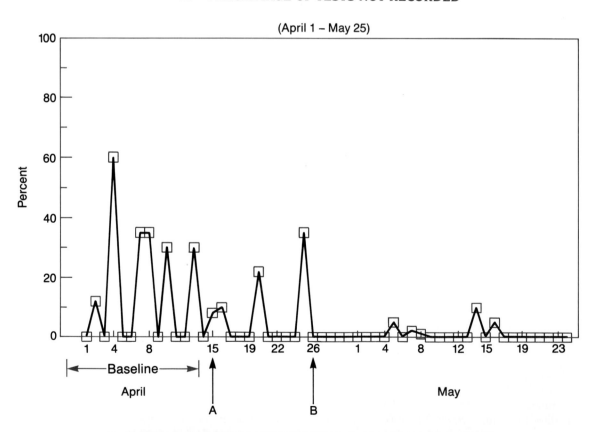

A: Problem first discussed with technicians after baseline was recorded.

B: Positive reinforcement is initiated.

therefore, to monitor behavior changes on a less frequent but ongoing basis and to take corrective action (reanalyze, reconsider strategy, etc.) when necessary.

Modeling and Shaping Behavior

Not all behaviors are easy to change. The more important or complex the behavior, the more likely a manager may need to use techniques such as modeling and shaping.

Modeling

Modeling is an excellent technique for helping individuals acquire new behaviors. **Modeling** is learning by imitation and is based on the premise that learning can occur by observing the behaviors and consequences of others as well as by direct personal experience.

For example, an admired co-worker who comes to work on time and is complimented by the boss, will be an effective model if others believe that their own on-time behavior will lead to similar compliments. Conversely, if a supervisor "fudges" on his expense account and is not reprimanded, a subordinate may adopt a similar practice, expecting that she too can do so without being punished.

Modeling is valuable to managers for a number of reasons. First, behaviors acquired through modeling do not have to be learned through a tedious process of trial and error. Second, modeled behavior can be learned by many people at once because learning takes place vicariously; each individual does not have to experience the behavior personally. Third, even when it is possible to establish new patterns of behavior through other means, the acquisition process can be shortened through modeling.[25]

In addition to facilitating the learning of **new** behavior, modeling can strengthen or weaken previously learned behaviors. For example, a person who occasionally returns late from work breaks may do so less often if he observes someone else being reprimanded for doing the same thing. Modeling may also prompt already-learned behaviors. Telethons designed to raise money for charities often announce the names of contributors, which serve as social cues for others to make contributions. Similarly, one employee's offer to work late may prompt other employees to make the same offer.

Effective modeling

Four factors can influence the effectiveness of modeling. These factors include (1) properties of the modeled activities; (2) observer determinants; (3) functional value of the modeled behavior; and (4) attractiveness of the model.[26] (See Exhibit 4.16.)

1. Properties of the modeled activities   refer to such characteristics as the importance of the behavior to the learner, how clearly the modeled behaviors can be distinguished from other behaviors, and the complexity of those behaviors.

2. Observer determinants   refer to the readiness and ability of an observer to learn a modeled behavior. A person's perceptions may prepare or otherwise predispose her to observe some behaviors accurately and others inaccurately.

3. Functional value   refers to the usefulness of the modeled behavior to the observer. An observer is more likely to focus his attention on those behaviors he believes will

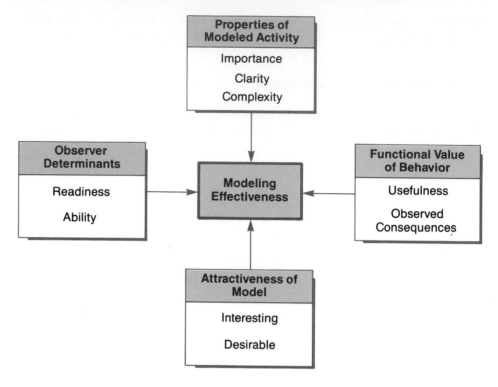

EXHIBIT 4.16   FACTORS INFLUENCING MODELING EFFECTIVENESS

be employed in the future than those he perceives to be less relevant to his situation. An observer may also be influenced by the behavior consequences experienced by the model. Modeled behaviors that have either positive or negative outcomes increase the observer's attention; behaviors that produce no noticeable outcomes are more likely to be ignored. Direct outcomes cannot always be observed. In such cases, observers may be influenced by symbols of successful outcomes.

For example, a group of new salespeople attending a seminar conducted by the company's leading salesman do not actually see him receive his sales comissions. However, they may observe symbols of his success such as his Rolex watch, expensive clothing, and good reputation. The higher the probability that the behavior-consequence relationship will be the same for the learner as for the model, the more effective the model.

4. Attractiveness of the model is also important. Observers tend to be more responsive to models who are interesting or otherwise attractive. Given the option, the new salespeople in the example above will be more inclined to attend a successful salesperson's presentation on "What I Did Right" than an unsuccessful salesperson's presentation on "What I Did Wrong"! Of course, attractiveness is in the eye of the beholder. An advertiser of cosmetics may want to use a handsome celebrity to model the use of a product, while the promoter of a family theme park may wish to use models whose attractiveness lies in their "just plain folks" image.

Shaping

In **shaping,** a complex behavior is learned as successive approximations of that behavior are reinforced.[27] In other words, a shaped behavior is one that is learned incrementally over time rather than all at once. An employee who is required to learn how to perform a complex task may find it easier if the task is broken down into smaller behavioral segments and reinforcement is received as each segment is learned than if the entire task must be mastered before any reinforcement is received.

In some cases, a related technique known as **chaining**[28] may be employed. Recall the first time you tried to write a computer program. At first, you may have thought you would never reach a point where you could run a program successfully. In order to build your confidence, your instructor probably gave you a simple assignment which allowed you to complete an entire program (task). You felt good about being able to write a "finished program." Later, as your confidence increased, you learned to write more complex programs. This was a form of chaining, a behavior-change strategy in which the final step (in this case, a completed, although simple, program) in the chain of events is learned and reinforced first. When that step has been learned, the next-to-last step is learned, and so on.

Behavioral Self-Management

This chapter has focused on the fundamentals of learning theory and on how learning theory can be applied by managers in organizational settings. Another area that is currently receiving considerable attention is that of **behavioral self-management.** Behavioral self-management, also known as self-regulation and self-control, is concerned with the systematic application of learning theory to the management of one's own behaviors. Self-management calls for the conscious regulation of a person's behavior by internally controlled rather than externally controlled reinforcement and punishment.

Self-management represents more than an individual's motivation or desire to change. Instead, it is concerned primarily with the *means* for exercising influence over behavior.[29] Self-management assumes that an individual is capable of self-observation, the ability to judge her own behaviors, and the ability to act or react in a manner that will increase, decrease, or maintain the level of a given behavior. Exhibit 4.17 describes the three behavioral elements of Self-management: self-observation, self-evaluation, and self-reaction.

The primary focus of behavioral self-management has been on self-influence processes themselves. These processes fall into two main categories, stimulus management and consequence management.

Stimulus management occurs when an individual increases or decreases the appearance of antecedent cues responsible for certain behaviors. A manager who feels that too much of her time is spent reading junk mail may simply ask her secretary

EXHIBIT 4.17 ELEMENTS OF BEHAVIORAL SELF-MANAGEMENT

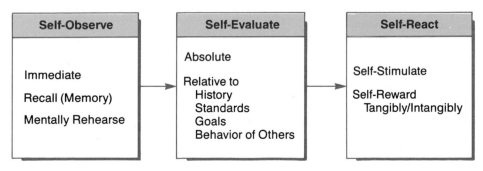

Self-Observe	Self-Evaluate	Self-React

Immediate
 	
Recall (Memory)
 	
Mentally Rehearse
	Absolute
	
	Relative to
	  History
	  Standards
	  Goals
	  Behavior of Others
		Self-Stimulate
		
		Self-Reward
		  Tangibly/Intangibly

not to place the mail on her desk with other important correspondence. Removal of the stimulus (the junk mail) should lessen her compulsion to examine it. Conversely, taping a note to the telephone may cue her to return an important call. In both cases, wishing to regulate her own behaviors, she initiated the actions herself.

Consequence management occurs when an individual initiates control over the consequences of his own behaviors by rewarding or punishing the occurrence of those behaviors. Such a strategy may be used as an incentive to behave in a certain way (e.g., "I'm going to take a day off when I complete this report"). In addition, systematic self-reinforcement of behavior can increase the probability of similar behaviors occurring in the future. Authors often adopt a consequence-management strategy by permitting themselves to "do other things" only after they have written a certain number of pages each day. Consequence management may involve a number of self-reinforcement variations including other cognitive forms of reinforcement such as feelings of increased self-esteem, feelings of greater competency (self-efficacy), and good feelings about the task.

Another variation of consequence management involves self-punishment. Although self-punishment has proved to be a viable way to decrease behaviors, it tends to be less effective than self-reward. Self-punishment can discourage work on desired behavior changes, and can even reverse gains in productivity achieved through previous decreases in undesirable behavior. Finally, it is more difficult to administer self-punishment than self-reward. The experience is not unlike trying to pull your own tooth or to give yourself a shot.

Let's look at the case of Joe Ziegler. Joe was increasingly perplexed by his situation at work. Six months earlier, he had agreed to head up a special task force to investigate an unusually high rate of equipment failure in plants located in the Eastern Region. At first, due to the large number of orders being processed in his own plant, Joe had been reluctant to undertake the assignment. However, Thomas McKinnon, the corporate vice-president for manufacturing, had assured him that the task force would not take too much time. He also pointed out to Joe that he himself had many irons in the fire. McKinnon commented, "I take on little extras like this all the time, and there's really nothing to it. Just approach these things the way I do."

Unfortunately, Joe had not spent that much time around McKinnon, and now he had even less time to learn from him. He wasn't sure exactly how he was going to give enough time to the work of the task force and still keep his own operation going. But one thing was sure: he knew that he'd better find a way and find it fast.

Under more ideal circumstances, McKinnon might train Joe, possibly employing modeling or shaping techniques, to prepare him for his new assignment. However, the present circumstances appear to require Joe to use some form of behavioral self-management strategy to acquire the behaviors necessary to successfully complete the additional work. Joe may decide to structure his task force activities using such stimulus-management tools as schedules, timetables, and deadlines to initiate task-force-related activities. In addition, a consequence-management strategy using self-reinforcement techniques should increase the likelihood that Joe completes the project in a timely manner.

Self-management emphasizes self-reinforcement that is linked to the completion of a task. An expansion of the Self-management concept, known as self-leadership,[30] can add to the range of intrinsic or "natural" reinforcements in a number of ways including

1. choosing a naturally rewarding work environment (e.g., taking paperwork to a more pleasant work area);

2. performing the task in an intrinsically satisfying manner in which variations in the performance process are possible (e.g., sending a memo concerning a problem to the boss rather than confronting him in person); and

3. altering thought processes about the work (e.g., focusing on certain enjoyable aspects of a job rather than on how long it will take).

Maintaining Changed Behaviors

Changes in behavior, whether organizational or individual, are sometimes difficult to maintain. One strategy for overcoming this problem is relapse prevention.[31] Such a strategy begins by acknowledging and accepting that *relapses will take place.* (Even the most adamant dieter is likely to nibble "just once.") Accepting this inevitability allows an individual to *identify high-risk situations* when relapses are most likely to take place and to *formulate coping strategies.* These strategies, in turn, can be practiced in simulated high-risk situations. Practicing coping strategies in this manner can increase a person's sense of mastery of the coping skills as well as of the changed behavior itself. Learning, strengthening, or weakening behaviors is the immediate goal of self-management. However, maintaining behavior change over time is the ultimate objective.

LEARNING, REINFORCEMENT, AND BEHAVIOR ANALYSIS: CONCLUSIONS

Learning is concerned with how individuals acquire, strengthen, and weaken specific, overt behaviors. Many authorities and a growing number of managers believe that it is these overt behaviors, rather than internal cognitive states, that lead directly to the attainment of organizational goals.

Classical learning theory assumes that behavior is brought about by external cues or stimuli. Operant theory, on the other hand, explains the occurrence of specific behaviors on the basis of their immediate consequences. In both cases, learning depends on an individual's firsthand stimulus→behavior→consequence experiences.

The third theory of learning, social cognitive theory, holds that learning is the result of a continuous interaction between behaviors, environment, and cognitive processes. It is this last area, human cognition, that sets SCT apart from classical and operant theory. According to SCT, individuals play an important part in their own learning through their observations, interpretations, and mental rehearsals of specific behaviors.

The concept of reinforcement is central to all three approaches to learning and tends to be the focus of many management applications. In many instances, however, managers confuse reinforcement with a more traditionally held view of reward. Managers are in a position to reward desired behaviors and often do so by providing financial bonuses, verbal recognition, and other benefits. Remember, however, that a reward reinforces behavior only if the recipient values it and perceives it to be a positive consequence of that behavior. Similarly, punishments used by managers will influence behavior only to the extent that they are seen by the employee as undesirable consequences of the behavior.

The timing and pattern of the reinforcement (reinforcement schedule) also influence the rate, strength, and retention of learning. Reinforcement schedules should be selected based on the type of behavior to be learned. For example, certain behaviors (administrative) lend themselves to interval schedules; other behaviors (machine- or unit-related) might be more easily reinforced according to a ratio schedule. Schedules can also be designed for more rapid learning (continuous and fixed) or to minimize halting of the learned behavior (variable). Both reinforcement and scheduling strategies can be altered during the learning period to accomplish desired learning goals.

Learning theory can be applied in specific situations through a variety of approaches to behavior change. One comprehensive approach to changing organizational behavior is Organizational Behavior Modification. OB Mod combines classical and operant principles of learning with organizational systems analysis and provides managers with specific tools for affecting critical performance-related behaviors. Organizational behavior modification, then, focuses attention on behaviors that lead directly to accomplishing the organization's goals and objectives.

Other applications of learning theory gaining popularity include behavior modeling and shaping and Behavioral Self-Management. In the section on self management, you read about a plant manager, Joe Zeigler, who seemed unable to satisfy many competing demands on his time. Although his superior suggested that Ziegler approach the situation as the superior would, the necessary behaviors had not been modeled effectively. Therefore, Ziegler may have to develop an appropriate self-management strategy employing the use of stimulus or consequence management, or otherwise create intrinsic value in the behaviors necessary to complete all of the tasks before him. Such an approach accompanied by a relapse prevention strategy may help him to meet many of his present and future needs.

On the other hand, Tim Roberts, whom we met in the opening vignette, felt that he was no longer being reinforced for doing his job. From his point of view, the failure of either Julie or the line foremen to acknowledge his positive contributions is responsible for his changed behavior. Remember, reinforcement is a vital part of the learning process and must be present if behaviors are to continue over time.

Managers who understand learning theories and principles, and are able to use related behavior management techniques, possess valuable tools for influencing both individual and organizational behavior.

QUESTIONS FOR REVIEW AND DISCUSSION

1. In what ways are classical learning theory different from operant learning theory? Give an example of each in a work setting.
2. What are the three components in the social cognitive theory model?
3. How can SCT by useful to a manager?
4. What conditions must exist for learning to take place? Do all of these conditions apply to the SCT model? Explain.
5. Restate the principle elements of the law of effect. What is the significance of each element?
6. How are positive reinforcement, negative reinforcement, and punishment different from one another?

7. Explain the importance of the history of a reinforcer.
8. Why are self-reward and self-punishment important, and how does each influence self-control?
9. What are the five steps of organizational behavior modification, and why is each important?
10. What are the four factors that can influence the effectiveness of modeling?
11. When and how should shaping be used by a manager?
12. Can self-management techniques be used by any employee? Why or why not?
13. Why is it necessary to plan for maintaining changed behaviors?

REFERENCES

1. Ivan P. Pavlov, *Conditional Reflexes,* trans. G. V. Anrep (London: Oxford University Press, 1927).

2. John B. Watson, "Psychology as the Behaviorist Views It," *Psychology Review,* Vol. 20 (1913): 158–177.

3. B. F. Skinner, *Contingencies of Reinforcement* (New York: Appleton-Century Crofts, 1969).

4. A. Bandura, *Principles of Behavior Modification* (New York: Holt, Rinehart & Winston, 1969), 32–33; P. G. Ginter and D. D. White, "A Social Learning Theory of Strategic Management," *The Academy of Management Review,* Vol. 7 (April 1982): 254–255.

5. M. Snyder, "Seek, and ye shall find: Testing hypotheses about other people," in E. T. Higgins, C. P. Herman, and M. P. Zanna, Eds., *Social Cognition: The Ontario Symposium on Personality and Social Psychology,* Vol. 1 (1980): 105–130.

6. Tom Peters, "Disney's Illusion Reinforces Image," *On Achieving Excellence,* 4 (September 1989): 8.

7. Bandura, *Social Foundations of Thought and Action* (Englewood Cliffs, N.J.: Prentice-Hall, 1986).

8. Donald D. White and David A. Bednar, *Organizational Behavior* (Boston: Allyn & Bacon, 1986), 221.

9. T. Cassidy, "Interview with Joseph Baum," on "Pinnacle" (New York: Cable News Network), 19 March 1988.

10. E. L. Thorndike, *Educational Psychology: The Psychology of Learning* (New York: Columbia University Teachers College, 1913), vol.II.

11. L. W. Fredericksen, *Handbook of Organizational Behavior Management* (New York: John Wiley and Sons, 1982), 77.

12. Bandura, *Principles of Behavior Modification,* op. cit.

13. C. E. Thorensen and M. J. Mahoney, *Behavioral Self-Control* (New York: Holt, Rinehart & Winston, 1974); C. C. Manz and Henry P. Sims, "Self-Management as a Substitute for Leadership," *The Academy of Management Review,* Vol. 5 (July 1980): 361–367.

14. Cassidy, op. cit.

15. "Incentives Can Be Bad for Business," *Inc.,* January 1988, 93–94; E. L. Deci, "Notes on the Theory and Metatheory of Intrinsic Motivation," *Organizational Behavior and Human Performance,* vol. 13 (1975): 130–145; M. Ross, "Salience of Reward and Intrinsic Motivation," *Journal of Personality and Social Psychology,* vol. 22 (1975): 245–254; T. L. Daniel and J. K. Esser, "Intrinsic Motivation as Influenced by Rewards, Task Interest, and Task Structure," *Journal of Applied Psychology,* vol. 65 (1980): 566–573.

16. R. M. Ryan, et. al., "Relation of Reward Contingency and Interpersonal Context to Intrinsic Motivation: A Review and Test Using Cognitive Evaluation Theory," *Journal of Personality and Social Psychology,* vol. 45 (1983): 736–750; Z. Kunda and S. H. Schwartz, "Undermining Intrinsic Moral Motivation: External Reward and Self-Presentation," *Journal of Personality and Social Psychology,* vol. 45 (1983): 763–771.

17. F. Luthans and D. D. White, "Behavioral Modification: Application to Manpower Management," *Personnel Administration,* vol. 34 (July-August 1971): 43.

18. D. K. Fox, B. L. Hopkins, and W. K. Anger, "The Long-Term Effects of a Token Economy on Safety Performance in Open-Pit Mining," *Journal of Applied Behavior Analysis,* Vol. 20 (Fall 1987): 215–224; R. A. Reber, J. A. Wallin, and J. S. Chhokar, "Reducing Industrial Accidents: A Behavioral Experiment," *Industrial Relations,* Vol. 23 (Winter 1984): 119–125.

19. Luthans and R. Kreitner, *Organizational Behavior Modification and Beyond* (Glenview, Ill.: Scott, Foresman, 1985).

20. Ibid.; D. D. White and B. Davis, "Behavioral Contingency Management: A Bottom-Line Alternative for Management Development," *Personnel Administration* (April 1980): 676–75; B. M. Carlson and J. A. Collins, "Motivating Managers with Positive Reinforcement," *Management Accounting,* Vol. 67 (March 1986): 48–51; W. Dierks and K. A. McNanny, "Incentives You Can Bank On," *Personnel Journal,* Vol. 64 (May 1985): 60–65.

21. J. N. Marr and B. L. Means, *Behavior Management Manual* (Fayetteville: Arkansas Rehabilitation Services, 1980).

22. Ibid., 3–6.

23. S. Weiss, "The Sad Saga of Variable Pay," *Business Month,* April 1990, 74, 77.

24. Kreitner and Luthans, "A Social Learning Approach to Behavioral Management: Radical Behaviorists 'Mellowing Out,' " *Organizational Dynamics,* Vol. 13 (Autumn 1984): 47–65; Luthans and K. Thompson, "Theory D and OB Mod: Synergistic or Opposite Approaches to Performance Improvement," *Journal of Organizational Behavior Management,* Vol. 9 (1987): 105–124.

25. An excellent discussion of modeling can be found in Bandura, *Social Foundations.*

26. Fredericksen, *Handbook,* 528–529.

27. L. W. Miller, *Behavior Management* (New York: John Wiley & Sons, 1978), 138–144.

28. F. H. Kanfer and A. P. Goldstein, *Helping People Change* (New York: Pergamon Press, 1980).

29. C. C. Manz, *The Art of Self-Leadership* (Englewood Cliffs, N.J.: Prentice-Hall, 1983).

30. Manz, "Self-Leadership: Toward an Expanded Theory of Self-Influence Processes in Organizations," *Academy of Management Review,* Vol. 11 (July 1986): 585–600.

31. R. D. Marx, "Relapse Prevention for Managerial Training: A Model for Maintenance of Behavior Change," *Academy of Management Review,* Vol 7 (July 1982): 433–441.

CASE 4.1

The sociable salesman

STEVEN G. MOON   *University of Arkansas*
DONALD D. WHITE   *University of Arkansas*

Barry Stone worked as a salesman in the Menswear Department of Holt's Department Store. He obtained a degree in retail management from a small state college and immediately took a job with Holt's. He had been with the store about one year.

Barry was raised as one of two children in an upper-middle-class home. He had always been a bright student in school and graduated in the upper ten percent of his class. Barry had purposely chosen to attend a small college. While there, he was well liked by many members of the student body. His popularity and interactions with his fellow students were enhanced by the fact that he was actively involved in many clubs and organizations. He was vice-president of his fraternity and a three-year member of the

student government association. During his senior year he actively campaigned for and was elected president of the student body. He was also voted "Big Man On Campus" that year. Barry was a member of the debate team. He attended college on a full football scholarship and was an all-conference tailback.

Holt's was a one-level department store containing 44,000 square feet of floor space, located in the downtown area. The store was organized into four main selling departments, including Menswear, Ladies' Wear, Cosmetics, and Shoes and Accessories. In addition, there were two sub-departments, Young Men's Wear and Young Ladies' Wear (see Exhibit 4.18). All working departments operated within designated sections of a single, primarily open, area. All

EXHIBIT 4.18   HOLT'S DEPARTMENT STORE FLOOR PLAN

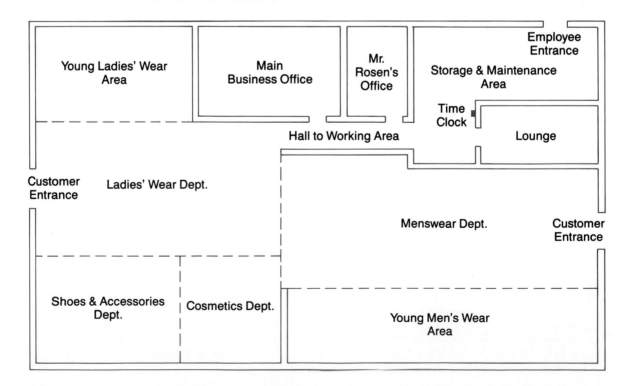

employees regularly worked in a particular department. Interdepartment transfer of personnel was sometimes necessary during periods of worker shortages and increased demand. Once on the sales floor, employees were not permitted to leave their assigned departments except on official business or when traveling to and from the time-clock area for lunch and scheduled breaks. Each major department operated under the direction of a department manager who also performed the usual everyday functions of all other salespeople.

The store itself was owned and managed by Stuart Rosen. Mr. Rosen maintained an office within the store but generally was not involved in the day-to-day activities of salespeople. He left direct supervision of the salesforce to the department managers and concentrated his own efforts on the overall operation of the store. Rosen was a well-educated man, respected by employees for his fairness and knowledge of the retail business.

Barry was pleasant and sociable on the job. He enjoyed conversing with customers and other employees in the store. His confident, outgoing behavior seemed to draw respect and admiration from his co-workers. This was reflected in his sales, which, on average, were the highest in the department. He had consistently turned in high daily sales totals, and his value to the store had never been disputed. Lately, however, Barry's sales had been slowly dropping and had become erratic.

Joe Pennington, Barry's department manager and close friend, noticed the decrease in Barry's sales. As he observed Barry more closely, he also began to recognize certain patterns in his workday behaviors. For example, when Barry came to work in the mornings or returned from his lunch hour, he would "punch in" on the time clock. For several minutes thereafter, he would stand around in the storage room, hall, or office area and joke with the office or maintenance personnel before actually starting work. Often he would find unimportant things to do in the office before going to his department. After observing Barry's regular delays in getting to the sales area, Joe called Barry aside and explained, "Barry, I know you enjoy visiting with the other workers, but in the future, please see that you come directly to the sales area. You know, Christmas is almost here and we need all available personnel on the floor. We need you every minute out there to sell and restock, and we have to keep an eye out for shoplifters! You can't do that from the office or back room." Barry replied, "All right Joe, I'll be on time tomorrow. I just wanted to keep you guys on the floor busy." Barry and Joe then headed back to the salesfloor

talking about the basketball game the two had gone to that weekend. Barry reported to work on time the next day and continued to be prompt for almost a week, when he resumed his pattern of procrastination.

As time passed, Barry's backroom conversations attracted a greater number of workers. Delays in personnel getting to their respective departments were evidenced in temporary manpower shortages. Joe Pennington began to hear a growing number of customer complaints, most of which reflected the feeling that, "You can never find a salesman when you need one." And several salespeople who had good sales records in the past were submitting lower daily sales, negatively influencing the total sales of the department.

Once again, Joe decided to speak to Barry. Barry, however, seemed undaunted by Joe's friendly reminder. Not only did he not return to the sales floor, but instead he struck up a new conversaton with Joe himself. Barry's "sociable" behavior continued even though Joe spoke with him on several different occasions. It seemed that Joe's warnings only affected Barry's behavior temporarily, if at all, and they had no lasting impact. Moreover, prolonged conversations began occurring between Barry and other employees during afternoon breaks. Each worker was allowed one daily break lasting fifteen minutes. Every fifteen minutes in succession one worker would leave as another returned. Employees traveling to and from their work areas during the scheduled breaks would stop and talk as they met outside their departments or around the lounge. These sometimes prolonged encounters caused delays in getting back to the salesfloor and thus resulted in worker shortages and increased idle time.

Stuart Rosen's office was located off a hallway adjacent to the employee lounge. He would occasionally and unexpectedly leave the office while Barry and the other employees were talking. Upon seeing Rosen, the workers usually went directly to their departments before he had a chance to detect their loitering. Barry was no exception.

One Friday, Rosen called Barry into his office. "I just wanted you to know, Barry, that we appreciate your fine work around here. Starting today you will receive an increase of 10 percent in salary." Barry was elated with Mr. Rosen's praise and the salary increase. "I'm glad you are pleased with my work, sir," Barry said, "and I'll try even harder in the future." "Oh, by the way," exclaimed Rosen, "I'm going to need an extra hand here at the store the next two Saturdays. We need to run a partial inventory. Can you help us out?" Barry gladly accepted Rosen's request. He arrived early both Saturdays. In addition, Barry was punctual the next two weeks and turned in his highest sales totals in two months. Thereafter, Barry's backroom loitering slowly resumed and production again began to slip off.

Joe observed Barry's dawdling, its effect on the efficiency of the various departments and consequently on the store as a whole. With understandable concern, he decided to meet with Barry again to further discuss the problem and any disciplinary action he might have to take. "Perhaps," he thought, "I'm going to have to stop being so friendly with Barry myself."

CASE 4.2   Ron Brown's problem

GEORGE COBB   *Firestone Tire and Rubber Company*
DONALD D. WHITE   *University of Arkansas*

Ron Brown managed the Tire Building Department in a large tire manufacturing plant in the Southwest. The plant was a modern facility producing bias passenger, radial passenger, and light truck bias tires. The daily production ticket (number of tires produced) was 24,000 tires. Production was divided equally between the three strategic business units. The plant operated twenty-four hours a day and five days a week with occasional Saturday work during peak periods. A typical work week at the plant began at 11 P.M. Sunday night and ended at 11 P.M. Friday night. The three shifts ran from 11 P.M. until 7 A.M., 7 A.M. to 3 P.M., AND 3 P.M. to 11 P.M., respectively.

The function of the Tire Building Department was to receive the various tire components from other processing departments and assemble those components into a "green tire" carcass. The department employed approximately three hundred hourly Tire Builders to achieve its production goals. In addition to production workers, the department had three shift foremen and twenty-seven line supervisors.

The Tire Building Department used an incentive or piecework compensation system. Basically, builders were payed according to the number of tires they assembled during their eight-hour shift. Industrial engineers did time studies on each type of tire constructed, and a production standard was assigned. A tire builder who could produce at a rate faster than the standard without sacrificing quality could earn additional income. (Thus, a builder who built at 120 percent of standard could receive an additional 20 percent wage for the day.) A tire builder who could

not build on standard due to machine or component conditions was payed at a fixed rate for the period during which his or her machine was down (not running). This rate used to be considerably less than the builder could have earned under normal conditions. However, a recently negotiated clause in the union contract raised down-time pay to 95 percent of the builder's average pay for the period. For example, a builder who could establish a rate of $12.00/hour based upon effectiveness would be payed at a rate of $11.40/hour for that time during which the machine was down.

MEASURING PERFORMANCE

The performance of each foreman and supervisor in the Tire Building Department was measured against a set of objectives. All management employees had unit performance criteria they were expected to achieve in the areas of employee relations, quality, productivity, safety, and cost. Specific quantified parameters for each of these areas were established and were monitored continuously.

At the beginning of each month, Ron Brown reviewed with the Shift Foremen the performance of their respective shifts against established objectives. The Shift Foremen in turn conducted similar reviews with each of the Line Supervisors. Monthly performance figures were accumulated for each foreman and line supervisor once a year, and a formal performance assessment was completed and forwarded to the Personnel Department. This annual assessment was used to determine each respective salary increase.

The area of productivity was one of the most critical to Ron Brown. Since tire manufacturing is a mass production operation, it is critical to the department and the plant that tire-builder productivity be maximized. Ron knew that recent changes in the tire-builder payment system had reduced the per-tire incentive and that a different management approach to improving productivity at the department level was necessary.

MEASURING BUILDER PERFORMANCE

Productivity on the supervisor's and foremen's objectives was broken down into three parts: builder effectiveness, builder use, and tires per builder. These were the areas in which foremen and supervisors were considered to have the greatest impact.

Builder **effectiveness** is the rate at which a builder produces against the standard. If the production standard is one hundred and fifty tires per shift for a particular type of tire, and the tire builder is able to build two hundred tires during the shift, then that worker's effectiveness is 133 percent.

The ability to earn extra pay generally is considered to be the driving force toward high builder-effectiveness levels. However, the foreman and supervisor actually play an important role in terms of the tire builder's ability to achieve high builder effectiveness. If managers are not efficient in handling the production problems, whether machine- or component-related, the builder will be unable to build at a rate higher than standard or will not be motivated to do so. Furthermore, union-negotiated nonincentive payments have reduced the impact of the incentive system. If line managers do not project high expectations relative to builder effectiveness, tire builders are often more likely to build at a lower rate.

Builder **use** is of utmost importance to high productivity. builder use is defined as the percentage of time the tire builder spends working against the standard versus being in an off-standard condition. If a builder is on standard for 6.5 hours of an 8.0 hour shift, then the builder use would be 81 percent. The builder effectiveness level is a result of the efforts of both the tire builder and the supervisor/foreman; builder use is primarily under the control of the line managers. To achieve high levels of builder use, the supervisor and foreman must be efficient at handling the conditions that result in the tire builder being off

standard (e.g., equipment failure, lack of raw material inventory, etc.). Line managers are further challenged by the supervisor in that some workers are not motivated by the incentive system. In such cases, an off-standard condition actually allows the builders to work at a greatly reduced pace and still draw a set level of pay.

Total builder productivity is determined through the following equation:

$$\text{productivity} = \text{builder effectiveness} \times \text{builder use} \times \text{production standard}$$

This productivity results in a tires-per-builder figure and serves as the basis for an overall measurement of the department's productivity. Since the production standard is not within the direct control of the supervisors and foremen, Ron Brown measures his line managers only on builder effectiveness and builder use. At the end of each shift, the foreman calculates builder effectiveness, builder use, and tires per day using the data collected from individual builders by each line supervisor. Ron then reviews the data from all three shifts and calculates month-to-date figures for the shifts and the department. Any abnormal shifts away from the averages are noted and investigated. Exhibit 4.19 is an accumulation of these figures for a typical month.

As Ron Brown sat in his office, he reviewed a series of events that led him to believe he had a serious problem. Simply put, he was not getting the production from his tire builders that he needed. He believed the problem stemmed from the fact that the builders were paid on the basis of their effectiveness rather than of their use. The department, on the other hand, was evaluated on the basis of its overall performance.

Ron knew that the builders sometimes played games with the system by driving their effectiveness rating up and then going down. Those who were discovered intentionally underproducing were reprimanded by their supervisor or foreman. However, many violations were subtle, and they continued to occur. Moreover, even small abuses (3–5 minutes at a time) cost the department significant amounts of money in a month's time.

As he looked out of his office window at the tire builders below, he thought, "The foremen and supervisors try to keep tight controls on machine use. They get on some workers pretty hard, but they can't catch everybody. Frankly, I'd like to see builder effectiveness improve as well. I've got a problem; I just don't have an answer!"

EXHIBIT 4.19   TYPICAL PRODUCTION FIGURES FOR ONE MONTH

	BUILDER EFFECTIVENESS				BUILDER USE				TIRES PER BUILDER		
Date:	1st	2nd	3rd	Date:	1st	2nd	3rd	Date:	1st	2nd	3rd
01	115	119	117	01	92	90	93	01	112	115	116
04	116	120	117	04	90	89	95	04	111	115	115
05	118	125	120	05	91	89	93	05	112	114	117
06	116	121	120	06	89	89	95	06	112	116	115
07	116	123	115	07	90	87	95	07	110	114	113
08	117	122	119	08	90	88	93	08	111	115	115
11	110	119	123	11	87	88	91	11	113	116	114
12	116	118	120	12	88	90	92	12	112	115	115
13	119	120	122	13	88	91	94	13	113	117	116
14	120	122	119	14	89	87	94	14	112	115	116
15	119	127	118	15	89	89	94	15	113	114	117
18	118	122	120	18	86	89	92	18	111	116	116
19	118	123	117	19	88	88	91	19	110	115	115
20	117	120	117	20	87	83	93	20	113	116	114
21	116	122	118	21	89	89	96	21	112	114	116
22	117	122	114	22	88	90	94	22	109	115	115
25	115	121	118	25	90	89	92	25	113	116	115
26	119	120	119	26	89	89	92	26	113	115	116
27	117	121	119	27	87	88	95	27	112	117	117
28	118	121	119	28	88	88	92	28	112	115	116
29	116	124	117	29	89	90	91	29	112	115	116
Average:	117	122	118	Average:	89	89	93	Average:	112	115	115

EXERCISE 4.1

BEHAVIORAL ANALYSIS: "FROM A TO C"

Organizational goals can only be met when individual behaviors that lead to attaining those goals are practiced regularly. As you have learned, behaviors are related to either antecedent cues or specific consequences. That is, a stimulus may cause a behavior to take place, or a behavior may come about in order to achieve some specific consequence or to keep that consequence from happening. If we are to understand why behaviors occur, we must first understand their relationship to these cues and consequences. The purpose of this exercise is to help you identify the relationship of behaviors to antecedent cues and/or behavioral consequences.

INSTRUCTIONS

Part I

Identify three important performance-related behaviors in your present class. Behaviors are considered to be performance-related only if they contribute directly to the grade you receive in your class.

1. Discuss why these behaviors were selected.
2. These behaviors were identified by you as being important. Does that mean that they are practiced regularly? Why or why not?
3. What consequences do these behaviors have for your organizational unit (this class)?

Part II

The frequency of these behaviors is related to antecedent cues and/or consequences of the behaviors.

1. Analyze each behavior as to the reason for its occurrence.
2. In what way could you increase (or decrease) the frequency of these behaviors for (a) yourself, or (b) others?
3. Based upon your understanding of the A→B→C behavioral model, discuss why you and your fellow students either practice or fail to practice those behaviors that will lead to successful class performance.

Part III

Formulate a specific strategy for bringing about or maintaining performance-related behaviors in your class. Base your approach on the five behavioral contingency management steps described in this chapter. Discuss your intervention strategy with classmates.

EXERCISE 4.2
DESIGNING A TRAINING AND DEVELOPMENT PROGRAM: APPLYING LEARNING THEORY ON THE JOB

INTRODUCTION

You have been hired as a consultant to help an employer design a training and development program for a group of workers soon to be hired. These new employees have little work experience. For the most part, they consist of high school dropouts attempting to find their first full-time job and a group of individuals identified by the local Employment Security Office as hard-core unemployed. As you design the program, keep in mind the learning principles you studied in this chapter.

SITUATION

Jobs for which the training program is to be designed include machinery operators, stockpersons, and janitors. Machinery operators are to be trained to start, stop, and operate a five-step tube bender. Copper tubing must be cut to an appropriate length, placed on the machine, secured on the machine, bent by the machine, removed from the machine, and placed in an appropriate bin. Minor maintenance (adjusting calibrations according to dials on the machine and lubrication) also must be performed. Stockpersons must pick up stock from the designated storage area and keep raw material bins three-fourths full at each of twenty-eight machine locations. Records of pick-up and delivery times and quantities must be maintained by stockpersons. Janitorial activities include keeping the work area clean and free from safety hazards. The company employs 175 persons on each of three shifts, and you are responsible for training 24 new employees—14 machine operators, 6 stockpersons, and 2 janitors.

Machine operators are expected to produce 1,200 units an hour by the end of the first week and to attain a rate of 2,400 units an hour within two months. You have available off-the-job as well as on-the-job training facilities. Videotape equipment can also be provided by the company. Newly hired employees all will receive the same entry-level wage ($3.50/hour). Janitors and stockperson will remain on an hourly wage, which can be increased incrementally to $4.20/hour in the first three months. Machine operators will be paid on a piece rate basis at the end of the training period and will receive .25 cents per/piece.

You and your consulting group will present your final recommendations in a brief report to the plant manager.

QUESTIONS TO BE ANSWERED IN YOUR REPORT

1. What steps will you include in the training sequence for each job?
2. What form of reinforcement will you use?
3. What type of reinforcement schedules will be used for each job category?
4. How might modeling or shaping be used during the training?
5. What recommendations will you make to line supervisors once training has been concluded and the new workers are on the job?

CHAPTER **5**

THE MOTIVATION TO WORK: CONTENT THEORIES

LEARNING OBJECTIVES

1. To understand factors that contribute to employee motivation.
2. To learn ways in which content motivation theories can be applied on the job.
3. To distinguish differences between motivation and satisfaction.
4. To learn strengths and weaknesses of content motivation theories.
5. To understand the impact of intrinsic, extrinsic, and vicarious motivators.

CHAPTER OUTLINE

Why Study Motivation?

Intrinsic, Extrinsic, and Vicarious Motivation
Intrinsic and Extrinsic Motivation
Vicarious Motivation

Content Theories of Motivation
Needs and Need Hierarchies
Two Factor Theory of Work Motivation
Affiliation, Achievement, and Power
Applying Content Theories in Managerial Situations

The Motivation to Work: Conclusions

Questions for Review and Discussion

References

Cases: 5.1 Going Back Home
        5.2 What Ever Happened to Professional Pride?

Exercises: 5.1 Understanding Work Motivation
            5.2 Applying Content Theories

KEY TERMS

Motivation

Intrinsic motivation

Extrinsic motivation

Vicarious motivation

Maslow's need hierarchy

ERG theory

Motivators

Hygienes

Affiliation need (n aff)

Achievement need (n ach)

Power need (n pow)

A ndrea had been with Therma-Dor's marketing research team for nearly six years. Most of the team members had joined the company at the same time. They worked closely with one another and sometimes socialized away from the job. Andrea liked her co-workers and had consistently been recognized as a "highly motivated" employee. Recently, she was promoted to become new products coordinator and relocated from the suburban research park to the central office in downtown Los Angeles.

Everyone was sure that Andrea was right for the job. She was bright, enthusiastic, and highly regarded by her co-workers. In fact, praise from her team members had played an important part in her promotion decision. After six weeks on the job, however, members of the executive group as well as Andrea herself had begun to question her new assignment. Her performance was fair at best and she seemed to those around her to be unhappy with her situation. She talked by phone almost daily with her former co-workers and often expressed her dissatisfaction with the downtown office.

In a recent meeting with Andrea, Ted Vinson, the vice-president of marketing, confronted her directly saying, "Andrea, you haven't seemed very motivated since you came here, and frankly, you appear to be getting less enthusiastic every day." After a moment Andrea replied, "I just don't know; the job's not what I expected. Most of the people in our group spend their time on the road, and I follow their progress through their faxed reports. When they get back for the monthly meetings, we have so much to do that no one seems to care about anyone else's problems; it's everyone for himself."

Ted Vinson probably wonders if earlier perceptions of Andrea were accurate. Was she *ever* highly motivated? Has Andrea changed since she took her new job, or are changes in her environment responsible for her lack of motivation? Ted certainly isn't the only manager who has ever wondered about these problems. The questions of what actually does motivate people and how motivation levels can be increased face all managers.

WHY STUDY MOTIVATION?

Motivation is the term we use to describe the act or process of initiating and sustaining behaviors toward certain goals. Executives and managers at all levels have long recognized the importance of motivation and have used a variety of means in attempts to stimulate it. Some view motivation like the king in Exhibit 5.1. More enlightened leaders, however, place greater value on individuals and tend to use more constructive approaches to motivate employees.

The issue of motivation has taken on added significance as explanations for poor workmanship and declining productivity have been sought. According to Alan Smith, executive vice-president of General Motors Corporation, we are involved in a people revolution: "It's a revolution in which each side recognizes that people, not fixed assets or technology, are the deciding factor in the bottom line."[1] This focus on human assets has led to a reexamination of motivation theories and the develop-

EXHIBIT 5.1   WHAT IS THE KING'S ATTITUDE TOWARD MOTIVATION?
SOURCE: By permission of Johnny Hart and News America Syndicate, Inc.

ment of new techniques to influence the performance of managers, workers, and professionals alike.

Motivation has been defined as "those psychological processes that cause the arousal, direction, and persistence of voluntary actions that are goal directed."[2] This definition identifies a number of important elements related to motivation and is broad enough to encompass the wide range of theories used to explain the subject today.

Each of the theories we will explore treats motivation as an individual phenomenon and should be viewed in light of whether or not it

1. allows for the uniqueness of each person;
2. views motivation as intentional;
3. answers questions about what initiates a particular behavior and gives it direction; and
4. helps us to predict behavior in the future.

From a practical point of view, this chapter should help you understand and influence your own motivation and the motivation of those you manage.

Our discussion of motivation has been separated into two chapters. In the present chapter, we will concentrate on approaches to motivation known as content theories. In the following chapter, we will examine three additional types of motivation theories: (1) process theories; (2) goal setting theory; and (3) reinforcement theory.

INTRINSIC, EXTRINSIC, AND VICARIOUS MOTIVATION

Internal processes can also be influenced by external events and the actions of other individuals, however. In order to understand more fully how motivation occurs, it is helpful to examine three concepts:

1. Intrinsic motivation,
2. Extrinsic motivation, and
3. Vicarious motivation.

Intrinsic and Extrinsic Motivation

The terms intrinsic and extrinsic motivation refer to the source of motivation and the nature of its consequences. The source of **intrinsic motivation** is a need or other stimulus that occurs *within* an individual. **Extrinsic motivation,** on the other hand, is caused by incidents or stimuli that occur *externally.* Consequences can occur either *naturally* (as a direct result of the motivated behavior) or *arbitrarily* (indirectly through the actions of another person). A natural consequence, for example, might include positive feelings about a job well done. An example of an arbitrary consequence would be praise given by a supervisor, because its existence depends on the actions of another person. Exhibit 5.2 shows the contingent relationships of behavior consequences and the source of those consequences.

Intrinsic motivation commonly refers to three behavior–outcome relationships:

1. A behavior produces naturally occurring outcomes that are internal to the person (e.g., deep breathing relieves nervous tension).
2. A behavior produces self-reactions to a person's own performance (e.g., completing a difficult report produces a good feeling).
3. A behavior produces consequences that originate externally but are naturally related to the behavior (e.g., when sales exceed a predetermined level, a desired bonus *automatically* becomes effective).[3]

Extrinsic motivation takes place when outcomes occur externally and their relationship to the motivated behavior is arbitrary rather than natural. Examples of extrinsic motivators include paychecks, special privileges, and compliments.

Vicarious Motivation

The term **vicarious motivation** is relatively new to the motivation literature, and refers to the fact that seeing others rewarded or punished functions as a motivator by arousing a person's expectations that he is likely to experience similar outcomes for his own comparable performances.[4] For example, you might be motivated to use

EXHIBIT 5.2   FACTORS RELATED TO INTRINSIC AND EXTRINSIC MOTIVATION

Adapted from: A. Bandura, *Social Foundations of Thought and Action* (Englewood Cliffs, N.J.: Prentice-Hall, 1986), 240.

		Consequence	
		Natural	Arbitrary
Source	Internal	Intrinsic	Intrinsic
	External	Intrinsic	Extrinsic

The classification of Intrinsic vs. Extrinsic motivation depends upon a consequence's source (internal or external) and whether it is a natural or arbitrary consequence of the behavior.

a piece of fitness equipment such as a stationary bicycle because someone else who uses it appears to be healthy.

Vicarious motivators that are indirectly linked to consequences tend to increase motivation only for short periods of time. Direct experience of outcomes, however, is more likely to sustain motivation. (If you use the exercise bicycle and personally experience its benefits, you are likely to continue to use it.) An earlier pairing of vicarious and direct outcomes may cause behavior to be sustained even longer, even in the absence of a present direct outcome. (You decide to continue to use a stationary bicycle because you observed a healthy person using it and because your own earlier use produced positive results.)

Let's look at two work-related examples that further clarify intrinsic, extrinsic, and vicarious motivation. Diane feels good when she is left alone to complete a special assignment. We can conclude that she is *intrinsically* motivated since her work, or what it enables her to achieve, is personally gratifying. If her motivation is linked to praise or other recognition she receives from her supervisor, we can conclude that she is motivated *extrinsically*. Allen, a fellow employee, has observed Diane working diligently on an assignment and has overheard the supervisor praise her for her hard work. If Allen's observation motivates him to take on a similar project, we may conclude that he has been motivated *vicariously*.

Of course, it is difficult to know what actually motivates either Diane or Allen. Although indications may exist as to the source of a person's motivation, our assessment of what is *actually* motivating someone (even ourself) may be little more than an educated guess or feeling. Nevertheless, recognizing these three types of motivators can help a manager to understand the forces that influence individual motivation and to respond accordingly.

CONTENT THEORIES OF MOTIVATION

There appears to be no single cause of motivation. Many factors are believed to influence a person's desire to perform work or to behave in a certain way. Content theories explain motivation as primarily a phenomenon occurring within an individual. One view suggests that motivation is linked to need satisfaction. This view is tied closely to a concept known as the need-drive-goal cycle. According to the need-drive-goal cycle, motivation occurs when a felt *need* (or deficiency) within an individual initiates a *drive* toward a specific *goal*. For example, a salesperson who desires recognition (need), may work long hours and contact additional clients (drive) in order to receive the annual sales award (goal). (See Exhibit 5.3.) Achievement of the goal will temporarily satisfy the need and the behavior will subside until that same (or some other) need is again activated. The need-drive-goal cycle provides a simple, although not comprehensive, explanation of motivation. It helps us to understand the relationship of motivation to behavior and, indirectly, to job performance.[5] But questions must still be answered concerning what specific needs individuals have and how those needs influence job performance.

Needs and Need Hierarchies

Content theories suggest that motivation is intrinsic (initiated within the individual) and focus on what stimulates or arouses individual behavior. These theories are usually concerned with individual needs or the arrangement of those needs in

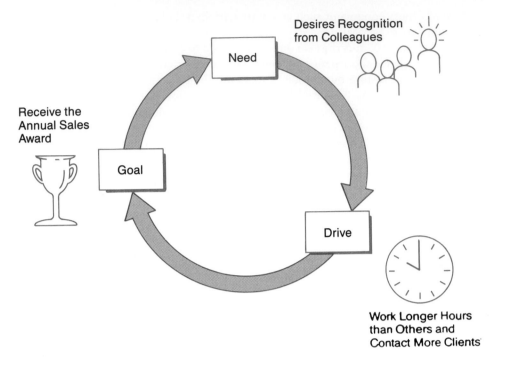

EXHIBIT 5.3   NEED-DRIVE-GOAL CYCLE

some *hierarchy* or order of importance. We will explore two such theories, Maslow's hierarchy of needs and Alderfer's ERG theory. In addition, we will examine a related approach to work motivation, Frederick Herzberg's two factor theory of motivation.

Maslow's Hierarchy of Needs

Maslow's hierarchy of needs[6] is perhaps the most cited of all need theories. The theory served as the basis for much of the early literature about motivation in organizational settings and continues to influence many management and supervisory training programs.

According to psychologist Abraham Maslow, five basic needs (or motives) are common to all mentally healthy adults. These needs include

▶ Physiological needs: Life necessities, such as food, liquid, and air, essential to our existence.
▶ Safety needs: The assurance that basic physiological needs will be satisfied in the future (also known as security needs).
▶ Love and belongingness needs: Social needs such as the need for affection or the need for acceptance by others.
▶ Esteem needs: Needs for self-respect and for respect from others.
▶ Self-actualization needs: The need for self-fulfillment; the need to reach one's potential.

Exhibit 5.4 presents Maslow's five needs along with examples of how each might be satisfied in an organizational setting.

Maslow's theory contends that each of the five needs, either by itself or in combination with other needs, is capable of motivating behavior. However, the needs

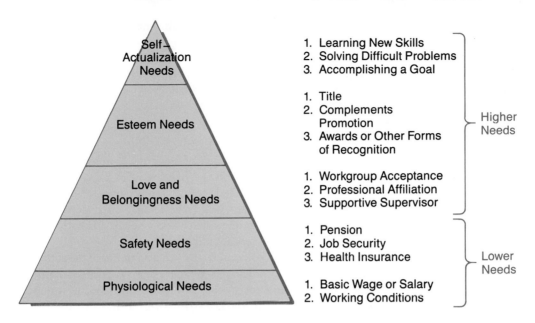

EXHIBIT 5.4   MASLOW'S NEEDS HIERARCHY AND ORGANIZATIONAL EXAMPLES

are arranged in a distinct hierarchy with the appearance of one need resting upon full or partial satisfaction of other more "prepotent" needs. Thus, according to Maslow's needs hierarchy, a clear pattern of *needs progression* exists.

For example, a factory worker receiving the minimum wage is likely to be motivated by the promise of a larger pay check (to cover basic physiological needs) rather than a larger contribution to her pension plan (safety). However, if her take-home pay fully meets her personal and family needs, "putting a little away for the future" will probably become more attractive, and more motivating. Similarly, a worker whose income and security needs are fully met by his job might be more inclined to join an evening social group (belongingness) than to seek additional part-time employment simply to gain extra income.

In our opening case, Andrea was promoted in part because she was believed to be highly motivated. As you rethink Andrea's behavior, to what do you attribute her early motivation? If you based your assessment on Maslow's need hierarchy, you may have concluded that Andrea had a high need for belongingness. Her apparent motivation in her first job could possibly be attributed to her close relations with co-workers. After her promotion, members of Andrea's new department were usually away from the office and maintained their independence from one another. It is possible that Andrea felt isolated and therefore lacked motivation.

Maslow's needs hierarchy is intuitively logical and provides managers with a means for conceptually understanding human motivation. Many studies have supported the existence of Maslow's need categories, although not all have supported Maslow's rigid hierarchy. One authority, for example, has upheld the prepotency of the basic physiological and safety needs but has suggested the existence of two broad groups of needs which may be referred to as *higher needs* (belongingness, esteem, and self-actualization) and *lower needs* (physiological and safety).[7]

Maslow himself concluded in his later writings that two broad groups of needs, those which reduce deficiencies and those which seek personal growth, may in fact exist.[8] Although few researchers have studied these two categories, managers commonly use the phrases *higher needs* and *lower needs* when discussing worker motivation.

Empirical research has not consistently upheld the precise order of the needs hierarchy, the needs progression hypothesis, or the theory's ability to predict behavior. Nevertheless, the theory remains an important contribution to our understanding of motivation and continues to influence management thinking around the world.

ERG theory

ERG theory, another important need theory, presents human needs in terms of three categories: existence, relatedness, and growth.[9] (See Exhibit 5.5.) Existence needs refer to basic physiological needs and safety needs of a material nature. Relatedness needs encompass "interpersonal" safety needs (e.g., the security that comes from group membership), social needs, and interpersonal esteem needs. Growth needs are concerned with self-esteem as well as self-actualization needs.

ERG theory reformulates the need hierarchy in an attempt to reflect more accurately research findings about hierarchical needs progression. A number of propositions concerning the categories and their relationships to one another are set forth. Some of these are consistent with Maslow's thinking, although others are significantly different.

ERG theory holds that if both existence and relatedness needs are relatively dissatisfied, then

1. the *less* relatedness needs are satisfied, the *more* existence needs will be desired; and
2. the *less* growth needs are satisfied, the *more* relatedness needs will be desired.

These conclusions suggest that a person's desire to satisfy lower needs will increase if higher needs cannot be satisfied. This phenomenon is known as *frustration-regression* and typically leads to the over compensation of lower needs when higher needs are blocked. Exhibit 5.6 describes the sequences of need satisfaction → progression and need frustration → regression found in ERG theory.

ERG theory also suggests that

1. if relatedness needs are relatively satisfied, then the *more* they are satisfied, the *more* they will be desired; and
2. when growth needs are relatively satisfied, the *more* they are are satisfied, the *more* they will be desired.

EXHIBIT 5.5 ALDERFER'S ERG THEORY

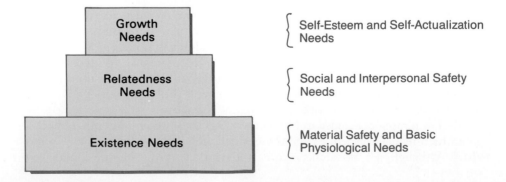

Growth Needs — Self-Esteem and Self-Actualization Needs

Relatedness Needs — Social and Interpersonal Safety Needs

Existence Needs — Material Safety and Basic Physiological Needs

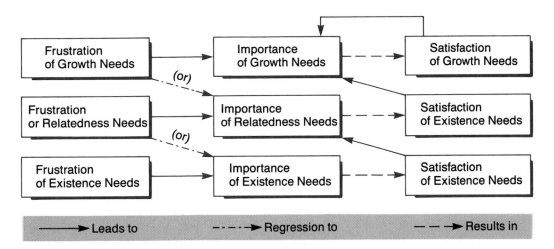

E R G Theory holds that need satisfaction can lead to the desire to attain a higher need; frustration of a higher need can cause regression to a lower need.

**EXHIBIT 5.6   FRUSTRATION, REGRESSION, AND SATISFACTION
                IN ERG THEORY**

Source: From *Psychology of Work Behavior*, 4th Edition, by Frank J. Landy. Copyright © 1989 by Wadsworth, Inc. Reprinted by permission of Brooks/Cole Publishing Company, Pacific Grove, California.

In other words, relatedness and growth needs may become more, not less, important as they are satisfied.

EASTERN AIRLINES

The lengthy strike of Eastern Airlines employees, which began on March 4, 1989, may be explained, in part, by such a frustration-regression reaction. Employees officially struck over wages and working conditions, and negotiators focused on contractual improvements concerning traditional economic issues at the bargaining table. However, rank and file members directed their anger primarily at Texas Air Chairman Frank Lorenzo rather than at the issues being negotiated. Signs and lapel buttons they displayed signaled their frustration concerning the lack of respect shown them by Lorenzo. This frustration, in turn, may have resulted in union personnel holding more firmly to contract demands.

It may be helpful to contrast predictions of future behavior based on ERG theory with those based on Maslow's needs hierarchy. According to Maslow, an individual who is satisfied by her membership in numerous clubs and other types of groups will not be motivated to join yet another organization. Instead, she might be drawn toward an opportunity to take a leadership role in an organization of which she is already a member in order to satisfy her *emerging* esteem need. According to ERG theory, she may seek a leadership position, but if unsuccessful, may become frustrated and develop an even greater appetite for affiliation opportunities (relatedness) with others.

ERG theory has been supported by much of the research on needs hierarchies and has contributed further to our understanding of the three needs themselves. For example, one study found that (1) existence needs were significantly greater for men than for women; (2) relatedness needs were significantly greater for women than for men; and (3) growth need strength for individuals correlated positively with the growth need strength of their parents.[10] Although a considerable amount of research on ERG theory has been conducted, further study and validation is necessary before it will be widely accepted.

Two Factor Theory of Work Motivation

The **two factor theory of work motivation** (also known as the motivator-hygiene theory) added an additional dimension to motivation theory and focused attention on motivation in the work place.[11] While studying managers in engineering and accounting firms, psychologist Frederick Herzberg concluded that two separate and distinct sets of factors influence individual motivation. Herzberg referred to these groups of factors as satisfiers and dissatisfiers. The terms were eventually renamed *motivators* and *hygienes*. (See Exhibit 5.7.) Early research suggested that factors in the work *environment* (hygienes) such as working conditions, pay, and technical supervision could prevent dissatisfaction but did not contribute to an employee's motivation. Instead, factors related to the job itself (e.g., opportunities for achievement, recognition, meaningful work, growth, responsibility, and advancement), known as motivators, influenced work motivation.

Let us look at a work-related situation and how it might be interpreted using the two factor theory. Joel Lyons had been enthusiastic about accepting a job at the home office of a large northeastern bank. The salary was well above that offered by smaller, local banks, and the benefits package also seemed excellent. Just walking into the ornate lobby made Joel feel important. His official title was management trainee, but he was disappointed that most of his time seemed to be spent running errands for an assistant vice-president.

After almost four months on the job, Joel had been given little responsibility, but he knew that the supervisors under whom he worked were bright "fast trackers" who always seemed to have the answers to his questions. Joel was satisfied with his job, but something still seemed to be missing. He had not yet thought seriously about leaving the bank, but he knew that he wasn't as motivated as when he first took the job.

Basing your analysis on the two factor theory, you might conclude that Joel was *attracted* to his job by *hygiene factors*, and he did not particularly want to give up a

EXHIBIT 5.7   HERZBERG'S MOTIVATOR AND HYGIENE FACTORS

MOTIVATORS	HYGIENES
• Work Itself	• Company Policies and Administration
• Recognition	• Salary
• Responsibility	• Working Conditions
• Achievement	• Relationships with Superiors
• Growth	• Relationships with Peers
• Advancement	• Relationships with Subordinates
	• Security
	• Status

good salary and benefits. On the other hand, neither the nature of his work nor his opportunities for achievement and responsibility were being met. According to the two factor theory, these *motivators* must be present in his job if Joel is to be motivated. Two factor theory suggests that work motivation and employee maintenance are separate and distinct dimensions. Thus, factors like improved working conditions or better security may attract or even help to retain employees but may not sustain long-term, directed effort.

Numerous questions have been raised about the plausibility of the two factor theory. These questions have focused on the research techniques used, interpretation of research findings, and concern that groups in early studies (primarily professionals) represented too narrow a segment of the work force for the theory to be applied to all workers. Later studies of satisfaction and dissatisfaction patterns in other groups have produced mixed results. The overall structure of two groups of factors continues to be found, although individual items that make up each group are sometimes different. The International Dimension below describes the results of one study designed to explore the two factor theory in another cultural setting.

In any case, the two factor theory has had a notable impact on management practices and work design. For example, the terms *motivators* and *hygienes* have found their way into the workplace. Managers often speak of hygiene factors when referring to fringe benefits and other perquisites (e.g., plush working environments or prestigious titles) and acknowledge that such factors are generally less likely to contribute to worker motivation than factors related directly to the work itself (motivators).

Although some valid criticisms of the two factor theory can be made, it has offered valuable contributions to our effort to understand motivation. Delineation of the two sets of factors has caused managers to question traditionally held views about

INTERNATIONAL DIMENSION
Motivation in the Republic of Korea

The Republic of Korea is having an increasing impact on world trade. Korea is an important off-shore producer for major manufacturers from North America, Europe, and even Japan. During the past decade, Korean manufacturers have also successfully marketed their own products, such as Hyundai automobiles and Gold Star appliances, around the world.

Researchers studying Korean public employees found that achievement and recognition were the two factors most frequently mentioned when workers were asked to recall favorable aspects of their jobs. These same two factors were also mentioned most frequently by a comparable group of public employees in the United States. Though the sample of one hundred interviewees was small, study results were similar to those predicted by Herzberg's two factor theory.

Questions
In what ways did the findings of this study surprise you?

Would the fact that respondents in both countries were public employees significantly affect the findings?

How do you interpret these research findings?

SOURCE: C. Park, N. Lovrich, and D. L. Soden, "Testing Herzberg's Motivation Theory in a Comparative Study of U.S. and Korean Public Employees," *Review of Public Personnel Administration*, Vol. 8 (Summer 1988): 40–60.

the importance of such things as fringe benefits, technical supervision, and working conditions on job performance and productivity.

Perhaps the theory's most significant contribution has been its impact on the design of job enrichment programs. Job enrichment involves the redesign of jobs in order to provide workers greater autonomy and responsibility for planning and controlling their own performance. Such efforts focus on the social-psychological aspects of work rather than solely on the technical or engineering aspects of the job, and are intended to increase opportunities for achievement, responsibility, recognition and growth (i.e., motivators) in each individual's work. (Job enrichment will be discussed in greater detail in Chapter 14, "Work Design.")

BEN & JERRY'S

An increasing number of organizations are looking for ways to enrich both work and the environment in which that work is performed. One such company is Ben & Jerry's Homemade, Inc. A little over ten years ago, Ben Cohen and Jerry Greenfield spent five dollars on a correspondence course to learn how to make ice cream. Today, Ben and Jerry have stores in thirty-five states, revenues of $30 million, and recently opened the first shop of its kind in the Soviet Union. Ben and Jerry, friends since the seventh grade, decided to start a business that would be a fun place for people to work: "Our entire motivation was to be our own bosses. We saw ourselves as having fun. It's important to do something that reflects who you are as a person. Be true to yourself rather than try and do what is expected of you." In short, Ben and Jerry seem to be motivated by the need to fulfill their own dreams and to enjoy their work and one another.

Ben and Jerry are interested in extending their sense of personal satisfaction to those who work for them. One way they have accomplished this is to ensure that salary differences throughout the organization are minimized. Although CEO salaries in the United States are on average ninety-three times greater than those of factory workers, at Ben & Jerry's the CEO salary is only five times greater. Ben and Jerry have worked hard to maintain a family atmosphere throughout the organization despite its rapid growth. That will be more difficult to sustain in the future, but employee involvement, all workers' opportunity to choose the tasks they wish to perform each day, and occasional free back rubs, all seem to have so far provided a highly motivating environment in which Ben & Jerry's employees have prospered. Other companies, such as Patagonia Sportswear and Alagasco, are, like Ben and Jerry's, part of a new wave of firms that are trying to find ways to sustain highly motivated work forces. Alagasco's "Don't Be a Dinosaur" program encourages employees to be creative problem solvers, and Patagonia encourages its employees to take time off work to relax. These and similar programs are intended to contribute to higher motivation, productivity, and job satisfaction.[12]

Affiliation, Achievement, and Power

A number of content theorists have focused their efforts on the study of specific needs and how those needs influence behavior in the work place. Many motives are believed to underlie behavior. However, management researchers, following the lead of Harvard psychologist David C. McClelland,[13] have generally agreed that three motives are particularly important in the workplace. These motives (or needs) include affiliation, achievement, and power, and they affect the behavior of managers and nonmanagers alike.

Affiliation (n aff)

The **need for affiliation** (n aff) refers to a person's need for friendly relationships, group acceptance, and being liked by others. Maintaining positive interpersonal relationships within an organization is an important function. Studies have indicated that managers who have a high need for affiliation spend more time communicating than do other managers[14] and are most likely to be found in jobs where maintaining relationships is more important than making decisions.[15] Although promoting and maintaining positive relationships is important, managers must also insure that work-related tasks are performed. Research findings indicate that managers who have high levels of n aff may be ineffective in accomplishing organizational goals due to their strong desire to preserve harmony.[16]

United States and Canadian companies, following the lead of their Japanese and European counterparts, are today engaged in the widespread adoption of work teams. Organizations ranging from Caterpillar and Digital Equipment to the United States Postal Service are investing considerable resources in team-based management systems.[17] Effective teamwork requires that employees work together cooperatively and pursue goals that are common to the group as a whole. Work-group members with high needs for affiliation are likely to demonstrate higher levels of group commitment and loyalty, two conditions necessary for the success of a sustained teamwork effort. Recognizing employee affiliation levels and using this knowledge in the selection and placement of work-team members can ultimately contribute to work-team success.

Achievement (n ach)

The **need for achievement** (n ach) refers to "the desire to do something better or more efficiently than it was done before."[18] N ach has long been recognized as a need that significantly affects the performance of individuals in certain roles and jobs.

Managers high in n ach tend to exhibit similar characteristics. First, goal setting and control over the goal-setting process are both important to high achievers. In other words, they like to work toward goals that they have personally set for themselves. High n ach individuals are concerned primarily with maximizing their sense of achievement rather than the specific rewards, such as pay and promotion, that may result from goal attainment. High n ach individuals do not simply establish and pursue high goals; rather they calculate goals carefully and set them at challenging but attainable levels. Second, high achievers require immediate, concrete feedback on progress toward goals. Only through feedback of this type can they gauge their accomplishments. Third, people with high n ach are more likely to choose tasks for which they are solely responsible rather than those which require the participation of others. Fourth, high achievers prefer to rely on their own performance rather than the performance of others. They are usually more comfortable in jobs in which they work alone than those in which close coordination and teamwork are required.

N ach has a number of implications for organizational behavior. The effectiveness of an organization is measured largely in terms of its ability to achieve its objectives. Individuals who have a high need to achieve and who in turn are able to align personal and organizational goals can make significant contributions to their organizations.

Careful placement of high n ach persons is likely to influence their work-related success. High n ach employees tend to be satisfied in jobs in which goal attainment and self-discipline are important. A job involving commission sales, for example, would permit an employee to set and directly influence the achievement of her personal goals. On the other hand, a high n ach bank teller who repetitively processes transactions and cannot regulate the flow of customers will probably be frustrated and become dissatisfied with his work. Finally, as we indicated above, high n ach persons function best in situations that require individual rather than group effort, and therefore, may not prove to be the team players needed in certain organizational positions.

A need closely related to, and sometimes confused with, achievement is failure avoidance. The need for an individual to avoid failure may produce outcomes similar to those attained by someone with a high need for achievement. However, such outcomes are attained through distinctly different goal-setting behaviors. Unlike high n ach individuals who set challenging but attainable goals, individuals who have a high need to avoid failure tend to set goals either so low that they cannot fail to achieve them or so high that they will not be expected to achieve them.[19]

Needs are individual in nature. Because a manager has a high level of n ach does not insure that his or her work unit will be productive. On the other hand, a group equivalent of n ach, **desire for group success** (Dgs), has been found to exist in some organizations. Dgs is a unique blend of n aff and n ach that produces a strong sense of group involvement and can help overcome lack of individual n ach and personal fear of failure.[20]

The characteristics of groups having high Dgs and individuals who have high n ach are strikingly similar in terms of goal setting and the need for concrete feedback. Managers who are capable goal setters and can also instill a sense of unity in their work groups may employ goal-oriented management systems to create a stronger desire for group success in their organizations.

RICK WILLIAMS

Richard "Rick" Williams, who claims his motivation comes from deep within himself, is the owner/operator of the Famous Amos Cookie Shop at Mitchell International Airport in Milwaukee, Wisconsin. Williams's business venture was the first of its kind in any major airport in the United States. Although he was told by many that his idea would never work, Williams knew he had what it took to succeed in the business world. "Success depends on reaching down inside yourself and finding a dream to hold onto," says Williams.

Williams has always been a high achiever. He was raised in Chicago and went on to receive a B.A. in economics and business and an M.B.A. Later, he received additional training at the University of Miami and Dartmouth's Tuck School of Business. Working with Operation Push (the minority advancement program founded by Jesse Jackson), the Milwaukee Urban League, and McDonald's Corporation has given Rick Williams a unique perspective on success. The Famous Amos operation at Mitchell International is only the tip of the iceberg, and when it comes to motivation, Williams cooks up more than chocolate chip cookies. His company, The Williams Partnership, has been the base from which other entrepreneurial endeavors have been launched, and it is one of those endeavors, Dare to Dream, he finds most motivating, even though he derives no financial benefit from it.

Williams conducts Dare to Dream tours for minority and other children throughout the Milwaukee area to help them find and capitalize on the motives that lie within them: "These children must be able to see their dreams and know that they can accomplish them. It all depends on the way they see the world and whether or not they believe that their dreams can be achieved," says Williams. "I get a rush out of making something happen, and something *is* happening for these youngsters."[20]

Power (n pow)

The **need for power** (n pow) is defined here as a concern for obtaining and maintaining control over others. While a manager high in n ach may be expected to try to influence the achievement of a goal, a manager high in n pow is more concerned with controlling the human, information, and other resources necessary to accomplish a goal. The term *power* is often associated with those who have misused it. It is natural, therefore, for us to look with suspicion at individuals who have a high need for power. But such a manager can attempt to gain control over his or her environment without necessarily resorting to coercive or autocratic means.

In one study, high n pow managers were judged to be more successful in terms of organizational performance and employee morale than those who were high in either n ach or n aff.[21] However, the researchers concluded that a manager's need for power must be socialized or controlled. In other words, high n pow is beneficial in a managerial sense when it is directed toward organizational rather than personal ends. When it is so directed, it is known as institutionalized power.

Some individuals appear to be motivated by the thrill of manipulating or otherwise controlling resources whether or not their power contributes positively to the organization's purposes. A manager whose power is *institutionalized*, on the other hand, is motivated to manipulate resources in an organizational context such that the organization as a whole will benefit. The Ethical Dilemma presented on page 158 raises a question concerning Apple Computer co-founder Steve Jobs's desire to retain personal power over Apple's operation even though most corporate insiders considered this not to be in the best interest of the organization.

Affiliation, achievement, and power needs are all important influences on individual behavior, although other motives can also influence people in organizational settings. Each need tends to be characterized by a certain behavior profile. Although such profiles may not guarantee specific performance outcomes, they can provide additional information on which to base logical job placement decisions (see Exhibit 5.8).

EXHIBIT 5.8   LINKING SPECIFIC NEEDS TO JOB PLACEMENT

NEED	IMPACT ON BEHAVIORS	LOGICAL JOB PLACEMENT
Affiliation (n aff)	Associates with Others; Joins Groups, Clubs, etc.	Nursing Ombudsman Counselor
Achievement (n ach)	Sets Goals; Seeks Feedback; Prefers to Work Alone	Commissioned Salesperson Piece-Rate Worker
Power (n pow)	Assertive, Controlling; Attempts to Influence People and Other Resources	Manager Consultant Teacher

ETHICAL DILEMMA
Whom Should Power Serve?

The growth of Apple Computer is legendary in business circles. Apple became a Fortune 500 company just six years after computer wizards Steve Jobs and Steve Wozniak began assembling computers in Jobs's garage. Jobs served as chairman and chief operating officer but felt torn between business responsibilities and his first love, developing computer systems. Soon, the company experienced severe growing pains and the board of directors began its search for someone to oversee Apple's business affairs. Ultimately, Apple recruited Pepsi-Cola president John Sculley as its new president and CEO. Steve Jobs retained his former position as chairman.

Sculley was attracted to Apple in large part by Jobs's enthusiasm and vision. He believed that working with the Apple team would provide him with an exciting and rewarding opportunity to grow a successful company. But the honeymoon was short-lived. Apple continued to falter. Many attributed the company's problems to Jobs, who by now held the positions of chairman and general manager of the Macintosh Division. Jobs and Sculley were frequently at odds over operating decisions. Jobs also appeared to others to behave arbitrarily and to be more interested in his own pet projects than the corporation's overall performance.

Finally, Sculley felt compelled to approach the board of directors about a major reorganization of Apple. Under his plan, Jobs would be divested of all responsibility for operations. Jobs strongly opposed the idea. He demanded that he be shown greater respect as the founder of Apple and proposed that he and Sculley simply switch roles: he would become president and CEO and Sculley would take over as chairman. The board sided with Sculley, and Jobs was stripped of all operating responsibility.

Questions

Does it appear that Steve Jobs's need for power was personal or institutional? Explain.

What ethical question did Jobs face as he attempted to retain his control at Apple?

What ethical dilemma did John Sculley face when he decided to approach Apple's board of directors with the proposed reorganization?

SOURCE: John Sculley, *Odyssey* (New York: Harper and Row, 1987); J. Kaplan, "John Sculley's Last Roundup: Rethinking the Feel-Good Manager," *Businesss Month*, March 1990, 32–35, 38–39.

Applying Content Theories in Managerial Situations

Content theories can provide managers with useful insights into employee behavior. Understanding *need patterns*, for example, may help to explain unrest among secure, well-paid workers when a manager fails to address the workers' higher needs. In such a case, workers may seek greater recognition or self-determination as might be predicted using Maslow's needs hierarchy or, if blocked from satisfying those higher needs, may demand even better wages or conditions of employment as might be predicted using ERG theory.

Recognizing individual needs may help us to use an employee's talents in a manner consistent with his underlying motives. For example, in our opening vignette, Andrea's needs for affiliation seemed to be more important to her than the prestige or power associated with her new position. Consideration of her need to work closely with others no doubt should play an important part in any decisions about her future assignments.

This example demonstrates how content theories can be used to analyze and interpret behavior. Nevertheless, a manager must use his knowledge of needs and need hierarchies carefully. Content explanations of behavior may be conveniently used to explain existing situations. But accurately identifying an individual's needs and then linking them to specific performance outcomes may be difficult. For example, managers with high needs for achievement and those with high needs for power are both likely to appear successful to the casual observer. Only by carefully examining their actual behaviors can we differentiate between their underlying motives. Furthermore, content motivation theories fail to establish the important link between motivation and performance. This link is an important focus of expectancy motivation theory discussed in the following chapter.

Of course, the existence of a common need in itself does not lead to common behaviors among all individuals. Specific behavioral responses to a felt need may be related to earlier learning or to the perceived consequences of a particular behavior. Certain behaviors, for example, may be more acceptable in one culture than another. Physical closeness in formal social relationships is normal in Mediterranean countries but considered an invasion of personal space among many Asians. A Japanese businessman, therefore, may satisfy a need to be close to others while still "maintaining his distance."

Nevertheless, understanding human needs (or motives) may enable us to assess underlying causes of behavior more accurately. Our ability to recognize our own needs and the needs of those with whom we work can enhance performance and job satisfaction through more appropriate job placement and improved interpersonal relations.

THE MOTIVATION TO WORK: CONCLUSIONS

In this chapter we reviewed incidents involving two individuals, Andrea and Joel. Both seemed to lack motivation in their jobs. Andrea had proven herself to be highly motivated in her earlier job but failed to perform well when promoted to a new, high-prestige position. Joel, on the other hand, was attracted to his job by the status and the opportunity to work for talented supervisors in a pleasant work environment. Yet he too has begun to show signs of disenchantment and lack of motivation.

Content theories of motivation may help us to explain Andrea's and Joel's behavior. We concluded, for example, that Andrea may have been more motivated by her need to work closely with associates than by a need for prestige or for a greater challenge. Joel's situation was somewhat different. The motivator-hygiene theory suggests that factors like prestige and technical supervision may attract an individual to a job but that these same factors may not be important when it comes to bringing about sustained motivation on the job. Thus, we concluded that Joel's lack of motivation might be found in the nature of the work that he was being asked to perform.

Content theories emphasize the importance of inner needs and their role in initiating the motivational cycle. Some researchers have focused selectively on specific needs such as affiliation, achievement, and power in an attempt to understand how they may influence human behavior in the workplace. Others, including Maslow,

Alderfer, and Herzberg, have looked for logical arrangements of needs and categorized them accordingly. Exhibits 5.9 and 5.10 compare the major content theories and present some of the strengths and limitations of each.

In addition to the various content theories presented in the chapter, we have explored other important concepts related to motivation. The goal or outcome phase of the need-drive-goal cycle is an important part of any need theory. Determining the source of those outcomes, whether intrinsic, extrinsic, or vicarious, provides additional information to a manager which in turn can be used to predict and manage the behavior of others. Finally, we have briefly explored the relationship between satisfaction and motivation. Satisfaction and motivation are often confused. Yet, their differences must be understood if we are to use our knowledge of motivation to influence employee morale and performance effectively.

Many managers, through formal training and development programs, have become familiar with content theories of motivation. This exposure, in turn, has given rise to widely held perceptions of work motivation that are consistent with needs and need hierarchies.

Unfortunately, most content theories oversimplify the motivation process and assume that employees are generally motivated by the same broad groups of needs. Moreover, while the theories recognize that each person may have a unique need profile, inability to accurately measure need strength makes their application difficult. Nevertheless, content theories do increase our awareness of important internal forces in motivation and provide a framework for understanding (if not always predicting) human behavior. These issues and others important to our understanding of motivation in the workplace are addressed more extensively in the following chapter, "Process, Goal-Setting, and Reinforcement Theories of Work Motivation."

EXHIBIT 5.9   MAJOR CONTENT THEORIES OF MOTIVATION

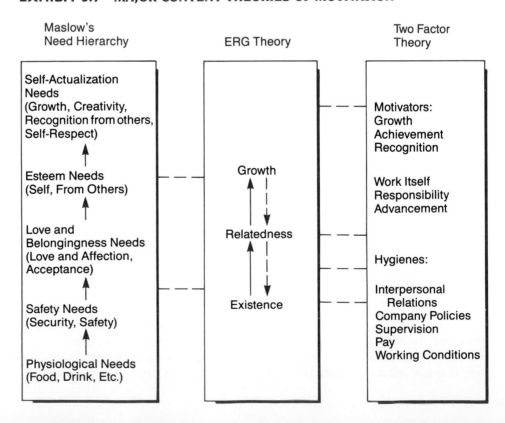

EXHIBIT 5.10   A COMPARISON OF SELECTED MODELS OF MOTIVATION

	UNDERLYING PREMISE	STRENGTHS	LIMITATIONS
Content Theories			
Maslow's Need Hierarchy	Motivation depends on a series of needs arranged in order of prepotency. Satisfaction of a need leads to emergence of next higher need.	Easy to understand. Intuitively appealing. Shows similarities among different individuals.	Tends to focus on similarities rather than individual differences. Lacks widespread empirical support.
ERG Theory	Reduces Maslow's needs hierarchy to 3 more-general need categories.	Has received empirical support.	Tends to focus on similarities rather than individual differences. Further research and testing are necessary.
Two Factor Theory	Certain factors related to the nature of work are responsible for motivation; other factors related to the work environment may attract and hold workers but do not motivate them.	Intuitively logical. Easy to put into practice. (Job enrichment)	Ignores/minimizes individual differences. Assumes all persons are alike. Inconsistent empirical support.
Affiliation, Achievement, Power and Other Needs	One or more needs is primarily responsible for preponderance of behavior.	Easy to understand. Can be used to explain past behaviors.	Difficult to identify individual needs accurately. Overemphasis on singular, nonchanging cause of behaviors.

QUESTIONS FOR REVIEW AND DISCUSSION

1. How do intrinsic and extrinsic motivation differ from one another and why are such differences significant?

2. What is meant by the term *vicarious motivation* and why is it particularly important to a manager?

3. How do the need theories of Maslow and Alderfer differ from one another and why are such theories significant?

4. Give at least two examples in which Alderfer's ERG theory is used to explain motivation in a work setting.

5. What factors are most important to motivation according to the two factor theory of work motivation?

6. How might a high need for affiliation (n aff) affect managerial performance differently from the performance of a work-team member?

7. How does the need for power (n pow) differ from the need for achievement (n ach)?

8. How might differences in motivation between individuals from different cultures be explained by content theories of motivation?

9. What advantages do you see to the use by managers of content motivation theories?

10. What disadvantages do you see in the use by managers of content motivation theories?

REFERENCES

1. Alan Smith, "The 'People Factor' in Competitiveness," address presented at the University Club of Chicago, Chicago, Ill., 6 December 1988; "Is Another Smith Headed for the Top at GM?" *Business Week*, 26 March 1990, 78, 80.

2. T. R. Mitchell, "Motivation: New Directions for

Theory, Research, and Practice," *Academy of Management Review*, Vol. 7 (1982): 80–88.

3. A. Bandura, *Social Foundations of Thought and Action* (Englewood Cliffs, N.J.: Prentice-Hall, 1986), 240–241; Jim Braham, "A Rewarding Place to Work," *Industry Week*, 18 September 1989, 15–19.

4. Ibid., 303.

5. W. F. Charsley, "Management, Morale, and Motivation," Vol. 17 (July-August 1988): 27–28.

6. Abraham Maslow, "A Theory of Human Motivation," *Psychological Review*, Vol. 50 (1943): 370–396.

7. L. B. Barnes, *Organizational Systems and Engineering Groups: A Study of Two Technical Groups in Industry* (Boston: Division of Research, Harvard Business School, 1960).

8. Maslow, "Deficiency Motivation and Growth Motivation," in M. R. Jones, ed., *Nebraska Symposium on Motivation* (Lincoln: University of Nebraska Press, 1955).

9. C. P. Alderfer, *Existence, Relatedness, and Growth: Human Needs in Organizational Settings* (New York: Free Press, 1972); Clayton P. Alderfer, R. R. Kaplan, and K. K. Smith, "The Effect of Variations in Relatedness Need Satisfaction on Relatedness Desires," *Administrative Science Quarterly*, Vol. 9 (1974): 507–532.

10. C. P. Alderfer and R. Guzzo, "Life Expectancies and Adults' Enduring Strength of Desires in Organizations," *Administrative Science Quarterly*, Vol. 24 (September 1979): 347–361.

11. Frederick Herzberg, B. Monsner, and B. Snyderman, *The Motivation to Work* (New York: John Wiley and Sons, 1959).

12. C. Clurman, "More Than Just a Paycheck," *USA Weekend*, 19 January 1990, 4–5.

13. D. C. McClelland, *The Achieving Society* (New York: Van Nostrand, 1961); R. Leach, "Motivation: Turn-Offs and Ons," *Industrial Marketing Digest*, Vol. 14 (First Quarter, 1989): 49–55.

14. K. Noujaim, *Some Motivational Detriments of Effort Allocation and Performance* (Ph.D. thesis, Sloan School of Management, Massachusetts Institute of Technology, 1968).

15. D. A. Kolb and R. Boyatzis, "On the Dynamics of Helping Relationships," *Journal of Applied Behavior Science*, Vol. 6 (1970): 272.

16. McClelland and David H. Burnham, "Power Is the Great Motivator," *Harvard Business Review*, Vol. 54, March-April, 1976, p. 103.

17. "The Payoff from Teamwork," *Business Week*, 10 July 1989, 56–62.

18. McClelland and Burnham, op. cit., 1; McClelland, "That Urge to Achieve," *Think Magazine*, Vol. 32 (November-December 1966): 19–23.

19. H. L. Tossi, A. Rizzo, and S. Carroll, *Managing Organizational Behavior* (Marshfield: Pittman Publishing, 1986), 226–227.

20. Interview with Richard Williams, Milwaukee, Wis., 23 April 1990.

21. A. F. Zander, "Team Spirit versus the Individual Achiever," *Psychology Today*, Vol. 8 (November 1974): 64–68.

22. McClelland and Burnham, op. cit., 102–103; J. Hall, "Putting Your Power to Work," *Management World*, Vol. 17 (November/December 1988): 21–23.

CASE 5.1   *Going back home*

DONALD D. WHITE   *University of Arkansas*

Jerry Warren had been with the Carrolton Fire Department for only fourteen months. He was twenty-two years old and the youngest fireman ever hired into the department. Now, for the first time, he wasn't sure he wanted to remain in firefighting, at least not in Carrolton!

Jerry grew up in Carrolton, an Arkansas community with a population of about eleven thousand. He liked the town, but thought he could "make more out of his life" if he got to a bigger city. Once he told his father, "I want to accomplish something in my life-

time. I'd like to be able to look back at what I've done some day and know that I've made someone or something better." Before graduating from Carrolton High School, Jerry was captain of the school basketball and baseball teams and had a B average in his classwork. He attended the University of Arkansas for one year but decided that he was more interested in being a fireman than in obtaining a college degree.

His interest in firefighting had been supported by his service on the Carrolton Auxiliary during his junior and senior years in high school. Before leaving the university, Jerry wrote his uncle, who was captain in the St. Louis Fire Department. Jerry thought that if he went to St. Louis, his uncle might be able to get him a job with one of the city firefighting units. Instead, his uncle suggested that he apply to the city's Firefighting Academy and "learn to be a modern firefighter from the start."

Jerry was excited and decided to follow his uncle's advice. He immediately obtained letters of reference from the local fire chief, Frank Hanson, and his uncle and applied to the St. Louis Firefighting Academy. He was surprised and pleased when he received a letter from the Academy accepting him for the fall class. He immediately called his uncle and made arrangements to live in his home during the year he would spend attending the Academy.

Jerry worked hard and graduated near the top of his class. At his graduation ceremonies, one of his instructors approached him and his uncle and said, "You've got a fine boy here, Ted. He not only learns fast, but he also has a lot of good ideas. I'm sure he will make a helluva firefighter before he's through. Why, I'll bet he is a lieutenant in two years."

Jerry remained in the St. Louis area for two years. There, he worked with a newly created department in a small suburb and had an opportunity to use much of his training. After two years with the department, his name was placed before the city board for promotion to lieutenant. Two days before the board was to make a decision, Jerry received the distressing news that his father was ill and was unable to take care of the farm at home. His mother had written to ask Jerry if he could come home and help out. She thought there was an opening in the Carrolton Fire Department and he might be able to take the job and still have some time to help out around the farm. Jerry was disappointed at having to leave what appeared to be a great opportunity. However, he knew that he was needed at home and immediately turned in his resignation.

Shortly after arriving in Carrolton, Jerry went to the fire chief's home. There he explained what had taken place and asked the fire chief if he had an opening in the department. Fortunately, there was an opening. Chief Hanson knew Jerry well from his high school days. In addition, Jerry had kept in touch while in St. Louis by occasionally sending the chief articles about new firefighting techniques and equipment. In his job interview, Jerry asked the chief if he had received the articles. The chief said that he had, but nothing else was said about them. Jerry got the job in the department.

During Jerry's first two months with the department, he quietly went about doing his job. Although he had been considered for lieutenant at his previous position, the opportunity wasn't available in Carrolton. He didn't have any seniority with the department (the average age of his fellow firemen was forty-seven, and most had been with the department twelve years or longer). At one point, he asked that his time with the Auxiliary or perhaps that with the St. Louis area fire department be considered as experience on the seniority roster. However, the fire chief stated, "We've never had a situation like this before. I really don't see how we can give you credit when you weren't here with the department."

After a few months, Jerry began to get restless. He had continued to take a firefighter's bulletin published in the St. Louis area and on occasion passed on the bulletin to others in the station if an article contained a new idea he thought would benefit the department. From time to time, he had made suggestions to the chief and captain concerning training and firefighting techniques. However, few of his ideas were acknowledged and even fewer tried out.

The captain at one point asked Jerry, "Why do you keep taking that paper? It must cost you something, and you know that we can't use those city ideas down here." After fourteen months with the Carrolton Fire Department, Jerry was confused. He honestly thought he would like to be a firefighter, but lately he wasn't so sure. That week he received a reprimand for failing to show up for his shift on time. He arrived at the station only to find the last truck pulling out of the garage on its way to a brush fire. Jerry followed the truck to the fire and helped fight it. However, he was still rebuked for his failure to get to work on time.

He decided to discuss the matter with the chief, and the following discussion ensued:

Jerry: Chief Hanson, I just wanted you to know that I am sorry about last week. But, I couldn't do much about it. I was looking over the "specs" on the new truck we were considering, and my watch stopped. I'll be more careful the next time.

Chief Hanson: You don't need to read about fire trucks or anything else, Jerry. I'll make that decision when the time comes.

Jerry: I just thought I could give you some ideas . . .

Chief Hanson: You've got a lot of bright ideas— you always did. But I need firefighters, not idea men. Wait until you are a chief yourself. That's something I don't understand about you young guys. You're too impatient. You all want to be supervising and changing things before you learn enough about the way things are around here. You know, I had to let a couple of fellas go two years ago for almost the same thing. Just take orders and do your job and everything will work out all right.

When Jerry left the chief's office, he was lost in thought. He knew that his father and mother still needed help with the farm. But he wasn't sure he could remain with the Carrolton Fire Department much longer. "What's the future in it?" he thought.

CASE 5.2
What ever happened to professional pride?

H. WILLIAM VROMAN   *Towson State University*
DONALD D. WHITE   *University of Arkansas*

Air Frame, Inc., is an established producer of small aircraft. As in any aircraft company, the engineering group plays an important role in the company's performance. The service engineering division (SED) at Air Frame is a staff organization whose primary function is to submit recommendations concerning equipment design changes, technical procedural changes, and all other matters requiring analysis and study of an engineering nature. Studies are not instigated by the division. Rather, they are conducted only on request by project managers. Recommendations that accompany the final reports are nonmandatory.

The service engineering division is organized along two primary lines: (1) according to engineering discipline or speciality, and (2) according to the technical systems serviced.

PRODUCTIVITY AND JOB SATISFACTION IN SED

Productivity within the service engineering division has always been difficult to assess accurately. Quantity is easily measured, but the division's output is closely related to the quality of its final reports. Unfortunately, quality of the reports is not always easy to judge. For instance, the production time for an engineering investigation can be varied or controlled according to the depth of an analysis undertaken. The

end product is used by nonengineering line managers. The quality of the reports is often only evident to users in the long run and sometimes not even then.

Most of the engineers recognize the inadequateness of any measure of their own performance. As one senior member of the division stated, "When the work load is heavy, pressures increase to meet deadlines. Quality is ultimately sacrificed as these pressures increase. Our work isn't poor, but sometimes you have to wonder." Some engineering sections have attempted to create a better means for evaluating their own contributions. However, no standard means for evaluation exists throughout the division.

Phyllis White, the division chief, is pleased with her division's productivity and recently noted:

Productivity is sufficient; it meets the demand. I suppose it varies substantially among individual workers. However, quality, thoroughness of work, and the extent to which individual projects need be pursued preclude the development of any standards of comparison along the traditional lines of output versus input or output per available worker hour.

Neither can productivity be accurately judged by complaints received from the recipients of the final reports. The general policy at Air Frame is not to complain or reject an engineering report. Instead, line managers tend to accept, ignore, or modify the recommendations. Occasionally, an engineering decision or recommendation will result in an accident, failure, or some other easily identifiable calamity. However, the lag time involved between the completion of the report and the implementation of recommendations, together with alterations and changes which are normally introduced, rarely result in the engineering group being held directly responsible. A recent employee interview program conducted by the personnel division at Air Frame indicated that satisfaction among engineers was close to being nonexistent. On more than one occasion, an engineer has been heard to say that accepting a position in "this" organization was like selling one's professional soul to the devil. On the other hand, higher-than-average salary offers have attracted and helped to hold qualified engineers in the company. Job security at Air Frame is good, and the firm's location in a small community thirty miles east of Kansas City is considered by most employees to be very favorable.

PERSONAL AND PROFESSIONAL GROWTH

Although an engineering degree entitles the holder to a "quasi-professional status," a truly professional status is achieved only after the engineer has pursued his or her education past the undergraduate level or has acquired a license to practice. There is little recognition at Air Frame of engineers as professional employees except on the basis of their pay differentials. Engineers in the service engineering division are forced to clock in and out of the plant, as were production employees, up until six months ago, when Phyllis White, under considerable pressure, had the practice discontinued. Neigher Phyllis nor other executives at Air Frame have encouraged their employees to further their education or to obtain appropriate engineering licenses. Two years ago, considerable interest was shown by members of the division in a series of engineering seminars conducted by a nearby state university. However, production demands at Air Frame caused requests for time off to be refused.

Last year, an evening MBA program was offered by the state university. A large number of engineers enrolled in the program, with some departments having as many as 60 percent of their people participating. Shortly thereafter, a small group of engineers from the design department began a movement to encourage a greater number of their associate engineers to obtain professional registration. This was done in spite of the fact that there was no organizational reward for doing so.

A younger engineer who was preparing to leave Air Frame made the following comments to Phyllis White:

"The management here seems more interested in meeting deadlines than with the competence demonstrated on each job. My work in many cases was not even professionally challenging. When it was, I sometimes found facilities like the test laboratory not to be available when I needed them. That resulted in a delay and what I thought was a poor job. You know, no one even told me that my work was under par."

PHYLLIS WHITE'S CONCERN

Phyllis White was more than a little concerned with the general disinterest among her engineers. She reflected upon the conditions within the division and noted some of the shabby work that had been done of late. Phyllis recognized that many of the higher level engineering jobs were currently held by persons with no college education. At the same time, she knew that many of these employees would be leaving the firm through attrition or retirement over the next four to six years. She had communicated this fact to younger engineers, but some of them still seemed to be impatient.

Phyllis believed that one of her biggest problems was the work rules at Air Frame. The same work rules applied to engineering positions that applied to many of the unskilled, hourly, blue-collar employees. It had been a long-standing policy at Air Frame that all employees would be treated alike. Upper management personnel shared the same eating facilities with other workers in the company and no special privileges as far as parking or other fringe benefits were given on the basis of rank or department.

Phyllis White noted the interest shown by many of the engineers in the MBA program as well as the increased interest in gaining professional registration. Turnover in certain departments within the division had been as high as 35 percent, with the average for the total division being about 23 percent. In her final analysis, she concluded that there were three types of engineers working at Air Frame:

"We have a few incompetents who don't care and are doing as little as possible. We also have some professionally minded people here who recongize some of the limitations of their jobs and who make the best out of their situations. Last are those who are using their positions as project engineers as a stepping-stone to higher management jobs either here or elsewhere. I'm not really sure what can be done about some of these people. Sometimes I think they've lost their professional pride."

EXERCISE 5.1
UNDERSTANDING WORK MOTIVATION

The objective of this exercise is to uncover the many practical dimensions of motivation. As you will see, motivation covers most facets of the work situation.

INSTRUCTIONS

1. Go through each of the questions and draw on your experience to support or reject the statement. Place an A or D to indicate whether you agree or disagree with each statement.
2. Underlying the question is an assumption about human nature. In some cases, the questions say that people are basically lazy. In other questions, the assumption is that people are essentially motivated, and what stops them from working hard are poor supervisory practices and jobs that are too simple. Try to determine the assumption in the questions and check them against your answer.

QUESTIONS

1. Work that an employee considers interesting is an important source of motivation. _____

2. The opportunity to experience achievement on the job is an absolute necessity if a person is to be motivated at work. _____
3. To be a good supervisor, it is more important to be a good designer of work than to be skillful at human relations. _____
4. Shorter hours of work (for example, the four-day week) is one good motivational tool. _____
5. Incentive-pay plans, if tied directly to individual productivity, are an effective motivational tool. _____
6. Improved two-way communications can greatly enhance job satisfaction of employees. _____
7. Plans that push decision-making responsibility down in an organization will be met with resistance by most employees. _____
8. Improved working conditions often affect employee attitudes significantly and contribute to their level of job satisfaction. _____
9. Excessive absenteeism may be due to poor supervision, inadequate pay, or boring work, among other things. _____
10. Elimination of the sources of job dissatisfaction, whatever they may be, will result in improved job satisfaction and motivation. _____
11. A major responsibility of supervisors and managers is to motivate their people to achieve. _____
12. In most cases, extending more decision making to employees involves more risk than gain. _____
13. One effective way to reduce employee dissatisfaction is to see that people are informed about the reasons for decisions that affect them. _____
14. Employees on routine or repetitive jobs are often more motivated and satisfied with their jobs if they understand how their work contributes to overall company goals and objectives. _____

15. Common sources of dissatisfaction at work are personality clashes and disagreements. If these conflicts can be minimized, job dissatisfaction will be reduced, but employee motivation and interest in the work will probably not improve. _____

16. A supervisor's or manager's task is best defined as that of providing people opportunities for achievement so that they will become motivated. _____

17. Most employees would prefer to have their supervisors take over the more complex and difficult tasks in their jobs as long as their pay would not be reduced. _____

18. Boring, uninteresting work may make some employees more demanding about such things as pay, working conditions, holidays, etc. _____

19. Most employees would prefer not to have their work identified because they do not want to receive feedback on their errors. _____

20. Indicators of status and/or seniority such as well-furnished offices, privileges of various kinds, and service awards are very important to some employees and provide a strong source of motivation and job satisfaction. _____

EXERCISE 5.2
APPLYING CONTENT THEORIES

INTRODUCTION

In this chapter, four different content theories were presented. Maslow's needs hierarchy examined five basic needs. Alderfer's ERG theory concerned existence, relatedness, and growth needs. Herzberg's two factor theory addressed motivation at work in terms of motivators and hygienes, and McClelland's theory identified three types of needs that are believed to be particularly important in the workplace (affiliation, achievement, and power).

Each of these content approaches to motivation provides a unique frame of reference, and can lead to a different explanation of individual behavior. Managers encountering motivational problems are likely to select a particular course of action depending upon which theory they embrace.

INSTRUCTIONS

Your instructor has divided the class into four or more groups, and assigned one of the four content theories to each group.

1. Meet briefly in your group and discuss the assigned motivation theory and its implications for managing in the workplace.
2. Read the passage entitled, "What's A Person To Do?" on the following page.
3. After reading the passage, your group should discuss the problem and formulate a solution based on the theory you have been assigned.
4. A representative from each group will present the group's solution to the class as a whole.
5. Classroom discussion should focus on the differences among the four strategies presented.

WHAT'S A PERSON TO DO?

Background

Juanita had supervised a small group of computer programmers at a large insurance company. Upon the birth of her daughter, she chose to leave her job and do free-lance programming from her home. After her daughter entered school, Juanita decided to take a more traditional job once again. She was both surprised and excited when she was offered a position as head of the data processing department at Keating State Bank.

Juanita has twelve employees reporting to her. Three have technical degrees from a local junior college and the rest are recent college graduates. Although Juanita did not complete her college education, you have been impressed with her experience and know-how and believe she can get the job done.

Present Situation

You know that Juanita Rodriguez has become increasingly frustrated in her new job. Recently she has been spending more time by herself. She has failed to complete her last two monthly reports on time, and the department's overall performance has been declining. In a recent conversation, she told you, "No one around here listens to me, and my ideas and suggestions are usually received with skepticism or outright opposition. There seems to be a lot of animosity toward me in the department. I think my employees have lost their motivation, and I know I'm losing mine." What's a person to do?

CHAPTER **6**

 PROCESS, GOAL-SETTING, AND REINFORCEMENT THEORIES OF WORK MOTIVATION

LEARNING OBJECTIVES

1. To learn the differences in major approaches to motivation.
2. To learn the strengths and limitations of differing approaches to work motivation.
3. To learn ways in which process, goal-setting, and reinforcement motivation theories can be applied on the job.
4. To understand how motivation theories can be usefully combined.

CHAPTER OUTLINE

Process Theories of Motivation
Expectancy Theory
Equity Theory
In Summary

Goal-Setting Theory
Setting Goals
In Summary

Reinforcement Theory
Behavior and Reinforcement
In Summary

Process, Goal-Setting, and Reinforcement Theories of Work Motivation: Conclusions

Questions for Review and Discussion

References

Cases: 6.1 It's Not My Job
     6.2 The Need to Listen

Exercises: 6.1 Understanding the Expectancy Theory of Motivation
        6.2 Applying Motivation Theories

KEY TERMS

Expectancy theory   **Outcomes**
Effort   **Benevolents**
Perform   **Entitleds**
Reward   **Equity sensitives**
Expectancy   **Goal-setting theory**
Instrumentality   **Goal specificity**
Equity theory   **Goal difficulty**
Inputs   **Reinforcement theory**

S eth seemed to possess all the characteristics of a good salesman. He was outgoing, knowledgeable about his products, and had demonstrated the ability to use the sales techniques he had learned in his training program. Seth and his wife, Tracy, were both active in their church and community. They sponsored an area youth group and shared leadership in the local Parent-Teacher Organization.

Seth's employers had told him that performance was a key factor in moving up in the company and the vice-president of sales had given Seth's sales record as one reason for his recent move to a larger district. The move was considered to be a promotion, but increased demands on his time had caused Seth and Tracy to weigh the new assignment's impact on their personal lives.

Recently, Seth's employers informed him that an even larger district on the East Coast might be open to him if his sales continued to grow. A fellow salesperson, Angela McWethy, wasn't so sure. In a conversation with Seth she observed, "That plum has been held out to others before, and anyway, most of us here really don't want to leave. After all, this is where the action will be in the future." How motivated will Seth be to increase his productivity? What factors will influence his motivation?

Seth, like many others in the work world, is faced with a decision about how much effort he should put into his job. Although every person's circumstances are unique, the processes that influence these decisions are essentially the same.

Content theories like those presented in the preceding chapter add to our understanding of human behavior. But they tend to oversimplify motivation and fail to examine the complex relationships that exist in the motivation process. In this chapter, we will examine three additional types of motivation theories: (1) process theories; (2) goal-setting theory; and (3) reinforcement theory.

PROCESS THEORIES OF MOTIVATION

Process theories equate motivation with the decision to act or put forth effort. These theories are concerned with the means by which individuals gather and analyze information and the "process" by which effort-related decisions are made. We will examine two such theories, expectancy theory and equity theory, in this section.

Expectancy Theory

Expectancy theory is based on the assumption that the amount of effort put forth in a situation depends on (1) the valence (or value) to the individual of the anticipated outcome of his effort, and (2) the perceived probability that the desired outcome will actually be obtained.[1] Put another way, expectancy theory addresses the question, "How much **effort** must I expend in order to **perform** in such a way that I can receive a desired **reward**?"

Expectancy theory is outcome- (rather than need-) oriented. Central to expectancy theory is the belief that motivation (effort) is a function of the extent to which it is instrumental in attaining a valued outcome and that effort expenditure is a rational decision. Expectancy theory, therefore, is concerned with: (1) making a decision to expend a given level of effort, (2) based on the value (to the individual) of the outcome derived from that decision, and (3) the likelihood that the outcome will actually follow.

Valence and perceived probability

According to expectancy theory, motivation depends on both the *valence* (or value) of a desired outcome and the *perceived probability* that effort will lead to that outcome. The value of a reward may lie in its ability to satisfy a drive-creating need, the innate pleasure it brings, or the extent to which it is seen as contributing to a higher-level goal (secondary outcome). Valence, in other words, is in the eyes of the beholder. *Individual* needs and goals are important determinants of what will or will not be valued by an employee in a work setting. For example, one worker may place a high value on financial rewards while another is more concerned with personal recognition.

Effort-related decisions also depend on the perceived probability that the desired outcome can actually be obtained. In one study of supervisors and employees in a federal agency, researchers found that individuals who valued promotion were willing to increase their effort on the job, but also that their willingness decreased when promotion opportunities were perceived to be low.[2]

Our perceptions of the likelihood that certain outcomes will occur are based on our knowledge of past performance-reward relationship as well as on what we believe about the future. In our opening case, Seth was told that higher sales would lead to a promotion. His past experience supported that effort-outcome relationship. Seth's dilemma stemmed from conflicting evidence provided by his co-worker, Angela, and from what he saw as a negative valence attached to a promotion that would mean moving to another location.

Expectancy and instrumentality

Two important relationships contribute to effort-related decisions. The first of these, **expectancy,** refers to the likelihood that a given level of *effort* will lead to a given level of *performance*. The second, **instrumentality,** is concerned with the likelihood that a given level of *performance* will lead to a desired *outcome*. Exhibit 6.1 on page 174 shows the relationships of the five fundamental elements of the expectancy model: effort, expectancy, performance, instrumentality, and outcome.

Let us look at an example. An engineer has decided to work late (effort) to complete a project on time (performance). She does not know that working late will lead to the desired performance outcome, but she perceives—perhaps based on past experience or some present calculation—that such a relationship exists (expectancy). She also perceives that completion of the project will result in one or more outcomes such as praise or feelings of self-worth (instrumentality). The example is shown graphically in Exhibit 6.2 (on page 174).

Remember that neither effort-performance nor performance-outcome relationships are absolute. Instead, the *perceived* relationships between effort and performance (expectancy) and performance and outcome (instrumentality) influence the engineer's effort decision.

The expectancy model sets forth the five fundamental components of expectancy theory. However, questions concerning the factors that affect perceived probabilities

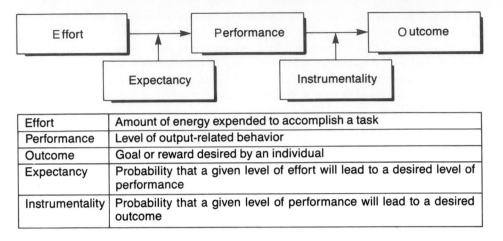

Effort	Amount of energy expended to accomplish a task
Performance	Level of output-related behavior
Outcome	Goal or reward desired by an individual
Expectancy	Probability that a given level of effort will lead to a desired level of performance
Instrumentality	Probability that a given level of performance will lead to a desired outcome

EXHIBIT 6.I   THE EXPECTANCY MODEL

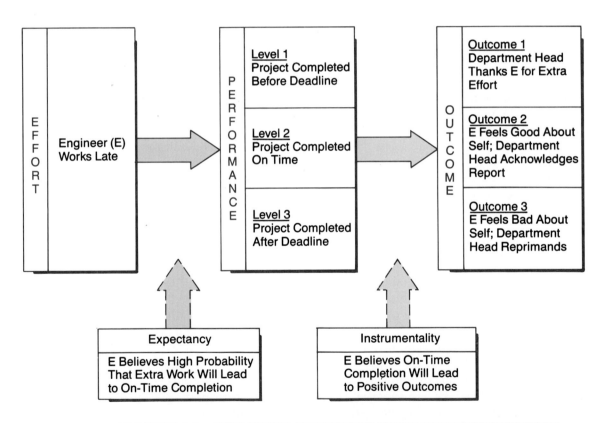

EXHIBIT 6.2   EXPLAINING MOTIVATION USING EXPECTANCY THEORY

as well as those that influence the value placed on outcomes are better explained by the modified model shown in Exhibit 6.3.

The modified model expands on many of the process relationships and helps to clarify why effort alone does not lead to performance. In addition to effort, important factors such as *abilities* and *traits* and *role perceptions* (all of which also influence

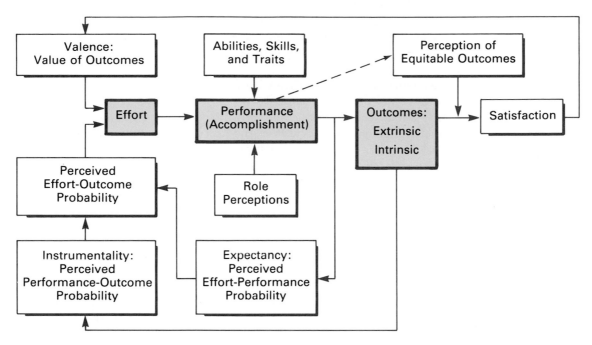

EXHIBIT 6.3   MODIFIED EXPECTANCY MODEL

performance) are identified. A person may put forth considerable effort and fail to accomplish a given task if he lacks the necessary ability or skill to do the job. Similarly, job knowledge and effort may contribute toward one's ability to perform; however, perception of how, when, and where that knowledge and effort should be applied (role perception) will also affect performance.

The engineer in the earlier example who chose to work late on a project may not have the necessary ability to complete the entire report, or she may not understand (role perception) how best to use her training in this particular instance. In either case, putting forth the necessary effort will not permit her to complete the project on time.

Performance, therefore, is contingent on many input variables. A manager is in a position to influence some of these factors. Skills and role perceptions may be altered through training and coaching respectively. However, a manager may have little or no power to alter other factors like intelligence or hand-eye coordination.

Three factors are particularly relevant to the effort-performance relationship. First, an outcome will only affect performance if an individual sees it as being closely tied to performance. A person will work hard for a promotion, for example, *only* if he believes that hard work will, in fact, lead to a desired promotion. Second, the outcome must be positively valued by the recipient. An employee who doesn't want to be promoted, for example, will not gain satisfaction from such an outcome. In cases where outcomes have both positive and negative valences, effort-related decisions can be further complicated. For example, a manager's promotion might be personally gratifying but also lead to an unwanted transfer. This appears to be Seth's case in our opening example; he is interested in advancement but has strong personal ties to his present geographic area.

Third, satisfaction with rewards received for performance also depends on whether those rewards are perceived to be equitable. ("Will what I receive *adequately* compensate me for what I do?") As Exhibit 6.3 suggests, satisfaction results from the absolute value placed on an outcome as well as from the perceived outcome equitability. Satisfaction with the outcome, in turn, leads to effort in similar future situations.

The essence of expectancy theory lies in the premise that effort will ultimately lead to the achievement of a particular outcome or reward. There are two broad categories of outcomes, extrinsic and intrinsic outcomes. Extrinsic outcomes are those obtained by one individual from another. They are indirectly related to an employee's behavior and are dependent upon someone or something else. A paycheck or a compliment from the boss would be examples of extrinsic outcomes.

Intrinsic outcomes, on the other hand, are natural consequences of a specific behavior that generally come from within the individual. A feeling of self-satisfaction resulting from accomplishing an important goal and a feeling of personal growth after solving a difficult problem are examples of intrinsic outcomes.

Recent insights on expectancy theory

Research on expectancy models of motivation continues to expand our understanding of its strengths and limitations and has shed additional light on the relationship between motivation and job satisfaction. Recent findings, for example, indicate that not all individuals are equally sensitive to expectancies. While personal expectancies rationally influence the behaviors of some individuals, perceived social norms are more likely to influence the behavior of others.[3] Serious questions have also been raised concerning the widely held belief that satisfaction leads to high performance. Expectancy research generally supports the hypothesis that performance leads to job satisfaction, and that job satisfaction appears to be directly related to employee behaviors such as absenteeism and turnover. According to one leading authority on motivation, "satisfied workers are most likely to remain members of the organization, to go to work regularly, and to get there on time"; however, "satisfaction just doesn't seem to lead to high job performance."[4]

Do individuals calculate valences and probabilities mathematically or consciously determine the amount of effort they will put forth in every situation? Certainly not! However, the factors outlined in our discussion of expectancy theory logically influence effort-related decisions and are no doubt evaluated more fully in some situations than others. Expectancy processes are most likely to influence motivation when necessary information is available and when an individual can understand and process that information.

In recent years, managers have begun to pay more attention to compensation and other reward programs that are consistent with expectancy theory's effort→performance→reward relationships. Most wage and salary plans fail to link compensation directly to either effort or performance. Organizations usually pay employees for how long they work (hourly wage or salary); only in a few cases are they paid for what they actually produce (piece rate) or sell (commission).

But one approach to compensation, broadly known as "gainsharing," develops direct links along expectancy model lines. At Bayport, Minnesota-based Andersen Corporation, manufacturer of wooden windows and patio doors, profit-sharing distributions amounting to 84 percent of wages and salaries, are tied directly to reduction in expenses and improvements in quality. Increased effort in either area is likely to lead directly to higher profit-sharing payouts. Lincoln Electric, a manufacturer of arc welding equipment, has successfully employed such a system for many years, and newcomers like Fisher-Price Toys have taken special steps to insure that employees are fully aware of the direct link between their performance and the financial benefits they receive from the company.[5]

SPRINGFIELD REMANUFACTURING COMPANY

John P. "Jack" Stack, CEO of Springfield Remanufacturing Corporation (SRC), has also adopted such an approach to motivating his employees. SRC reworks gas and diesel automotive engines, fuel injection pumps, and other engine-related accessories for such companies as Chrysler, General Motors, and Navistar. Stack operates on the simple premise that business is essentially a game and that everyone in the organization must understand the rules. Eighty-one percent of SRC is owned by Stack's employees, who therefore share in the risks and the rewards. Importantly, however, Stack believes that individuals must understand how their rewards can be achieved. He has taught plant employees how to read the company financial reports and provides them with weekly income statements so they can react as necessary to achieve their desired goals. According to Stack, providing employees with statistics, basic know-how, and incentives makes them aware, stimulates them, and gives them the opportunity to use their intelligence to achieve something worthwhile.

How successful has the SRC program been? In less than six years, the company's workforce and sales have tripled and the quality of work is so high that Daimler-Benz AG recently began shipping all Mercedes-Benz engines requiring rework from Stuttgart, West Germany, to Springfield, Missouri. Says SRC human resource vice president, Gary Brown, "We're trying to create a working environment that involves ordinary, blue-collar workers in more than just day-to-day job routines. We firmly believe employees are capable of doing more than coming to work just to grind crankcases. We are appealing to a higher level of thinking."[6]

LOVEJOY MEDICAL, LTD.

Going a step further, Lorie and Matthew Lovejoy, owners of the $2.3 million Lovejoy Medical, Ltd., have offered their employees an opportunity to benefit from the equity growth of the company. Employees receive profit-sharing dividends on annual revenues exceeding 10 percent of pretax profit. Dividends are graduated (1 percent at 10 percent profit, 2 percent at 12 percent to 15 percent, and 3 percent on profits over 15 percent). However, two key managers also share in the increase of the business's book value. Although they are not actually awarded stock, these increases can be cashed in if they leave the company for any reason, even if they are fired.[7]

A relatively new form of compensation known as pay for knowledge (PFK) rewards employees for learning more about their own jobs and more about other jobs in their work area.[8] Under PFK, a worker who can perform his own job may receive $6.25 per hour; however, he may make $6.50 per hour if he can perform two different jobs and even more when he learns to perform others. Pay for knowledge is attractive to employers because they have greater flexibility in assigning work and therefore can more easily accommodate changes in daily schedules and make better use of the work force should equipment break down. Given your understanding of expectancy theory, why and how might employees be motivated by gainsharing and pay for knowledge systems?

Equity Theory

Equity theory (ET) represents a second process approach to motivation. ET is concerned with decisions about the *exchange* of individual contributions for organizational rewards.

According to Equity Theory, an individual's motivation relies on three important variables:

1. the inputs an individual perceives he is contributing;
2. the outcomes (rewards) an individual perceives he is receiving; and
3. the way in which an individual's inputs and outcomes compare to the inputs and outcomes of another person.[9]

Consider how salespeople, athletes, or students determine the value of their own efforts. According to equity theory, they first consider the benefits they have achieved in light of the effort they have invested. They are then likely to compare their own efforts and results to the efforts and results of other salespeople, athletes, or students. This *social comparison* process depends on each individual's perception of events and outcomes and in turn influences his or her satisficaton and subsequent actions.

Perceived inputs and perceived outcomes

The relationship between an employee's **inputs** and **outcomes** (input-outcome ratio) affects his or her willingness to contribute on the job. However, the relationship must first be recognized (perceived) by the employee. Thus, if Linda does not recognize that her performance is well above average, her superior work will not affect her perception of the pay that she thinks she should receive. On the other hand, if Alan fails to notice the favorable treatment (e.g., special privileges) that he has received from his boss, that treatment will not directly affect what he is willing to invest in his job. Remember, only those inputs and outcomes you perceive to exist will affect your input/outcome (I/O) ratio and therefore your motivation to work.

Relative input/outcome ratios

Individuals evaluate their contributions and rewards on the basis of what seems fair. You may be willing to turn in the exercises at the end of this chapter if your professor offers you an adequate reward—let's say twenty bonus points. Equity theory, suggests, however, that what is considered to be a "fair" input/outcome ratio is relative. For example, twenty bonus points may look less attractive if you find out that your instructor has offered the person sitting next to you thirty points to complete the same material. You may still be willing to read the chapter, but at some point your motivation to do so will alter. Would you change your mind if you discovered that someone else in the class was receiving fifty points to do the same work? Exhibit 6.4 depicts how equity theory might explain your different reactions.

Each of us compares our own input/outcome ratio with the I/O ratio of another individual or group. This "referent other" may be a specific individual (e.g., the person working next to you, a neighbor, or even yourself in another time or situation) or a number of persons you view as similar to yourself. A student employed in a

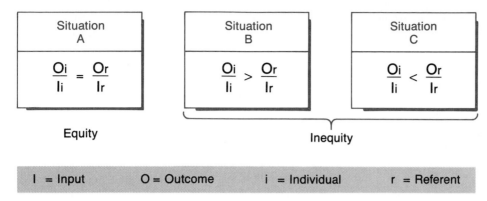

Situation A: Individual's input-outcome ratio ($\frac{Oi}{Ii}$) perceived to be equal to input-outcome ratio ($\frac{Or}{Ir}$) of referent

Situation B: Individual's input-outcome ratio perceived to be greater than input-outcome ratio of the referent

Situation C: Individual's input-outcome ratio perceived to be less than input-outcome ratio of referent

EXHIBIT 6.4   EQUITY THEORY RELATIONSHIPS

supermarket, for example, may consider other employees in the store, other super-market employees in the community, or other working students as his referent other. Whether an individual or a group, referent others are those individuals we typically perceive to be similar to ourselves.

Not everyone in an organization will look for a referent in the same way. In a study of data processing employees working in a large state government, selection of a referent other with regard to compensation and job complexity issues was influenced by length of tenure within the organization. Those with longer tenure tended to look within the organization for their referent, while newer employees tended to look outside the government.[10] A wage-related study of blue- and white-collar workers in Israel found a dual orientation. Both groups first compared their earnings with referents in similar occupations outside their organization. Then, an average-earnings figure for all employees in the organization served as a second frame of reference.[11] A study of white-collar employees in a manufacturing firm revealed that workers may even use themselves as referents. When across-the-board pay cuts were made, workers compared themselves in their present situation to themselves at an earlier time.[12]

Work situations may also influence perceptions of equity and inequity. Research-ers studying a two-tier wage system in a unionized retail store found that lower-paid employees perceived significantly greater pay inequity than higher-paid employees, although they were less likely to perceive the inequity if they worked primarily with other lower-tier employees. Researchers concluded that selection of a referent other was more a function of the work situation than of individual characteristics of the employee.[13] Finally, perceived equity and workplace status have been found to influ-ence job performance among insurance underwriting employees. Employees were temporarily moved to different offices while their own offices were refurbished. Those who were assigned to "higher status" offices increased their performance, while those who were assigned to lower status offices decreased their performance.[14]

The underlying premise of equity theory is that a person will be motivated to reduce a discrepancy between what she perceives to be her own input/outcome ratio and the input/outcome ratio of her referent other. Equity theory, therefore, might be thought of as "inequity theory," since it is primarily concerned with motivation resulting from the *reduction* of perceived inequities.

In order for a manager to use equity theory to understand employee behavior, he must first recognize when and how inequity is being reduced. Six methods for reducing inequity and work-related examples are presented below.

1. A person may decrease her inputs if they are high relative to the inputs of another. (E.g., she may choose to work fewer hours if a co-worker works less than she does but receives the same pay.)
2. A person may increase his outcomes if they are low relative to the outcomes of another. (E.g., he may ask for a raise or seek other job benefits if he does the same amount of work as a co-worker but is paid less.)
3. A person may psychologically distort her inputs and/or outcomes. (E.g., she may rationalize that she "really is" receiving more or doing less than her referent other.)
4. A person may psychologically distort the inputs or outcomes of another. (E.g., he may rationalize that his colleagues are having to work harder or are getting less than he is.)
5. A person may change the referent person or group. In such cases, an individual may simply compare herself to another person. (E.g., she may not be able to reconcile the inequity between the way she and a fellow employee are being rewarded and therefore concludes that the co-worker is really not comparable to her (the co-worker has more seniority); this could lead to the selection of a different referent person.)
6. A person may "leave the field." (E.g., he may find it easier to quit the job than to alter either of the input/outcome ratios.)[15]

In each of the preceding examples, the person being motivated to act believed that his or her I/O ratio was *less* favorable than that of the referent other. However, equity theory also provides explanations of behaviors occurring when an individual's I/O ratio is *more* favorable than that of a referent. Thus, a person may increase his inputs or even ask for a reduction in his compensation if he believes that he is being paid more than someone doing comparable work. Needless to say, the likelihood of either of these two behaviors actually taking place (especially the latter) does not seem very large. In fact, research using pay as a measure of outcome inequity has supported the theory in cases of underpayment but has failed to provide substantial evidence to support the overpayment hypothesis. Individuals, then, generally appear less likely to recognize over-reward than under-reward.

Equity sensitivity

Equity theory increases our understanding of motivation by refocusing on the importance of environmental influences in the motivation process. The **equity sensitivity** construct may help explain why individuals react differently to equity and inequity.[16] Equity sensitivity presupposes that individuals "react in consistent but individually different ways to both perceived equity and inequity . . . because they have different preferences for equity.[17] In other words, some individuals may actually prefer maintaining inequity to maintaining equity with their referent other. Three types of individuals, called *benevolents*, *entitleds*, and *equity sensitives*, each hold different equity preferences.

Benevolents tend to think more in terms of giving than receiving and thus prefer that their input/outcome ratios be less than the input/outcome ratios of their referents. **Entitleds,** on the other hand, assume that they deserve more than their referents and therefore prefer that their input/outcome ratios exceed those of their referents. **Equity sensitives** fit the traditional equity theory model and prefer that their input/outcome ratios be comparable to those of their referents. (See Exhibit 6.5.)

Equity sensitivity may moderate relationships between perceptions of equity and organizational outcomes and influence how individuals actually perceive inputs and outcomes. The construct can help a manager explain consistent patterns of employee behavior while accounting for individual differences regarding equity preferences. For example, entitleds may have higher levels of absenteeism or put out less effort than referent others under conditions of equity (e.g., equal pay). Conversely, benevolents are likely to have low levels of absenteeism and put forth more effort than referent others under conditions of equity.

The concept of equity sensitivity is relatively new. However, a recent study of 519 undergraduate students at a large university found that benevolents preferred lower input/outcome ratios than their equity sensitive and entitled counterparts and appeared to be willing to provide higher inputs than members in the other two groups. Although differences were found between equity sensitives and entitleds, those differences were not statistically significant. Researchers concluded that (1) individual differences appear to influence the way in which persons define equity for themselves, and (2) benevolents could be expected to produce significantly more work at salaries slightly lower than equity sensitive or entitled employees.[18]

Whether equity sensitivity is a state likely to vary with the situation or a relatively stable trait that remains constant from one setting or job to another is not known. It may also be possible that individuals will show different equity preferences during the different life stages discussed in Chapter 2, "Individuality in the Workplace."

EXHIBIT 6.5 EQUITY SENSITIVITY CONSTRUCT

Equity Exists When:

$$\frac{O_i}{I_i} < \frac{O_r}{I_r}$$

Benevolents

$$\frac{O_i}{I_i} = \frac{O_r}{I_r}$$

Equity
Sensitives

$$\frac{O_i}{I_i} > \frac{O_r}{I_r}$$

Entitleds

I = Input	O = Outcome	i = Individual	r = Referent

Benevolents perceive equity when their $\frac{O}{I}$ ratio is less than the referent other's. Equity sensitives perceive equity when their $\frac{O}{I}$ equals the referent other's. Entitleds perceive equity when their $\frac{O}{I}$ ratio is greater than the referent other's.

Equity theory can explain a variety of employee behaviors, although most applications relate directly to compensation. Two important compensation issues, wage compression and two-tier wage and salary systems, provide excellent examples of the impact of perceived inequity on motivation and behavior.

Wage compression occurs when the gap between salary levels of "senior" and "junior" employees narrows. Wage compression is likely to affect motivation negatively when higher-paid workers compare the two salary levels.

Let us look at an example. Steven Riley has spent nine years as a bioengineer with Ergotech. He likes his work and most of his co-workers but has become disgruntled with what he considers unjustifiably high salaries of newly hired engineers. The quality of his work has slipped noticeably, and he has talked about looking for a job with another company. Recently, he confided to a friend who joined the company at about the same time he did, "I'm just not motivated anymore. When I came here, I made a lot less than the old heads and was told to be patient; now that I'm a senior engineer, I find that the new people are making almost as much as I am." How does equity theory help to explain Steven's behavior?

Two-tier wage systems can also create perceived inequities for some employees. A number of companies, including Kaiser Permanente Medical Care Program, American Airlines, and Giant Foods, have adopted two-tier wage plans to try to hold down labor costs. Two-tier plans maintain higher wages and salaries for present employees while paying newly hired workers, who perform the same jobs, at a substantially lower rate. But according to Roger Olsen, Giant's vice-president for labor relations, two-tier scales create unhappiness among employees. Hughes Aircraft dropped its two-tier plan after experiencing numerous quality problems. Labor leaders at Hughes attributed at least some of those problems to low morale among second-tier, lower-paid workers.[19] Do two-tier wage plans represent equity or inequity in a compensation system? How might your knowledge of equity theory be used to facilitate successful implementation of a two-tier wage plan?

Equity theory provides us with general guidelines about rewarding employee performance. First and foremost, employees do not receive rewards, whether tangible (e.g., pay or promotion) or intangible (e.g., attention, praise, or recognition), in a vacuum. Each person considers personal outcomes in relation to personal investments in the job. Moreover, those investments and outcomes are then compared to the investments and outcomes of others who are in comparable life situations. The value of work-related rewards and benefits, therefore, should be viewed as relative, not absolute.

The propositions of equity theory can help us to better understand the behaviors of individual employees, including their responses to perceived inequity. Understanding the sources of inequity and how inequity can be managed effectively will add to your own motivational skills as a manager.

In Summary

Expectancy theory and equity theory each contribute significantly to our understanding of work motivation. Both explanations account for the individual nature of motivation and help us to understand how and why individuals decide to put forth effort in a given situation. The effort→performance→outcome relationships of expectancy theory, together with the concepts of expectancy and instrumentality, suggest that managers can engage in certain types of behaviors in order to affect employee motivation. Equity theory helps us to unravel further the complex puzzle of human motivation. The theory reminds us that, while individual in nature, motivation takes place in a social setting and is influenced by our perceptions of the relatively equitable or inequitable treatment that we and those around us experience.

Both expectancy and equity theory are concerned with the outcomes that individuals expect to receive in exchange for their effort in a particular situation. Formal reward systems are intended to provide such outcomes. Sometimes, rewards are clearly different according to the performance of individual workers. Such is the case when piece-rate wages are paid to factory workers or commissions are paid to sales personnel. However, reward systems that treat all workers the same and fail to differentiate on the basis of individual output also exist. The International Dimension below describes such a system in the People's Republic of China.

GOAL-SETTING THEORY

A famous athlete addressing a convention of young people gave the following advice: "Set a goal for yourself. You may not reach it, but you will go a lot farther in life than if you don't know what you want to achieve." Perhaps without realizing it, the athlete had just presented one of the underlying tenets of **goal-setting theory.** Goal-setting theory is concerned with the effect of goals or targets on individual performance.[20] Goal-setting theory is an approach to motivation that focuses on *intended*

INTERNATIONAL DIMENSION
Factory Towns in China: From Cradle to Grave

Panzhihua is a "factory town." Chairman Mao located Panzhihua Iron and Steel Company, like many of China's vital factories, in China's remote interior to protect it from invading enemy forces. The town's population, almost all of which works for the company, is isolated from the rest of the world. Realizing that its workers must be given incentives to make what is often a lifetime commitment to it, the company heavily subsidizes housing, food (breakfast for three costs about twenty-five cents), and education (tuition for a child is $1 a semester), and provides free medical coverage. On top of this, there are no layoffs.

Each morning, workers are greeted at the front gate by a sign that reads, "Happily, Happily Come to Work," but many are not completely happy with their situation. They complain that promotions are rare and trans-fers are difficult to obtain. While practically no one is fired, it is also difficult to leave. In fact, when workers once were given such an opportunity, the company lost almost all of its college graduates and engineers.

Questions

How can worker behavior at the Panzhihua factory be explained by expectancy and equity theories?

In motivational terms, what do you believe would be the primary weaknesses of a "cradle to grave" reward system in the United States?

What are the weaknesses of such a system anywhere?

SOURCE: A. Ignatius, "Cradle to Grave: In This Factory Town, China's Welfare State Is Still Alive and Well," *Wall Street Journal,* 17 October 1989, pp. A1, A24.

outcomes rather than internal needs or motivational processes. It has received widespread support from researchers and practicing managers alike.

The main premise of goal-setting theory is that goals, whether set for or by an individual, will influence performance. Such influence is related to a person's self-efficacy (i.e., one's judgement about one's capability to accomplish a certain performance outcome) and feelings about being able to function at a given performance level.[21]

Setting Goals

Among the earliest findings about goal settng were (1) that individuals who sometimes set goals achieved higher levels of output when they did than when they did not set goals, and (2) that individuals who set goals outperformed those who did not.[22] These findings have been developed further to include other factors such as the specificity of goals, goal difficulty, feedback, and expected versus unexpected evaluation (see Exhibit 6.6).

Goal specificity

Goals come in all shapes and sizes. However, researchers have found that the more specific the goal the greater the likelihood that it will be achieved. Goal specificity can be facilitated by setting quantitative rather than qualitative goals. A goal to make fifteen customer calls a day, for example, is preferable to a goal to make "a lot" of calls each day. Although one researcher found that specific goals in group settings impeded coordination,[23] studies have generally concluded that setting specific goals reduces the variability of performance[24] and can lead to more predictable levels of output.

Goal difficulty

Generally speaking, the more difficult a goal, the higher the level of performance that can be expected. However, evidence suggests that this relationship does not

EXHIBIT 6.6   FACTORS AFFECTING THE RELATIONSHIP BETWEEN GOALS AND PERFORMANCES

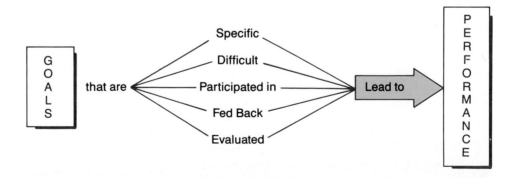

Goals influence performance, but their effects are moderated by their specificity, difficulty, and acceptance, the type and amount of feedback provided, and whether a person knows that goal attainment will be evaluated.

hold true in all situations. For example, goals that have been set at relatively high levels may fail to gain the acceptance or commitment necessary to bring about high levels of performance. Levels of achievement motive, confidence, and self-assurance have also been found to influence the relationship between goal difficulty and performance.[25]

Participation

During the 1980s and 1990s, many management authorities have called for increasing participation of subordinates in goal setting and decision making. They reason that greater involvement in such activities is likely to heighten goal commitment and employee motivation. In fact, research suggests that subordinate participation in goal setting is beneficial in that tasks are clarified and individuals have a clearer sense of where to direct their efforts. But empirical evidence does not support the contention that participation increases commitment. Thus, participation's impact on goal setting is usually more cognitive than motivational.[26]

On the other hand, researchers have found that cultural differences can influence the effects of assigned versus participatively set goals. Performance levels for Israeli students were higher when goals were set participatively than when they were assigned. No difference was found among American students.[27] In yet a another study, researchers found that assigned goals increased performance of Israeli workers in the private sector, while participation led to higher performance in the trade-union sector and the more collectivist kibbutz.[28]

Feedback

The use of goal setting might be likened to shooting at a target. The target gives the marksman something to aim at. Concepts such as goal specificity, goal difficulty, and goal acceptance influence performance before the trigger is pulled. Feedback, on the other hand, is concerned with the effect of goals as they contribute to our knowledge of results. Thus, a goal is set, action is taken, feedback is obtained, and that feedback in turn influences subsequent performance.

Although goal setting alone can influence performance, goal setting coupled with feedback can enhance performance still further.[29] The effects of goal setting and feedback used together as a single motivation technique have also been examined. Evidence suggests that goal setting facilities motivation while feedback provides direction, although "generally [it] is difficult to separate the directional from the motivational function in practice."[30]

Feedback may come from a number of sources including the supervisor, the job, and co-workers. The supervisor represents the traditionally accepted source of work-related feedback. Feedback from the job itself is important because it can occur without the presence of the supervisor; however, its nature and timing will influence its impact on the employee. Co-workers can also provide work-related feedback, although workers are likely to seek out feedback from more supportive rather than less supportive peers.[31]

Expected and unexpected evaluation

According to goal-setting theory, goal attainment increases an individual's motivation. But questions have been raised concerning the interrelated effects of goal difficulty and expected evaluation on motivation.[32] In an experiment involving one hundred male business undergraduates, intrinsic motivation increased when easy goals were attained and evaluation was expected, but decreased when evaluation was not expected. Conversely, the attainment of difficult goals resulted in higher intrinsic motivation when evaluation was not expected than when it was expected. In other words, a manager's unexpected evaluation may inadvertently decrease feelings of self-satisfaction if goals are easily attained. (A possible explanation is that an employee may be embarrassed to accept praise for accomplishments that she does not consider praiseworthy.)

For example, if Julie has more than enough time to complete a report and turns it in early, her intrinsic motivation may actually be decreased if her supervisor unexpectedly compliments her promptness. On the other hand, Julie's intrinsic motivation will be increased whether it was easy or difficult for her to meet a deadline if she expects her supervisor to acknowledge her timeliness. Her intrinsic motivation is even more likely to be increased if the deadline is difficult to meet and the supervisor's comments come unexpectedly.

In Summary

The positive impact of goal setting on performance has been recognized by managers for some time, and it is generally considered to be a highly effective motivational technique. Goal setting has become a fundamental part of many reward and recognition programs of firms such as Bank of America and Pacific Gas and Electric.[33] Many manufacturing plants, like Firestone's Oklahoma City facility, have also made widespread use of goal setting and feedback by posting daily goals and performance results on large charts clearly visible to all production workers. Such systems have also been used to increase the number of hours spent by mental health clinicians in direct client contact,[34] and, in one particularly interesting case, to increase the "body checking hit rate" for a hockey team having a chronic losing record. In the latter case, the hit rate increased 82 percent in the first year of system implementation and 141 percent over two years. The team had winning records in both years.[35]

Goal setting also is the focal point of a widely used management system known as Management by Objectives (MBO). MBO contributes to long-range planning and facilitates performance appraisal. The process involves joint manager-employee goal setting and evaluation of performance in terms of goal accomplishment. MBO's concrete performance measures enable extrinsic rewards to be linked directly to performance. A more detailed discussion of Management by Objectives is contained in Chapter 15, "Organizational Change and Development."

RICK WILLIAMS

In the previous chapter, you met Rick Williams, the Milwaukee entrepreneur whose Dare To Dream program has been presented to over six thousand minority children throughout the greater Milwaukee area. Williams is a young but important civic leader in Milwaukee and a tireless pursuer of economic opportunities for minorities throughout Wisconsin. He is particularly concerned about the opportunities available to young people, but believes that these young people must reach down within *themselves* to find success. Williams also believes that minority children must be able to see their dreams, to have personal goals, and to know that those goals can be obtained. Dare to Dream presentations ask young people to "hold onto your dreams and never let them go."

Williams's "you can do it" message couples a necessary belief in young people's own self-worth with the equally important knowledge that they can and will achieve their goals through personal commitment and hard work. That means learning the necessary skills and putting forth the effort to achieve their personal goals and other important outcomes. To help children achieve the opportunities that await them, Rick Williams puts into practice and shares with others many of the underlying elements of motivation theory that we have discussed in this chapter.

REINFORCEMENT THEORY

In Chapter 5, motivation was described as "the act or process of initiating and sustaining behavior toward goals." Some authorities question the validity of classifying **reinforcement theory** as a theory of motivation; however, others view the use of rewards and punishment to increase or decrease specific behaviors as an obvious form of motivation.

Traditional process theories of motivation are primarily concerned with effort-related decisions. Reinforcement theory tends instead to focus on the performance of discrete, measurable behaviors. These might include tardiness, absenteeism, safe or unsafe behaviors, or behaviors that directly affect output. Learning theory, out of which reinforcement theory has emerged, was covered in depth in Chapter 4. We will, therefore, only briefly review the foundations of reinforcement theory here and focus on the motivational implications of reinforcement and rewards.

Behavior and Reinforcement

Reinforcement can affect behavior in one of three ways:

1. Reinforcement of a behavior at the time of, or immediately following, a behavior will increase the likelihood that the behavior will occur again in the future. Thus, a manager who reinforces a worker for his politeness might view his act as promoting (or motivating) further politeness. This view of reinforcement is consistent with classical learning theory.
2. Some behaviors take place in order to obtain specific outcomes that the individual perceives to be reinforcing. A salesperson might make a greater number of customer calls each day if she believes that sales will increase as a result. In this case, we assume that increased sales in some way will reinforce the salesperson and that she will be motivated to make the calls in anticipation of the reinforcing outcome. This second view of reinforcement is consistent with operant learning theory.
3. Behaviors can be influenced by cognitive activities such as mental rehearsal, self-reward, and observation of the behavior-reinforcement pairings of others (vicarious learning). A student may be motivated to study harder by anticipating the personal pleasure gained from making good grades or by anticipating a reward he will receive from someone else (e.g., a new car from his parents), or even by

seeing the benefits accruing to others from making good grades. This third view of reinforcement is supported by social cognitive theory.

Work-related rewards and punishment

Most managers have heard the statement, "Behavior is a function of the rewards associated with that behavior." But what rewards are available in an organizational setting? And will those rewards be meaningful (reinforcing)? Exhibit 6.7 lists a variety of rewards managers may have available to them.

Rewards fall into two basic categories: (1) contrived rewards, and (2) natural rewards. Contrived rewards are those which are indirectly related to the work itself (consumables, manipulatables, visual and auditory rewards, and tokens). Such rewards may be associated with certain behaviors or the accomplishment of some end result, but normally are not considered part of the work setting itself. Natural rewards, on the other hand, include such things as attention, praise, and special privileges known as premack rewards.[36]

Premack reward simply means that a person will be permitted to participate in a second activity that she considers more desirable (reinforcing) after a prior activity is completed. For example, a manager may announce that those attending a special problem-solving meeting will be permitted to return to their own work as soon as the problem is resolved. The premack principle presumes that certain activities perceived by an individual to be rewarding can be used to reinforce the completion of other "less" rewarding activities. Generally, the second set of activities would also be work related, although rewards such as contingent time off may also be useful.

Reinforcement theory, like learning theory, emphasizes positive reinforcement rather than punishment. Nevertheless, punishment is viewed as a means for initiating and, when coupled with clear explanations, directing behavior. As we concluded in the previous chapter, punishment may not be an efficient long-term solution to a problem and may also create negative side effects for both the employee and the manager. Punishment may provide some short-term motivation to either terminate or initiate a behavior, but as the "hot stove rule," known to many managers, suggests: if punishment is to be effective it should (1) "burn" immediately; (2) be preceded by a clear warning; (3) be administered consistently to everyone; and (4) be imper-

EXHIBIT 6.7   ON-THE-JOB REWARDS

CONTRIVED REWARDS				NATURAL REWARDS
Consumables	Manipulatables	Visual and Auditory	Tokens	Social
Free Lunches	Desk Accessories	Office with a View	Money	Friendly Greetings
Food Baskets	Personal	Piped-in Music	Movie Passes	Feedback About
Dinners	Computers	Redecoration of	Trading Stamps	Performance
Thanksgiving	Wall Plaques	Work	Entertainment	Requests for
Turkeys	Watches	Environment	Tickets	Advice
	Trophies and	Private Office	Vacation Trips	Recognition in
After-Work	Commendations	Larger Desk	Coupons	House Organ
Wine and	Service Pins		Redeemable at	Pat on the Back
Cheese Parties	Shirts, Caps, etc.		Local Stores	Smile

SOURCE: From ORGANIZATIONAL BEHAVIOR MODIFICATION AND BEYOND: An Operant and Social Learning Approach by Fred Luthans and Robert Kreitner. Copyright © 1985, 1978 by Scott, Foresman and Company. Reprinted by permission of HarperCollins, Publishers.

ETHICAL DILEMMA
Preaching and Practicing at Amway

Richard DeVos and Jan Van Andel founded Amway Corporation in 1958 in a basement in Ada, Michigan. Today Amway ranks among the largest privately held companies in the United States with sales of over a billion dollars. DeVos and Van Andel attribute much of their success to rewarding the right behaviors and actions of their employees. They have long touted their company's high ethical standards. So strongly did they feel about their philosophy that they wrote a book about it titled *Believe*, which they distributed to all Amway corporate members. *Believe* stressed continuously that good behavior should be automatically rewarded and bad behavior automatically punished. Richard DeVos was given *Industry Week's* Excellence in Management award in 1977 for promoting free enterprise and high standards for doing business. At that time DeVos said about his work force: "Our only plea is ethical. We have a code of ethics they must subscribe to. It includes honesty and integrity."

Subsequently, Amway was convicted in Canada on charges of evading customs duties for products imported into the country. Amway had set up a dummy corporation that underpriced its products for shipment into Canada, thereby allowing the company to pay lower duties.

Faced with this seeming inconsistency between their professed beliefs and their actual business practices, DeVos and Van Andel suggested that the problem Amway had encountered stemmed simply from the economics of trade. They denied complicity in the company's actions and strongly denied that avoiding payment of duties in any way constituted unethical behavior.

Soon *Believe* was redistributed throughout Amway. The reissued book made no mention of Amway's legal entanglement.

Questions
What effect do you suppose Amway's conviction might have had on its workforce?

Must a company's internal reinforcement systems be consistent with its external actions?

SOURCE: C. Grant, "Giving Ethics the Business," *Journal of Business Ethics*, Vol. 7, No. 7, (July 1988) 489–495; "Excellence in Management Awards," *Industry Week*, 7 November 1977, 54–56.

sonal (i.e., directed at the behavior rather than the person). Clearly, a manager should think carefully about the pros and cons of using punishment in terms of both motivating an employee's present behavior and its impact on other future behaviors.

Reinforcement as a means for motivating employee behavior has been widely espoused and adopted in the business community. Two business leaders, Amway founders Richard DeVos and Jan Van Andel, embraced the philosophy so strongly that they wrote a book addressing the subject and distributed it throughout their organization. However, Amway's business practices came under scrutiny when the corporation became the subject of a Canadian investigation and trial questioning certain international business activities. The Ethical Dilemma above raises questions concerning how employees may view company behavior that seems inconsistent with corporate business philosophies.

In Summary

Reinforcement theory of motivation has gained popularity due to the relative ease with which it can be used and evaluated. In practical terms, reinforcement theory is concerned with rewarding behaviors that will lead to improved performance in order to increase the probability of these behaviors' future occurrence. Conversely, behaviors that detract from desired organizational outcomes are either ignored or punished in order to bring about their termination. Reinforcement theory is related directly to learning theory, and should be applied in a manner consistent with learning principles if it is to be effective.

Many managers believe that they already use rewards and reinforcement to motivate their employees. Praise, promotions, incentive travel, trinkets, and even pay, however, must be used in a timely and systematic fashion if they are to contribute effectively to the motivation of individual behavior. Among the most versatile reinforcement programs now in use are "cafeteria plans," which allow individuals to select from a "menu" of rewards those that are most important to them. These rewards are then systematically provided as work is successfully completed or as goals are met. Cafeteria plans often include rewards such as financial bonuses, additional insurance coverage or pension benefits, gifts, special vacation packages, and additional time off.

PROCESS, GOAL-SETTING, AND REINFORCEMENT THEORIES OF WORK MOTIVATION: CONCLUSIONS

We began this chapter by relating a brief incident. Seth had demonstrated his ability to perform well on the job. He was informed that even greater rewards awaited him if he continued to be productive. However, another employee told Seth that he should not be too sure about getting the promised rewards and that those rewards might not be all that they were cracked up to be anyway. Expectancy theory provides us with one means for predicting Seth's future motivation. He might *value* yet another promotion to a district where higher sales could be obtained. However, questions raised concerning the *probability* that the promotion would actually follow his extra effort and indications that the *value* of the move might not be as great as he had been led to believe may cause him to decide not to expend his effort toward the goal at the present time.

Later, we considered Steven Riley. Steven had become disturbed with the salary structure at Ergotech and stated that he was no longer motivated to work there. Here, we used knowledge of equity theory to explain his lack of motivation. Steven believed that the wage structure at Ergotech did not reward (*outcome*) him for his greater years of service with the company (additional *input*). In other words, his input/outcome ratio was smaller than that of the newly hired engineers and he was therefore motivated to reduce his effort.

Each of the approaches to motivation covered in this chapter gives us additional insight into work motivation. Remember, however, that motivation is a complex process that can be viewed from a number of different perspectives. The models presented in this chapter reflected three such perspectives: motivation linked to information processing and decision making; motivation associated with goal setting; and motivation that resulting from reinforcement. Although each of these perspectives may lead to unique managerial actions, all three can contribute to our understanding of employee behavior and to our ability to manager that behavior more effectively.

Process theories of motivation equip managers with analytic tools for understanding and managing employee motivation. Both expectancy theory and equity theory encourage managers to "think" like their employees in order to better understand their effort-related decisions. The modified expectancy model, for example, can help managers recognize the complex relationships between effort, performance, and rewards. As a result, they may alter the probabilities of each relationship by aligning organizational rewards with outcomes sought by organizational members.

Equity theory adds yet another piece to the motivation puzzle. First, a manager can only expect an employee to contribute to the organization if that person receives something in exchange. Keep in mind that it is the perception of the employee, not the manager, that determines whether or not what is received is equitable. Second, rarely do the actions of a manager affect the behavior of one employee at a time. People tend to view themselves in terms of those around them. Their own motivation is, at least in part, a function of whether or not they believe that they are being treated fairly. Organizational rewards should be administered equitably, and managers

EXHIBIT 6.8   A COMPARISON OF CONTENT THEORIES OF MOTIVATION AND PROCESS, GOAL-SETTING, AND REINFORCEMENT THEORIES

	UNDERLYING PREMISE	STRENGTHS	LIMITATIONS
Content Theories			
Maslow's Need Hierarchy. ERG. Herzberg's Motivators and Hygienes.	Needs initiate behavior and may take on a specific order arrangement.	Easy to understand. Intuitively appealing.	Assume all persons have similar need patterns. Minimizes individual differences. Limited empirical support.
Process Theories			
Expectancy.	Effort is expended if a person believes that (1) effort leads to performance, and (2) performance will lead to desired rewards.	Views motivation as a natural process. Lends itself to application.	Complex to apply. Seems to have descriptive rather than predictive qualities.
Equity.	People compare their input/outcome ratio to inputs and outcome of referent others.	Recognizes the influence of social comparison processes on individual motivation.	Does not predict for increased effort resulting from overpayment.
Goal-Setting Theory	People are purposive and will exert effort toward goals.	Extensive empirical support for the positive influence of goal setting on performance.	Assumes all persons are affected by goal setting in the same way.
Reinforcement Theory	Rewarding behaviors that lead to improved performance will increase the probability of their occurrence.	Lends itself to easy application. Intuitively logical and appealing.	Requires that rewards be constantly given. Negative rewards (punishment) provide shortlived benefits.

should be aware of the impact that reward-related decisions directed toward one employee or group will have on others.

Goal setting appears to be a sound managerial technique for motivating employee performance. Managers who set goals with (or for) their employees will generally experience higher productivity from their work force than will those who do not set goals. Moreover, research results indicate that such goals should be specific, challenging (though not overly difficult to attain), and accompanied by feedback. Although goal setting may be more effective for some employees and in some situations than others, it is a managerial technique that is likely to produce improved performance for managers who use it correctly.

Finally, scholars and managers alike are giving increased attention to the reinforcement of organizationally desirable and undesirable behaviors. Reinforcement theory helps to explain such behaviors and provides managers with a direct means for influencing employee motivation.

The models of motivation presented in this chapter have certain strengths and limitations. Exhibit 6.8 briefly describes each model.

Motivating an individual, much less a group of employees, can be a complex undertaking. However, understanding and applying theories of motivation such as those presented in this and the preceding chapter can greatly enhance your managerial effectiveness. The models of motivation presented in this chapter have certain strengths and limitations. Exhibit 6.8 briefly describes each model.

QUESTIONS FOR REVIEW AND DISCUSSION

1. What are the primary ways in which process theories of motivation differ from content theories?
2. What is meant by the terms *expectancy* and *instrumentality* and why are these two terms important to understanding motivation?
3. According to the modified expectancy model, factors other than effort influence performance. Name and discuss the impact of these factors.
4. What factors influence a person's motivation according to equity theory?
5. Use equity theory to explain employee reactions to (a) wage compression, (b) two-tier wage systems.
6. Name and discuss at least three factors that influence the relationship between goals and performance.
7. Feedback in the form of evaluation influences the impact of goal setting. How do expected and unexpected evaluation influence goal setting differently?
8. Explain the relationship between behavior and reinforcement as it relates to employee motivation.
9. What types of rewards are available to managers and what factors influence the choice of such rewards?
10. What ethical questions arise concerning the use of reinforcement theory as an approach to employee motivation?

REFERENCES

1. V. Vroom, *Work and Motivation* (New York: John Wiley and Sons, 1964).
2. P. M. Baker, W. T. Markham, C. M. Bonjean, and J. Corder, "Promotion Interest, and Willingness to Sacrifice for Promotion in a Government Agency," *Journal of Applied Behavioral Science*, Vol. 24 (1988): 61–80.
3. L. E. Miller and J. E. Grush, "Improving Predictions in Expectancy Theory Research: Effects of Personality, Expectancies, and Norms," *Academy of Management Journal*, Vol. 31 (March 1988): 107–122.
4. Edward E. Lawler III, "Developing a Motivating Work Climate," *Management Review*, Vol. 66 (1977): 26.

5. P. T. Taplin, "Profit Sharing Plans as an Employee Motivator," *Employee Benefit Plan Review*, Vol. 43 (January 1989): 10–12; "Gainsharing'" in Lawler, *High-Involvement Management* (San Francisco: Jossey Bass Publishers, 1986), 144–169; K. Penrar and M. Mandel, "The New America," *Business Week*, (25 September 1989): 162.

6. F. T. Adams, "Motivation and the Bottom Line," *Human Capital* (July 1990): 19–22; Adams, "The American Dream: Alive and Well in Missouri (an interview with Jack Stack)," *Human Capital* (July 1990): 23–26; B. Burlingham, "Being the Boss," *Inc.* (October 1989): 49–65.

7. B. G. Posner, "Owner's Rights," *Inc.* (January 1990): 114–115.

8. G. D. Jenkins, Jr., and N. Gupta, "The Payoffs of Paying for Knowledge," *National Productivity Review*, Vol. 4, No. 1 (Spring 1985): 121–130.

9. J. S. Adams, "Toward an Understanding of Inequity," *Journal of Abnormal Psychology*, Vol. 67 (1963): 422–436. The foundations of equity theory can be found in the theories of social justice and cognitive dissonance; see G. C. Homans, *Social Behavior: Its Elementary Forms* (New York: Harcourt, Brace, & World, 1961) and L. Festinger, "The Motivating Effect of Cognitive Dissonance," in Gardner Lindzey, ed., *Assessment of Human Motives* (New York: Rinehart & Co., 1958), 65–86.

10. G. R. Oldham, C. T. Kulik, L. P. Stepina, and M. L. Ambrose, "Relations Between Situational Factors and the Comparative Referents Used by Employees," *Academy of Management Journal*, Vol. 29 (September 1986): 599–608.

11. M. Dornstein, "Wage Reference Groups and Their Determinants: A Study of Blue-Collar and White-Collar Employees in Israel," *Journal of Occupational Psychology*, Vol. 61 (September 1988): 221–235.

12. J. Greenberg, "Cognitive Reevaluation of Outcomes in Response to Underpayment Inequity," *Academy of Management Journal*, Vol. 32 (March 1989): 174–184.

13. J. E. Martin, and M. M. Peterson, "Two-Tier Wage Structures: Implications for Equity Theory," *Academy of Management Journal*, Vol. 30 (1987): 297–315.

14. Greenberg, "Equity and Workplace Status: A Field Experiment," *Journal of Applied Psychology*, Vol. 73 (November 1988): 606–613.

15. Adams, op. cit., 77–80.

16. R. C. Huseman, J. D. Hatfield, and E. W. Miles, "A New Perspective on Equity Theory: The Equity Sensitivity Construct," *Academy of Management Review*, Vol. 12 (April 1987): 222–234.

17. Ibid., 223.

18. E. W. Miles, J. D. Hatfield, and R. C. Huseman, "The Equity Sensitivity Construct: Potential Implications for Worker Performance," *Journal of Management*, Vol. 15 (December 1989): 581–588.

19. A. Bernstein, "Why Two-Tier Wage Scales Are Starting to Self-Destruct, *Business Week* (16 March 1987): 41.

20. E. A. Locke and G. P. Latham, A *Theory of Goal Setting and Task Performance* (Englewood Cliffs, N.J.: Prentice-Hall, 1990); Edwin A. Locke, "Toward a Theory of Task Motivation and Incentives," *Organizational Behavior and Human Performance*, Vol. 3 (1968): 157–189.

21. M. G. Evans, "Organizational Behavior: The Central Role of Motivation," *Journal of Management*, Vol. 12 (Summer 1986): 203–222; A. Bandura, *Social Foundations of Thought and Action* (Englewood Cliffs, N.J.: Prentice Hall, 1980), 391.

22. Locke, op. cit.

23. J. V. Baumler, "Defined Criteria of Performance in Organizational Control," *Administrative Science Quarterly*, Vol. 16 (February 1971): 340–349.

24. E. A. Locke, D. Chah, S. Harrison, and N. Lustgarten, "Separating the Effects of Goal Specificity from Goal Level," *Organizational Behavior and Human Decision Processes*, Vol. 43 (April 1989): 270–287.

25. J. B. Miner, *Theories of Organizational Behavior* (Hinsdale, Ill.: The Dryden Press, 1980), 180–187.

26. Locke and Latham, op. cit., 154–172.

27. M. Erez, "The Congruence of Goal Setting Strategies with Socio-Cultural Values, and its Effect on Performance," *Journal of Management*, Vol. 12 (December 1986): 585–592.

28. M. Erez and P. C. Earley, "Comparative Analysis of Goal-Setting Strategies Across Cultures," *Journal of Applied Psychology*, Vol. 72 (November 1987): 658–665.

29. J. S. Kim and W. C. Hamner, "Effect of Performance Feedback and Goal Setting on Productivity and Satisfaction in an Organizational Setting," *Journal of Applied Psychology*, Vol. 61 (1976): 48–57.

30. J. S. Kim, "Effect of Behavior Plus Outcome Goal Setting and Feedback on Employee Satisfaction and Performance," *Academy of Management Journal*, Vol. 27 (1984): 139–149.

31. S. J. Ashford and L. L. Cummings, "Feedback as An Individual Resource: Personal Strategies for Creating Information," *Organizational Behavior and Human Performance*, Vol. 32 (December 1983): 32, 370–398.

32. C. E. Shalley and G. R. Oldham, "Effects of Goal Difficulty and Expected External Evaluation on Intrinsic Motivation: A Laboratory Study," *Academy of Management Journal*, Vol. 28 (September 1985): 652–640.

33. H. Rollinson, "Make Awards Count," *Personnel Journal*, Vol. 67 (October 1988): 139–157.

34. J. P. Calpin, B. Edelstein, and W. K. Redmon, "Performance Feedback and Goal Setting to Improve Mental Health Center Staff Productivity," *Journal of Organizational Behavior*, Vol. 9 (1988): 35–58.

35. D. C. Anderson, C. R. Crowell, M. Doman, G. S. Howard, "Performance Posting, Goal Setting, and

Activity-Contingent Praise as Applied to a University Hockey Team," *Journal of Applied Psychology,* Vol. 73 (February 1988): 87–95.

36. F. Luthans and R. Kreitner, *Organizational Behavior Modification and Beyond* (Glenview, Ill.: Scott, Foresman and Company, 1985), 126–130.

CASE 6.1　*It's not my job*

BARRY L. WISDOM　*Southwest Missouri State University*

Dennis was not surprised to hear the company CEO, Tom Hughes, say that the time for change had come. Though the Hughes Motor Company was financially sound, its profits were being eaten away be a growing quality problem. Both scrap and rework were up by 7 percent over the past year and, Hughes being a small company operating on a narrow profit margin, the pinch was being felt.

"If the problem is not solved quickly," said Tom Hughes to the assembled department heads, "we will have to pass the cost of our quality problem along to our consumers and that is likely to weaken our competitive position in the marketplace. With several Japanese firms planning to introduce products into this market, our share will be hard to hold even without a price increase." Dennis understood the situation. He had worked his way up the ladder during his ten years with HMC. He knew the business from the ground up and thought he knew where the company's quality problems were coming from.

HMC had been in business for almost nineteen years, and as the demand for their product (fractional horsepower electric motors) had grown so had the company. The plant now employed about four hundred people, mostly from the nearby community of Elkton, a small town having a population of about three thousand. In many ways the assembly-line process employed today was not much different from when the plant first opened. Due to the small size and delicate nature of the components going into the motors and a lack of investment capital, the company had never made the transition to high tech. The production process was still labor intensive and the performance and durability of the motors was in large part a function of the assemblers' skill and care. It was a growing lack of care on the part of the workers that Dennis thought was the problem. However, not everyone shared his view.

OPERATION QUALITY

After Tom Hughes had finished expressing his concerns about rising costs and increasingly competitive markets, he presented his plan of action. The last hour of the department heads' meeting was spent outlining a new quality plan to go into effect next Monday. The key theme of "Operation Quality," as the plan came to be called, was improved inspection. All department heads were to start the ball rolling by meeting the following day with their section foremen. Once briefed, each foreman would be responsible for selling the program to the fifteen or so employees under his or her supervision.

At Dennis's staff meeting the next day, his six section foremen seemed receptive enough to Dennis's presentation. They listened patiently as he talked about the reasons behind the plan, yet they seemed much more interested in the mechanics of the operation. The department heads were to analyze each assembly job on the line and prominently post a list of the four to six checks each employee should make on every assembly produced before the components were placed in a common bin and moved to the next work station.

It was also noted that the twelve quality inspectors employed by HMC were to be much more conspicuous than in the past, with most of them now roving through the plant and doing random quality spot checks. As an additional means of making quality more visible, all outgoing products would have a bright green sticker affixed proclaiming "This product meets quality standards" if the motor had in fact been cleared by the final inspector.

First thing Monday, foremen throughout the plant met with their workers to lay out the details of Operation Quality. After all the line personnel were thoroughly briefed on their new responsibilities, the plan was off and running.

FOUR WEEKS LATER

At the end of four full weeks of Operation Quality, the effects of the plan were being felt by almost everyone, though not in the way Tom Hughes had intended. It was true that everyone had become more aware of quality and some departments had even shown reductions in waste after the first two weeks, but Dennis saw little if any improvement in the quality reports for the last two weeks. In fact, conversations he had overheard among the foremen and workers had increased his doubts about the long term success of the plan.

Passing by the break room at lunch on the Friday following the introduction of the plan, Dennis had overheard Mike and Sara, two of his foremen, saying the following:

Mike: I'm really worried about my year-end bonus. With all this quality stuff coming down, it sure doesn't look good. The way they tie our bonuses to meeting monthly production schedules and with the additional burden of riding my people about their assembly checks, I'm eight hundred units behind on this week's quota.

Sara: I know what you mean. With my son going off to college next year, this is not the time for me to start sacrificing for the sake of the company. Besides what are they paying the quality control people for anyway?

Mike: You got me. I'll keep it up a little longer, but as soon as the heat is off, I'll meet my quota first and let the quality cops worry about the rest.

Just this past Wednesday, Dennis had observed a heated exchange between Hal, one of the senior workers, and his foreman. Almost in tears, Hal had said, "Look, Mister, you pay me to do two hundred brush assemblies an hour. You can't expect me to do that and all these quality checks too! I'm pretty good at what I do, and if I do make mistakes the inspector will catch them. If ole Mr. Hughes is worried about quality, tell him not to bother me. It's not my job!" Other workers listening to Hal's speech had clapped and whistled in support, and as the day went by, many of them came by his work station to pat him on the back.

Dennis was bothered by what he saw. In his interactions with his foremen, Dennis had been complimentary whenever he had found them promoting better quality. However, on only a few occasions had he seen the foremen doing the same with their workers. Dennis often felt powerless in his ability to add more support to the program, given the structure at HMC.

As the compensation plan was presently designed, the foremen were salaried with a bonus awarded at the end of each year based on the ability of each section to meet its production schedules. Each line worker was also paid on an incentive basis with his or her wages based on a standard hour plan. Under this plan, the daily wage for a worker was calculated by dividing his or her total daily output by the standard number of units per hour expected for the given assembly operation to determine the number of standard hours of output achieved. Standard hours were then multiplied by the hourly wage to get daily gross pay.

THE YEAR-END MEETING

At the year-end meeting, Dennis could see defeat in Tom Hughes's eyes as he announced the introduction of price increases throughout the product line for the coming year. Though every box leaving the plant now wore a bright green quality sticker, and the inspectors were better than ever at spotting defects, the costs from scrap and rework were still out of hand.

Dennis couldn't bring himself to blame the workers or the foremen for the failure of Operation Quality, for he understood why they had reacted the way they had. How could he expect them to see the severity of the problem with Japan such a long way from the quiet little town of Elkton? He had some ideas about how the quality program might work but it would require some major changes in the reward and accountability systems.

Dennis couldn't help but wonder if the company could have had more success with the quality program if it had put its money where its mouth was. He struggled to build up the courage to talk with Mr. Hughes as he walked back to his office after the meeting.

CASE 6.2

The need to listen

INTRODUCTION

Keith Dunn, president of McGuffey's Restaurants, Inc., had just received questionnaires filled out by his employees on how they felt about working at Mc-Guffey's. Excitedly, he ripped open the first envelope. His gaze zoomed to the question in which employees had been asked to rate his performance on a scale of one to ten. He already knew that the rating would be a nine or a ten.

A zero!

He ripped open the next envelope.

Another zero!

Of 230 employees, over 10 percent rated Keith Dunn's performance a zero, and none rated him higher than three. What had happened?

MCGUFFEY'S

Dunn started McGuffey's in 1983 out of frustration with the employee abuse he saw and experienced while working for big restaurant chains. He had vowed to provide his employees a place to work where they felt valued, involved, and appreciated. His mission in life was to prove that restaurants could succeed without mistreating their employees. Now, this!

McGuffey's had been quite a success. The company had expanded from one to three restaurants in its first year of operations. The original restaurant alone had had sales of over $2 million in the first year. Although yet to show a profit by the second year, company sales had reached nearly $3.5 million. In the process it had managed to put two competitors (including a franchisee of a national chain) out of business. But in the wake of apparent success, problems began to surface.

In order to accomplish this kind of growth, Dunn spent much of his time away from the restaurant. He travelled to trade shows looking at state-of-the-art

SOURCE: J. Hyatt, "The Odyssey of an 'Excellent' Man," *Inc.*, February 1989, 63–69.

equipment, met bankers who might finance his expansion plans, and sponsored street festivals to build goodwill. Dunn's world was growing, but that of his employees was sliding. They were busy busing tables or cooking burgers and being ordered around by their managers. Employees had also begun to leave in great numbers. The company gave them better benefits (e.g., health and dental insurance) than other restaurants and planned to set up a profit-sharing program. Still, dissatisfaction grew.

Even Dunn's personal relationship with employees had degenerated badly. He was described as a guy "with his nose in the air" who "never said hello" and "just came through the restaurant once in a while." These were the same people talking who had joined the company because they had heard that it was "real employee-oriented." Now, it seemed that Dunn had turned McGuffey's into exactly the kind of organization that he had once abhorred, one where employees had no say in running the company.

Keith Dunn had originally hoped to hold turnover to around 50 percent. Yet he had taken McGuffey's actual turnover rate of 220 percent for granted. Several departing employees had told him that he didn't care about his people and that he was turning out to be like other restaurant company bosses; but Dunn had ready answers; "We're a big company, and we've got to do big-company things," and "Its inevitable, since we can only grow if we use their tried-and-true methods."

In its third year, the company posted profits of $75,000 on sales of $4 million. But a successful start was rapidly falling apart. Sales were dwindling; employees felt ignored, resentful, and abandoned. Restrooms didn't get scrubbed so thoroughly, the food didn't arrive quite as hot, and the servers didn't smile so often.

Again Dunn had an answer. He decided to improve sales by tying his managers' compensation to their performances. Managers had previously received bonuses based on their relative performance toward goals. The new plan laid out an all-or-nothing approach. Managers would have to achieve their goals completely before any bonus was received.

Other steps were taken as well. Bartenders were told to learn and perform magic tricks for customers, and a contest to motivate employees was begun. The work force was divided into six teams, and teams could win special bonuses for the exceptional performances of their members. The desired effects of Dunn's scheme were shortlived.

In order to achieve their objectives and receive their bonuses, managers reduced staff, let supplies run short, and neglected equipment maintenance and repairs. Others did not even try to reach their objectives, believing that they were unrealistic. The employee contest also met resistance. Teams which began to lag behind simply gave up trying to perform better, since they felt they could not win the rewards anyway. As for the bartenders, few of them bothered to try and learn magic tricks. Even feedback sessions held by Dunn were a flop. Only three people showed up for the first meeting he held!

One day during a managers' meeting, Keith Dunn asked if anyone knew why employees were not showing up for his feedback sessions. He was told that they were required to come on their day off and were not paid to do so. Furthermore, many felt that their suggestions would not be implemented anyway. Regarding apparent failure of the contest, he was told the employees wanted a win–win situation where everyone would benefit rather than just a few. As for the magic tricks, he learned that the bartenders were never asked if they liked the idea or if it was even practical. One manager went further: "It was just another thing you shoved down their throats."

For the first time in years, it dawned on Keith Dunn that he hadn't been listening. What was missing in his company was the voice of his employees. In his zeal to succeed he had attempted to superimpose his view of an employee-oriented management style without consulting the very people to whom he thought he was oriented. Once again, it was time for a change. But this time, he thought, "It will be different!"

EXERCISE 6.1
UNDERSTANDING THE EXPECTANCY THEORY OF MOTIVATION

In this chapter, you learned about a theory of motivation known as expectancy theory. Expectancy theory explains motivation in terms of the amount of effort a person is willing to put forth in order to accomplish a given outcome (or reward). This exercise has two parts. Part I requires you to design an experiment that will allow you to examine expectancy theory. Part II allows you to take a closer look at expectancy theory in an organizational setting.

PART I

In a group of three to five individuals, design an experiment that will allow you to examine more closely the concepts associated with expectancy theory of motivation. As you formulate your ideas, remember that you must develop a means for measuring the perceived values of outcomes as well as the perceived likelihood that they will occur. Explain your experiment to another group in the class and conduct three trial runs. When you have completed your trials, critique your experiment as well as the predictive ability of the model.

PART II

A. Together with one other member of your class, interview two managers in two separate organizations concerning various aspects of the institutions's reward system. Attempt to assess the nature of the rewards (tangible and intangible) used, why they have been selected (or used), and how successful the manager believes them to be.
B. Interview at least two employees in each organization and ask them how effective they believe each reward is (1) for others, and (2) for themselves. As you probe their responses, ask questions about what will reflect perceived value, perceived probability, and perceived equitability of rewards.

After Completing the Interview

1. Prepare a brief report on your interviews and present your findings to a small group of your classmates. (Groups of six—three two-person teams—are recommended.)
2. Discuss the effectiveness of reward systems relative to expectancy theory.
3. As a group, develop a general set of recommendations to managers concerning the effective use of rewards.

EXERCISE 6.2
APPLYING MOTIVATION THEORIES

In this chapter, four different theories of motivation were presented. Expectancy theory views motivation as a natural process that is determined by links between outcomes and performance. Equity theory explains motivation in terms of social comparisons that individuals make. Goal-setting theory views motivation as resulting from consciously set goals. Reinforcement theory suggests the use of rewards and punishments as a way of influencing motivation.

Each of these approaches to motivation provides a unique frame of reference, and can lead to a different explanation of individual behavior. Managers encountering motivational problems are likely to select a particular course of action depending upon which theory is embraced.

INSTRUCTIONS

Your instructor has divided the class into four or more groups, and assigned to each group one of the four content theories.

1. Meet briefly in your group and discuss the assigned motivation theory and its implications for managing in the workplace.
2. Read the passage "What's A Person To Do?," on page 168 at the end of Chapter 5.
3. After reading the passage, your group should discuss the problem and formulate a soluton based on the theory you have been assigned.

4. A representative from each group will present the group's solution to the class as a whole.
5. Classroom discussion should focus on the differences between the four strategies presented.
6. What differences do you see between your present solutions and those that you formulated using the content theories discussed in the previous chapter?

CHAPTER 7

 # DECISION MAKING

LEARNING OBJECTIVES

1. To appreciate the central importance of decision making in the managerial role.
2. To know the distinction between decision making and problem solving.
3. To describe the steps in the problem-solving process.
4. To understand two models of the decision-making process.
5. To identify barriers to the decision-making process.
6. To recognize both the advantages and disadvantages of group decisions.
7. To describe the various forms of participative decision making.

CHAPTER OUTLINE

The Managerial Role and Decision Making
Managerial Decision Making and Problem Solving

Models of the Decision-Making Process
The Rational-Economic Model
The Administrative Model

Barriers to Effective Decision Making
Tunnel Vision
Previous Commitments
Implicit Favorites
Lack of Creativity

Individual Versus Group Decision Making
Advantages of Group Decision Making
Disadvantages of Group Decision Making

Participation in Decision Making
Participation versus Delegation
Putting Participation to Work

Decision Making: Conclusions

Questions for Review and Discussion

References

Cases: 7.1 Changing the Shuttle Launch Decision Process
        7.2 Dilemma of a Young Manager

Exercises: 7.1 NASA Exercise
            7.2 Creative Thinking

KEY TERMS

Decision making	**Anchoring and adjustment**
Problem solving	**Overconfidence**
Programmed decisions	**Tunnel vision**
Nonprogrammed decisions	**Previous commitments**
Rational-economic model	**Implicit favorites**
Administrative model	**Creativity**
Bounded rationality	**Groupthink**
Maximizing/Satisficing	**Group polarization**
Representativeness	**Participative decision making**
Availability	**Delegation**

Janice knew she had to make her decision quickly; Greg Weiss was waiting anxiously for a reply to his offer. Janice worked in the corporate accounting department of Fayarb, Inc., a large manufacturing firm headquartered in Columbus, Ohio. She had been employed by Fayarb since graduating from college eight years ago, and she enjoyed the challenges of her work, her colleagues, and the life-style available to her in Columbus.

Greg was a mechanical engineer who had recently developed a new braking system for large trucks. Initial tests performed by an independent agency comparing Greg's system with traditional brakes indicated that his system offered significant improvements in braking performance and equipment wear. Several trucking firms had learned about the test results and expressed interest in experimenting with the new system on their trucks. Greg had formed a new company, SafeBrake, Inc., to manufacture and market the brake system. With the positive test results and growing demand for the new system, the prospects for SafeBrake looked good.

Greg was well aware that he was an engineer and not an experienced businessperson. He had met Janice in a local civic organization and learned of her excellent accounting and financial work at Fayarb from Joe Reed, a personal acquaintance who was a consultant to Fayarb. After investigating Janice's background and conducting an interview with her, Greg had offered Janice a job in his new company. He wanted her to guide the company through the complicated start-up phase and develop a successful business organization and staff.

The offer from SafeBrake was appealing to Janice; it provided a new challenge and the chance to participate in the creation of a new product and company. It might be a once-in-a-lifetime opportunity. But Janice also felt a sense of loyalty to Fayarb. Did she really want to give up the secure job she already had? What if SafeBrake encountered some unexpected difficulties? Would she have a chance like this again? These and other questions raced through Janice's mind as she tried to make this important decision.

Some decisions, like the one faced by Janice, can have a major impact on our personal and organizational lives. Other decisions may be more routine, yet still require that we select an appropriate course of action. Think about some of the decisions you have already made today—what to eat, what to wear, how to spend your money, where to go, and what to do with your time. Now, consider some of the major decisions you may make that will significantly affect your future—decisions about family, career, and life-style. We make decisions frequently, and the effects of our decisions have both short- and long-term consequences. Despite extensive personal experience, however, most people are generally unaware of how they make decisions or why they prefer one alternative to another. This chapter introduces concepts and models that can help you more fully understand the important process of making decisions.

THE MANAGERIAL ROLE AND DECISION MAKING

Have you ever wondered what managers actually do? To answer this question, Henry Mintzberg investigated the nature and content of managerial work and identified three general roles or types of activity in which managers engage.[1] These basic roles were defined by (1) activities concerned primarily with developing and maintaining interpersonal relationships; (2) activities dealing principally with the transfer of information; and (3) activities essentially involving decision making. The most crucial part of the manager's work—the part that justifies great authority and powerful access to information—is performed in the role as a decision maker. The essence of managerial work involves the exercise of judgment and the making of decisions.

According to a noted management authority, "a decision is a judgment. . . . a choice between alternatives."[2] **Decision making,** then, is the process of selecting from among available alternatives. Upon graduation, for example, you will have to choose from among the various job offers you receive. Exhibit 7.1 shows how difficult some career choices can be. As a manager, you may have to select the most deserving employee to receive a service award. The key feature of decision making thus is the process of selecting or choosing.

Managers usually make two basic kinds of decisions—programmed and nonprogrammed.[3] A **programmed decision** is made repeatedly according to established principles and policies applicable to all similar situations. The decision to reprimand an employee formally for three unexcused absences, for example, is a programmed decision. Similarly, a decision to expel a student for unsatisfactory performance (in terms of minimum GPA) usually is based on established guidelines and practices.

A **nonprogrammed decision** is new or unique. Established guidelines or procedures usually do not exist to direct decision making in novel or exceptional cases. The decision maker explores new territory in making a nonprogrammed decision. For example, many policy decisions made by senior level executives in response to rapidly changing market conditions (e.g., the personal computer industry) are nonprogrammed.

Mintzberg's research indicated that managers work at a fast, action-oriented pace. Half the activities in which managers engaged lasted less than nine minutes, and only 10 percent exceeded an hour. He concluded that managers and executives are action-oriented and have little time for reflective thinking. Given this description of managerial activity, programmed decision-making is essential to efficient manage-

EXHIBIT 7.1   THE DIFFICULTIES OF DECISION MAKING!

SOURCE: © 1976 Newspaper Enterprise Association, Inc. Reprinted by permission of NEA, Inc.

FRANK AND ERNEST   **by Bob Thaves**

ment. It should also be obvious, however, that one determinant of successful nonpro-grammed decisions is the decision maker's creativity. Thus, managers and executives must work continuously to achieve a balance between the needs for structured, routine decision-making procedures and for flexibility and creativity.

Managerial Decision Making and Problem Solving

Choosing from among available alternatives is only one step in the overall problem-solving process. This more encompassing process involves six basic steps: (1) identifying and defining the problem; (2) searching for and developing alternatives; (3) evaluating and comparing alternatives; (4) making a choice; (5) implementing the choice; and (6) monitoring, reviewing and following up.

Identifying and defining the problem

Recognizing and defining a problem clearly are the first and, according to many researchers, the most important steps in the problem-solving process. A manager frequently becomes aware of a problem by comparing a current situation or state of affairs with some desired goal. For example, sales in a particular department of a retail store during the month of November may have increased only 2 percent, while the goal for the month was 10 percent. The discrepancy between actual sales and the goal may indicate a problem that needs attention.

Reliable information is very important during problem identification and defini-tion. Inaccurate information or data can cause time to be wasted working on a problem that does not actually exist, or it can lead a manager to miss the underlying causes of a situation. Faulty identification and definition of the problem can therefore lead to a poor or counterproductive solution.

Unfortunately, problem definition is easier said than done when considering human behavior in organizations. The true nature of a problem may be deeply rooted in an individual's past experience, in the complexity of the organization itself, or in some combination of individual and organizational factors. Therefore, a manager must pay particular attention to this first step of the problem-solving process in order to identify a problem as accurately as possible.

Searching for and developing alternatives

Once a problem has been identified and defined correctly, the manager can develop alternative courses of action that may result in goal attainment. This stage of the problem-solving process requires creativity and imagination. Ideally, a manager should attempt to develop many alternatives and should also try to make the set of alternatives as varied as possible. In this way, the problem solver increases the likelihood that many good potential alternatives will be considered and evaluated.

Managers may rely on their education and training, personal experience, and knowledge of the situation to generate alternatives. Input also can be solicited from other people such as peers, employees, supervisors, and other groups within the organization. In some cases, customer-focus groups are also asked to supply infor-mation that can be used in the decision-making process. Such groups may be external to the organization or simply represent other user groups within the company. Idea

EXHIBIT 7.2   SOURCES OF CURRENT INFORMATION ABOUT BEHAVIOR IN ORGANIZATIONS

Problem situations deserve first-hand attention. At the same time, managers can draw on existing solutions and do not necessarily have to "reinvent the wheel." Problems involving human behavior in organizations are studied regularly by scholars and confronted daily by managers. As researchers and practitioners broaden their understanding of organizational behavior, they often share their findings with others through academic and professional publications. Articles contained in such publications are an excellent source of information about the nature of problems, their causes, and in some cases, possible decision alternatives. Suggestions obtained from such periodicals may even provide relatively complete solutions to some problems.

These publications usually fall into one of two categories: (1) academic/scholarly journals, and (2) periodicals and journals intended for practicing managers. Articles printed in scholarly journals usually report the findings of original empirical research on such topics as work motivation, compensation practices, organizational structure, job design, decision making, leadership, and so on. Publications intended for managers provide practical information about such topics as those mentioned, as well as current business trends and management techniques. Both types of periodicals are important sources of the latest information about human resource management.

Listed below are a number of journals. This list is not intended to be exhaustive. Rather, our purpose is to make you aware of some specific sources of information about management theory and practice. These periodicals may be helpful in researching a problem or in starting your own ongoing reading program.

PUBLICATIONS FOR PRACTICING MANAGERS	ACADEMIC/SCHOLARLY JOURNALS
Business Week	Organizational Behavior and Human Decision Processes
Business Month	
National Productivity Review	Administrative Science Quarterly
Personnel Administrator	Academy of Management Journal
Academy of Management Executive	Academy of Management Review
Supervisory Management	Journal of Management
Organizational Dynamics	Journal of Applied Psychology
Harvard Business Review	Personnel Psychology
Training and Development Journal	The Journal of Vocational Behavior
Fortune	The Journal of Applied Behavioral Science
Forbes	
Personnel Journal	

generation techniques such as brainstorming or the nominal group technique are particularly effective in this stage of the problem solving process (See Chapter 9, "Putting Groups to Work," for detailed descriptions of these techniques).

Evaluating and comparing alternatives

A problem solver evaluates alternatives by comparing the relative advantages and disadvantages of each alternative under consideration. Predetermined decision criteria such as the following are used in the evaluation process: (1) Will this alternative bring us nearer to the goal? (2) What is the anticipated cost of this alternative? (3) What are the uncertainties and risks associated with this alternative? (4) What is the anticipated benefit of this particular alternative? The product of this evaluation process should be a ranking of the alternatives from best to worst according to their likelihood of leading to the attainment of the problem solver's goals.

Making a choice

Choosing an alternative is the crucial step in the problem-solving process. Making a choice is quite straightforward, however, if the problem has been properly defined and alternatives have been evaluated systematically and comprehensively. Ideally, the problem solver selects the alternative that will most likely lead to the attainment of the desired state or goal.

Although choosing an alternative may seem rather simple, difficulties can frequently arise. For example, two or more alternatives may be equally attractive or have a similar likelihood of leading to the achievement of a goal. In such a situation, the problem solver might need to gather additional information or use some other criterion to make the choice. Some complicated problems may even require the simultaneous implementation of two or three alternatives in order to achieve a desired outcome.

Implementing the choice

A manager may feel that her job has been accomplished once a particular alternative is selected. However, the problem-solving process is nothing more than a mental exercise if the chosen alternative is not implemented. The selected alternative is put into action to reduce the disparity between the current situation or level of performance and the desired goal. It is in this phase of the problem-solving process that a choice is changed from a cognitive abstraction into an operational reality.

Monitoring, reviewing, and following up

Managers are faced with numerous problems and decisions every day. It is therefore understandable that many feel the job of problem solving is complete once a final decision is made and a particular plan of action implemented. No problem-solving process is complete, however, until the impact of the selected alternative has been monitored and evaluated. The problem solver should not be expected to enforce the decision under any and all circumstances; rather, he should observe the impact of the decision as objectively as possible and take further corrective action if it becomes necessary.

The process of following up permits a manager to determine the effectiveness of his decision. If a problem still remains, and some disparity continues to exist between the current situation and the desired goal, another cycle in the problem-solving process may be initiated. If the problem appears to be resolved, the manager can turn his attention to other problems with the knowledge that similar situations encountered in the future may be dealt with in a like manner.

Although the terms **problem solving** and **decision making** are often used synonymously, in this book we refer to problem solving as a broader and more systematic process that includes decision making. Problem solving is characterized by the activities of searching, inventing, reacting, and creating, with the major objective being the identification of acceptable alternatives. Decision making, on the other hand, requires skill in evaluating, judging, critiquing, and choosing, with emphasis on selecting the most appropriate alternative. Problem solving and decision making are related but different processes that effective managers must understand and successfully apply. Exhibit 7.3 illustrates the relationship between problem solving and decision making.

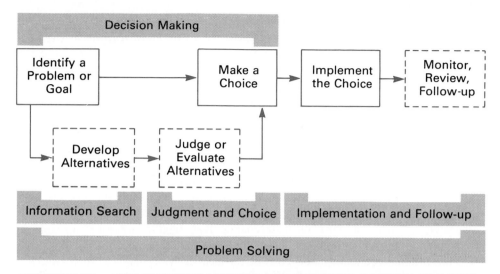

EXHIBIT 7.3   THE DECISION-MAKING AND PROBLEM-SOLVING PROCESS
SOURCE: Reprinted by permission from *Understanding Organizational Behavior* by Denis D. Umstot,
Copyright © 1984 by West Publishing Company. All rights reserved.

MODELS OF THE DECISION-MAKING PROCESS

Many models of the decision-making process can be found in management literature. Although these models vary in their scope, assumptions, and applicability, they are similar in that each focuses on how a decision maker processes information before making a final choice. In this section, we discuss two well-known models of the decision-making process—the rational-economic model and the administrative model.

The Rational-Economic Model

The **rational-economic model** is prescriptive of how decisions should be made rather than descriptive of how decisions actually are made. The model posits that people are economically rational and that a decision maker seeks to **maximize** outcomes by systematically searching out and evaluating all possible alternatives and then selecting the single best alternative. In addition, people are assumed to have perfect information about all available alternatives and the consequences of those alternatives. Individuals are also believed to process information in a logical, objective, and systematic manner.

Maximizing outcomes places great demands upon a decision maker's cognitive abilities. In order to maximize an outcome, a manager is required to develop a complete set of possible courses of action, specify all possible outcomes resulting from any of these actions, and judge the actions according to appropriate criteria. Thus, the decision maker requires a well-specified set of alternatives and a clear basis for choosing the alternative that will best achieve the goal or desired outcome.

According to this model, for example, a consumer shopping for a new car equipped with air conditioning, stereo, power windows, and all of the latest options, would search out all possible alternatives (e.g., all of the automobiles in the town or county that met the criteria) and select the car with the most features at the least cost. Such a decision-making strategy would thus maximize the usefulness of the outcome to the consumer.

The rational-economic model portrays decision making as a straightforward process. In practice, however, making a decision is never that simple. Several reasons explain this disparity between theory and practice. First, people rarely, if ever, have access to complete and perfect information. For example, a consumer shopping for a car will undoubtedly bypass some alternatives or obtain only partial information about others. Second, even if the information were available concerning all possible alternatives, an individual's cognitive limitations would make it difficult to process accurately the vast amount of material. Third, decision makers seldom have adequate knowledge about the future consequences of alternatives (e.g., can the consumer accurately predict the cost of maintenance and repairs for each automobile considered?).

The rational-economic model portrays the ideal decision-making process and has provided the foundation for much of the empirical research and current knowledge we have about decision making. Unfortunately, however, this model is seriously limited as a tool for understanding many day-to-day decision-making situations.

The Administrative Model

The **administrative model**[4] is descriptive and provides a framework for understanding the process that decision makers actually use when selecting from among alternatives. This model also assumes that people generally attempt to find the best possible alternative when confronted with a decision. Unlike the rational-economic model, however, the administrative model acknowledges human limitations that make rational decisions difficult to achieve.

This model suggests that a person's cognitive ability to process information is limited. In other words, a human being can handle only so much information before overload occurs. Herbert Simon, a noted authority on human decision making, suggested:

> The capacity of the human mind for formulating and solving complex problems is very small compared with the size of the problems whose solution is required for objectively rational behavior in the real world— or even for a reasonable approximation of such objective rationality.[5]

Even if complete information were available to a decision maker, these cognitive limitations would impede making a completely rational decision. According to the administrative model, then, decision makers have **bounded rationality.**

Managers usually attempt to behave rationally within their limited perception of a decision situation. When confronted by the complexity of most organizational situations, however, people are forced to view problems within sharply restricted bounds of rational decision making. Decision makers frequently try to compensate for their limited ability to cope with the information demands of complex problems by developing simple models of those problems. Their behavior can be considered rational, but only in terms of their simplified views of the problem. Bounded rationality is generally accepted in theories of administrative decision making and helps to explain departures from the maximizing choice mode specified in the rational-economic model.

The concept of bounded rationality affects several key aspects of the decision-making process. First, the decision maker does not search out all possible alternatives and then select the best one. Rather, various alternatives are identified and evaluated only until an acceptable solution is found. Having found a satisfactory alternative, the search for additional solutions then stops. Other and potentially better alternatives may exist but will not be identified or considered because the first workable solution has been accepted. Therefore, only a fraction of the available alternatives may be considered because of a decision maker's information processing limitations.

Second, bounded rationality implies that decision makers *satisfice* instead of maximize. **Satisficing** occurs when an alternative is selected that meets minimum rather than optimum standards of acceptance. In other words, a decision maker, because of various constraints (time, cost, inability to process large amounts of information), chooses an alternative that is satisfactory rather than continues to search for the ideal. For example, as a college graduate entering the labor market, you may accept the first available job that pays $30,000 a year rather than continue the search for a job that provides better pay, pleasant working conditions, and significant opportunities for advancement.

Finally, the search for alternatives is guided primarily by past experiences or rules of thumb that provide a shorthand method for quickly identifying solutions with the greatest likelihood of succeeding. Researchers have identified several important heuristics (rules of thumb) and behavioral biases affecting the way people search for alternatives and make decisions.

Representativeness

The **representativeness** heuristic reflects the tendency to make decisions based on the belief that object A belongs to class B.[6] For example, the job of an employment recruiter working for a large corporation is to select candidates with the greatest likelihood of succeeding on the job. The representativeness heuristic suggests that the recruiter's training and years of experience have taught the characteristics essential to a new employee's successful job performance. In judging the probability that a particular candidate will be a successful employee, the recruiter simply compares the candidate (object A) to successful employees previously interviewed (class B). When B and A are very similar, then the probability of A is usually judged to be very high (e.g., "Jane Williams looks like an excellent candidate to me").

Availability

The **availability** heuristic suggests that the ease with which events can be remembered or imagined is an important factor in making judgments about frequency.[7] For example, what is the likelihood of a strike by the United Auto Workers next year? If contract negotiations between the major automobile companies and the UAW have led to strikes in recent years, you would be more inclined to remember these events and attribute a high probability to another strike. Similarly, a male executive may be requested to estimate the proportion of female managers in the United States work force. If the executive's personal experience is such that he recalls more males than females in the managerial role, this may cause him to underestimate the relative number of female managers. Even though the number of female managers in the United States has increased significantly during the last decade, the executive may not estimate the proportions accurately because historically there have been more male managers (and he most easily remembers this characteristic).

Anchoring and adjustment

People generally believe they can review decision alternatives and adjust their judgments as additional information is obtained. Research indicates, however, that this belief is not true. In fact, decision makers tend to use a natural starting point or **anchor** as a first approximation to the judgment. The anchor is then **adjusted,** often imprecisely, to accommodate the implications of additional information. This decision-making rule of thumb is referred to as anchoring and adjustment.

For example, an employment recruiter typically forms an initial impression of a candidate when they first meet in the interview. Such an impression can be based on the candidate's physical appearance, style of communication, confidence, and other factors. This initial impression is adjusted (supposedly) as the recruiter receives additional information about the candidate's background and qualifications. Research conducted in a variety of decision situations, however, indicates that adjustments based on new information usually are imprecise and insufficient.[8]

Overconfidence

Research also suggests that people tend to be more confident in their ability to assess probabilities and make judgments than is justified by their actual performance.[9] In fact, we tend to (1) disregard the data on which judgments are based, and (2) overestimate our own abilities on tasks requiring skill. This heuristic can have a significant impact on such managerial activities as planning and forecasting. In preparing a budget proposal, for example, an executive may ignore or overlook relevant information because of confidence in personal forecasting ability. Similarly, a manager may commit serious errors while planning a marketing strategy because of overestimating her ability to anticipate future trends in the marketplace.

The administrative model presents a realistic description of how decisions often are made. Some situations require a rational-economic approach to decision making,

EXHIBIT 7.4   A COMPARISON OF THE RATIONAL-ECONOMIC AND ADMINSTRATIVE MODELS OF DECISION MAKING

SOURCE: Robert A. Baron, *Behavior in Organizations: Understanding and Managing the Human Side of Work* (Boston: Allyn and Bacon, 1983), 357. Used by permission.

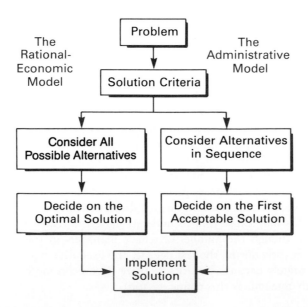

but most people probably *satisfice* more than they maximize. Exhibit 7.4 summarizes the differences between the rational-economic and administrative models of decision making.

BARRIERS TO EFFECTIVE DECISION MAKING

Decision making can be a complex and confusing process. Many barriers inhibit our ability to make informed and effective decisions. An awareness of such barriers as tunnel vision, previous commitments, implicit favorites, and the lack of creativity can help improve the process by which we search for and choose among multiple alternatives.

Tunnel Vision

When horses were used for pulling wagons and carriages, they often wore blinders. The blinders served to block distractions that could frighten or distract the horse. In similar fashion, people often have mental blinders that can restrict the search for an acceptable solution to a relatively narrow range of alternatives. An executive with a negative stereotype about women managers, for example, may only consider men for important assignments and exclude competent female candidates. An industrial engineer, by virtue of specialized training and experience, may view new technology as the best method of improving a factory's productive capacity instead of supervisory training or rigorous quality control. To the extent that **tunnel vision** inhibits identifying additional and worthwhile alternatives, it has a detrimental effect on the decision-making process.

Tunnel vision and the mental blocks it can cause are the result of many factors: individual biases or prejudices, past experience, assumptions, specialized training or education, or the culture of a particular group or organization. The problems in Exhibit 7.5 are not difficult, although your ability to solve them may be limited by tunnel vision. Try to solve both problems. Did tunnel vision affect your solutions?

EXHIBIT 7.5   AVOIDING TUNNEL VISION IN PROBLEM SOLVING

Problem 1
Six ordinary drinking glasses are standing in a row. The first three are empty, and the next three are full of water. By handling and moving only one glass, you can change the arrangement so that no empty glass is next to another empty glass, and no full glass is next to another full glass. How can you do this?

Problem 2
Draw four straight lines that pass through all nine dots without picking up your pencil and without retracing any lines.

Previous Commitments

Another barrier to effective decision-making is commitment to an idea or position resulting from previous decisions. On a personal level, we are all familiar with situations in which a course of action is not working, but where we are unsure whether withdrawal or persistence is the best solution. An obvious example is being placed on hold on the telephone; you may soon become uncertain about how long to wait before hanging up. An investor deciding between selling or buying a stock after a significant price drop is faced with a similar dilemma.

Decisions are rarely made in isolation and without an impact on other decisions. Instead, decisions usually occur in interrelated sequences. Perhaps the most difficult decisions a person ever makes are not choices about what to do in a single incident, but choices about the fate of an entire sequence of decisions or a course of action. Research indicates that people who feel personally responsible for a bad decision often tend to commit additional resources to the previously selected alternative.[10] If you purchased a used car that was a lemon, for example, you may continue to spend money to repair the car in order to justify your initial decision. In essence, good money follows bad in an attempt to salvage the original investment.

Escalation situations appear to have three common factors.[11] First, the situations involve some loss or costs that have resulted from an original course of action (e.g., the initial decision to invest in the stock market). Second, the predicaments are not one-time affairs, but dilemmas involving ongoing courses of action and decision sequences (e.g., preparing for retirement by investing in a variety of stocks). Third, simple withdrawal is not an obvious solution to the problem, either because withdrawal involves substantial costs (e.g., selling out means a loss) or because persistence holds at least some prospect of eventual gain (e.g., the market is likely to rebound by the end of the year).

Some of the worst losses suffered by corporations are attributable, in part, to continued expenditures in escalation situations (e.g., large banks extending non-performing loans to some financially shaky Latin American countries). The important implication is that the escalating commitment to a particular decision makes it increasingly difficult to evaluate other alternatives objectively and to change the course of action already initiated by that choice.

Implicit Favorites

Bounded rationality suggests that a decision maker selects the first satisfactory alternative and then stops searching for additional solutions. However, research indicates that many people select a favorite alternative early in the decision-making process and continue to evaluate additional solutions.[12] Subsequent alternatives are distorted perceptually and evaluated using decision criteria that emphasize the superiority of the favorite solution. Information is therefore processed in such a way that selecting the **implicit favorite** is virtually guaranteed.

For example, a study of the process used by students graduating from MIT's Sloan School of Management to select a job found that most students rapidly identified the job they most wanted but continued the job search even after receiving an offer from the desired company. Additional jobs were used to compare and justify the implicit favorite alternative as the best possible selection. Eighty-seven percent of the students studied eventually chose their implicit favorites. The findings of this study suggest that individuals may attempt (perhaps unconsciously) to create the appearance of rational decision making when in fact they are simply rationalizing irrational decisions.

Lack of Creativity

We often associate creativity with artists, inventors, authors, and musicians and assume that such people have an innate genius that makes them different from us. Creativity, however, is not a rare gift possessed by a few individuals. Most people possess creative ability that can be developed through training and practice.[13]

Creativity is the ability to generate ideas that are both new and useful. Such ability is an obvious requirement for managerial effectiveness and is especially important in making nonprogrammed decisions. Unfortunately, this particular skill rarely receives adequate attention within organizations. There are several reasons for this neglect. First, organizational policies and procedures usually are designed to promote order, consistency, and uniformity. The nature and climate of the organization itself may exert pressure inhibiting a manager's willingness to experiment or play with new ideas. Second, managerial work is fast-paced and action-oriented. Creativity, on the other hand, requires a significant investment of time, effort, and energy. Many managers simply do not have or make time for creative activities. Finally, most people do not understand creativity and therefore ignore rather than encourage or reinforce it.

The creative process involves four basic steps or stages: preparation, incubation, inspiration, and validation.[14] Each of these steps is described briefly below.

Preparation

A creative decision or discovery is not something that just happens. Rather, creativity is the result of hard work and effort. A decision maker must read, observe, study, collect data, solicit opinions, and analyze evidence. This information also must be assembled and organized in such a way that the problem or decision situation is thoroughly understood.

Incubation

Incubation follows preparation and usually is described as a period of relaxation of conscious effort. In other words, the decision maker stops thinking solely and intensely about the decision at hand. This may involve the redirection of effort to another task or to a completely unrelated activity (e.g., playing tennis or going swimming). The information obtained in the "preparation" step is allowed to "simmer" in the mind of the decision maker.

Inspiration

Inspiration occurs when an idea, solution, or decision alternative first enters the decision maker's mind. You may have experienced, for example, the "flash of insight" that brings an idea to your consciousness. Such insight typically is the result of repeated hard work (e.g., rewriting a report several times). It is in this step, then, that the decision maker realizes the "payoff" for the effort expended in preparation and incubation.

Validation

In this final step, the decision alternative or solution is tested for its usefulness and applicability. A manager, for example, may "bounce an idea off" his subordinates, co-workers, and superiors in order to obtain feedback. This process of sharing and discussing helps to "fine tune" the new solution and make it workable.

3M

As a means of remaining competitive in the international marketplace, many contemporary organizations are working to encourage and facilitate the creative process. 3M Corporation, for example, has long been recognized as a leader in innovative product development and production.[15] The following simple rules are key elements in 3M's approach to creativity.

1. *Permit everyone to innovate.* When a 3M employee comes up with a product idea, he or she recruits an action team to develop it. Salaries and promotions are tied to the product's progress. The employee has a chance to run his or her own product group or division someday. If an idea cannot find a home in one of 3M's divisions, an employee can devote 15 percent of his or her time to prove it is workable. For those who need development money, as many as ninety Genesis grants of $50,000 are awarded each year.

2. *Avoid punishments for innovations that fail.* By encouraging experimentation and risk taking, there are more chances for a new-product success. Divisions must derive 25 percent of sales from products introduced in the past five years.

3. *Stay close and be sensitive to the needs of employees and customers.* Division managers are expected to know each employee's first name. Researchers, marketers, and managers visit with customers and routinely invite them to help brainstorm product ideas.

Other companies such as Rubbermaid, Hewlett-Packard, Dow Corning, Merck, General Electric, Johnson & Johnson, and Black & Decker are also successful in fostering innovation throughout the organization.

INDIVIDUAL VERSUS GROUP DECISION MAKING

Do individuals or groups make better decisions? The answer to this question is, "It depends!" In some cases, individual choices are preferable. On other occasions, a group may make a decision more effectively than an individual. We now examine the advantages, disadvantages, and appropriate conditions for group decision making.

Advantages of Group Decision Making

Group decision making is an integral part of daily life in most organizations. Committees, task forces, and ad hoc groups are frequently assigned to identify and recommend decision alternatives, or, in some cases, actually to make important decisions. The greater total knowledge of a group is one important reason managers often use groups to make decisions. In essence, a group is a tool that can focus the experience and expertise of several people on a particular problem or situation. The combined knowledge of an accountant, a marketing specialist, and a financial planner, for example, clearly is superior to that of most individuals. The varied backgrounds, training, and expertise of group members also provide different perspectives or approaches to a decision situation. Interaction among group members helps overcome tunnel vision by providing the opportunity to view the problem in more than one way. Similarly, group interaction can stimulate more and better decision alternatives (i.e., the synergistic effect of $1 + 1 = 3$) than could be produced by the same individuals working alone.

People tend to have greater acceptance of and satisfaction with a decision when they are involved in making that decision. Group decision making provides a means of achieving this participation and increased acceptance. For example, a group of six managers probably would find a training program that they had helped select more acceptable than one pushed on them by the personnel office. In addition, the implementation of a decision is affected by the degree of acceptance among group members. People will better understand and be more committed to a decision in which they have had a say than to one made for them. As a result, such a decision is more likely to be implemented successfully.

Disadvantages of Group Decision Making

Perhaps the most obvious disadvantage of group decision making is the time required to make a decision. The time needed for a group discussion and the associated arguing, compromising, and selecting of a decision alternative can be considerable. Thus, group decision making should be avoided when speed and efficiency are the primary considerations.

A second disadvantage is domination of the group discussion by an individual or individuals. Such dominance by a few participants can stifle other group members' willingness to participate and thus cause decision alternatives to be ignored or overlooked. Also, the dominant individuals' suggestions may be accepted without adequate discussion or debate.

Groups can exert tremendous social pressure on individuals to conform to established or expected patterns of behavior. This pressure can be a formidable problem in the group decision-making process. A newly hired supervisor, for example, may quickly learn that sticking together is an important expectation among all plant supervisors. He may have serious reservations about a decision alternative proposed by another supervisor in a meeting but go along in the interest of maintaining group solidarity and togetherness. In this instance, pressure to conform to the expectation of cohesiveness might inhibit the critical evaluation of a decision alternative.

Intense pressure within a group for conformity and cohesiveness can lead over time to a phenomenon known as groupthink. **Groupthink** is "a deterioration of mental efficiency, reality testing, and moral judgment" that can negatively affect the quality of a group decision.[16] A group experiencing this effect may not examine a full range of decision alternatives, may discount or avoid information that threatens the group's preferred choice, and may ignore possible roadblocks to a decision. Eight conditions are normally associated with groupthink:

1. An illusion of invulnerability, or group-wide overconfidence, that hides risks and may lead to unrealistic optimism.
2. Collective rationalization, or group-wide efforts to rationalize negative information and discount warnings.
3. An illusion of morality, or a group-wide belief that the group is inherently moral and does what is right.
4. The stereotyping of those outside the group as weak, incompetent, and/or evil.
5. Direct pressure is applied to any member who disagrees with the group's illusions, stereotypes, commitments, etc.

6. Self-censorship, or members tending to be silent when they see their views as differing from the group's view.

7. An illusion of unanimity, or an illusion that everyone in the group is in agreement.

8. *Mindguarding,* or the attempts of certain self-appointed group members to protect the leader, members, or group itself from negative information or feedback.

The groupthink phenomenon has been used to explain numerous group decisions that have resulted in fiascoes.[17] Examples of such decisions include the Kennedy administration's decision to initiate the Bay of Pigs invasion, the Watergate cover-up, and NASA's decision to launch the Challenger space shuttle. Most people who watched the explosion of the Challenger on January 28, 1986, later listened as scientists and engineers described the failure of the rubber O-ring seals that led to the space shuttle disaster. Many observers consequently saw the tragedy as a failure of modern technology. Another dimension of the incident, however, raises important questions about how the launch decision itself was made.

In his testimony before the House Committee on Science, Space, and Technology, NASA official Lawrence Mulloy concluded that the space agency "got into a groupthink situation" when it decided to launch the shuttle despite concerns raised by some individuals about the safety of such an action. Deputy NASA administrator William Graham added to the groupthink hypothesis: "As an activity becomes more successful . . . , it certainly becomes more difficult to challenge and to raise questions."[18] Group pressures to ignore threatening evidence at Morton-Thiokol, builder of the failed booster rockets, and to achieve a successful launch at NASA may well have been critical elements in the shuttle disaster.

Finally, group decisions often are more extreme (e.g., more risky or conservative) than decisions that might have been made by the individual members. This tendency, called **group polarization,** essentially involves the accentuation or exaggeration, through group discussion, of the initial positions that individual members bring to the group. For example, when group members are initially somewhat inclined to take a risk, the opportunity to discuss and diffuse responsibility for a decision to all participants may encourage an even riskier decision by the group. This polarizing effect specifically is manifested in the risky shift (a more risky decision by a group than by an individual) and the cautious shift (a more cautious decision by a group than by an individual). A group decision thus can be substantively different from an individual decision because of this polarizing effect, even if both decisions are based on identical facts and information.

Group decision making is an inevitable part of organizational life. A group decision per se is not necessarily always better or more effective than an individual decision. The advantages and disadvantages of group decision making are summarized in Exhibit 7.6. The group decision-making process should be used in appropriate

EXHIBIT 7.6   GROUP DECISION MAKING

ADVANTAGES	DISADVANTAGES
Greater Total Knowledge	Time
Different Perspectives and Approaches	Domination by an Individual or Individuals
Increased Acceptance	Social Pressure
	Groupthink
	Group Polarization

situations and managed so that the advantages are maximized and the disadvantages minimized. Specific techniques for managing the group decision-making process are discussed in Chapter 9.

PARTICIPATION IN DECISION MAKING

In Chapter 1, we discussed the managerial revolution presently taking place in the United States and other industrialized countries. No single issue or concept reflects the changes in managerial philosophy and practice more than participation in decision making. The current emphasis on participation has occurred partly because of interest in the management philosophy and techniques that sparked Japan's economic miracle (see Chapter 1). Decision making by consensus, or *ringisei,* is one hallmark characteristic of Japanese management.

According to the *ringisei* method of group decision making:

> . . . changes in procedures and routines, tactics, and even strategies are originated by those who are directly concerned with those changes. The final decision is made at the top level after an elaborate examination of the proposal through successively higher levels in the management hierarchy that results in acceptance or rejection of a decision only through consensus at every echelon. The decision process is best characterized as bottom up instead of top down, which is the essential characteristic of the decision-making process in a U.S. corporation.[20]

The acceptance, commitment, and sharing of responsibility that *ringisei* promotes are key elements in the formula for organizational effectiveness in Japan.

The success of the Japanese and the inevitable comparisons between Eastern and Western decision-making processes have produced an increased willingness on the part of managers and executives to use participation in traditionally autocratic organizations. Today in magazines, newspapers, and on television, corporate executives frequently extol the virtues of more effectively using human resources through such participative methods as quality circles, worker involvement groups, and project teams.

FORD MOTOR COMPANY

The climate in many organizations seems to be changing from "I'm the boss and *I* will decide" to "Let's see if *we* can work together to make this decision." One example of such a change occurred at the Ford Motor Company.[21]

At the beginning of the 1980s, Ford was losing billions of dollars. Although Ford's troubles were overshadowed by Chrysler's brush with bankruptcy, the company was facing serious problems in 1980 and 1981. To deal with the crisis, Ford management went on simultaneous cost-cutting and quality-improvement campaigns in which worker involvement teams were used at every level and in every area of the company.

The company closed fifteen plants worldwide and cut 49,800 United States blue-collar jobs. These cuts went hand-in-hand with a drastic change in Ford's culture. Once a nearly militaristic, top-down organizational structure, it now became team-oriented and participative. Ford and the United Auto Workers established what may still be the most extensive worker participation program in a major, unionized company. Thousands of teams of workers and supervisors at Ford's plants and depots met weekly to deal with production, quality, and work-environment problems. The participation process at Ford was labeled Employee Involvement (EI).

Plant managers reported that EI had a huge impact on quality and cited improvements in warranty repairs above 40 percent for many products. An independent research firm reported that a survey of sixty-five hundred buyers of 1984 Ford cars showed that "things gone wrong" had declined 55 percent since 1980. Employee participation also helped to reduce production costs by providing a mechanism for employees to suggest cost-cutting changes in equipment, production flow, and work procedures.

Ford executives worked to involve employees in the decision-making process. For example, executives started listening to design teams, which advised styling cars based on aerodynamics. Ford first tested the new look by altering its classic Thunderbird. Introduced in 1983, the sporty, "aerodynamic" T-Bird was a big hit that helped to revitalize the financially troubled company. The Taurus, Ford's biggest triumph, was designed by a team of stylists, engineers, and manufacturing employees working together to develop the best possible car. Ford even involved assembly workers, customers, and the competition. When it came time to produce the new cars, workers had authority to stop the line if quality was being compromised. In fact, the Taurus debut was delayed several months as Ford worked out quality glitches. Ford called the development process "Team Taurus," and it became the model for how Ford automobiles are developed today.

Participation versus Delegation

The example of participation at Ford helps clarify the distinction between participation and delegation. **Participative decision making** is defined as "joint decision making."[22] This definition emphasizes a shared decision-making process that can occur between a supervisor and a subordinate, within a single group, or among many groups of subordinates. Participative decision making differs from delegation in that **delegation** implies only the assignment of specific duties or responsibilities to an individual. The result of delegation is not a sharing in common with others but rather a division of labor usually determined by someone in the organizational hierarchy. Participation, on the other hand, suggests (1) a shared or mutual responsibility for the decision-making process, and (2) involvement by the individuals or parties who will be directly affected by a decision.

Putting Participation to Work

Participative decision making means different things to different people. To one manager, participation may mean listening to employee complaints. To another, it may mean giving one or two key individuals an opportunity to provide input on an important decision. To other managers, participation means that all employees in a department or organizational unit have an equal voice in decisions (perhaps through a democratic vote).[23] No single approach to participative decision making is best, nor is one type of participation most effective in all situations.

A manager can elect to make a decision alone (an individual decision) or choose to use one of several participative methods like those described next.[24]

INTERNATIONAL DIMENSION
Scandinavian Airline Systems

In 1981, Jan Carlzon was appointed president of Scandinavian Airline Systems (SAS), which was losing $17 million per year. After a single year of Carlzon's leadership, SAS was earning $54 million.

The core of the SAS story, and the central theme of Carlzon's management approach, is a strong belief in the ability and innate integrity of the people on the front line. Carlzon acted on the premise that the people who actually do the work of an organization are best able to think, make decisions, and act in the organization's, and the customer's, best interest.

When Carlzon took over the airline in the midst of a worldwide airline recession, he determined that the course of salvation lay in making SAS "the businessperson's airline." The company's assets, he reasoned, were not airplanes but the millions of satisfied customers on those airplanes. In SAS's case, however, there were not enough of those satisfied customers in the seats. There was clearly room for service improvement.

Carlzon moved decision-making responsibility for serving the customer down several levels, from middle managers who seldom made contact with the traveling public to the front-line people—flight attendants, ticketing clerks, and customer service representatives—who made the contacts minute-by-minute in the "moments of truth." SAS customers, Carlzon told everyone from baggage handlers to executives, judged the airline on the quality of those contacts. If the experience was positive, they would fly SAS again. If negative, they would take their business to competitors who treated them better.

Moving decision-making responsibility down in the organization created a major cultural change for both managers and front-line employees. Carlzon himself took the lead in communicating the message that the front-line people were directly in charge of satisfying the customer's needs. SAS managers' new role was to assist the people on the front lines, not to dictate to them, in the accomplishment of that task. "If you're not serving the customer," Carlzon told his managers flatly, "your job is to serve those who are."

The customer-driven and decentralized decision-making approach at SAS has been extremely successful and has become a model for other airlines and industries as diverse as retailing, manufacturing, and banking.

Questions
What barriers may have been encountered within SAS during the effort to decentralize decision-making authority?

What cultural (i.e., Scandanivian, European) factors may have hindered or helped the decentralization of decision-making authority?

SOURCE: "Scandinavian Management—A Look At Our Future?" *Management Review,* July 1988, 44–47.

Participation in work decisions (PWD)

Participation in work decisions includes programs and processes through which workers influence decisions about the work itself. This form of participation tends to be formal, direct, and long-term. The Employee Involvement (EI) program at Ford is an example of this form of participation. The influence of workers is high and they typically focus on how work is organized, what is done, and who does what. Employees may have veto power over certain decisions or, in some cases, even make the final decisions. Employees may also have considerable influence on pay and other personnel decisions.

PLUM CREEK

Management at Plum Creek sawmill in Belgrade, Montana,[25] instituted PWD several years ago when worker discontent at the mill led management to consider new ways of working with employees. Today, when plant manager Dave Morgan hears about an equipment break-down, he asks employees how *they* are solving the problem and making decisions.

The one hundred fifty employees, in teams of three to eighteen, not only maintain equipment, but also decide by consensus who to hire, what jobs to work on a particular day, and the kinds of lumber to produce. "We tell our teams, 'Here are some expected goals. It's your job to figure out how you're going to do that. If you need help, management will be glad to help. It's not important to us whether you do x job or y job. What we want is a level of quality, safety, productivity.'"

Consultative participation (CP)

Consultative participation is similar to participation in work decisions in that it is also formal, direct, and long-term. However, CP involves a lesser degree of employee influence and involvement. Employees may be requested to share their opinions and input, but they do not have veto or complete decision-making power.

Scanlon plans and quality circles are examples of consultative participation programs. A Scanlon plan is a method of distributing monetary bonuses to employees for productivity-enhancing suggestions and innovative work methods. Quality circles are small groups of employees that identify and analyze work-related problems and formulate recommended solutions for consideration by management. Unlike Scanlon plans, quality circles do not typically provide a monetary bonus or incentive to participants.

Short-term participation (STP)

Short-term participation is characterized by programs and processes of limited duration, ranging from a single group meeting to training sessions of several days. For example, a marketing manager may bring staff members together during a two-day retreat to formulate a strategy for attracting new clients. Similarly, an office staff might meet with a manager or executive to review and improve work procedures. Like participation in work decisions, STP is formal, direct, and focused on the work itself; workers also have significant influence in the decision-making process. Time (temporal) duration is the principal difference between STP and PWD.

Informal participation (IP)

Many organizations do not have formally established participation programs or groups involved in the decision-making process. However, participative decision making may still occur informally through the interpersonal relationships that exist between managers and employees. For example, the opinions and beliefs expressed during an informal discussion in the break room may influence a manager's decision concerning the scheduling of work assignments. Although not as systematic or formal as the other forms of participation already described, IP still enables employees to have an impact on decisions that directly affect them.

Representative participation (RP)

Representative participation is formal, indirect, and of medium-to-low influence. Through RP, employees participate indirectly through representatives elected to a governing council or through representatives on the board of directors. The placement of a union official on the board of directors at Chrysler Corporation is an example of representative participation. The power of a representative can vary from having a vote on the board of directors to a purely advisory voice on a worker's council.

Representative participation has been practiced for many years in various European countries. Worker councils in West Germany, for example, exert considerable influence on the decisions of private corporations and government agencies. Similarly, elected representatives have played important roles in organizations throughout Eastern Europe, the Soviet Union, and the People's Republic of China.

Employee ownership (EO)

Employee ownership is a formal and indirect approach to participation. EO is formal in that the employee, as a part owner of the enterprise, has as much right to participate as any stockholder; it is indirect in that most such organizations are operated conventionally by managers who make both daily and strategic decisions. Employees can influence the decisions made by management through mechanisms such as stockholder meetings and board of directors elections.

Some employees in these organizations may participate directly, but the typical employee does not. The focus of participation can be a wide range of topics and is not restricted to the work itself. The level of influence is high, although employees may not always exercise this control. Many companies such as Avis, Procter & Gamble, Texaco, U.S. West, Polaroid, J. C. Penny, and Epic Healthcare have instituted Employee Stock Ownership Plans (ESOPs) as one form of employee ownership.

AVIS

Avis has established a broad-based involvement program that provides examples of several forms of participation: employee ownership, representation, and direct involvement in the management of the firm.[26] Avis implemented its ESOP in the late 1980s when employees bought the company from Westray Capital Corporation for $1.75 billion. Joseph V. Vittoria, chairman of Avis, now works for 12,700 employee shareholders who have a long-term investment in the success of the company. Vittoria spends three or four days each month visiting Avis offices around the country briefing employees on business developments and answering their questions. Such visits are just a small part of an elaborate system that gives Avis workers a significant say in how their company is managed.

At the heart of the system are employee participation groups (EPGs), consisting of representatives from every area of the company, from mechanics to rental agents. EPGs, established in each city where Avis has an office, meet once a month. Employees are encouraged to suggest ways of improving customer service and running the business more effectively. EPG representatives also meet frequently at the zone and district levels to monitor the process and carry suggestions throughout the system. A national meeting of EPG members with Vittoria and other managers is held annually at the company's headquarters in Garden City, New York. Avis employees thus have an unusual ability to influence management decisions through these forms of participation and the rights granted to them through stock ownership.

The various forms of participation discussed in this section can have different impacts on organizational outcomes such as performance and satisfaction.[27] For example, empirical evidence indicates that informal participation (IP) and employee ownership (EO) are effective in terms of increasing both performance and employee satisfaction. Participation in work decisions (PWD) has also produced relatively consistent and positive improvements on performance; increases in satisfaction have not been demonstrated consistently. Short term participation (STP) appears to have a negligible affect on both performance and satisfaction. Each form of participation and its impact on organizational outcomes is summarized in Exhibit 7.7.

Is participation effective? As the results reported above indicate, the answer is "it depends." Participation can take many forms, and the cost/benefit constraints, existing technology and culture, and criteria of effectiveness in a given situation will determine which particular form should be selected and used. A manager must be aware of these conditions when deciding to make a decision using an individual, group, or participative method.

EXHIBIT 7.7   FORMS OF PARTICIPATION

FORM	DESCRIPTION	LEVEL OF INFLUENCE	IMPACT
Participation in Work Decisions (PWD)	Formal, direct, and long-term involvement in decisions about the work itself. Employees may have veto power and responsibility for final decisions.	High	Increases performances. Mixed impact on satisfaction.
Consultative Participation (CP)	Formal, direct, and long-term input in the decision-making process. Employees share opinions and provide input.	Medium to Low	Research findings are inconclusive for both performance and satisfaction.
Short-Term Participation (STP)	Formal, direct, and short-term involvement in decisions about the work itself. Employees may have veto power and responsibility for final decisions.	High	No impact on performance or satisfaction.
Informal participation (IP)	Informal, indirect influence through interpersonal relationships.	Variable	Increases both performance and satisfaction.
Employee Ownership (EO)	Formal, indirect involvement as a part owner of an enterprise through mechanisms such as stockholder meetings and board of directors elections.	High	Increases both performance and satisfaction.
Representative Participation (RP)	Formal, indirect influence through representatives on worker councils, boards of directors, and/or governing councils.	Medium to Low	No impact on performance or satisfaction.

Adapted from: John L. Cotton, David A. Vollrath, Kirk L. Froggatt, Mark L. Lengnick-Hall, Kenneth R. Jennings, "Employee Participation: Diverse Forms and Different Outcomes," *Academy of Management Review*, Vol. 13, No. 1 (1988): 8–22.

ETHICAL DILEMMA
Burroughs Wellcome Co.

In 1986, Burroughs Wellcome Co. officers stood shoulder-to-shoulder with federal officials at a Washington, D.C., press conference proudly announcing the first major breakthrough against acquired immune deficiency syndrome (AIDS)—Wellcome's life-prolonging drug AZT. Three years later, activists in San Francisco, London, and New York staged demonstrations attacking Burroughs Wellcome and its parent, London-based Wellcome PLC, as corporate extortionists. Five AIDS activists chained themselves to a balcony inside the New York Stock Exchange, sounded a horn to drown out the opening bell and unfurled a banner that read "Sell Wellcome." Protesters also invaded pharmacies and pasted other Wellcome products with stickers reading "AIDS Profiteer."

The company was accused by activists and some health-care providers of reaping unseemly profits from AIDS patients and federally funded Medicaid by keeping the price of AZT—about $8,000 for a one-year supply—at a level that made it one of the most expensive drugs ever sold. "Wellcome is involved in shameless profiteering," contended Curtis Morriss, administrator of the infectious disease clinic at Atlanta's charity hospital, Grady Memorial. "They ought to be ashamed."

Particularly galling to Wellcome's many critics was the fact that the AZT profits were something of a windfall for the company. Wellcome had acquired AZT years ago; however, it had *not* (1) developed the compound; (2) discovered its effectiveness against AIDS-type vuruses; (3) ascertained its effectiveness against AIDS itself; or (4) conducted the first human tests. Much of that work had been done by other scientists, some at the National Institutes of Health with federal financing. Driven in part by AZT, Wellcome's profits more than doubled between 1986 and 1988 to $198 million. Moreover, a recent study confirming that AZT helps people who are in-

fected with the lethal virus but not yet showing symptoms could mean that the Food and Drug Administration will soon authorize the compound for sale to hundreds of thousands of people rather than to just the tens of thousands who show symptoms. At the current price, Wellcome could generate $1.2 billion of AZT sales in 1992, with about half of that amount flowing to the bottom line as net profit.

In its defense, Wellcome pointed out that most of its dividends go to charity and much of its retained profits are used for research and development. The company is 75 percent owned by the Wellcome Trust, a charitable organization that has spent millions of dollars aiding pharmaceutical research and other causes. Twenty-five percent of its earnings are paid out to the trust. Wellcome also invests heavily in research and development of experimental drugs for a wide range of diseases, including cancer, sickle cell anemia, and multiple sclerosis.

Some analysts believe that Wellcome's gross profit margins on AZT (70 percent to 80 percent) are high but in line with what other companies achieve on major new drugs. High returns are needed to finance research and development and pay for the many drugs that never reach the market. Wellcome's main defense has been that it needed to recoup its upfront investment in AZT, which included paying for a major clinical trial in which the drug was given free to as many as five thousand AIDS patients, and spending $80 million on a new plant and raw materials.

"There is a myth out there that we're robber barons, ripping people off," contends David Barry, vice-president for medical affairs and research and development of the Wellcome unit based in Atlanta. "It would be theoretically possible for us to give away all our drug," Barry says. "Everyone would get it for a while, and then we'd go bankrupt."

(Continued on next page)

(Continued from p. 223)

Demonstrations and talks with activists notwithstanding, he said there will be no "knee-jerk" concessions on AZT's price. He cautioned that Wellcome's potential bonanza may be offset by several recent studies suggesting the drug may be just as effective at half the dose, thus cutting the annual cost to the patient to $4,000 or less. "If there were a decision to lower price," Dr. Barry said, "it would be on a rational, quantitative basis."

What started out as a triumph for Wellcome has turned into a public relations disaster and sparked a raging debate that raises troubling questions about medical ethics, government policy, and the role of private enterprise in drug development and the decisions made by corporate executives.

Questions
Was Wellcome's pricing strategy unethical? What ethical questions or concerns about decision making does the Wellcome case raise?

SOURCE: "Burroughs Wellcome Reaps Profits, Outrage from Its AIDS Drug," *The Wall Street Journal,* 15 September 1989.

DECISION MAKING: CONCLUSIONS

Decision making, the process of selecting among alternatives, is an integral part of a manager's work. In fact, exercising judgment and making decisions constitute the essence of managerial activity. Skill as a decision maker, therefore, is a distinguishing characteristic of most successful managers.

Decision making is a crucial component in the overall problem-solving process. When approaching a problem situation, a manager should (1) identify and define the problem correctly; (2) search for and develop acceptable alternatives; (3) evaluate and compare alternatives; (4) make a choice; (5) implement the choice; and (6) monitor, review, and follow up. Managers who systematically follow these guidelines, within the constraints of time, information, and ability, increase the likelihood that they will make sound decisions and effectively solve problems.

A manager should remember that the ideal approach to decision making portrayed in the rational-economic model is not always used in practice. Although this model suggests that people are rational and seek to maximize outcomes, human limitations make it impossible to achieve complete rationality. Instead, people often exhibit bounded rationality and *satisfice* by selecting satisfactory rather than optimum alternatives. The fast-paced and action-oriented nature of managerial work suggests that satisficing is more prevalent than maximizing in many organizations.

The inability to achieve complete rationality is an important factor affecting the decision-making process. Other barriers such as tunnel vision, previous commitments, implicit favorites, and the lack of creativity also hinder an individual's ability to make informed and successful decisions. A manager who understands these difficulties can attempt to minimize their negative impact on the decision-making process. For example, recognizing the potentially harmful affects of escalating commitment to a previous decision may lead an executive to change methods of evaluating decision alternatives. The executive may consciously seek out diverse and independent (and hopefully more objective) opinions before making a final decision. Or, to overcome tunnel vision, a production manager may consult with the marketing, accounting, and finance departments to obtain a broader perspective on a decision alternative.

A decision managers frequently make is how best to make a decision—individually or with the assistance of a group. Group decisions have a number of specific advantages (greater total knowledge, a variety of perspectives, synergy, increased acceptance by subordinates) and disadvantages (time required, domination of group discussion by an individual or individuals, social pressure, groupthink, group polarization). A decision maker, therefore, should carefully analyze a situation to determine the most appropriate method. In addition, the decision-making process must be managed so the advantages are maximized and the disadvantages minimized.

Finally, the widespread use of participative decision making reflects the major changes occurring today in organizations. Participation is not a panacea for the ills of all modern organizations. However, it can significantly affect (1) the performance and satisfaction of employees, and (2) the quality of decisions that are made. As a manager, you need to identify participative decision-making situations in order to realize these important advantages. You must also learn to select the appropriate form or method of participation to meet the demands of a particular situation and to achieve maximum effectiveness.

QUESTIONS FOR REVIEW AND DISCUSSION

1. Define decision making.
2. What is the difference between decision making and problem solving?
3. Compare and contrast the rational-economic and administrative models of decision making.
4. How does bounded rationality affect the decision-making process?
5. Describe four heuristics and behavioral biases that can affect a manager's decisions.
6. What can a manager do to overcome the effects of an implicit favorite?

7. What are the steps in the creative process?
8. What are the advantages and disadvantages of group decision making compared to individual decision making?
9. What is groupthink? What can a manager do to overcome the effects of groupthink?
10. What is the difference between participative decision making and delegation?
11. Describe the various forms of participative decision making.

REFERENCES

1. Henry Mintzberg, *The Nature of Managerial Work* (New York: Harper and Row, 1973).
2. Peter Drucker, *The Effective Executive* (New York: Harper and Row, 1966), 143.
3. Herbert Simon, *The Science of Management Decisions*, 2nd ed. (Englewood Cliffs N.J.: Prentice-Hall, 1977).
4. Simon, *Models of Man* (New York: Wiley, 1957).
5. Ibid., 198.
6. Daniel Kahneman and Amos Tversky, "A Subjective Probability: A Judgment of Representativeness," *Cognitive Psychology*, Vol. 3 (1972): 430–454.
7. A. Tversky and D. Kahneman, "Availability: A Heuristic for Judging Frequency and Probability," *Cognitive Psychology* Vol. 5 (1973): 207–232.
8. A. Tversky and D. Kahneman, "Judgment under Uncertainty: Heuristics and Biases," *Science*, Vol. 185 (1974): 1124–1131.
9. Paul Slovic, Baruch Fischhoff, and Sarah C. Lichtenstein, "Behavioral Decision Theory," *Annual Review of Psychology*, Vol. 28 (1977): 1–39.

10. Barry M. Staw, "The Escalation of Commitment to a Course of Action," *Academy of Management Review*, Vol. 6, No. 4 (1981): 577–587.
11. Barry M. Staw and J. Ross, "Behavior in Escalation Situations: Antecedents, Prototypes, and Solutions," in L. L. Cummings and B. W. Staw, eds., *Research in Organizational Behavior* (Greenwich, Conn.: JAI Press, 1987), 39–78.
12. P. O. Soelberg, "Decision Making," *Industrial Management Review*, Vol. 8 (1967): 19–29; D. J. Power and R. J. Aldag, "Soelberg's Job Search and Choice Model: A Clarification, Review, and Critique," *Academy of Management Review*, Vol. 10, No. 1 (1985): 48–58.
13. D. J. Treffinger and J. C. Gowan, "An Updated Representative List of Methods and Educational Programs for Stimulating Creativity," *Journal of Creative Behavior*, Vol. 5 (1971): 127–139.
14. C. Patrick, *What Is Creative Thinking?* (New York: Philosophical Library, 1955); T. A. Matherly and R. E. Goldsmith, "The Two Faces of Creativity," *Business*

Horizons, Vol. 28, No. 5 (1985): 8–11; E. T. Smith, et. al., "Are You Creative?" *Business Week* (30 September 1985): 80–84; Teresa M. Amabile, "A Model of Creativity and Innovation in Organizations," in Staw and L. L. Cummings, eds., *Research in Organizational Behavior* (Greenwich: JAI Press, 1988), 123–168; Charlene Marner Solomon, "What an Idea: Creativity Training," *Personnel Journal* (May 1990): 65–71.

15. Russell Mitchell, "Masters of Innovation: How 3M Keeps New Products Coming," *Business Week* (10 April 1989): 58–63; Joe Flower, "The 3M Credo—Innovation: Where Do You Get That Spark," *Healthcare Forum*, Vol. 29, No. 4 (July/August 1986): 8–11; Sophie Wilkinson, "Insight Into Inhouse Innovation," *Chemical Week* (27 December 1989): 8–58.

16. I. L. Janis, *Victims of Groupthink; A Psychological Study of Foreign-Policy Decisions and Fiascoes* (Boston: Houghton Mifflin, 1972), 9.

17. Glen Whyte, "Groupthink Reconsidered," *Academy of Management Review*, Vol. 14, No. 1 (1989): 40–56.

18. Testimony before the House Committee on Science, Space, and Technology, June 17, 1986. (U.S. Documents Y4, Sci. 2:99–137+).

19. H. Lamm and D. G. Meyers, "Group-Induced Polarization of Attitudes and Behavior," in L. Berkowitz, ed., *Advances in Experimental Social Psychology*, Vol. 11 (1978).

20. S. P. Sethi, C. L. Namiki, and C. L. Swanson, *The False Promise of the Japanese Miracle: Illusions and Realities of the Japanese Management System* (Boston: Pitman, 1984), 34.

21. Peter Yates, "What's Creating an Industrial Miracle at Ford," *Business Week* (30 July 1984): 80–81; James B. Treece, et al., "Can Ford Stay On Top?" *Business Week* (28 September 1987): 78–86; Alex Taylor, "Why Fords Sell Like Big Macs," *Fortune* (21 November 1988): 122–125; Patricia P. Mishne, "A Passion For Perfection," *Manufacturing Engineering*, Vol. 101, No. 5 (November 1988): 46–58; Taylor, "Caution: Bumps Ahead at Ford," *Fortune* (18 December 1989): 93–96.

22. E. A. Locke and D. M. Schweiger, "Participation in Decision-Making: One More Look," in B. Staw, ed., *Research in Organizational Behavior* (Greenwich, Conn.: JAI Press, 1979), 265–340.

23. W. Woodworth, "Managing from Below," *Journal of Management*, Vol. 12, No. 3 (1986): 391–402.

24. John L. Cotton, David A. Vollrath, Kirk L. Froggatt, Mark L. Lengnick-Hall, Kenneth R. Jennings, "Employee Participation: Diverse Forms and Different Outcomes," *Academy of Management Review*, Vol. 13, No. 1 (1988): 8–22; Katherine I. Miller and Peter R. Monge, "Participation, Satisfaction, and Productivity: A Meta-Analytic Review," *Academy of Management Journal*, Vol. 29, No. 4 (1986): 727–753.

25. Tom Peters, "Employees Open the Way to a Management Revolution," *On Achieving Excellence*, Vol. 4, No. 10 (1989): 2–3.

26. Christopher Farrell and John Hoerr, "Employee Ownership: Is It Good for Your Company?" *Business Week* (15 May 1989): 116–123; David Kirkpatrick, "How the Workers Run Avis Better," *Fortune* (5 December 1988): 103–114; Corey Rosen, "Values of Ownership," *Executive Excellence*, Vol. 6, No. 2 (February 1989): 14–15.

27. Cotton et. al., op. cit., 16–17.

CASE 7.1 *Changing the shuttle launch decision process*

DONALD D. WHITE *University of Arkansas*

Date: January 28, 1986
Time: 11:38 A.M. eastern standard time
Event: Space shuttle Challenger lifts off from Cape Canaveral.

Exactly one minute and fourteen seconds later, NASA's worst fears were realized when the Challenger

SOURCE: "NASA's Challenge: Ending Isolation at the Top," *Fortune*, 12 May 1986, 26–28; "NASA Overhauls Shuttle Launch Decision Process," *Aviation Week and Space Tecnhology*, 23 May 1988, 20, 21.

exploded in a huge ball of fire, killing all seven crew members. Prior to the disaster, there had been twenty-four shuttle flights without injury to any crew member, and NASA had been confident in its procedures. Since then, however, the procedures and processes surrounding shuttle missions have been thoroughly reexamined.

Technically, the Challenger explosion was caused by the failure of an O-ring on one of the solid-fuel booster rockets. Subsequent investigations, however, have placed the responsibility squarely on NASA's launch decision. That decision was made despite repeated warnings by engineers at Morton Thiokol, the company that manufactured the boosters, that it would be dangerous to launch the shuttle in cold weather. Lawrence Mulloy, chief of the solid rocket booster program at the Marshall Space Flight Center, repeatedly refused to accept their arguments. He told them that he required "proof of probable failure" to abort a launch. When they stood their ground, he went over their heads and convinced Joe Kilminster, Thiokol's vice-president for space booster programs, to sign a launch go-ahead. The rest is history.

CHANGING THE DECISION PROCESS

In the aftermath of the disaster, NASA significantly overhauled the decision-making process that leads to shuttle launches. The new system involves a number of reviews by several committees and uses much more information than in the past. Under new procedures, the deputy director of National Space Transportation System Operations, astronaut Robert L. Crippen, has the final responsibility to launch or to hold a shuttle. He receives support and management inputs from the Launch Team, the Mission Management Team, and the Space Shuttle Management Council. The Management Council is composed of the directors of the Kennedy, Johnson, and Marshall Space Centers and in turn receives inputs from the National Space Technology Laboratories.

Once a preliminary launch decision has been made, a number of critical reviews take place before the terminal countdown is started. The most important of these reviews is the Flight Readiness Review (FRR), which addresses all aspects of flight preparation, especially any that can cause problems at the time of launch or during the flight. Technical matters that are likely to endanger the flight in any way are addressed by a committee of NASA engineers with inputs from relevant outside contractors. The engineering committee assesses the likely impact of the technical problems and decides how to solve them. Their assessment is then considered by the review committee, which decides whether to proceed with or delay the launch and makes a formal recommendation to the Mission Management Team.

The FRR also takes into account the preparedness level of the crew. Special attention is given to crew members who will be going into space for the first time. The crew members are also assessed on their ability to handle problems that might occur in space. If a particular crew member is believed not sufficiently

capable of handling his or her duties, especially in a crisis, the committee recommends that either the individual be dropped from the flight or the launch be delayed until such time as the astronaut is fully trained.

Another important review is the constraints review. This review involves all supporting organizations (the National Space Technology Laboratories and the three Space Centers); possible constraints on a particular launch are analyzed and ways are devised to cope with them. Constraints might include inclement weather causing a risky launch or landing, solar flares that may disrupt communications, or other aspects of the mission such as a satellite deployment involving unusual shuttle maneuverings. The constraints committee also reviews the preparedness of alternative landing sites if their use is considered possible.

Two days before the scheduled launch date, a final review, under Crippen, takes place. At this time, the Mission Management Team verifies that all actions recommended by the FRR and any other review committees have been completed successfully. Finally, nine minutes before launch, the Launch Director and head of the Launch Team, Robert B. Sieck, polls the engineering support team, Air Force meteorologists at Cape Canaveral, NASA's test director, and the chairman of the Space Shuttle Management Council for final concurrence. Sieck then formally recommends to the Mission Management Team Chairman, Crippen, that they go ahead with the launch. However, all members of the Launch Team are authorized to interrupt the mission countdown right up until the moment of launch (T minus zero).

In retrospect, the Challenger disaster is seen by many experts as the result of top management's isolation from the technical personnel closest to the launch. The Presidential Commission that investigated the accident concluded that those who gave the launch order did not have a clear understanding of the engineering and weather objections that should have stopped the launch.

The current decision-making process involves checks and verifications by over three hundred NASA personnel as well as by numerous outside contractors. Though viewed by some as cumbersome, the system has been adopted in order to insure the safety of NASA personnel and equipment. The current process is intended to keep NASA's management in touch with lower-level engineers and others with technical expertise.

To date, revised launch procedures appear to be working succesfully. However, there are indications that NASA is lapsing into its old ways. The recent launching of the Galileo space probe to Jupiter was carried out despite strong objections raised by some scientists and reservations voiced by some NASA personnel. Galileo is a probe powered by fifty pounds of highly radioactive plutonium. Should a plutonium-powered probe launch fail and the probe crash to earth, it is likely to contaminate vast areas, posing extreme danger to millions of people. Galileo was launched from the space shuttle Atlantis, which, like all NASA space shuttles, was launched from Cape Canaveral, a point close to several highly populated areas.

NASA officials claimed that the risks associated with such a launch have been greatly exaggerated and that there is minimal danger. They say that a disaster on board the shuttle would not contaminate anything farther than fifty miles from the launch site and would pose negligible risks of cancer to anyone.

Several efforts were made to stop the launch. Some scientists implored President Bush to intervene and a public-interest group, the Christic Institute, even tried to obtain a court order to prevent NASA from launching Galileo. A physicist appointed by the White House to look into the matter, while approving a launch, did state that NASA's procedures to evaluate safety left much to be desired.

CASE 7.2   *Dilemma of a young manager*

BILL D. FORTUNE   *Fortune Management Consultants*
BRIAN BELT   *University of Missouri—Kansas City*

"Where will it all end?" ponders Johnny Woods as he sits at his desk recalling the events of the past six weeks.

He thinks of what he studied about human relations in college. He wishes he had a workable and equitable solution to his problem.

Johnny thinks to himself, "I know I've been fair enough with those two guys—maybe, too fair at times. More than once I've jeopardized my job to protect them."

He momentarily remembers a question raised by one of his college buddies one day during the discussion of a case assigned in his personnel/human relations management course, "What if your subordinates don't like you?" Johnny wonders if being liked is really worth it and if being liked is the answer to his problem.

"Maybe," Johnny thinks, "Professor Bates can given me some advice as to how I might solve this problem."

Johnny decided to give Professor Bates a call and see if he could discuss this problem with the professor. Johnny called Professor Bates and she agreed to discuss Johnny's problem with him the next day.[1] The following is an account of Johnny's discussion of his problem with the professor.

EVENTS OF THE PAST SIX WEEKS

Johnny Woods, age twenty-four, started to work for the Futuristic Automotive Electrical Corporation six weeks ago, immediately upon completing all the requirements for "A Certificate of Completion" in electrical theory and practice at The Community Technical Institute.[2] Johnny is the supervisor of the

---

1. Professor Bates was the instructor of the personnel/human relations management course mentioned. Johnny took the course under Professor Bates at Lack University (LU), a four-year academic university. Johnny dropped out of LU during his junior year after making the decision to attend The Community Technical Institute located in his hometown.

2. The Futuristic Automotive Electrical Corporation rebuilds automobile, truck, and farm tractor starters, generators, alternators, distributors, and voltage regulators that are marketed all across the United States. Its products are distributed primarily through automobile and truck parts and accessories shops. However, approximately 25% of its sales are to a national mail-order company. The corporation also provides machine-shop service, such as turning armatures, to local automobile and truck garages.

lathe-machines shop where he supervises the work of seven lathe operators. (Exhibit 7.8 presents a description of Johnny's job.) He has had problems with Billy Adams and Charles Pierce almost from his first day on the job. For instance, at the end of the first week on the job, Johnny overheard the following parts of a conversation among Adams, Pierce, and another of the lathe operators as he walked into the shower room this Friday morning:

Adams Those kids think they're just it! Why, I bet he isn't twenty years old. What do they teach these kids today—how to comb their sideburns? All that schoolboy ever thinks about is work.

Pierce I remember when old man Jones had his [Johnny's] job.[3] He let us do our own thing. What's happening to the company when they'll

let a kid come in here and boss around seven experienced machinists? Billy, you and me are at the top of our labor grade.

Laroque Hey, you guys better shut up! Mr. Woods is standing over there. Let's go to work; it's time to punch in.

The following conversation ensued when Johnny conferred with his professor:

Professor Bates How would you describe your relationship with the other lathe operators and with your boss, the general supervisor?

3. Mr. Jones held Johnny's job for eight years. Johnny was selected to replace Jones when he retired from the corporation.

EXHIBIT 7.8 THE FUTURISTIC AUTOMOTIVE ELECTRICAL CORPORATION

POSITION DESCRIPTION

Position: Supervisor
Department: Lathe-Machines Shop

Primary function: Under the supervision of the General Supervisor, supervises 7–12 (varies) lathe operators and through them provides the highest quality machine services that he is capable of to the entire plant.

Position content:
1. Seventy-five percent: Performs supervisory duties as follows:
    a. Observes all work of subordinates to ascertain that the work conforms to work orders, as generated by Production Control.
    b. Supervises the machining of work pieces and directs the general work assignments made to his department.
    c. Schedules assignments as determined by work orders received from other activities and sees that tools, materials, equipment, and personnel are available as needed for best performance.
    d. Inspects equipment and tools to insure proper conditions and use; requests repairs as needed.
2. Ten percent: Performs managerial duties as follows:
    a. Conducts safety meetings; revises work practices and equipment to alleviate hazards; sees that safety regulations are observed; procures, issues, or inspects individual safety equipment.
    b. Interprets standard practices and procedures for unusual conditions and checks for compliance with standard practices and procedures applying to machining activities.
    c. Initiates notices of employees' performance; reprimands for violations of regulations or for deficient work; participates in settlement of step-1 grievances, rates probationary employees.
    d. Transfers or promotes personnel to fill temporary vacancies in hourly positions; grants employees time off; prepares employee working schedules.
    e. Signs time cards; originates labor distribution; originates and signs Supervisor's accident reports, requests for medical attention, reports on unsafe practice of condition, safety charts, and safety meeting report.
3. Fifteen percent: Performs technical and administrative duties as follows:
    a. Originates and signs work orders as needed for repair of equipment.
    b. Originates and signs material requisitions for supplies, tools, etc.
    c. Collaborates with various operating and maintenance personnel regarding work orders pertaining to jobs requiring services of Lathe-Machines Shop.
    d. Analyzes work orders and determines labor and equipment requirements for efficient operation. Assigns overtime according to company policy.

Working conditions:
1. Works day shift.
2. Works overtime during emergencies.
3. Subject to normal plant and Lathe-Machines Shop conditions.

Johnny   I get along well with all the men except Adams and Pierce. With the exception of these two guys, everyone goes about doing his job without causing problems for me or anyone else. Adams and Pierce, no doubt, are good at their work. My boss seems to be satisfied with my work and the work of my shop. In fact, she complimented me several times for "getting the work out." But I don't know how long this will last if those two guys keep fouling things up for me.

Professor Bates   How would you characterize your boss?

Johnny   As I pointed out, she seems to be satisfied with my work. However, when she interviewed me for this job, she emphasized several times that she takes a "hands-off approach" to the people who work under her. She said that she thinks a supervisor should be capable of handling his [the supervisor's] problems without intervention from her [the General Supervisor]. This is why I've tried to work out my own problems.

Professor Bates   Are there other events of the past six weeks you would like to discuss?

Johnny   Five times within the past six weeks, twice during my first week on the job, Billy Adams has been from 10–35 minutes late for work. Each time, I reminded him that it was important for all the men to be at work on time because of the high volume of work that had to be turned out by our shop in order to meet delivery dates set by Production Control. On each occasion, I told Adams that I saw no need to report his being late to the Personnel Office, as long as he was not late to work again.

Twice I have seen Adams leaving work early. Both times I checked his time card to see if he had punched out. He had not. On both occasions, I checked his time card again after 5 P.M., the shop's regular quitting time, to see if it had then been punched. As I suspected, someone had punched the time cards at 5 o'clock so that Adams' leaving early was not reflected on the cards. Although I realized that it was a Class A offense,[4] according to the existing labor contract, for a person to punch another employee's time card, I made no attempt to find out who punched the card. I have no evidence of it, but I suspect Pierce of punching Adam's card. Again, although

I have no evidence of it, I suspect the other lathe operators are aware of Adams' leaving early and having someone else punch his time card. I just have a feeling the others are aware; it's the way they act.

Professor Bates   Johnny, are there other incidents similar to the ones you have just described?

Johnny: Yeah, I'll tell you about a few of them.

Both Adams and Pierce have missed the last three biweekly safety meetings. In other words, they haven't attended a single safety meeting since I started to work here at Futuristic. I did not report their absence to either the General Supervisor, even though she is a stickler for safety, or to the Personnel Office. Each time I didn't think it would be necessary. After each of their first two absences, I reminded them of the company rule that requires their attendance at the safety meetings. They sounded so sincere each time when they told me they wouldn't miss another meeting and when they asked me please not to report them. I noticed at the last safety meeting that they were both absent again. Also Laroque was absent. He had never been absent before during my time here. The next morning I was able to catch Adams and Pierce in the shower room before work and after everyone else had left to go to the shop. I started out by asking them why they were absent from the safety meeting. Boy! Did they blow up! Pierce told me quite frankly that he had been working at Futuristic for three years and he already knew everything that was ever said at the meetings.

There are two more incidents I can tell you about.

One day, the manager of Stores, who fills requisitions for materials, parts, and hand tools, called me and pointed out that Adams and Pierce had come to him several times requesting various hand tools without first having me sign the requisition forms, which I'm supposed to do. He very carefully explained to me, as if I didn't already know, that company policy required me to sign the requisition for all hand tools. This incident really made me look like a fool. I called this incident to the attention of Adams and Pierce. In no uncertain terms, Pierce was quick to tell me what I could do with the requisition forms.

But, wait until you hear about what happened yesterday a few hours before I called you, Professor Bates. After this incident, I just knew I had to ask someone for advice.

The bananas really hit the fan yesterday! It is

---

4. A Class A offense is an infraction of company rules considered so serious as to warrant summary dismissal on the first offense, regardless of mitigating factors. Each of the seven lathe operators in Johnny's shop is a member of the United Automobile, Aircraft, and Agricultural Implement Workers Union.

company policy that working overtime be assigned to the people in the shop on a revolving basis. That is, each lathe operator in the shop works overtime in an emergency as his turn comes up. Well, yesterday I needed three people to work a few hours overtime in order to get out a rush order for one of the local garages. I checked the overtime schedule and found that Adams' name was among those persons whose turn it was to work overtime. I went to each of the three men just before quitting time and pointed out to them that we had to get out a rush order and that their names had come up to work overtime. [According to Johnny, he was informed of the rush order just a few minutes before he talked to the three lathe operators.] After a few seconds of the normal grumbling that always comes from the people who are asked to work overtime, the first two said they would work late. Adams' reaction was something else, though. He said he was tired and didn't want to work late. He turned and walked out of the shop. I had to get another person to work in his place. Adams showed up for work this morning and acted as if nothing had happened.

Professor Bates   Johnny, tell me something about the characteristics of Adams and Pierce.

Johnny   Adams is 32 and Pierce is 29 years old. Adams has been with the company five years and Pierce, three years. Both of them are at the top of their labor grade. Both are high school graduates. Neither one of them is married, although I think Pierce used to be. I, quite naturally, would characterize them both as being smart alecks to say the least. That's about all I can tell you about them.

Professor Bates   Was either of them a candidate for your job?

Johnny   No. From what I've been able to pick up, neither one was interested in the job. Besides, my boss wanted a graduate of The Community Technical Institute for the job. So, I don't think there's any hard feelings because I got the job.

Professor Bates   Johnny, tell me something about yourself.

Johnny   As you know, my father has owned a machine shop and garage for more than twenty years. I started helping my father in the shop when I was about ten years old. I learned to operate every machine in the shop—lathe, boring and honing machines, milling machines, valve grinding machines, and so on. I learned to completely rebuild any part of a car, truck, and tractor such as the motor, starter, generator, carburetor. You name it,

and my father taught me how to rebuild it. However, I've always been most interested in automotive electronics. That's the reason I went to The Institute for formal training in electrical theory and practice. I learned things there in two years that I could never have learned in my father's shop. My interest in and desire to learn more about automotive electronics is what prompted me to take this job with Futuristic. Too, if I work up to General Supervisor, then I will have an opportunity to learn about the entire field of automotive electrical systems. I would like someday to be the owner-manager of my own shop. The experience I get at Futuristic will help me realize this long-run goal.

Professor Bates   I gather you know a great deal about the technical side of your job. What would you say are your qualifications as a manager of people? That is, what are your qualifications as they pertain to the human side of your job?

Johnny   As far as formal training goes, I had a course in working with people and a course in shop management at The Community Technical Institute. Also, I had your personnel/human relations course at LU. As a matter of fact, recalling some of the things we discussed in the course is what prompted me to call you.

Professor Bates: Such as?

Johnny   Well, things like Theory X and Theory Y; role behavior and conflict; Chester Barnard's acceptance theory of authority; making unpopular decisions; and, taking disciplinary action.

Professor Bates   What about practical experience in directing people?

Johnny   This job with Futuristic is what I would consider to be the first job I've had where I am formally responsible for directing people. When I worked for my father, I helped him oversee the machinists and mechanics who worked in his shop. But, that's not quite the same as here at Futuristic. I guess I've got a lot to learn.

How do I solve this dilemma? I've only been here six weeks. What do I do? Do I take the problem to my hands-off boss who thinks I'm doing such a good job? Do I do nothing and jeopardize losing my job because I fail to meet production schedules or fail to carry out some other job responsibility? Maybe I should quit my job?

Professor Bates   You've told me something about Billy Adams and Charles Pierce. What about the other lathe operators in your department? Is there anything you can tell me about them that might have a bearing on the resolution of your problem?

Johnny   Not much. I've not had time in only six weeks to learn much about them. My job is not the kind that requires that I directly supervise and interact with the people in my department or shop. It's not really necessary; they all know their jobs and more or less take orders from the situation at hand. Also, because of the tight production schedules in my department, my people do not have a great deal of time away from their jobs so that I could get to know them better.

I do know that all the other lathe operators are married and have families and are older than I am. They all are experienced lathe machine operators. They seem to accept me. Other than this, there's not anything more I can tell you about them.

RESOLUTION OF THE PROBLEM

Professor Bates   You alluded to your concern as to whether being liked was the answer to your problem. Do you think this is your problem? Why don't you reflect on all you've told me and then do the following, which should help to guide your thinking in determining a solution to your problem.

1. Define the problem(s).
2. Analyze the cause(s) of the problem.
3. Develop alternative ways of removing the causes and thus solving the problem. Remember that these alternatives should deal with causes, not symptoms of the problem.
4. Evaluate the alternatives, according to criteria such as these:
   a. How well does the alternative meet the corporation's objectives?
   b. How much time and organizational resources are required?
   c. Does the alternative conform to personal and organizational values for equitable and responsible behavior?
   d. What are the ramifications of each alternative?
   e. What is the probability of success?
5. Select an alternative.
6. Develop a detailed plan of implementing the solution to the problem. Who should do what? How? When?

EXERCISE 7.1
NASA EXERCISE

As you approach the moon for a rendezvous with the mother ship, the lateral dissimilar malfunctions, forcing your ship and crew to land some 17 craters, or 145 earth miles, from the mother ship. The touchdown results in a great deal of damage to the ship but, luckily, none to the crew. Survival is dependent upon reaching the mother ship. The most critical items must be chosen for the trip.

INSTRUCTIONS

Below are the only fifteen items left intact after the landing. Rank order the items in the importance they hold to you and your crew in reaching the rendezvous point. Place *1* by the most important item, *2* by the next most important, and so on, through all fifteen items. You should complete this section in ten minutes.

Your Decision	Articles	Group Decision
_____	box of matches	_____

_____ food concentrate   _____

_____ 50 feet of nylon rope   _____

_____ parachute silk   _____

_____ portable heating unit   _____

_____ two .45 caliber pistols   _____

_____ one case dehydrated pet milk   _____

_____ two 100-pound tanks of oxygen   _____

_____ stellar map (of the moon's constellation)   _____

_____ self-inflating life raft   _____

_____ magnetic compass   _____

_____ 5 gallons water   _____

_____ signal flares   _____

_____ first aid kit containing injection needles   _____

_____ solar powered FM receiver-transmitter   _____

GROUP INSTRUCTIONS

Because you have to survive as a group, the most appropriate decision making is group consensus. The rank order has to be agreed upon by each member of the group. Because the consequences of a wrong decision are so severe—death—you want to be as logical as you can and avoid arguments. In addition, you want to be sure only to agree with that ranking that somewhat meets your solution. Be sure not to employ any voting, averaging, or trading techniques that might stifle and embitter one of your companions on this survival journey.

SCORING

1. Subtract the group score on each item from your individual score on each item. Write down the difference. For example, you put down an item as 3 on your list, and the group ended up ranking it 6. There is net difference of 3.
2. Add all the net differences together to get your pair score.
3. Collect all the scores in the group, add them, then divide by the number of people in the group.

YOUR NET DIFFERENCE SCORE _____

AVERAGE INDIVIDUAL SCORE _____

0–20   Excellent
20–30   Good
30–40   Average
40–50   Fair
over 50   Poor

Now take the correct NASA computed rankings and compare the group ranking with it, computing the net difference between the group and the correct ranking.
NET DIFFERENCE SCORE—GROUP AND CORRECT _____
What do these differences mean?

EXERCISE 7.2
CREATIVE THINKING

INSTRUCTIONS

Part I

Each student will work alone and try to solve the following problems:

1. A ping-pong ball is in a hole. The circumference of the hole is just slightly bigger than the ball. The hole is deeper than your arm is long. There are no long sticks or other objects available for you to use. What can you do to get the ball out of the hole?
2. Suppose you have two containers. One container holds five liters of liquid; the other container holds three liters of liquid. You need *precisely* four liters of liquid. How can you get exactly four liters?
3. Each word below is missing two letters. The two letters can appear in any order, but each will appear at least twice in the word. The missing letters are A, E, I, N, O, R, S, T; now it is up to you to fill them in, in the right blanks—and to figure out which two missing letters appear in more than one word.

   B __ __ __ __ __
   __ __ __ __ __ G
   A __ __ __ __ __ __ __
   H __ __ __ __ __
   __ A __ __ __ __

Part II

Now divide the class into small groups (i.e., three or four students). Have each group work together to solve the following problems.

1. Find the connection between the following words:
    anyone
    panic
    change
    clean
    bemoaned
    salamander
    chairman
    barbarian
2. There is a women's washroom directly across from the nurse's station at County General Hospital. But Nurse Jones always walks to the far end of the corridor to use the facilities. Why?
3. For each group of three words, find the three definitions that sound alike but are spelled differently. For example, if the word group consisted of *erode, location, merchandise,* the answers would be *wear, where,* and *ware.*
    journeyed, highway, paddled
    atmosphere, before, inheritor
    rude person, pierce, swine
    harness, shower, rule
    tree trunk, pod, dish

Part III

After students have worked individually and in groups to solve the problems, discuss the following questions. What barriers or difficulties did you encounter while working on these problems? What difference did you notice between working individually and in a group? Do you think creativity can be learned or improved?

CHAPTER **8**

UNDERSTANDING GROUP BEHAVIOR: ORIGINS AND DYNAMICS

LEARNING OBJECTIVES

1. To understand how a group develops and matures.
2. To learn the manager's role in group development.
3. To examine the effects of groups on organizational behavior.
4. To understand how intergroup competition can be managed.
5. To understand how managers can facilitate the socialization process.
6. To recognize factors that influence the effectiveness of group members.

CHAPTER OUTLINE

Groups Defined

Types of Groups
Task Groups / Project Groups / Informal Groups

Stages of Group Development
Forming / Storming / Norming / Performing / Adjourning
Timing and Environmental Influences on Group
Development

Socialization: The Process of Fitting In
Three Phases of Socialization
Managing the Socialization Process
Socialization in Perspective

Factors Influencing Group Effectiveness
Individuality / Leadership
Group Norms / Group Cohesiveness
Task / External Factors

Understanding Group Behavior: Conclusions

Questions for Review and Discussion

References

Cases: 8.1 Executive Retreat: A Case of Group Failure
8.2 Division E

Exercises: 8.1 Two-Four-Eight: Building Teams
8.2 Group Member Roles

KEY TERMS

Group

Primary groups

Secondary groups

Task groups

Forming / Storming

Norming / Performing

Adjourning

Socialization / Encounter

Change and acquisition

Realistic job preview

Role

Emergent leader

Group norms

Dave Peters and Jim Scott had known one another professionally for a number of years. One day, Dave called Jim and asked if he would be interested in co-authoring a major book for a new company. Jim initially showed interest in the project but later questioned whether he had the time to do the book justice. Dave assured him that his expertise was necessary and that he was the right person for the job, but Jim remained hesitant to accept the offer.

As Jim considered the opportunity, he thought of a mutual friend and colleague, Jeff Kimball. Kimball's background would complement that of Dave and Jim. Although the men had never worked together on a project of this magnitude, contacting Jeff seemed like a good idea. Jeff, too, was at first hesitant to commit to the undertaking. After a long discussion, however, he concluded that the opportunity to work with his friends on the book would be fun and would also further his career.

The three men worked closely with one another during the next two years and completed the book to everyone's satisfaction. Did the task of writing the book really require that all three men work together if it was to be accomplished successfully? Or did they pursue the project together primarily because they were good friends? In either case, all three decided to act together (as a group) rather than individually.

Most human activity is linked in one way or another to group behavior. Groups satisfy our needs for affiliation, camaraderie, and status. They also allow us to perform certain tasks that might be more difficult or even impossible to accomplish alone. Groups are the fundamental building blocks of organizations as well as of society itself. People discovered long ago that associating with others enabled them to hunt, build, and defend themselves better than if each individual tried to survive alone.

Sociologists and social psychologists have studied groups and group processes for many years, focusing on the development, structure, and dynamics of small groups. In this and the following chapter, we discuss concepts and research results that can help you better understand and manage small group behavior.

Academic interest in groups and their importance to organizational success can be traced back to the now famous Hawthorne studies[1] (see Chapter 1). Those studies, conducted by Harvard University researchers at Western Electric's Hawthorne Plant, raised far more questions than they answered. Importantly, however, researchers' investigations revealed the substantial and complex impact of groups in work settings. Since then, considerable attention has been given by managers and researchers alike to the nature and dynamics of group behavior.

In recent years, there has been a resurgence of interest in groups in business and other organizations. This interest has been spurred by the success of self-managed work groups in northern Europe and small problem-solving groups known as quality control circles which many observers associated with the "Japanese Miracle" of the 1980s. (See Chapter 9, "Putting Groups to Work.") Most managers today agree that groups of all kinds, both formal and informal, significantly influence the behavior of individuals and the larger organizations for which they work. So pervasive is their impact that rarely will employees or managers complete a workday without attending at least one meeting, and some individuals spend the better part of their organizational lives involved in a variety of group endeavors. This spread of groups has created problems for managers who have previously viewed their jobs as being primarily concerned with the management of individuals. Kerney Laday, a senior executive with Xerox Corporation, shares his view on the importance of groups and the unique problems that groups can present to managers in the Ethical Dilemma below.

Some students of behavior have maintained that groups merely represent a collection of individuals and thus can best be understood by studying the aggregate behaviors of their individual members. Today, however, most authorities on groups recognize that group behavior is distinctly different from individual behavior and more than just the sum of the behaviors of group members.

This last statement can be best understood if we return to an important definition associated with systems theory. You may recall that in Chapter 1 we defined synergy as a unique combination of system inputs resulting in the creation of something greater than the mere sum of those inputs. Stated another way, the whole is greater

ETHICAL DILEMMA
Rewarding Groups or Rewarding Individuals: Through the eyes of Kerney Laday, Vice-President, Operations, Southern Region, Xerox Corporation

The reward and recognition systems of companies such as Xerox Corporation are based primarily on individual accomplishments. Recently, however, competition from abroad has taught us that solutions to complex problems can often best be solved by groups rather than by individuals alone. Traditionally, work has been divided among groups of individuals who perform similar tasks or depend on each other to complete a job. When work is segmented this way It becomes easy to see the interdependencies of individuals and why the individual role becomes subordinated to that of the group.

Given this new view of the work place, there is potential for conflict and sub-optimization of the ultimate work objective. The team concept allows little room for individual competition. Therefore, the role of the traditional manager changes from that of a director of activities to an enabler of actions. Further-more, the team's attention must turn from meeting internal objectives to satisfying external customer requirements.

As more and more focus is placed on understanding and satisfying customer requirements, there will be an even greater expansion of the role of work groups. Managing in this new environment emphasizes the need for balancing individual and group recognition. Our objective at Xerox is to maximize group effectiveness through individual excellence—a goal that will produce new challenges and new dilemmas.

Questions
What ethical dilemmas are posed when we attempt to manage new philosophies and adopt new orientations to performance?
Is changing and reorienting existing reward systems to emphasize group instead of individual performance fair?

than the sum of its parts. This concept represents an important, unique phenomenon associated with group behavior.

Consider, for example, a situation in which a manager wishes to draw on the ideas of subordinates when solving a particular problem. The manager may ask each employee for personal ideas in a series of one-on-one meetings or may bring everyone together to discuss their ideas about the problem. In the latter case, the manager probably will find that solutions generated by one or more employees will spawn additional ideas by others. These new solutions may not have been conceived had the group not come together. Furthermore, these solutions are not necessarily the mere combination of existing proposals but may be unique in their own right. This interesting dynamic is only one quality distinguishing group behavior from the behavior of individuals.

Groups are complex social systems capable of developing their own identities. In turn, they affect the behavior of individual members, interpersonal relationships, and the performance of larger organizations.

HARLEY-DAVIDSON

Vaughn L. Beals, Jr., is proud of Harley-Davidson, and well he should be. Harley-Davidson is one of only two major United States companies (the other is Xerox) that has regained control of a major market taken over by the Japanese. For years, Harley-Davidson was *the* name in motorcycles throughout the world. By the mid-1970s, however, poor quality, high prices, and competition from aggressive Japanese manufacturers spelled disaster for Harley-Davidson. In 1969, the company commanded 100 percent of the heavy motorcycle market in the United States. By late 1970, market share had dropped to 40 percent, and following record losses in 1981 and 1982, eventually bottomed out at 23 percent. Today, Harley-Davidson, under Beal's leadership, has made a miraculous recovery claiming 59 percent of the heavy bike market in 1989 and running well over 70 percent through the first quarter of 1990. The company has increased productivity by 40 percent, increased inventory turns to twenty times (versus a 3.5 national average), reduced scrap and rework by two thirds, and tripled delivery of defect-free motorcycles.

Changes did not come about from any one course of action. Redesign of manufacturing and marketing systems have played an important role in the Harley-Davidson turnaround. However, according to Beals, it took "turning the corporation upside down" to make the changes happen. Employee involvement, or what Beal terms getting white-collar workers to listen to blue-collar workers, was necessary to achieve Harley's success. One hundred and seventeen quality circle groups (small problem-solving groups), involving about 50 percent of all Harley employees, were established throughout the plants and administrative areas and managers became team leaders rather than bosses. Quality-focused employee involvement using the power of these small, committed groups of workers has been the cornerstone that has sparked Harley-Davidson's turnaround, and it is upon these groups of dedicated Harley workers that Vaughn Beals believes the company's future will continue to rest.[2]

GROUPS DEFINED

For our purposes, a **group** is defined as two or more individuals who communicate, have some sense of history or future, and function interdependently in the pursuit of a common goal or a mutual interest or interests. Let us briefly examine the four primary components of this definition.

Size

Two or more people are needed to form a group. However, groups of different sizes may behave differently. The number of persons in a group affects its dynamics as well as the feelings of individual members. For example, sentiments tend to be emphasized more in two-person groups than in larger groups. A three-person group significantly alters the power relationships and dynamics among members by permitting "two-against-one" coalitions.[3]

The optimal size of a small group appears to be five members. In five-person groups (1) decision deadlocks are not possible; (2) individual members are not isolated when the group splits into a majority of three and a minority of two; and (3) the group is large enough for members to shift roles or withdraw from awkward positions before an issue is resolved.[4]

Your own experiences probably confirm these observations about group size. When you get together with a friend or someone at work, plans can usually be made or differences resolved without a great deal of difficulty. The addition of one other person, however, may complicate the relationship if the third person sides with either you or the other individual. Adding two more people to the group permits a majority decision but affords some personal protection as long as the minority consists of at least two members of the group.

Generally, group members find it easier to get to know one another and identify common interests in smaller groups. Due primarily to the limitations placed on the amount and quality of communication as group size increases, groups become less personal as they increase in size. "Small groups encourage more participation proportionately than larger ones."[5] This, in turn, tends to influence feelings of member satisfaction. In a recent study of volunteer board members and task force groups, members of large boards reported low levels of satisfaction while members of smaller task forces reported greater satisfaction.[6]

In some small groups, members may even wear special hats or T-shirts or adopt group names. Quality teams at Northrup Corporation, for example, have chosen names like "Team-Hornet" and "Tiger-by-the-Tail";[7] at Xerox you may encounter members of the "Releasers," "Hot Sox," or "Problembusters." Such names give groups a greater sense of identity.

Group size can reach an upper limit beyond which rules and regulations tend to be established to formalize and maintain associations. The generally accepted upward limit for a small group is twenty persons, although this number can vary depending on several factors such as the location of group members or the extent to which group members share common sentiments. Few informal groups reach this size before splintering into smaller social units.

Communication

Group members communicate with one another and function interdependently. The concept of a group presupposes some social interaction and mutual dependency. Interaction usually takes the form of face-to-face contact, although groups can come together as the result of other media such as teleconferences or the exchange of written correspondence.

In some cases, communication can be less conventional. For example, undercover agents during World War II reported developing a special sense of camaraderie with other agents with whom they communicated even though they knew one another only by code names and never actually met. Similarly, prisoners of war in Korea and

Vietnam who were visually isolated from others developed special relationships with fellow captives by tapping out coded messages on the floors or walls of their cells. In whatever context, however, group members interact and work interdependently toward mutually satisfying ends that either cannot be attained alone or can be accomplished more easily through the members' association with one another.

Sense of history or future

The existence of most groups extends beyond a single meeting or project. Group membership implies some continuity over time and reflects either a history or an anticipated future. Even so, it may not be possible to identify the specific point at which a group forms or when it ceases to exist. This is particularly true of small, informal groups such as friendship cliques. Perhaps you have been part of such a group while working on a summer job. It may be difficult to identify exactly when you and your new-found associates really became a close-knit group. Similarly, the point at which you realized that the closeness of the group no longer existed (probably shortly before or after you returned to school) is somewhat fuzzy.

The boundaries of a group, both in terms of *who* are considered members and *when* membership is actually initiated or terminated, may be unclear. This lack of clarity can be due to the fact that awareness of group membership, commitment to the group, and acceptance (or rejection) of members all gradually evolve over time.[8]

For example, Elizabeth worked as a programmer in a large downtown bank. She became close to those with whom she worked. The group often ate lunch together and gathered at a nearby "watering hole" each Friday after work. Her hard work and social skills resulted in a promotion and transfer to a large facility in the suburbs, and her contact with her former co-workers has become less frequent. She continues to receive occasional invitations to join the group for lunch or after work on Fridays, although she has not done so in a number of months. In fact, she recently confided to a co-worker, "I hate to always say no, but I just don't feel like I'm still part of the group."

Common goals

The impetus for joining and retaining membership in a group is often the shared beliefs, interests, motives, or goals of group members. Individuals tend to seek out other people with whom they have certain things in common and build relationships around those similarities. Employees may affiliate with one another, for example, because they perform the same kind of work (office workers tend to take breaks and eat lunch with other office workers rather than with plant personnel) or if they enjoy the same type of leisure activities (e.g., bowling, softball, having a beer after work). Mutual concerns or fears also can be important in bringing and holding a group together. In the now classic study of group activity at Harwood Manufacturing,[9] researchers reported that concern about changes introduced by outsiders (management) resulted in group pressures that significantly influenced productivity. They found that when new ways of performing a job were introduced to work groups, group pressures could decrease, as well as increase, output depending on certain conditions existing at the time the changes were introduced. Concern about the external threat was so great that individual differences in levels of production declined significantly. See Exhibit 8.1.

In the experiment, this decline was true for the control group and for experimental group 1, in which productivity decreased signficantly and stabilized below the prechange level, as well as for experimental groups 2 and 3, in which an initial downturn in productivity was followed by significant productivity improvements that ultimately exceeded prechange levels. The decline in individual differences is reflected in the standard deviations shown in Exhibit 8.1, which dropped from approximately ten units before the change to as few as 1.9 units afterward.

Although group members generally share certain similarities with one another, each individual may have a personal reason for joining a group. Five reasons people join groups include:

1. Security: Individuals may join a group to protect themselves from a perceived threat from outsiders.
2. Affiliation: Some individuals find the opportunity to associate with others to be rewarding and thus a reason to join a group.
3. Esteem: Group membership can provide a person with esteem either from other members or from outsiders who perceive the group to have high status.
4. Power: Groups can enable a person to accomplish external objectives by providing resources that the person alone is incapable of generating. In addition, some individuals may derive a sense of personal power from group experiences through their role as a leader.
5. Goal accomplishment: Joining a group allows an individual to take advantage of the collective experiences and synergy of group members, thereby leading to more creative approaches to goal attainments.[10]

As we can see, individuals choose group membership for a variety of reasons. In all cases, however, they do so to attain an outcome that can be best achieved through their association with other people.

TYPES OF GROUPS

Groups can be classified in a number of different ways. Understanding the characteristics associated with each type of group can affect a manager's expectations of relationships among group members and of the group's performance. For example, primary and secondary groups are differentiated on the basis of group size. This distinction is important because the two terms reflect certain qualities of the relationship of group members.

Primary groups are relatively small and are characterized by intimate face-to-face associations among members. The closeness of these associations directly influ-

EXHIBIT 8.1   CHANGES IN OUTPUT DEVIATIONS FOR WORK GROUPS BEFORE AND AFTER EXTERNAL THREATS

GROUP	Standard Deviation Before Change	Standard Deviation After Change	Overall Productivity Change
Experiment I			
Control Group	9.8	1.9	Decrease
Experimental 1	9.7	3.8	Decrease
Experimental 2	10.3	2.7	Increase
Experimental 3	9.9	2.4	Increase

Adapted from: L. Coch and J. R. P. French, "Overcoming Resistance to Change," *Human Relations*, Vol. 1 (August 1948): 531.

ences the behaviors of group members. **Secondary groups,** on the other hand, are larger and less intimate than primary groups. Relationships tend to be impersonal and often are formalized. Because of the large size of secondary groups, members have only intermittent contact with one another, and that contact may be restricted to certain job-related functions. Members of secondary groups, therefore, tend to participate in delimited and special capacities (e.g., contributing a particular skill) rather than committing their personalities and full range of talents.[11]

All of us participate in both types of groups. Primary groups exert a greater influence on our day-to-day activities through the presence of other group members and their ability to immediately and continually reinforce our behaviors. Secondary groups rely instead on sanctions that must be imposed through impersonal control systems (rules, regulations, policies, etc.) or that are exercised by designated individuals such as group leaders or a sergeant at arms.

A manager may be less likely than co-workers to influence an employee's behavior directly if the co-workers make up the employee's primary group. For example, a technician in AT&T's Orlando microchip manufacturing facility may be told by his supervisor that his tardiness will have to stop immediately. The technician is always in the plant on time but is often delayed by close friends who like to talk in the dressing room before going into the "clean" area where they work. In such a case, the employee may resist the suggestions of his supervisor and even a threat of disciplinary action rather than violate the expectations of his primary group.

Groups also can be classified according to their function or the circumstances under which they gather. These differences influence group goals and activities. Three types of groups you may encounter in an organizational setting are task groups, project groups, and informal groups.

Task Groups

Task groups (or functional groups) are determined by formal job requirements. They are brought together for the purpose of transforming some inputs (raw materials, ideas, objects) into an identifiable output such as a physical product, a decision, a report, or some other "detectable environmental change."[12] Task group members usually interact with one another on a day-to-day basis and take the form of departments or ongoing work teams.

Project Groups

Project groups are determined by formal but temporary job requirements. Assignment to project groups characterize organizational life, especially for managers. All organizations have some activities requiring grouping across functional lines (e.g., an interdepartmental planning committee). In addition, many high technology organizations are characterized by groups consisting of specialists brought together for the life of a special project. Large manufacturers, for example, often create project groups to develop and market new products. These groups may be disbanded when the product is manufactured or when it is no longer a significant part of the company's marketing strategy. Project group members return to their routine work activities or go on to another temporary project group after that project has been completed. Examples of project groups include research and development teams, internal consultant groups, and medical teams.

The organization best known for its use of project groups is the National Aero-nautics and space Administration (NASA). The practice is also widespread through high-tech companies such as Apple Computer, IBM, and Eastman Kodak, where the timely introduction of new concepts and products is essential. Project groups have often been adopted by companies who feel competitive pressure from smaller, more flexible organizations.

Informal Groups

Informal groups are those that satisfy the needs of individual members but do not exist in order to accomplish a formal goal. Membership criteria in informal groups are normally unstated. In some cases, such groups occur because people find themselves in a common location. For example, the first group of close friends made by college freshmen usually consists of students who live in the same dormitory or apartment complex. Similarly, new employees often associate closely with employees located in the same work area. Common interests or activities also are important. Informal groups emerge around activities (e.g., athletics, lunch, or card playing), commonly held beliefs ("we're all in this together"), or a common fear or enemy ("we've got to stick together").

Informal groups can come about as the result of a need to solve organizational problems outside regular channels. They also can arise when people within an organizational unit (such as a department) get together to achieve informal goals. As Chester Barnard, a noted organization theorist, observed, " . . . when formal organizations come into operation, they create and require informal organizations."[13] Thus, similarities within groups as well as differences among them can lead to informal activities in organizations.

STAGES OF GROUP DEVELOPMENT

When is a group a group? This question is central to our understanding of how and when groups become effective contributors to organizational success. Too often, managers and group members themselves become dissatisfied with a group that never gets the job done right or fails to satisfy its members' needs. The following scenario may sound familiar.

Gretchen, along with five of her classmates, was assigned to do a group project. She was enthusiastic about the assignment, although not everyone in the group felt as she did. She expressed concern to her roommate that "they all might not pitch in and do their part. . . . I don't know them all, and I'm not sure that they are very excited about having to do this project. I sure would like to see us do a good job and get a high grade." The final report was due three weeks after the group first met. A flurry of activity the weekend before that deadline produced the group's final product. The paper was given a grade of B − , and Gretchen again confided to her roommate, "We never seemed to get it together. Aaron and Sandy didn't even bother to come to our last meeting. I don't think we ever *had* a group!"

Effective groups do not simply occur. They evolve through identifiable stages of development. These stages have been likened to stages of personality development similar to those we discussed in Chapter 2. In fact, the term **syntality** is used to describe the personality of a group.[14]

Perhaps the most extensive analysis of group development has been conducted by Bruce Tuckman[15] of the Naval Medical Research Institute. Tuckman has identified five distinct stages in that developmental process: forming, storming, norming, performing and adjourning. Each stage is characterized by unique features and activities (see Exhibit 8.2).

Forming

Forming refers to the initial period of development in which group members attempt to orient themselves both to the task and to each other. Behaviors characterizing the forming stage might include conversations intended to identify participants ("Hi, my name is Joyce; what's yours?") and reasons for being present in the group ("I'm a new auditor in the accounting department. What's your specialty?"). Individuals also may gather information on group structure or expectations (e.g., leaders or standards) that already may exist for the group. The personalities of group members have a particularly significant effect during this initial stage.

Storming

Storming is the stage during which members are likely to vie with one another for group as well as task roles. Conflict is likely to arise concerning leadership of the group, and a pecking order will begin to emerge. Agreeing on the group purpose and identifying the roles necessary to accomplish group goals may result in polarization around personal positions. Finally, questions must be resolved about who will perform each of the varied group tasks.

EXHIBIT 8.2   CHARACTERISTICS OF TUCKMAN'S FIVE STAGES OF GROUP DEVELOPMENT

Stage 1: *Forming*	Members feel out one another to determine actual desire for group membership. Members seek information about nature and boundaries of task.
Stage 2: *Storming*	Interpersonal conflict leading to coalitions and establishment of a pecking order.
Stage 3: *Norming*	Emergence of a sense of oneness. Concern for maintaining relations. Emphasis on cohesion and conformance to group standards. New roles are adopted.
Stage 4: *Performing*	Integration and synthesis of members. Relationships internalized. Insight gained into task or problem. Solution emerges.
Stage 5: *Adjourning*	Norms may become lax. Members begin to withdraw from one another. Group dissolves.

Norming

Norming is the stage during which a feeling of oneness begins to emerge in the group. Personal views and group-related individual behaviors give way to patterns generally accepted by the group as a whole. During this stage, the group gives up its appearance of a collection of individuals and becomes an entity in and of itself. Norms are behavior patterns endorsed and reinforced by group members and reflect overt signs of individual conformity to group standards. We will discuss norms in greater depth later in this chapter.

The norming stage is particularly significant, since it is at this point that the group's self-concept or "socioconcept" becomes clearly defined. This socioconcept represents group members' conscious self-awareness of the group's purpose, structure, processes, and relationship with the environment.[16]

Performing

Performing is the stage in group development during which meaningful activity directly related to the group's goals actually takes place. All groups accomplish some outcome. Task and project groups are typically created to achieve specific organizational goals such as producing a product or delivering a service within a specified period of time. Even informal groups achieve certain outcomes, although those outcomes may be different for different group members.

During the performing stage, the group's energy is channeled into the task at hand. The group's structure, which emerged during the storming stage, now contributes directly to task performance.[17] It is at this stage that the group reaches maturity. Of course, further changes in goals, processes, and relationships are likely to occur, since groups are dynamic social systems. However, much like a mature adult, the group has now reached a point at which it can function and perform.

Adjourning

Adjourning is the final stage of development during which members begin to separate themselves from the group. Groups typically form to accomplish some common goal or meet the needs of individual members. Once goals are achieved or needs are met, the common interests that hold the group together are likely to weaken or disappear. At this point, the focus of group members changes from group maintenance to termination of group membership.

In one study, for example, developing groups were found to pass through three intervals as they attained satisfactory performance levels:[18]

1. Inclusion: activities influenced by members' needs to be included.
2. Control: activities influenced by members' needs to control others or to be controlled by them.
3. Affection: activities influenced by a liking for other people and a desire to be liked by them.

The sequence was reversed, however, as the group moved toward its anticipated termination. As Exhibit 8.3 indicates, interpersonal behavior during the final three

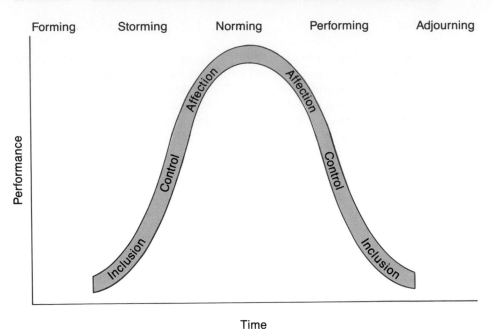

EXHIBIT 8.3   GROUP LIFE CYCLE

intervals took the form of affection, control, and inclusion, in that order. Preparing for a group's "death" and handling its reality are important issues to people who have been committed to a group, especially in those groups that have achieved a strong socioconcept.[19]

The adjourning stage is particularly significant in that activities that once strengthened the group and enabled it to perform now interfere with that performance. Energy directed at goal attainment is spent on maintenance activities, and managers must pay close attention to insure that the task at hand is completed. Perhaps you have worked with a similar group that achieved a high level of performances for a period but then saw that performance diminish as the group approached adjournment.

All types of groups may experience adjourning. Members of a close group of high school seniors (informal group) are likely to sense changes in one another's behaviors as they prepare to leave for college or take a job. Members of special project groups created to achieve a particular goal (e.g., a new product start-up) may also experience a sense of separation. Project managers in matrix or project organizations (see Project Organization and Matrix Organization in Chapter 13) must cope regularly with this phenomenon. Finally, individuals who leave a group that otherwise remains intact are likely to experience similar feelings and behaviors as they approach the end of their association.

According to stage theories of development, groups need to mature if they are to reach their full potential. Earlier, Gretchen questioned whether the group to which she belonged had ever really become a group. Based on what you now know about group development, her question appears to be legitimate and may be a major reason her group was unable to produce a better class project.

Timing and Environmental
Influences on Group Development

Not all research supports stage theories of group development. One recent study found that groups with deadlines quickly became engaged in their activities. Each group exhibited a distinctive approach to its task but experienced a major transition almost precisely halfway between its first meeting and its official deadline. A framework of behavioral assumptions and patterns emerged during the first meeting and guided the group's activities during the first half of its life. At this midway point, however, communication with outsiders increased and new approaches and frameworks were adopted where necessary. Thus, three phases were observed for groups with deadlines:

1. Initial phase—frameworks and activities growing out of the first meeting.
2. Transition phase—occurring at midpoint of the group's calendar life; group members reexamine environment and requirements placed on them by outside parties.
3. Final phase—resurgence of activity using reaffirmed or new frameworks to complete the task and prepare for transfer of group outcomes to outside parties.

This research raises questions about the smooth, on-going stages of more popular group development theories and focuses attention on timing and group-environment relationships on group performance.[20]

SOCIALIZATION: THE PROCESS OF FITTING IN

Socialization refers to the process by which individuals "learn the ropes" and are incorporated into groups and larger organizations. Just as groups may develop through certain stages before they are able to perform effectively, individuals also go through certain phases as they assume membership in groups and organizations.

Three Phases of Socialization

The socialization process involves three distinct phases:[21] 1) anticipatory socialization; 2) encounter; and 3) change and acquisition. (See Exhibit 8.4).

Anticipatory socialization

An individual's adjustment to a group begins before he or she actually becomes a member.[22] In fact, the first step in the socialization process is one in which "outsiders" *anticipate* what will be expected of them after they join the group. Information from different sources (observation, rumor, written documents, etc.) creates expectations about group or organizational membership. In some cases, groups intentionally create particular beliefs and images in order to attract certain types of members. At the organization level, recruiting brochures or other information released to the public are used to strengthen and reinforce those images. Whatever the sources of information, individuals use them to create "perceived realities" about the group.

Anticipatory socialization involves two specific phenomena. First, individuals selectively perceive certain characteristics of the group. Second, these perceived

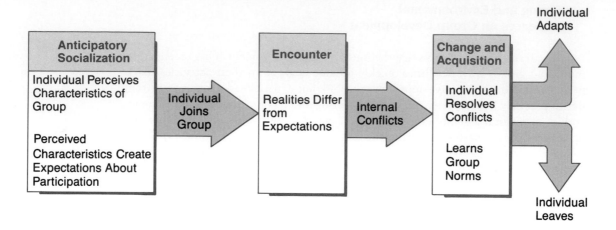

EXHIBIT 8.4   THE SOCIALIZATION PROCESS

characteristics, whether true or not, create expectations of what participation in the group will entail.

Encounter

Encounter occurs after an individual joins a group and begins to identify differences in his premembership beliefs and conditions that actually exist within the group. These differences lead to internal conflicts for new group members. For example, a working mother who is told that her job should not interfere with her home life may find her supervisor is not sympathetic to her leaving work early to attend her child's recital or basketball game.

Change and acquisition

Change and acquisition represent the final phase of the socialization process. Here, individuals adapt to group expectations and work through conflicts experienced during the encounter phase. New behaviors are learned and norms governing those behaviors are generally accepted. Individuals who are unable to adapt to the group's "way of life" are likely to leave voluntarily, be terminated, or be informally asked to leave the group. Persons who choose to remain in the group out of desire or necessity, but who are unwilling to accept group norms, are likely to be isolated by most if not all remaining group members.

Managing the Socialization Process

Socialization is an individual experience. However, the nature and efficiency of that process can influence group performance.[23] Managers and other leaders, therefore, can and should employ techniques to help facilitate the socialization process.

Four techniques that may help group leaders manage the socialization process are: (1) realistic job previews; (2) training and counseling; (3) behavior modeling; and (4) sponsor or "buddy" systems.

Realistic job preview

More than one individual has joined a group and found colleagues or conditions to be quite different from what he had expected. Often, group members (or other organizational representatives) convey unrealistic expectations about an organization or a job. A **realistic job preview** (RJP) involves giving those who are considering joining a group a realistic impression of the roles, conditions, and relationships that are likely to be found.

Realistic job previews not only permit those looking for specific organizational realities to accurately identify them and thus join the group with confidence, but will also provide realistic expectations for persons who decide to join the group *despite* their failure to find a "perfect fit." In the long run, RJPs enable new members to discover the true nature of the groups they are about to join and can help to minimize dissatisfactions brought about by unfulfilled expectations.

Counseling

Counseling may help new group members adjust their perceptions of group conditions and bring about certain changes in their behaviors. Counseling provides a means of verbally communicating group expectations in a manner acceptable to the new group members while answering questions and otherwise clarifying issues that may be producing anxieties.

Behavior modeling

Earlier, in Chapter 4, "Learning, Reinforcement, and Behavior Analysis," we discussed the nature and importance of behavior modeling. Behavior modeling in a group setting occurs when specific, desirable behaviors are demonstrated by group members and leaders. Those modeling the desired behaviors must do so in an appropriate manner and meet the other requisites of a good model (i.e., the modeled behavior is clear, distinguishable, and useful, and the model is interesting and desirable).

Sponsor or "buddy system"

New group members are frequently teamed with a sponsor or "buddy" in order to learn the ropes of the organization. The new member accompanies her sponsor for a specified period of time, during which she can observe and ask questions about the behaviors and activities in which the sponsor engages. It is the sponsor's responsibility to describe and/or demonstrate those behaviors that will be required of the new member when she is on her own. Although buddy systems can be extremely beneficial, sponsors must be carefully selected and be familiar with the group or organization's needs.

THE BODY SHOP

In Chapter 2, you met Anita Roddick, CEO of the London-based The Body Shop International. Roddick, you may remember, feels strongly about social causes and introduces her values and beliefs into the workplace. Needless to say, working for The Body Shop is not for everyone, and acclimation of new employees is an important job for company managers.

Roddick makes sure that potential employees are interested in working not only for a company that sells personal grooming aids but also for one that supports selected social causes ranging from saving a nearly extinct Brazilian native tribe to opposing animal testing for cosmetics and other products. In addition, The Body Shop is interested in hiring people who are customer centered rather than merely sales centered. Training is formalized and extensive, and information about products and performance is displayed liberally throughout the company. Anita Roddick is creating an exciting atmosphere at The Body Shop, where employees are fully aware of what she and the company stand for and which permits each individual to choose whether or not she or he will fit into the company's culture.[24]

Socialization in Perspective

Socialization programs like those described above can facilitate the entry of new members into group or other organizational settings. Studies suggest that formalized attempts to socialize new members lead to greater job satisfaction and commitment and lower intentions to quit.[25] In addition, socialization of newcomers can positively affect existing group members by reaffirming the importance of their own membership.[26] Managers are clearly in a position to facilitate the entry of new members into groups and thereby influence both individual and group performance.

FACTORS INFLUENCING GROUP EFFECTIVENESS

Whether the decision is that of an individual to join a group or that of a manager to form or otherwise make use of a group, the decision is based on the belief that the group will be *effective*. Group effectiveness is therefore critical to our understanding of how and why groups function in organizations.

A group is effective if (1) the group's task output is acceptable to those who receive or review it; (2) the capability of members to work together in the future is maintained or strengthened; and (3) members' needs are more satisfied than frustrated by the group experience.[27] Thus, work group effectiveness may be defined as the group's ability to attain a goal or produce an output that will satisfy a manager or some other outside party, to satisfy its own existence needs, and to motivate its members toward continued participation.

Other effectiveness criteria, depending upon the type of group, might include the ability of the group to interact with other work groups or organizational units, the group's cost/performance ratio (efficiency) and the long-term versus short-term impact of the group.[28] Project group members may place greater value on short-term goal attainment than on the potential for group activities to satisfy individual needs or maintain longer-term relationships between members. Conversely, a work team may be able to perform at a high level only if group maintenance needs (personal satisfaction and positive interpersonal relations) are satisfied. Many Japanese managers attribute the success of their organizations, for example, to their ability to nurture and maintain long-term work group relations.

Many factors influence group performance. As Exhibit 8.5 suggests, individuality (skills, values, other personal qualities), leadership, group norms, group cohesiveness, and task and certain external factors contribute to group performance.

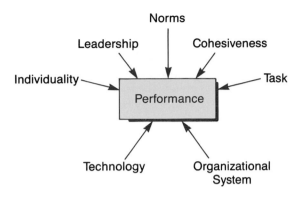

(Internal Factors)

(External Factors)

EXHIBIT 8.5   FACTORS INFLUENCING GROUP PERFORMANCE

Individuality

As we discussed earlier, groups are more than a mere collection of individuals, more than the sum of their members. Yet the personalities and physical abilities of all members are essential group inputs. Each person occupies a given position within the group. Whether that position is set apart from others (e.g., team captain) or is similar to positions held by others in the group (team member), it is accompanied by a set of expectations group members have about the behavior of each member. This set of expectations is known as a **role.**

A person's behavior is influenced by his or her role. However, the individual qualities a person brings to the group also affect actual behaviors. For example, research indicates that dominant individuals tend to have a high rate of interaction in groups and are likely to take on task leadership roles. Similarly, people with high self-esteem tend to play an active part in groups; those with low self-esteem are less willing to participate.[29] Considerable research exists concerning the relationship of personality to group participation and interpersonal relations. However, two factors complicate using personality as a predictor of group success. First, each individual has a number of interrelated traits. Second, groups represent unique combinations of an almost infinite number of separate personalities.

Leadership

Leadership is another important variable influencing group performance. A leader may be assigned to a group by some higher authority or may be selected informally by group members (**emergent leader**). Emergent leaders possess certain characteristics. First, they are socially compatible with group members. Second, they tend to be prominent in the eyes of group members. Third, the emergent leader is perceived by group members as being able to help the group attain its objectives. The first characteristic helps satisfy the group's socioemotional needs; the second and third characteristics help satisfy its needs for structure and goal attainment.

Task group leaders have two primary responsibilities: (1) to complete the task or achieve the goal, and (2) to maintain the group and satisfy its members' needs. Effective leaders accomplish these sometimes conflicting roles by understanding the responsibilities associated with each role and matching their leadership style to the specific situation. The role of the informal group leader is complicated because the leader has no formal authority to require group members to act in a particular manner. An informal leader has attained that position by best representing the group's central interest (e.g., the highest status person in a status group, the friendliest person in a personal attractiveness group, etc.). Although the leader may be allowed to deviate somewhat from the accepted patterns of the group (thus providing leadership), too great a deviation will differentiate the leader from the others and cause group members to no longer view that leader as the exemplary group member.

As we discussed earlier, such conforming factors as similar interests, education, and personality characteristics can cause an informal group to emerge. These or other factors also can cause informal subgroups to form within larger task or functional groups. They also can have a major impact on the leadership style that will be most effective in that group. For example, a group might consist of many persons with a distinct need to work in a well-defined environment (authoritarian personalities). Group members looking to someone (a manager or informal leader) to generate such an atmosphere would function most effectively under a directive leadership style.[30] Groups consisting primarily of nonauthoritarian personalities, on the other hand, would likely prefer a democratic leader.[31]

Group Norms

Group norms are the informal rules groups adopt to regulate the behaviors of their members. Although norms also may influence member attitudes and perceptions of important aspects of the environment, they most significantly affect the *behavior* of group members. These accepted standards of behavior become part of a group's socioconcept and can influence groups to be either highly productive or to restrict output. During the development process, the group comes to accept (possibly even require) certain behaviors. Attendance, timeliness, and cooperation with supervisors are examples of important organizational behaviors that can be significantly influenced by group norms.

Norms serve various functions in organizations. For example, they facilitate group survival, clarify and simplify the behaviors expected of group members, and provide the group with a sense of identity.[32] Norms tend to develop gradually and informally for one or more reasons. According to Feldman, norms can develop as a result of explicit statements by supervisors or co-workers, critical events in the group's history, primacy (the first or early behavior pattern that emerges in the group), and carry-over behaviors from past situations.

Norms have five major characteristics:

1. Norms summarize group influence processes. They state the rules for joining and maintaining membership in the group.
2. Norms apply to behavior rather than private thoughts and feelings. Concurrence while in the group is required, but private acceptance is unnecessary.
3. Norms apply only to behaviors seen as important by most group members. Not all individual behaviors in a group are regulated.
4. Not all norms apply equally to everyone. High-status group members often have more privileges and leeway than low-status members of the same group. Simi-

larly, group leaders may be allowed to deviate (within limits) from the norms followed by other group members.

5. Norms generally develop slowly and subtly. however, they can form more quickly if supervisors or co-workers, in the interest of time, wish to be more explicit about acceptable behaviors.[33]

Norms are significant to the extent that group members conform to them. The willingness of an individual to adopt a group's norms will be influenced by the real or imagined consequences administered by other group members. Individuals are also likely to conform if they fear punishment from the group or actually seek information about what constitutes acceptable group behavior.[34]

The nature of the individual as well as that of the group also influences the likelihood of conformity to group norms. For example, individuals with low self-esteem, little previous success with a task, or believing they have no ability for the task are more likely to conform. On the other hand, a group is better able to bring about conformity if (1) it is made of of experts; (2) its members are important to the individual; and (3) its members are comparable to the individual in some way.[35]

A group can use both positive and negative methods for bringing about conformity to norms. A slap on the back (friendly or otherwise), sarcastic comments, conversations, and looks or other nonverbal cues are a few ways a group openly or subtly can enforce the behavior standards on which it has agreed. Picketing strikers, for instance, may attempt to damage vehicles passing through the protestors' lines or carry signs labeling nonconformists as "traitors" or "scabs." A few National Football League Players Association members brought shotguns to the picket line during their 1987 strike against the owners as a symbolic display of their opposition to strike breakers. Group members, simply by their immediate presence, are also a constant source of pressure toward conformity to established standards.

The impact of norms depends on (1) who is aware of them; (2) how and to what extent they are enforced; (3) the types of behaviors with which they are concerned; and (4) the types of groups in which they exist. For example, norms governing social behavior are probably more important in informal groups than are norms concerning the allocation of resources. For task groups, allocation and output norms would tend to be most important. Differences in norms may also exist between different types of task groups. For example, a project team that relies heavily on integration and interpersonal cooperation may emphasize norms concerning social relationships, while such norms may be less important in a setting where a group of data entry clerks work independently of one another. These examples reveal the complex impact of norms in the work setting. A manager must attempt to understand the norms that influence workers if he expects to effectively manage group behavior.

Earlier in the chapter, we referred to the study of group activity at the Harwood Manufacturing textile mill. The findings of the research provide an excellent example of how pressures to conform influenced one employee. The following account describes the behavior of a presser in the mill who was part of a small work group but was later removed from the group and permitted to work on her own.

> For the first twenty days after she joined the group, the group was producing at the rate of about fifty units per hour. Starting on the thirteenth day, when she reached standard production and exceeded the production of others, she became a scapegoat of the group. During this time her production decreased toward the level of the remaining members of the group. After twenty days the group had to be broken up and all the other members were transferred to other jobs, leaving only the scapegoat operator. With the removal of the group, the

group standard was no longer operative, and the production of the one remaining operator shot up from the level of about forty-five to ninety-six units per hour in a period of four days. Her production stabilized at a level of about ninety-two.[36]

Why do you suppose the presser's productivity decreased after she exceeded standard production? How do you explain the ninety-two unit output she was able to maintain after being removed from the work group?

Norms influence the behavior of most, if not all, group members. An individual's response to informal pressures, of course, depends upon his or her personal traits and characteristics. On the other hand, the influence of pressures to conform to group norms may be particularly strong in certain countries or cultures. The International Dimension below describes cultural factors infuencing the strong group orientation in Japan and the extent to which Japanese businessmen may be willing to go to meet group and organizational expectations.

INTERNATIONAL DIMENSION
The Role of Groups in Japan

Most Western businesspeople know or quickly learn about the importance of groups in Japanese organizations. Many business decisions are made by groups rather than by individuals, and worker groups known as Quality Circles identify and solve problems and then take it upon themselves to implement their new ideas in the workplace. Few non-Japanese, however, realize the full extent to which group membership influences the way Japanese workers think and behave.

Japan is a nation of groups and factions, and the Japanese learn at a young age that you must be a loyal group member if you wish to be heard. Feelings about groups run deep. Obligations to society are met only after responsibilities to the immediate group are fulfilled. Even the moral codes that govern an individual's behavior are more likely to be tied to the group to which he belongs rather than to a broader set of societal or religious expectations.

Seemingly blind loyalty to the group or company has sometimes led Westerners to question the ethical values of Japanese businesspeople. Industrial espionage, though widespread around the world, is given an added dimension in Japanese firms, where employees may view such activities as legitimate simply because they promote the interests of the group or company. Such was the case in San Francisco when officials from Hitachi and Mitsubishi Electric were arrested for attempting to bribe IBM employees in order to obtain technical secrets. The situation, according to the "spies," was simple. When attempts to license IBM technology from the corporation failed, it was only "logical" to dispatch industrial espionage teams to obtain it.

Questions

What other examples can you give of the influence of groups on Japanese business or other activities?

Of what importance is the emphasis on groups to businesspeople outside of Japan?

Are you aware of other countries where groups play an important role in business organizations?

SOURCE: M. Zimmerman, *How To Do Business with the Japanese* (Tokyo: Charles E. Tuttle Company, 1985).

Group Cohesiveness

The extent to which members of a group "stick together" can influence group performance. This closeness is known as **cohesiveness** and consists of three important elements: (1) the degree to which group members are attracted to the group; (2) the degree to which group members are motivated to remain in the group; and (3) the degree to which group members mutually influence one another.[37] Cohesiveness is important to group performance. As we read earlier, leadership and norms influence the *direction* or focus of group behavior. Cohesiveness, on the other hand, can affect the *energy* and *effort* that group members are willing to put forth toward a common goal.

Three factors are particularly significant to cohesiveness, although certain factors may be more important in one type of group than another. These factors include (1) the group's attractiveness to individual members; (2) its instrumental value (use of the group to accomplish a task); and (3) the risk taking that occurs in the group.[38] These factors can be managed. For example, managers can affect intermember attractiveness by paying attention to group composition and staffing work units carefully. A group's perceived instrumental value can also be increased by helping each member clarify what he can expect to receive from group membership.

The factors underlying cohesiveness can affect patterns of group behavior as well as the likelihood that goals will be attained.[39] For example, cohesiveness arising from the shared attractiveness of a group's goals influences task accomplishment. On the other hand, cohesiveness that is a consequence of the personal attractiveness or friendliness of group members may encourage behaviors directed toward maintaining group membership rather than those facilitating goal attainment.

The relationship of cohesiveness to group performance is more complex than it may appear at first. Keep in mind that cohesiveness is concerned with attraction to the group and the subsequent power of the group to maintain that attraction. Cohesiveness, alone, however, provides no assurance that the groups will be productive or will attain goals set by group members or leaders. Other factors such as the ability of group members to perform the necessary tasks, understanding how tasks are to be performed and how they are to be integrated with one another, and individual commitments to the task (not simply to the group) will all influence the group's overall performance.

Task

The nature of group activities and the way such activities are performed are also important variables affecting group performance. The term *task* refers to the things a group must do to accomplish its goal. Four broad types of group processes are performed in groups: generate, choose, negotiate, and execute.[40] The "group task circumplex" shown in Exhibit 8.6 describes these group activities according to two dimensions, Conflict-Cooperation and Conceptual-Behavioral, and further breaks the processes down into eight specific task types while presenting the different types of tasks performed by groups. In addition to identifying these tasks and distinguishing them from one another, it suggests that the unique dynamics of each group may have a distinctive impact on the group's performance. Let us look briefly at two examples.

A committee has been established to plan an upcoming meeting for middle managers. The group must plan an agenda that will be meaningful to all those in attendance and must allocate meeting times and facilities according to agreed-upon priorities. There is no best program design, and the final product will depend upon

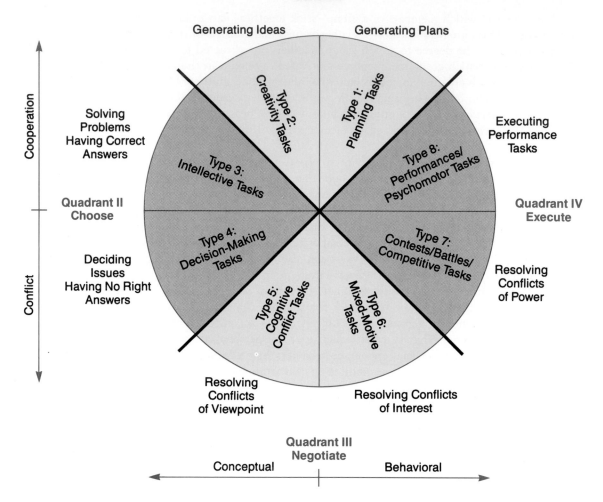

EXHIBIT 8.6   GROUP TASK CIRCUMPLEX

SOURCE: Joseph E. McGrath, GROUPS: Interaction and Performance, © 1984, p. 61. Reprinted by permission of Prentice Hall, Inc., Englewood Cliffs, New Jersey.

the ability of group members to reach a consensus on the overall program content. The group's task requires generating and sharing information as well as solving a problem for which there is no right or wrong answer. Participation in the group involves little, if any, personal risk.

A totally different dynamic exists within a group that competes against another group. For example, one aerospace company, knowing that it will be bidding against another major company for a contract, has set up two competing teams of engineers to develop the company's final proposal. It is understood by those in both groups that the winning team will be guaranteed participation in the new project if its design is accepted by the outside buyer. Those in the "losing" group may have an opportunity to work on the new project or may be transferred to a division in another part of the country.

Risks are high and success at the expense of the "opponent" is understood. The dynamics and activities of the two competing groups is likely to be quite different from those of the planning group described in the previous example. Likewise, other types of groups can also be expected to behave and perform activities differently depending upon their unique purposes and resources.

External Factors

In addition to the factors discussed above, group performance may be affected by external factors.[41] These factors include technology and the organizational system of which the group is a part. Technology includes components such as the equipment, the material to be worked on, and the physical environment. A group of accountants working with inexpensive calculators, for example, would approach a project and perform differently than if they were able to use personal computers on the same project. Access to resources, including information, the authority to act or to cause others to act, or the responsibilities of group members not related directly to the task at hand, are examples of organizational system variables that can influence group performance.

UNDERSTANDING GROUP BEHAVIOR: CONCLUSIONS

In the earlier chapters of this book, we concentrated on the individual aspects of managing organizational behavior. Yet, much of our daily lives is spent working in and with small groups. These groups are not simply collections of individuals. They represent potent organizational forces capable of developing their own personalities. Although groups can influence the behaviors of their members, some groups are more likely to do so than others. Primary groups usually are small and, due to their intimacy, often have greater influence on member behaviors than do the actions of a manager to whom the group reports. Your effectiveness as a manager can increase significantly if you understand the nature of important primary groups in your organization and the impact those groups have on their members.

Not every group can be counted on to be a highly productive organizational force. Groups, like individuals, pass through a distinct developmental sequence and are only likely to reach their potential when they have entered the performing stage. Each stage of development is accompanied by certain structural and behavioral characteristics. You may be better able to understand the nature of a group's behavior and how the group should be managed if you can correctly identify where it is in the developmental process.

You may also find that certain management actions can facilitate the speed and completeness with which a group develops. For example, attention to group composition might help create a desirable atmosphere during the forming stage and minimize counterproductive conflict during the storming stage. Other management actions that might facilitate group development include modeling and rewarding desirable behaviors and helping members recognize the relationship of their individual inputs to the objectives of the group as a whole.

In addition to the developmental process through which a group passes, other factors (both internal and external) influence group performance and therefore require your attention as a manager. For example, staffing decisions in certain work areas require that you consider the potential impact of individual personalities on the group process. Similarly, the effectiveness of your own leadership style depends on the composition of the group being led. Your activities as a manager may also help facilitate the formation of norms consistent with organizational objectives, and decisions regarding group composition, clarification of the relationship of group behaviors to group goals, and the use of a reward system that reinforces individual risk taking can affect group cohesiveness.

Finally, a manager must be conscious of external forces that influence group behavior. Such factors as available technology and the organizational system (suprasystem) of which the group is a part may impose constraints on group behavior over which neither group members nor their leader can exercise control.

Clearly, groups are an important and relatively complex element of organizational behavior. In the following chapter, "Putting Groups to Work," we will examine a number of ways groups can be effectively used in organizations.

QUESTIONS FOR REVIEW AND DISCUSSION

1. In what ways are group behaviors different from the behaviors of a collection of individuals?
2. For what reasons do people join groups?
3. How can a project group be distinguished from other task groups?
4. What are the five stages of group development? Why are these stages important?
5. What is the significance of the adjourning stage of group development?
6. Why is a knowledge of group developmental stages important to a manager or group leader?
7. How do the four techniques for managing the socialization process help facilitate the entry of new members into groups?
8. What factors influence group effectiveness? Why is each factor important?
9. What are the five major characteristics of norms?
10. What do studies like those at Harwood Manufacturing illustrate about the influences of groups on their members?
11. What factors influence group cohesiveness?
12. What important decisions must managers make about groups in their organizations?

REFERENCES

1. F. J. Roethlisberger and W. J. Dickson, *Management and the Worker* (Cambridge: Harvard Press, 1939).
2. "How Harley Beat Back the Japanese," *Fortune*, 25 September 1989, 155–165; Vaughn F. Beals, speech delivered at the 1990 Midwest Academy of Management meeting, Milwaukee, Wis. 20 April 1990; Vaughn L. Beals, "Harley-Davidson An American Success Story," *Journal for Quality and Participation*, Vol. 11, (June 1988): a19–a23; Beals, "Quality and Productivity: The Harley-Davidson Experience," *Survey of Business*, Vol. 21 (Spring 1986): 9–11.
3. C. R. Shephard, *Small Groups: Some Sociological Perspectives* (Scranton: Chandler Publishing Co., 1964), 3–4.
4. A. P. Hare, *Handbook of Small Group Research*, 2nd ed. (New York: The Free Press, 1976), 229.

5. R. W. Napier and M. K. Gershenfeld, *Groups: Theory and Practice*, 4th ed. (Boston: Houghton Mifflin Co., 1989), 40.

6. S. Huberman, "Making Jewish Leaders," *The Journal of Jewish Communal Service*, Vol. 64, No. 1 (Fall 1987): 32–41.

7. E. E. Lawler III, *High Involvement Management* (San Francisco: Jossey-Bass, 1986), 48.

8. J. E. McGrath, in P. S. Goodman, *Designing Effective Work Groups* (San Francisco: Jossey-Bass, 1986), 362–369.

9. L. Coch and J. R. P. French, "Overcoming Resistance to Change," *Human Relations*, Vol. 1 (August 1948): 32–33.

10. L. N. Jewell and H. J. Reitz, *Group Effectiveness in Organizations* (Glenview, Ill.: Scott, Foresman & Co., 1981), 8–9.

11. M. Olmstead, *The Small Group* (New York: Random House, 1967), 17–19.

12. D. M. Herold and S. Kerr, "The Effectiveness of Work Groups," *Organizational Behavior* (Columbus: Grid Publishing, 1979), 96.

13. Chester I. Barnard, *The Functions of the Executive* (Cambridge: Harvard University Press, 1938), 120.

14. R. B. Cattell, "Concepts and Methods in the Measurement of Group Syntality," *Psychological Review*, Vol. 55 (1948): 48–63.

15. Bruce W. Tuckman, "Developmental Sequence in Small Groups," *Psychological Bulletin*, Vol. 63 (1965): 384–399; Tuckman and M. A. C. Jensen, "Stages of Small Group Development Revisited," *Group and Organizational Studies*, Vol. 2, No. 4 (1977): 419–427.

16. R. B. Levy, *You and Your Behavior* (Boston: Holbrook Press, 1975), 341.

17. Tuckman, op. cit., 396.

18. W. C. Schutz, *Firo: A Three-Dimensional Theory of Interpersonal Behavior* (New York: Holt, Rinehart, 1958), 168.

19. T. M. Mills, *Group Transformation* (Englewood Cliffs, N.J.: Prentice-Hall, 1964), 67–80.

20. C. J. G. Gersick, "Making Time: Predictable Transitions in Task Groups," *Academy of Management Journal*, Vol. 32, No. 2 (June 1989): 274–309.

21. D. C. Feldman, "The Multiple Socialization of Organization Members," *The Academy of Management Review*, Vol. 6, No. 2 (April 1981): 309–318; Feldman, *Managing Careers in Organizations* (Glenview, Ill.: Scott, Foresman, 1988); J. P. Wanous, A. E. Reichers, and S. D. Malik, "Organizational Socialization and Group Development: Toward an Integrative Perspective," *The Academy of Management Review*, Vol. 9, No. 4 (October 1984): 670–683.

22. D. Birnbaum and M. J. Somers, "The Influence of Occupational Image Subculture on Job Attitudes, Job Performance, and the Job Attitude-Job Performance Relationship," *Human Relations*, Vol. 39, No. 7 (July 1986): 661–672.

23. A. E. Reichers, "An Interactionist Perspective on Newcomer Socialization Rates," *The Academy of Management Review*, Vol. 12, No. 2 (April 1987): 278–287.

24. B. Burlingham, "This Woman Has Changed Business Forever," *Inc.*, June 1990, 34–38, 41–47.

25. S. A. Stumpf and K. Hartman, "Individual Exploration to Organizational Commitment or Withdrawal," *Academy of Management Journal*, Vol. 27, No. 2 (June 1984): 30329; J. E. Hebden, "Adopting an Organization's Culture: The Socialization of Graduate Trainees," *Organizational Dynamics*, Vol. 15, No. 1 (Summer 1986): 54–72; G. R. Jones, "Socialization Tactics, Self-Efficiency, and Newcomers' Adjustments to Organizations," *Academy of Management Journal*, Vol. 29, No. 2 (June 1986): 272.

26. R. I. Sutton and M. R. Louis, "How Selecting and Socializing Newcomers Influences Insiders," *Human Resource Management*, Vol. 26, No. 3 (Fall 1987): 347–361.

27. J. R. Hackman, "A Normative Model of Work Team Effectiveness," *Tech Rept. No. 2* (New Haven: Yale School of Organization and Management, November 1983).

28. D. Gladstein, "Model of Task Group Effectiveness," *Administrative Science Quarterly*, Vol. 29, No. 4 (December 1984): 499–517.

29. Hare, op. cit., 183–184.

30. T. W. Adorno et.al., *The Authoritarian Personality* (New York: Harper and Company, 1958).

31. M. Rokeach, *The Open and Closed Mind* (New York: Basic Books, 1960).

32. D. C. Feldman, "The Development and Enforcement of Group Norms," *The Academy of Management Review*, Vol. 9 (March, 1984): 47–53.

33. Ibid.

34. J. R. Hackman, "Group Influences on Individuals," in M. P. Dunette ed., *Handbook of Industrial and Organizational Psychology*, (Chicago: Rand McNally, 1976), 1495–1496.

35. E. Aronson, *The Social Animal*, 4th Ed. (New York: W. H. Freeman and Company, 1984), 25–28.

36. Ibid., 23–24.

37. J. R. P. French and L. Coch, op. cit., 520.

38. J. P. Stokes, "Components of Group Cohesion: Intermember Attraction, Instrumental Value, and Risk Taking," *Small Group Behavior*, Vol. 14 (May 1983): 163–73.

39. Herold and Kerr, op. cit., 111.

40. J. E. McGrath, *Groups: Interaction and Performance* (Englewood Cliffs, N.J.: Prentice-Hall, 1984).

41. H. F. Kolodny, "Toward the Development of a Sociotechnical Systems Model in Woodlands Mechanical Harvesting," *Human Relations*, Vol. 33, No. 9 (1980): 623–645.

CASE 8.1   Executive retreat: A case of group failure

DONALD D. WHITE   *University of Arkansas*
H. WILLIAM VROMAN

John Matthews was a young executive at the divisional level of a large corporation. John, like a number of other young businesspeople throughout the United States, had been selected by higher-ups in his firm to attend a two-and-one-half-week executive development retreat.

The retreat was held at a remote camp in northern Minnesota. Although all of the necessary facilities for an enjoyable vacation were present, the structure and demands of the retreat left little time for relaxing and enjoying the surroundings. John was among sixty executives who were registered to attend the retreat. They would spend fifteen days living, working, and competing with one another.

ORGANIZATION AND ACTIVITIES

The sixty participants were divided into five groups of twelve. Each group was provided with a group leader, a senior corporate executive who had previously attended the retreat. For fifteen days, the executives were involved in a variety of academic and athletic activities.

Selected sessions of the retreat were designated for "educational activities." The executives participated in seminar sessions designed to deepen their understanding of central management decision making. These sessions involved a limited amount of lecture by either the group leader or a visitor. However, the majority of time devoted to academic pursuits was spent in case studies and a business game. Athletically, a good deal of the executive's time was spent in physical fitness training and athletic competition. Finally, a few sessions were conducted along the lines of sensitivity training.

Although a considerable amount of time was spent in intragroup activities, intergroup competition was also fostered. In particular, groups competed athletically and through the business game.

The remaining portions of this case represent the reflections of John Matthews on his experiences at the executive retreat.

FIRST IMPRESSIONS

It is hard to express the emotions or thoughts that were going through my mind, let alone the minds of others, when I first met the members of my group. Until now, I had been working with business acquaintances in my company's San Francisco office. When I learned of my selection for the retreat and the manner in which it would be conducted, I wondered what my new associates would be like. Would we all remain the full two and one-half weeks of the retreat? Would I be able to take the criticisms of others? How would our group do athletically and academically? And would the other members of my group resent the fact that I could not participate in the sporting events due to an old knee injury? Subconsciously, I had been establishing the criteria by which I would accept others and they would accept me.

During the first group meeting, I tried to learn the backgrounds of others who were with me. I went through the following processes. I tried to find out where the others were from, what their education was, and the kind of experience they had accumulated. I discovered that the level at which one had worked within a firm together with whether he or she had held down a "home office" job were important because they created identification and solidarity between individuals; i.e., financial officers interacted with other financial officers, production managers with production managers, marketing people with others from marketing departments, and so forth. Our group leader made sure that he allowed enough time for all of us to meet each other before he walked in the door.

The group leader was the faculty member who had over-all responsibility for administrative functions in the group. He also graded papers and presentations, conducted all of our counseling sessions and was the all-around nursemaid for the group. Our leader, Mark, was a top-level corporate executive out of New York. This posed an immediate threat to some in the group when they first met him. After a few minutes of informal chit-chat, Mark called everyone into a seminar room.

Mark made a low-key introduction of himself and the retreat. He emphasized that to be a success individually at "the camp," everyone had to cooperate and function as a group. He explained that no group always dominated intellectually or athletically. He related that his last group was not especially great in academics or athletics yet their cumulative scores both in tests and games enabled them to become the top group at the retreat. This allowed certain privileges over other groups. The point Mark kept trying to make was that we could no longer think of ourselves as individuals. "The school theme," he said, "is 'Think—Communicate—Cooperate' and I suggest that you too adopt it as your guiding principle while you are here."

GROUP MEMBERS

The following are my recollections of the other members in our group.

Wally

Wally was an older member of the group and became the group student leader. He was a middle-level manager in a large company and had no formal technical training. This may have made him reluctant to assume a leadership role in the group. He appeared to be afraid of hurting other people's feelings even though his actions were usually justified.

Donna

Donna also did not have formal technical training; however, she was one of the few who had had experience as a corporate president. She was an average student and speaker and above average in her writing ability.

Jim

Jim was a financial analyst. He was one of two bachelors and was considered to be the playboy of the group. His goal was just to finish the retreat and get back to his home office.

Bob

Bob was a manager of production and operations for a leading producer of men's apparel. He too was a bachelor and considered himself to be a "ladykiller." To most of us he appeared to be conceited and boisterous. He claimed to be an authority on most subjects. He was also suspected of cheating in the twenty-five-mile jogging club (cheating on anything was strictly forbidden).

Laurie

Laurie was a director of public relations for a major steel producer. She had a liberal arts background and turned out to be our only distinguished graduate. Although she participated in everything, she never really assumed a leadership role and her contribution to the section was minimal. She was the only one (with the exception of me) who was not able to run a mile and a half in twelve minutes. She was a good speaker but a below-average writer.

Rich

Rich was an internal financial consultant. He had attended Harvard Business School and was later to be considered as one of the better executive prospects at the retreat. He was a good speaker and writer. Although he was very outspoken, he did make a lot of sense. He assumed the leader's role in two major exercises; however, he never did maintain his hold as leader over the group.

Wayne

Wayne was a personnel director. He was an average student, writer, and speaker. He never did assume a leader's role, possibly because he was the most naïve member of the group.

Ollie

Ollie was a marketing manager and was considered the "country boy" of the group. He was an average student, good speaker, and good writer. He performed many odd jobs for us and was successful in leading us to two victories in athletics.

Gary

Gary was an executive vice-president for a pipeline supplier whom I thought, at the beginning, would emerge as the leader of the group. He was poor academically, an average writer, and a good speaker.

His additional duty was that of athletic chairman. Although he encouraged everyone to run twenty-five miles (twenty-five-mile club) during this period, he himself failed to achieve this goal.

Burrell

Burrell was a personnel and public relations manager. He was also considered to be among the more promising people at the retreat. He was a fair speaker and an average writer. His additional duties were academic chairman and basketball coach. He was the type of guy that, if something were to go wrong, he would be in the middle of it.

Paul

Paul was manager for engineering for an electronics manufacturer. He had to spend three days of the first week of the retreat in the infirmary with a virus. This may have been one of the reasons he was always trying to promote group functions when he got back. One thing I remember in particular about Paul is that he was always complaining about the "developmental rotation" program in his company. The program placed technically trained managers in functional areas other than their own for up to six months to provide them with career broadening. He saw the program as a threat to his own career but failed to see it as a threat to "general managers with no technical expertise." Over-all, Paul was an average speaker, writer, and student.

John (myself)

I did not have formal technical education for my job as division director of industrial relations. I was an average student and writer and above average speaker. I considered myself to be a harmonizer of the group. I was the only member who was excused from sports because of an injury. Although I disagreed many times with decisions that were made, I usually went along with the group in the end.

The group members lived in three locations during the school. Living in Cabin II were Donna, Wally, Jim, Bob, John, and Laurie. Wayne, Burrell, and Paul lived in Cabin II, while Ollie, Rich, and Gary lived in Cabin III. Bob and John generally walked to seminar sessions together as did Wally and Laurie, Wayne, Burrell, and Paul and Ollie, Rich, and Gary. Donna and Jim walked separately to the sessions. Rich and

Burrell studied together regularly. Laurie, Rich, and Paul generally studied together.

GROUP ORGANIZATION AND ACTIVITIES

For convenience, Mark arranged the seating alphabetically around the table (see Exhibit 8.7). There was only one exception; Wally, the designated leader by virtue of age and experience, sat near the front. Following some brief introductions and a few administrative actions, goals of the group were established.

After much haggling about the goals, which ranged from totally idealistic to extremely pragmatic, the group decided on the following goals:

1. Everyone in the group would strive to complete the program and would seek to assure that our group was ranked first among various competing groups.
2. We would strive to be the best in sports.
3. Everyone would run at least 25 miles.
4. We would strive to maintain a harmonious atmosphere in the group.

Of immediate importance to the group was developing athletically rather than academically. (In final group ratings, athletics ranked a very close second to academics in total possible points that could be scored.) In fact, it wasn't until the latter part of the school that the section would come together in academics.

A couple of incidents that occurred during the retreat illustrated the extent of the group's success.

Toward the end of the first week, an entire afternoon was set aside for self-evaluation. The session resembled a T-group session. Most groups had lunch followed with a little beer drinking to "loosen things up." After our loosening up we started our discussion. Several comments were made that should have provoked a fiery discussion, but for some reason they never did.

I don't believe we were open that afternoon. We looked at our leadership in academics, but none of us was willing to tell Burrell that he had a weak academic program. None of us would tell Gary that our athletics program was bad and that our group looked worse than most other groups with whom we competed. We all knew these things, but were unwilling to place the blame on anyone. Our group leader must have been totally frustrated at the end of the day. How could a

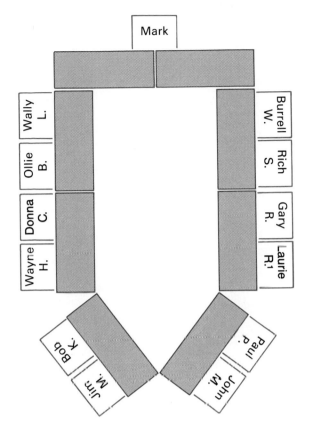

EXHIBIT 8.7   SEATING ARRANGEMENT FIRST DAY

group that had such high goals and such mediocre results have allowed such an opportunity to pass by?

A few days later another group project was scheduled. An obstacle course, intriguingly called "Project X," consisted of a series of tasks to be performed by six people at a time. It was supposed to test the group's ability to recognize the problem, decide on a solution, and carry it out in a fifteen-minute period. During the break, we tallied our score, 0 for 5. Mark seemed very upset. It was the first time he got upset with the entire group. Laurie commented on the episode:

We didn't see "Project X" or even the rest of the retreat as a life or death situation. In a retreat where no one fails to graduate, it can hardly be considered as a threat to anyone's career if these group goals go unaccomplished.

Personally, I saw us as a group of individuals in search of a real leader. We were strong in our own individual specialties in our own organizations, but couldn't muster up the same vitality and enthusiams to carry forth this synthetically designed group toward goal achievement. Although we wouldn't openly admit it, we were not committed to our goals. Yet, even though we lacked this commitment, we still maintained the goals. Going back to the afternoon encounter session, someone suggested that we revise our goals in light of our successes and failures to date. Even though it was impossible to achieve the original goals set, they were still unchanged!

The seating as depicted in Exhibit 8.8 was the arrangement for the last few days.

GROUP PERFORMANCE

Our group finished the two-and-one-half-week session having accomplished the following: Out of twelve individuals, one finished as a distinguished graduate and a total of three finished in the top third of the class. Ollie made the observation, "Lacking strong

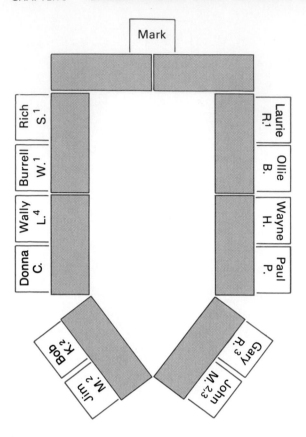

[1]These individuals finished in top third of class.
[2]These individuals never changed their seats.
[3]Gary and John sat next to each other during the last seven weeks.
[4]Wally never did assume the leader's position at the end of the table except when he led the two seminars.

EXHIBIT 8.8   SEATING ARRANGEMENT, LAST TWO WEEKS

leadership in education, we each went our separate ways in trying to wade through all the material."

Our second goal also shared defeat. At the beginning of the program it was felt that our group had a chance to do well in sports. During practice sessions, we appeared to be relatively good. However, practice sessions reflected one characteristic of the group. Generally, we were disorganized, and there was always a lot of joking going on. I believe this carried over to the games and resulted in less than full commitment to winning. Gary would get frustrated and try to motivate the team at times, but his sudden surge of spirit usually was short-lived.

The third goal also fell short of being successfully accomplished. Only six of the members of our group actually finished the twenty-five miles. Another important factor regarding the twenty-five-mile club centered on the ethics of one individual. Bob had been suspected of not running all the miles that he logged. At first Wally and Laurie had suspected this, as later all the group members living around Bob did. One member noted, "We all felt that Wally should have confronted him with our suspicions." However, because the evidence against Bob was circumstantial, Wally didn't formally say anything to Bob about the incident. One change that did develop out of the episode was that the entire group ceased to listen to or trust Bob once they suspected his cheating.

The group came closest to achieving the final goals that involved the maintenance of harmonious relationships between one another. An example of this was our mutual respect for each other's territory. As one member stated it, "When Paul went to the hospital, his seat remained vacant even though we didn't have permanently assigned seats. When he returned, everyone made a special effort to make him feel a part of the group. Even when we suspected Bob of not really completing his running, we tried not to make too big of a deal out of it.

Personally, I think I got a lot out of the retreat. I learned a lot in the academic sessions and even discovered some things about myself that I hadn't realized before. But, truthfully, I never figured out our group. Sometimes I think it was a near disaster.

CASE 8.2 *Division E*

H. William Vroman

O'Hara Aeronautics was a highly integrated aircraft maintenance organization. Division E was a special engineering branch at O'Hara. It was staffed by four electrical engineers, five engineering technicians, a project engineer, a clerk, a secretary, a quality control specialist, and a chief engineer. The office was involved with the engineering and production of software for automatic computerized testing equipment. Division E was responsible for staff engineering support, which meant they were not involved directly in production. The division was two years old.

O'Hara had contracted for software development with outside firms prior to Division E's formation two years ago. A number of factors caused O'Hara to decide that they could develop in-house capability. Under the pressure of the imminent undertaking of some new contracts, O'Hara set about staffing Division E.

All technicians' positions were filled by transferring people from other divisions (see Exhibits 8.9, 8.10, 8.11). Therefore, none of the technicians had less than fourteen years experience in either his or her field or some closely related electronics specialty. On the other hand, only one of the four engineers who were needed (Lenny Stokes) was available from within the present organization, and he had only been with O'Hara for about one year. The other engineers eventually hired had varied backgrounds. One had worked for O'Hara for about six months before leaving

for military service; he was given an engineering position in Division E upon his return. Two other engineers and one clerk were newly hired when Division E was established.

The remainder of the division was composed of Leslie Smithers, a project engineer; Harry Yates, a senior technician and quality control specialist; Jason Ventures, a secretary; and Luke Iler, the Division Chief. Leslie Smithers and Luke Iler were engineers who had supervised and worked in conjunction with the original contractors and Harry Yates had been a technician involved in automatic testing since its inception. All of these people were associated in some way with the firm's previous contract work. It was not unusual to hear comments around the office about these four persons such as, "They seem to know all the right people," and "Those people were really made for this place." Some of the comments were aimed more directly at Jason. For example, "If you need something done, ask Jason for help. He knows all the people and all the ways to get things done."

When announcing the establishment of Division E, Michael O'Hara, president of O'Hara Aeronautics, Inc., described its purpose as, "to get projects and develop their test programs and associated test equipment interfaces as thoroughly and as quickly as possible so that the shop and production facilities will have that knowledge." Mr. O'Hara also expressed hope

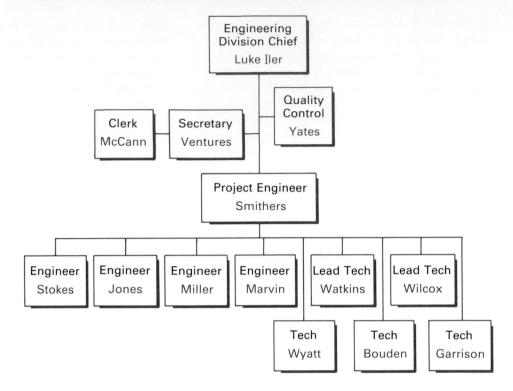

EXHIBIT 8.9   ORGANIZATIONAL CHART

that Division E would provide assistance to the people in the shop when they encountered technical difficulties. All of the members of Division E seemed to take pride in delivering a complete, neat, and error-free product at all times, as indicated in the following exchange.

Harry: Leslie, I think our division is probably the most conscientious at O'Hara. In general, I'd say we put out some darn good products.

Leslie: I think you're right. Everybody here seems to be trying to set an example for the people down in production.

EXHIBIT 8.10   ORGANIZATIONAL LIST OF EMPLOYEES

NAME	POSITION	AGE	YEARS OF SERVICE
Luke Iler	Division Chief	35	12
Harry Yates	Quality Control	48	23
Jason Ventures	Secretary	32	10
Jane McCann	Clerk	21	2
Leslie Smithers	Project Engineer	38	13
Lenny Stokes	Engineer	28	3
Art Jones	Engineer	30	3
Jan Miller	Engineer	34	2
Clete Marvin	Engineer	41	2
Troy Watkins	Lead Technician	43	17
Jeff Wilcox	Lead Technician	53	26
Greg Wyatt	Technician	37	16
Emma Bouden	Technician	34	14
Bill Garrison	Technician	41	17

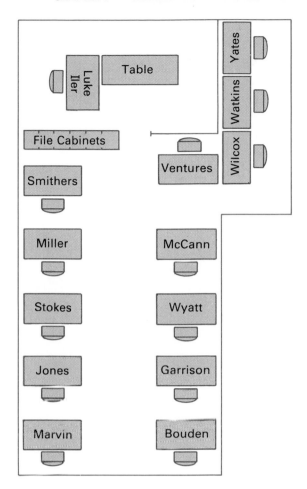

EXHIBIT 8.11   SEATING CHART

The four older technicians were good friends away from the office, and they often socialized at one another's homes. Harry Yates, a former technician, often joined in this socializing. One night, the four technicians and Harry were at Troy Watkins's house (the most frequent meeting place). The conversation turned to the office.

Troy: Those engineers sure are cocky, aren't they?

Jeff: Yeah, and they average about two years' experience between 'em.

Troy: That compares with our minimum fourteen years' experience. 'Course, they have that degree and that gives you all the know-how you need.

Jeff: Yeah, well I've had them come five–six times a week looking for short-cuts and help in programming problems. They know where to come on problems even if they don't acknowledge it.

Harry: I'm glad I'm out of the way in the office, that way half the problems miss me. I must confess that I'm confused by their approaches to problems. They just seem to miss the point. Where you guys and the engineers present proposals to the same problem, I'll bet I approve yours most of the time.

Troy: Boy, Jason is feeling out of it. Maybe we should have invited him over tonight. He was telling me that he doesn't work well with the engineers. Seems they are more compatible with Jane McCann.

Jeff: She came in with them—maybe that's why.

Harry: One thing though, Troy. Luke Iler has a lot of confidence in you. You're about the first person he talks to when he has a problem.

A DIFFERENT VIEW

The engineers usually did not socialize outside the office, even though they got along well at work. Most of their conversations about the office took place over lunch. The following conversation took place at one of their favorite lunch spots.

Lenny: Clete, I had what I thought was a beautiful plan for that new project we have been working on. I asked Bill Garrison what he thought of it, and he showed me his plan. Clete, I swear that thing was really ragged. We ended up taking them both to Harry Yates, and guess which plan he approved. Bill's, of course.

Clete: I know, Lenny. I would be the first to admit that those technicians have a lot of years of experience, but experience doesn't mean a thing when it comes to new work like you have been doing. That requires free thinking. In some cases their fifteen years' experience is like one year's experience fifteen times.

Lenny: The thing that kills me is the way Luke Iler always asks Troy Watkins for his opinion. He never asks any of us.

Jan: Well, you know how it is, Lenny. We can't win for losing. Sometimes it seems that no matter what we do our work won't be accepted.

Art: Well, I'm not sure I'd go that far, but it sure is frustrating when we get our work rejected so frequently. By and large, the technicians are pretty good guys.

Lenny: I guess you're right, Art. I can see where they could be a lot harder to work with than they are. Say, we've got to get back to the office.

EXERCISE 8.1

TWO-FOUR-EIGHT: BUILDING TEAMS

GOAL

To divide a large group into workable subgroups in such a way as to increase group cohesiveness and identity.

GROUP SIZE

Any number. The example is based on thirty-two participants who are divided into four groups. This design is easily adaptable to groups of other sizes.

TIME REQUIRED

Approximately thirty minutes.

PHYSICAL SETTING

Participants should sit on chairs that can be moved easily as groups form.

PROCESS

1. Participants are asked to number off using "one, two, one, two," etc., in order to form two large groups.
2. Participants labeled "one" are asked to stand on one side of the room and those labeled "two" on the other side.
3. Each number one invites a number two to form a dyad. Number ones are asked to invite someone they do not know or, if they know all participants, someone they do not know well. Dyads move to a neutral location until all have been formed.
4. The facilitator divides the dyads into two groups of eight dyads each, which relocate on opposite sides of the room.
5. After a consultation, which should take no more than three minutes, a dyad from one side of the room invites a dyad from the opposite side of the room to form a quartet. A dyad may not decline an invitation to join another dyad. One by one, dyads from the same side of the room issue invitations until all eight quartets are formed.
6. The quartets then caucus for no more than three minutes to determine which other quartet they would like to join.
7. Quartets successively ask another quartet to join them. Invitations to join *may* be declined. If an invitation is declined, the next group makes its offer. This process continues until all quartets have been chosen.
8. The octets are now ready to work. Their first task is to discuss the experience of choosing and being chosen.

VARIATIONS

1. Invitations to join may be rejected in forming the various groupings.
2. To achieve maximum heterogeneity, participants are urged to invite only the persons they know least well. After octets are formed, the facilitator shifts membership to get an even representation in each group based on some relevant criteria, such as no supervisor and subordinate in the same group, proportional representation by males and females, or age. The criteria can be announced prior to or following the invitations.
3. Open-ended statements can be provided at each stage of the teams' formation to heighten the developmental process. Examples:

   Dyads—I chose you because . . .

      When you chose me, I felt . . .

   Quartets—We chose you because . . .

      Our reaction to being chosen was . . .

   Octets—My first impression of you was . . .

      Right now I'm feeling . . .

EXERCISE 8.2
GROUP MEMBER ROLES

GOALS

1. To provide feedback to the group member on the roles that his fellow members have perceived him as playing.
2. To study various types of roles in relation to group goals.
3. To demonstrate that leadership in a small group consists of several functions that should be shared among members.

GROUP SIZE

Six to twelve members.

TIME REQUIRED

Approximately one and a half hours.

MATERIALS UTILIZED

1. Role Nominations Forms.
2. Pencils.

ROLE NOMINATIONS FORM

DIRECTIONS: For each member, place check marks in the column corresponding to the roles he or she has played most often in the group so far. Include yourself.

Roles   Members

Group Task Roles	A	B	C	D	E	F	G	H	I	J	K	L
1. Initiator contributor												
2. Information seeker												
3. Information giver												
4. Coordinator												
5. Orienter												
6. Evaluator												

Group Growing and Vitalizing Roles	A	B	C	D	E	F	G	H	I	J	K	L
7. Encourager												
8. Harmonizer												
9. Gatekeeper and expediter												
10. Standard setter or ego ideal												
11. Follower												

Anti-Group Roles	A	B	C	D	E	F	G	H	I	J	K	L
12. Blocker												
13. Recognition seeker												
14. Dominator												
15. Avoider												

PHYSICAL SETTING

Participants should be seated comfortably for writing, preferably at tables or deskchairs.

PROCESS

1. The facilitator gives a lecturette on roles that group members often play. He explains that some roles relate to the group's task, some maintain and enhance the functioning of the group, and some detract from the group's work. He distributes the Role Nomination Forms and explains each of the fifteen roles included. (Names of members should be written in on each of the forms in the same order in advance of the meeting.)
2. Pencils are distributed, and participants follow instructions on the form.
3. When all have completed the form, a tally is made of all of the check marks. Each member calls out all of the marks he put down, and each participant makes a complete tally for the entire group. Variation: the facilitator collects the forms and reads them aloud anonymously.
4. The group has a discussion of the array of tallies. Individual members are encouraged to solicit feedback on their distributions of nominations. Attention may be given to the presence or absence of adequate numbers of persons playing various functional roles and to how disfunctional roles are to be coped with.

CHAPTER **9**

PUTTING GROUPS TO WORK

LEARNING OBJECTIVES

1. To see how groups can be used in problem solving and decision making.
2. To examine different types of task and project groups that are used in organizations.
3. To understand the nature of quality groups and self-managed groups.
4. To recognize the unique challenges posed by interorganizational groups.
5. To determine how intergroup competition can be managed.

CHAPTER OUTLINE

Techniques for Managing Group Decision Making
    Committees and Interacting Groups
    Brainstorming
    Nominal Group Technique
    Synectics
    Delphi Technique

Expanding the Role of Groups in Organizations
    Quality Groups
    Self-Managed Work Groups
    Interorganizational Groups

Managing Intergroup Competition
    Group Activities During Competition
    Consequences of Competition
    Insights into Managing Competition

Putting Groups to Work: Conclusions

Questions for Review and Discussion

References

Cases: 9.1 The Case of Q.C. 5
        9.2 Consumer Airlines: A Study in Autonomous Work Groups

Exercises: 9.1 The Bomb Shelter
          9.2 Using the Nominal Group Technique

KEY TERMS

Committee management	**Quality groups**
Interacting groups	**Quality circle facilitator**
Brainstorming	**Self-managed work groups**
Nominal group technique	**Interorganizational groups**
Synectics	**Intergroup competition**
Delphi technique	

C harles Britton leaned back and thought about his problem. He knew that he had to make an important decision that would affect the course of the marketing division for the next two years. The decision needed to be correct, and he wasn't sure that he had all the necessary information at his fingertips. In addition, he was convinced that having the support of those throughout the division and the cooperation of influential parties in the manufacturing sector was critical if the decision was to be implemented successfully.

Charles had recently read a lot about participative management, but he wasn't sure that he had either the time or the patience to let a group of individuals, each with their own agenda, labor over this issue. "After all," he wondered, "wasn't it a committee that set out to build a horse and wound up with a camel!" He really felt the need to get others involved, but he wondered what options he had available. "I just don't know if there is a way to get the right people together and arrive at a good decision that everyone can live with."

In the previous chapter, we examined the nature of groups, how groups develop, and how they affect the behaviors of their members. Although individuals have different personal reasons for belonging to groups, we concluded that their common interests and concerns bring them together in a particular setting.

Groups of all kinds have a major impact on organizational behavior. This is particularly true when they become directly involved in problem-solving and decision-making activities traditionally left to individual managers. Of course, a group's existence alone (even in the cases of a project or task group) does not insure that it will be productive or achieve organizational goals. In our opening example, Charles Britton wanted to involve others in his decision but was concerned about drawbacks to group problem solving and decision making. In this chapter, we will examine how small groups can be effectively used in organizations and look at a number of group options that are available to managers.

TECHNIQUES FOR MANAGING GROUP DECISION MAKING

A variety of group techniques have emerged over the last few years and are being applied in organizations of all types. In this section, we examine a number of these techniques. But first, let us look at how groups traditionally have functioned in organizations.

Commitees and Interacting Groups

The most common form of group participation is the committee. **Committee management** occurs when responsibility and authority are placed in the hands of committee members. Committee management can be found in different types of organizations and at various hierarchial levels. In some cases, such committees may be responsible for decisions that are important but limited in scope.

A product development committee at Proctor & Gamble, for example, may have the authority to develop and test-market new products, while approval for faculty members to conduct certain types of research on a university campus may have to be obtained from a human subjects committee. Committee management can even be found at the executive level in some companies. The president of Du Pont, for example, reports directly to an executive committee.

Committees are widely used (if not always widely appreciated) in organizations. Many criticisms concerning committees have been raised. "Nothing ever gets done," some say. "No one takes responsibility for the group's decision. No one gets what they want!" Perhaps the most common reaction to committee management was summed by Charles Britton in our opening example when he recalled the adage that a camel was a horse designed by a committee. However, committees are not necessarily at fault; the customary nature of group interaction (i.e., distribution of power, dominance of certain group members, and influence on norms) may inhibit their effectiveness. Consider, for example, the last group meeting you attended. Did everyone participate? Probably not.

Research indicates that group leaders and dominant individuals in conventional meetings (also known as **interacting groups**) consume a disproportionate amount of time and that some people rarely if ever contribute to the group process.[1] Moreover, a considerable amount of time spent in such groups revolves around personalities rather than issues. Criticisms of ideas are sometimes taken personally, and discussions often reflect ego involvement in personal positions rather than focus on the problems or decisions at hand.

Managers have focused attention on group problem solving and decision making in order to improve the performance of committees and other small groups. As we observed in Chapter 7, "Decision Making," problem solving has two critical dimensions.[2] The *quality dimension* is the requirement that the decision be technically correct. The *acceptance dimension* is the degree to which the support of people

EXHIBIT 9.1   TIME WASTERS!

Source: *The Wall Street Journal*, October 28, 1986, p. 31. Reprinted by permission of *The Wall Street Journal*, © Dow Jones & Company, Inc., 1986. All Rights Reserved Worldwide.

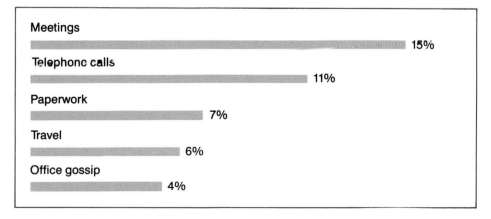

In a *Wall Street Journal* survey, managers identified group meetings as the activity that accounted for the greatest amount of their nonproductive time. Their observations may say a lot about how well many organizations conduct certain group activities.

carrying out a decision is needed for its successful implementation. The quality of a decision is clearly important. However, attempts to improve the quality of group decisions by closely supervising the problem-solving process have sometimes been frustrated when the decision was not implemented properly because it lacked group support.

Most literature on decision making emphasizes the quality dimension and ignores the acceptance dimension.[3] However, group techniques have emerged in recent years that satisfy both considerations. In this section, we explore four such approaches to group decision making—brainstorming, nominal group technique, synectics, and Delphi technique.

Brainstorming

Brainstorming is a technique developed by advertising executive Alex Osborn in order to increase creativity in the group problem-solving process.[4] A typical brainstorming group is conducted in the following manner. Group participants are given a topic and asked to generate a large number of specific ideas or problem solutions. Participants are encouraged to be freewheeling; no idea is considered too off base. Items are recorded on flip charts or some other medium for later reference. After all ideas have been shared, participants are asked to combine and improve on the items generated.

The period during which ideas are shared is relatively unstructured. The group leader does not direct the group but instead acts as a recorder while participants present their suggestions. All criticism or other comments regarding ideas must be withheld until after the item-generation phase of the meeting is completed. Occasionally, the leader may step in and enforce this important rule of brainstorming. Discussion of individual items takes place *only* after all ideas from the group have been recorded. Exhibit 9.2 lists the four principle rules of brainstorming.

Brainstorming can be used in both small and large groups. The technique attempts to remove inhibiting factors such as leader influence, structure, and ego involvement from the group process. All members are given an equal opportunity to contribute and are encouraged to do so. Research indicates that more group members play an active role and more ideas are generated in brainstorming groups than in traditional interacting groups.[5]

Nominal Group Technique

The structure and procedures of brainstorming create a unique atmosphere in which group members are encouraged to contribute their own ideas and are stimulated

EXHIBIT 9.2   RULES FOR BRAINSTORMING

1. Judgment and criticism of ideas is withheld until later.
2 Freewheeling is encouraged.
3 The greater the number of ideas the better.
4 Combination and improvement of ideas takes place only after all ideas are presented.

SOURCE: Alex F. Osborn, *Applied Imagination* (New York: Charles Scribner & Sons, 1953), 300–301.

by their interaction with others. Brainstorming also affects decision acceptance by raising the level of group member participation in the problem-solving and decision-making process. Nevertheless, it is difficult to insure that everyone present will participate in the process. **Nominal group technique** (NGT) is essentially a variation of brainstorming that broadens member participation and even further reduces group pressures to conform.[6] The term *nominal* refers to a process that brings individuals together but regulates their opportunities to communicate verbally. This unique approach to group decision making works in the following way.

Participants are first presented with a question that reflects some problem or decision the group has been asked to consider. Group members are presented with the question written on a flip chart before them. Each person then writes personal answers on a sheet of paper. Every participant is asked to provide as many answers as possible but usually is encouraged to generate some minimum number of items (e.g., ten) that is sufficient to stretch his or her thinking.

When everyone has completed a list, the facilitator (group leader) asks each person to share one idea with the group. Each item is recorded on a flip chart until every member has had an opportunity to present an idea to the group. This process is continued on a round-robin basis until all items on everyone's list have been recorded. At no time during the feedback phase are individuals permitted to endorse, criticize, or question the answers being shared. Some individuals may run out of ideas earlier than others. They are encouraged to continue thinking of new ideas and will be asked for their input again during subsequent rounds. This technique, known as hitchhiking, provides a means for keeping all group members actively involved and brings *synergy* to the group process.

When participants have shared all of their respective items, the individual lists are disposed of and a period of editing takes place. At this time, recorded items may be clarified, reworded, combined or (if duplications exist) eliminated. The final edited list is then voted on by all group members. The voting procedure requires each person to list personal choices of the best answers (e.g., the top five) and to use a reverse weighting system (first choice, 5 points; second choice, 4 points, etc.) as a means for valuing the items. Each participant's preferences are then read aloud and recorded on the flip chart. Finally, points for each item are totaled, thereby providing a *group perception* of the best answers to the problem at hand. Exhibit 9.3 presents the steps followed in the nominal group technique.

Nominal group technique is a powerful tool for including and balancing the contributions of all group members in the problem-solving process. NGT can also facilitate the generation of many ideas without the negative social forces present in

EXHIBIT 9.3   STEPS FOR USING THE NOMINAL GROUP TECHNIQUE

1. Presentation of nominal group question.
2. Silent generation of ideas in writing.
3. Round-robin feedback from group members; ideas recorded on flip chart.
4. Editing of recorded ideas through group discussion.
5. Individual prioritizing of "most important" ideas; rank order voting.
6. Group's votes "weighted" and tallied by leader.
7. Group decision made as mathematically derived outcome of voting.

SOURCE: A. L. Delbecq, A. H. Van de Ven, and D. H. Gustafson, *Group Techniques for Program Planning* (Glenview, Ill.: Scott, Foresman and Company, 1975), 40–82.

interacting groups. The technique has been used in a wide range or organizations, including such companies as the retailing giant Wal-Mart Stores Inc., and the nation's largest long-term care corporation, Beverly Enterprises.

Synectics

Synectics[7] is an approach to group problem-solving and decision-making that uses unconventional methods to examine a problem. Although synectics is associated with a particular set of procedures, it is more concerned with the frame of reference from which a group attempts to resolve an issue. Synectics makes extensive use of analogies and metaphors, thereby allowing problems to be viewed in a unique manner. This approach was used by the Gillette Company when members of a product development team were told to imagine themselves as a piece of hair and to think about what would make them feel good. Their efforts resulted in the creation of Gillette's Silkience Shampoo.

Even more unusual charges may be given a group. Members of a product improvement team, for example, may be asked to think of themselves as magic elves and told that there are no limits on what they can do to make a product better. Other analogies such as likening a problem to an item or event in nature or examining it symbolically can also be used. Whimsical as some of these techniques may seem, they permit problems to be viewed in entirely unrelated contexts, reduce tunnel vision, and encourage creativity. Exhibit 9.4 describes an actual situation in which a nature-related analogy was used to solve an industrial problem.

EXHIBIT 9.4   HOW IS A ROOF LIKE A FLOUNDER'S BACK?

An engineering group was faced with the problem of developing a new kind of roof that would insulate a dwelling from summer heat as well as from colder temperatures during the winter. An analysis of the problem suggested that a white roof would reflect the summer's heat thus cooling the building, while a black roof would absorb the rays of the sun and help to heat the building during the winter.

After considerable discussion, the group leader raised a question. "What in nature changes color?" The first was, "A weasel—white in winter, brown in summer." However, someone quickly pointed out that the weasel must lose its white hair in order for the brown hair to grow in. Another member of the group observed, "Not only that. It's not voluntary and the weasel only changes color twice a year. . . . I think our roof should change color with the heat of the sun . . . There are hot days in the spring and fall . . . and cold ones, too." Soon after, someone suggested a flounder, and a discussion commenced concerning the way in which a flounder changed colors.

"This is how the switching works: in the deepest layer of the cutis are black pigment chromatophores. When these are pushed toward the epidermal surface the flounder is covered with black spots so that he looks black. . . .

When the black pigment withdraws to the bottom . . . then the flounder appears light colored."

Finally, someone else spoke up.

"Let's flip the analogy over onto the roof problem. Let' say we make up a roofing material that is black, except buried in the black stuff are little white plastic balls. When the sun comes out and the roof gets hot the little white balls expand according to Boyle's law. They pop through the black roofing vehicle, now the roof is white . . . just like a flounder. . . . Is it the black-pigment-imparted chromatophores that come to the surface of the flounder's skin? Okay. In our roof it will be white pigment in plastic balls that come to the surface when the roof gets hot."

SOURCE: W. J. J. Gordon, *Synectics* (New York: Harper and Row Publishers, 1961), 54–56.

Not all individuals function well in groups using synectics. Creativity depends somewhat on an individual's ability to connect with the analogy used. In addition, certain persons (e.g., those with high internal locus of control*), are able to generate more ideas than are others (externals).[8] Nevertheless, a variety of organizations, including such companies as Lotus, Kimberly-Clark, and Fisher-Price, have successfully employed the synectics process to solve problems ranging from new product development to improved quality control.

Synectics may require considerable preparation. Participants must be carefully selected and trained. In addition, group members may be asked to meet at on off-site location to remove them still further from the actual problem being considered. The steps required to put synectics into practice are described in Exhibit 9.5.

Brainstorming, nominal group technique, and synectics all provide means for enriching group decision making and problem solving. They also can facilitate creative thinking at the group level. Exhibit 9.6 compares the procedures associated with each of these three group techniques.

Delphi Technique

Delphi technique is a unique approach to group problem solving that does not require participants to meet in a common location. Instead, questionnaires are used to provide the inputs necessary for decision making. The ultimate purpose of the Delphi technique is to move group members (typically experts on some subject) toward a consensus. Let us look at an example in which the Delphi technique could be used and consider the steps that would be undertaken.

*External and internal loci of control were discussed in Chapter 2, "Individuality in The Workplace."

EXHIBIT 9.5   SIX STEPS IN THE SYNECTICS PROCESS*

Step 1: Problem stated as a given.	The problem is stated; all parts are revealed and clarified.
Step 2: Problem restated in terms of what actually is sought.	The problem is restated in order to focus on possible solutions.
Step 3: Analogies or metaphors are used.	The use of analogies/metaphors allows participants to take a unique view of the problem and its elements.
Step 4: Answers emerge in the analogy/metaphor.	Comparable problem in the analogy (or metaphor) is understood in terms of the analogy.
Step 5: Solutions to the original problem emerge.	Solutions to the problem as given are revealed due to unique insights produced by analogies.
Step 6: Solution is tested.	Selected alternative is tested or otherwise reintegrated with existing knowledge.

SOURCE: Adapted from W. J. J. Gordon, *Synectics* (New York: Harper and Row Publishers, 1961), 158–160.
*Synectics, according to Gordon, involves nine distinct phases through which the process passes. These phases overlap with the steps outlined above.

EXHIBIT 9.6   A COMPARISON OF BRAINSTORMING, NOMINAL GROUP
TECHNIQUE, AND SYNECTICS

BRAINSTORMING	NGT	SYNECTICS
1. Problem presented to group.	1. Presentation of nominal group question.	1. Problem stated as given.
2. Members share ideas that come to mind. a. Unstructured b. Criticisms withheld	2. Silent generation of ideas in writing.	2. Problem restated in terms of what actually is sought.
	3. Round-robin feedback from group members; ideas recorded on flip chart.	3. Analogies or metaphors are used.
3. Ideas recorded on flip chart.		4. Answers emerge in the analogy/metaphor.
4. Ideas combined and improved on by group.	4. Editing of recorded ideas through group discussion.	5. Solutions to the original problem emerge.
	5. Individual ranking of most important ideas; rank-order voting.	6. Solution is tested.
	6. Group's votes weighted and tallied by leader.	
	7. Group decision made as mathematically derived outcome of voting.	

Today, there is a high level of interest among government officials and business leaders concerning international trade between Europe and its world trade partners in and beyond 1992. (Trade barriers between European Economic Community member countries will be removed entirely in 1992, creating an economic "United States of Europe.") In order to better anticipate the impact of these major changes, we may wish to bring together the views of leading experts from around the world. Using the Delphi technique would permit us to pull together the views of these experts without the expense or inconvenience of everyone traveling to a single location.

The first step in the Delphi technique is to develop and send to our experts a questionnaire that will provide information relevant to our central issue, trade relations after 1992. Group members are normally asked to return their responses within a relatively short period of time (usually one week). The completed questionnaires will then be analyzed.

Upon completion of the analysis, group members are sent a second questionnaire. In addition, participants are given results, in the form of ranges and averages, for each item on the original questionnaire. This feedback permits respondents to consider the views of other group members before they complete the second questionnaire. When responses from the second round are returned, they are tabulated and the results redistributed in the same manner. Normally, from three to five rounds are required before a consensus is reached. When results from the final round are tabulated, a report reflecting the group's opinion is prepared.[9]

The use of multiple rounds of information gathering, each with the benefit of feedback from the group as a whole, enables the leader to narrow and refine the answers, thereby enhancing the ability of the group to reach consensus. But the technique suffers from certain limitations. Because questionnaires are mailed to participants, the leader has little or no control over who completes the instruments or whether they are completed. Moreover, Delphi is particularly subject to the attrition of participants. The amount of time elapsing between rounds, the aversion some individuals have to completing lengthy questionnaires, and loss of interest in the process all contribute to decreased participation (and therefore to some bias) in the final group product. Advances in technology including fax machines and computer networks (such as the BITNET System, which links many university faculty members and other users nationwide) may substantially reduce such time lags and facilitate use of the Delphi technique.

EXPANDING THE ROLE OF GROUPS IN ORGANIZATIONS

The techniques we discussed in the first part of this chapter can enhance group problem solving and decision making. Other forms of group management have further expanded the role of groups in organizations and given employees at the lowest levels a greater opportunity to become involved in management activities. We will now examine two such types of groups, quality groups and self-managed work groups.

Quality Groups

Quality groups are small groups of employees who meet on a regular basis to identify, analyze, and solve problems that occur within or affect their own work areas. Such groups are an outgrowth of perhaps the best-known aspect of Japanese management, **Quality Circles**.

In the early 1950s, two American quality consultants, W. Edwards Deming and Joseph M. Juran, introduced many quality-related concepts to the Japanese. These ideas were adopted and implemented by Japanese companies in the unique form of quality control circles. The first circle was registered in Japan in 1962. With the support of JUSE (the Japanese Union of Scientists and Engineers), the concept spread rapidly throughout the country. By 1980, estimates placed the number of circles in Japan at nearly 1 million.

Development of comparable quality groups in Canada and the United States progressed more slowly. In 1974, Lockheed Missiles and Space Company, a division of Lockheed Aircraft, implemented the first major quality circle (QC) program in the United States. The number of such programs has grown rapidly since then.

As we will see later in this chapter, the quality circle movement has given rise to a variety of other quality groups. In fact, the term *quality circles*, while still used in many organizations, has lost some of its early appeal. Still, extensive development of QCs and their support systems merits a closer examination.

The structure of circle programs

Quality circles are more than just another group meeting. They represent a unique attempt to blend both human resource and technical orientations at the lowest organizational level by delegating to first-line workers the authority to investigate and solve work-related problems. Circle programs are part of an elaborate network that includes a steering committee, facilitator(s), leaders, and members.

Steering Committee.   The steering committee is made up of representatives from all levels of the organization, including line and staff managers, supervisors, circle members, and the program facilitator. Its purposes are to oversee the overall quality circle program and to support circle activities.

Facilitator(s).   The quality circle facilitator plays a key role in the program. It is the facilitator's responsibility to coordinate the overall circle program, train circle leaders, and assist in training individual circle members. Facilitators represent the primary source of circle expertise in the organization. They also help maintain interest and enthusiasm in the program and see to it that circles receive the necessary management support. Time requirements along with the responsibilities of the position limit the number of circles a facilitator can coordinate effectively. Therefore, larger programs may require more than one facilitator.

Leaders and Members.   Each quality circle consists of a leader and from ten to fifteen members (although this number can vary depending on the circle). Circle leaders may be first line supervisors or they may be selected from the ranks of employees in a work area. Leaders are responsible for training circle members and running the meetings. Although it is not the leader's job to direct the activities of members, the leader does set the agenda, insure that meetings begin and end on time, and encourage all members to participate actively. Finally, the circle leader acts as a liaison with middle management, other circles, and other expert groups (e.g., industrial engineers or computer experts) from whom outside help on a problem might be secured.

Training and techniques

Circle members approach their tasks of identifying, analyzing, and solving problems only after they receive training designed to facilitate these activities. Circles often go through eight to ten weeks of training (conducted during regular weekly meetings). Participants learn skills and techniques that will enable them to identify problems and collect and analyze information.

Some basic techniques used by quality circles include brainstorming, cause-and-effect diagrams (also known as fishbones), pareto diagrams, check sheets, and graphs. More advanced circles may be trained to use such tools as pn control charts, X-R control charts, stratified sampling, and scatter diagrams. Exhibit 9.7 describes some of the problem-identification and problem-solving techniques used in quality circles.

Two visual techniques, the Cause-Effect Diagram and the Pareto Diagram, are shown in Exhibit 9.8. Circle members are even taught formal presentation techniques (organization, visual aids, etc.) so that they can effectively offer their findings and suggestions to upper-level managers. Such training increases the participants' confidence and no doubt is partly responsible for the high degree of acceptance of ideas reported for most circle programs.

Circle meetings

The structure of circle meetings is a major factor differentiating quality circles from other groups. Unlike special project groups and certain committees, circles are not convened only when a problem arises and then disbanded when it is solved. Meetings are conducted regularly (usually once a week) and last one hour. They become a normal part of the employees' work week. In addition, problems for which solutions are sought are part of the circle members' immediate work environment. These two factors, continuous involvement and problems directly affecting participants, are

EXHIBIT 9.7 SELECTED QUALITY CIRCLE TECHNIQUES

Basic Techniques	Brainstorming	A technique used by groups to generate ideas, decision alternatives, and problem solutions; encourages free thinking and broad-based participation.
	Cause-Effect Diagram	A schematic diagram showing root causes that contribute to a specific problem.
	Pareto Diagram	A combination bar chart and line graph used to show the cumulative impact of different root causes of a problem.
	Check Sheet	A chart used to record the occurrence of operations, events, etc.
	Graph	A tool used to present areas of interest in picture form; commonly used graphs include line, bar, and pie.
Advanced Techniques	pn Control Chart	A chart that shows if a unit of production is inside or outside acceptable quality control limits.
	X-R Control Chart	A control chart that graphically reflects the average measurement of the sample and the range of dispersion around that average.
	Stratified Sampling	Collecting data in a manner that insures the representation of all subclasses of the population.
	Scatter Diagram	A plot of many points that represent the relationship between two different variables (e.g., time and units produced); used to determine whether a systematic relationship exists between the variables and what that relationship may look like.

important reasons for quality circles' success in organizations of all types. In essence, circle members look for opportunities to improve the existing situation rather than ignore problems or wait until they must be solved.

Success and failure in quality circles

Over a decade has passed since quality circles were first introduced in Canada and the United States. During that time, much has been learned about successful and unsuccessful QC programs. (Estimates place the failure rate of new circles as high as 70 percent.[10]) Success, of course, depends on what managers and employees hope to achieve through circles. Some who adopt quality circles seek to influence *performance* by improving quality or raising *productivity* (hard measures). Others see quality circles

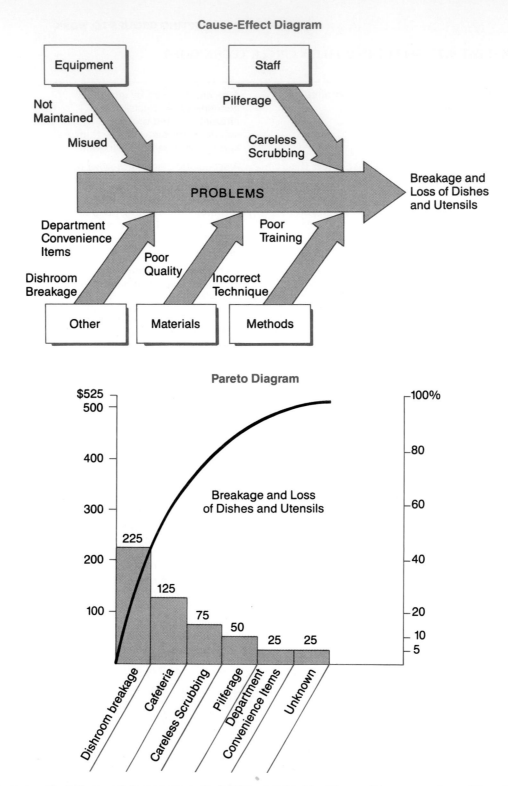

Cause-Effect Diagram

Equipment

Not Maintained

Misued

Staff

Pilferage

Careless Scrubbing

PROBLEMS

Breakage and Loss of Dishes and Utensils

Department Convenience Items

Dishroom Breakage

Poor Quality

Poor Training

Incorrect Technique

Other

Materials

Methods

Pareto Diagram

Breakage and Loss of Dishes and Utensils

225
125
75
50
25
25

Dishroom breakage
Cafeteria
Careless Scrubbing
Pilferage
Department Convenience Items
Unknown

The cause-effect diagram (also known as the fishbone) helps identify possible causes of a problem. The pareto diagram illustrates the relative and cumulative significance of problem causes, enabling circle members to prioritize them more easily. These and other quality circle tools help members visualize problem situations and facilitate implementation of solutions.

EXHIBIT 9.8   EXAMPLES OF QUALITY CIRCLE TOOLS

as a way to improve *labor-management* relations and generally contribute to the organization's quality of work life (soft measures).

Results in all three areas have been mixed. Reports of improved quality and productivity are abundant; however it is sometimes difficult to link "bottom-line" savings or gains directly to circle activities. For example, one automobile rental agency was able to reduce by twenty-seven seconds the time required to locate an available vehicle in the system. This can be translated into direct savings *if* more customers can be booked or fewer operators are required to handle reservations. However, the actual impact on profits may be more difficult to monitor if the work force is not reduced or if there exists no way to measure the number of clients who, refusing to wait for an operator, choose instead to call another rental company.

Likewise, the impact of changes in quality of work life (QWL) on an organization is difficult to measure or even determine. One recent study found that participation in quality circles had a strong impact on QWL issues related directly to circle activities but did not affect attitudes toward job challenge, overall job satisfaction, or communication through the entire organization.[11] Nevertheless, behavioral indicators such as productivity and absenteeism improved significantly for QC members, but remained about the same for nonparticipants.

Failure Factors   Some QCs experience problems which, if left unchecked, can lead to the failure of a single circle or an entire quality circle program. One examination of 193 QC programs concluded that quality circle problems could be traced to a number of different sources.[12] Some problems originated within the circle or circle programs themselves, others occurred in the circle (or program) environment, and still others occurred at the interface between circle activities and the organization. In addition to a lack of management support, the most often cited problems included: staffing program positions (steering committee, facilitators, leaders), nonmember feelings of jealousy and exclusion, scheduling and logistical problems, and disruptions due to personnel transfers and changes in the economy.

Success Factors   A number of studies have examined factors that are related to the success of quality circle programs. It appears that programs are more likely to succeed if they focus on long-range plans, are concerned with ongoing problems, have volunteer facilitators, measure cost savings, are cost effective, involve a significant number of employees at the work site, meet at least once a week, and provide managerial incentives for supporting circles.[13] In a study of two British firms, circles were most likely to succeed when managers received information on the success of circles in their work areas and were personally given credit for the success of circles.[14]

Organizational Impact.   Questions have been raised concerning the impact of quality circles on the overall organization. One study of circle programs suggested that circles are likely to bring about substantial organizational change when (1) there is sufficient training of participants; (2) attention is given to group dynamics (interpersonal relations, group development, cooperation versus competition, etc.); (3) goals for each QC are set and accurate records of their activities are kept; and (4) circles are created out of existing, intact work teams.[15] Furthermore, evidence exists that circles often experience early success, but may begin to decline after the "honeymoon" period (approximately two years) is over.[16]

Individual Impact   Of course, not everyone wants to participate in a quality circle. Those who do tend to believe that QCs will allow them greater involvement at work and an opportunity to accomplish meaningful changes in the organization. Factors such as age, tenure, and wanting a break from the job do not appear to play an important role in why workers choose to participate.[17]

Second generation circles and other quality groups

The quality circle movement grew rapidly after its introduction in North America. Unfortunately, however, this growth was accompanied by a high rate of program failure. These failures were often due to the establishment of QC programs in unhealthy labor-management environments or the misuse of circles by managers. Problems with early QC programs has lead to a reassessment of the manner in which these and similar employee involvement groups perform. As a result, the structure of quality circles has generally remained intact, although their names and functions have in many cases changed.[18]

Second generation circles are today known by a number of different names, including employee involvement teams, worker participation groups, employee performance and recognition groups, and quality improvement teams. These groups sometimes operate on a broader scope than the original QCs and may even try to *prevent* problems rather than wait to respond until they have occurred. Two additional variations that appear to have met with success include (1) required rather than voluntary participation in circles, and (2) giving QCs the authority to implement their own ideas.

Circles at McDonnell Aircraft Co. of St. Louis, for example, now include over two thirds of all employees, and everyone from the president to the newest employee at the Paul Revere Insurance Group belongs to at least one quality team. At Paul Revere, over fifty-seven hundred ideas with an annual value of $7 million were reportedly implemented before they were approved formally.[19]

XEROX

One of the leading proponents of quality groups is Xerox Corporation, the 1989 winner of the prestigious Malcolm Baldrige National Quality Award. Xerox has created a national network of quality improvement teams which identify important quality improvement needs and seek to solve related quality problems. District, regional, and national competitions are held to encourage trained Xerox quality teams to achieve significant quality improvements in their own areas and for the company as a whole.

One Houston-based Xerox team concerned with a Customer Service Support Representatives (CSSR) recognition program investigated the existing program and redesigned it to better meet CSSR needs. An evaluation of monthly performance reports along with data gathered directly from those affected by the program revealed that customer calls per day and quality of work both increased significantly. Team members estimated that adoption of the program would result in nearly $900,000 in savings for the company's Southern Region alone. Other Xerox teams addressed such problems as redesigning the billing system to increase the accuracy of customer invoicing, increasing the availability of information necessary to improve customer service, reducing overtime, and reducing bad debts.

Arguments surrounding the nature and function of "true" quality circles continue to rage. Some proponents suggest that a narrow view of QCs, similar to the definition presented on page 283, remains viable and that attempts to change either the purpose or process of circles will diminsh their effectiveness.* Others, however, are likely to support variations or hybrids that meet the respective needs of each organization. Although this latter 'contingency'' approach to the use of QC-type groups may be viable, there still remains a need for attention to group goals, structure, and procedures.

Finally, it has been suggested that quality circles and similar groups may best be viewed as techniques which can lead to a more participative culture in the organization.[20] In this context, such groups are likely to be seen as a single step toward the implementation of a broad-based participative philosophy.

Self-Managed Work Groups

Quality groups place a significant amount of responsibility for problem identification and solution, activities that traditionally have been reserved for managers and other specially trained staff members, in the hands of first-line employees. **Self-managed work groups** are another way of involving workers in traditional management activities. However, the purpose and functions of these groups are considerably broader in scope than either quality circles or the group decision-making techniques we discussed earlier.

The nature and functions of self-managed work groups

Members of self-managed work groups work in the same area and perform related tasks. They are given responsibility for producing an entire product or service or a significant part of it. Groups typically consist of from five to as many as twenty members and operate as self-contained organizational units. These factors contribute to the group's **syntality** (group personality) and its cohesiveness. Team members learn several jobs to increase the group's flexibility and members are often paid according to their ability to perform a variety of tasks rather than on the basis of seniority or because they hold a single job title.

Self-managed groups perform the day-to-day functions normally associated with their respective work areas (e.g., production, service, sales). Such groups differ from other task groups, however, in that they are also responsible for performing traditional business activities (budgeting, scheduling, and maintaining records) and personnel functions (assigning jobs, skill training, performance evaluation of group members, and dealing with tardiness, absenteeism, and on-the-job motivation).[21]

Conducting group meetings

Group meetings can be conducted on a regular (weekly) basis or called when specific problems arise. Meetings can be attended by an outside coordinator or an upper-level manager known as a support team member. However, they normally are conducted by a team leader selected by the group. Meetings also can be attended by members of other teams when the problems being addressed require coordination between two or more groups. Meetings are not structured or technique-bound, although decision-making techniques like those discussed earlier in this chapter can also be used.

---

*These individuals maintain the distinction between quality circles and other forms or worker participation. Although not necessarily disputing the worth of alternative types of group participation, they generally believe that QC's are most effective when organizations adhere strictly to the original model.

Challenges to group effectiveness

Self-managed work groups, like all management innovations, must overcome problems that can potentially inhibit their effectiveness. Two areas that merit particular attention include (1) potential problems with group decision making, and (2) problems with leading self-managed groups.

Group Decision Making   Certain problems related to group decision making have been observed in self-managed work groups. In one organization, for example, individuals who held views inconsistent with those of the majority were pressured by co-workers to conform to the group's belief patterns. Group leaders also tended to ignore differences of opinion and assume, through their actions, that all group members were in agreement. This occurred despite nonverbal indications by some participants that they were not in complete agreement with the group. Thus, in addition to creating an illusion of unanimity, the groups observed tended to censor their own activities.[22] These patterns are part of the more broadly based phenomenon known as group-think, discussed in Chapter 7.

Leadership.   The leadership of self-managed work groups can also be a source of confusion. The introduction of such groups into our industrial culture requires that traditionally schooled managers reexamine leadership behaviors both within and outside the group. Delineation of the roles of external coordinators and internal group leaders potentially can lead to misunderstandings and conflict. Group leaders, in particular, find themselves in the delicate position of providing direction without appearing to lead. Group leaders can use such specific self-management strategies as group self-observation, group self-goal setting, and group self-reward to minimize this problem.

Recent experiences with self-managed work groups

Self-managed work groups first received wide attention when they were introduced to the automobile industry by the Swedish manufacturer Volvo in the 1960s. A number of companies in the United States and Canada briefly experimented with the idea, but few attempted to employ it on a widespread basis. Today, there has been a renewed interest in such groups. This interest is primarily due to (1) emergence of a strong participative management philosophy in many companies, and (2) reorganizations resulting in the elimination of many lower- and middle-management positions.

To date, reports on the success of these groups have generally been favorable. Lower administrative costs, a reduction in number of job classifications, greater flexibility in scheduling and assigning work, and improved quality and productivity have all been reported.[23] Some organizations, like Skippy's Little Rock plant and the LTV Steel Co. plant in Cleveland, have had widespread success with such teams. Both Chrysler and General Motors view teamwork in general and self-managed teams in particular to be central to their future competitiveness.

The concept has today spread even further into such industries as food processing, electronics, insurance and financial services. But opposition to such teams does exist. Some managers feel threatened by their loss of influence or the possible loss of their job. Opposition also exists in some labor unions which view work teams as union-busting devices.[24]

The impact of self-managed groups has been felt for some time in northern Europe and has been incorporated into the work system of at least one Eastern Bloc country, Yugoslavia. In fact, it appears that wider use of these and other forms of group participation may become common in the Soviet Union and some of the formerly Communist Eastern European states. The International Dimension below provides an interesting insight into the impact of Perestroika and Glasnost on such changes.

Interorganizational Groups

Quality groups and self-managed work groups solve problems and accomplish other tasks within a single organization or organizational unit. Circumstances arise, however, and lead to groups being established to facilitate cooperation, resolve differences, or jointly undertake projects involving two or more organizations. These

INTERNATIONAL DIMENSION
Perestroika and Group Participation

A fundamental concept of Soviet ideology is the participation of people in their own governance. Worker participation on the local level, however, was largely discredited under administrative command systems of the past. According to one Soviet expert, Vladimir Shlepentokh, it was not until the implementation of Mikhail Gorbachev's policies of glasnost and perestroika began that progress was made toward involving workers in job-related decision-making processes.

Following a five-day tour of Yugoslavia, President Gorbachev indicated that the self-management approach used in such enterprises as Iskra and Ivo Lola might provide a model for the involvement of worker groups in the management of Soviet enterprises. However, at least one Soviet experiment in worker participation has failed to achieve its intended results. Workers in a number of plants were given legislative authority to elect their own executive personnel. But according to Soviet management expert Gennady B. Kochetkov, inefficiencies and a general lack of satisfaction with the procedure's impact on organizational performance have resulted in a rethinking of the practice and proposed legislation that will curtail or eliminate the practice.

Most observers conclude that the ongoing restructuring in the Soviet Union and Eastern Europe is likely to be accompanied by dramatic changes in the level of employee participation and group influence in the Eastern Bloc's manufacturing and service sectors. Only time will tell what form such participation will take and the extent to which it will alter labor-management relations. One thing seems certain, however; the impact of perestroika and glasnost will be felt in the workplace.

Questions

What problems are Eastern Bloc enterprises that experiment with group self-management and other forms of worker participation likely to encounter?

What companies in countries outside the Soviet Union and Eastern Europe learn from the experiences of firms like those in Yugoslavia?

SOURCE: "Seeing the Future," *The Wall Street Journal*, 21 March 1988, p. 18; Interview with G.B. Kochetkov, Head of Department of Management Studies, Institute of the USA and Canada, USSR Academy of Science, 5 March 1990.

interorganizational groups are made up of members who represent more than one *parent* organization and who meet periodically to make decisions that are relevant to the common interest of all the organizations represented.

For example, an interorganizational group might be formed when a state legislature mandates that a performance-based evaluation system be implemented in all state-supported colleges and universities. Representatives could be appointed from each institution to develop uniform procedures for meeting that mandate. Similarly, a number of non-affiliated hospitals deciding to undertake a joint, community mental health program could form an interorganizational group consisting of health professionals and other interested parties from each participating hospital to identify and solve potential problems.

CLARK AND VOLVO

In an actual case, an interorganizational group was created when Clark Equipment Corporation, a United States-based firm, and AB Volvo of Sweden joined forces to compete with industry giants Caterpillar and Komatsu. The first step was the formation of a ten-person team consisting of the production, marketing, financial, engineering, and general managers from both Clark Michigan and Volvo BM, two participating divisions. The team's task was to produce a detailed feasibility study and design the mechanisms of cooperation that would be necessary for the joint venture to succeed.

When their work had been completed, group members not only had produced a design acceptable to both companies but had also "welded themselves into a tightly knit management team." In just six months, group members had anticipated nearly all problems the joint venture would encounter, had overcome most cultural obstacles, and had even agreed on who should occupy executive positions in the new company.[25]

Interorganizational groups can be classified along two dimensions, (1) group origin (mandated versus voluntary), and (2) degree of externally imposed task structure (high versus low).[26] In one of our examples the committee representing state colleges and universities was mandated and had high externally imposed task structure. The mental health group, on the other hand, was made up of volunteers whose exploratory activities were low in externally imposed task structure.

The behavior and satisfaction of group members as well as the quality of the group's output can be affected by its respective classification characteristics.[27] Exhibit 9.9 provides examples regarding the expected development and outcomes in different types of interorganizational groups. Notice, for example, that the "forming" stage of group development is relatively brief in mandated groups and requires more time in voluntary groups, especially in those groups whose tasks are less structured (i.e., members have greater influence over their own goals and activities). Conversely, mandated groups with high external task structure are more responsive to external demands than either Type II or Type III groups and are considerably more responsive than Type IV (voluntary, low task structure) groups.

Initial studies of interorganizational groups provide preliminary insight into the costs and benefits of different types of interorganizational groups. For example, members of Type I groups are generally clear on what is expected of them; they are likely to perform at least at the expected level and attend to work efficiently. Members of Type II groups may be frustrated by their required but structureless participation, but they are likely to be responsive to those who have appointed them to membership.

EXHIBIT 9.9 EXPECTED DEVELOPMENT AND OUTCOMES IN INTERORGANIZATIONAL GROUPS

Group Origin	EXTERNAL TASK STRUCTURE	
	High	Low

Mandated	Type I: Reliable Compliance
	Brief Formative Phase
	Low Level of Overt Problems in Group
	Decision Making: Efficient Participation
	Low Member Satisfaction
	High Agreement on External Evaluation
	Minimal Quality of Output
	High Compliance to External Demands
		Type II: Frustrated vs. Responsive
		Brief/Moderate Formative Phase
		Low/Moderate Level of Problems in Group
		    Decision Making: Confusion, Covert Conflict
		Low/Moderate Member Satisfaction
		High/Moderate Agrement on External
		    Evaluation
		Minimal/Moderate Quality of Output
		High/Moderate Compliance to External
		    Demands

Voluntary	Type III: Directed vs. Inner Conflict
	Moderate/Longer Formative Phase
	Moderate/High Level of Problems in Group
	Decision Making: Manipulation, Open
	    Conflict
	Moderate/High Member Satisfaction
	Moderate/Low Agreement on External
	    Evaluation
	Moderate/High Quality of Output
	Moderate/Low Compliance to External
	    Demands
		Type IV: Creative Commitment
		Longer Formative Phase
		High Level of Problems in Group Decision
		    Making: Open Conflict Over Specific Ends
		    and Most Appropriate Means
		High Member Satisfaction
		Low Agreement on External Evaluation
		High Quality of Output
		Low Compliance to External Demands

SOURCE: J. H. Shopler, "Interorganizational Groups: Origins, Structure, and Outcomes," *Academy of Management Review*, Vol. 12 (October 1987): 704.

Type III group members may experience inner conflict because they have volunteered for the group but are subject to external structuring of their activities. Since membership is voluntary, if designated leaders do not exist, power plays are likely. Finally, members of Type IV groups are likely to be active and highly committed, although their output may have greater relevancy to the group members themselves than to their parent organizations.

Interorganizational groups present special challenges to managers. The complexity of interpersonal relations and group dynamics is significantly greater in such groups than in groups that exist within a single organization. Multiple constituencies, diverse goals and differing organizational-related behavior patterns all contribute to understanding how and why interorganizational groups function as they do. Finally, not all interorganizational groups may be officially recognized and the ethical implications of individuals from more than one organization working together may be questioned by competitors and others. The activities of one such group, known as The Clique, are described in the Ethical Dilemma on page 294. This group's interorganizational relationships and activities were found to be not only unethical but also illegal.

MANAGING INTERGROUP COMPETITION

Businesses, by their nature, compete with other organizations. Even nonprofit enterprises (e.g., some hospitals and schools) may find themselves in competition for resources with institutions that provide similar products or services.

ETHICAL DILEMMA
Self-Interest and
the Law

Interorganizational groups are normally created to achieve benefits for members of more than one enterprise. Although they often succeed, their actions may not always be in the public's best interest and may go further than is desirable for the parent organizations themselves.

In 1985, a highly classified document pertaining to the United States Government's "Star Wars" program was sent from the President's Office to the secretaries of State and Defense and the Chairman of the Joint Chiefs of Staff. A midlevel Boeing budget analyst named Richard Fowler also received a copy of the memo, which he hand-delivered to executives at Boeing. Fowler was praised by Boeing executives for his good work and named Marketing Employee of the Quarter the following year. The government took another view of his activities, however, and on January 12, 1990, sentenced him to two years in prison for his role in what has become known as "The Clique."

The Clique is a tight-knit group of various Defense Department insiders and executives from at least five major corporations who compete for defense contracts. According to government prosecutors, members of The Clique have regularly conspired to acquire and misuse government documents, many specifically labeled "Not Releasable to Contractors."In fact, entry to The Clique was gained by demonstrating that fresh information could be offered to existing members. As for Fowler, he contends that he was only doing his job and maintains that he won't testify against other members of The Clique: "I simply would never subject anyone else to the things I've gone through."

Questions
Are interorganizational groups intended to fulfill roles like that of The Clique?
Do organizations that encourage interorganizational groups increase the likelihood that they will experience ethical problems?
How can the risk of ethical dilemmas be reduced for interorganizational groups?

SOURCE: A. Pasztor, and R. Wartzman, "The Clique: How a Spy for Boeing and His Pals Gleaned Data on Defense Plans," *The Wall Street Journal,* 15 January 1990, pp. A1, A6.

The belief that competition is healthy has carried over to the internal management of many organizations. It is not uncommon, for example, for individual companies' regional sales organizations, different shifts, or even plants to compete with one another informally or as part of a management-sanctioned program. Xerox Corporation has built its team-based quality improvement program around sector, regional, and national competitions, with winning teams at each level receiving awards, cash prizes, and corporate-wide recognition. The competition concludes with winning teams from throughout the company coming together for a corporate quality fair.

Although **intergroup competition** can contribute to organizational goal attainment, it can also have unintended impacts within and between the groups involved. In this section, we will examine group activities that occur during competition, the consequences of such competition, and how intergroup competition can be effectively managed.[28]

Group Activities During Competition

Intergroup competition has an impact within, as well as between, competing groups. Group members tend to close ranks (within their own groups) and set aside differences when they are involved in competition. Task-related behavior becomes more prevalent, groups become more highly structured, and leadership patterns become more directive. Each group tends to demand more loyalty and conformity from its members, and participants are inclined to accept their new roles.

Competing groups, even though they are part of the same parent organization, begin to see one another as the enemy rather than as neutrals. Perceptions become distorted, with members looking at their own group as good and fair and viewing the other group(s) more negatively. Communication between the groups decreases, and hostility increases. Finally, when interaction between the groups is required, group members tend to selectively perceive what is taking place, listen to fellow members and disregard the views of people in other groups.

Consequences of Competition

Competition normally ends with one party winning and another party losing, and studies suggest that different post-competition patterns emerge within winning and losing groups. Winning groups, for example, are likely to retain their cohesiveness and show a high degree of concern for member needs. At the same time, winning can also lead to feelings of complacency. Group members are likely to want to reap the benefits of their victory and show little concern for evaluating why or how they were able to succeed.

Losing groups, on the other hand, are characterized by a significantly different pattern. The group's perceptions of its invincibility and rightness have been shattered and must be reexamined. Feeling towards other group members can deteriorate, and interpersonal conflicts can cause the group to splinter. The remaining group members may blame others for their defeat but also may be ready to work harder together in the future. Losing groups thus can use defeat as a learning experience.

Let us look at the example of Armortech, a manufacturer of construction siding for homes and commercial use. The company was approached by a national distributor of home improvement products and asked to develop a new generation of insulated siding. The company suspected that others in the industry might soon attempt to develop a similar product. Therefore it was decided that two teams would be formed and each asked to develop the best possible product.

At the end of six weeks, both teams presented their new products to top management, and a product was chosen. This product, in turn, was submitted to the national distributor. The distributor evaluated the new siding, but requested that certain modifications be made. At first the members of the winning team headed by Bob Taylor resisted the distributor's suggestions and argued that their product, "the clear winner" of the internal competition, remain unchanged. When top management insisted that the modifications be examined more closely by the team, progress was slow.

Members of the losing Armortech team viewed the request differently. Although they recognized that their original product proposal had not been accepted, the decided to modify their own design in a manner that would satisfy the distributor's concerns. Spending a few evenings and a weekend at the plant, they presented their revised proposal to top management just twenty-four hours after Taylor's group reported back that, "some of the changes can be made, but others cannot be incorporated, as they will violate the integrity of the original design." After examining the second, unsolicited proposal, Armortech's CEO accepted the revision.

Early the following morning, Bob Taylor's team held a brief meeting to talk about what had happened. Some members were indignant. Others, however, looked at what had happened more philosophically. Said one somewhat bemused team member, "We were too busy planning our victory party; maybe there's a lesson here for all of us!"

Insights into Managing Competition

In this section, we examined the impact of intergroup competition and pointed out some of its weaknesses. Such competition can also be beneficial to an organization. Group members can acquire a greater sense of cohesiveness and identity, and the competition itself can result in an improved end product. Furthermore, a manager can take certain steps to reduce the negative consequences of intergroup competition.

Effectively managing intergroup competition requires competing groups to find common goals and establish and maintain a viable means of communicating with one another. Three tactics for accomplishing these ends include

1. locating a common enemy;
2. conducting intergroup negotiations on a subgroup level; and
3. identifying and working toward a superordinate goal.

First, a manager can help competing groups locate a common enemy. Identifying such an external threat often brings the groups closer together. Second, interaction can be facilitated through intergroup negotiations conducted on a subgroup level. Such negotiations establish a forum for exchanging ideas and provide another group environment (the negotiation teams) for achieving a common goal (intergroup cooperation).

Finally, identifying a superordinate goal toward which both groups can aspire can refocus attention away from one another and toward some mutually beneficial end. Goals can be redefined to reflect the interests of both groups (e.g., outselling the competition throughout the country rather than one regional sales group out-performing another), or a goal may be established to increase cooperation between groups. For example, two shifts in a production plant may seek ways to improve the change-over during the shift change or to establish a liaison group to iron out differences impeding productivity in the department as a whole.

Intergroup competition can benefit organizations and lead to improved performance. However, such competition can and must be managed if those benefits are to be fully derived and if the potential problems of intergroup competition are to be minimized.

PUTTING GROUPS TO WORK: CONCLUSIONS

As we discussed in the previous chapter, it is important to understand the nature of groups and how they influence behavior. It is equally important to know how groups can be used effectively in organizations.

Many managers have resisted the widespread use of groups because of problems they have encountered with committees and other forms of group activities. It is not necessarily the nature of groups, however, that is responsible for such problems. Too often, group failure can be traced to poor management of the group process.

In this chapter, we described a number of ways groups can be used effectively in organizational settings. In particular, groups can contribute to the decision-making process by increasing the quality of decision as well as the likelihood that those decisions will be implemented enthusiastically.

Four useful techniques for improving group problem solving and decision making (brainstorming, nominal group, synectics, and Delphi) were discussed. As a manager, you must learn to use the appropriate technique in the given situation. For example, either brainstorming or the nominal group technique can be used to set goals, identify problems, or arrive at solutions when group members can meet in one location. NGT might be chosen over brainstorming when it is particularly important to minimize the influence of status differences between participants or to reduce unusually strong pressure to conform. Delphi technique, on the other hand, might be chosen when group members cannot meet face-to-face and when you want the overall group to affect participant opinions subtly. These decision-making techniques, along with synectics, probably are more likely to be used by groups of managers than by first-line employees.

Managers in organizations have recently begun sharing decision-making and problem-solving responsibilities with lower-level employees. Two types of groups particularly effective in this regard are quality groups and self-managed work groups. Once again, decisions about whether to use such groups and which type of group might be most appropriate for your organization must be made carefully.

Although both quality groups and self-managed groups have met with success, problems must be anticipated and dealt with. Managing these groups also may require a careful evaluation of your managerial philosophy and a substantial commitment of personal and organizational support if their full contribution is to be realized.

While many group activities take place within a single organization and may even be confined to a single organizational unit, increasing attention is being given to groups whose members represent more than one parent organization. These interorganizational groups can be found in business and governmental organizations and are especially prevalent in the health and human services sector. Interorganizational groups can present unique demands on group members and must be understood if your management responsibilities require that you cooperate with those in organizations other than your own.

Finally, you may find yourself in an environment in which groups within your organization compete with one another. Competition can be beneficial to group performance. As you have seen, however, difficulties can arise between, as well as within, competing groups. Your responsibility as a manager is not simply to allow or encourage intergroup competition, but rather to *manage* it when it occurs.

It is difficult to imagine an organization in which you as a manager will not spend considerable time in group settings. Now that you have completed this chapter, you should be in a better position to select and use group techniques that meet your situational needs.

QUESTIONS FOR REVIEW AND DISCUSSION

1. What is an interacting group and what are its shortcomings?
2. What are the quality and acceptance dimensions of organizational problem solving and why are they important?
3. What are the important characteristics of brainstorming?
4. What are the advantages of the nominal group technique over other forms of group meetings? What, if any, shortcomings does NGT have?

5. What techniques are used in the synectics approach to group problem solving?

6. Under what conditions might you use the Delphi technique? What problems are you likely to encounter using this approach?

7. How do quality groups differ from project and other types of groups?

8. How successful are quality groups and what types of problems are they likely to experience?

9. What are self-managed work groups and how are they different from other types of groups?

10. How do groups behave during and after they have been in competition with other groups?

11. What are interorganizational groups and how may their behaviors differ from other types of groups?

REFERENCES

1. D. D. White, D. S. Cochran, and D. R. Latham, "Enhancing Academic Research Through the Consulting Engagement," in G. J. Gore and R. G. Wright, *The Academic Consultant Connection* (Dubuque: Kendall-Hunt, 1979), 276–285.

2. N. R. F. Maier, *Principles of Human Relations* (New York: John Wiley & Sons, 1952).

3. F. C. Miner, Jr., "A Comparative Analysis of Three Diverse Group Decision Making Approaches," *Academy of Management Journal*, Vol. 22, No. 1 (March 1979): 88–93.

4. Alex F. Osborn, *Applied Imagination: Principles and Procedures,* (New York: Scribner's Sons, 1953), 297–307.

5. White, et al., op. cit.

6. A. L. Delbecq, A. H. Van de Ven, and D. H. Gustafson, *Group Techniques for Program Planning* (Glenview, Ill.: Scott Foresman and Company, 1975); William F. Fox, Anonymity and Other Keys to Successful Problem Solving Meetings, *National Productivity Review*, Vol. 8, No. 2 (Spring 1989): 145–156.

7. W. J. J. Gordon, *Synectics* (New York: Harper and Row Publishers, 1961); G. M. Prince, "The Operational Mechanism of Synectics," *The Journal of Creative Behavior*, Vol. 2, No. 1 (1968): 1–13.

8. D. Ireland, *The Problem Solving Procedure, Group Composition Classification, and Locus of Control Orientation on Idea Genereation Performance and Group Participant Perceived Satisfaction Levels* (Ph. D. thesis, Texas Tech University, 1977), 64.

9. Delbecq, op. cit., 83–107.

10. W. Imberman, "Why Quality Circles Don't Work," *Canadian Business* (May 1982): 103–104, 106.

11. M. L. Marks, "The Question of Quality Circles," *Psychology Today*, Vol. 20 (March 1986): 36–46.

12. D. D. White, and D. A. Bednar, "Locating Problems with Quality Circles," *The National Productivity Review*, Vol. 4 (Winter 1984–85): 45–52.

13. H. N. Seelye, and J. A. Sween, "Critical Components of Successful U.S. Quality Circles," *The Quality Circles Journal*, Vol 6, No. 1 (1983): 14–17.

14. K. Bradley, and S. Hill, "Quality Circles and Managerial Interests," *Industrial Relations*, Vol. 26 (Winter 1987): 68–82.

15. E. E. Lawler, S. A. Mohrman, and G. E. Lawler, "Quality Circles: After the Fad," *Harvard Business Review*, Vol. 63, No. 1 (1985): 65–71.

16. E. E. Lawler, and S. A. Mohrman, "Quality Circles: After the Honeymoon," *Organizational Dynamics*, Vol. 15, No. 4 (1987): 42–54; R. Griffin, "Consequences of Quality Circles in an Industrial Setting: A Longitudinal Assessment," *Academy of Management Journal*, Vol. 31, No. 2 (March 1988): 238–258.

17. J. W. Dean, "The Decision to Participate in Quality Circles," *Journal of Applied Behavioral Science*, Vol. 21, No. 3 (1985): 317–327.

18. B. Gofer, "Quality Circles: The Second Generation," *Training*, Vol. 3 (December 1986): 10.

19. J. C. Horn, "Making Quality Circles Work Better," *Psychology Today*, Vol. 20 (August 1986): 10.

20. Lawler and Mohrman, op. cit.

21. J. R. Hackman "Work Design," in J. R. Hackman and J. Suttle, eds., *Improving Life at Work* (Santa Monica: Goodyear Publishing, 1977), 96–162; H. P. Sims and C. C. Manz, "Conversations Within Self-Managed Work Groups," *National Productivity Review*, Vol. 1, No. 3 (1982): 261–269.

22. C. C. Manz, and H. P. Sims, Jr., "The Potential for 'Groupthink' in Autonomous Work Groups," *Human Relations*, Vol. 35, No. 9 (September 1982): 773–784.

23. A. Bernstein and W. Zeller, "Detroit vs. the UAW: At Odds Over Teamwork," *Business Week*, 24 August 1987, 54–55; Brian Dumaine, "Who Needs a Boss," *Fortune*, 7 May 1990, 52–60.

24. J. Hoerr, "Is Teamwork a Management Plot? Mostly Not," *Business Week*, 20 Februrary 1989, 70. N. M. Tichy and M. A. Devanna, *The Transformational Leader*, (New York: John Wiley & Sons, 1986), 140–142.

25. J. H. Shopler, "Interorganizational Groups: Origins, Structures, and Outcomes," *The Academy of Management Review*, Vol. 13, No. 3 (October 1987): 702–713.

26. Ibid.

27. E. H. Schein, *Organizational Psychology*, 2d ed. (Englwood Cliffs, N.J.: Prentice-Hall, 1970), 96–103.

CASE 9.1 *The case of* Q.C. 5

DON ADAY   *Firestone Tire and Rubber Co.*
DONALD D. WHITE   *University of Arkansas*

Firestone Tire and Rubber Company is one of the world's largest producer of tires. The company has manufacturing facilities throughout the world, including five plants in the United States. Among the most progressive of the Firestone facilities is the forty-acre facility located in Oklahoma City, Oklahoma.

The Oklahoma City plant had long been a leader in the area of human resource programming. Therefore, it came as no surprise when the plant manager announced that a quality circle program would soon be operational at the plant.

PROBLEMS AT THE 5-ROLL CALENDER

The manufacture of automobile tires involves a complex process combining carefully prepared materials, the use of heavy industrial equipment, and the attention and skills of well-trained personnel. Among the most important of the operations is that of the calendering. The calender is a piece of equipment that is used to make the rubber innerliner for a tire. The calender squeezes hot rubber between large rolls, producing sheets which are cut, cooled, and later wound on spools.

Ever since the 5-roll calender operation was introduced in the plant, problems were encountered with the feed chutes jamming up. The problem was compounded further when radial tire production placed additional demands on the system. Despite efforts by the engineering group to correct the problem, feed chutes continued to come loose and the rollers continued to fail. This, in turn, caused the rubber strips being fed into the calender to ball up and jam on the chutes.

When jam-ups occurred, operators were forced to slow down or stop the calender and remove the material causing the problem. In addition to interrupting the normal flow of product, the only rubber coming off the calender was graded as pigs (scrap). These pigs then had to be returned to a large mixer known as the banbury and reprocessed into the product flow.

Workers responsible for calender operations had long been frustrated by the problem. Pressure from the production manager and foreman to "straighten things out down there" coupled with the inability of the engineering staff to correct the problem only further frustrated the operators. One operator confided, "they expect us to keep this damn thing running, and blame us when it goes down, but no one in the office has any answers. It's not my fault I'm not an engineer."

FORMATION OF Q.C. 5

In September, Q.C. 5 was formed in the 5-roll calender department. Although other quality circles had been in existence for some time in the plant, Q.C. 5 was the first circle in the calender work area. The circle had seven members including the supervisor of the 5-roll calender operation.

Circle members began their activities by participating in an eight-week training program, during which they received instruction in various information gathering and analysis techniques. Following the training, they began to explore the problems they were experiencing at the 5-roll calender.

Members immediately agreed that their problem was with the calender jam-ups. They used a technique known as brainstorming and compiled a list of probable causes responsible for the pigs. (See Exhibit 9.10.) These problems were then transferred to a cause-effect diagram similar to that shown in Exhibit 9.11.

One problem was seen as the varying width caused by the automatic knives, which sometimes oscillated. After identifying the problem, the supervisor contacted the maintenance department, which calibrated the knives. This seemed to help correct the problem. A second problem, too much departmental maintenance, also was corrected immediately. After examining the rest of the list, the circle agreed that the design of a free-falling feed system probably was the major cause of the excess pigs. As the nature of the problem and its causes became clearer to the group, a decision was made to collect data on the job that would more accurately indicate the true impact of each of

EXHIBIT 9.10   BRAINSTORMED CAUSES OF PIGS ON FIVE-ROLL CALENDER

1. Product size changes that require adustments.
2. Feed strip jam-up due to bad chute design.
3. Operator running material (rubber) at too low a temperature.
4. Varying width of stock because cutting knives are oscillating.
5. Mechanical breakdown.
6. Operator error at wind-up machine.
7. Bad stock from banbury mixer.
8. Calender run-out due to rubber breaking.

the projected causes on the problem. These data are contained in Exhibit 9.12.

Some problems were encountered in gathering the data on the floor. The operator of the 5-roll calender kept track of the number of feed chute jam-ups. At first, pig check data was gathered by individuals running wind-up machines. After the rubber was cooled, it was put into fabric liners and onto spools. The good rubber was later used for the inside lining of the tire. If pigs rather than good rubber came off the calender, the pigs were wound and later reprocessed. Since wind-up operators are supposed to identify the pigs anyway, it seemed logical that they could keep a record for the project.

Unfortunately, the wind-up operators were not members of the circle. In addition, they did not always know what was going on at the calender. This resulted in the circle's encountering a considerable amount of difficulty gathering the data. It was finally decided that the checklist should be kept by the calender operator.

ANALYSIS AND PRESENTATION

Q.C. 5 collected jam-up cost data for a four-month period. The data revealed an average monthly cost of $1,789 (an annual cost of $21,478). The circle recommended that the feed chute system be redesigned. In fact, circle members attempted to redesign the feed chute themselves. However, they encountered considerable resistance from the engineering staff. The industrial engineers express doubt about the qualifications of circle members to design such a chute. Moreover, they stated that they believed that there really was no need to change the existing feed system.

In time, the quality circle program facilitator was able to convince the engineering staff to assist the group, and they provided sufficient support to permit the job to be finished. Upon completion, Q.C. 5 presented its proposal to management, and it was accepted.

EXHIBIT 9.11   CAUSE-EFFECT DIAGRAM

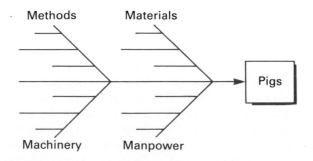

Hour	Product Size Changes	Calender Run-out	Jam-up in Chute	Banbury Delay	Oscil-lating Knives	Mechanical Breakdown	Wind-up Operator Error	Calender Operator Error	Other
7-8 A.M.	ЖЖ ЖЖ //	ЖЖ	////						
8-9 A.M.	////	ЖЖ ///	ЖЖ ЖЖ ЖЖ ЖЖ						
9-10 A.M.	///	ЖЖ ///	ЖЖ /	/	/		//		
10-11 A.M.	//		///	//			/	ЖЖ /	
11-12 noon	ЖЖ	ЖЖ ЖЖ //	ЖЖ ЖЖ /	/	/				
12-1 P.M.	//	///							
1-2 P.M.	ЖЖ ///	////	ЖЖ ЖЖ ЖЖ //		//				
2-3 P.M.	Ø	Ø	Ø	Ø	Ø	Ø	Ø	Ø	Ø
Totals	36	40	61	4	4	0	3	6	154
% of Total	23	26	40	3	3	Ø	2	4	

Checklist reflects number of pigs by cause. Data were collected on a per-hour basis for one week.

EXHIBIT 9.12 DATA COLLECTED ON CAUSES OF PIGS

EPILOGUE

Although the proposal was approved, a three- to four-month delay occurred before the new chute was installed. Some members blamed the engineers for standing in the way of the changes, but the department manager was satisfied that the delay was mainly due to red tape. Unfortunately, the problem with the pigs continued to occur at a slightly reduced level. Another six to eight weeks were required by the engineers and machinists to work out the remaining problems. In the meantime, Q.C. 5 began to brainstorm for a new problem, but disbanded after a few weeks when the members were unable to agree on another project.

CASE 9.2
Consumer Airlines: a study in autonomous work groups

AUBREY CRAMER *Kasten-Cramer*

Consumer Airlines was one of the many new airlines born soon after the airline industry was deregulated. It was founded on principles which support autonomy and interdependence; commitment to the development of employees; all employees as both decision makers and stockholders; industry role models; and each person working both line and staff functions. These values have guided the airline's efforts.

The initial team consisted of a twenty-person managing officer group plus a dozen other managers representing key areas of expertise in the airline industry. Most of the start-up team had worked for

industry. Most of the start-up team had worked for the same, more traditional, airline prior to this venture. By the end of year one in this southwestern airline, there were 1,000 employees and a half dozen planes with additional planes and employees on the way. The spirit of start-up, unexpected rapid growth, and the PATCO* strike helped to create an intense working community. Everyone pitched in to do whatever was needed to get the fledgling enterprise "off the ground."

From this start-up mode evolved the strong norm that task forces** would become a corporate way of life as time-limited vehicles formed to address critical organizational issues and needs. The recognition and impact of these groups were first made obvious by the start-up team managers (i.e., excluding officers) who influenced a major change in organizational structure at the end of the second year.

The airline's organizational structure had been designed to have very few levels. This resulted in a greater reliance on horizontal rather than vertical relationships in the enterprise. This configuration easily promotes the proliferation of simultaneous self-managing work groups. It also allows for multiple access points and information flow through all levels of the corporation. The continuous rotating of staff and line functions contributes to a potentially balanced mix of experience represented in these self-managed work groups.

FORMATION OF THE TRAINER DEVELOPMENT SELF-MANAGING WORK GROUP

The training and education function in the airline industry is pivotal to the success of the business. At the heart of the body of knowledge imparted is safety. Training at Consumer Airlines is an on-going process. It begins with an initial two-month period and is considered a keystone for orientation and acculturation. As with all airlines, pilots and flight attendants alike are required by the FAA to participate in annual recurrent classes to update and refresh their skills and knowledge.

In its third year, Consumer Airlines had hired a total of 6,000 employees. The flow of those employees to be trained never ceased. At the same time, more

and more seasoned trainers were being rotated out on to the line. This situation created a shortage of experienced educators. Several senior trainers from the flight attendant area expressed their concern and proposed the idea to their group managers of creating a work group.

The group managers gave full sanction for them to go ahead and solve the problem. They were free to invite those they considered key players, take as much time as they needed and were offered external resources in the form of a consultant to help design the program content.

The trainers invited their own flight attendant group managers, several group managers from the pilot group and two members from the leadership development area to participate in a problem-identification session. They agreed the problem affected all three functions and decided jointly to have area representatives in the work group.

The original group of seven dwindled to an active group of four. This was due, in part, to the use of a cross-utilized work force. Under such an arrangement, employees frequently were "pulled" from support areas (marketing, recruiting, accounting, etc.) to staff line positions. For example, an employee whose primary responsibility might be training and development could be relocated to another city to "work on the line" selling tickets or handling baggage. Thus, the flexible working arrangements reduced the number of group members who remained at the home office. The strongest participation came from the coordinating trainers, including the group-appointed leader, Lana, and her training colleagues, Chuck and Signe. Dwight, the leadership development member, participated more actively during the first six months of the group. The consistently invisible members were the pilots.

ORGANIZATIONAL INTEGRATION AND ITS EFFECT ON WORK GROUPS

While the Trainer Development Work Group was forming, the organization-at-large was focusing on issues of integration. The rapid growth made it increasingly difficult to maintain the close, community atmosphere that once typified Consumer Airlines. Officers and employees alike were concerned about this. Separate departments became more "compartmentalized" than was deemed desirable. Top management began encouraging more teamwork and integration rather than polarization. (Polarization in the airline

---

*Air Traffic Controllers' Strike ended by President Reagan when he fired the entire organization and "broke" the union.

**In this organization, task forces are typically self-managing work groups.

industry typically occurs between attendants and pilots.)

Shared ownership, absence of unions, and organizational values all were created to decrease the potential polarization at Consumer Airlines. However, history and professional socialization do not suddenly vanish in the face of a new environment. These issues seeped into and ultimately surfaced in the Trainer Development Group.

The pilot group managers, Ben and Phil, expressed their interest and support in the joint work group task. However, Phil was always too busy to attend. Ben was also overwhelmed by other responsibilities, but was more positive, visible, and accessible than Phil. In addition, their general manager, Gary, was also continually invited but declined attendance.

The work group provided the first tangible project on which both training areas could begin to collaborate. As such, it signaled a key change to the entire company. Managing officers had been pushing for cooperation of this type and now were watching carefully to see what its impact would be.

Frustrations began building as Lana and her flight attendant colleagues continued meeting, designing, and experimenting with the new program. The pilot group kept promising to be involved but always had other pressing priorities. Managing officers were pressuring flight attendants (F.A.) to be stronger in confronting the pilots.

The F.A. group clearly had mixed feelings about their position. They wanted more cooperation from the pilot group; they sought more equal colleagueship. Yet, they also experienced resistant and slightly elitist pilots. The F.A.'s also believed that they were more progressive and flexible than the pilot group and shouldn't have the corporate burden placed on them for this critical integration. Simultaneously, these dilemmas were being played out on the group management level and were visible to each areas' employees.

Despite the coordinating problems, the program itself was moving along and being taught quite successfully. Other departments heard about the program and requested help in adapting it for their own use. However, only a few pilots had become exposed to the program. Therefore, some of the managing officers viewed it as a partial failure due to the lack of integration. A meeting was scheduled with the active work group, their respective group managers, the managing officer for the human resource area, and the two pilot group managers.

EXERCISE 9.1
THE BOMB SHELTER

THE SITUATION

Your group is the Area Civil Defense Council located in an underground headquarters in charge of several bomb shelters. The area has just withstood a nuclear attack with a very high incidence of Strontium 89. There are now people in the fallout shelters. You have radio communication with most of the shelters under your jurisdiction.

In one shelter, which has oxygen, supplies, and equipment for a maximum of seven people, there are twelve people. The supplies and equipment, however, will sustain life for the anticipated shelter stay of four to five months.

The only information you have about the occupants of the shelter in question are contained in sketchy personnel files on each of the persons.

THE TASK

First, make your own decision as to who should be ejected form the shelter. Then, as a group, reach a decision on which seven people may remain in the shelter. Five persons *must* be ejected from the shelter. (You do have means of ejecting them.) You must decide who may stay and who must leave. In addition, be prepared to explain your reasons for choosing the persons who must leave and the persons who may stay.

BIOGRAPHIC INFORMATION

1. Dr. Eileen Bernstein, M.D., is 36 years old and a renowned surgeon. Her husband and child are reported to be safe in another shelter.
2. Fr. James Miller is the pastor of a Catholic Church. He is 64 years old. Previously, he taught theology at a Catholic university.
3. Collins Green, a computer technician, was honorably discharged from the army six years ago. He has a thorough understanding and knowledge of electronic components and equipment. During Mr. Green's attendance at a vocational high school, he was considered a "militant black activist." He is 34 years of age and is not married.
4. Cathy Brian is 21 years old and seven months pregnant. No one knows whether her husband survived the attack. Cathy seems very upset and somewhat emotionally unstable. She has become hysterical on two occasions. Dr. Bernstein had to sedate her. She continually screams that she must "save her baby."
5. Georgia Stuart is a black businesswoman. She is very prominent in the black business community and an influential member of the state legislature. Last year, she reportedly gave $20,000 to a local charity. She is also noted for her contributions to the poor.
6. Shelly Johnson is a 14-year-old student. Evidently, she had slight brain damage in an automobile accident which has put her in a "slow learner" category. For the past two and a half years she has caused a lot of problems for her parents—she has become a "problem child." Her parents and two younger sisters are in another shelter.
7. Colonel Thomas Kelley, age 45, is one of the top military advisers in the Department of Defense. He has assumed command of shelter activities and seems to have activities and duties organized and assigned. In our last communication with the people in the shelter, Col. Kelley said people were somewhat upset by his rationing of food and water, but he felt they should conserve it "just in case."
8. Alex Saslov was the military adviser to the Russian ambassador in Washington. About five years ago, however, he defected to the West. At 39, he is an outstanding authority on radioactive materials.
9. Jim Tyler, who supposedly has cancer, is the only person who has experience in operating and maintaining a radio transmitter. Mr. Tyler has one son who lives in California.
10. Anna Wigner, a Jew, is a graduate of a West German university whose academic background is in physics. Several years ago she was nominated for a Nobel Prize in science. She is 67 years old.
11. Raymond Dexter is a very husky 29-year-old man who was convicted of rape. He was recently released on parole after having served eight years of a life sentence, with time off as a result of being considered a "model prisoner." He has been attending a local junior college where he is learning fish hatchery operations and management.
12. George Arnet is a healthy, robust 66-year-old widower. Even at his age, he is very much concerned with physical fitness. He exercises daily and maintains his job as an auto mechanic. Mr. Arnet is also a health food advocate and eats mostly organic foods. It is noted that he has four children and seven grandchildren.

POST-EXERCISE DISCUSSION

1. What means did you use for arriving at a decision?

2. Was your process a smooth one? Discuss this.
3. Is the final decision acceptable to everyone in the group? Ask each member of the group to describe his or her feelings about the decision now that it has been made.
4. What other approaches exist to arriving at a group decision? If other groups in the class also participated in this exercise, share with one another the various approaches taken and the positive and negative aspects of each.

EXERCISE 9.2
USING THE NOMINAL GROUP TECHNIQUE

This chapter outlined the steps used in nominal group technique (NGT). This exercise is designed to permit you to use NGT and observe its impact on group members and group output.

PREPARATION

Form groups of seven to ten persons. Have access to flip chart, masking tape, magic marker, wall space. (A large blackboard may be used.) Groups should be separated to prevent interference with one another.

PROCEDURE

1. As a group, decide on a topic about which you would like to generate information or a problem you would like to solve. You might, for example, attempt to better understand problems faced by new students entering the university for the first time or ways to improve ticket distribution for major sporting events on campus. (The topic may be provided by your professor.)
2. Once a topic has been selected, each person in the group should write down a nominal group question that will produce the information desired. Now, compare the questions and briefly discuss the strengths and weaknesses of various questions.
3. Randomly select one person to facilitate each step of the NGT process:
   1. Initial orientation and instructions.
   2. Recording feedback (two or more persons may play this role, sequentially).
   3. Editing
   4. Voting
4. When you have completed the exercise:
   a. Discuss each step of the process and constructively critique the performance of respective facilitators.
   b. Ask facilitators to share their perceptions of their respective activities.
   c. Survey participants to determine their reactions to each step in the NGT process.
   d. Discuss individual feelings about inclusion in the group, in the quality of the group's output, and in the general acceptance of the final decision/solution.
   e. Identify ways in which NGT improves on traditional group processes.

CHAPTER 10

COMMUNICATION

LEARNING OBJECTIVES

1. To appreciate the central role of communicating in organizing.
2. To recognize the elements in the communication process.
3. To identify barriers and problems that inhibit effective communication.
4. To develop skills that increase communication effectiveness.
5. To understand the types of networks existing within organizations.

CHAPTER OUTLINE

The Nature of the Communication Process
　　What Communication Is and Is Not
　　Verbal and Nonverbal Communication
　　Communication Channels and Media

Barriers to Effective Communication
　　Perceptual Differences / Language and Meaning / Noise /
　　Lack of Control over the Communication Process

Overcoming Barriers to Effective Communication
　　Listening / Soliciting and Giving Feedback

Organizational Communication
　　Networks
　　Barriers to Effective Organizational Communication
　　Auditing Organizational Communication

Communication: Conclusions

Questions for Review and Discussion

References

Cases: 10.1 The Chief
　　　　 10.2 The J. R. Reston Company, Inc.

Exercises: 10.1 One-Way versus Two-Way Communication
　　　　　　 10.2 Serial Communication

KEY TERMS

Communication / Encode /
Decode / Channel
Feedback
Verbal messages
Nonverbal messages
Media
Perceptual differences
Noise / Listening
Feedback receptiveness

Feedback responsiveness
Downward communication
Upward communication
Horizontal communication
Gatekeeper / Liaison / Bridge
Isolate / Distortion
Overload / Timeliness
Communication audit

M ichael Stone walked back to his office at Randeb, Inc., with a brisk step and a bright smile. His proposal to modify the benefits package for all company employees had just been accepted by the executive committee.

As Mike reflected on the presentation he had made to the committee, he felt a sense of personal satisfaction. He had worked for several months investigating new ways of administering health, insurance, and other fringe benefits. While collecting information and comparing alternatives, Mike became convinced that a cafeteria style benefits package, which allows employees to choose from a menu of benefits, was the way to go. The company would save money, and each employee could tailor a benefits program to his or her particular situation. The members of the executive committee agreed with his thinking and evidence, and they instructed him to implement the new program as rapidly as possible.

Mike now faced the most challenging part of the assignment—how to communicate to hundreds of employees the changes in and details about the benefits program. As Mike walked into his office and sat down at his desk, he realized the hardest part of this job was just beginning.

THE NATURE OF THE COMMUNICATION PROCESS

Imagine yourself in a large room with ninety-nine other people. You have specifically been brought together to accomplish a particular task. Now, further imagine that everyone can talk with anyone, anytime, about anything pertaining to the methods and procedures for performing the assignment. What would it be like in that room? You are probably correct if you imagine a state of total confusion or chaos. The relationship between *communicating* and *organizing* is best understood in just such a situation.

An organized state of affairs in a group or larger social system implies the regulation of communication among its members.[1] In this situation, for example, there are 4,950 potential communication channels among the 100 people.[2] The unrestrained use of all or most of these available channels clearly would hinder coordinated effort directed toward completing the assigned task. Organizing thus involves specifying who can communicate with whom, about what, and when. This crucial function led a noted management authority to suggest that "in any exhaustive theory of organization, communication would occupy a central place, because the structure, extensiveness, and scope of the organization are almost entirely determined by communication techniques."[3] Communication is the very essence of an organization.[4]

Because communication is so integrally related to organized activity, we will define communication and discuss the components of the communication process.

What Communication Is and Is Not

Communication is the process of sending and receiving messages. A **sender encodes** (translates a thought or idea into symbols) and transmits a **message** through a **channel** (a means of conveyance) to a **receiver** who **decodes** (interprets symbols and assigns meaning) the message and provides **feedback** (a response to the original message). A basic model of the communication process is presented in Exhibit 10.1.

This seemingly simple definition of communication—the process of sending and receiving messages—directs our attention to several important issues. First, communication involves the transmission and reception of *messages.* As communicators, we use symbols (e.g., letters, numbers) to create messages representing the reality we experience. We cannot literally communicate to another individual a meaning, attitude, perception, belief, or feeling.[5] Rather, we use a message or messages to represent what we see, feel, or experience. Just as an artist uses a brush and paint to depict a beautiful sunset or landscape, so, too, do communicators use messages to represent their perceptions, thoughts, and feelings.

People receive and interpret messages and then create meanings. Meanings are not found in words, messages, or events themselves. Rather, meanings are in people. Frequently, however, many people assume that communication simply involves the transfer of meaning from one individual to another. This *meaning transfer assumption* can have a negative effect on the process of sending and receiving messages. For example, this assumption may cause a person to believe that the following statement should have the same meaning to both a sender and a receiver: "Please get a copy of the latest report, and meet me in the conference room in twenty minutes." Because the sender meant a copy of the sales projections for the current quarter, she may be surprised when the receiver of the message shows up with a sales report for the recently concluded quarter. If the sender mistakenly believed that meanings are transferred, she may be perplexed and even irritated at the receiver's inability to follow simple instructions. In the mind of the sender, the message was clear, concise, and direct (the misunderstanding was obviously the receiver's fault!). Because of this incorrect assumption, we frequently tend to blame others when communication is ineffective.

The second important issue highlighted by this definition is that communication involves *both sending and receiving* messages. Communication does not consist of a single message shot from a sender to a receiver, to be evaluated in terms of how far

EXHIBIT 10.1   BASIC MODEL OF THE COMMUNICATION PROCESS

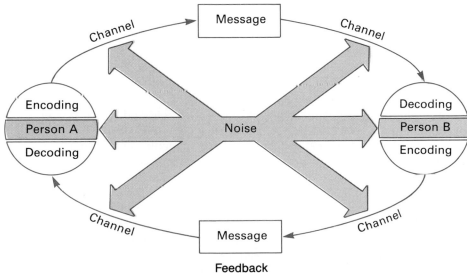

Feedback

it missed the target. An individual involved in the communication process must act as both a sender and a receiver, sometimes changing roles in rapid succession and often operating in both capacities simultaneously. Traditionally, much emphasis is given to sending communication skills (e.g., writing and speaking) in our formal education system. It is important to note, however, that receiving skills (e.g., reading and listening) are equally necessary for successful communication. Skill and effort in both sending and receiving, by both sender and receiver, are required for effective communication.

Finally, *the process nature of communication* is emphasized in our definition. Communication is best described as a process because it is active, continuous, reciprocal, and dynamic. For convenience, we can discuss separate elements of the communication process such as senders, receivers, or messages as if they were static and discrete. However, any model that portrays communication as beginning with a sender and proceeding until it reaches a receiver inadequately represents the actual communication process.

Verbal and Nonverbal Communication

Verbal communication is message exchange through the use of written or spoken symbols. **Nonverbal** communication, on the other hand, refers to anything that transcends written or spoken symbols. For example, a person's tone of voice, facial characteristics, gestures, eye behavior, and physical size are all nonverbal cues. Similarly, the style of print (e.g., handwritten, typed) and kind of paper (e.g., scratch pad, official stationary) used in a written message are important nonverbal characteristics. (Verbal and vocal are often confused. A scream, for example, is a nonverbal but vocal cue. Verbal refers to the use of written and/or spoken symbols; vocal refers to sounds uttered by the voice.) Nonverbal cues can accent, complement, repeat, or contradict verbal messages or can act as substitutes for verbal messages.

Some experts estimate that between 70 and 85 percent of an individual's day is devoted to communication-related activity. But can you guess the amount of time you spend talking each day? One noted authority on nonverbal behavior estimated that the average person spends only ten to eleven minutes actually speaking each day.[6] He further suggested that in a normal two-person conversation, more than 65 percent of the messages are conveyed nonverbally. Clearly, understanding the non-verbal component of the communication process is very important.

Although verbal and nonverbal messages often are described or analyzed separately, it is important to remember that they occur simultaneously in actual communication. The complexity of the communication process becomes much more apparent as we recognize that the nonverbal qualities of a message, many of them subtle, cannot be separated from the verbal aspects. The verbal part of a message conveys content or information. The nonverbal component indicates how the verbal message should be interpreted and thus is a metacommunication. If, for example, in response to a request from your co-worker for help in preparing a budget report, you answer, "You bet!" the nonverbal cues of an enthusiastic voice and rolling up your sleeves help the friend to interpret your message as "sincerely willing to help." If, on the other hand, your response to the request is, "You bet," accompanied by a yawn, eyes rolled upward, and a sarcastic tone of voice, then the co-worker is probably correct in interpreting the message as meaning "No way!" Any message, then, is the product of a complex interaction between both verbal and nonverbal components.

Whenever verbal and nonverbal messages contradict each other, we are more likely to believe the nonverbal. In fact, it has been suggested that the total impact of a message is a function of the following formula:[7]

$$\text{Total Impact} = .07 \text{ verbal} + .38 \text{ vocal} + .55 \text{ facial}$$

The sobering implication of this finding is that *what* we communicate will almost always be overshadowed by *how* we communicate it. It should be remembered that, while the spoken or written symbols we use may convey an intended message, non-verbal cues may suggest quite a different and more believable interpretation of that message.

Sensitivity to both verbal and nonverbal messages is particularly important for a manager or executive because managers are almost constantly communicating. Based on systematic observations of the daily work routines of high level executives, one researcher calculated that verbal interaction accounted for 78 percent of the managers' time and 67 percent of their activities.[8] This research indicates that communicating is what managers do; it is an integral aspect of managerial work. Since so much of the work a manager does is accomplished nonverbally, an effective manager must be aware of and sensitive to both the verbal and nonverbal messages he sends, as well as to those received from others.

Communication Channels and Media

A **communication channel** is an avenue or pathway through which a message moves from a source to a receiver. People send and receive messages with and through the five senses (seeing, hearing, smelling, tasting, touching). The senses thus provide the link between the sender and the receiver of a message and are the primary channels used in human communication. We tend to rely most heavily on the visual, audio, and tactile channels of communication.

The term *media* frequently is associated with particular methods of mass communication (e.g., radio, television). In a more general sense, however, **communication media** include all the mechanisms used to transmit messages. Posters, reports, bulletin boards, letters, and memos are common types of written/graphic media. Spoken media include face-to-face and telephone conversations, loudspeaker systems, videotapes, committee meetings, and so on.

Communication media vary considerably in terms of speed, formality, intensity, cost, and opportunity for and immediacy of feedback. Consequently, the choice of a particular medium can have a significant impact on both the effectiveness and efficiency of the communication process. Furthermore, the type of medium used to transmit a message determines the "richness" of that message, or its information-carrying capacity.[9] Thus, the actual impact of a message is greatly influenced by the medium used to convey it. Exhibit 10.2 shows the information-carrying capacity of various communication media.

BARRIERS TO EFFECTIVE COMMUNICATION

Effective communication occurs when both sender and receiver share a common interpretation of a message. Sounds simple, right? In fact, communication is one of

Communication Medium	Information Richness
Face-to-Face	Highest
Telephone	High
Written, Personal (e.g., Letters, Memos)	Moderate
Written, Formal (e.g., Bulletins, Documents)	Low
Numeric, Formal (e.g., Computer Output)	Lowest

EXHIBIT 10.2   COMMUNICATION MEDIA AND INFORMATION RICHNESS

Adapted from: Richard L. Daft and Robert H. Lengel, "Information Richness: A New Approach to Managerial Behavior and Organizational Design," in B. Staw and L. Cummings eds., *Research in Organizational Behavior* (Greenwich, Conn.: JAI Press, 1984) 196. Used with permission.

the most complex processes in which we human beings engage. Moreover, we never completely share a common interpretation of a message with another individual. A process that sounds so simple—sending and receiving messages—is complicated by a number of factors. An extensive list of communication barriers could be generated. We have chosen, however, to limit our discussion to several primary barriers that inhibit effective communication.

Perceptual Differences

As defined in Chapter 3, perception is the process whereby an individual selects, organizes, and interprets stimuli from the environment. An individual's physiology, psychology, and past experiences combine to create a unique frame of reference through which that person perceives the world. In a sense, every individual exists in a continually changing world of experience of which he or she is the center.[10] It follows, then, that since no two people have exactly the same frame of reference, we each perceive events and actions around us differently.

The fact that people have varied frames of reference and perceive differently has a profound impact on the communication process. What we communicate about is our perception of what the world is like. Having created for ourselves a perception of people and events, we re-create for others, through oral, written, or nonverbal messages, what we perceive. The point to remember is that we can never exactly re-create in another person's mind our own original perceptions. Interpretations and meanings thus are more negotiated than absolute.

Managers must be particularly aware of perceptual differences when communicating with individuals from other countries and cultures. Verbal and nonverbal messages commonly accepted and understood in one country can suggest different meanings to a person from another culture.

In Japan, for example, English classes begin in junior high school, and the first thing students learn is that in English, **hai** is "yes." When the Japanesse telephone system was reconstructed after World War II, the system had many technological problems. There was constant clicking and buzzing in the background, and conversation would frequently be cut off in the middle. **"Moshi moshi?"** a person would say, meaning "Hello, can you hear me?" **"Hai hai,"** the other party would respond.

This habitual response pattern has persisted, and a Japanese manager communicating with a foreign manager will frequently say "Yes" when the person he is talking with has finished a sentence or has come to the end of a thought. The

INTERNATIONAL DIMENSION
Going Beyond Berlitz

The growth in international trade is challenging United States managers to learn unfamiliar languages and customs in order to communicate effectively overseas. Although English is commonly used in industrialized countries, nearly a third of the Fortune 500 companies do business in less developed countries where English is seldom spoken. Fast-paced language courses such as those offered by Berlitz give United States executives a few basic foreign language skills, but managers in international businesses are being urged to become more proficient in several languages.

With the opening of trade with the People's Republic of China, new associations with Singapore and Malaysia, and the growing power and influence of Japan in international trade, the Japanese and Chinese languages have become more important for English-speaking managers. Language studies are now being coupled with cross-cultural studies because ignorance of subtle differences in language and insensitivity to cultural differences can result in serious communication problems.

In Asian countries, for example, sexually oriented messages are not used to advertise or sell products; Asian marketing is based on product performance. When a Swiss businessman tried to land an import contract in Japan for watches that he claimed were "alluring," he therefore was turned down. Going after the same contract in Singapore with a video campaign showing a glamorous woman model-

ing an expensive watch, the Swiss failed again. By the time he went to Beijing, he had learned his lesson: he presented his product as an "accurate timepiece." Unfortunately, after a late afternoon meeting, he took his departure by saying in Chinese, "See you later." To the Chinese, that meant he would return shortly to continue the discussion. They waited, he didn't come back, and the infuriated Chinese ended negotiations.

In a similar incident, an American, eager to impress Chinese buyers with his firm's four-year experience in China, described his company in a communiqué as an "old friend." The Chinese characters he used for "old" meant "bygone," carrying the connotation of "used" or "former." The message to the Chinese was that the American firm wanted nothing more to do with trade in China.

Questions
What can a manager do before conducting business in a foreign country to become acquainted with the culture and customs of that country?
Can you identify specific nonverbal gestures or cues that have different meanings in different countries and cultures?

SOURCE: René White, "Beyond Berlitz: How to Penetrate Foreign Markets Through Effective Communications," *Public Relations Quarterly* (Summer 1986): 12–16.

intended meaning of "yes" in this context is "I hear you; I am listening to you." Frequently, however, the foreign manager will hear "Yes" and interpret it to mean "Ah, he agrees with me." A manager may be quite surprised when, after hearing all of the "yes" responses, the conversation or negotiation ends with an unexpected "No."[11]

If there is such an opportunity for misunderstanding at this very basic level involving "yes" and "hai," how much greater the opportunity for confusion at a more substantive level involving complex business issues in the international marketplace? The International Dimension above provides additional examples of how particular words, phrases, and images are perceived in different countries.

Language and Meaning

Language is an invaluable tool for describing and mapping our perceptions. Like a map, language can describe people and events accurately and precisely. However, just as an inaccurate map can mislead, so, too, imprecise language can cause error, distortion, and confusion in sending and receiving messages.

Many people assume, much like Humpty Dumpty in Lewis Carroll's *Through the Looking Glass*, that "when I use a word it means just what I choose it to mean—neither more nor less." A word, however, does not literally have a meaning but rather an accepted usage or usages. The true meaning of a word resides in the person using it, not in the word itself. Words, then, do not have meanings; people do.

The fact that a word or symbol potentially has as many meanings as there are people using the word has obvious implications for the communication process. The potential for misunderstanding and erroneous interpretation is compounded when individuals have different meanings for the same words (e.g., "I know you believe you understand what you think I said, but I am not sure you realize that what you heard is not what I meant!"). Such difficulties with language and meaning can often have devastating consequences, as the following example illustrates.[12] The Japanese word *mokusatsu* can be used to communicate both *ignore* and *withholding comment until a decision can be made*. When this term was used by the Japanese government in response to the Potsdam Ultimatum near the end of World War II, it was translated by the Donei news agency as *ignore* instead of the intended *withholding comment*. It was subsequently learned that this misinterpreted message contributed significantly to the Allies' decision to drop the atomic bombs on Hiroshima and Nagasaki. Clearly, significant consequences can occur because of a word and the meaning(s) associated with a word. Exhibits 10.3 and 10.4 provide additional examples of confusing language usage.

Noise

Have you ever made a long-distance telephone call and had difficulty understanding the other person because of static in the line? If so, you have experienced some of the negative effects that noise can have on the communication process. **Noise** is anything that interferes with or disrupts the accurate transmission and/or reception of messages. It can occur at many or all points within the communication process (e.g., during encoding, decoding, or within a channel as a message is being transmitted).

EXHIBIT 10.3   HOW'S THAT AGAIN?

A plumber wrote the Bureau of Standards to ask about using hydrochloric acid for cleaning pipes. The Bureau replied: "The efficacy of hydrochloric acid is indisputable, but the chlorine residue is incompatible with metallic permanence." The plumber indicated his pleasure at the Bureau's agreement, whereupon the Bureau quickly wrote him another letter: "We cannot assume responsibility for the production of toxic and noxious residues with hydrochloric acid, and suggest that you use an alternate procedure." Again, the plumber indicated his satisfaction with their agreement. Finally, they wrote the plumber: "Don't use hydrochloric acid; it eats hell out of the pipes." That he understood!

SOURCE: Stuart Chase, *The Power of Words* (New York: Harcourt, Brace & Jovanovich, 1954), 259.

EXHIBIT 10.4   "ENGLISCH AS SHE IS GOODLY SPOCKEN"*

NINO LO BELLO

Fractured English is the name of the game. It's fun to play, and all you have to do is travel with pad at the ready. Here is a sampling from my flip-of-the-tongue collection gathered abroad, beginning with an Italian doctor's sign: *Specialist in Women and Other Diseases.*

Even the British, who speak English themselves, muff one occasionally, as in this hospital sign in London: *Visitors. Two to a Bed and Half-an-Hour Only.* Or this linguistic lapse: *Our Establishment Serves Tea in a Bag Like Mother.*

One hotel in France lists an egg on its menu as *extract of fowl.* It can be ordered *peached* or *sunside up.*

Then there is the dentist in Istanbul whose doorway proclaims: *American Dentist, 2th Floor—Teeth Extracted by Latest Methodists.* At least he picked the right floor.

The problem extends to communist nations courting tourists. In Belgrade's state-owned skyscraper hotel, the Slavija, the elevator instructions say: *To move the cabin push button of wishing floor. If the cabin should enter more persons, each one shoud press number of wishing floor.* Posted in another Yugoslav hotel: *Let Us Know About Any Unficiency As Well as Leaking On The Service. Our Utmost Will Improve.*

I found this piece of prose in the office of one of Czechoslovakia's state travel bureaus: *Take One Of Our Horse-Driven City Tours—We Guarantee No Miscarriages.* And these lifesaving instructions aboard a Soviet ship in the Black Sea: *Help savering apparata in emergings behold many whistles! Associate the stringing apparata about the bosoms and meet behind. Flee then to the indifferent lifesavering shippen obediencing the instructs of the vessel chef.*

On the elevator door in a Romanian hotel I found my all-time favorite: *The lift is being fixed for the next days. During that time we regret that you will be unbearable.*

---

*From a sign in the Netherlands advertising a Dutch-English grammar.

Noise is a principal source of error in communication and can be either external or internal. External noise can be anything from a purely physical sound—a child crying or a jackhammer pounding in the street—to an ambiguous or misused word. Internal noise, on the other hand, can be a headache, hunger pains, anxiety, stress, biases, and/or prejudices that inhibit a person's ability to send and receive messages accurately. As a practical matter, noise cannot be eliminated completely from the communication process. Effective communicators can, however, control or eliminate the negative impacts of noise by avoiding distractions, communicating in appropriate settings (e.g., conducting an interview in a private office instead of a busy work area), and concentrating.

Lack of control over the communication process

Communication is often considered something a sender intentionally does to a receiver—a controlled, planned, and carefully executed process resulting in a desired outcome. As we more fully understand the process nature of communication, however, we recognize that an individual does not communicate, but *engages in communication.*[13] The nature of the communication process is dynamic and continuous and does not necessarily start, stop, or occur as we might wish. A noted communication consultant has suggested:

> Whether management likes it or not, it must face the fact that all actions, by all people, on all levels, in all functions of the organization, constantly communicate: that all actions create impressions in employees, judged by each employee from his peculiar frame of reference. It

> makes little difference whether the employee's interpretation is correct—this is "his world" and he looks out of "his window." What he wants to see and hear is the impression he gains from the words and actions around him.[14]

Not only do we have relatively little control over exactly what people perceive and attach meaning to, but we also cannot determine precisely when communication will occur.

> Communication takes place every time human beings use their natural faculties to listen, think, observe, be impressed (for better or worse), have doubts, feel neglected, etc. This common trouble occurs when management takes the rather naive stand that "this is not the time to talk."[15]

The point to remember, then, is that when you are with at least one other person, you cannot *not* communicate. Anything and everything an individual does, or fails to do, may be perceived as a message and given meaning by someone.

OVERCOMING BARRIERS TO EFFECTIVE COMMUNICATION

Achieving a degree of shared meaning and understanding does not necessarily produce agreement. Susan and Lane may understand each other but disagree about a particular issue or strategy. Understanding, however, must precede an attempt to resolve a difference of opinion or to reconcile two different approaches to a problem situation.

Effective communication is not easy. A person who desires to improve her communication effectiveness must (1) understand the nature of the communication process; (2) learn skills that can be used to increase mutual understanding; and (3) practice and develop those skills conscientiously. We now focus on two specific skills a manager or executive can learn and practice in order to increase communication effectiveness: (1) listening, and (2) soliciting and giving feedback.

Listening

Hearing and listening are terms often used interchangeably. However, becoming aware of the differences between these two processes is essential to an understanding of the communication process. Hearing is a physiological process and the forerunner of listening; it involves changing acoustical energy outside the body into energy sources within the body that the brain can act on. In other words, hearing is the perception of sound. **Listening,** on the other hand, refers to the active processes of receiving and interpreting aural stimuli. Listening is the attachment of meaning to aural symbols.[16]

Many managers mistakenly associate effective communication only with skillful message-sending. They concentrate on message-sending skills such as writing and speaking and the techniques that make messages clear, concise, and memorable. Such managers may believe that effective message-sending determines the outcome of a communication episode and, consequently, pay little attention to the process of message receiving.

Exhibit 10.5 contains a brief listening quiz. Take a minute or two right now to complete the quiz before you read further.

Each statement in the quiz is false and helps to identify common misconceptions people have about listening. The first misconception is that listening is easy and takes little energy. In fact, effective listening is quite demanding and requires a substantial expenditure of effort. Listening is not just being quiet while another person talks. Effective listening is as active as talking.

A second misconception about listening is that smart people do it better. Poor listening habits are found among people of all intelligence levels, age levels, and at every level of an organizational hierarchy.

A final misconception about listening is that good listeners can do it faster than poor listeners. Such a listener is likely to finish a speaker's sentences for him, or prematurely complete ideas for others. Listening is a job that requires concentration, and there are no easy shortcuts to effective listening.

Listening skills can be developed and practiced. Four guidelines are particularly helpful in improving listening effectiveness: (1) prepare to listen; (2) stay on track; (3) listen for central ideas; and (4) avoid judging too quickly.

Prepare to listen

An effective listener must be physically and mentally prepared. Before listening to a grievance from an employee, for example, a manager might review all of the documents related to the case. Similarly, an individual might prepare to listen to an unexpected request for information from a colleague by asking her to state briefly the nature and extent of the problem on which she is working; such a request can prepare the individual to focus on and listen more effectively to her exact request.

Stay on track

As you listen, it is important to focus on what is being said and to give the other person complete and undivided attention. Distracting influences such as physical and mental distractions should be avoided. A manager may reduce distractions, for ex-

EXHIBIT 10.5 LISTENING QUIZ

Please mark each of the statements below with "Agree" or "Disagree."

1. _____ Listening is a matter of being quiet while the other person talks.

2. _____ Listening takes much less energy than talking.

3. _____ Intelligent people listen more effectively than less intelligent people.

4. _____ Older people listen better than younger people.

5. _____ I sometimes find myself daydreaming while others are describing their problems to me.

6. _____ I usually know within a minute or so what another person is leading up to, even though it may take ten minutes to get the message across.

7. _____ I cut off people a lot; otherwise I would spend most of my day listening to others ramble on.

8. _____ I listen pretty well because I have been doing it all my life.

9. _____ The listener's personality is not relevant to the listening task.

10. _____ People practice listening every day; daily practice eliminates the need for listening training.

Adapted from: Robert Hopper, *Between You and Me: The Professional's Guide to Interpersonal Communication*, (Glenview, Ill., Scott, Foresman and Co., 1984), 21

ample, by not taking phone calls or accepting messages during a conversation with a client in his office.

Resisting mental distractions is perhaps the biggest obstacle to effective listening. The human brain is capable of processing words at between 500 and 700 words per minute. However, the average person speaks at a rate of approximately 125 words per minute. Consequently, the difference between how fast people can think and talk leaves plenty of time for daydreaming or detouring during a conversation. Energy must be expended to concentrate during a conversation and to avoid the tendency to "fade in and out."

Listen for central ideas

It is quite difficult, if not impossible, to remember everything another person may say during a discussion, conversation, or meeting. An effective listener focuses on the central ideas and points the speaker is attempting to convey. Generally, there are just one or two central ideas and rarely more than three or four major points that a person will want to remember from a conversation.

Good listeners mentally summarize and paraphrase the main points a speaker is making. The listener should not mentally debate or argue with the speaker; rather, effort is expended in an attempt to understand the speaker's key idea or concern. Asking questions is also a good strategy when an individual has missed some details or cannot grasp the speaker's main idea. For example, John may ask Michael during a meeting, "How would you summarize your position?" The speaker's summary may help you to better understand the main point and organize your thoughts more effectively.

Avoid judging too quickly

We evaluate and judge other people all the time. Managers, as a part of their work, must constantly make difficult decisions about employee behavior and work performance. Unfortunately, however, such judgments and decisions are frequently made too quickly and with incomplete or insufficient information. The following example demonstrates how the tendency to judge prematurely can inhibit listening effectiveness.

Bill Curington walked into his supervisor's office and began describing a problem he was having with his equipment. "I've tried three times to adjust the nozzle," he reported, "but the attachment is worn slick, and I . . ." Mr. Jenkins interrupted, "Bill, that equipment is not even nine months old, and the attachment was replaced just three weeks ago. It is not worn out, and we do not need to replace it."

Did Mr. Jenkins ever really find out what Bill's problem was? Before Mr. Jenkins adequately understood the problem, he made a snap judgment and indicated that the part did not need to be replaced. In fact, however, Bill was not asking for a replacement part; he was simply coming to ask Mr. Jenkins about the proper procedure for using a new tool to adjust the nozzle.

Mr. Jenkins began formulating and giving his rebuttal before he had listened to the complete message. Consequently, he missed the most important part of Bill's statement. Mr. Jenkins could become a better listener by "holding his fire" and suspending judgment until he listens to and understands a problem more completely.

Soliciting and Giving Feedback

Feedback, as we indicated earlier, is a receiver's response to a sender's original message. Feedback is the only means by which a message sender may discover what kind of response his message is getting, or even whether the message has been received. Consequently, effective communication is impossible without feedback.

Feedback enables a message sender to assess the effect of an initial message and to improve the quality of subsequent messages. A manager should become aware of and sensitive to two basic dimensions of feedback: receptiveness and responsiveness.[17] **Feedback receptiveness** refers primarily to a manager's willingness to receive incoming feedback from others. **Feedback responsiveness,** on the other hand, indicates a manager's willingness to give feedback to others. Most managers are much better at giving than receiving feedback. Effective managers, however, are both feedback receptive and responsive.

Perhaps the most important thing a manager can do to solicit feedback from others is to establish and maintain a supportive work climate or culture. Exhibit 10.6 presents a series of characteristics typically associated with supportive and defensive climates in interpersonal relationships, small groups, and organizations.[18] A defensive climate stifles the openness and trust necessary for effective feedback. A supportive climate, on the other hand, promotes honest and timely message exchange and feedback.

The guidelines described in Exhibit 10.7 are helpful for facilitating supportive communication and soliciting feedback. A manager who follows these guidelines indicates that she is feedback receptive. Directly asking for and genuinely listening to feedback, especially negative feedback, are also indicators of receptiveness.

Sam Walton, founder of Wal-Mart, is famous for his open style of communication, methods of soliciting feedback, and willingness to be available to employees. It is not uncommon for "Mr. Sam," as he is referred to by Wal-Mart employees, to make an unannounced visit to a store and spend the majority of his time working and visiting with check-out clerks, department managers, and hourly workers. He routinely asks employees for input about company policies, pricing and promotional strategies, and other relevant issues. He actively encourages employees to call or write to him with suggestions or complaints, and he has established an open-door policy

EXHIBIT 10.6   CHARACTERISTICS OF DEFENSIVE AND SUPPORTIVE CLIMATES

DEFENSIVE CLIMATE	SUPPORTIVE CLIMATE
Evaluation (Negative and Positive Judgments)	Description (Clear, Specific Statements of Fact)
Control (Attempts to Change Individuals Who Are Seen as Problems)	Problem Orientation (Focuses on Problem Situation)
Strategy (Manipulations Stemming From Hidden Motives)	Spontaneity (Honest Responses and Openness About Motives)
Neutrality (Indifference)	Empathy (Respect, Understanding, and Caring)
Superiority (More Powerful and Better than Others)	Equality (Equal Partners in Mutual Problem Solving)
Certainty (Knows It All and Closed to Other Alternatives)	Provisionalism (Conclusions Tentative and Open to Change)

EXHIBIT 10.7　GUIDELINES FOR SUPPORTIVE COMMUNICATION

To Reduce *Evaluation*	Avoid criticizing or evaluating another person *as a person*.
To Improve *Description*	Focus on accurately describing specific behaviors or ideas that need to be improved or further developed.
To Reduce *Control*	Avoid dominating or coercively regulating other people.
To Improve *Problem Orientation*	Focus on creating a spirit of teamwork and collaboration.
To Reduce *Strategy*	Avoid using manipulation and trickery to obtain what *you* want.
To Improve *Spontaneity*	Focus on developing openness and candor.
To Reduce *Neutrality*	Avoid being cold, calculating, and impersonal.
To Improve *Empathy*	Focus on understanding how others feel and on showing an attitude of interest and concern.
To Reduce *Superiority*	Avoid creating the impression of believing you are better than other people.
To Improve *Equality*	Focus on the worth, contribution, and integrity of others.
To Reduce *Certainty*	Avoid giving the impression of knowing all of the answers.
To Improve *Provisionalism*	Develop a willingness to listen to new information and points of view.

throughout the company. One of the hallmarks of Walton's management style is the significant amount of time he spends soliciting and listening to feedback from employees throughout the company.

5–15

A specific method used to solicit feedback in Patagonia, Inc., and Esprit de Corps is the "5–15 report," so named because it requires no more than fifteen minutes to write and five minutes to read. Handwritten or typed, it is submitted every Friday by almost all employees of these companies.

　　Each 5–15 report contains three basic parts. The first part is a simple account of what the employee did during the week (e.g., "I continued to work on the fall catalog; our department is putting together product details for Robert and has given him vendor information."). The second part is a candid description of the author's morale, and the morale of his or her department (e.g., "I'm frustrated with purchasing—can't believe we back ordered a product as easy to get as jackets. However, I feel things went well this week in the department."). The third part consists of an idea for improving the job, the department, or the company (e.g., "My idea for the week is to replace the present copier with a new one. No one likes the present machine; copy quality is bad and the machine is down far too often."). A 5–15 report provides a snapshot of its author at the end of a given week and is an invaluable source of information and suggestions for employees throughout the organization.[19]

Giving feedback to another person may appear to be quite easy. In practice, however, giving feedback is not simple. The characteristics presented in Exhibit 10.8 should be considered when giving feedback to another person. Following these basic guidelines can increase a manager's effectiveness when soliciting and giving feedback. Developing and practicing these skills are important steps in the overall process of achieving shared meaning and understanding with fellow members of an organization.

ORGANIZATIONAL COMMUNICATION

Much of our discussion thus far has focused on the dynamics of communication as it occurs in interpersonal and group settings. As we turn to organizational communication, our attention is now directed to the process of sending and receiving messages through patterned pathways called **networks.** In the organizational context, the communication process becomes more complex, and additional problems can impede effective message exchange.

Networks

Organizations are comprised of people occupying certain positions or roles. The flow of messages between and among these people occurs through pathways called **communication networks.**

EXHIBIT 10.8   CHARACTERISTICS OF EFFECTIVE FEEDBACK

FEEDBACK SHOULD BE SPECIFIC, NOT ABSTRACT

Feedback should be detailed and provide the recipient with an understanding of the issue that must be clarified or restated. A statement such as "your report does not make sense" is not specific enough to do the author of the report much good. The following statement identifies more clearly a possible concern about the accuracy of the report: "The economic assumptions you use as a basis for the projections in your report are not clear to me." Concrete statements that identify specific concerns or behaviors are easier for the receiver of feedback to understand, accept, and act upon.

FEEDBACK SHOULD BE TIMELY RATHER THAN RANDOM

Frequently, feedback about a message or a particular work episode is not received until days, weeks, or even months after it occurs. In most instances, feedback should be given as close to the event it relates to as possible.

FEEDBACK SHOULD PROVIDE DESCRIPTIVE INFORMATION ABOUT WHAT THE PERSON SAID OR DID AND SHOULD AVOID INFERENCES ABOUT MOTIVES, INTENT, OR FEELINGS

Effectively describing ("I heard you say 'um' twelve times during your presentation."), as opposed to evaluating or judging ("You lack self-confidence."), helps to minimize receiver defensiveness.

FEEDBACK SHOULD NOT BE FORCED ON ANOTHER PERSON

Feedback tends to be more effective when the other person requests it. A manager's job requires that she provide feedback to many people, many of whom may not want to receive it. Nevertheless, an employee or colleague is more likely to consider feedback objectively and be responsive when he has requested it. Forcing feedback on someone or insisting he receive it may put that individual on the defensive.

One readily discernible feature of an organization's communication system, as it is examined over time, is that repetitive patterns of information and communication exchange take place. Some members of the organization interact with one another, but not with other members. They interact more often some times than at other times. Their interaction may cover certain topics; at other times it doesn't. Certain topics never occur in the interactions among some members of the organization. When management sends out messages to subordinates, the messages travel various pathways or networks—some intended and some not.[20]

Networks thus function to guide the flow of messages and information within the organization. Exhibit 10.9 summarizes and illustrates the results of several important research studies on communication networks.

General types and functions of networks

Five basic types of organizational networks have been identified and described.[21]

The **authority network** is often thought of as the organization's formal chain of command. Messages primarily flow upward and downward in this network and pertain to goals, procedures, policies, and suggestions. In theory, the authority network

EXHIBIT 10.9   RESEARCH ON COMMUNICATION NETWORKS

What effect does an individual's position within a communication network have on his or her morale and job satisfaction? What effect does the structure of a group have on the the efficiency of message exchange? Such questions provided the focus for several important research studies conducted during the 1950s and 1960s on communication networks in small groups. Investigators commonly used the five networks illustrated below.

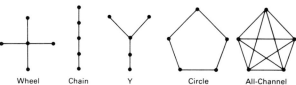

Wheel   Chain   Y   Circle   All-Channel

The results of these studies indicated that:

1. The structure of a network elevates certain individuals into leadership positions. For example, the central person in a network such as the wheel (who can communicate with any of the other group members) usually becomes the leader and experiences greater satisfaction with the position than those on the periphery (who must direct all of their comments through the center).
2. Occupying a key position in a network also frequently leads to message overload for the leader, through whom all the messages must pass.
3. Centralized networks such as the wheel contribute to rapid performance of simple tasks. Often, however, the error rate is high because two-way communication and feedback are restricted.
4. Decentralized networks such as the circle are associated with member satisfaction.
5. The all-channel network may be relatively slow but is superior in terms of idea-sharing and member satisfaction. Feedback is more immediate and, as a result, accuracy of communication is better. When the problem to be solved is complex, the decentralized networks such as the circle and all-channel are most desirable.

provides for the quick and efficient movement of messages throughout the organization. In practice, however, this efficiency is seldom the case.

Messages transmitted through the **information network** deal primarily with internal organizational operations and changing conditions in the environment. This network provides the information necessary for effective problem solving and decision making. The formal information network operates through such standardized reporting procedures as progress reports, staff meetings, and newsletters. An informal information network (the grapevine) is also active in most organizations.

The **task-expertise network** carries the messages and information needed for task accomplishment. Specifically, this network provides technical information on how jobs should be done, how problems should be handled, and where expert knowledge and assistance are located within the organization.

A fourth type of network, a **friendship network,** often develops among various organizational members. Such a network or networks can result from routine organizational operations (e.g., managers with adjacent offices) or from extracurricular activities (e.g., participation on an after-work softball team). Messages conveyed in the friendship network tend to be more informal, candid, and less directly purposeful than messages in the three networks already described.

The fifth network is the **status network,** which carries messages about the status and prestige of organizational members. These messages are often conveyed nonverbally through such cues as the size of a manager's desk, the location of an office (next to the V.P.!), or a reserved parking place.

In actuality, an organization is a network of networks, each operating with a specific function and purpose. This list of networks is not intended to be exhaustive. Rather, these networks are examples of the generic types of networks operating in an organization.

The formal network

Messages following official paths dictated by the organizational hierarchy or by job function flow through the **formal communication network.** Within the formal network of every organization, messages pass downward, upward, and horizontally. Messages typically proceed down and up the formal network if the scalar principle of authority and hierarchy (chain-of-command) is used, and across if the functional principle of job classification is adhered to.[22] Even though downward, upward, and horizontal messages may follow similar paths within the network, the nature and content of each are quite different.

Downward communication refers to messages transmitted from superiors to subordinates. Five basic types of messages are sent downward through the organization:[23]

1. Specific task directives—job instructions.
2. Information designed to produce understanding of the task and its relation to other organizational tasks—job rationale.
3. Information about organizational procedures and practices.
4. Feedback to the subordinate about his or her performance.
5. Information of an ideological character to inculcate a sense of mission—indoctrination of goals.

All five types of downward communication are task oriented; that is, how one does the job, why one does it, details about the job, how one is doing on the job, and attempts to motivate.

Upward communication involves message exchange between a subordinate and a boss. General categories of upward messages have been summarized as what people say:[24]

1. About themselves, their performance and their problems.
2. About other people and their problems.
3. About organizational practices and policies.
4. About what needs to be done and how it can be done.

Subordinates thus communicate with their boss about what they have done, what those under them (in the hierarchy) have done, what peers have done, what they think needs to be done, their problems and the problems of their work unit, and about matters of organizational practice and policy. They also can seek clarification about general goals and specific directives. Upward communication is usually limited to the immediate superior unless the organization's structure provides more direct access to higher management levels. Open-door policies, grievance systems, quality circles, and other formal programs can be used to expand an employee's upward communication opportunities beyond the immediate superior.

Horizontal communication refers to sending and receiving messages between people at the same level of the organizational hierarchy. Messages exchanged laterally usually relate to joint problem solving, coordinating work flow, information sharing, and resolving conflicts. Messages communicated among peers are also important in providing emotional and social support.

The informal network

As any person with experience in organizations can testify, the sending and receiving of messages does not always occur within organizationally specified networks. Messages not following scalar or functional pathways flow through the informal communication network, or **grapevine.** The grapevine has been a subject of curiosity and concern to managers for decades. Recent research has produced some interesting findings about this informal network.

First, the grapevine is accurate. Researchers have carefully analyzed messages received through the grapevine and found the accuracy to range between 78 and 90 percent. Accuracy was especially high when the messages did not deal with highly emotional or controversial information.[25]

A second significant finding is that the grapevine is fast. Messages are disseminated rapidly because the informal network is both flexible and personal. In one organization, for example, 46 percent of the management personnel knew about a plant supervisor's newborn child within thirteen hours of the event.[26] It has also been reported that 92 percent of the American public knew about the assassination of President John Kennedy within ninety minutes of the shooting.[27] Although the mass media obviously played a major role in communicating this message, research indicates that the patterns of interpersonal message exchange about this event were similar to the operation of the organizational grapevine.[28]

Finally, the grapevine is active and carries large amounts of information. Messages traveling through the grapevine seldom fit into the pattern of a long chain (e.g., A tells B, who tells C, who then tells D, etc.). Rather, most messages follow a cluster pattern (e.g., A tells three or four others. Only one or two of these receivers actually pass the message on, but usually to more than one person.).

The informal network is a fact of life in all organizations and cannot be avoided or eliminated. An awareness of and sensitivity to the dynamics of the informal network can help a manager deal more effectively with the complex process of sending and receiving messages within organizations.

Individual roles in communication networks

A person can take many different roles in a network. However, an individual is likely to occupy a specific communication role. The communicative function a person performs in a network determines his or her particular role. Not all individuals perform the same function, nor are the functions of equal importance. We will now discuss the specific roles of gatekeeper, liaison, bridge, and isolate.

A **gatekeeper** is an individual who, because of his or her position within the network, can screen, filter, or control the flow of messages and information. Jane Burdock, for example, was attempting to get an urgent memo to her boss, Mr. Hampton. Jane delivered the memo to Mr. Hampton's secretary and asked that it be forwarded "immediately." The secretary indicated that Mr. Hampton was "in conference" and could not be disturbed until later in the afternoon. Since the secretary controlled the items that were brought to her bosses' attention, she was acting as a gatekeeper. Gatekeepers serve a vital communication function by (1) screening out unimportant messages and (2) allowing important messages to pass through the network or some portion of the network.

A **liaison** interpersonally connects two or more groups or departments in an organization. The liaison is usually not a member of either group but joins or links the groups communicatively. For example, William Goodall is employed as a research scientist in the R&D department at a major tire and rubber company. For the last six months, he has been working on a new design for steel-belted radials that would increase the life of a tire by 10,000 miles. Since he knows this new development will affect both the marketing and production departments, he frequently meets with members of both departments to solicit ideas and inform them of the latest project developments. William is the interpersonal link or connection between the marketing and production departments and functions as a liaison. Thus, liaisons are positioned at the crossroads of message flows in an organization and provide the cement that holds the structural bricks of an organization together.[29]

Bridges also perform a linking and connecting function between two or more groups. Unlike liaisons, however, bridges are actual group members who communicate with members of other groups. If, for example, the respective managers of the production and marketing departments at the tire and rubber company provide the communication link between their departments concerning the new tire design, then they are acting as bridges. Bridges provide another form of communicative connection between two or more groups.

Finally, an individual who has few or no communication contacts with the rest of the organization is an **isolate.** Such an individual may be relatively young and inexperienced within the system and would seldom be found in a position of power. In a study of isolation and participation in a military organization, researchers found that isolates tended to be younger, lower-ranking, and less-educated personnel.[30] They were also less satisfied with their jobs, less committed to the military, and had poorer job performance than more active participants. Exhibit 10.10 shows the four individual communication roles within a network.

A knowledge of these individual communication roles is extremely valuable to a manager or executive. A substantial number of isolates within an organization, for example, might be cause for concern. Isolation could be an indication of an individual's dissociation and alienation from the organization. A manager who is aware of

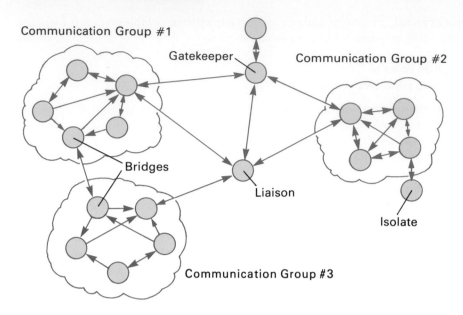

EXHIBIT 10.10   GATEKEEPER, LIAISON, BRIDGE, AND ISOLATE COMMUNICATION ROLES

this possibility can take steps to involve isolates more effectively and improve their job performance.

Barriers to Effective Organizational Communication

The barriers we discussed earlier—perceptual differences, problems with language and meaning, noise, and lack of control over the communicative process—are also associated with ineffective organizational communication. However, we now want to focus on several distinctive problems that arise when messages flow through a network.

Distortion occurs when an intended message is changed or altered as it passes through a network. Changes in messages can result from the personality characteristics of sender and/or receiver, status differences, power, or the sheer number of communication links in the network. Exhibit 10.11 shows just how much distortion can occur when a message is transmitted through the "chain of command."

Message distortion is often even more serious when different organizational levels are involved. Opinion Research Corporation conducted studies examining the extent of distortion as messages flow from one hierarchical level to another.[31] One such investigation, conducted in a metals producing company to measure the degree of understanding about a problem with declining profits, produced some surprising results about the accuracy of messages communicated downward:

Of the top corporate officers:	91% understood
Of upper middle management:	48% understood
Of lower middle management:	21% understood
Of first-line supervisors only:	5% understood

EXHIBIT 10.11 THE CHAIN OF COMMAND

The Colonel told the Major: At nine o'clock tomorrow, there will be an eclipse of the sun, something which does not occur every day. Get the men to fall out in the company street in their fatigues so that they will see this rare phenomenon, and I will explain it to them. In case of rain, we will not be able to see anything, so take the men to the gym.

The Major told the Captain: By order of the Colonel, tomorrow at nine o'clock there will be an eclipse of the sun. If it rains, you will not be able to see it from the company street, so then, in fatigues, the eclipse of the sun will take place in the gym, something that does not occur every day.

The Captain told the Lieutenant: By order of the Colonel in fatigues tomorrow at nine o'clock in the morning the inauguration of the eclipse of the sun will take place in the gym. The Colonel will give the order if it should rain, something which occurs every day.

The Lieutenant told the Sergeant: Tomorrow at nine, the Colonel in fatigues will eclipse the sun in the gym, as it occurs every day if it is a nice day. If it rains, then in the company street.

The Sergeant told the Corporal: Tomorrow at nine, the eclipse of the Colonel in fatigues will take place by cause of the sun. If it rains in the gym, something which does not take place every day, you will fall out in the company street.

This is what the Privates understood: Tomorrow, if it rains, it looks as if the sun will eclipse the Colonel in the gym. It is a shame that this does not occur every day.

SOURCE: Personal recollection of author David Bednar of story told by Professor W. C. Redding, Purdue University, 1978.

Other researchers have also found that distortion of messages traveling upward, caused by distrust or a fear of punishment, is a major problem in many organizations. Since the flow of accurate and timely messages is vital to an organization's health, it may be that working to minimize distortion in the communication networks is a manager's most important job.

GENERAL ELECTRIC

Distorted messages within General Electric Co. seriously affected the development of a new refrigerator compressor during the 1980s. GE's engineers had developed a revolutionary compressor (the pump that creates cold air) and a futuristic factory to manufacture it. Executives were so confident about the success of the product that they staked the company's $2 billion refrigerator business on the innovative compressor design. However, blunders were committed at almost every organizational level during the design, development, and testing of the new product. Managers, eager to meet deadlines and cut costs, failed to ask the right questions about the new compressor and shortened or eliminated some aspects of the testing procedure. The new compressor flopped so badly that the company had to take a $450 million pretax charge in 1988. Since early 1989, GE has voluntarily replaced nearly 1.1 million defective compressors.

Ultimately, the problems at GE stemmed from poor corporate communication. Several low-level salaried employees at GE, the technicians who actually did the preproduction testing, reported that they had thought the compressor might be defective and had told their superiors. However, senior executives six levels removed heard only *good news* about the new product.[32]

A second major barrier to effective organizational communication is overload. **Overload** occurs when an individual receives more messages than she has the capacity or ability to handle. Given the vast number of potential message sources within a large organization, it should not surprise you that communication overload is a constant problem.

Seven basic strategies for handling overload have been suggested:[33]

1. Omission: a person can simply fail to handle all of the incoming messages. Many messages are ignored.
2. Error: a person can overlook or fail to correct mistakes. The processing of messages gets sloppy.
3. Queuing: a person can allow incoming messages to stack up for processing at a later time.
4. Filtering: a person deals with incoming messages according to an established priority system (e.g., customer complaints receive first attention).
5. Approximation: a person may lower the standard of precision used in processing incoming messages.
6. Multiple channels: a person may delegate or decentralize message-processing procedures in order to reduce the load.
7. Escape: a person may refuse to process any messages or may simply leave.

Most of these methods of dealing with overload have potentially negative impacts (e.g., increased error, delay). Communication networks should therefore be structured to minimize the problems associated with overload.

Effective communication within organizations also is affected by **timeliness.** Even accurate and complete messages are of little use unless they reach a receiver at the proper time. Detailed instructions about the procedures for accomplishing a task, for example, have no value if they are received after the deadline for completing the task. Further, such instructional messages may not have the intended impact if they are communicated two months before the deadline. The length of time between task instruction and task performance may inhibit comprehension and retention of the information. A manager thus must work to maintain a communication system that can consistently transmit both timely and accurate messages throughout the organization.

POLAROID

"What's Happening" is a program designed to promote timely and accurate message exchange at R-2, the largest plant in Polaroid's Integral Film Assembly division. A generous amount of time is set aside each month for supervisors from each shift to meet with the plant manager and his staff. The night and swing shifts share one meeting; the day shift has its own regularly scheduled meeting time. The plant manager and his top aides attend both meetings to (1) explain "what's happening" in the plant; (2) discuss goals, plans, and timetables; (3) respond to questions; and (4) solicit ideas and information. These meetings are an ongoing part of the overall communication strategy at R-2 and have been instrumental in fostering teamwork and in helping management achieve important organizational goals.[34]

Recent developments in communication technology are helping managers to deal more effectively with distortion, overload, and timeliness problems. Computerized information processing systems, telecommunication systems, electronic information networks, fax machines, and microcomputers are altering traditional methods of organizational message exchange. For example, many managers can today send and receive memos, notes, and other messages via electronic mail. This medium eliminates the practice of drafting a document or dictating a message to a secretary who then prepares the final document and mails it. Many managers can also directly access production, sales, or personnel information, thereby improving timeliness and reducing the number of intermediaries through whom a message must pass. It is important to remember, however, that the likelihood of overload is also increased by such direct communication opportunities.

New communication technologies are having a significant impact on the daily activities of individual workers, the communication networks, and the social systems within organizations. These technologies will provide users with more, though not necessarily better, information and may place even more responsibility on managers to use information properly.

Auditing Organizational Communication

An accountant audits an organization's books to determine the financial health of the enterprise. The information obtained from such an audit can be used to determine future markets for goods and services, plan growth strategies, and manage cash flow. Audit data thus help identify organizational strengths and weaknesses and prevent financial crises.

A **communication audit** is a systematic appraisal of communication effectiveness within an organization. Just as a financial audit supplies a client with the information necessary to assess the status of an enterprise, so a communication audit provides a means of analyzing and improving the flow of messages in an organization. A number of methods are available for collecting information about the various levels of the communication system (individual, interpersonal, network). Exhibit 10.12 lists and briefly describes several diagnostic methods.

A communication audit can provide reliable and valid data about the flow of messages in an organization. Such information can be used to analyze current practices and procedures and possibly to identify potential problems in the networks of communication. Managers thus can be equipped to deal proactively with the organizational communication system, rather than reactively or defensively as communication problems occur.

COMMUNICATION: CONCLUSIONS

Communication, the process of sending and receiving messages, is the essence of organized activity. In any organization, two of a manager's foremost responsibilities are the development and maintenance of an effective communication system.

Many managers perceive their role as a communicator primarily as one of sending messages. Effective managerial communication, however, requires skill in both the sending and receiving aspects of message exchange. In addition, many barriers can affect the interpersonal communication process. A manager must (1) recognize such barriers as perceptual differences, noise, and imprecise language, (2) understand the

EXHIBIT 10.12   SOME DIAGNOSTIC METHODS USED IN COMMUNICATION AUDITS

LEVELS	DIAGNOSTIC TOOLS	USES
Individual/Personal	Cognitive Stretch Test	Focuses on problem-solving styles of individual managers
	Kirkpatrick's Supervisory Inventory on Communication	Assesses individual's listening, speaking and writing skills
	Communication Apprehension Tests	Indicates individual's tendency to avoid communication
	Rokeach's Dogmatism Scale	Measures individual's closed-mindedness versus open-mindedness
Interpersonal	Disparity Tests	Tests for differences between bosses' and subordinates' perceptions of authority, ability, and responsibility
	Accuracy Tests	Measures degree of accuracy of managers knowledge about how information is disseminated in the organization
	Falcione's Credibility Test	Examines subordinates' perceptons of their supervisors' credibility
Network	Observational Studies	Selected individuals or trained observers record communication activities in diaries
	ECCO Analysis	Charts episodic communication channels in the organization by tracking a message or set of messages through the organization
	Network Analysis	Computer-generated comparisons of patterns of communication pathways (such as actual versus expected, regulative versus innovative)
Multilevel	The ICA Communication Audit	Uses these five instruments: questionnaires, interviews, experience descriptions, diaries, and network analysis. Data are collected, analyzed, and fed back to the organization in a planned way
	The OCD Audit System	Uses one questionnaire to try to locate dissatisfaction and problems related to many aspects of communications in the organization

For further descriptions and sources of these and other instruments, see Richard V. Farace et al., *Communicating and Organizing* (Reading, Mass.: Addison-Wesley, 1977), 209–225; Gerald Goldhaber et al., *Information Strategies* (Englewood Cliffs, N.J.: Prentice-Hall, 1979), 222–250, 270–280; and Gerald Goldhaber, *Organizational Communication* (Dubuque, Ia.: Wm. C. Brown, 1979), 338–380.

conditions under which such difficulties are most likely to occur, and (3) learn skills and methods that can help to minimize such problems.

The process of communicating (message exchange) does not necessarily result in shared meanings between sender and receiver. Effective communication occurs when a sender and receiver achieve a degree of mutual, shared understanding. Achieving a level of shared meaning is hard work and requires the development of interpersonal skills such as listening and soliciting and giving feedback. Managers must devote time and effort to preparing to listen, concentrating and staying on

ETHICAL DILEMMA
Up-Front Negotiations?

Dick Wilson had been involved with computers all his working life. He had just started his own data-processing firm two months ago after leaving DataCo, where he had worked for five years. Dick had been an excellent sales manager and a key member of DataCo's management team. However, he had always dreamed of founding and building his own company. Dick made the break from DataCo after months of late evenings running spreadsheets, developing customer lists, and otherwise preparing for the new venture.

As Dick looked out the window in his new office, he noticed Jerry Abram getting out of his car. Jerry represented the best office-furnishings company in town, Furniture-Mart, and Dick had several new offices and work areas to outfit. Jerry had scheduled an appointment to discuss his company's products and services. "Thanks for coming out, Jerry," Dick greeted him. "Let's take a little stroll and you can see the space we're talking about."

Walking through the vacant rooms, Dick knew he had Jerry right where he wanted him. Dick had already done business with Jerry's company, paying Jerry promptly with his start-up capital. Dick also knew that a credit check would show plenty of cash on hand and a good payment record. There was no reason for Furniture-Mart not to cooperate on this one; Jerry would ship the furniture and equipment out and bill in thirty days. Dick figured that Furniture-Mart would not even pick up the phone to inquire about payment until forty-five or sixty days had passed.

Granted, Jerry did not know exactly what Dick was planning. He did not know, for example, that the rooms he inspected would soon be occupied by several highly paid programmers and many expensive machines. Having already landed two big accounts, Dick was expanding more rapidly than outlined in his original business plan. The cash drain on Dick's company would likely be severe. He estimated that it would be approximately six months before Furniture-Mart would get all of its money. Dick planned on sending them just enough each month to show good faith, and to keep the moving trucks away from the door.

As they walked back to his office, Dick considered telling Jerry about the whole situation. He wondered, "Would it sink the deal?" Maybe, and then Dick would be left with unfurnished offices and the word out that he was short of cash. On the other hand, who would be hurt if Dick said nothing? Jerry's company would eventually get its money, and Dick would be ready for the new business he took on. Even in the worst situation, all Furniture-Mart would need to do would be to pick up its furniture.

Questions
What should Dick do? Should he tell Jerry about his plans or keep quiet?

Should Dick postpone the order for more furnishings until he can pay for it?

SOURCE: "Honest Business," *Inc.,* January 1990, 65–69.

---

track, listening for central ideas, and avoiding snap judgments. In addition, effective managers must become both feedback receptive and responsive.

At the organizational level, messages are communicated through a variety of networks. Managers usually rely most heavily on the authority, information, and task expertise networks. However, information can be conveyed through friendship and status networks. Barriers also exist, however, that can impede the flow of accurate messages within a system. Important aspects of a manager's job, therefore, are the ongoing assessment and treatment of such message-related difficulties as distortion, overload, and timeliness. Regular communication audits provide one means of proactively rather than reactively dealing with obstacles that can encumber the flow of messages in an organization.

QUESTIONS FOR REVIEW AND DISCUSSION

1. What is the importance of communication in organizations?
2. Define communication.
3. What are the components of the communication process?
4. Discuss the relationship between verbal and nonverbal messages.
5. What is the difference between communication channels and media?
6. How much control does a manager have over the communication process?
7. What is the difference between hearing and listening?
8. What can a manager do to improve listening skills?
9. What are the five general types of organizational networks? Describe the function of each network.
10. What types of messages are usually communicated downward?
11. What is a gatekeeper?
12. What are the major barriers to effective organizational communication?

REFERENCES

1. H. A. Thelen, "Exploration of a Growth Model for Psychic, Biological, and Social Systems," Mimeographed paper, no date.
2. The following formula was used to obtain this figure: n(n − 1)/2, where n = number of people.
3. Chester I. Barnard, *The Functions of the Executive* (Cambridge: Harvard University Press, 1938), 91.
4. D. Katz and R. L. Kahn, *The Social Psychology of Organizations*, 2nd ed. (New York: Wiley, 1978).
5. Stephen R. Axley "Managerial and Organizational Communication in Terms of the Conduit Metaphor," *Academy of Management Review*, Vol. 9, No. 3 (1984): 428–437.
6. M. L. Knapp, *Nonverbal Communication in Human Interaction* (New York: Holt, Rinehart and Winston, 1972), 12.
7. A. Mehrabian and M. Wiener, "Decoding of Inconsistent Communication," *Journal of Personality and Social Psychology*, Vol. 6 (1967): 109; A. Mehrabian and S. R. Ferris, "Inference of Attitudes from Nonverbal Communication in Two Channels," *Journal of Consulting Psychology*, Vol. 31 (1967): 248–252.
8. H. Mintzberg, *The Nature of Managerial Work* (New York: McGraw-Hill, 1973).
9. R. L. Daft and R. H. Lengel, "Information Richness: A New Approach to Managerial Behavior and Organization Design," in B. Staw and L. Cummings, eds., *Research in Organizational Behavior* (Greenwich, Conn.:

JAI Press, 1984), 191–233; R. L. Daft and R. H. Lengel, "Organizational Information Requirements, Media Richness, and Structural Design," *Management Science*, Vol. 32, No. 5 (1986): 554–563.
10. Paraphrased from C. R. Rogers, *Client-Centered Therapy* (Boston: Houghton Mifflin Co., 1951), 483, 484, 487, 494.
11. Akio Morita, "Doing Business Without Blame: Miscommunication and Misperceptions in U.S.-Japan Trade," *Speaking of Japan*, Vol. 8, No. 80 (August 1987): 28.
12. Stuart Chase, *Power of Words* (New York: Harcourt, Brace & Jovanovich, 1954), 259.
13. E. M. Rogers and R. Agarwala-Rogers, *Communication in Organizations* (New York: The Free Press, 1976), 26.
14. W. Wiesman, *Wall-To-Wall Organizational Communication* (Huntsville, Ala.: Walter Wiesman, 1973), 4.
15. Ibid., 3.
16. Ralph G. Nichols, "Listening: Questions and Problems," *Quarterly Journal of Speech*, Vol. 33 (February 1947): 83.
17. W. Charles Redding, *The Corporate Manager's Guide to Better Communication*, (Glenview, Ill.: Scott, Foresman and Company, 1984), 94–95.
18. Jack R. Gibb, "Defensive Communication," Journal of Communication, Vol. 11, No. 3 (1961): 141–148; Louis P. Cusella, "Feedback, Motivation, and Performance," in Frederic M. Jablin, Linda L. Putnam, Karlene H.

Roberts, and Lyman W. Porter, eds., *The Handbood of Organizational Communication* (Beverly Hills, Cal.: Sage Publications, 1987), 624–678.

19. Paul Hawken, "The Employee as Customer," *Inc.*, November 1987, 21–22.

20. R. V. Farace and D. MacDonald, "New Directions in the Study of Organizational Communication," *Personal Psychology*, Vol. 27 (1974): 7.

21. H. Guetzkow, "Communication in Organizations," in J. March, ed., *Handbook of Organization* (Chicago: Rand McNally, 1965), chapter 12.

22. G. M. Goldhaber, *Organizational Communication*, 3rd ed. (Dubuque: Wm. C. Brown, 1983), 154.

23. Katz, op. cit., 440.

24. Ibid., 446.

25. K. Davis, "Management Communication and the Grapevine," *Harvard Business Review*, September-October 1953): 44.

26. K. Davis, *Human Behavior at Work*, 4th ed. (New York: McGraw-Hill, 1972), 263.

27. P. B. Sheatsley and J. J. Feldman, "The Assassination of President Kennedy: A Preliminary Report on Public Reactions and Behavior," *Public Opinion Quarterly*, Vol. 28 (1964): 189–215.

28. B. S. Greenberg, "Diffusion of News of the Kennedy Assassination," *Public Opinion Quarterly*, Vol. 28 (1964): 225–232.

29. Rogers, op. cit., 135.

30. K. H. Roberts and C. A. O'Reilly, "Some Correlates of Communication Roles in Organizations," *Academy of Management Journal*, Vol. 22 (1979): 42–57.

31. *Avoiding Failures in Management Communications*, Research Report of the Public Opinion Index for Industry (Princeton, N.J.: Opinion Research Corporation, January 1963).

32. Thomas F. O'Boyle, "GE Refrigerator Woes Illustrate the Hazards in Changing a Product," *Wall Street Journal*, 7 May 1990, p. 4.

33. J. G. Miller, "Information Input, Overload, and Psychopathology," *American Journal of Psychiatry*, Vol. 116 (1960): 695–704.

34. Ruth G. Newman, "Polaroid Develops a Communications System—But Not Instantly," *Management Review*, January 1990, 34–38.

CASE 10.1   *The chief*

GEORGE EDDY   *University of Texas–Austin*
JERRY SAEGERT

"I never thought that b——would try a stunt like that!" Alex Brown angrily exclaimed, striking his desk with a clenched fist so hard he winced.

Startled by the outburst, Anne Stevens looked up from her desk where she had been trying to type the minutes of the last safety council meeting. Astonished and concerned by this unexpected action from her boss, Anne realized that something quite serious must have occurred in the plant manager's office. Mr. Brown had rushed over there as soon as Mr. Arrowsmith called over the office intercom. She had always regarded Mr. Brown as a quiet and fairly restrained type of person who never blew his top. She believed most people would agree with her view of Mr. Brown as a competent and highly motivated individual whose considerable energies were devoted to developing ways to increase the efficiency of the plant safety office at Southwestern Arsenal.

As his secretary, Anne knew Mr. Brown was experimenting with some new approaches that he was confident would resolve a number of problems created by the newly organized firefighter-guard force at Southwestern. For several weeks, Mr. Brown had been trying to define responsibilities and authorities of several new supervisory positions. The force was an amalgamation of two formerly separate organizations: a security force and a firefighting force. Both had existed for several years. Selected to head this new combination was William Sprague, who had been the chief of the fire department at Southwestern almost since the organization's inception at the commencement of the Vietnam War. An aggressive, outspoken person,

Sprague's substantial physique seemed particularly consonant with a brusk, authoritarian manner.

Constructed in the early 1960s, Southwestern Arsenal was typical of scores of industrial plants the federal government had built to produce explosives of all sorts and to load, assemble, and pack (lap) a great variety of small arms, artillery shells, and bombs. Encompassing some 15,000 acres of relatively flat and treeless terrain, this installation was divided into two principal areas: one devoted to administrative purposes and the other designed to provide the extensive areas needed for working with explosives. Each area was separately fenced, with entrance and egress controlled by guards of the internal plant security force. Activities in the explosive operational areas were closely supervised and performed in accordance with detailed written procedures commonly referred to as Standard Operating Procedures (SOPs).

Because of the potential catastrophic results that could ensue from a fire involving explosives, the plant firefighting personnel required special knowledge of the important characteristics of explosives and the principal chemical reactions to high temperatures associated with conflagrations. Training and drills for such personnel received continual emphasis, and frequently the plant manager, Henry Arrowsmith, either participated himself or observed in the company of the safety officer. Supplementing these drills were detailed critiques held with the objective of improving performance. During Vietnam, all firefighting had been the responsibility solely of the fire department, while the separate guard force concerned itself with the aspects of physical security of the administrative

and operational areas of Southwestern. Not considered qualified to fight fires involving explosives, the guards did get some training in the subject of explosives characteristics and were expected to assist the fire department during emergencies.

After the war, Southwestern continued in production (the majority of such government facilities were closed and sold) under the same general management, although the scope of its activities was substantially reduced and there was considerable turnover of personnel. Included in the numerous organizational realignments necessitated by the significantly lessened need for the plant's products was the decision to merge the guard force with the fire department. Shortly after Henry Arrowsmith chose William Sprague to become the chief of this new organization of some fifty people, Alex Brown joined the staff as the plant safety officer. After reviewing the organization chart (Exhibit 10.13), Brown realized his arrival was coincidental with probably the maximum degree of turbulence engendered by the considerable shifting and reassignment of both former guards and firemen.

Following his initial meeting with Chief Sprague, a tour of the firefighter-guard facilities and an opportunity to talk with most of the supervisors and men on duty, Brown began to assess what he had observed. When he first visited the central station, located about the middle of the restricted area, Brown noticed that Arrowsmith was in the kitchen, pouring himself a cup of coffee. Each station operated on a twenty-four-hour basis, had sleeping quarters, a small kitchen and eating area, an office, supply and armory facilities, general equipment area, washing and toilet facilities,

EXHIBIT 10.13　SOUTHWESTERN ARSENAL ORGANIZATION CHART

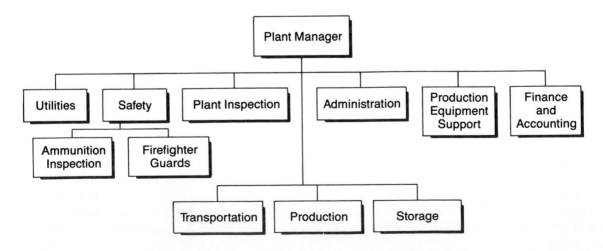

and an area that could be used for a variety of purposes, such as conferences, classes, and the like. There was always a pot of coffee brewing.

"Hello, Alex," said Arrowsmith, "I see you are making the rounds. What do you think of our setup?"

"I think I've seen just about everything that's under the Chief's control, Hank. Of course, I'm trying to sort things out, but it shouldn't take long. Already, I can appreciate [that] this reorganization of security and firefighting elements requires a 'new look' in a lot of aspects," replied Brown, as he concluded with a comment that he thought that the realignments would place a premium on flexibility in attitudes.

"Well, okay, Alex," Arrowsmith noted as he got up to leave, "I've got to get back to the office. It sure makes a nice break to get out in the area and stop off here and shoot the bull with the Chief. It'll soon be hunting season again, so I'll be out here a lot."

As the Chief walked out to the car with Arrowsmith, Brown noted that the conversation seemed quite informal and jovial. He wondered how often the plant manager visited the station and what sort of relationship existed between the manager and the station staff. Recalling each time the Chief had come to visit him in the administrative area, some six miles distant, Brown realized that the Chief had yet to come on his own initiative. Further, Brown realized that he either stopped by Hank's office before coming to see him or went there right after Brown had concluded their discussion about some matter on firefighting or security.

Soon after Brown had proposed a major change in the training schedule to the Chief, the subject had been mentioned by Arrowsmith. Surprised at first by the extent of Hank's knowledge of some of the details which he had not yet discussed with the plant manager, Brown quickly learned that the Chief had spoken to Hank about it, voicing various apprehensions of certain provisions. Arrowsmith told Brown that he had agreed with several of the Chief's concerns. Due to the manner in which Arrowsmith related his conversation with the Chief, Brown was convinced that the plant manager did not know these were matters that had originated with the safety officer, not the Chief. "Yeah, Alex, I told him the idea to increase the amount of time spent on security training by 40 percent was screwy," remarked Arrowsmith offhandedly. "After a bit, the Chief said he had to agree with me."

It was about this time that Brown recognized with growing irritation that the Chief seemed to be getting more disputatious on changes or innovations that

Brown proposed. As he reflected on the past three sessions with the Chief, Brown had to note that the Chief disagreed with every new idea the safety officer suggested was worth trying out. While the Chief did not say so directly, he managed to convey the impression that he felt these recommendations were absurd. The Chief began to emphasize that since his long tenure as the fire chief had run smoothly, there was no need to get tangled up in schemes of questionable merit. Clearly, the Chief was nettled by what he believed to be meddling in his affairs by a newcomer who had not been at Southwestern when "things were really tough" and who furthermore had probably never even held a firehose in his hands.

Even Hank suggested that perhaps Brown was pushing the Chief too hard and that he should give him a little more time to adjust to the requirements of the new firefighter-guard organization. The hunting season had commenced, and Brown learned that the plant manager spent several hours every day "out in the area." While some of these hours occurred right after daybreak, and were thus before the normal working day started, it seemed apparent that Arrowsmith stopped at the firefighter-guard station at least once every day for coffee and conversation. Brown was convinced the Chief always managed to be present when the plant manager appeared. Not a hunter himself, Brown never went out with Arrowsmith, who did not lack for company. Usually he took the mayor of Midvale, a small town nearby, as his guest.

"That must be quite a chore, Hank, to clean all those birds you seem to shoot so expertly," Brown remarked at the height of the season.

"Oh hell, Alex, I don't do that!" exclaimed Arrowsmith, "the Chief always takes care of it for me."

Some four months after he assumed the duties of safety officer, Brown was dismayed to recognize that whatever changes he had succeeded in getting implemented in the firefighter-guard organization had been "by direction." It no longer seemed possible to discuss matters of importance with the Chief, who never failed to find something wrong with anything new or different—Brown concluded—and who had become so intractable that Brown had grown weary in his repeated attempts to get him to focus on central issues instead of personalities. Even the relatively simple matter of determining the vacation schedule for supervisory personnel had become a contentious matter. The schedule the Chief had presented bothered Brown as he believed it unduly "favored" the supervisors with the longest tenure, giving them a disproportionate share of the most desirable vacation periods, simultaneously leaving the force under the newest and least experienced hands. After a heated discussion, the Chief reluctantly agreed to modify the schedule, but remained vague concerning his own plans.

Pointing to the wall calendar, Brown remarked that there were several periods available to the Chief. "Just let me know when you want to take off, Chief," Brown declared as the Chief got up to leave. "Yeah," replied the Chief and departed.

Brown picked up the latest training schedule and tried to concentrate on those portions that pertained to leadership and the general aspects of how to improve supervision. Based on his observations of the firefighter-guard organization, Brown was convinced the supervisory personnel, both relative newcomers and most oldtimers, were significantly deficient in performance in that capacity. They seemed reasonably proficient technically, and the continuing program to upgrade the force in this respect had progressed without major difficulty. He had spoken at length on leadership matters with the Chief, but since the latter had not shared his concern about such an emphasis, Brown went ahead and prepared a detailed and comprehensive program. At the time of the session on the vacation schedule, Brown had just concluded the last details, including lesson plans and the preparation of reference material he proposed to hand out for further study by the firefighter-guard supervisory personnel. Scheduling himself as the instructor for the majority of the lessons, Brown believed he had developed something significant that was long overdue.

Still smarting over his last discussion with Hank Arrowsmith about the Chief, who had complained again directly to the plant manager over a matter that Hank seemed disposed to regard as minor but was considered by Brown as most important, Alex was astounded by this contention:

"The Chief says you are trying to get him, Alex," Hank began, "He claims you've never stopped attacking him since the day you first arrived. He does not understand why this is happening as he has done his job for years without prior criticism. Then you appear and nothing is right. Why? Suddenly he figures it out. You are trying to act like your father!"

"What?"

"Let me finish, Alex," continued Hank Arrowsmith. "That's the way the Chief looks at it. He thinks you are so impressed with your father's methods that you can't help imitating him."

"You've got to be kidding, Hank. He's never even met my father, who has never been to Southwestern.

I know that my father is fairly well known as a forceful plant manager elsewhere. I'm not trying to 'get' the Chief—unless you regard trying to persuade him to follow reasonable instructions as something intolerable. I've given him every chance to cooperate, Hank, and he has chosen to fight me instead."

"Now, Alex, I don't think it's quite that," interjected Hank.

"Yes it is, Hank. The Chief has decided that he's going to override my authority and that he doesn't have to listen to anyone but you! It's now gotten to the point that it's either him or me . . . "

Arrowsmith had risen from his chair while Brown was speaking agitatedly. Now he went over to the window, turning his back to Brown in silence. After a few minutes of waiting for Arrowsmith to turn around, Brown abruptly left the office.

When he returned to his own office, Brown required some moments to regain his composure. Finally he picked up the telephone and dialed the number of the central firefighter-guard station.

"I want to speak to the Chief," he said to the person who answered.

"Golly, Mr. Brown, I thought you knew."

"Knew what?"

"That he's gone on vacation."

"Oh . . . ah, yes. Must've forgot." He hungup, fuming.

The day the Chief returned he found a message to report to Brown's office right away. Just as he started to leave the central station, the telephone rang. He picked it up and recognized Hank Arrowsmith's voice: "Say, Chief, glad you're back. I've got an errand I'd like you to run for me. It's quite important and you'll have to go right now."

"Sure, Mr. Arrowsmith, just tell me what you want and I'll be on my way."

"I feel like a damned fool, Chief, but I know I can count on you. You see, I just realized that when I sent my suit to the cleaners in Midvale this morning I forgot to take out the master key I have to all the gates at the plant. You've got to get it back immediately and quietly without tipping anybody off what the key is. Got it?"

"I understand, Mr. Arrowsmith. I'll get it, you can be sure. Don't worry about a thing. I'm on my way."

Wondering what was keeping the Chief, Brown reread the letter of reprimand he had prepared to give him as soon as he arrived.

It was the strongest disciplinary letter he had ever written, and he thought grimly it would probably lift the Chief right out of his chair.

CASE 10.2 *The* J. R. Reston Company, Inc.

SCOTT MARKHAM *University of Central Arkansas*
DALE A. LEVEL *University of Arkansas*

BACKGROUND

The J. R. Reston Company, Inc., like many of today's giants of American industry, had a modest beginning. It all started back in 1915 when John Reston, known in later years in the company as "the old man," quit the bank for which he was working over a dispute about the way stocks, bonds, and other securities were physically being transferred from the bank to other banks, customers, brokerage houses, and other financial institutions.

Reston opened his own private courier service, specializing in fast, dependable, and confidential transferring of various types of important printed documents between all of the banks in Denver and the various places to which these instruments needed delivering. Reston expanded rapidly and opened the first branch office in Los Angeles in 1920. By this time the name "John Reston" had become synonymous with integrity and confidentiality in Western financial circles. Using this well-deserved reputation, Reston hired several of his former colleagues away from their banking positions and incorporated the first of several wholly owned subsidiaries—J. R. Reston & Partners, Ltd., a stock brokerage firm.

About the time Reston had completed negotiations to purchase all of the outstanding stock of Bowles & Son, Inc., a printing concern, he started getting some feedback about the need for another type of business which would fit in well with his rapidly growing company. It seemed that many of the banks for which the Reston company delivered were approached from time to time by parties with whom they were familiar who would ask for financing. The prevailing practice at the time was for the bank loan officer to forward the request to the bank's "new business" department. This department would then begin an investigation to determine the credit worthiness of the applicant.

It appeared that this was taking too long for most of the banks, and they were losing some business from impatient businessmen, many of whom turned out to be excellent credit risks. If ever was there a man with a "nose for opportunity," it was Mr. J. R. Reston. He called his board of directors together and asked its opinion of the forming of a third wholly owned subsidiary. The corporate title suggested was Reston Services Company, Inc. A motion was made to proceed, a person was hired to lead this new venture, and thus Reston was launched into the providing of information to financial institutions.

The venture proved profitable and led Reston to expand his services to include all types of businesses that might have need for the same data he had been furnishing exclusively to banks. The expense had been incurred by the time the report went to a bank, so Reston thought, why not make extra copies of the report, lower the price to all customers, and share the data with other parties who had legitimate business reasons for needing it?

The stock market crash ruined J. R. Reston & Partners, Ltd.; the printing and delivery and business information companies managed to break even. By 1935 they were going strong once again. With the general boom in American industry following World War II, Reston decided to retire. John, Jr., was ready to take the helm. His first major decision was to go public. The stock issue was well accepted. It sold out within three weeks of its issue date.

With this increased capitalization, J. R. Reston Company, Inc. moved into other fields, including a 20 percent ownership of a small Western railroad, a 50 percent ownership of a large California farm, and another wholly owned subsidiary—Reston Real Estate, Inc.

ORGANIZATION

Transportation, communication, information, food, and shelter—five industries that J. R. Reston felt would always be winners in the United States economy. One way John, Sr., had rewarded "his people" was to give them a title. Thus, the organization had "grown up" and been expanded with each new division. Lines of authority and responsibility often overlapped. John, Jr., kept most of the men who had worked for his father, and, in fact, he observed the same basic management style: "give them the ball and tell them to run with it as far as they want to." A partial organization chart is shown in Exhibit 10.14.

TAKE THE BALL AND RUN

Ben Smith, VP Marketing for all the Reston Companies, called a 10:00 A.M. meeting in his office for Tuesday. Present at the meeting were Glenda Humphrey, Walter Brown, and Smith.

Smith opened the meeting cordially: "Everybody, glad you could make it. What we have to talk about today could be the thing that really puts the name of Reston Services Company on the tongue of every business person in the country. You are both aware that we have completed putting all of the information

on all of the companies in our files into the computer—there are over 1,000,000 companies—the businesses America does most of its business with. What I am proposing is that we develop a program whereby any organization can use our data for purposes other than just checking to see if someone is a good credit risk."

"What sort of uses did you have in mind, Ben?" Glenda Humphrey asked.

"I was especially thinking of uses in the area of prospecting for new business. We could have our computer programmers develop programs to print-out the critical information on each business; name, address, who to see, what they do, and size. Instead of the long reports we are now selling, I could see this new service being offered on 3 × 5 cards and disks so our customers could plug our data directly into their data processing equipment, or give it directly to their salespeople in the field."

"Sounds tremendous to me," Walter Brown added.

"I'm glad we're all in agreement. Walter, I'd like you to develop some ideas for promotional tools to push this concept, and Glenda, you will be in charge of

EXHIBIT 10.14   ORGANIZATION CHART

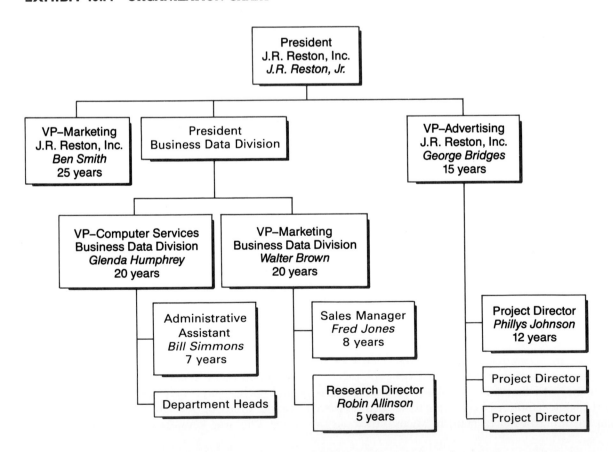

developing the computer programs. All clear?" Smith asked.

"Clear to me," responded Brown.

"Yes, quite clear," Humphrey echoed.

For the next several months, rumors were running rampant throughout the company's headquarters, based initially upon the meeting just described.

One of the rumors was that the basic information division of the company was going to be completely computerized and that many of the lower level jobs now being performed by high school graduates with some experience and recent college graduates would be eliminated.

Bill Simmons, administrative assistant, brought this to Humphrey's attention during coffee one morning: "Ms. Humphrey, I've heard quite a bit of talk lately, from several sources, that a lot of the people who gather our raw data are afraid there is some move afoot to discontinue their jobs. I know this is because of the work we're doing to develop computer programs and formats for Smith's new-product idea, and that, when completed, it won't affect their jobs one way or the other, but they don't know that. Do you think it would be a good idea for you to distribute a memo to that effect to the department heads in our division, and maybe ask Mr. Brown if he would like to do the same in his division?"

"Hell no, Simmons, the less we pamper those people on the bottom, the better off the company will be. If we start sending out memos every time we hear a rumor, that's all this office will end up doing: sending out memos. And as far as Brown is concerned, we'll let him make his own mistakes, understood?"

"Yes, ma'am," replied Simmons.

WHO'S IN CHARGE?

A formal letter outlining what a great opportunity this was for the company was issued from Ben Smith's office about four months after the initial meeting. It was addressed to the department heads in the information division. Humphrey was a bit miffed, as she received her copy at the same time the department heads who reported to her received theirs. But this was not unusual.

When Humphrey was leaving work, it was inevitable that on some afternoons she would be in an elevator with some of the line people in her division. Even though these people all worked for the same company, Humphrey never carried on much of a conversation with any of them. A few of these people

who had been with the company almost as long as Humphrey, would always try and talk with her anyway. On the few occasions when she would respond with more than a "yes" or "no," it really "made their day." Humphrey's general attitude and her "great stone face" only served to reinforce the younger line employees' opinion of her.

Even though an unusually large number of employee turnovers hampered the progress of developing the computer outputs, Humphrey managed to make headway on her part of the project. Walter Brown, in the meantime, was forging ahead on the promotional tools which he hoped would be a major factor in causing the success of this program. His first step was to call a meeting between himself, George Bridges, in advertising, and Fred Jones, sales manager. In the meeting, Bridges seemed distracted, even though it would be his department's responsibility to actually produce the physical promotional items.

"Is it O.K. with Smith if we bring in the ad agency guys on this one?" Bridges asked.

"I don't really know, George," Brown responded. "I just don't know."

"Well this looks like a helluva lot more work than I can handle, especially considering the other projects we're working on," Bridges added. "What did Smith mean when he said 'promotional tools' anyway?"

"He didn't really spell it out, George. I suppose pamphlets, brochures, some 'leave-behinds' for the salesmen, some direct mail, you know, that sort of thing."

"Yeah, my people will need all the help they can get when they go into this area. You know, it will be a whole new ball game out there. They may be calling on the same types of firms, but they'll be talking to different people once they get inside," Jones added.

"I know, I know, but let's get back to Smith's 'promotional tools,'" Bridges states. When he pronounced "promotional tools," he had an unmistakable sneer in his voice.

"He doesn't want any radio, or magazine, or newspaper, is that what you're saying?" Bridges asked. "Not even the *Journal* [Wall Street Journal]?"

"I don't know for sure, George. Why don't you go up there and ask him?" Brown retorted, this time raising his voice just a bit.

"Anyway, George, if you would work on some ideas for us I would appreciate it, and I'm sure Fred and his people would too. If you need to talk to Smith, just go up there and talk to him, or if you think he would say he's too busy, then just work up what you think is best. At any rate we've got a meeting with his people, my people and your people and Humphrey's crew in the Board Room, June 1. O.K.?"

"O.K.," Bridges grunted.

George Bridges didn't return directly to his office. Instead, he walked around the block a few times. His mind was racing. "Why didn't Smith invite me to the initial meeting? Why didn't he put in writing what kind of promotion he wants, or at least why didn't Brown put in writing the kind of promotion he would like to see. If either or both of them had, that would at least give me something more concrete to go on." He returned to his office and called in Phyllis Johnson, one of his project directors.

"Phyl, we've a real job coming up. What it involves is producing some direct mail and some pamphlets for Smith's latest brainstorm."

"You mean the computerized sales aids Humphrey's people have been working on?"

"One and the same. You get down to Humphrey and find out what you can about the product and the market, and write me up some stuff. Have somebody in the art department 'dummy up' some samples of what you think the brochures should look like."

Phyllis Johnson followed through on her part of the assignment, collecting most of the data from various people in Humphrey's area, not getting much help from Humphrey herself. Johnson developed a direct mail campaign consisting of three letters, each accompanied by a different brochure. The brochures could also be used separately as "leave-behinds" by the sales force, or could be used with personal letters written by the sales people to preferred customers. She went in to explain what she had developed to George Bridges. About midway through, Bridges stood up from where he had been seated and looking out of the window and asked Johnson to leave the material on his desk and that he would get to it as soon as he could. Johnson left Bridges' office a very confused young woman.

HIDDEN AGENDAS

June 1 rolled around and found Ben Smith and his top two assistants in the Board Room on the twentieth floor thirty minutes before the meeting was to start. Smith had seated himself at the end of the table farthest from the door. His two people flanked him.

Brown, Jones, Allinson, Bridges, and Johnson arrived at about the same time. Brown, Jones, and Allinson seated themselves on the side of the table nearest the door, with Brown sitting nearest Smith.

There was one empty chair between Brown and the person on Smith's right. Johnson followed Bridges to the opposite side of the table and they arranged themselves similarly to Brown and his people. Humphrey, Simmons and two more business data people arrived about five minutes after 1:00.

Humphrey reported that work was progressing nicely on the computer programs. She passed around samples of what the 3×5 cards would look like, and explained what data would be available on the disks. Brown reported on the field work he and Jones had done with their sales force, working through their department heads, as well as the instructions he had given Bridges in regard to promotion.

Bridges then passed around Johnson's letters and brochures, never mentioning who did them. They were well received. Bridges then asked Smith's opinion of some ads in the *Wall Street Journal.* Smith responded favorably and also mentioned he thought some "things in the business sections of the *Los Angeles Times* and *New York Times* plus *Fortune* would be nice." Bridges mentioned that he had been thinking the very same thing.

Humphrey then mentioned that what she saw and heard was good but that it seemed to her something was missing. Some type of brochure that was more extensive, something that would contain some useful data that would really whet the businessperson's appetite for more. Smith consented and asked Brown and Bridges to work on it.

Bridges and Brown met. Brown tried to give the project to Bridges. Bridges said that it was Humphrey's idea, so "Why didn't she do it?" In the end, it was delegated as a group project to Johnson from Advertising, Simmons from Business Data, and Robin Allinson from Marketing Products.

During their first meeting, Simmons suggested their second meeting could easily be held in his division's conference room, as it was in the center of the building, and accessible for both Johnson and Allinson. Allinson countered with the statement that "Yes, but our place has the new video equipment, and it might make it easier for Phyllis if we met there, because she will probably want to have slides made of her stuff anyway, and that way she would have all the equipment she needs already in the room."

Simmons did not make a verbal reply; he simply raised the palms of both hands upward and shrugged his shoulders.

It was decided that the booklet would contain grouped data on the businesses in the Reston file. The data were to be arranged first by type of industry and second by geographic area, that is, by each of the fifty states. The data were compiled after several more months' work, and rough copies were hand-delivered to Smith, Brown, Bridges, and Humphrey.

SUCCESS IN SPITE OF?

In a subsequent Board meeting, Smith, Humphrey, and Brown were present. The computer programs, formats, and all promotional materials (letters, bro-

chures, newspaper and magazine advertisements, and the booklet) were presented. All met with the Board's approval, with minor modifications.

The product and its accompanying promotion were presented later at a major meeting at the Denver Hilton. All of the parties previously mentioned were present, as was J. R. Reston, Jr., and all of Reston Service Company's Regional Managers. Brown, Bridges, and Humphrey were all thinking to themselves, "There must be a better way. . . . "

EXERCISE 10.1
ONE-WAY VERSUS TWO-WAY COMMUNICATION

The process of interpersonal communication is sometimes complicated by our failure to secure feedback. The verbal and nonverbal form of feedback available to the sender is also an important factor in communication. The purpose of this exercise is to demonstrate the impact of various types of feedback on goal attainment. It may also be used to illustrate the importance of organization structure on communications effectiveness.

INSTRUCTIONS

1. A sender must be selected from the group. He or she will be given some time in which to examine a diagram provided by the instructor. The diagram consists of well-known geometric forms that have been linked to one another.
2. The sender will demonstrate a "one-way" communication format by describing the diagram to other members of the group without receiving *any form* of feedback. (This can be accomplished by placing the sender behind a screen or by turning his or her back to the group.) Members of the group are not permitted to ask questions or provide any feedback (statements, laughing, etc.) to the sender.
3. After Step 2 is completed, the sender faces the group and describes a second diagram. Group members still may not ask questions about their instructions. In this case, however, the sender is in a position to pick up nonverbal feedback from the group.
4. A third diagram is provided to the sender. This time he or she may observe the group and receive verbal feedback (questions, comments, etc.) directly from group members.
5. Step 4 may be repeated more than once.
6. Measure (count percent of errors) the accuracy for each variation in format.

VARIATIONS

Rules may be established that govern the type of feedback given, the number of times a step is repeated, and who may communicate with the sender. In the last case, the group may be structured in a manner that requires information to flow through or around certain individuals. Many other variations can be added to the exercise.

QUESTIONS

1. What differences exist for the sender in one-way versus two-way communication? The sender may want to describe his or her experiences or feelings in each situation.
2. How did different types of feedback affect the efficiency and the effectiveness of the total communication process?
3. What were your experiences as a receiver under different communication arrangements (frustrations, confusion, sense of competence, accuracy, etc.)?
4. What were the advantages and disadvantages of each communication format? Is two-way communication better than one-way communication? Is unstructured feedback better than structured feedback? Discuss.

EXERCISE 10.2
SERIAL COMMUNICATION

OBJECTIVES

To allow the student to:

1. Observe the process of distortion in the serial reproduction of information.
2. Determine the effect of serial communication in the world of work.

PROCEDURES

1. Have six members of the class leave the room and remain far enough away so that they cannot hear what is going on in the room.
2. Call one of the six students back into the room. The instructor reads a short story to the student.
3. Call in the next student and have student #1 reproduce the story or report as accurately as possible. Student #2 should listen very carefully because he or she will be asked to reproduce the message for the next student. No questions or discussion should occur before, during, or after the reproductions.
4. Call in the third student. Have student #2 tell the story as close to verbatim as he or she heard the story to student #3 while the class listens.

5. As student #2 returns to his or her seat, call in the next student. Have student #3 tell the story to the fourth student, and so on until all six students who left the room have heard and repeated the story.

6. Each time the story is repeated, class members should note what changes occur. Finally, when the last student tells the story, have the class record it verbatim.

7. Lead a discussion concerning the following questions:

   a. What kinds of information were reproduced accurately, omitted, added, and changed to conform to "what makes sense"?

   b. What methods could be used or devised to improve the accuracy with which information was reproduced?

   c. How much should a person depend on the accuracy of information reproduced from memory through several individuals?

   d. How do the circumstances of this exercise differ from normal rumor transmission on the job? Do these differences make the reproductions in the exercise more or less accurate than would occur in business settings?

CHAPTER 11

POWER AND CONFLICT

LEARNING OBJECTIVES

1. To recognize the role of power in organizational behavior.
2. To become familiar with different types and sources of power.
3. To identify strategies for obtaining power.
4. To understand the process of empowering.
5. To understand conflict as a process.
6. To recognize the functional and dysfunctional effects of conflict.
7. To identify strategies for managing conflict.

CHAPTER OUTLINE

Distinctions Among Influence, Power, and Authority
Determinants of Power

Individual Bases of Power

How Power Is Obtained
Doing the Right Things and Knowing the Right People
Coalescing / Co-opting

An Alternative Perspective on Behavior in Organizations
A Strategic Contingencies Approach

Empowerment and the Managerial Revolution

Understanding and Managing Conflict

Conflict as a Process
Frustration / Conceptualization
Behavior / Outcome

The Functional and Dysfunctional Consequences of Conflict

Strategies for Managing Conflict
Negotiation / Establishing Superordinate Goals
Using a Third-Party Intervention
Removing Personnel and Restructuring the Organization

Power and Conflict: Conclusions

Questions for Review and Discussion

References

Cases: 11.1 Just Who Runs This Show?
       11.2 Dissension at RANDEB

Exercises: 11.1 Win as Much as You Can
        11.2 Disarmament Exercise

KEY TERMS

Influence / Power / Authority

Reward power / Coercive power

Legitimate power

Expert power / Referent power

Information power

Coalescing / Co-opting

Organizational politics

Strategic contingencies theory

Empowerment / Conflict

Functional and dysfunctional consequences of conflict

Negotiation

Negotiation stages

Distribution negotiation

Integrative negotiation

Superordinate goals

Third-party intervention

Conciliator / Mediator
Arbitrator

Susan was confused and upset. She had been a marketing executive at Tip-Top Corporation for almost six years. Her performance evaluations indicated that she was conscientious, creative, and dedicated. Susan could not understand why Harold James had received an important promotion instead of her. "I have more experience and am better qualified for that position—and almost everyone around here knows it," she confided to a colleague. "You are indeed better qualified," the colleague responded, "but you must remember that Harold is a master of organizational politics. He has cultivated the right connections within the company, knows the proper people, and can push the correct buttons to get what he wants. You were not denied the position because of inadequate qualifications; you were outmaneuvered by an expert who knows how to use power and influence to get what he wants."

Darrell Henderson had recently resigned as the dean of a well-known college of business administration. The central administration of the university was about to promote to the deanship one of the college's most noted professors—a man with considerable administrative experience. A group of the college's full professors visited the president to deliver a petition requesting that he give the job to another candidate—a rather meek man of moderate talent. The president acquiesced. For years thereafter, the college of business administration stagnated. The professors owned the dean, and they opted for maintaining the status quo.

These two examples highlight a common phenomenon in organizations: the exercise of power and influence. In fact, power is a fundamental reality of organizational life. Many people, however, consider power to be a dirty word and inappropriate as a topic of discussion or study. Rosabeth M. Kanter, a noted specialist in organizational behavior, suggests that:

> It is easier to talk about money—and much easier to talk about sex—than it is to talk about power. People who have it deny it; people who want it do not want to appear hungry for it; and people who engage in its machinations do so secretly.[1]

Despite this bad reputation, power is an essential element in the formula for effective managerial behavior. Management scholars and researchers have increasingly focused on issues associated with power and influence in the last ten to fifteen years, having recognized the importance of these concepts to the study of organizational behavior. As a result, the emerging large body of literature can help us understand what power is, how power can be obtained, and how the dynamics of power affect both managers and organizational members.

DISTINCTIONS AMONG INFLUENCE, POWER, AND AUTHORITY

People often use words such as *influence, power,* and *authority* as if they were synonymous. These concepts are closely related, but important conceptual distinctions do exist among them.

Influence, the most general of the three terms, is the process of producing certain intended effects in individuals, groups, or organizations. At least two parties are involved in any influence process, an agent and a target. The agent (an individual, group, or organization) initiates the process and attempts to produce certain intended effects in the target (another individual, group, or organization). Such intended effects can include changes in the target's behaviors, attitudes, beliefs, or values. For example, as part of an overall strategy for altering the culture of an organization, a chief executive officer (agent) may attempt to influence all organizational members (targets) to adopt a participative style of decision making (intended effect).

Power is the ability or capacity to influence, usually obtained by controlling an important resource upon which other individuals or groups depend. Information and money, for example, are resources frequently linked to power and the exercise of influence but control over other resources, such as job assignments and promotion opportunities, may also affect a person's ability and capacity to influence the actions of others. For example, the instructor who determines your grade in this class has the capacity to affect your behavior. Similarly, the department head or dean who evaluates the performance of your instructor can affect his or her behavior. An individual with power has the potential to alter decisions, actions, and outcomes.

A characteristic frequently associated with power is a private goal orientation rather than a group or collective goal orientation. In other words, power enables a person to promote personal goals without the knowledge, understanding, or consent of the target.[2] This private or personal goal orientation makes many people uneasy about the subject of power. For example, one writer has indicated that "power is poison," and Lord Acton, when writing to Bishop Mandell Creighton, made the well-known statement that "Power tends to corrupt and absolute power corrupts absolutely."[3] Remember, however, that power is not inherently evil or bad; neither is it used exclusively to achieve selfish interests. Power can be used responsibly to accomplish a variety of objectives, both selfish and selfless.

Power is the ability to bring about changes in the behavior and attitudes of others (intended effects). **Authority,** on the other hand, refers to a particular type of relationship in which the intended effects are produced with the knowledge or by the consent of the target. In other words, the exercise of authority is based on legitimacy. Managers, police officers, teachers, and supervisors, for example, have the *right* to influence the actions of other people. The right of such agents to exert influence is legitimate when it is granted or accepted by the target. Authority can be conferred on an individual by an organization (e.g., a manager by virtue of position has authority to direct the work of subordinates) or by a group of people (e.g., an elected official has authority to represent constituents) and is used to direct the behavior of others for the promotion of collective goals.[4]

In practice, the concepts of influence, power, and authority are very much interrelated. As a corporate executive, for example, Diana Stewart has the authority of her position and the willingness of subordinates to accept directives. She obtains power through control of corporate resources. The executive uses both power and authority to influence customers, competitors, suppliers, and employees. In addition, the executive can use this control of the corporation's resources as a means of enhancing her career (pursuit of a private goal) and can pursue policies designed to keep the firm financially sound and competitive (pursuit of a collective goal).

Determinants of Power

Power primarily is determined by three factors: resources, dependency, and the availability of alternatives.[5] Understanding these antecedents of power is especially useful in our study of organizational behavior.

As we discussed earlier, power is obtained through the control of resources. To have power, however, another individual or party must depend on the resource an agent controls. Oil, for example, is an important resource in industrialized countries. Oil-producing countries have power to influence the affairs of other nations to the degree that such nations depend on oil to fuel their economies. Similarly, an employer may have more power to influence employees during a recession because jobs are tight and difficult to find (increased employee dependency). Thus, the stronger the dependency, the greater the power.

Power is also determined by the availability of alternatives. Even if an agent possesses or controls an important resource on which another party depends, power is weakened if alternative sources of the resource exist. For example, Bill Tyler, a skilled employee, may threaten to quit his job if he does not receive an equitable pay increase. However, the power of Bill's threat is greatly reduced if many other skilled workers are available in the labor market. The availability of alternative resources is thus a significant determinant of an agent's power.

It is important to remember that perception significantly affects these determinants of power. In many instances, it is not the actual control but the *perceived* control of a resource that gives an individual power. For example, a staff manager like Herb Wilcox may have relatively little control over the pay or promotion opportunities of line managers. If, however, a line manager thinks Herb has power to influence decisions about these important matters, then Herb has power over that line manager. Ultimately, then, power is given to an agent by a target, and a target's perceptions of resource control, dependency, and alternatives are critical.

In summary, power is determined by (1) the actual and/or perceived control of resources (2) on which a target depends and (3) for which few if any alternatives exist. To obtain or increase power, an agent can acquire and/or create the perception of greater control of a valued or important resource, increase a target's dependence on that resource, and reduce or eliminate alternative suppliers of the resource. (Specific strategies for acquiring power are discussed in this chapter after the following discussion on individual bases of power.)

INDIVIDUAL BASES OF POWER

Six major types or bases of power have been identified: reward power, coercive power, legitimate power, referent power, expert power, and information power.[6]

Reward power exists when an agent controls reinforcements, incentives, and outcomes that are important to another person (target). A manager, for example,

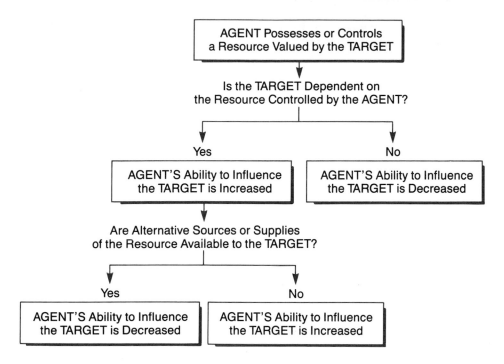

EXHIBIT 11.1   DETERMINANTS OF POWER

may have substantial reward power because he makes decisions about promotion opportunities, pay raises, vacation schedules, and job assignments. To the extent that these rewards are important to subordinates, the manager has power to affect or alter subordinates' behavior.

Coercive power is based on the ability to punish, frighten, or bully a target into compliance with a request or a directive. Such power can be exerted through threats, physical force, withholding emotional support, and other types of punishment. For example, a manager may cut a salesperson's pay for failing to make a sales quota during the previous month. Similarly, a supplier can put a "late charge" on an overdue bill to a customer. Coercive power is also referred to as punishment power.

Legitimate power exists when a target submits to the control of an agent because the agent is perceived to have the right to exert influence. Authority, as defined earlier, is similar to this particular type of power. Managers have certain legitimate powers (e.g., to evaluate performance; to provide positive and negative feedback; to direct, counsel, and coach) due to their hierarchical positions. An individual can also acquire legitimate power through designation or appointment. For example, a manager can be appointed chairperson of a special committee by the boss and given the power to get the job done.

Expert power stems from specialized knowledge or expertise. Medical doctors, for example, have considerable power due to their detailed knowledge of and experience with specific types of health problems. Similarly, an executive who speaks and writes Japanese, Korean, or Chinese may acquire power within an organization that is attempting to market products in Pacific Basin countries.

Advances in technology, office automation, and data processing have caused many organizations to experiment with new businesses and procedures centered on the computer. For example, J.C. Penney now processes credit card transactions for

EXHIBIT II.2   INDIVIDUAL BASES OF POWER

Shell Oil and Gulf Refining and Marketing as a way to leverage its investment in information technology. In contemporary organizations, the expertise of the data processing manager will enable him or her to become increasingly powerful as information technology becomes a strategic tool rather than simply a support function. The information manager who can speak management's language and explain how these new tools can be used to compete effectively in the marketplace will be an invaluable organizational asset.

Referent power usually results from a target's strong attraction to or identification with an agent. Movie stars and professional athletes, for example, frequently have the ability to influence the behavior of adults and young people due to the visibility and status associated with their professions. Advertisers often use well-known figures such as Michael Jordan, Chris Evert, and Michael J. Fox to promote products and causes, hoping consumers will imitate the behavior of these admired celebrities.

Information power is obtained through access to information about particular situations or problems within an organization or about the organization's relationship to its external environment. A secretary, for example, can have a lot of power in a department or organization because of access to sensitive information about projects, deadlines, and people. It is important to remember that expert power is based on accumulated knowledge, expertise, and experience. Information power, on the other hand, stems from access to sources of important information. A secretary may not know much about the process of making strategic personnel decisions, but because of his position he may know exactly who in the department is being considered for an important promotion. Access to information or sources of information is thus an important source of power.

In practice, the six bases of power are rarely separate and distinct. In fact, they are interrelated. An executive's referent power, for example, may increase if the executive accurately evaluates subordinate performance and equitably distributes rewards. Conversely, a manager who unfairly or capriciously uses reward power may weaken his or her referent power. In a similar manner, an executive's expert power can enhance both legitimate power (increased employee willingness to accept authority) and referent power (increased identification with and imitation of the individual). Remember—an individual's power usually is derived from several different bases and is affected by characteristics of both the individual and the organization.

HOW POWER IS OBTAINED

How do people obtain power? Are some individuals just lucky? Do they just happen to be in the right place at the right time? Can power be given to or bestowed on a person by someone else? How can an individual expand personal bases of power? We now discuss several specific methods and strategies for acquiring power.

Doing the Right Things and Knowing the Right People

Individuals in organizations obtain power by engaging in activities that are highly visible, extraordinary, and related to accomplishing organizational goals.[7] For example, Jeff Wilkens may receive an assignment as head of the production department in a manufacturing plant that has had only a mediocre record of performance during the past three years. Increases in output and product quality are imperative since this facility accounts for a substantial portion of the profits for Acme Corporation, and upper level management will be watching Jeff's performance carefully as he attempts to turn the situation around. The job poses considerable risk for Jeff, but the potential payoff is significant. He has been given an important, goal-related, and highly visible task to perform. If his efforts to improve the production department are successful, he will have done much to enhance his career and expand his personal bases of power in Acme Corporation. Individuals thus can seek out, volunteer for, and even create such opportunities in organizations as a means of increasing personal power.

A statement frequently heard in many organizations is, "It's not what you know but who you know that's important around here." Cultivating relationships with the right people, or **networking,** is another method of obtaining power. Such relationships can be with superiors, subordinates, and peers in the organization and also with key individuals outside of the organization. For example, a young doctor may become acquainted with a respected surgeon at a professional meeting. As a result of their initial meeting, they may correspond frequently to exchange ideas about surgical procedures and techniques. This association with a nationally respected figure may enhance the young doctor's personal power within the hospital. Similarly, relationships developed over time with superiors, influential peers, or competent subordinates can enhance one's personal bases of power.

Coalescing

Another strategy frequently used to acquire or enhance power is **coalescing**— the process of forming coalitions. Individuals or groups frequently combine their resources to pursue common goals and objectives. The basic reason for joining together in such alliances is an increased capacity to influence, achieved through greater control of resources. A labor union, for example, is comprised of many individuals seeking to promote the collective interests of workers (e.g., pay, safety, benefits). A single worker may be relatively powerless in dealing with an organization's management (e.g., "If the working conditions around here don't improve, I'll quit!"). However, a coalition of employees can exert considerable influence in pursuit of workers' rights and privileges ("If the working conditions around here don't improve, we'll all strike!"). Similarly, competing automobile companies may coalesce and lobby together for legislation imposing restrictions on the number of foreign imports allowed into the United States domestic market. Thus, individuals and groups coalesce and combine resources to wield more influence collectively than they could separately.

The recent move by the 1.6 million-member International Brotherhood of Teamsters to rejoin the AFL-CIO is an example of how power can be increased through coalescing. The economic and political strength gained by the AFL-CIO through the merger is significant. For example, the Teamsters began paying monthly dues of thirty-one cents per member to the AFL-CIO, adding more than four million dollars a year to the organization's $53 million dollar budget. The Teamsters also brought along one of the United States's fastest growing political action committees, which has several million dollars in its fund. The merger has heightened labor's bargaining strength and enabled the two organizations to coordinate attempts to organize workers more effectively.

Co-opting

Another method of increasing power and creating alliances is co-opting. **Co-opting** is accomplished by absorbing people or groups whose support is needed into positions of limited influence. This tactic differs from coalescing in that it specifically seeks to eliminate threats and opposition to an individual's base of power. A manager, for example, may recognize that Sam Jones is a potential threat to her pet project and thus to her ability to exercise power and influence in the marketing department. Sam has expressed reservations about the project on two different occasions. To minimize or eliminate this potential source of opposition, the manager can co-opt Sam by inviting him to participate on a task force given the responsibility of implementing the project. The expectation is that Sam's involvement in the project with other people committed to it will neutralize or even reverse his opposition and resistance.

Doing the right things and knowing the right people, coalescing, and co-opting are specific strategies for acquiring power. Individuals or groups frequently use these tactics to (1) gain control of an important resource (e.g., information as a result of knowing the right people); (2) foster or increase dependence on a resource (e.g., the labor of a coalition of employees); or (3) eliminate alternative suppliers of a resource (e.g., eradicating a competitor through co-opting). Of course, these are not the only strategies for obtaining or increasing power, but they are representative of the methods commonly used and observed in organizational settings.

AN ALTERNATIVE PERSPECTIVE ON BEHAVIOR IN ORGANIZATIONS: ORGANIZATIONAL POLITICS

Many management scholars and theorists assume that organizations are rational. In other words, organizational behavior and processes are believed to be logical and have purpose. Consider the instances, however, when behavior in organizations appears to contradict this assumption. For example, how does a less qualified individual receive a promotion over someone with more expertise and experience? (Remember the case at the beginning of the chapter involving Susan?) Or, why does a particular department in an organization consistently receive more than its appropriate share of the annual budget? Why are organizational goals often replaced by individual and group goals? One explanation for these seemingly irrational actions is the concept of organizational politics.

Organizational politics refers to intentional acts of influence designed to enhance or protect the self-interest of individuals or groups.[8] In other words, organizational politics involves activities and behaviors through which power is acquired, developed, and used in organizations to obtain what one wants. Politics is power in action or the use of power to get something accomplished.

An important characteristic of this definition is the emphasis on the self-interest of individuals and groups. In the section on influence, power, and authority, we suggested that power often is considered a dirty word. This negative connotation arises not so much from the concept of power itself but from the tactics and strategies sometimes used in the exercise of power (politics). The following characteristics are frequently associated with political behavior in organizations:

1. Such behavior usually occurs outside the legitimate systems of influence and often in opposition to them. In other words, such behavior is technically illegitimate and often clandestine.
2. Such behavior is designed to benefit the individual or group, ostensibly at the expense of the organization at large (although not always).
3. Such behavior, as a result of the two previous characteristics, is typically divisive or conflictive in nature, pitting individuals or groups against the organization at large, or against each other.[9]

Several key conditions tend to stimulate political behavior by individuals, groups, and organizations: uncertainty, the allocation of scarce resources, and conflicting goals and interests. Assume, for example, that a state government has received a large and unexpected amount of revenue because of a change in federal tax laws. As the directors of various state-funded agencies learn about the availability of these funds, each is interested in obtaining as much of the money as possible to support his organization's activities and projects. The need for additional funds is especially critical because the budgets of each of these organizations have been either reduced or held constant over the past few years. In this example, the priorities for deciding where and how the money should be spent (e.g., on highways, education, the prison system, human services) may not be obvious to or accepted by all of the interested parties; in other words, a great degree of *uncertainty* is present. Furthermore, this example clearly involves important decisions about the *allocation of a scarce resource*. Since the agencies have different areas of focus and typically compete for resources, they also have *conflicting goals or interests*. Consequently, the likelihood of political behavior occurring in such a situation is high because of the high demand for funds by all of the departments, the significant amount of money to be distributed, the lack of established allocation guidelines or clear spending priorities, and the inherent conflicts about goals and interests that arise among the organizations.

Viewing an organization as a political system presents a unique perspective on organizational behavior. The traditional assumptions of rationality and purposive behavior are replaced by the reality of political maneuvering, infighting, and games. Thus, the seemingly irrational examples presented at the beginning of this section are more easily understood when seen through a political framework of competing self-interests, goals, and objectives.

A Strategic Contingencies Approach to Intraorganizational Power

This chapter has thus far emphasized power at the individual level of analysis. The dynamics of power also occur between and among groups, departments, and organizations. We now examine strategic contingencies theory,[10] a framework for understanding the process through which organizational departments or subunits acquire, develop, and exercise power in organizations.

Strategic contingencies are critical problems affecting an organization's basic mission and behavior. The theory's premise is that the organizational subunits or departments best able to cope with such problems will acquire power. The theory suggests three major determinants of a department's or subunit's power: (1) uncertainty; (2) substitutability; and (3) centrality.

Uncertainty

Subunits and departments that effectively reduce uncertainty acquire power in an organization. **Uncertainty** originates in an organization's internal and external environments and is caused by a lack of information about future events that makes outcomes and alternatives unpredictable (e.g., the status of the economy, the impact of the Treasury Department's proposed changes in tax policy). Organizations must deal with environmental uncertainties in order to perform tasks and achieve goals successfully. The more a department or subunit provides the means of coping with uncertainty (e.g., the accounting department formulates a strategy to deal with new tax laws), the greater its power in the organization.

Substitutability

Groups or departments that cannot be easily replaced also are likely to acquire power in an organization. For example, a purchasing department would have relatively little power if all of its activities and tasks could be performed by other people or departments inside or outside the organization. Similarly, a personnel department would lose its influence if its functions could be accomplished by employment agencies and line managers. The lower the **substitutability** of the activities of a subunit, then, the greater its power in the organization.

Centrality

The **centrality** of a department or subunit is the degree to which its activities are integrated into the entire organization. Two basic factors affect centrality: (1) pervasiveness (the extent to which a department's activities are interconnected with those of other departments throughout the organization), and (2) immediacy (the extent to which a department's activities are required immediately by other work units and would quickly impede the primary workflow of the organization if stopped). An accounting or finance department, for example, can affect the work of most other subunits in an organization through budgeting and cost-control procedures (pervasiveness). Problems in the production department, on the other hand, can affect the organization's primary workflow in a short period of time (immediacy). It is important to remember that the pervasiveness and immediacy of a department's workflow are not necessarily related. Thus, the higher the pervasiveness and/or the immediacy of the workflows of a subunit, the greater its power in the organization.

When examined as a whole, strategic contingencies theory suggests that subunit power is a function of (1) the ability to reduce or cope with uncertainty;

(2) replaceability; and (3) centrality. The more these three conditions exist in a department or subunit, the greater the influence that subunit can exert within the organization. A careful balancing of all three factors is needed to explain how an organizational department or subunit acquires and maintains power.

In the container manufacturing industry, for example, outputs must fit varying customer requirements for containers. Scheduling for production departments and design problems for research departments are therefore completely subject to the contingencies of orders brought in by the sales department. Sales has not only the opportunity to cope with such uncertainty as may exist over customer requirements, it is also highly central; its activities connect it directly to both the other departments (workflow pervasiveness) and if ceased, production of containers would stop (work flow immediacy). The effects of centrality are probably bolstered by nonsubstitutability, since the sales subunit develops a specialized knowledge of customer requirements. Production and research are, therefore, comparatively powerless when facing the strategic contingencies controlled by the sales subunit. In short, these three factors help explain the patterns of contingencies from which power strategically flows.[11]

EMPOWERMENT AND THE MANAGERIAL REVOLUTION

Historically, the study of power and influence has focused on who gets power, how power is acquired, how power is used, and methods for maintaining and enhancing power once it has been obtained. This traditional approach to power grows out of and closely parallels the control-oriented model of work-force management discussed in Chapter 1. In fact, most of the concepts and models discussed so far in this chapter have been heavily influenced by this traditional view of power.

In Chapter 1, we described an important shift that is occurring in contemporary management thinking and practice, a shift from a control- to a commitment-based model of management. The significance of this managerial revolution is reflected clearly in changing attitudes about and practices concerning power. An increasing number of executives and companies are experimenting with the idea that effectiveness depends on the sharing and distribution of power throughout an organization, rather than on rigid hierarchical control and the hoarding of power.[12]

Ralph Stayer, for example, is one executive who has taken this new view of power to heart. As CEO at Johnsonville Foods, a rapidly growing specialty foods and sausage maker in Sheboygan, Wisconsin, he believes that

> flattening an organization does not work if you do not also transfer power. Before, I did not have power because I had people wandering around not giving a damn. Real power is getting people committed. Real power comes from giving it up to others who are in a better position to do things than I am. Control is an illusion. The only control you can possibly have comes when people are controlling themselves.[13]

In organizations such as Colgate, Sara Lee, Chesapeake Corporation, and Heinz USA, emphasis is placed on **empowering** managers and employees. Empowering, the process of instilling a sense of power, can affect important organizational outcomes. For example, recent studies suggest that empowerment is a key element in organiza-

ETHICAL DILEMMA
The Slow Death of E.F. Hutton

Even at age sixty-three, Robert Fomon cannot sit still. For five hours, he paced his living room trying to explain to a *Fortune Magazine* reporter the demise of E.F. Hutton, the brokerage house he ran for sixteen years. A haze of cigarette smoke clouded the English antiques and sporting paintings decorating his Fifth Avenue apartment. "Did I let the firm down?" he asked. "Did I let the employees down? No, I don't think so." In Fomon's view, there were no good explanations for Hutton's collapse and subsequent sale to Shearson Lehman Brothers; no large lessons to be learned.

Was Hutton's collapse inevitable? Had the eighty-four-year-old franchise outlived its usefulness? The answer to each question is "No." Hutton's problem, said a former managing director, was that it "made every mistake in the book, and no one was ever punished."

The Hutton saga is a managerial morality tale that revolves around mismanagement, selfishness, arrogance, and greed. The blunders ranged from the ridiculously extravagant (investing $100 million in a glitzy new headquarters when the firm was losing money) to the downright illegal (check kiting). However, the seminal error was allowing Robert Fomon to wield absolute power for so long. He hired and promoted whomever he wanted, including close friends. He personally reviewed the salaries and bonuses of more than one thousand employees. "His whole life was holding court, making all the large and small decisions," says a former Hutton managing director and Fomon confidant. As Hutton grew, it became far too complex to be run so autocratically. After suffering a broken leg and two small strokes between 1983 and 1985, Fomon, said a former Hutton officer, "lost control of the firm and no one ever regained it."

Hutton's senior officers contributed to the chaos because so many lacked managerial skills. In the firm's entrepreneurial culture, executives usually came up through the ranks as brokers or dealmakers; they did not regard the work of day-to-day managing as particularly important. In addition, the firm's vaunted but poorly organized retail brokerage, which produced about 75 percent of Hutton's revenues, had problems. Executives focused so much on increasing revenues that they lost sight of costs. Profits slipped steadily at the retail brokerage, starting in 1981. Still, Hutton's legendary perquisites continued. Though the firm lost $90 million in 1986, according to a former top executive, it spent $30 million to send its best-producing brokers and spouses on all-expense-paid trips.

Between 1980 and 1982, Hutton did not just squander its own money; it also used funds from a $4 million check-kiting scheme. Hutton managers intentionally overdrew the firm's checking accounts for a day or two to earn additional interest income. The firm pleaded guilty to two thousand counts of mail and wire fraud in 1985 and never recovered from the scandal.

After the Shearson takeover, Hutton's board voted itself more than $2.5 million in retirement benefits. Some members of the management team, who refused to join the new Shearson Lehman Hutton without contracts, did even better, collecting from $1 million to about $5 million each. Almost forgotten in the rush to divide the spoils, however, were Hutton's other employees. Because of the way the board had structured the company's profit-sharing plan, they were not permitted to sell the Hutton shares held for them in trust. Most walked away with little more than the right to collect unemployment checks.

(Continued on next page)

(Continued from p. 356)

Although the director's special treatment of themselves seemed unfair, it was in keeping with the tradition of "me first" at Hutton. "People around here believed that if they could get away with something, they should do it," said a former Fomon associate. At Hutton, selfishness was a way of doing business. The company lived—and died—by it.

Questions

What are the ethical issues in the E. F. Hutton case?

What role does power play in these ethical dilemmas?

SOURCE: "The Slow Death of E. F. Hutton," *Fortune,* 28 February 1989, 82–88.

---

tional effectiveness, particularly during times of transition and transformation.[14] Further, studies of control and power within organizations indicate that the more productive forms of organizational power increase when superiors share power and responsibility with subordinates.[15]

What can leaders and managers do to build a sense of power among organizational members? The following guidelines provide an initial answer to this question.[16]

Distribute power and opportunity widely

Employees are empowered when they can influence decisions and policies that directly affect them. As part of the effort to empower employees at Johnsonville Foods, for example, the personnel department became the Personal Development Lifelong Learning Department. Employees meet with a counselor who helps them to articulate their goals and dreams, whether these dreams include becoming a senior vice-president, putting kids through college, or learning to grow roses. Each employee receives a cash allowance to spend on a personal-growth project that will assist in achieving his or her goal(s). In addition, volunteers from the shop floor write the manufacturing budget. At first a financial expert guided the employees through the process; now the finance department serves as a resource. When the sales department aimed at increasing volume 40 percent, the manufacturing group set and achieved a goal of providing the additional output while holding cost increases to 20 percent. Another group of volunteer workers designed and continue to modify the manufacturing line. If the workers want new equipment, they do the discounted cash flow analysis to justify the request themselves. In each of these instances, employees have real power to affect decisions concerning their work and personal lives.

Maintain an open and Decentralized communication system

Such a communication system enables employees to be informed about problems, opportunities, and resources so that they can make responsible decisions and implement them effectively. Wal-Mart, for example, uses an open door policy whereby all employees have direct access to any manager or executive in the company. Many employees initiate direct contact with executives to make suggestions and discuss product or consumer trends. Executives and employees also spend time "managing by walking around" in an attempt to stay informed about consumer preferences and store needs. Heinz USA promotes open communication across the company through interdepartmental task forces that share knowledge and make policy on subjects such as purchasing and media buying. Thus, empowering organizations do not safeguard or hide information; rather, information is shared with and distributed to employees so that tasks can be performed more effectively.

Use integrative problem solving

Traditional management theory tends to encourage the use of localized or segmented problem-solving strategies. Such strategies typically dictate that responsibility for problem solving rests with the smallest functional unit. Concerns about product quality, for example, have historically been viewed as the responsibility of the quality control department. Production produces, marketing markets, and quality control (QC) takes care of quality.

An integrative problem-solving approach assigns responsibility for a problem *among* functional work units; it is the classic task-force approach to problem solving. The combination of people assembled in such task forces increases the likelihood that an innovative solution to the problem will be found. Further, task forces involve more people as problems solvers and encourage a "we" attitude *among* functional units rather than a "we/they" attitude *between* units.

W. L. Gore and Associates, a twenty-eight-year-old firm founded to exploit the properties of Teflon as an insulator for electronic wire, uses integrative problem solving extensively and encourages employees to involve others in the defining and solving of problems. Gore uses task forces when dealing with a wide array of problems from manufacturing processes within a plant to benefits policy across the corporation.

Ford's Team Taurus provides another example of integrative problem solving. All functional units of the company were involved simultaneously in the design and development of the Taurus; manufacturing unit employees worked with employees from the design, engineering, sales, purchasing, legal, service, and marketing units. The result was (1) a process that helped to reduce the traditional barriers between design, engineering, and production, and (2) a car that received recognition for its design and quality.

Reward and recognize people so as to encourage high performance and self-responsibility

Outstanding employee performance should be rewarded in highly visible and confidence-building ways. Positive encouragement, bonuses, words of praise, and other meaningful rewards are important sources of empowerment.

One executive established the "I Make A Difference Club" within his organization. Each year two or three outstanding employees are selected for recognition and induction into the club. Inductees are invited to dinner in New York City but are not told beforehand that they have been selected for the club. They arrive and meet with other staff members whom they believe are simply attending a staff dinner. During the dinner, each individual is asked to speak about what is going on in his or her part of the company. Only after the presentations are the inductees informed about their selections. As one manager said, "It was one of the most wonderful moments of my life."[17]

The guidelines described above are not the only methods that can be used to empower employees and organizations. They do, however, provide a basic sense of what a leader or organization might do to begin the process of empowerment. Other factors, such as organizational culture, the methods used to select, socialize, and train employees, and leadership style, can also affect the positive use of power by employees and organizations.[18] As more individuals and organizations experiment with a commitment-based approach to power, further knowledge will be gained about this important process.

This discussion of power, organizational politics and empowerment sets the stage for a discussion of another important phenomenon—conflict. In contemporary organizations, conflict is pervasive and a potential barrier to the effective use of human resources. In fact, the primary functions of a manager are to (1) coordinate the various groups and subgroups in his or her jurisdiction, and (2) resolve conflicts among them. Therefore, it is absolutely essential that a manager learn to manage conflict effectively.

UNDERSTANDING AND MANAGING CONFLICT

Bill Jackson sat at his desk thinking about the day's events. As vice president for human resources at ABC Trucking Company, he had been assigned the responsibility of preparing for contract negotiations with the Teamsters' Union. He and his staff had worked and researched for fifteen months to prepare a set of proposals and anticipate the demands of the union representatives. The formal negotiations had started six weeks ago but were not going as expected. Labor and management seemed to be moving farther apart rather than closer together. The chief negotiator for the union had today stated that if satisfactory progress toward a settlement was not made by the end of the week, a strike would be inevitable. Bill knew that an acceptable settlement probably could not be hammered out in that period of time. He wondered, "Why are we constantly in conflict with the union? We should be able to resolve our differences instead of constantly going at each other. I thought this round of negotiations might be different."

Power and conflict are different but related concepts. It is thus difficult to discuss power without also considering conflict. In Bill's situation, for example, labor and management are in conflict over the terms of the contract, and both parties are using their respective resources and power to obtain an agreement on their own terms. The union is threatening to withhold its principal resource (labor), and management appears willing to take the consequences of a strike in order to win concessions. Both parties are using their respective powers to prepare for the upcoming battle.

CONFLICT AS A PROCESS

Conflict is the interaction of interdependent people or groups who perceive incompatible goals and interference from each other in achieving those goals.[19] This definition emphasizes several key characteristics of conflict.

Conflict is a *dynamic,* interactive process. Its nature is cyclical, with one conflict episode setting the stage for another. Further, conflicts are initiated, sustained, and resolved by the behaviors of the parties involved and their reactions to one another. Conflict interaction can take many forms (e.g., shouting, open struggling), and each form presents special problems and requires special handling.

Conflict is affected by the *interdependence* of the parties. For conflict to occur, the behavior of one or both parties must have consequences for the other. A conflict at ABC Trucking Company, for example, would not occur if management's and labor's separate demands did not influence and threaten each other. In addition, any action taken in response to the conflict has consequences for each party. A decision to strike, for example, affects both the workers and the company.

The goals of the conflicting parties are *perceived* to be incompatible, and the other person or group *is seen* as a source of interference in achieving those goals.

Regardless of whether goals really are incompatible or whether interference actually is present, conflict is probable if the parties perceive that such conditions exist. Thus, the interpretations and beliefs of the parties involved play a key role in conflict.

Finally, conflict involves *goal incompatibility* and *mutual interference* in efforts to achieve goals. In other words, conflict implies an attempt to frustrate, block or interfere with the other party's achievement of an objective. This characteristic of interference distinguishes conflict from competition. In competition, parties may perceive incompatible goals but do not necessarily interfere with each other in attempting to accomplish those goals (e.g., each participant in a sales contest wants to win but does not obstruct the progress of or interfere with the other contestants). In conflict, however, the parties have incompatible goals, and each party seeks to block the other party's efforts (e.g., two computer companies attempting to capture the majority share of the home computer market).

PITTSTON COAL

On a Sunday afternoon in late 1989, ninety-nine unarmed men clad in camouflage fatigues entered a Pittston Coal Company plant in southwestern Virginia. Company guards, taken by surprise, retreated to an office building while the intruders—ninety-eight miners and one minister—took over the plant to draw attention to the United Mine Worker's five-month-old strike against Pittston. For three days, two thousand supporters blocked the entrance gates to the plant and kept state troopers away while miners occupied the facility and kept Pittston from processing coal. The miners finally departed peacefully to comply with a court order.[20]

The Pittston/UMW example highlights the key characteristics of conflict described above. The conflict is *dynamic* in that the takeover of the plant was one in a long series of events between two *interdependent* parties, the UMW and Pittston, concerning *goals* that were *perceived to be incompatible.* Negotiators had attempted for several years to reach agreement about health care benefits, job security, and work rules. The inability to reach agreement on these key issues, however, produced frustration and *interference* in the form of strikes, the plant takeover, and legal actions. In fact, the dispute between Pittston and the UMW produced one of the most confrontational strikes of the 1980s.

Conflict is a pervasive characteristic in organizations and an inevitable consequence of the interactions and interdependencies among organizational members. Conflict stems from differences in goals, values, beliefs, and attitudes and from similar requirements for such scarce resources as money, people, equipment, and information. Conflict occurs at four levels in all organizations and social systems:

1. Intrapersonal: conflict within an individual (e.g., Should I accept the job offer from the bank or from the insurance company?).
2. Interpersonal: conflict between two or more individuals (e.g., You can't use those tools right now. I need them to finish this job today by 4:30.).
3. Intragroup: conflict among members of the same group (e.g., Bill, Jane, and I don't think increasing our rate of production is important right now. We should be more concerned about improving the quality of our products.).
4. Intergroup: conflict between two or more groups (e.g., The R&D people are

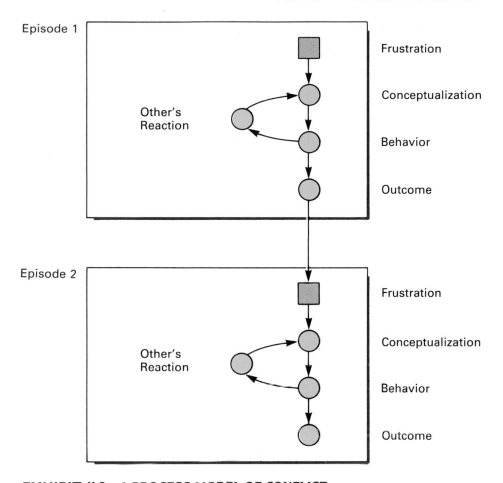

EXHIBIT 11.3   A PROCESS MODEL OF CONFLICT

SOURCE: Kenneth Thomas, "A Process Model of Dyadic Conflict Episodes," in *The Handbook of Industrial and Organizational Psychology,* (New York: John Wiley & Sons, 1976), 895. Used with permission.

always trying to change how we do things around here. Why can't they just leave us in the production area alone!).

Conflict can also arise between departments or subunits in an organization (intraorganization) and between different organizations (interorganization).

Exhibit 11.3 above presents a process model of conflict between two parties.[21] This model suggests that conflict is an ongoing and dynamic process consisting of four primary phases: frustration, conceptualization, behavior, and outcome.

Frustration

Conflicts usually arise from one party's perception that another party is frustrating the accomplishment of one of its objectives or goals. Such frustration can be caused, for example, by scarce economic resources, promotion, interpersonal needs, rules, or values. Specific events leading to such frustration can include the denial of a request, disagreement, insult, ignoring one's feelings, violating an agreement, or active interference with goal-related performance.

Conceptualization

In this phase of the conflict process, the parties attempt to (1) define and understand the problem at hand and (2) become aware of various action alternatives and their potential outcomes. Conceptualization is a subjective, not objective, process. Biases, beliefs, and opinions strongly influence an individual's conflict-handling behavior. Most conflicts arise from real differences in interests or goals. However, the perception and conceptualization of those conditions play an important role in determining the intensity and magnitude of the conflict episode.

Behavior

Following the frustration and conceptualization phases, the parties engage in conflict behavior. Five different types or styles of conflict behavior have been identified (see Exhibit 11.4).

A *competitive* style is high in assertiveness and low in cooperativeness. The person places great emphasis on personal concerns and ignores those of others. This style represents a desire to defeat the other, and has also been called the forcing or dominant style.

An *accommodative* style is unassertive and cooperative. The person gives in to the other party at the cost of his or her own concerns. This orientation has also been called appeasement or smoothing and those who use it attempt to avoid conflict for the sake of maintaining the relationship.

An *avoiding* style is unassertive and uncooperative. The person simply withdraws and refuses to deal with the conflict. In this orientation the person is indifferent to the outcome of the conflict and can be described as apathetic, isolated, or evasive. This style has also been called flight.

A *collaborative* style is high in both assertiveness and cooperation. The person works to attain a solution that will meet the needs of both people. This orientation seeks full satisfaction for all and has also been called the problem-solving or integrative style.

A *compromising* style is intermediate in both assertiveness and cooperativeness. Both people give some ground and split the difference in order to reach an agreement. In this orientation, both parties are expected to give up something and keep something. It has also been called sharing or horse trading.

EXHIBIT 11.4   FIVE TYPES OF CONFLICT BEHAVIOR

Competitive		Collaborative
ASSERTIVENESS Behaviors Intended to Satisfy Own Concerns	Comprising	
Avoiding		Accommodative

COOPERATIVENESS
Behaviors Intended to Satisfy Others' Concerns

Outcome

The outcome of any conflict episode involves more than a settlement or an agreement. Frustation, respect, hostility, or trust can result from a particular conflict. Furthermore, such outcomes set the stage for future conflict episodes.

THE FUNCTIONAL AND DYSFUNCTIONAL CONSEQUENCES OF CONFLICT

The traditional view of conflict within organizations suggests that conflict negatively affects goal accomplishment and should be avoided at all costs. To classical management theorists, conflict was an indication of inadequate control, planning, and execution. For the human relations theorists, it was the result of faulty leadership or a lack of participative management. In both cases, however, the goal was to eliminate conflict. Cooperation and harmony among different subunits or individuals in an organization were ideas to be fostered and promoted.

Systems theory (see Chapter 1) helps us understand that conflict is an inevitable aspect of behavior in organizations. The interrelatedness, interdependencies, and complexities of systems and subsystems suggest that conflict is unavoidable. For example, the nature and function of the research and development department (to promote innovation and change) often conflicts with the production department (stability and efficiency). In the same way, the various colleges within a university system frequently conflict over the distribution of economic resources. A contemporary view of conflict, therefore, suggests that conflict is neither good nor bad; it is inevitable. Thus, the manager's or supervisor's task is not to avoid or eliminate conflict but to manage it so its positive aspects can be realized. One authority concluded:

> The most important single thing about conflict is that it is good for you. Perfect organizational health is not freedom from conflict. On the contrary, if properly handled, conflict can lead to more effective and appropriate adjustments. The way conflict is managed—rather than suppressed, ignored, or avoided—contributes significantly to a company's effectiveness.[22]

Conflict can lead to positive effects such as innovation and change and a search for new ideas; it can also help in developing proposals, decision alternatives, and solutions. The conflict dynamic can be particularly helpful when focused on such substantive issues as policies, procedures, objectives, or methods of resource allocation. As an idea or proposal is challenged and fully articulated, weaknesses can be identified and corrected. Tensions, difficulties, and conflict cannot be avoided. Instead, they should be used to improve the problem-solving and decision-making processes.

The increased use of teams in contemporary organizations is one method of promoting the positive aspects of conflict. At Milliken, a major textile manufacturer, over one thousand Customer Action Teams have been established. Each team is a self-contained effort to identify new market opportunities in partnership with an existing customer. Team members from a customer are joined by Milliken representatives from manufacturing, sales, finance, and marketing to seek creative approaches to better serve current markets. Conflict about ideas and proposals that occurs between Milliken and its customer and between both organizations' various departments has produced numerous improvements in product quality and service.

Conflict can also have negative or dysfunctional consequences. Conflict based on emotional issues or negative feelings can produce distrust, fear, resentment, and anger. Prolonged conflict can divert individuals and groups from task performance and can also create a negative climate in a work group or organization.

In practice, substantive and emotional issues are frequently interrelated. Emotional issues tend to produce more negative results, are more difficult to resolve than substantive issues, and require a manager's skillful handling. Thus, any conflict situation can produce either functional or dysfunctional outcomes, depending on how it is managed. In today's complex organizations, resolving conflict is one of a manager's most important responsibilities.

STRATEGIES FOR MANAGING CONFLICT

A number of strategies can be used to deal with conflict situations involving individuals, groups, organizations, communities, and nations. We now discuss four general strategies particularly useful at the organizational level: negotiating, establishing superordinate goals, using a third-party intervention, and removing personnel and restructuring the organization.

Negotiation

People often use and hear the word **negotiation.** For example, a consumer negotiates with a salesperson about the price of a car or appliance, lawyers negotiate over plea bargaining, and diplomats arrange negotiations between competing groups or nations. Essentially, negotiation is a process whereby two or more parties attempt to settle what each will give and take, or perform or receive, in a transaction between them.[23] In other words, negotiation is a process involving the presentation of demands or proposals by one party, the evaluation of these by the other party, followed by counterproposals and concessions. The ultimate objective of bargaining is a settlement acceptable to both parties that spells out how a specific resource is to be divided and/or how a particular issue is to be resolved.

Negotiation occurs when the following basic conditions exist:[24]

1. A conflict exists between two or more parties; in other words, what one party wants is not what the other party wants.
2. No established rules or procedures exist for resolving the conflict, or the parties prefer to work outside a set of fixed rules and procedures to achieve a solution to the conflict.
3. The parties, at least for the moment, prefer to search for agreement rather than to fight openly, to have one side capitulate, to break off contact permanently, or to take their dispute to a higher authority to resolve it.

In a conflict situation, then, negotiating is a means of achieving a settlement satisfactory to both individuals or parties.

In an organizational context, negotiation is most often associated with the discussions that take place between union officials and management representatives.

However, negotiating is also a method for managing and resolving conflict among individuals, groups, and departments. The key requirements for successful negotiation are (1) the possibility of an agreement in which each party is better off (or at least no worse off) than if no agreement is reached, and (2) both parties' willingness to give and take.

BOEING

When one negotiating party is unwilling to modify its initial position or proposal or attempts to bully the other party into making concessions, the conflict is usually intensified rather than reduced. For example, officials at Boeing began contract negotiations with 58,000 machinists in late 1989 determined to hold down wages and to pay more in the form of one-time bonuses. In 1983 and again in 1986, as a means of helping Boeing through economic difficulties, the company had persuaded machinists to take yearly bonuses instead of wage increases. Improved profitability and a large backlog of orders for Boeing's planes in 1989, however, convinced the machinists that the company could afford wage increases.

The machinists considered Boeing's first wage proposal in the negotiations too low. The machinists presented a counter-proposal, but Boeing, overestimating the strength of its position, did not respond.[25] The conflict escalated, and eventually resulted in a costly five-week strike. The "give and take" of negotiation, therefore, must be managed carefully when the parties in conflict are already emotionally charged, extremely defensive, or when the nature of the conflict is particularly intense.

Negotiations usually proceed through three distinct stages: (1) establishing the negotiation range; (2) exploring and probing the negotiation range; and (3) moving toward agreement or impasse.[26]

Establishing the negotiation range

During the first stage of negotiations, the parties identify the relevant issues or problems and then establish the range or ranges within which they will negotiate. For example, in the first stage of disarmament talks between the United States and the USSR, negotiators may establish that they will discuss heavy missiles, light missiles, and bombers. The United States' opening proposal may include a limit of 150 heavy missiles, and the Soviets may counter with a demand for 300. Thus, the range for the subsequent negotiations has been established.

Exploring and probing within the negotiation range

Once the negotiating parties have identified the major issues or problems and established the parameters for discussion, they then explore and probe within the negotiation range. Negotiators ask questions, exchange information, retreat from initially stated positions, and observe each other carefully for signs of agreement or concession. During this stage, negotiators explore and decide among several potential agreements, but do so without the pressure of selecting the one course of action that they will have to defend and live with in the future.

Moving Toward Agreements or Impasse

During the final stage, the negotiators attempt to reach an agreement. The parties probe for true resistance points, examine the flexibility and rigidity of their respective positions, and reduce general agreements to specific ones. An impasse occurs when the two parties are deadlocked and unable to reach a mutually satisfactory settlement.

The atmosphere and nature of interaction in each phase of negotiation can vary significantly. As the negotiation range is established, for example, negotiators typically threaten their opponents, emphasize the conflict between them, and stress their loyalty to their respective positions. The parties use more congenial behavior, ask more questions, and present fewer threats, however, as the negotiation range is explored and probed. Conflict about issues and procedures is normal and to be expected during the first phase of negotiation; such conflict should be less dominant during the second phase. Conflict and some tension are also quite normal during the third phase as the parties move toward a final agreement or impasse. Just as a knowledge of group development phases can aid a manager in diagnosing and working with groups (see Chapter 8, "Understanding Group Behavior"), so can an understanding of these three basic stages help a manager become more aware of and effective in the negotiation process. (The International Dimension below describes several customs, rituals, and stylistic characteristics that can affect the negotiation process that occurs between managers from different countries.)

The outcome of any negotiation depends on both the nature of the conflict and the strategy used to negotiate a resolution. Two basic strategies are frequently used in negotiations: *distributive* (or win-lose), and *integrative* (or win-win).

In **distributive negotiation,** the goals of one party and the attainment of those goals are in fundamental and direct conflict with the goals of the other party. Resources are fixed and limited, and each party seeks to maximize its share of the resources. For example, management (on behalf of stockholders) and labor (on behalf of rank-and-file employees) may believe that they deserve the larger share of a company's profits. Both may want to "win" on issues such as wages, work rules, or control of certain policy decisions. To the extent one party wins in the negotiation, the other party loses.

INTERNATIONAL DIMENSION
Negotiation Styles Around the World

Seven executives are trying to do business in a Tokyo conference room—four Americans (a vice-president in charge of sales and his associates) and three Japanese middle managers. The Japanese are deferring to their visitors, nodding and listening with pointed respect, especially to the vice-president. The Americans respond with the same formality even though they tend to avoid hierarchical behavior, preferring to put everyone on an equal footing. Things are off to a bad start—and about to get worse.

(Continued on next page)

(Continued from p. 366)

Three more Japanese enter the room, all senior executives in their late 50s, all obviously outranking their compatriots, and all treated with due respect. This puts the Americans in a bind. Having worked hard to be the middle managers' equals, they must readjust to a new situation. In the midst of their efforts, in comes another Japanese person, the president of the corporation. The Americans are now caught in an escalating confusion of statuses, and sure enough, the rattled vice-president makes a major tactical blunder, suggesting an inappropriate meeting at an inappropriate time and place, as negotiations grind to an embarrassing halt.

One of the Americans, a thirty-one-year-old graduate student, never forgot this debacle. John Graham, presently a professor of marketing at the University of Southern California, has made a career of studying negotiation styles throughout the world. He has gathered a mass of data from direct observation, interviews, questionnaires, and, above all and uniquely, from videotapes of executives role playing with real-life fervor. His library contains 150 cassettes recording behavior not only in the United States and Japan, but also in ten other cultures.

Professor Graham has noted the following negotiation rituals, customs, and styles:

- Americans tend to be quite comfortable with "nontask sounding"—the light, personal conversation that takes place before getting down to the immediate business at hand—provided it does not take too long. For Americans, approximately ten to fifteen minutes seems appropriate. For the Japanese, however, such conversation is the heart of the matter and an essential element in the negotiation process, at least as important as the final deal itself. Concerned with long-term, personal relationships, Japanese negotiators are ready to chat for an hour, for an entire morning, or for even longer. The bigger the deal and the more important the dealers, the longer the preliminaries.

- The buyer is king in all countries, but more so and with a vengeance in Japan. Special courtesy words mark the difference in status between the buyer and seller. A buyer refers to the seller's firm as *otaku* (your company), while the seller tradionally responds with *onsha* (your great company). Americans, who rarely mind being deferred to, tend to do fine as buyers. However, being deferential is rarely their customary style.
- The Japanese tradition is to avoid a direct "no" at practically any cost. A Japanese negotiator may ask a counterquestion, promise an answer at some later date, change the subject, and even occasionally leave the room. Another common response is no response at all, a dead silence.
- A key characteristic of negotiations with Mexicans is that the buyer enjoys high status, just as he or she does among the Japanese, although not quite to the same degree. Furthermore, kinship weighs heavily in Mexican business circles, often at least as heavily as economics.
- South Koreans resemble the Mexicans and Japanese in giving the buyer superior status. They often speak out even more frankly and bluntly than Americans and tend to be more emotional than the Japanese.
- Brazilian negotiators tend to make frequent physical contact with an opponent and talk more often and rapidly. Japanese and American negotiators never touch one another, while the Brazilians make a habit of touching, poking, and patting.

Questions

How can a manager learn about his or her negotiation style?

What factors should a manager consider when preparing to negotiate with a businessperson from a different country?

SOURCE: John Pfeiffer, "How Not to Lose the Trade Wars by Cultural Gaffes," *Smithsonian*, January 1988, 145–156.

Integrative negotiation, on the other hand, involves identifying a common goal and achieving a settlement that enables *both* parties to maximize their desired outcomes. One party's gain is not necessarily achieved at the other party's expense. For example, the relationship between the United Auto Workers (UAW) and the major United States automobile companies has historically been adversarial in nature (win-lose). In order to compete internationally against strong foreign competition, however, these traditional rivals have attempted, in some instances, to achieve mutual benefit through integrative negotiation.

Negotiation is a process that requires preparation, planning, and skill. When determining how to negotiate, a manager must consider the nature of a particular conflict situation, the history between the involved parties, and the importance of the key issues. In addition, it is important to recognize that integrative negotiation is not as simple as it may initially appear; only by working to facilitate mutual understanding and an open flow of information and ideas can the integrative process work successfully.

Establishing Superordinate Goals

One major cause of conflict between two individuals or groups is goal incompatibility. Conflict stemming from goal incompatibility often occurs because the parties fail to recognize the interdependence of their goals. One strategy for resolving conflict arising from this cause is establishing a superordinate goal.[27]

A **superordinate goal** is a goal more important to each party than his or her independent goals and requiring mutual dependence to achieve. For example, two groups of employees in a production department may be in conflict over scheduling unpopular work assignments (e.g., cleanup). One group, comprised primarily of experienced workers, wants the assignments made on the basis of seniority. The other group, workers with less time on the job, thinks these duties should be scheduled on a rotating basis. To reduce this conflict, a manager may establish a superordinate goal such as improving the department's overall quality rating or reducing the amount of scrap produced during an eight-hour shift. Cooperation resulting from the achievement of these superordinate goals can improve communication, trust, and friendship between the parties. These factors, in turn, increase the likelihood that the parties will also cooperate on the incompatible goals.

A **common enemy** is a negative form of superordinate goal. Participants in a conflict often find new motivation to resolve their differences in order to defeat a common enemy or to avoid intervention by a third party. Labor and management may behave more cooperatively, for example, when threatened with government intervention in their dispute.

In order to have a significant impact on negotiations, superordinate goals must be jointly desired by both parties and must not be seen as benefiting one side more than the other. It is important to remember that superordinate goals are an addition to existing group goals. They do not replace or substitute other group goals, and the underlying incompatibility is not changed. Superordinate goals do, however, provide a means for working through and overcoming conflict caused by goal incompatibility.

Using a Third-Party Intervention

On some occasions, conflict is such that the parties cannot resolve it themselves (even through negotiation or superordinate goals). The participants may adopt a tough position and make an agreement difficult to achieve. Or, individuals may be adamant in believing their position is correct and therefore unwilling to make any concessions. Such stalemate situations often require using a neutral third party.

A neutral third party can help resolve a conflict by introducing an objective, positive attitude to the conflict situation. Participants in a conflict frequently become entrenched in their positions and unwilling to give at all. The intervention of an objective third party can help reduce the tension by promoting increased openness, trust, and understanding of opposing positions.

A third party usually functions in one of three roles: conciliator, mediator, or arbitrator. A *conciliator* intervenes when the parties have stopped all bargaining and tries to get the opposing sides to talk to each other again. Conciliation can be accomplished by breaking deadlocks in order to promote continued discussions, steering discussions away from highly emotional or risky issues (until the parties are ready to handle them), and providing the needed emotional support and encouragement.

A **mediator** uses many of the conciliator's procedures and tactics but assumes a more active role in the conflict. A conciliator is a peacemaker who tries to establish or repair the channels of communication; a mediator offers original alternatives and encourages the parties to adopt a particular solution. The mediator thus is a problem solver who tries to bring the conflicting parties to an agreement.

Arbitration is probably the most common and well-known form of third party intervention. After parties in conflict have reached a deadlock or a deadline without successfully resolving their differences, they present their respective positions to an arbitrator. An **arbitrator** acts as a judge and, after collecting relevant information and analyzing alternatives, actually has authority to impose a settlement on the parties. The arbitrator usually does little to reduce the underlying conflict between the parties but does resolve the particular issue at hand. The likelihood that an arbitrator can successfully resolve a dispute is increased when the parties in conflict agree on who the arbitrator should be and that the arbitrator's decision will be accepted as the final judgment.

The ultimate objective of any third-party intervention is the resolution of conflict. Careful analysis is necessary, however, before a manager can decide which approach is most appropriate for a given situation.

Removing Personnel and Restructuring the Organization

When a conflict cannot be resolved through bargaining, superordinate goals, or some form of third-party intervention, more drastic methods may be necessary. One method is actually removing key persons in the conflict. Such a change can be accomplished by transferring the conflicting parties to different jobs or by firing one or both of them. This severe method of handling conflicts should be used only as a last resort.

Restructuring a group or organization can also effectively resolve conflict when the source of conflict is structural. Conflicting groups can be relocated, task responsibilities redefined, and resources reallocated. Restructuring effectively removes the conflicting parties from one another by altering their formal interaction patterns. For example, two conflicting work units reporting to different supervisors can be placed under the jurisdiction of the same supervisor. Such a structural change may produce an increased incentive to cooperate. Redesigning jobs and creating linking or coordinating positions in the organizational structure are also viable methods for reducing conflict.

Negotiating, establishing superordinate goals, using a third party, removing personnel, and restructuring the organization are strategies for managing conflict that can be used in most organizations. Implementing any of these strategies in a conflict situation can be difficult and requires that a manager be sensitive and tactful. Because the conflict process can lead to dysfunctional behavior and strong emotional responses, a manager must be familiar with these strategies and must develop the interpersonal and decision-making skills necessary to use them effectively.

POWER AND CONFLICT: CONCLUSIONS

To execute their duties effectively, managers must know how to influence subordinates in achieving organizational goals. They must also be able to coordinate the activities of different groups and subgroups in the organization and manage the conflicts among them. Understanding the concepts of power and conflict discussed in this chapter can help a manager successfully accomplish these important managerial tasks.

Power, the ability or capacity to influence, is acquired through the control of resources. Managers, for example, use the power derived from their control of information, rewards, and punishments to influence employees. They can also use the legitimate power of their positions (authority) to affect the behavior and job performance of subordinates. In the minds of many people, power has a bad reputation because it is commonly associated with the pursuit of private goals rather than group or organizational goals. In other words, power is seen as the means of getting what *I* want. Remember, however, that power is not inherently bad or selfish. In fact, the responsible and timely use of different types (bases) of power is an important ingredient in the formula for managerial effectiveness.

Organizations have traditionally been viewed as rational, logical, and purposive in nature. It is important to remember, however, that organizations are also arenas for the exercise of power. The concept of organizational politics provides a helpful framework for understanding the seemingly illogical and irrational behavior that often occurs in organizations. In addition, strategic contingencies theory is useful in helping explain how organizational subunits or departments acquire and use power.

The study of power in organizations has historically focused on how power is acquired, how it is used, and how it can be maintained and enhanced once it is obtained. In many modern organizations, this traditional approach to power is being challenged. An increasing number of executives and companies are experimenting with the idea that effectiveness depends on sharing and distributing power throughout an organization, not on rigid hierarchical control and the hoarding of power. Empowerment is the process of instilling a sense of power in organizational members through open and decentralized communication, integrative problem solving, and rewards that encourage high performance and self-responsibility.

Many managers and executives believe that conflict is negative and should be reduced at all costs. Conflict, however, is the inevitable result of interactions and interdependencies among organizational units and members. Therefore, the objective should not be totally eliminating conflict (which cannot be achieved anyway), but managing conflict to realize its positive effects.

Different strategies a manager can use to manage conflict include bargaining, establishing superordinate goals, using a third party, and removing personnel and restructuring the organization. Because conflict can produce serious dysfunctional consequences, a manager should be familiar with these strategies and develop the interpersonal and decision-making skills necessary to implement them successfully.

QUESTIONS FOR REVIEW AND DISCUSSION

1. What are the differences between influence, power, and authority?
2. What are the three primary determinants of power? How does the perception process affect these determinants of power?
3. Explain the difference between coalescing and co-opting as strategies for obtaining power.
4. Define the concept of organizational politics. How and why are interpretations of organizational behavior altered when an organization is viewed as a political system?
5. According to the strategic contingencies theory, what factors determine a department's or subunit's power? Explain the significance of each factor.
6. What can a manager do to empower employees within a department or organization?
7. Why is goal incompatibility usually identified as a major cause of conflict?
8. What are the four phases in a conflict episode?
9. How is conflict beneficial to an organization?
10. Explain how establishing a superordinate goal can reduce conflict between two individuals or groups.
11. What is the difference between a mediator and an arbitrator?

REFERENCES

1. Rosabeth M. Kanter, "Power Failure in Management Circuits," *Harvard Business Review*, Vol. 57 (July/August 1979): 65–75.
2. A. J. Grimes, "Authority, Power, Influence and Social Control: A Theoretical Synthesis," *Academy of Management Review*, Vol. 3 (October 1978): 724–735.
3. G. E. G. Catlin, *Systematic Politics* (Toronto: University of Toronto Press, 1962), 71.
4. Grimes, op. cit., 727.
5. D. Katz and R. Kahn, *The Social Psychology of Organizations*, 2nd ed. (New York: Wiley, 1978).
6. J. R. P. French and B. H. Raven, "The Bases of Social Power," in D. Cartwright, ed., *Studies in Social Power* (Ann Arbor: University of Michigan Press, 1959); B. H. Raven, "A Comparative Analysis of Power and Preference," in J. T. Tedeschi, ed., *Perspectives on Social Power* (Chicago: Aldine, 1974).
7. Rosabeth M. Kanter, *Men and Women of the Corporation* (New York: Basic Books, 1977).
8. R. W. Allen, D. L. Madison, L. W. Porter, P. A. Renwick, and B. Mayes, "Organizational Politics: Tactics and Characteristics of Its Actors," *California Management Review*, Vol. 22 (Fall 1979): 77–83.
9. H. Mintzberg, *Power In and Around Organizations* (Englewood Cliffs, N.J.: Prentice-Hall, 1983).
10. D. J. Hickson, C. Hinings, C. Lee, R. Schneck, and J. Pennings, "A Strategic Contingencies Theory of Intraorganizational Power," *Administrative Science Quarterly*, Vol. 16 (June 1971): 216–227.
11. Ibid, 225.
12. P. Block, *The Empowered Manager* (San Francisco: Jossey-Bass, 1987); W. W. Burke, "Leadership as Empowering Others," in S. Srivastva, ed., *Executive Power* (San Francisco: Jossey-Bass, 1986), 51–77; R. M. Kanter, *The Change Masters* (New York: Simon & Schuster, 1983); Jay A. Conger, "Leadership: The Art of Empowering Others," *Academy of Management Executive*, Vol. 3, No. 1 (1989): 17–24.
13. Thomas A. Stewart, "New Ways to Exercise Power," *Fortune*, 6 November 1989, 53.
14. W. Bennis and B. Nanus, *Leaders* (New York: Harper and Row, 1985); R. M. Kanter, "Power Failure," *Harvard Business Review*, 1979, 65–75.
15. A. S. Tannenbaum, *Control in Organizations* (New York: McGraw-Hill, 1968); R. M. Kanter, "Power Failure," Endnote 3.
16. M. Pacanowsky, "Communication in the Empowering Organization," in J. A. Anderson, ed., *Communication Yearbook 11* (Beverly Hills: Sage Publications, 1988), 356–357; R. M. Kanter, "The New Managerial Work," *Harvard Business Review*, Vol. 57 (November/December 1989): 85–92.
17. J. Conger, "Leadership: The Art of Empowering Others," *The Academy of Management Executive*, Vol. 3, No. 1 (1989): 17–24; J. A. Conger and R. N. Kanungo, "The Empowerment Process: Integrating Theory and Practice," *Academy of Management Review*, Vol. 3, No. 3 (1988): 471–482.
18. R. J. House, "Power and Personality in Complex Organizations," in B. M. Staw and L. L. Cummings, eds., *Research in Organizational Behavior* (Greenwich, Conn.: JAI Press, 1988), 305–358.
19. J. Frost and W. Wilmot, *Interpersonal Conflict* (Dubuque, Iowa: Brown, 1978).
20. "The Mine Workers Must Win This Fight to Survive," *Business Week*, 9 October 1989, 144–148.
21. K. W. Thomas, "Conflict and Conflict Management," in M. D. Dunnett, ed., *Handbook of Industrial and Organizational Psychology* (Chicago: Rand-McNally, 1976), 889–966.
22. J. Kelly, "Make Conflict Work for You," *Harvard Business Review*, Vol. 48 (July/August 1970): 103–113.

23. J. Z. Rubin and B. R. Brown, *The Social Psychology of Bargaining and Negotiation* (New York: Academic Press, 1975), 2.

24. Roy J. Lewicki and Joseph A. Litterer, *Negotiation* (Homewood, Ill.: Richard D. Irwin, Inc., 1985), 4.

25. Aaron Bernstein, Leslie Helm, and Maria Shao, "The Boeing Strike: Both Sides Are Flying Blind," *Business Week,* 6 November 1989, 44; Bernstein, "Why Boeings Hard Line Didn't Pay Off," *Business Week,* 4 December 1989, 33; Richard O'Lone, "No Progress Reported in Second Week of Strike," *Aviation Week and Space Technology,* 16 October 1989, 18–19; Richard O'Lone, "Boeing Machinists Strike Hits Economy, Airline Fleet Plans," *Aviation Week,* 20 November 1989, 126–127.

26. A. Douglas, *Industrial Peacemaking* (New York: Columbia University Press, 1962).

27. M. Sheif, "Superordinate Goals in the Reduction of Intergroup Conflict," in B. Hinton and H. Reitz, eds., *Groups and Organizations* (Belmont, Calif.: Wadsworth Publishing, 1971), 392–401.

CASE 11.1

Just who runs this show?

CALVIN KELLOGG   *Illinois State University*

WXYZ-TV is a medium-sized commercial television station located in a rural/suburban section of the Southeast. The station primarily serves a city of 150,000 and a large surrounding area including rural towns and villages.

In its thirty-year history, the station has been through three ownership changes. The present owner is a closely held corporation with diverse interests in banking, oil, and communications. The president has a great personal interest in the television industry. Thus, the corporation is making an effort to reestablish a tradition of excellence within the station, as well as to make it profitable. Part of the plan to revitalize station operations is to replace and update much of the worn-out equipment with new equipment. The plan has produced a considerable cash drain on the organization.

The chain of command is one typical of a broadcast facility. The general manager sets broad guidelines for station operation. Under him and responsible for the daily activities are the department heads: Chief Engineer; Production manager; Sales Manager; News Director; and Business Manager. The organization chart in Exhibit 11.5 shows each manager's formal position and authority within the corporate structure.

STATION MANAGER

Ray Wilkins has been station manager for about five years. He joined the station soon after the corporation bought it. Ray has been in television advertising and sales since graduating from college in the early 1960s. He is a close friend of the corporate president. Before coming to WXYZ, he was sales manager for a station in a neighboring city. Although strong in the sales area, Ray has little understanding of the operation or management of the station. To help combat this deficiency, a consulting firm was hired to provide research and operations expertise.

CHIEF ENGINEER

Ben Roberts, the chief engineer, has recently moved up to department head after almost twenty years with the company. His background and training are similar to that of his staff: military experience, technical school, then special training offered by broadcast equipment manufacturers. The engineering department is responsible for maintaining, installing, and operating the station's electronic equipment according to standards set by the Federal Communications Commission. The staff also keeps the electronic news gathering (ENG) equipment, studio camera, support apparatus, and mobile-to-station communications links in good repair. Most of the engineers and technicians have graduated from vocational schools specializing in broadcast electronics. Like Ben, the staff feels the best way to learn about the equipment is to tear it apart and then put it back together. The station's investment in new digital equipment has

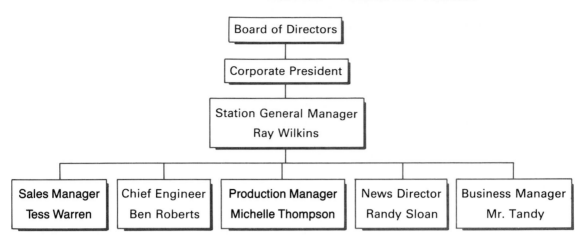

EXHIBIT 11.5   TABLE OF ORGANIZATION: WXYZ–TV

received a mixed reception among the technical corps. Many of the older engineers feel threatened by the new technology while the younger engineers are pushing for complete replacement of the station's equipment with state-of-the-art gear.

PRODUCTION MANAGER

Michelle Thompson, the production manager, also worked her way up the company ladder. Eight years after starting out as a studio cameraman, she was promoted to production manager. Her department is primarily responsible for putting together commercials for station advertising clients. Production is also saddled with the time-consuming task of providing the news department with technical support and the actual production of three daily newscasts.

Unlike the other operations departments, most of the production staff are unskilled high school graduates. Their skills are taught as part of on-the-job training. Low pay and unpredictable work hours result in high turnover. For those who stay with the company, advancement within the department can be rapid. For example, the director of the six o'clock newscast started out as a cameraman just a year ago.

NEWS DIRECTOR

Within a span of fifteen years, Randy Sloan, the current news director, has worked for the station on three different occasions. Now he runs the news department. His staff of twelve are mostly college graduates with less than three years of experience. The news department, like engineering and production, is considered a training ground. Turnover is high as the more talented move to higher paying jobs with larger stations.

The news department's reporter/cameraman teams cover events in a large part of the state and sections of three adjoining ones. It is not unusual for reporters to spend fifty to sixty hours a week working on stories and covering "spot" news. Intense loyalty and pride is involved in their work. Arriving at a major news event and getting the story on the air first, with the most accuracy, is the foremost goal of the staff. Top management encourages this combination of professionalism and youthful enthusiasm.

BUSINESS MANAGER

Mr. Tandy (out of respect no one calls him by his first name) has been with the station as business manager since the radio days of the late 1930s. His department handles the billing, accounting, and payroll. Mr. Tandy supervises a work force of eight. Mostly high school graduates, the workers are the most restricted within the company. The clerical nature of their work demands they stay near their desks, thereby greatly limiting their interaction with the other departments. The business department alone keeps regular hours and observes legal holidays.

Mr. Tandy has gained a unique position within the corporate structure due to his department and personality. The business section has more communication with the corporate headquarters than any other department within the station. Because of the nature of the work, corporate visitors frequently make their way to his office soon after arriving in town. Often when a problem occurs, Mr. Tandy discusses it with the station manager or an executive at the corporate headquarters. Since the business department is not actually an operations division, Mr. Tandy considers it a waste of time to attend the daily management meetings. He feels there is no need to defend his department's policies before the other managers. An accountant by training, his personality demands diligence, precision, and little concern for anything not connected with the business side of the firm.

SALES MANAGER

Tess Warren was a salesperson for twenty-two years before moving up to Sales Manager about seven years ago. Contacts in the community have made her invaluable to previous as well as the current owners.

Tess's long association with WXYZ has developed into a loyalty to the station but not to the owners. It is her judgment that station and personal image must come before the corporate one. "One day they will decide to sell . . . if the offer is good enough . . . and I want to keep my job after the new owners have taken over."

Her staff of three make sales calls, write commercials, schedule commercial running times, and receive input on station operations from the business community.

The staff's dramatic increase in sales has made her one of the most powerful forces within the company. Other station department heads must clear their request for extra personnel, replacement equipment, even supplies through the sales manager. It is her recommendation that carries the most weight with the station manager and the president. As a reward for increased sales, the department has been given a generous pay hike. The raise makes them the highest paid department within the station.

THE MEETING

Each morning, the department heads meet in the sales manager's office. All of the station's departments are represented here on a regular basis with the exception of the business department. The four remaining department heads look over and discuss the discrepancy sheet. This document is a running account of "goofs" in station operations. Missed commercials, equipment malfunctions, or unusual operating events, such as the loss of a network feed, are reported by engineers and/or production personnel.

It is not uncommon, at these meetings, for department head battles to escalate into shouting matches. At these times, each blames the other for causing problems and not wanting to cooperate.

At the staff level, there are some hard feelings toward the other departments. Engineers believe newspeople could tear up an anvil. Production sees the news department as always causing problems, making demands and keeping them away from important work. The news department feels the engineers are incompetent and production is lazy and unwilling to work with them. The salespeople think of themselves as superior, viewing the other departments as necessary evils. "After all," a salesperson said, "all you do is spend the money. . . . we earn it!"

Recently, suppressed interdepartmental conflicts exploded when the station management ordered the news director to "kill" or prevent an exclusive story from being aired. A reporter had just completed an investigation of possible conflicts of interest and fraud in a local bank. The story pointed out possible inept handling of trust funds, misleading of investors, and possible criminal conspiracy to defraud.

The bank, fearing a scandal, pressured the station's sales department to stop the story or lose their advertising account. They claimed the charges were false, misleading, and injurious to their public image.

Within the station, backlash to management's unilateral action was unprecedented. The newspeople considered their professional purity tainted. Some threatened to quit or have a work slow down. Mostly, they were hurt by management's thoughtless treatment of the situation. The salespeople thought the reaction was outrageous. They had used good business judgment in dealing with the matter. Each side would later use this incident to justify and reinforce their conception of the other as an enemy.

Ray, the station manager, had long been aware that interdepartmental fighting was taking place. He knew many on the station payroll didn't totally trust him because of his close ties to and background in sales. Yet his immediate problem is to enlist the employee's cooperation and hard work in pulling the station's ratings up at the expense of its competition. A key part of his plan is intense coverage of the upcoming general election day. Thinking aloud, he says, "How can I get them to stop bickering long enough to work together?"

CASE
II.2   *Dissension at* RANDEB

DONALD D. WHITE   *University of Arkansas*

Sol Axton was upset but felt like he didn't have anywhere to go to get the whole mess straightened out. His associate Leslie Thompson was also disturbed, but neither one could do much more than complain to the other. Both of them had joined RANDEB as design engineers shortly after receiving their Ph.D.s in electrical engineering. Each had been highly recruited by leading corporations in the telecommunication industry after graduation, but they had selected RANDEB largely on the strength of a dynamic vice-president for engineering, Randal Kern.

Both Axton and Thompson felt good about their choice, even though RANDEB was a small and relatively unknown firm. Kern had assured them that the company, under the leadership of a a new CEO, Beverly Broyles, was on the verge of prying loose the "Big Three" telecommunications giants' stranglehold on the industry. Now, however, it was rumored that Kern might resign as vice-president, and the division seemed to be in disarray.

RANDAL KERN JOINS RANDEB

Randal Kern joined RANDEB in the Fall of 1983. He had come to the division highly recommended by the senior design engineer, Bud Holloway. Holloway was an eccentric genius whose reputation in the field of superconductivity was widely known. He demanded and received respect from all those who worked in the engineering division and was a powerful figure in the corporation.

Prior to coming to RANDEB, Holloway had established himself as a nationally known research scientist at a leading university. It was there that he had met and trained Randal Kern. When Beverly Broyles sought to fill the position of vice-president for engineering, Holloway recommended his former star pupil.

Kern was brought to company headquarters where he met with members of the engineering division and was interviewed by Broyles. Everyone took an immediate liking to Randal Kern. He was strong, dynamic, and literally "sold himself" to everyone. He surprised everyone, including Beverly Broyles, when he asked if he could depart from the original interview schedule and make a brief presentation. The presentation lasted an hour and forty-five minutes and outlined his projected development and growth plans for the engineering division. Everyone present was impressed, although privately, Broyles quipped with board members, "We'll have to keep a lid on this guy; he's already restructured our production group and no doubt has his eye on the sales force."

Prior to leaving, Randal told Broyles, "I've got to know something within two weeks. I am considering a couple of other positions and want to make a decision right away." Athough Broyles had no intention of moving quite this fast, and she had planned to interview additional candidates, she decided that Randal Kern was the man for the job. The offer was extended and accepted within the week.

Randal returned just two weeks later to "get things ready for the family." Bud Holloway insisted that Randal stay with him: "I've got a big house, bigger than anyone else in the division, so I insist you stay with me." Randal accepted the offer and spent the next week looking for a permanent place to live. Although Holloway recommended a couple of "nice" neighborhoods to Randal, he was somewhat surprised when Randal purchased a large home with a scenic view. When Randal asked Bud what he thought, Bud responded, "It's nice, but I think it's a little over your head, don't you?" In fact, the home would place a significant financial strain on Randal, but as he was later fond of saying, "I just had to have it!"

Shortly thereafter, Randal's wife and daughter arrived in town. Both were impressed with the beautiful home, and his wife was equally pleased when she walked into the garage and found an expensive foreign car that Randal had "picked up" for her.

LEADING THE WAY

Randal's first few months on the job appeared to go smoothly. He was a strong leader, stronger than most had expected, and was able to bring to the division corporate resources that his predecessor had never been able to obtain. His successes, however, were not without some cost. Positions promised to other divisions were redirected to engineering, much to the frustration of other division vice-presidents. In addition, some on the executive committee were getting tired of listening to Randal tell of his successes since coming to RANDEB and hearing him refer to the engineering staff as "my little family." Nancy Ellerman, vice-president for sales and promotion, even told Randal, "Cool it if you want to have any friends left around here."

By this time, problems within the engineering division had also begun to develop. According to Randal, "They began the first week I was here. Bud Holloway stopped by my office and told me not to worry, that he would tell me everything I needed to do. He said that he had pretty much run the division before and probably would continue to do so. He told me to let him know before I made any major decisions."

It soon became evident that problems existed between Randal and Bud. Bud uncharacteristically began arriving at division meetings late. He had been a loner within the division but had lately been spending a good deal of time with two other, more senior, engineers. An open split occurred when Randal hired a new engineer over Holloway's objection and then assigned him to work with Bud on a special project. Bud let his anger be known to other members of the division, and in time word got back to Kern. Randal called Bud in to speak with him about the matter. "Dr. Holloway, if you have a problem with the way I run this division, bring it directly to me," he said. This is my division, and I make the decisions."

At first, Holloway denied that he had said anything to anyone in the division. However, unable to hold his temper, he finally blurted out, "Just remember, I brought you in here, and I can find someone to replace you. This division was doing fine before you came. Everyone here has always known who runs this division. Some of the more senior engineers feel the same way I do."

DRAWING THE BATTLELINES

On the surface, things in the division quieted down for the next six months. However, the engineering staff had become a house divided. Young engineers were being courted by the senior engineering staff under the informal leadership of Bud Holloway and also by Randal Kern. Not wanting to be caught in the middle, many of them had pulled away from both sides. Unfortunately, their actions were interpreted by both Holloway and Kern as disloyalty.

Finally, three of the engineers went directly to Beverly Broyles and described the division's plight. Broyles listened carefully and came away from the meeting perplexed. She knew that Randal Kern, or someone with his vision and energy, would be necessary to provide RANDEB technical leadership at this critical juncture. On the other hand, it was on Bud Holloway's technological breakthroughs that RANDEB was staking its future. Still, Holloway's actions were clearly disrupting the division. Finally, Broyles knew that the situation could not go on indefinitely as a number of the younger engineers were already talking about leaving the company.

Later that week she called both men into her office and discussed the problems that she had been hearing about. Neither Randal nor Bud had much to say. Randal's eyes were riveted on Beverly, although he occasionally glared at Bud. For his part, Bud minimized the problems and said that all he wanted to do was to get back to his work. Both men agreed to let the whole matter die down. When the meeting was over, both rose and hesitated as though they wanted to say something else to Beverly privately. Finally, it was Beverly who excused herself from the room.

Things remained quiet in the division for the next few weeks, although everyone could feel the tension. Bud Holloway continued to meet privately with the senior engineers. Kern became increasingly withdrawn. He abandoned the common practice of first name exchanges with his colleagues and began referring to each of them formally, using the title Doctor. In addition, he continued to place memos concerning Holloway and the other senior engineers in their personnel folders.

EXERCISE 11.1
WIN AS MUCH AS YOU CAN

PROCEDURES

1. Divide class into groups of eight, and have each group (cluster) divide into teams of two (dyads). (If numbers won't work out evenly, some dyads can be replaced by single individuals or teams of three.)
2. The goal of this exercise is to win as much money as you can.
3. Using the chart at the top of the tally sheet (Exhibit 11.6), each dyad is to decide whether it will chose an "X" or a "Y" (with the hope of winning money). The dyads then write their choices on their tally sheet for round #1, not letting any other dyad see their choices. No conversation among dyads should occur, except when provided for in rounds 5, 8, and 10.
4. After the time allotted for round # 1 (2 minutes) has passed, each dyad will show its choice to the other dyads in its cluster. Using the chart on the tally sheet, each dyad should determine how much money it won or lost in round #1, and record this amount on the tally sheet. No comments among dyads are allowed. Proceed immediately to round #2, then #3, and so forth as outlined on the tally sheet. Note that in rounds 5, 8, and 10, dyads can confer with each other at the beginning of the round. Note also that the amounts won in these rounds (or lost) are multiplied by 3, 5, and 10.
5. At the end of the exercise, determine which dyad won the most and which ended up furthest behind. Then compare clusters.

EXERCISE 11.2
DISARMAMENT EXERCISE

INSTRUCTIONS

You and your team are going to engage in a disarmament exercise in which you can win or lose points. In this exercise your objective, as a team, is to win as many points as you can.

THE EXERCISE

1. Each team will be given 20 cards or "weapons." Each card will be marked on one side with an "X" to designate "armed" condition. The blank side of the card signifies that the "weapon" is "unarmed." To begin the exercise, each of the two teams will place 10 "weapons" in an "armed" condition and 10 in an "unarmed" condition. During the course of an exercise, these cards will remain in your possession and out of sight of the other team.

4 X's:	Lose $1.00 each
3 X's: 1 Y :	Win $1.00 each Lose $3.00
2 X's: 2 Y's:	Win $2.00 each Lose $2.00 each
1 X : 3 Y's:	Win $3.00 Lose $1.00 each
4 Y's:	Win $1.00 each

STRATEGY: You are to confer with your partner(s) on each round and make a joint decision. Before rounds 5, 8, and 10, you confer with the others in your cluster.

Round	Time Allowed	Confer With	Your Choice	Cluster's Patterns of Choices	Payoff	Balance	
1	2 mins.	partner					
2	1 min.	partner					
3	1 min.	partner					
4	1 min.	partner					
5	3 mins. 1 min.	cluster partner					Bonus round payoff × 3
6	1 min.	partner					
7	1 min.	partner					
8	3 mins. 1 min.	cluster partner					Bonus round payoff × 5
9	1 min.	partner					
10	3 mins. 1 min.	cluster partner					Bonus round payoff × 10

EXHIBIT 11.6   WIN AS MUCH AS YOU CAN TALLY SHEET

2. Each "set" consists of no more than five moves for each team. Each move may consist of changing two, one, or none of the "weapons" from "armed" to "unarmed" status or vice versa.

   Each team has two and one-half minutes to make a move and thirty seconds between moves. At the end of two and one-half minutes, you must have decided to turn two, one, or none of the weapons from "armed" to "unarmed" or from "unarmed" to "armed" status. If you fail to decide on a move in the allotted time, none will be turned.

3. There will be two or more sets depending on the time. Scores will be calculated after each set.

POINTS AND SCORING

1. Teams will have an equal number of players. Each team gets 150 points per player. The world bank begins with as many points as each team.

2. "Attack"
   a. Each team may announce an attack on the other team during the thirty seconds following any two and one-half minute decision period (including the last one). The choice of each team made during the previous decision period counts as a move. You may not "attack" during "negotiations" (see below).
   b. If there is an "attack," the set ends. The team with the geater number of "armed" weapons will win five points (per member) for each "armed weapon" they have over and above the other team's number of "armed weapons." This money will be paid directly from the treasury of the losing team to the treasury of the winning team. However, attacks also cost both the attacking and the attacked team five points (per member) payable to the world bank.

3. If there is no "attack"
   a. At the end of each set, your team's treasury will *receive* from the "world bank" two points per member for each "unarmed weapon" and your treasury will *pay* to the "world bank" two points per member for each "armed weapon."
   b. If both teams win points, they will be awarded by the "world bank." If both teams lose points, they will be awarded to the "world bank."

NEGOTIATIONS

1. Between moves you will have the opportunity to communicate with the other team through negotiators.
2. You may call for negotiations during the thirty seconds between any decision period. The other team may accept or reject your initiation. Negotiations can last no longer than three minutes.
3. When the negotiators return to their teams, the two and one-half minute decision time will start again.
4. Negotiators may say whatever is necessary to most benefit their team.
5. The team is not bound by agreements made by their negotiators, even when made in good faith.
6. Your negotiators *must* meet with those of the other team after the second and fourth move.

SPECIAL ROLES

You will have fifteen minutes to discuss and plan your team strategy. During this time before the exercise begins, you must select persons to fill the following roles. The persons can be changed at any time by a majority of the group.

1. Two negotiators—activities stated above.
2. A group spokesperson—communicates group decisions to referees regarding initiation and acceptance of negotiations, moves in game, attacks, etc.
   a. You *must* elect a spokesperson.
   b. The referees will listen only to the spokesperson.
   c. Spokespersons cannot be negotiators.
3. One recorder—records moves of team.

CHAPTER 12

EFFECTIVE LEADER BEHAVIOR

LEARNING OBJECTIVES

1. To learn more about the factors that influence effective leader behavior.
2. To become familiar with leadership models that can be applied on the job.
3. To understand the situational nature of effective leadership.
4. To recognize differences between transformational and transactional leadership activities.
5. To be able to choose an effective leadership style.
6. To appreciate alternative explanations of the leadership role.

CHAPTER OUTLINE

Early Approaches to Leadership
The Great Man Approach / The Trait Approach
Early Approaches in Perspective

Behavioral Theories of Leadership
Iowa Studies / Michigan Studies
Ohio State Studies / Managerial Grid
Behavioral Theories in Perspective

Situational Theories of Leadership
Contingency Theory / Path-Goal Theory
Situational Leadership Theory / Normative Model
Situational Theories in Perspective

Transformational Leadership
Transformational Behaviors / The Transformational Process
Transformational Leadership in Perspective

Other Perspectives on Leadership
Substitutes for Leadership
Attribution Influences on Leadership

Effective Leader Behavior: Conclusions

Questions for Review and Discussion

References

Cases: 12.1 What It Takes to Be Number One: Lessons from
Wal-Mart's Sam Walton
12.2 Dogfight at Texas Air: Leadership the Lorenzo
Way

Exercises: 12.1 Selecting the Right Leadership Style
Assessing Your Leadership Style

KEY TERMS

Great man theory / Trait theory

Initiating structure

Consideration

Managerial Grid

Contingency theory

Contingency factors

Path-goal theory

Situational leadership theory

Follower readiness

Normative model

Transactional leaders

Transformational leaders

Substitutes for leadership

Mary Ellen always received good to excellent reviews for her performance and got along well with others in the department. Co-workers spoke highly of her, and other agency employees expressed little surprise when it was announced that she had been appointed to head an important task force recently created. Her appointment was publicized in the agency newsletter, in which the director pointed out, "Mary Ellen has what it takes to be a good leader . . . she knows how to get along with those around her." Mary Ellen, however, was less sure. She had seen good and bad managers, but she found it difficult to put her finger on why some succeeded as leaders while others failed. As she walked down the hall to her new office, she concluded, "I guess I'll just be myself . . . it's always worked before!"

Todd Bealer had just resigned his commission in the Marine Corps to take a job in private business. He had served as an infantry platoon leader and had also held a number of other responsible positions in the Corps. His last assignment required him to oversee a variety of noncombat training programs; this experience brought him to the attention of a large corporate vendor. Todd had enjoyed his years of military duty, but the job opportunity offered him by the company was too attractive to turn down. Although he had little work experience outside the military, he had been reassured by a company representative, "We like your style, Todd; you know how to get a job done; I guess it's that good Marine training." Todd thought about his new job. He had been asked to head a department that would assess training needs and develop new training techniques for the company's defense products line. His staff consisted of one retired Navy man, four highly trained technicians, and two recent college graduates whose degrees were in training and development. Todd was confident. He knew how to lead men and this was "another chance to put into practice what I have learned."

Mary Ellen and Todd were each given opportunities to be leaders. Both had been told that they possessed the leadership skills necessary for their new jobs. Yet, their backgrounds and approaches to leadership were quite different. What is the best leadership style? Can a leader be effective in one situation but encounter serious difficulties in another situation? When you complete this chapter, you should be able to answer these questions and better understand the problems and prospects Todd and Mary Ellen face.

Leadership is one of the most extensively researched constructs in the behavioral sciences[1] and is particularly important to the study of organizational behavior. Leadership is a complex topic and has been approached in a number of different ways. Despite the attention given to the subject by both managers and researchers, however, "the dimensions and definitions of the concept remain unclear."[2] We will examine leadership from a number of different perspectives; Exhibit 12.1 shows how each perspective contributes to leadership and ultimately to organizational outcomes. First, we look at early approaches to leadership that attributed success to a leader's

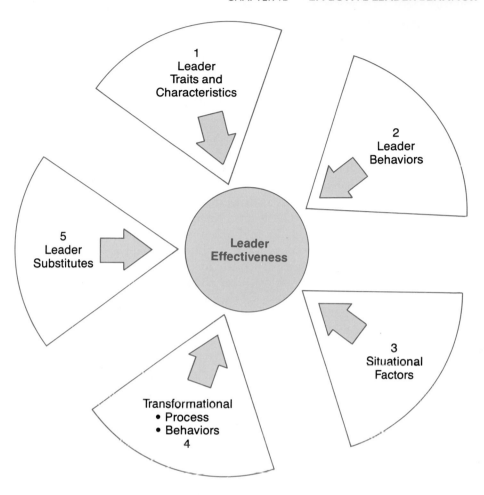

EXHIBIT 12.1   LEADERSHIP FACTORS CONTRIBUTING TO ORGANIZATIONAL OUTCOMES

inborn traits and other personal characteristics. Next, we examine leadership as a function of certain *necessary* leader behaviors. Third, we explore the situational nature of effective leadership and look at the need to systematically fit leader styles or practices to existing situational circumstances. Finally, we will look at recently emerging perspectives on leadership including the transformational school (which attempts to explain extraordinary leadership accomplishments), leadership substitutes, and attributional influences on leader actions.

EARLY APPROACHES TO LEADERSHIP

Early theories tended to explain leadership effectiveness in terms of the leader. The great man approach, as well as trait theories of leadership, focused on personal qualities of leaders and how those qualities influenced leader effectiveness.

The Great Man Approach

The **great man** or *zeitgeist* approach represented perhaps the earliest theory of leadership. Simply stated, the theory suggested that great leaders were born, not made. Such men and women were believed to possess certain qualities that lead them to greatness and no doubt would have done so at any time in history or under any set of circumstances. Great man theories were influenced by studies of such world leaders as Alexander the Great, Joan of Arc, Adolf Hitler, Winston Churchill, and Mahatma Ghandi.

Research studies produced little agreement on the qualities these and other outstanding leaders shared or on how individuals of such stature could easily be identified. However, some observers assumed that greatness passed through families from one generation to another. The Tudors, Adamses, and Roosevelts, for example, were sometimes identified as families into which great leaders seemed to be born. These assumptions were consistent with the doctrine of Social Darwinism—survival and the upward mobility of the most socially fit (see Chapter 1). However, little evidence exists to suggest that factors other than political, economic, or social opportunities have been responsible for the succession of influential leaders in families.

The Trait Approach

Trait theories of leadership were similar to the great man approach in that researchers attempted to identify specific traits and characteristics leaders held in common. In hundreds of studies, successful leaders were observed by researchers, rated by associates, or given sophisticated psychological tests. This research, however, produced an array of confusing findings. For example, one analysis of more than one hundred trait studies found that fewer than 5 percent of the traits thought to be important were common in four or more of the studies.[3] In time, hundreds of items were catalogued and ultimately reduced to twenty-six separate factors[4] (see Exhibit 12.2). Although leaders appeared to have marginal advantages over nonleaders in traits such as intelligence and certain physical dimensions (e.g., height), there were no characteristics in which all leaders were consistently found to be superior.

The trait approach fails to explain fully the source of effective leadership for a number of reasons. First and foremost, inconsistent research findings suggest that successful leaders, unsuccessful leaders, and even nonleaders sometimes possess the same traits. Therefore, one must seriously question whether a given trait causes an individual to become an effective leader.

Second, defining and measuring traits often present problems. Traits can be viewed differently by different individuals. In one study, for example, seventy-five executives defined the trait *dependability* in twenty-five different ways.[5] Measuring traits can also present a problem since many traits are psychological in nature and cannot be observed directly. Moreover, not even the valid measurement of a trait necessarily means that the information attained can be used to predict effective leadership. How much of a given trait is "enough"? Will someone who scores marginally higher on a trait than someone else be a more successful leader? Questions such as these are left unanswered by trait theories of leadership.

Third, leaders may be effective because they practice particular *leadership* behaviors rather than as the result of their physical or psychological traits. As we discovered earlier (see Chapter 4, "Learning, Reinforcement, and Behavior Analysis"), behav-

EXHIBIT 12.2   TWENTY-SIX TRAITS APPEARING IN THREE OR MORE STUDIES

TRAIT	FREQUENCY OF OCCURRENCE
Technical skills	18
Social nearness, friendliness	18
Task motivation and application	17
Group task supportiveness	17
Social and interpersonal skills	16
Leadership effectiveness and achievement	15
Emotional control and balance	15
Administrative skills	12
General impression (halo)	12
Intellectual skills	11
Ascendance, dominance, decisiveness	11
Willingness to assume responsibility	10
Ethical conduct, personal integrity	10
Maintaining cohesive work group	9
Maintaining coordination and teamwork	7
Communication, verbal abilities	6
Physical energy	6
Maintaining performance standards	5
Creative, independent	5
Conforming	5
Informal group control	4
Nurturant behavior	4
Experience and activity	4
Courage, daring	4
Mature, cultured	3
Aloof, distant	3

Adapted from: R. M. Stogdill, *Handbook of Leadership* (New York: The Free Press, 1974), 93.

iors can be acquired through reinforced practice or by observing the behaviors of others; they are not necessarily transmitted genetically.

Lastly, the qualities, characteristics, and skills of effective leaders may be determined largely by the nature of the situation in which they function. Simply stated, "leaders in one situation may not necessarily be leaders in other situations."[6]

A final observation about leadership and personal traits is worth noting. In one study, leaders and followers did not score as differently on trait scales as one might expect. Its findings suggested that the true opposite of a leader may not be a follower, but rather an indifferent person—one who is incapable or unwilling either to lead or to follow. The study concluded, "It may be that some individuals who under one situation are leaders may under other conditions take the role of follower, while the true 'opposite' is represented by . . . [one] . . . who neither leads nor follows."[7]

Early Approaches in Perspective

The simplicity of both the great man and trait theories of leadership is intuitively appealing. Neither, however, has withstood rigorous scholarly examination. Nevertheless, working managers may accept the tenets underlying both theories, which will distort their views of effective leaders. Remember, research fails to support either theory. No evidence exists that either family background or some limited number of personal characteristics will consistently contribute to an individual's ability to lead. Whether you are so endowed or not, you can still become an effective leader.

BEHAVIORAL THEORIES OF LEADERSHIP

Although some managers and researchers continue to look to personal traits for explanations of successful leadership, others have turned their attention to an examination of leadership behaviors or styles. **Behavioral theories** are primarily concerned with the things that effective leaders do and the activities in which they are involved. A good deal of our understanding of important leader behaviors can be traced back to three research programs at the University of Iowa, the University of Michigan, and Ohio State University.

Iowa Studies

In 1938, the first of many important studies to examine the impact of leadership style was conducted at the University of Iowa.[8] Researchers conducted a controlled experiment in which they observed the impact of three separate leadership styles—authoritarian, democratic, and laissez-faire—on the behavior of adolescent boys. The basic difference in the three styles was the location of the decision-making function in the group. Authoritarian leaders made decisions for their groups and communicated those decisions to group members. Democratic leaders allowed groups to make decisions about their own activities and helped them to arrive at a decision point. Laissez-faire leaders limited their interaction with group members to answering questions and providing materials when requested; group members made decisions independent of both the leaders and one another.

Data were gathered on the behavioral reactions of group members to each of the three leadership styles during two separate experiments. Research findings indicated that (1) group members preferred democratic over autocratic leaders, and (2) incidents of intragroup hostility were significantly higher in autocratic and lassez-faire groups than in democratic groups. In addition, the productivity of the groups with democratic leaders was higher than for either the autocratic or laissez-faire groups, although productivity was not a major factor of the study.

Findings of the Iowa studies generally supported the effectiveness of a democratic leadership style and no doubt contributed further to the human relations movement that had begun to gain momentum in management circles. On the other hand, the sample used (twenty adolescent boys), along with the narrow scope of the research, severely limited the application of the findings beyond the sample studied. Nevertheless, the Iowa Leadership Studies ushered in an era in which leadership behaviors rather than traits received increased research attention.

Michigan Studies

During the late 1940s and early 1950s, researchers at the University of Michigan[9] became concerned about which leadership style, employee-centered or production-centered, was most likely to result in improved performance. At first, the two styles were viewed as being at opposite ends of a single continuum (see Exhibit 12.3), and

Employee   Production
Centered   Centered

EXHIBIT 12.3   MICHIGAN STUDIES

initial findings seemed to indicate that employee-centered leaders were more effective than production-centered leaders.

Research designed to determine the precise nature of the relationship, however, was inconclusive. In one instance, for example, researchers found that production-centered leadership resulted in high productivity under certain conditions, although this productivity was accompanied by low worker satisfaction and high turnover.[10] Ultimately, the Michigan researchers abandoned their belief that employee-centered and production-centered leadership behavior represented separate ends of a single continuum and came to view them as independent of one another.[11]

Ohio State Studies

Among the most thorough and extensive leadership studies ever conducted were those begun during the late 1940s at Ohio State University. These studies have had a far-reaching impact on subsequent leadership theories and vocabulary. The Ohio State studies were conducted in an attempt to determine the most effective leadership style. Disappointed by the results of trait studies, the researchers attempted to document what leaders actually did and how they did it. Thousands of leaders in a wide variety of organizational settings were carefully studied. Exhaustive analysis of more then 1,700 behavioral descriptors resulted in identifying many factors that were reduced to two primary dimensions of leader behavior. Each dimension was strongly related to effectiveness. These dimensions of leader behavior were labeled "initiating structure" and "consideration."[12]

Initiating structure refers to the extent to which a leader is likely to define and structure a job for subordinates. A person high in initiating structure is oriented to scheduling work, assigning people to tasks, and determining performance levels. Such behaviors are task oriented. **Consideration**, on the other hand, deals primarily with psychological supportiveness and a leader's concern for group-member needs. A leader high in consideration is likely to place importance on such things as friendship, mutual trust, respect for employee ideas, and concern for the feelings of others.

Two findings from the Ohio State studies have been particularly important to our understanding of leadership. First, some effective leaders were found to be high in consideration; others were high in initiating structure. Second, initiating structure and consideration were discovered to represent two completely separate and distinct dimensions (see Exhibit 12.4). Thus, leaders did not have to be considered either employee oriented or task oriented. In fact, the findings implied the existence of at least four different leadership styles:

Style 1: high initiating structure, high consideration.
Style 2: high initiating structure, low consideration.
Style 3: low initiating structure, high consideration.
Style 4: low initiating structure, low consideration,

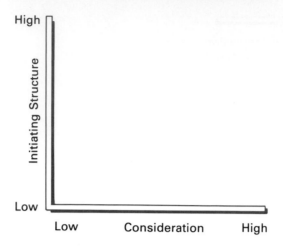

EXHIBIT 12.4   OHIO STATE STUDIES

Subsequent research on the two leadership dimensions suggested that high consideration (employee-oriented) leaders could expect low turnover and low absenteeism.[13] High task orientation, on the other hand, was found to lead to improved employee performance.[14] However, other studies have failed to support these findings consistently. Furthermore, some theorists have emphasized the importance of practicing the behaviors represented by both dimensions. Such managers are sometimes referred to as high/high (high in initiating structure and high in consideration) leaders. This position is held by those who support an approach to leadership known as the Managerial Grid.

The Managerial Grid

The **Managerial Grid** is a commercially marketed leadership model built on results of the Ohio State and Michigan studies.[15] The grid has received widespread attention from companies all over the world and has had a far-reaching impact on leadership training. In addition, its "high/high" leadership prescription poses important questions for today's leadership researchers.

Based on dimensions similar to those discovered at Ohio State and Michigan, the Managerial Grid goes further by identifying five leadership styles at each of five primary coordinates (see Exhibit 12.5). The name given to each style reflects the value placed on it by the Grid's originators. (Today, it is common for these five styles to be referred to by their numerical coordinates: Country Club Management is 1,9; Organization Man Management, 5,5; Team Management, 9,9; etc.)

The Managerial Grid represents what leadership theorists have come to refer to as a "one best style" approach to leadership—the 9,9 Team Builder (high concern for production and high concern for people). Supporters of the Grid have asserted that team builders are superior leaders regardless of the type of problem faced or the nature of the individuals or group being lead.[16]

Leadership training using the Managerial Grid requires that a manager's present leadership style first be identified on the Grid. A tailored program is then designed to move the manager from his present style to the most desirable style (9,9 Team Builder). This training is intended to develop a leader who achieves team-oriented

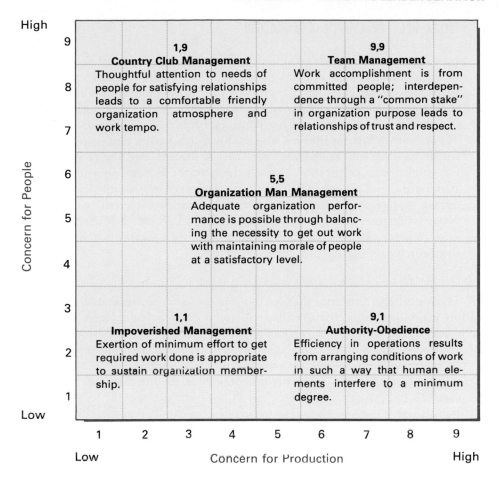

EXHIBIT 12.5 THE MANAGERIAL GRID®

SOURCE: Robert Blake and Jane S. Mouton, *The Managerial Grid* III (Houston: Gulf Publishing Company, 1985), 12. Reproduced by permission.

production through the use of such behaviors as openness, respect, participation, and win-win conflict resolution[17] (see Chapter 11, Power and Conflict).

Behavioral Theories in Perspective

According to behavioral theories of leadership, certain types of behaviors (or behavior dimensions) are related to effective leadership. Early studies such as those at the University of Iowa and Ohio State University, in particular, emphasized the importance of people-oriented, rather than task-oriented, behaviors. Some research, however, has suggested that no single style is necessarily best in all situations.

Our knowledge of both past and present leaders supports this notion. During World War II, for example, the hard-charging General George S. Patton and the mild-mannered "soldier's general" Omar Bradley both achieved notable victories in the field, despite their dramatically different leadership styles. Today, we see similarly diverse success stories in the world of business, ranging from hard-driving executives like Monsanto's Richard Mahoney to more employee-oriented leaders like Perot Systems' Ross Perot and Citicorp's John Reed.[18]

MYLLE BELL: BELLSOUTH CORPORATION

It has become increasingly clear to managers and researchers that neither technical nor interpersonal skills alone are sufficient for the exercise of effective leadership. Mylle Bell, director of corporate planning and development for BellSouth Corporation in Atlanta, is a rapidly rising star at BellSouth. Bell was first recognized when she and her immediate supervisor at General Electric's Transportation Systems Division were credited with a major turnaround that saw the division's market share grow from 12 to 70 percent. Bell was promoted into GE's upper management strata, but left the company for new opportunities with BellSouth. Since coming to BellSouth, she has served as assistant vice-president for new ventures and as the first president of the company's international division. Today, as director of corporate planning and development, Bell has found that most of her work is strategic and largely technical in nature, but, she says her degree in psychology has also been very helpful. [19]

Behavioral characteristics that lead to success in one international setting or culture may fail to be effective elsewhere. A case in point is that of Horst Schroeder. Schroeder was a highly regarded executive with Kellogg's European Division. He was later named president of the corporation but was dismissed after only a few months in the position. Horst Schroeder's rapid decline was attributed by insiders to his "European" leadership style. His story is contained in the International Dimension on page 393.

Evidence that concern for people and concern for production actually represent two separate and distinct behavioral dimensions contributes further to our appreciation of the complex nature of leadership. In practice, some managers attempt to develop their leadership skills along the lines suggested by behavioral theories, although no consistent evidence yet exists as to which leadership style is best.

SITUATIONAL THEORIES OF LEADERSHIP

One integrating theme in early attempts to understand leadership was a desire to identify qualities or behaviors effective leaders had in common. Researchers never achieved this goal; they were continually frustrated by the lack of consistent support for their findings and conclusions. The weight of evidence, in fact, suggested that leadership effectiveness depended on the specific situation in which an individual was called upon to lead. The latest generation of theories and research has pursued this lead and has attempted to fit leader style to selected situational variables.

Among these new-generation theories of leadership are Contingency Theory, Path-Goal Theory, and Situational Leadership Theory. A decision-making model, the Normative Model, has also been used to explain the situational approach to leadership. Each approach considers the influence of (1) the leader, (2) the followers, and (3) other environmental variables as it attempts to understand the true nature of leadership.

Contingency Theory

Contingency Theory represents the first major breakthrough in linking leadership style to the requirements of a particular situation. According to this theory, a

INTERNATIONAL DIMENSION
When in Rome . . . The Case of Horst Schroeder

Horst Schroeder was a successful executive with Kellogg Co. for many years. The German-born Schroeder joined the company in Bremen, West Germany, and later managed operations across much of Europe. By 1983, he was running all of Kellogg's non-United States business and ran it so impressively that he was named president of the company in early 1988. But nine months later, Horst Schroeder was fired.

Although he was a Kellogg star, Schroeder soon began to rub those around him the wrong way. Colleagues claimed he was demanding, abrasive, intolerant of dissent, and often unwilling to listen to subordinates. To others he seemed aloof and autocratic. According to one retired executive, "He was very abrupt—European; his personality was very different from what we consider normal executive manner."

Kellogg is widely known for its midwestern values and "family" culture. Referring to the situation with Schroeder, chairman and CEO William E. LaMothe concluded, "Not only do you come into a national culture, but a company culture that's nearly 100 years old; it may have been difficult for a foreigner to understand. What a tall order when you're foreign."

Chairman LaMothe may have been right. Studies of work-related values conducted by researchers from The Netherlands found German managers to be higher in power distance (acceptance of power differences in society) than managers in the United States, while similar studies of managers within the United States found midwesterners to be lower in power distance than managers in other regions of the country.

Questions
What factors other than Horst Schroeder's cultural background might have contributed to the difficulties he encountered as president of Kellogg?

Do you think the case of Horst Schroeder is unusual, or do you believe that cultural differences present a serious challenge for managers?

What steps should a company take to prevent or lessen problems like those experienced by Kellogg?

SOURCE: R. Gibson, "Personal 'Chemistry' Abruptly Ended Rise of Kellogg President," *Wall Street Journal*, 28 November 1989, pp. 1A, 8A; G. Hofstede, "The Cultural Relativity of the Quality of Life Concept," *Academy of Management Review* Vol. 9 (October 1984): 389–398; D. White and T. Jensen, "Redefining Cross National Comparison: The Case for Subcultural Analysis," paper presented at the Annual Meeting of the Academy of Management, New Orleans, August 1987.

leader can be effective only if his or her personal style is appropriately matched to a given set of situational variables.[20]

Leadership style assignment

Putting Contingency Theory into practice involves making two separate assessments. First, a person's natural leadership style must be determined. This is accomplished by having the leader complete the Least Preferred Co-worker Scale (LPC). The LPC identifies whether an individual is naturally relationship oriented (high LPC) or task oriented (low LPC). Thus, an underlying assumption of Contingency Theory is that every individual has a relatively stable leadership style that will generally remain unchanged.

Situational assessment

Second, the situation (group or organizational setting) must be measured. According to the theory, the level of leader control or influence depends on the nature of the situation. Some situations require a high degree of control; others may necessitate moderate or low control. Situational control is a function of three separate components: leader-member relations, task structure, and position power of the leader.

Leader-member relations refers to the willingness of group members to follow a particular leader. If little conflict or strain exists in the relationship between the leader and group members, then the situation is favorable (good relations). If conflict and strain exist in the relationship, the situation is unfavorable (poor relations). Leader-member relations, the most important of the three variables, has the greatest influence on situational control.

Task structure, the second most important variable, describes the clarity or ambiguity of the task. If there is only one way to perform the task or the correctness of the task can be determined quickly, then the task is clear (high task structure). If a number of approaches can be used to accomplish the task and time is required to determine its effectiveness, it is ambiguous (low task structure).

Position power is related to the authority vested in the leader because of his position in the organization. The ability to hire, fire, discipline, and reward determines a leader's position power. A football coach would have high position power. The chairman of a church committee, on the other hand, would have low position power.

These three components—leader-member relations, task structure, and position power—combine in a number of ways to create specific organizational situations. Exhibit 12.6 shows the eight possible combinations and indicates the relative degree of control required in each situation.

Determining the style-situation match

The final step in applying Contingency Theory is to determine the appropriate leadership style for the situation. Early studies provided a clearer picture of the appropriate match between leadership style and situational control (also known as situational favorableness). These studies found that task-motivated leaders (low LPC) perform best in situations requiring either high or low control. Relationship-motivated leaders (high LPC), on the other hand, perform best in situations requiring moderate control.[21] In high-control situations, leaders have a predictable environ-

EXHIBIT 12.6   EIGHT TYPES OF SITUATIONS ACCORDING TO CONTINGENCY THEORY

Type of Situation	I	II	III	IV	V	VI	VII	VIII
Favorableness	High ←						→ Low	
Leader-Member Relations	Good				Poor			
Task Structure	High		Low		High		Low	
Leader Position Power	Strong	Weak	Strong	Weak	Strong	Weak	Strong	Weak

EXHIBIT 12.7   LEADERSHIP STYLE, BEHAVIOR, AND PERFORMANCE UNDER VARYING LEVELS OF LEADER CONTROL

LEADERSHIP STYLE	SITUATIONAL CONTROL OF LEADER		
	HIGH CONTROL	MODERATE CONTROL	LOW CONTROL
Relationship-Oriented	Behavior: Somewhat autocratic, aloof, and self-centered. Primarily concerned with task. Effectiveness: Poor.	Behavior: Considerate, open, and participative. Effectiveness: Good	Behavior: Anxious, tentative, overly concerned with interpersonal relations. Effectiveness: Poor.
Task-Oriented	Behavior: Considerate and supportive. Effectiveness: Good	Behavior: Tense, task-focused. Effectiveness: Poor.	Behavior: Direct, task-focused, serious. Effectiveness: Relatively good.

Adapted from: Fred Fiedler, et al., *Improving Leadership Effectiveness: The Leader Match Concept* (New York: John Wiley & Sons, 1977), 136.

ment (e.g., support of group members, high task structure, high position power). In low-control situations, the task is unstructured or unclear, definite procedures do not exist, or leaders lack group support. Moderate-control situations lie somewhere between the extremes of high and low control. Exhibit 12.7 describes the behaviors and probable effectiveness of task- and relationship-oriented leaders to each of the three control situations.

One question remains: "What if the leader's style and the situational control requirements do not match?" This question is important in light of the contention that leader style is relatively stable and resistant to change. According to Contingency Theory, effectiveness can best be attained by engineering the job to fit the leader rather than expecting the leader to change a natural style. In most cases, situational variables can be adjusted. For example, a manager's leader-member relations might be altered by increasing (or decreasing) the leader's availability to employees or through the leader's use of selected rewards or punishments.

Similarly, task structure can be adjusted by delegating authority for job-related decisions or giving employees greater latitude in the way they do a job. For example, a manager might tell a group of workers, "You know what we're trying to accomplish; just do whatever you think is best!" Conversely, task structure might be increased by specifying the methods or procedures by which a job must be done. In some cases, a leader may not be able to alter the job sufficiently to fit a personal style. In such instances, the leader is advised to get out of the situation and find an alternative more consistent with his or her personal style.

Let us look at how Contingency Theory might be used. Tom Sitkowski has been concerned about the ability of a new regional manager, Cathy Parks, to provide effective leadership to the salespeople reporting to her. Tom decided to ask Cathy to complete the LPC and the situational control questionnaires.

The results of Cathy's LPC indicated that her natural leadership style was relationship-oriented. Based on the information she provided on the situational control instruments, Tom concluded that Cathy had good leader-member relations and a relatively unstructured task. In addition, constraints Tom had placed on Cathy because of her lack of experience as a regional manager left her in a low power position. Cathy's overall score revealed that she worked in a moderate control situation. Her LPC and situational control scores did, in fact, fit.

Tom still may not be completely satisfied with the performance of Cathy's region. However, according to Contingency Theory, he should probably look for explanations other than her leadership style to explain the problems he believes exist.

Despite the fact that many managers have been trained to use the assessment and job engineering techniques suggested by Contingency Theory, a number of questions have been raised about the theory's validity. Such questions focus on the stability of the LPC scale, the appropriateness of the three situational dimensions, and the research designs used to develop and test the theory. Some critics also object to the idea that individuals are unable to alter their personal leadership styles, although research results have supported the relative stability of style as it relates to personality.[22] Despite the questions that have been raised, there is general agreement that Contingency Theory has made a significant contribution to the evolution of empirically based situational leadership studies.

Path-Goal Theory

Path-Goal Theory focuses on leader behaviors that motivate subordinates to work more effectively. The theory has its origins in the path-goal explanation of productivity[23] and the expectancy theory of motivation (see Chapter 6). According to expectancy theory, motivation is viewed as a function of the degree to which an individual believes *effort* will enable him or her to *perform* sufficiently to accomplish a valued *outcome* (goal). Two important factors in determining the level of effort expended are (1) the *value* of the outcome to the individual, and (2) the *perceived probability* that the effort-related performance level will actually lead to the outcome. Path-Goal Theory builds on these concepts and is concerned with how a manager can influence employee motivation by using appropriate leadership behaviors.

According to Path-Goal Theory, "the motivational functions of the leader consist of increasing the number and kinds of personal payoffs to subordinates for work-goal attainment and making paths to these payoffs easier to travel by clarifying the paths, reducing road blocks and pitfalls, and increasing the opportunities for personal satisfaction enroute."[24] Leader behavior is effective, then, if it (1) is seen by subordinates as an immediate or future source of satisfaction; (2) makes subordinate rewards contingent on performance (work-goal attainment); and (3) supports goal attainment by removing obstacles.

Four leader behaviors

Path-Goal Theory proposes four specific types of leader behavior; directive, supportive, achievement-oriented, and participative. Unlike Contingency Theory, Path-Goal Theory suggest that a leader may *select* from among these four leadership styles a style that most appropriately fits the situation. Exhibit 12.8 describes the four leader behavior types associated with path-goal theory.

EXHIBIT 12.8   PATH-GOAL THEORY'S FOUR STYLES OF LEADERSHIP

LEADERSHIP STYLE	DESCRIPTION
Directive	Leader tells subordinates what is expected of them and gives specific directions. Leader may answer questions; however, leader does not solicit subordinate suggestions.
Supportive	Leader is open and shows a genuine concern for subordinates' well-being and comfort. Leader tries to create a friendly climate and to satisfy work-group needs.
Participative	Leader asks subordinates for information and encourages them to share their ideas. The leader considers inputs but still makes the decision.
Achievement-Oriented	Leader sets results-oriented, challenging goals and expresses confidence in subordinates' ability to achieve them. Responsibility for goal attainment rests with subordinates.

Contingency factors

Two groups of contingency factors influence the nature of the situation. The first group, *subordinate characteristics*, includes such things as authoritarianism (of the subordinate), locus of control (internal or external), and ability. The second group, *environmental factors*, includes the nature of the task, the formal authority system, and the primary work group. Subordinate characteristics (through individual perceptions) influence job satisfaction and the subordinates' acceptance of the leader. Environmental factors, on the other hand, affect motivational behavior (effort $\rightarrow$ performance $\rightarrow$ reward) (see Exhibit 12.9).

Choosing the appropriate leadership style

The style the leader adopts is the one that most effectively facilitates accomplishing a particular goal by clarifying the path to that goal in the subordinates' minds. In other words, subordinates must perceive the leader's behavior as aiding goal attainment. Exhibit 12.10 outlines some preliminary findings on path-goal studies.

Research on various elements of Path-Goal Theory generally supports its assertions. Unfortunately, however, the theory's complexity has led most researchers to examine isolated parts of the model rather than look at it as a whole. One observer concluded:

> Several studies have focused only on task variables while ignoring individual characteristics and other environmental variables. Researchers who ignore the personal characteristics of subordinates make the implicit assumption that task variables outweigh individual characteristics in all situations. This is neither stated not implied by the theory.[25]

The number of variables to be considered and a lack of conclusive research support for the theory as a whole complicates its application.

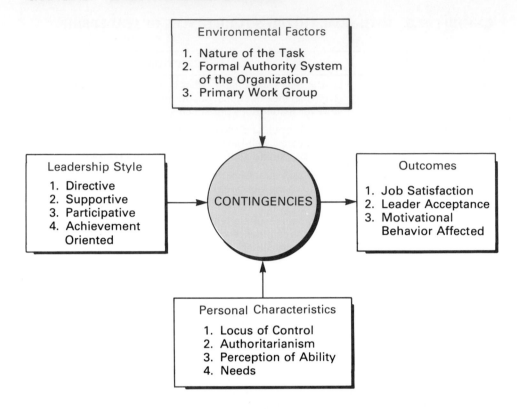

**EXHIBIT 12.9   FACTORS INFLUENCING EMPLOYEE OUTCOMES
ACCORDING TO PATH-GOAL THEORY**

JACK STACK: SPRINGFIELD REMANUFACTURING COMPANY

In Chapter 6, we described Jack Stack's philosophy and approach to employee motivation. His leadership style appears clearly consistent with some of the underlying tenets of Path-Goal Theory. Stack first teaches SRC employees how to read and use financial statements. Says Stack, "Thirty percent of the job is learning . . . we teach them about aftertax profits, retained earnings, equity, cash flow, everything." Next, he helps employees understand where they and the company are going and provides them with incentives to reach SRC goals, he says: "Our people know exactly where they show up on the income statement and how they contribute."

Eighty-one percent of the company is owned by the employee stock ownership plan (ESOP) and various employees, so it is not difficult to get people to focus on performance goals. By making information available that most other owners and managers "protect" from employees, Stack enables SRC employees to choose rational paths to personal and organizational goal attainment.

Situational Leadership Theory

Earlier in this chapter, we observed that the two dimensions identified through the Ohio State leadership studies (consideration and initiating structure) had a

EXHIBIT 12.10   PRELIMINARY FINDINGS ABOUT CONTINGENCY FACTORS AND LEADERSHIP STYLES IN PATH-GOAL THEORY

PERSONAL CHARACTERISTICS	APPROPRIATE LEADERSHIP STYLE
Locus of control	
External	Directive
Internal	Participative
1. Authoritarianism	
Authoritarian	Directive
Nonauthoritarian	Participative
2. Subordinate's perception of own ability	
Greater the perceived ability	Achievement-Oriented
3. Needs	
Achievement	Not known
Independence	Not known
Security	Not known
Affiliation	Not known

ENVIRONMENTAL FACTORS	APPROPRIATE LEADERSHIP STYLE
1. Nature of the task	
Routine	Nondirective
Ambiguous	Directive
Ambiguous, nonrepetitive	Achievement-Oriented
Frustrating, stressful	Supportive
Nonrepetitive, ego involving	Participative
Repetitive, less ego involving	
Low authoritarian	Participative
High authoritarian	Nonparticipative
2. Formal authority system of the organization	
Objective controls	Nondirective
3. Primary work group	
Clear group norms	Nondirective

NOTE: The effect of the leader on subordinate motivation is a function of how deficient the environment is with respect to motivational stimuli, constraints, and rewards.

significant impact on the development of subsequent leadership theories. **Situational Leadership Theory** (SLT) is one such theory.[26]

The two dimensions, relationship behavior and task behavior, provide the underlying structure for Situational Leadership Theory (see Exhibit 12.11). However, unlike the Managerial Grid, which was also based on the Ohio State studies, SLT does not prescribe one best leadership style. The model states that the effectiveness of leader behaviors is situational, and that a manager should choose the style most appropriate for each situation.

Leadership styles

As seen in Exhibit 12.11, each quadrant in the model represents a unique leadership style. These styles, in turn, have been fitted on a prescriptive curve to enable the leader to determine the type of behaviors most appropriate in a given situation. Each style reflects the behaviors necessary to meet the relationship and task requirements of the situation. The four styles and their respective behaviors are:

Style of Leader

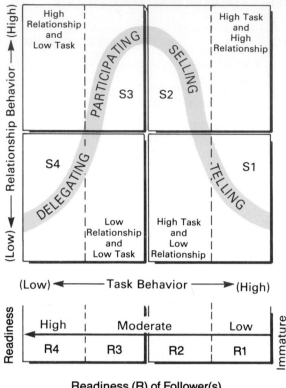

EXHIBIT 12.II   THE SITUATIONAL LEADERSHIP MODEL

Adapted from Paul Hersey and Kenneth H. Blanchard, *Management of Organizational Behavior*, 5th ed. (Englewood Cliffs, N.J.: Prentice-Hall, 1988), 71.

Telling (S1): Provide specific instruction to subordinates and closely supervise performance.

Selling (S2): Explain decisions to subordinates and provide opportunity for clarification.

Participating (S3): Share ideas with subordinates and facilitate the decision-making process.

Delegating (S4): Turn over responsibility for decisions and implementation to subordinates.

Follower readiness

According to the model, selecting the proper leadership style is contingent on the subordinate's **readiness level**. Readiness is viewed as consisting of two components—job-related readiness and psychological readiness. Job-related readiness refers to the ability to perform a task. It is influenced by the follower's level of achievement motivation (capacity to set challenging goals, desire for concrete feedback, etc.) and the task-relevant education and/or experience possessed. Psychological readiness refers to a follower's willingness to perform a job. It reflects an individual's self-confidence relative to some particular aspect of a job or area of responsibility. The four distinct levels of follower readiness range from low readiness (R1) to high readiness (R4). These four levels are expressed in terms of the follower's ability and willingness to perform a specific job:

R1: Person is unable and unwilling to perform the job.
R2: Person is unable but willing to perform the job.
R3: Person is able but unwilling to perform the job.
R4: Person is able and willing to perform the job.

Applying the model

The following example describes how the situational model might be applied. Ann Riley has recently been named as project manager for a new telemarketing program to be initiated by a large department store chain. The concept is relatively new to the organization; her subordinates thus have little or no experience in their new positions. Ann has distributed a brief description of the project to everyone, but all details have not yet been worked out. Based on her assessment of the members of her department, she has concluded that they rate low in terms of follower readiness (R1). Matching follower readiness to the appropriate leadership style, she should probably choose a telling style (S1). That it, she will want to provide specific instructions and closely supervise her employees' work.

Let us now assume that Ann can hire another employee, Mark. Mark has worked in telemarketing with another firm for about a year. He has acquired a considerable amount of knowledge about his job and usually (not always) has the self-confidence to pursue ideas independently. It appears to Ann that Mark can do the job and can usually be left alone to work. Ann has rated Mark at the R3 level. She should probably thus adopt a participating style (S3); she should share ideas and help him make decisions.

Increasing subordinate readiness

An employee's readiness level will probably change over time. Greater experience and reinforcement, for example, should lead to an increase in follower readiness. That is, the employee should become more able and more willing to perform the job. (Conceivably, certain conditions could result in decreased readiness.) Thus, the manager will need to adjust leadership style. In some cases, the manager may even wish to initiate steps to bring about such increased readiness. For example, although an employee's present readiness level may call for one style, the manager may choose to adopt a style that will require a higher level of readiness from the follower. This can be done by taking small steps along the curve instead of shifting too dramatically from one style to another.

For example, Derek has determined that Maria has low follower readiness (R1) and that a telling style (S1) should be used. However, he is interested in developing Maria so she will be more able and willing to perform her job without constant supervision. To bring about this readiness, Derek might provide a little less direction and follow Maria's performance with reinforcement or other attentive remarks. This process of loosening up and providing more support could be repeated until a selling style (S2) could be adopted.

It may appear from these examples that Situational Leadership Theory can be applied with relative ease. However, certain issues must still be addressed. Unlike other situational models which incorporate a range of contingency variables, SLT relies on a single factor, follower readiness. The factor is believed to be a solid benchmark for determining appropriate leadership style, although SLT proponents acknowledge that work and time pressures may also influence style decision. A second issue involves assessing individual as opposed to group readiness. Each individual is unique, but settings in which group members work closely with one another may require a leader to assess and address "group readiness" as a whole. Finally, even though Situational Leadership Theory has been used to train managers in organizations such as Xerox, Ford Motor Company, and the Federal Aviation Administration, neither the validity of measurement instruments nor the model's relationship to performance has been thoroughly investigated by independent researchers.

One study designed to assess the effectiveness of Situational Leadership Theory supported the SLT model's validity in situations involving low-readiness employees. However, it was not clear what style of supervision was most effective for subordinates of moderate readiness, and the model appeared unable to predict the best style for high readiness followers. In addition, the researcher suggested that the theory may be better suited to making predictions between, rather than within, job categories. In other words, greater ranges of readiness may exist between different jobs than for individuals at different stages within a single job.[27]

Business and government organizations have given considerable attention to Situational Leadership Theory. SLT's simplicity makes it appealing to many managers. Its "follower readiness" concept focuses managers' attention on those they lead and is consistent with the emphasis given to the nature and role of followers in current management literature.[28] As with most other recent leadership theories, however, the model requires much more study in a variety of settings.

Normative Model

In recent years, subordinate participation in decision making has become central to management philosophies espoused by an increasing number of organizations. Widespread support for participation, however, has been accompanied by questions concerning *when* participation is appropriate and *what form* it should take. The **Normative Model** directly addresses these questions. Leadership, according to the Normative Model, is defined in terms of the degree of subordinate participation that should be used when making management decisions under different sets of conditions.[29] In this section, we will examine the various leadership styles proposed by the model and discuss how and under what conditions a particular style should be selected.

Leadership styles

The Normative Model requires a manager to select from five separate leadership styles ranging from one allowing no subordinate participation to one stressing leader-facilitated group activities that enable the group as a whole to make the final decision. The five alternative styles are:

AI: The leader solves the problem or makes the decision personally, using the information available at the present time.
AII: The leader obtains necessary information from subordinates, then personally decides on a solution to the problem. The leader *may* or *may not* tell subordinates the purpose of the questions. Their input is limited to the leader's request for information.
CI: The leader shares the problem with relevant subordinates on one-to-one basis. After getting their ideas, the leader makes the decision. The decision *may* or *may not* reflect subordinate views.
CII: The leader shares the problem with subordinates in a group meeting during which he or she obtains their ideas and suggestions. The leader then makes the decision personally. The final decision *may* or *may not* reflect subordinate influence.
GII: The leader shares the problem with subordinates as a group. To-

gether, all parties generate and evaluate alternatives and attempt to reach consensus on a solution. The leader fcilitates the meeting, attempting to keep attention on the problem and moving the group toward a mutually acceptable solution. However, the leader *does not* try to influence the group to arrive at any particular solution.

Selecting the appropriate style

To select the appropriate style, the leader answers a series of questions. These questions address two important issues; (1) decision quality (whether or not the decision has a correct answer), and (2) acceptance (the likelihood the decision will be implemented if subordinates do not participate in its formulation). The questions shown at the top of Exhibit 12.12 address the quality and acceptance issues. The decision tree is then used to guide the leader to the most appropriate style or styles for a particular situation.

At first, the model may look confusing (most decision trees do). However, it is actually easy to use. A manager merely answers the questions along a path leading to an effective solution. The path's direction is determined by the answer to each question. For example, if the answer to question A is *yes*, the manager must answer question B. If the answer to question A is *no*, the manager will progress directly to question D—and so on until he or she arrives at the appropriate style.

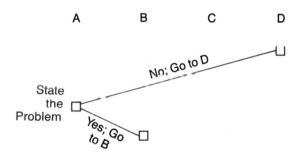

ANALYZING THE DECISION

According to the decision rules of the model (see Exhibit 12.14 on page 406), more than one style may be appropriate in a particular situation. In such a case, the model prescribes the most efficient style, that is, the style that will produce a solution in the least amount of time. If more than one solution will produce the same successful outcome, the leader is best served by the style that will require the least amount of time.

To see thc Normative Model in action, consider Carl's situation. Carl is confronted with a decision about the number and variety of new products his field representatives will be asked to carry during the next six months. Not all the new products are essential to support the existing line of merchandise, but a consulting firm recently recommended adding them to broaden the company's appeal to its customers and perhaps to improve salesforce morale. Let's help Carl address the appropriate questions by working through the decision tree (see Exhibit 12.13.)

A. Is there a quality requirement (i.e., does it appear that there is a best answer)? *Probably not.* Too many factors (including the number of items to be carried, what items would be carried, and how individual sales representatives would react to the new lines) make a best answer unlikely.

A. Is there a quality requirement such that one solution is likely to be more rational than another?
B. Do I have sufficient information to make a high-quality decision?
C. Is the problem structured?
D. Is acceptance of the decision by subordinates critical to effective implementation?
E. If I were to make the decision by myself, is it reasonably certain that it would be accepted by my subordinates?
F. Do subordinates share the organizational goals to be attained in solving this problem?
G. Is conflict among subordinates likely in preferred solutions? (This question is irrelevant to individual problems.)
H. Do subordinates have sufficient information to make a high-quality decision?

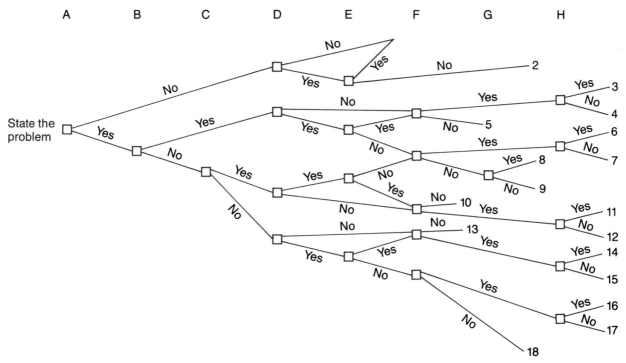

The recommended strategies for each problem type (1–18) for group (G) and individual (I) are as follows:

Group		Group		Group	
1	AI	7	GII	13	CII
2	GII	8	CII	14	CII
3	AI	9	CI	15	CII
4	AI	10	AII	16	GII
5	AI	11	AII	17	GII
6	GII	12	AII	18	CII

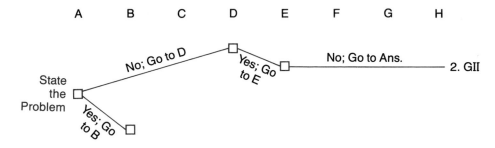

A. Is there a quality requirement such that one solution is likely to be more rational than another?

D. Is acceptance of the decision by subordinates critical to effective implementation?

E. If I were to make the decision by myself, is it reasonably certain that it would be accepted by my subordinates?

EXHIBIT 12.13   SELECTING CARL'S LEADERSHIP STYLE

B. Not appropriate since A was answered *no.*

C. Not appropriate since A was answered *no.*

D. Is subordinate acceptance important for effective implementation? *Yes;* sales representatives must be enthusiastic about new products if we expect them to push these products.

E. If Carl makes the decision alone, can he be reasonably sure everyone will accept it? *No;* because they are on the road a lot, the salesforce is an independent group. They usually decide individually how much support to give a particular product or new idea.

F. Not appropriate since E was answered *no.*

G. Not appropriate since E was answered *no.*

H. Not appropriate since E was answered *no.*

Carl would be advised to use a GII style—to share the problem with his subordinates as a group and attempt to reach consensus on the solution.

Of course, more than just selecting the correct management style is usually required to obtain a successful outcome. The results of a recent study of the Normative Model found that the impact of a chosen leadership style (in this case, on conflict resolution) differed depending on how the style was implemented. Thus, managers must be trained how to *use* as well as how to *select* each style effectively.[30]

Unlike many of the leadership approaches already discussed, the Normative Model has been tested extensively and has proved to be valid in both laboratory and field settings. It has been used to train managers in a variety of companies and public organizations, including General Motors, Hertz, the General Accounting Office, and the New Jersey court system. Nevertheless, the model continues to change. Applications now include leadership decisions involving only one subordinate. In addition, a revision in the format of the contingency questions has lead to the development of a more sophisticated version of the model and of hand-held calculator programs that facilitate on-the-job situational analysis.[31]

EXHIBIT 12.14 NORMATIVE MODEL DECISION RULES

1. THE LEADER INFORMATION RULE

If the quality of the decision is important and the leader does not possess enough information or expertise to solve the problem alone, then AI is eliminated from the feasible set.

2. THE GOAL CONGRUENCE RULE

If the quality of the decision is important and subordinates are not likely to pursue the organizational goals in their efforts to solve this problem, then GII is eliminated from the feasible set.

3. THE UNSTRUCTURED PROBLEM RULE

In situations in which the quality of the decision is important, if the leader lacks the necessary information or expertise to solve the problem alone, and if the problem is unstructured, the method of solving the problem should provide for interaction among subordinates likely to possess relevant information. Accordingly, AI, AII, and CI, which provide no interaction among subordinates, are eliminated from the feasible set.

4. THE ACCEPTANCE RULE

If the acceptance of the decision by subordinates is important for effective implementation, and if it is not reasonably certain that an autocratic decision will be accepted, AI and AII are eliminated from the feasible set.

5. THE CONFLICT RULE

If acceptance of the decision is important and is not reasonably certain if the decision is made autocratically, and disagreement among subordinates over possible solutions is likely, the methods used in solving the problem should enable those in disagreement to resolve their differences with full knowledge of the problem. Accordingly, under these conditions AI, AII, and CI, which permit no interaction among subordinates and therefore provide no opportunity for those in conflict to resolve their differences, are eliminated from the feasible set. Their use runs the risk of leaving some of the subordinates with less than the needed commitment to the final decision.

6. THE FAIRNESS RULE

If the quality of the decision is unimportant but acceptance of the decision is important—and not reasonably certain to result from an autocratic decision—the decision process used must generate the needed acceptance. The decision process should permit the subordinates to interact with one another and negotiate among themselves the method of resolving any differences with full responsibility for determining what is fair and equitable. Accordingly, under these circumstance AI, AII, CI, and CII are eliminated from the feasible set.

7. THE ACCEPTANCE PRIORITY RULE

If acceptance is important and not reasonably certain to result from an autocratic decision, and if subordinates are motivated to pursue the organizational goals represented in the problem, then methods which provide equal partnership in the decision-making process can generate far greater acceptance without risking decision quality. Accordingly, AI, AII, CI and CII are eliminated from the feasible set.

SOURCE: Reprinted from *Leadership and Decision-Making* by Victor H. Vroom and Philip W. Yetton, by permission of the University of Pittsburgh Press. © 1973 by University of Pittsburgh Press.

Situational Theories in Perspective

The situational leadership theories discussed in this section all have one thing in common. Each theory is based on the premise that an effective leader must use different leadership styles in different situations rather than rely on a single approach in all situations. This perspective requires that leaders be able to (1) differentiate between styles; (2) differentiate between situations; (3) match the appropriate style to a particular situation; and (4) be capable of using each style correctly.

Each theory approaches leadership from a different perspective and offers unique insights into how leaders can best influence follower behavior. Contingency Theory, for example, holds that each of us has a *natural*, and relatively *fixed*, style of management and must therefore either select situations in which we can lead effectively or engineer (i.e., alter) the situation to bring about a successful fit. Path-Goal Theory views the leader's job as enabling followers to identify desired outcomes (goals) and helping them determine how those outcomes can best be achieved (path analysis). The nature of the followers and certain organizational and job factors determine the leadership style. Situational Leadership Theory concentrates exclusively on the follower. The leader should evaluate followers on the basis of their *readiness* (i.e., job-related ability and psychological willingness) to perform. The leader then matches the appropriate leadership style to the follower's state of readiness. Finally, the Normative Model defines leadership in terms of choices between nonparticipative and various degrees of participative management. The leader selects the correct leadership style by answering a series of situationally relevant questions on a decision tree about decision quality and acceptance. Exhibit 12.15 presents the major elements of each of the four situational leadership theories discussed in this chapter.

You may find the number and variety of situational leadership theories confusing. Keep in mind, however, that there is usually more than one way to achieve a desired outcome, and this is also true of applying situational leadership models. Remember, different situations require different leadership styles and an appropriate match between style and situation must exist if a leader is to be effective.

TRANSFORMATIONAL LEADERSHIP

The leadership models discussed thus far have generally had one thing in common. Each is concerned with helping leaders find an effective way to bring about follower compliance or collaboration. In fact, leadership has been viewed by most researchers and writers as a process through which one individual (a leader) is able to bring about desired actions from others (followers) by using certain behaviors, rewards, or incentives. In essence, an exchange or "transaction" takes place between leader and follower.

David Beckmann, production manager in a small electronic fixtures factory, is a **transactional leader**. David is known at corporate headquarters as a guy who can always "meet the ticket" (attain daily production goals). When asked his secret, David explained, "It's easy; we explain the production goals each morning, and remind the crews that their take-home pay depends on getting the product out. Paying a few compliments here and there throughout the day doesn't hurt either."

David's transactional leadership style is an effective means for bringing about routine, expected levels of performance. However, students of leadership are continually looking for ways to bring about longer-term, higher-order changes in follower behavior. The term, **transformational leadership**, is used to describe the process of eliciting performance above and beyond normal expectations.[32] A **transformational**

EXHIBIT 12.15   FOUR SITUATIONAL APPROACHES TO LEADERSHIP

	KEY ELEMENTS
Contingency Theory	Effective leadership defined in terms of group effectiveness Three contingency factors: —Leader power position —Leader-member relations —Task structure Leader has a natural, stable style, either task-oriented or employee-oriented
Path-Goal Theory	Effective leadership defined in terms of leader's impact on subordinate goal setting and goal attainment Situational variables: —Environmental factors —Personal characteristics Leader selects from among four styles: —Directive —Supportive —Participative —Achievement oriented
Situational Leadership Theory	Effective leadership defined in terms of matching appropriate style to situation Subordinate readiness (job and psychological) Leader selects from among four styles: —Telling —Selling —Participating —Delegating
Normative Model	Effective leadership defined in terms of subordinate participation Situational variables: —Decision quality –Decision acceptance —Timeliness Leader uses decision tree to select from among five styles: —AI —CI —CII —GI —GII

leader is one who inspires others to reach beyond themselves and do more than they originally thought possible by raising their commitment to a shared vision of the future.

Janette Stuart is such a leader. Janette was hired as the president of a growing retail chain largely on the basis of her reputation in the industry as one who could solve tough problems. Shortly after she joined the company, however, those around her noticed that she had a "different" management style. Rather than respond to questions with answers, she held regular problem-solving meetings and encouraged others to do likewise in their own divisions. Janette spent little time in her office, and could usually be found talking with managers and other employees in their own work areas. Asked to describe Janette's leadership style, one division vice president confided, "She's given us a clearer picture of where we're going, and I think that most of us now think we have what it takes to get there."

Janette's transformational style differs from David's approach to leadership. David spends much of his time exchanging rewards for performance. Janette, on the other hand, is more concerned with setting the tone for high performance and inspiring those around her to draw on their own strengths and abilities to become part of the company's future.

Transformational leadership, then, involves (1) raising the follower's level of consciousness about the importance and value of particular outcomes and ways or reaching these outcomes; (2) Getting followers to transcend their own self-interest for the sake of a larger group or organization: and (3) raising the level or expanding the range of individuals' salient needs (e.g., enabling a person to recognize his need for self-actualization).[33] Exhibit 12.16 identifies differences between transactional and transformational leaders.

In a study intended to find evidence of transformational leadership, seventy senior executives were asked to describe in detail a leader who fit a transformational definition. Their responses revealed that such leaders created an environment where followers sometimes work "ridiculous hours" and give the leader all the support asked of them. Transformational leaders were described as being able to cause heightened motivation and awareness and elicit from followers such reactions as trust, admiration, loyalty, and total commitment to and belief in the organization.[34]

Transformational Behaviors

Transformational leadership involves three important factors: (1) charisma, (2) individualized consideration, and (3) intellectual stimulation.

Charisma, a special magnetic charm or appeal that gives a person power over others, has been found to be the most important of the three variables. A leader's charismatic qualities cause followers to place trust and confidence in the leader's vision and values and to develop intense emotional feelings about the leader. The concept of charisma is somewhat abstract; however, it may be possible to specify charismatic behaviors in terms of specific actions.[35] Exhibit 12.17 describes a number

EXHIBIT 12.16   DIFFERENCES BETWEEN TRANSACTIONAL AND TRANSFORMATIONAL LEADERS

	TRANSACTIONAL LEADERS	TRANSFORMATIONAL LEADERS
Status Quo	Essentially agrees with and strives to maintain status quo	Essentially opposes and strives to change status quo
Goal Orientation	Goals not too discrepant from status quo	Idealized goals usually highly different from status quo
Time Perspective	Has short-term perspective; primarily concerned with immediate results	Has longer-term perspective; motivates subordinates to strive for long-term goals
Motivation Strategy	Motivates subordinates with immediate tangible rewards	Motivates subordinates by inspiring them to aspire to higher-order personal goals (self-actualization)
Standardization of Behavior	Prefers that subordinates follow rules and conventions	Encourages subordinates to innovate and experiment
Problem Solving	Solves problems for subordinates or tells them where to find solutions	Asks questions; works with or encourages subordinates to develop own solutions

EXHIBIT 12.17

CHARISMATIC LEADERS PROJECT INNER STRENGTH AND SELF-CONFIDENCE BY

---

1. Identifying with popular subjects
2. Using stimulating verbal language
3. Using appropriate nonverbal language (body language)
4. Connecting with followers at their level, but transporting them to leader's level and toward leader's goals
5. Remaining independent but not isolated
6. Being committed to their own beliefs, but not being argumentative or adversarial

---

of actions associated with charisma. To the extent that such behaviors can be identified, they can be learned and practiced by managers.

The second important factor, **individualized consideration**, refers a leader's willingness to pay attention to, understand, and share in each subordinate's concerns. In addition, transformational leaders attempt not only to identify individual needs but to cause followers to be concerned about and responsive to higher-level needs (e.g., self-worth and self-efficacy).

In the preceding example, a vice-president in Janette Stuart's company said, "Most of us now think we have what it takes to get there [to achieve the company's vision]." His statement implies that Janette has reinforced managers' and other employees' beliefs in themselves and increased their confidence in their ability to help achieve a vision.

Finally, transformational leaders provide **intellectual stimulation** to subordinates by encouraging them to examine problems in new ways and by causing them to question their own beliefs and values as well as those of their leaders. In turn, followers are stimulated to identify and solve problems on their own. This was the approach taken by Janette Stuart in our example. Janette helped build self-confidence in subordinates by developing their problem-solving skills and inspiring them to make use of those skills on their own.

The Transformational Process

Although some authorities have focused on transformational behaviors such as those mentioned above, others have examined the process through which transformational leaders bring about significant changes in followers and organizations.[36] This process includes several key elements: (1) visioning, (2) articulating, (3) inspiring, and (4) empowering and ongoing communication.

Visioning

Perhaps the single most notable attribute of the transformational leader is his ability to envision, or "see," the organization's future clearly and completely. General Motors' Alfred P. Sloan, Polaroid's Edwin Land, and Wal-Mart's Sam Walton are among those industrialists who are often cited for their organizational vision. Similarly, political leaders such as Mahatma Gandhi and Martin Luther King, Jr., have been recognized as leaders with vision.[37]

Visioning may take on more than one form. Rather than require everyone in an organization to pursue a roadmap to his or her vision, an effective transformational leader might try to get each employee to have a vision of his or her own. As one executive concluded, the leader is responsible not only for the vision alone, but also for "an ongoing process of visioning throughout the organization."[38]

JAMES MORGAN, APPLIED MATERIALS

James Morgan is a business leader who has combined values and vision to build Applied Materials, now one of the fastest growing semiconductor-equipment manufacturers in the world, into a viable, hard-hitting corporation. From a young age, Morgan had a strong desire to be in charge. Full of self-confidence, he has added a sense of mission described by one observer as bordering on the Messianic: "Building a company is simply a matter of vision, of being able to look into the future."

Morgan has a strong sense of his own ability and is able to convey that sense and his vision to those around him. He is capable of making tough decisions, but prefers to push those who work for him to make up their own minds.

The semiconductor industry is erratic, at best, but its day-to-day instability has not altered James Morgan's style. He has remained focused and has generally been able to impart his energy and direction to those around him. Recently, he created ripples at Applied, as well as in the industry as a whole, when he embarked on a global strategy calling for Applied Materials to take on the Japanese in Japan. The company has been remarkably successful there in large part due to James Morgan's vision, hard work, and style.

His pay is relatively low, at the industry's 75th percentile, and most of his time is spent on a wide variety of company matters. Although he claims he would like to back away and turn even more over to his employees, those who know James Morgan think his ever-expanding vision and high level of personal commitment are likely to keep him in the middle of the action for a long time to come.[39]

Valuing

In a study of eleven transformational leaders, researchers found that each individual was "value driven."[40] That is, the leader was true to a set of core values around which the organizational transformation took place. These values were modeled by the leader and were consistently embraced as the leader and followers sought to fulfill the vision. For example, Sam Walton of Wal-Mart has repeatedly and publicly expressed his belief that "the customer is the boss." This *value* has lead to a company-wide practice of accepting any merchandise returned by a customer without question and of placing "greeters" at the front of every store to welcome each person who enters.

Leadership is not practiced in a vacuum. The leader's values and behaviors are likely to be felt throughout an organization. They will affect employees or other followers and impact relations with customers and vendors. In some cases, ethical dilemmas arise when the benefits of those decisions are not equitably distributed among members of the organization's various interest groups. Such was the case when F. Ross Johnson, chief executive officer at RJR Nabisco, found himself in the middle of history's largest leveraged buyout. Johnson's predicament is described in the Ethical Dilemma on page 412.

ETHICAL DILEMMA
Conflict of Interest at RJR Nabisco

He had served as chief executive officer at RJR Nabisco, Inc., for two years. Like all corporate officers, he was responsible to the board of directors for protecting the welfare of the company's shareholders. In 1989, however, F. Ross Johnson found himself in another position. He became the key figure in what has become the largest leveraged buyout (LBO) yet to be consummated on Wall Street. Johnson was in a unique position that many observers have suggested presented a clear conflict of interest. He represented not only RJR Nabisco shareholders but *also* the acquiring company.

Long before the board of directors finalized its decision to take the company private, Johnson arranged with Shearson Lehman Hutton, a primary financier for the proposed LBO, to allow him and six fellow managers to put up $20 million of their own money in order to acquire an 8.5 percent interest in the privatized company. This amount was substantially below what the stock would become worth when news of the decision to go private was released to corporate shareholders. In the meantime, Johnson and his associates would draw $18 million a year in salaries, stand to gain an additional $20 million in bonuses each year, and see the value of their stock increase by as much as 20 percent (approximately $2.5 billion) over five years.

However, the deal was not to be. When news of the arrangement leaked out, there was a massive public outcry. Johnson and

Shearson Lehman Hutton were forced to back off, and both parties were ultimately eliminated from the LBO. The company was later sold by RJR chairman Charles E. Hugel to Kohlberg Kravis Roberts for a reported $27.5 billion. F. Ross Johnson and his associates aren't the only executives ever to have arranged backroom deals that have affected leveraged buyouts. However, the RJR attempt was among the largest and most self-serving of all.

Questions

What values did the actions of F. Ross Johnson and other top managers at RJR convey to employees and how may those values be manifest in subsequent employee behavior?

Why is it important for managers and other leaders to sort out their ethical responsibilities and possible conflicts of interest? Is this the organization's responsibility as well?

What impact would actions like those taken by F. Ross Johnson and his associates have on (a) employees of the company, (b) customers?

SOURCE: B. Saporito, "How Ross Johnson Blew the Buyout," *Fortune*, 24 April 1989, 296–317; B. Inman, "Nabisco's Affable Executioner," *Business*, December 1988, 61–64; J.H. Dobrzynski, "Was RJR's Ross Johnson Too Greedy for His Own Good?" *Business Week*, 21 November 1988, 95; B. Morris, "Defeated RJR Chief Johnson Won't be Short of Consolations," *Wall Street Journal*, 2 December 1988, p. A10.

Articulating and inspiring

Visioning enables a leader to identify where the organization is headed and the events that will enable it to achieve those ends. Articulating, on the other hand, is concerned with clearly defining and communicating the vision to others. In addition to making others in the organization aware of her vision, the leader must clearly convey the values and beliefs in which follower behaviors are grounded. In other words, the transformational leader is one who can translate a vision into concrete operational terms and convey that reality to others. This ability often separates "dreamers" from "doers."

Articulating in itself may not be sufficient to bring about commitment to and enthusiasm for an idea. Transformational leaders also inspire their followers. Whether by word or action, they project qualities that excite followers or otherwise cause them to want to "join the team."

Empowering and ongoing communication

The essence of transformational leadership is the leader's ability to inspire in his followers the belief that they can contribute significantly to the attainment of the vision. This involves empowering followers by helping them achieve increased feelings of self-worth and enabling them to draw on the personal resources necessary to meet the new challenge. The leader develops followers through shared problem solving and delegation, thereby helping them to gain greater self-confidence.

Empowering is facilitated by the leader's willingness to work with followers individually, developing their skills when and where necessary and providing continual personal support by effectively communicating his belief in their worth and ability.

Transformational Leadership in Perspective

Transformatinal leadership offers an alternative to more traditional, transactional views of leadership. Transformational leaders are individuals who envision their organization's future, articulate that vision to organizational members, and inspire and facilitate a higher level of motivation than those members have thought possible. Although charisma plays an important part in the transformational process, such leaders are more than simply cheerleaders. They act out a "hands-on" philosophy, not by performing the day-to-day tasks of subordinates, but rather by developing and encouraging their followers individually.

HERB KELLEHER, SOUTHWEST AIRLINES

Herb Kelleher is such a transformational leader. Kelleher, president and chief executive officer of Southwest Airlines, is able to inspire his followers to pursue his corporate vision and reach beyond themselves to give Southwest Airlines that "something extra" that sets it apart from its competitors.

Kelleher recognizes that the company does not exist merely for the gratification of its employees; he knows that Southwest Airlines must perform and be profitable. However, he believes strongly that exceptional performance can best be attained by valuing individuals for themselves. If you fly Southwest Airlines, you may see Herb Kelleher: he travels frequently. But don't look in first class. You are much more likely to find him serving drinks, fluffing pillows, or just wandering up and down the aisle talking to passengers. The success of Southwest Airlines and the enthusiasm of its employees indicate that Herb Kelleher has achieved his goal of weaving together individual and corporate interests so that all who are members of the Southwest Airlines family benefit. Much of the research on transformational leadership has focused on major corporate and world leaders. Kelleher proves that transformational behaviors (visioning, valuing, articulating and inspiring, and empowering and ongoing communication) can be practiced by leaders in all types and at all levels of organizations.

OTHER PERSPECTIVES ON LEADERSHIP

As we indicated at the beginning of this chapter, not all authorities agree on the role that leaders play in organizations. Evidence of leader impact is inconsistent. We now consider two views on leadership that contrast with those we have previously examined. The first view holds that other factors exist in organizations that may neutralize or substitute for leadership. The second view suggests that leadership style may be the result, rather than the cause, of follower behavior and that style decisions are based on the perceived attributes of followers.

Substitutes for Leadership

Some researchers believe that inconsistent evidence linking leadership to organizational performance may be explained by certain conditions that neutralize or even counteract leadership. These characteristics may be sufficiently strong in their own right or may combine with one another to lessen a leader's influence.[41] For example, locating a manager's office away from the factory work floor is likely to reduce his ability to direct the actions of plant workers. Exhibit 12.18 lists a number of characteristics of the subordinate, the task, and the organization that can neutralize or moderate the impact of either relationship-oriented or task-oriented leaders.

Not all leadership substitutes will eliminate leader influences. However, their potential impact on task accomplishment and individual and group maintenance may

EXHIBIT 12.18　SUBSTITUTES FOR LEADERSHIP

SUBSTITUTE	WILL TEND TO NEUTRALIZE Relationship-Oriented, People-Centered Leadership	Task-Oriented Leadership
Individual		
1. Ability, experience, training	X	
2. Need for independence	X	X
3. Need for support	X	
Task		
1. Unambiguous and routine		X
2. Provides its own feedback concerning accomplishment		X
3. Intrinsically satisfying	X	
Organization		
1. Formalization of plans, goals, and responsibilities		X
2. Rigid rules and procedures		X
3. Closely knit, cohesive work groups	X	X
Other		
1. Organizational rewards not within the leader's control	X	X
2. Physical distance between superior and subordinates	X	X

Adapted from: S. Kerr and J. M. Jermier "Substitutes for Leadership: Their Meaning and Measurement," *Organizational Behavior and Human Performance*, Vol. 22 (December 1978): 379.

be substantial. Managers should be aware of these "functional equivalents" to traditional leadership behaviors and effectively balance the use of both. In some cases, leader behaviors and substitutes may mutually reinforce one another. In other cases, however, the existence of too many substitutes or behaviors performing the same function may overload followers and be counterproductive.[42]

Attribution Influences on Leadership

Characteristics attributed *to* a follower *by* a leader may cause that leader to practice a certain leadership style or select a particular substitute in order to cause certain follower behaviors. In fact, leadership is seen by some to be more a *result* than a *cause* of follower behavior. Attribution theory focuses on the leader's attribution activities and the important role they play in the selection of leadership style.[43]

Evidence suggests that the *perceived* characteristics of (1) individual followers, and (2) other situational factors cause a manager to behave in a particular way. A leader does not simply respond to what she observes. Rather, situational factors are interpreted according to a set of three observation cues: distinctiveness, consistency, and consensus. (At this point, you may wish to review the discussion of these cues on page 85 in Chapter 3, "Perception.") After initial observations are interpreted according to the three cues, causal attributions are made. These attributions may be internal (person-related: ability, effort, etc.) or external (environment-related: equipment, workload, etc.), and form the basis for subsequent leader decisions and actions. The causal attribution model in Exhibit 12.19 shows the relationship between situational factors, observation cues, causal attributions, and the leader's specific behavioral response.

Let us look at a brief example. Martin Fields has been late with his last two quarterly sales reports, although the sales figures themselves have been excellent. The controller has heard through the grapevine that Martin's previous employer experienced similar delays in obtaining important information from him and has communicated this information to Martin's sales manager. Martin claims that the large number of orders he must process and the amount of time he must spend on the road cause him to be late. The controller has expressed the opinion that Martin is disorganized and lacks commitment (internal attributions).

The sales manager has also evaluated the situation but views it differently. He has concluded that Martin's territory is large and that other salespersons in similar situations have also turned in late reports. In addition, he believes that staff support for the sales group as a whole is inadequate (external attributions). The sales manager's response will no doubt be quite different from that recommended by the controller. Rather than issue a reprimand and simply tell Martin to get the reports in on time (task-oriented response), the sales manager is likely to talk about the problem and attempt to work out a solution that meets both Martin's and the controller's needs (employee-oriented response).

Research supports the position that an attribution process does in fact influence subsequent leader behavior. One study of fifty-two M.B.A. students found that subordinates receiving performance feedback were approached differently depending on the superior's initial attributions.[44] Specifically, when subordinates' performance was seen as the result of lack of effort, superiors used a joint problem-solving style; when poor performance was attributed to lack of ability, superiors' style was more directive and had a "tell and sell" quality. Thus, preconceived attributions, regardless of their accuracy, appear to influence the way in which managers communicate with

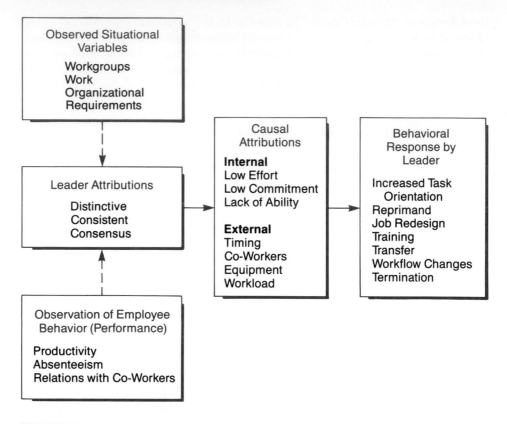

EXHIBIT 12.19   ATTRIBUTION MODEL OF LEADER BEHAVIOR

Adapted from S. G. Green and T. R. Mitchell, "Attributional Process of Leaders in Leader-Member Interactions," *Organizational Behavior and Human Performance,* 23 (1979): 429–458.

subordinates. Another study of 188 supervisors in 37 organizations further found that the nature of relationships between supervisors and subordinates influenced the supervisors' formation of attributions. Internal attributions were more likely to be made for "ingroup" members in effective performance situations, while internal attributions were more likely to be made for "outgroup" members when performance was ineffective.[45]

The process of forming causal attributions along with the specific nature of those attributions subtly influences leadership behaviors, including the selection of leadership style and decisions about the use of leadership substitutes. Further study and integration of attribution theory with other situational leadership theories may significantly alter our understanding of those theories and the way in which they are used by managers.

EFFECTIVE LEADER BEHAVIOR: CONCLUSIONS

The subject of leadership has received widespread attention from managers and researchers alike. Managers are interested in becoming more effective leaders and in identifying individuals who can lead other people toward organizational goals. Researchers, on the other hand, attempt to answer questions about the nature of leadership and how it can be used most effectively.

This chapter suggests that leadership is complex and requires more than an intuitive feeling for how to lead. Although you can identify certain traits or characteristics that most good leaders *appear* to have, a substantial amount of research indicates that no distinctive set of good leader traits exists. Some good leaders possess one set of traits; others possess another. Moreover, the same traits may characterize effective as well as ineffective leaders. In fact, certain types of behaviors rather than traits may be related to leadership effectiveness.

Researchers have identified two primary dimensions of leader behaviors. These dimensions, known by various names, are concerned with (1) the psychological support and concern shown for employees, and (2) the attention given to task performance and goal attainment. Interestingly, neither set of behaviors alone has been found to be most important to leadership effectiveness. Even though researchers disagree on the precise combination of these behaviors likely to result in effective leadership, practically all researchers agree that their effective use depends on the manager's specific situation.

The many models and theories presented in this chapter attest to the complexity of the leadership concept. Unfortunately for the day-to-day manager, each approach uses a different set of contingency factors (or independent variables) by which various situations are measured. In the same way, there is no universal agreement on the range of leadership styles available to managers. Nevertheless, existing models can guide a leader in selecting and using an effective style.

Additional factors affect our everyday leadership practices. Our "objectivity" in selecting what we believe to be an appropriate leadership style may be influenced by our interpretation of follower behaviors and other situational factors and by the subsequent causal attributions we make. In some cases, our leadership behaviors may be insufficient to influence employee behavior. Individual, group, and organizational factors may alter or even negate that influence. As a manager, you should attempt to identify those substitutes, and when possible, use them to enhance, rather than inhibit, your ability to lead.

The fact that there are a number of approaches to leadership does not mean that any particular theory or model is wrong. There is more than one way to achieve a desired outcome. In fact, each approach to leadership presented in this chapter raises important questions about the nature and impact of leadership behavior.

Finally, it is useful to distinguish transactional from transformational approaches to leadership. More conventional (transactional) leadership models may help you manage day-to-day activities and focus on situations as they arise. Transformational leadership, on the other hand, offers a means for significantly altering employee commitment and organizational direction. The question is not whether to take a transactional or a transformational approach to leadership, but rather how the two approaches can be integrated into a complete and effective leadership philosophy.[46] Understanding the variety of leadership perspectives addressed in this chapter should enrich your personal leadership philosophy and enable you to become a more effective leader.

QUESTIONS FOR REVIEW AND DISCUSSION

1. What is the current status of trait theories of leadership?

2. How do behavioral theories differ from the earlier great man and trait theories?

3. The Ohio State studies revealed the existence of two leadership dimensions, initiating structure and consideration. What was and continues to be the significance of that finding?

4. How do situational theories of leadership differ from other approaches?

5. How is the Path-Goal Theory of leadership related to expectancy motivation theory?

6. What is the role of the leader according to Path-Goal Theory?

7. How could you use the Situational Leadership Theory to manage two employees in different stages of readiness?

8. What two important issues are addressed by the decision-tree questions used in connection with the Normative Model? Explain their significance.

9. How do transformational leaders differ from transactional leaders?

10. What is meant by the term *substitutes for leadership*?

11. How do leader attributions influence the selection of leadership style?

12. Does self-management eliminate the need for leadership? Explain.

REFERENCES

1. R. M. Stogdill, *Leadership Abstracts and Bibliography: 1904–1973* (New York: MacMillan Free Press, 1981).
2. J. Pfeffer, "The Ambiguity of Leadership," *Academy of Management Review*, Vol. 2, No. 1 (January 1979): 104.
3. R. M. Stogdill, "Personal Factors Associated with Leadership: A Survey of the Literature," *Journal of Psychology*, Vol. 25 (1948): 35–71.
4. R. M. Stogdill, *Handbook of Leadership* (New York: The Free Press, 1974), 93.
5. P. Stryker, "On the Meaning of Executive Qualities," *Fortune*, June 1958, 116.
6. Stogdill, "Personal Factors," 63.
7. Ibid., 66.
8. K. Lewin, R. Lippitt, and R. White, "Patterns of Aggressive Behavior in Experimentally Created 'Social Climates'," *Journal of Social Psychology*, Vol. 10 (1939): 271–299.
9. D. Katz, N. Maccoby, and N. C. Morse, *Productivity, Supervision, and Morale in an Office Situation*, (Ann Arbor: University of Michigan, Survey Research Center, 1950): Katz et. al., *Production, Supervision, and Morale Among Railroad Workers* (Ann Arbor: University of Michigan, 1951).
10. N. C. Morse and E. Reimer, "The Experimental Change of a Major Organizational Variable," *Journal of Abnormal and Social Psychology*, Vol. 52 (January 1956): 120–132; R. Likert, *New Patterns of Management* (New York: McGraw-Hill, 1961), 62–71.
11. R. L. Kahn, "The Prediction of Productivity," *Journal of Social Issues*, Vol. 12, No. 2 (1956): 41–49.
12. R. M. Stogdill and A. E. Coons, eds., *Leader Behavior: Its Description and Measurement* (Columbus: Ohio State University Bureau of Business Research, 1957).
13. S. Kerr, et. al., "Toward a Contingency Theory of Leadership Based upon the Consideration and Initiating Structure Literature," *Organizational Behavior and Human Performance*, Vol. 12 (1974): 62–82.
14. Ibid.
15. R. R. Blake and J. S. Mouton, "An Overview of the Grid," *Training and Development Journal*, Vol. 29, No. 5 (May 1975): 29–37.
16. R. R. Blake and J. S. Mouton, "How to Chose a Leadership Style," *Training and Development Journal*, vol. 39 (February 1986): 39–46: Blake and Mouton, "Should You Teach There's Only One Best Way to Manage?" *HRD*, April 1978, 24.
17. Ibid.; Blake and Mouton, "Effective Crisis Management," *New Management*, Vol. 3 (Summer 1985): 14–17.
18. K. F. Girard, "Profiles in Power," *Business Month*, May 1989, 28–39; and P. Nulty, "America's Toughest Bosses," *Fortune*, 27 February 1989, 40–46, 50.
19. M. Billard, "Women on the Verge," *Business Month*, April 1990, 42–43.
20. F. E. Fiedler, *A Theory of Leadership Effectiveness* (New York: McGraw-Hill, 1967).
21. F. E. Fiedler, M. M. Chemers, and L. Hahhar, *Improving Leadership Effectiveness: The Leader Match Concept* (New York: John Wiley and Sons, 1977), 134–136; "How to Be a Successful Leader: Match Your Leadership Situation with Your Personality: An Interview With Fred Fiedler," *Leadership*, Vol. 1 (November 1979): 31.
22. R. G. Lord, C. L. DeVader, and G. M. Alliger, "A Meta-analysis of the Relation Between Personality Traits and Leadership: An Application of Validity Generalization Procedures," *Journal of Applied Psychology*, Vol. 71 (1986): 402–410; K. W. Kuhnert and P. Lewis, "Transactional and Transformational Leadership: A Constructive/Developmental Analysis," *Academy of Management Review*, Vol. 12 (October 1987): 648–657.

23. B. S. Georgopolous, G. M. Mahoney, and N. W. Jones, "A Path-Goal Approach to Productivity," *Journal of Applied Psychology*, Vol. 41 (December 1957): 345–353.

24. R. J. House and T. R. Mitchell, "Path-Goal Theory of Leadership," *Journal of Contemporary Business*, Vol. 3, No. 4 (Autumn 1974): 85.

25. C. E. Kellogg, *The Impact of Leader Behavior on Volunteer Satisfaction with Work*, (Ph. D. Thesis, University of Arkansas, 1985), 43; C. E. Kellogg and D. D. White, "Leader Behaviors and Volunteer Satisfaction with Work: The Effect of Volunteer Motivation Level," paper presented at the Annual Meeting of the Academy of Management, New Orleans, August 1987.

26. P. Hersey and K. Blanchard, *Management of Organizational Behavior*, 5th ed. (Englewood Cliffs: Prentice-Hall, 1982), 170–187.

27. R. P. Vecchio, "Situational Leadership Theory: An Examination of a Prescriptive Theory," *Journal of Applied Psychology*, Vol. 72, (1987): 445–451.

28. R. E. Kelley, "In Praise of Followers," *Harvard Business Review*, Vol. 66 (November-December, 1988): 142–148.

29. V. Vroom, "Can Leaders Learn to Lead," *Organizational Dynamics*, Vol. 5 (Winter 1976): 17–28.

30. A. Crouch, "Manager Behavior: Leadership Styles and Subordinate Performance," *Organizational Behavior and Human Decision Processes*, Vol. 39 (June 1987): 384–396.

31. V., Vroom, A. Jago, and B. Smith, "New Developments in the Vroom-Yetton Model: A Research Review and Model Revision," presentation at the National Meeting of the Academy of Management, Boston, 13 August 1984; personal interview with Art Jago, one of three authors of the current version of the Normative Model, 21 July 1989.

32. J. M. Burns, *Leadership* (New York: Harper & Row, 1978).

33. B. M. Bass, D. A. Waldman, B. J. Avolio, and M. Bebb, "Transformational Leadership and the Falling Dominoes Effect," *Groups and Organizational Studies*, Vol. 12 (March 1987): 73–87.

34. B. M. Bass, "Leadership: Good, Better, Best," *Organizational Dynamics*, Vol. 13 (Winter 1985): 26 10; Bernard M. Bass, "From Transactional to Transformational Leadership: Learning to Share the Vision," *California Management Review*, Vol. 18, No. 3 (Winter 1990): 19–31.

35. J. A. Conger and R. N. Kanungo, "Toward a Behavioral Theory of Charismatic Leadership in Organizational Settings," *Academy of Management Review*, Vol. 12 (October 1987): 637–647.

36. K. Labich, "The Seven Keys to Businesss Leadership," *Fortune*, 24 October 1988, 58–66; A. McNeil, "Containing Chaos," *Canadian Business*, January 1987, 62, 64–65; M. Sashkin, "True Vision in Leadership," *Training and Development Journal*, Vol. 40 (May 1986): 8–61; N. M. Tichy and D. O. Ulrich, SMR Forum: "The Leadership Challenge—A Call for the Transformational Leader," *Sloan Management Review*, Vol. 26, No.1 (Fall 1984): 59–68.

37. B. M. Bass, B. J. Avolio, and L. Goodheim, "Biography and the Assessment of Transformational Leadership at the World-Class Level," *Journal of Management*, Vol. 13 (Spring 1987): 7–19.

38. W. Kiechel III, "Visionary Leadership and Beyond," *Fortune*, 21 July 1986, 127–128.

39. John Sedgwick, "The Life and Times of a Fast Growing CEO," *Business Month*, May 1990, 32–35, 38–39.

40. N. M. Tichy and M. A. Devanna, "The Transformational Leader," *Training and Development Journal*, Vol. 40 (July 1986): 27–32.

41. S. Kerr and J. M. Jermier, "Substitutes for Leadership," *Organizational Behavior and Human Performance*, Vol. 22 (1978) 370–387.

42. P. Howell, P. W. Dorfman, and S. Kerr, "Moderator Variables in Leadership Research," *Academy of Management Review*, Vol. 11 (January 1986): 88–102.

43. S. G. Green and T. R. Mitchell, "Attributional Processes of Leaders In Leader-Member Interactions," *Organizational Behavior and Human Performance*, Vol. 23 (1979): 429–458; J. C. McIlroy, 'A Typology of Attribution Leadership Research," *Academy of Management Review*, Vol. 7 (July 1982): 413–417; T. R. Mitchell, "Attributions and Actions," *Journal of Management*, Vol. 8 (Spring 1982): 65–74.

44. K. W. Dugan, "Ability and Effort Attributions: Do They Affect How Managers Communicate Performance Feedback Information?," *Academy of Management Journal*, Vol. 32 (March 1989): 87–114.

45. R. L. Heneman, D. B. Greenberger, and C. Anonyuo, "Attributions and Exchanges: The Effects of Interpersonal Factors on the Diagnosis of Employee Performance," *Academy of Management Journal*, Vol. 32 (June 1988): 466–476.

46. Bass, "Transformational Leadership."

CASE 12.1

What it takes to be number one: Lessons from Wal-Mart's Sam Walton

DONALD D. WHITE   *University of Arkansas*
RAGHAV SINGH   *University of Arkansas*

Yes, its true: he's the wealthiest man in America, drives a ten-year-old pickup truck to work and once bumped into one of his own eighteen-wheelers while counting the cars in a Wal-Mart parking lot. Sam Walton is a unique, hard-working CEO who was named *Forbes'* Outstanding Executive of the Decade in 1989. His achievements are no accident. They are based on hard work and complete confidence in two very important groups of people, his customers and his "associates," the people other corporate leaders call employees.

Sam Walton opened his first store in 1962. By 1989, he had built his company into a $25 billion corporate empire. Wal-Mart is the sweetheart of Wall Street: the fastest growing major retailer, it has averaged nearly 40 percent return on equity for the past ten years.

To what does Wal-Mart owe its success? Some corporate analysts focus on Walton's early idea to offer brand-name merchandise at low prices. Others emphasize his location strategy. (Most Wal-Mart stores are located in small rural communities; the average host town population is 15,000.) However, those who know and work with Sam Walton will tell you there are a few simple keys to his enormous success. They include (1) employing people who work "with," not "for," him; (2) always putting the customer first; and (3) a lot of hard work.

Walton decided from the outset that he would be a hands-on manager who could be found on the sales floor with customers and associates. He believed there was no other way for him to make the best possible business decisions than to listen to those who knew. As the number of stores in the Wal-Mart chain grew,

Walton maintained his commitment to get out among the people who represented the company to the customer every day. In fact, until recently, Sam Walton visited every store at least once a year. His typical store visit is spent with associates rather than managers. Walking through every department, he addresses associates by their first names and listens carefully to their suggestions. He tells them he will consider their ideas and often ends store visits by reviewing with the manager and others from the general office many of the suggestions he has heard. Then it's off to another store.

Today, there are over fifteen hundred stores, and annual visits to each one are no longer possible. However, a top corporate executive visits every store at least once a year. Walton was one of the first executives to embrace the concept of Management By Walking Around (MBWA) and he sees to it that every Wal-Mart executive and every manager practices MBWA daily.

Sam Walton's enthusiasm is widely shared by Wal-Mart associates. Long ago, he concluded that associates who shared in the profits and had an ownership in the company were more likely to give the kind of effort it takes to outperform the competition. All Wal-Mart associates are eligible for these benefits and they exhibit a great deal of pride when they describe "our" company.

Another important key to Sam Walton's success is his never-ending attention to the customer. How important is the customer? Walton sums up his beliefs:

> There is only one boss, and whether a person shines shoes for a living or heads up the biggest corporation in the world, the boss remains the same. It's the customer! The customer is the person who pays everyone's salary and who decides whether a business is going to succeed or fail. In fact the customer can fire everyone in

SOURCE: John Huey, "Wal-Mart: Will It Take Over The World?," *Fortune*, 30 January 1989, 52–56, 58, 61; Keith F. Girard, "Profiles in Power," *Business Month*,) *May 1989, 38.*

the company from the chairman on down, and he can do it simply by spending his money somewhere else.

Wal-Mart views its commitment to the customer as an investment. Every Wal-Mart store has a full-time "people greeter" posted at the front door to welcome each and every customer who enters. "That job," confides one store manager, "may be the most important one in the store. Our greeter is the first link in a customer service chain that involves everyone in the company."

If you want to meet Sam Walton, get up early! His day begins at the crack of dawn and often runs into the late evening. At seventy-two years of age, his energy is only exceeded by his enthusiasm and commitment to make Wal-Mart the best it can be. When he's not on the road, Walton can be found at corporate headquarters in the small town of Bentonville, Arkansas. On Saturday mornings, he is usually having a 6:30 A.M. breakfast with associates. Breakfast is followed by a 7:30 meeting attended by regional managers, district managers, general office personnel, and visiting associates. If you miss breakfast, you'll

no doubt be late for the 7:30 meeting: meetings at Wal-Mart "always" start early. On Saturday, for example, you can expect to see Walton walking up and down the runway in the corporate auditorium talking business with personnel from every area in the company at 7:15 A.M.

If he's not on the road or attending the Saturday morning meeting, you may find Walton in his modest office. (There is no "executive look" to Walton's office or the office of any other top managers at Wal-Mart.) He will probably be talking with other managers or associates about new ways to improve customer service. He'll be easy to spot: Walton will be the one with the blue and white Wal-Mart baseball cap!

Sam Walton has been described as a business genius, a tent revivalist, a P. T. Barnum, all rolled into one. He's a tough negotiator, a customer-advocate, and everyone's favorite grandfather. "The Chairman," or "Mister Sam" to his associates, is a powerful business executive whose strength and influence are rooted in basic values including a strong work ethic, a belief in people, and the desire to "do it better today than we did it yesterday!"

CASE 12.2

Dogfight at Texas Air: Leadership the Lorenzo way

DONALD D. WHITE   *University of Arkansas*
RAGHAV SINGH   *University of Arkansas*

He has been described by his employees as a person who could scare cream into butter, by union leaders

SOURCE: G. F. Scib, "Eastern Pilots, Attendants End 264-Day Strike," *Wall Street Journal*, 24 November 1989, p. A3; M. Ivey and G. DeGeorge, "Lorenzo May Land a Little Short of the Runway," *Business Week*, 5 February 1990, 46–48; G. DeGeorge, "Fancy Flying Frank—But Not Fancy Enough," *Business Week*, 7 May 1990, 38–39; P. Nulty, "America's Toughest Bosses," *Fortune*, 27 February 1989, 40–54; K. Labich, "The New Master of the Skies," *Fortune*, 5 January 1987, 72–73; J. L. Bower and M. W. Weinberg, "Statecraft, Strategy, and Corporate Leadership," *California Management Review*, Vol. 30 (Winter 1988): 39–56.

as an evil presence and a malevolent wraith, and by his peers as a loose cannon who creates as much havoc among his own people as among the competition. Whatever the description, his reputation as an outstanding taskmaster earned him a place on *Fortune Magazine's* 1989 list of the seven toughest bosses in America. He is Francisco (Frank) A. Lorenzo, chairman of the board and chief executive officer of Texas Air.

Lorenzo routinely expects his managers to work fourteen hours a day, six days a week, and to go without vacations for years. He does not tolerate mistakes or performance that fails to match his high standards and expectations. A former employee of Texas Air described what happened when he made a mistake:

> When Frank found out, he stared at me, into me, through me. He stabbed me hard in the chest with his finger and he said, "You are going to take care of this, you are going to take care of this now." I can still feel his finger hitting my breastbone. That afternoon he put his hand on my shoulder, and I knew I would make it.

There are few executives at Texas Air who have worked for Lorenzo who have not, at one time or another, incurred his wrath and been through a similar experience. Many consider Lorenzo's attitude towards his employees incredible. But is hasn't prevented him from building a small regional carrier, Texas International, into Texas Air, the parent company to Continental and Eastern airlines among others. Today, Texas Air is the nation's second-largest airline company.

Lorenzo has created two chains of command at Texas Air. One is the official hierarchy of line managers; the other is a small cadre of executives he uses for special projects and to gather information. This special team does not officially exist; yet its members are almost always involved closely with Lorenzo's major decisions. Each member has long-standing relationships with Lorenzo and he trusts them. The group consists of lawyers, former government employees, and financial specialists, and Lorenzo chose its members carefully, selecting them over career airline employees.

The group has served him well in the past. In 1983, Continental Airlines filed for bankruptcy and the right to renege on its labor contracts, claiming that labor costs could force the company to liquidate. The group effectively smashed Continental's unions by successfully orchestrating the airline's bankruptcy and brought labor costs down until they were among the lowest in the industry. Group members admit that their success was due largely to the toughness instilled in them by Lorenzo.

Those outside the cadre see it as a source of intrigue that keeps the rest of the company off-balance. Lorenzo has often used the group to undermine the power of his senior executives. He frequently assigns lower-echelon people to projects their immediate bosses are unaware of or recommends to individual members of the group that they not support the plans of their superiors. In one case, an executive in charge of purchasing new aircraft bought several planes to meet Eastern route expansion and replacement needs. He later found that his subordinate had assigned the aircraft to another of the group's airlines. When he asked the subordinate why this was done without first informing him, he was told that it hadn't been considered necessary since Lorenzo had cancelled the route expansion plans. When he checked further, he found that none of the senior executives involved in the route expansion decision knew that they had been overruled. This style has led several executives to complain that planning is almost impossible because they are uncertain whether their subordinates will carry out their plans.

Surprisingly, turnover among Texas Air executives is low, despite this extraordinary state of affairs. On the other hand, a high divorce rate is reported among the executives: they have little time left for their families. Some managers attribute their feelings of loyalty and esprit de corps to Lorenzo himself. When quizzed about their motivation, many express little concern for job security, compensation, or formal position. Instead, they describe themselves as being driven by a fascination with the complexity of the tasks assigned to them and with Lorenzo's vision. But they also admit that the unrelenting pressure and Lorenzo's tenacious, insistent ways keep them off guard and never really leave them feeling safe.

Despite his successes, man of Frank Lorenzo's peers believe that he is unable to differentiate between constructive and destructive toughness. They say that his management style provides high gains but also carries high risks. Some observers believe that those high risks may lead to insurmountable problems. Labor strife and consumer uncertainty may ultimately take its toll on Lorenzo and his organization. But for now, Frank Lorenzo's unique executive style has enabled his company to survive in a tough, deregulated industry.

EPILOGUE

On November 23, 1989, 264 days after a walkout by employees of Texas Air's subsidiary Eastern Airlines, Easten pilots and flight attendants abandoned their strike. However, the machinists who had initiated the strike vowed to stand firm and to continue pressing for their demands. The strike, while initially effective, had been unable to shut Eastern down. The airline had managed to make almost eight hundred flights a day (about 75 percent of its prestrike schedule) with twenty thousand employees (two-thirds of the prestrike total). Although the machinists' strike continued, it posed little trouble for Eastern because the airline subcontracted most of the machinists' work.

The return of Eastern employees represented a personal victory for Texas Air chairman Frank Lorenzo, who had effectively smashed the unions at Eastern, repeating his earlier victory at Continental. Some observers believe that his approach—tackling labor head-on—has been vindicated.

However, the cost of Lorenzo's war with labor has been staggering. Over the last three years, the combined losses of Eastern and Continental have totalled over $2 billion, and Eastern was forced to sell off substantial assets in order to maintain operations. And Lorenzo himself has paid a price for Eastern's problems. Shortly after the strike began, the airline filed for bankruptcy protection and reorganization. On April 16, 1990, the bankruptcy court divested Frank Lorenzo of control of Eastern's affairs and appointed a trustee to oversee the reorganization.

EXERCISE 12.1
SELECTING THE RIGHT LEADERSHIP STYLE

INTRODUCTION

The Normative Model was discussed in the preceding chapter. This exercise will give you an opportunity to apply the Normative Model in three actual situations. Using the decision tree found in Exhibit 12.12, analyze each of the cases that follow. Variation: Cases can be analyzed in a small group setting.

CASE 1

Setting: Corporate Headquarters
Your Position: Vice-President

As marketing vice-president, you frequently receive nonroutine requests from customers. One such request, from a relatively new customer, was for extended terms on a large purchase ($2,500,000) involving several of your product lines. The request is for extremely favorable terms which you would not normally consider except for the high inventory level of most product lines at the present time due to the unanticipated slack period which the company has experienced over the last six months.

You realize that the request is probably a starting point for negotiations and you have proven your abilities to negotiate the most favorable arrangements in the past. As preparation for this negotiation, you have familiarized yourself with the financial situation of the customer using various investment reports you regularly receive.

Reporting to you are four sales managers, each having responsibility for a single product line. They know of the order and, like you, believe that it is important to negotiate terms with minimum risks and maximum return to the company. They are likely to differ on what constitutes an acceptable level of risk. The two younger managers have developed a reputation of being "risk takers" whereas the two more senior managers are substantially more conservative.

CASE II

Setting: Toy Manufacturer
Your Position: Vice-President, Engineering & Design

You are a vice-president in a large toy manufacturing company with responsibilities that include the design of new products that will meet the changing demand in this uncertain and very competitive industry. Your design teams, each under the supervision of a department head, are therefore under constant pressure to produce novel, marketable ideas.

At the opposite end of the manufacturing process is the quality control department which is under the authority of the vice-president, production. When Quality Control has encountered a serious problem that may be due to design features, their staff has consulted with one or more of your department heads to obtain their recommendations for any changes in the production process. In the wake of consumer concern over the safety of children's toys, however, Quality Control responsibilities have recently been expanded to insure not only the quality but the safety of your products. The first major problem in this area has arisen. A preliminary consumer report has "blacklisted' one of your new products without giving any specific reason or justification. This has upset you and others in the organization because you believed that this product would be one of the most profitable items in the coming Christmas season.

The consumer group has provided your company the opportunity to respond to the report before it is made public. The head of Quality Control has therefore consulted with your design people, but you are told that they became somewhat defensive and dismissed the report as "over-reactive fanatic nonsense." Your people told Quality Control that, while freak accidents are always possible, the product is certainly safe as designed. They argued that the report should simply be ignored.

Since the issue is far from routine, you have decided to give it your personal attention. Because your design teams have been intimately involved in all aspects of the development of the item, you suspect that their response is itself extreme and perhaps governed more by their emotional reaction to the report than by the facts. You are not convinced that the consumer group is totally irresponsible, and you are anxious to explore the problem in detail and recommend to Quality Control any changes that may be required from a design standpoint. The firm's image as a producer of high quality toys could suffer a serious blow if the report is made public and public confidence is lost as a result.

You will have to depend heavily on the background and experience of your design departments to help you in analyzing the problem. Even though Quality Control will be responsible for the decision to implement any changes you may ultimately recommend, your own subordinates have the background of design experience that could help set standards for what is "safe" and to suggest any design modifications that would meet these criteria.

CASE III

Setting: Corporate Headquarters
Your Position: Vice-President

The sales executives in your home office spend a great deal of the time visiting regional sales offices. As marketing vice-president, you are concerned that the expenses incurred on these trips are excessive—especially now when the economic outlook seems bleak and general belt-tightening measures are being carried out in every department.

Having recently been promoted from the ranks of your subordinates, you are keenly aware of some cost-saving measures that could be introduced. You have, in fact, asked the accounting department to review a sample of past expense reports, and they have agreed with your conclusion that several highly favored travel "luxuries" could be curtailed. Your executives, for example, could restrict first-class air travel to only those occasions when economy class is unavailable, airport limousine service to hotels could be used instead of taxis where possible, etc. Even more savings could be made if your personnel carefully planned trips such that multiple purposes could be achieved where possible.

The success of any cost saving measure, however, depends on the commitment of your subordinates. You do not have the time (nor the desire) to closely review the expense reports of these executives. You suspect, though, that they do not share your concerns over the matter. Having once been in their position, you know they feel themselves deserving of travel amenities.

The problem is to determine which changes, if any, are to be made in current travel and expense account practices in the light of the new economic conditions.

POSTEXERCISE QUESTIONS

1. Was your analysis and selection of appropriate leadership styles for each case the same as others in your group? Discuss any differences that exist.
2. What do you believe are the advantages and disadvantages of using the Normative Model in an actual leadership situation?

PART II

Select a leadership situation with which you are familiar. Write a brief summary of the situation. Now, analyze the appropriate leadership style based on the decision tree (Exhibit 12.12). Discuss with your group members the situation and your basis for selecting a leadership style. Each presentation should be followed by a brief group discussion of your selection analysis.

EXERCISE 12.2
ASSESSING YOUR LEADERSHIP STYLE

Please complete the following questionnaire. For each of the following 10 pairs of statements, divide 5 points between the two according to your beliefs and perceptions of yourself, or according to which of the two statements better characterizes you. The 5 points may be divided between the A and B statements in any one of the following ways: 5A 0B, 4A 1B, 3A 2B, 2A 3b, 1A 4B, 0A 5B, but not equally (2½) between the two. Weigh your choices between the two according to which one better characterizes you or your beliefs.

1. _____ A. I believe that a leader has a primary mission of maintaining stability.

   _____ B. I believe that a leader has a primary mission of change.

2. _____ A. I believe that a leader must cause events.

   _____ B. I believe that a leader must facilitate events.

3. _____ A. I believe that leaders should be concerned that their followers are rewarded equitably for their work.

   _____ B. I believe that leaders should be concerned about what their followers want in life.

4. _____ A. I believe that leaders' primary task is to mobilize and provide focus for their followers' needs.

   _____ B. I believe that leaders' primary task is to ensure clarity of responsibilities and roles for their subordinates.

5. _____ A. A primary value I hold is honesty in all matters.

   _____ B. A primary value I hold is equal justice for all.

6. _____ A. I believe leadership to be a process of changing the conditions of people's lives.

   _____ B. I believe leadership to be a process of exchange between leader and follower.

7. _____ A. I believe that leaders should spend considerable energy in managing separate but related goals.

   _____ B. I believe that leaders should spend considerable energy in arousing hopes, expectations, and aspirations among their followers.

8. _____ A. I believe that a significant part of leadership involves playing the role of a teacher, though not in the formal classroom sense.

   _____ B. I believe that a significant part of leadership involves playing the role of a facilitator.

9. _____ A. I believe that leaders should engage with their followers at an equal level of morality.

   _____ B. I believe that leaders should represent a higher morality.

10. _____ A. I believe that what power leaders have to influence others comes primarily from their ability to get people to identify with them and their ideas.

    _____ B. I believe that what power leaders have to influence others comes primarily from their status and position.

SCORING

The questionnaire is constructed according to two types of leaders—transactional and transformational. In other words, half of the A responses represent one type and half the other; the same is true for the B alternatives. The key is as follows:

Transformatinal	**Transactional**
1. B	1. A
2. A	2. B
3. B	3. A

4.	A	4.	B
5.	B	5.	A
6.	A	6.	B
7.	B	7.	A
8.	A	8.	B
9.	B	9.	A
10.	A	10.	B

By adding your responses for each of these two columns, you can determine what relative weight you are giving to one type of leadership as compared with the other.

CHAPTER 13

FORMAL ORGANIZATION: THE CONTEXT OF ORGANIZATIONAL BEHAVIOR

LEARNING OBJECTIVES

1. To understand the purpose of formal organization.
2. To learn how traditional organizational concepts influence human behavior.
3. To examine the role of formal organization.
4. To understand the nature of contemporary organizations and the unique impact they have on organizational behavior.

CHAPTER OUTLINE

Formal Organization: Fundamental Elements
Organizational Objectives
Division of Labor
Coordination
Differentiation and Integration

Organizational Structure: Traditional Concepts
Bureaucracy
Centralization and Decentralization
Span of Management
Line and Staff Organization
Recent Changes in Traditional Organizations

Contemporary Organization Structures
Project Organization / Matrix Organization
Organic Organization / Network Organization
Contemporary Structures in Perspective

Formal Organization: Conclusions

Questions for Review and Discussion

References

Cases: 13.1 Organizations in Transition:
From Taller to Flatter Structures
13.2 The Case of Two Masters

Exercises: 13.1 Division of Work
13.2 Organizing

KEY TERMS

Formal organization	**Authority**
Organizational structure	**Centralization**
Objectives	**Decentralization**
Goal displacement	**Entrepreneur**
Action goals	**Intrapreneur**
Division of labor	**Span of management**
Departmentalization	**Project organization**
Differentiation	**Matrix organization**
Integration	**Organic organization**
Bureaucracy	**Network organization**

Bill sat at his desk wondering how such a good idea had become such a mess. Three months ago, he and two colleagues from another department had obtained a major research contract from the Department of Energy. The three had their usual frustrations with the university bureaucracy, leading one of the researchers, Donna, to comment, "I don't think anyone else at this place really cares whether we get these contracts. Between the regulations and the endless channels, it's a wonder anybody here ever gets a dime."

The group had sought help from the university research office, a department created to assist faculty trying to acquire grants and contracts. The red tape they encountered, however, sometimes made the research office seem more trouble than it was worth. The group had also been told by an interested department head that she would spearhead an attempt to obtain computer software that would greatly facilitate the project. The research office had initially been concerned because the research would require coordination of persons from more than one department. However, all involved agreed that they needed to work together and would not permit anyone's special interests to dictate the course of the research. They also decided that no one would take the title of Principal Investigator; rather, they would all be equally responsible for coordinating the project.

The team had finally obtained the university's commitment to purchase the needed computer software. However, funds allocated to acquire the software had been diverted to another project. Bill quickly discovered that the problem was greater than he had first anticipated. He approached the director of the university research office but was told that the office could be of no further assistance. To make matters worse, the department head who had agreed to help the group acquire the software had been transferred, and it appeared that her replacement would not be named for some time. Bill and the other research-team members were becoming increasingly frustrated. Donna summed up the group's feeling when she concluded, "It's our job to do the research, not to buy pencils, paperclips, and computer software! What kind of an organization is this, anyway?"

In Chapter 1, we explained that organizational behavior is concerned with human behavior in organizations. Since then, we have concentrated primarily on the behavior of individuals and groups within organizations ("micro" approach) rather than on organizations themselves ("macro" approach). But problems like those encountered by Bill's research team can often be attributed to organizational rather than individual characteristics.

This chapter focuses on the organizational context in which group and individual behaviors occur. In particular, we will examine the purpose of formal organizations, their structures, and their impact on the behavior of individuals and groups. First, we will look at the fundamental building blocks of organizations (objectives, division of labor, and coordination) and address questions concerning why and how formal organizations evolve. We will then focus on concepts—such as hierarchy, rules, centralization and decentralization, span of management, and staff versus line positions—that define the structures of most organizations. Finally, we will examine the new structures that have emerged to meet the specialized needs of organizations having unique purposes and environments.

FORMAL ORGANIZATION: FUNDAMENTAL ELEMENTS

A **formal organization** is defined as the activities of a group of individuals who are pursuing some common goal through formalized structures and processes. Traditionally, formal organizations have been characterized by their structures (the relationships between their members) and by written guidelines (rules and policies) which clarify or enlarge upon those relationships.

Organizational structure is the system of relationships through which an organization is managed. Structure facilitates the performance of work as well as the flow of information throughout the organization and accomplishes four distinct functions. It

1. divides work logically among individuals and organizational subunits (work teams, departments, etc.);
2. recombines or coordinates the activities of those units to accomplish organizational objectives;
3. distributes formal power (authority) to direct or coordinate work; and
4. establishes channels of communication.[1]

In this section, we will examine three fundamental building blocks of formal organizations: objectives, division of labor, and coordination. We will also discuss differentiation and integration, two by-products of these processes (see Exhibit 13.1).

EXHIBIT 13.1   ORGANIZATIONAL BUILDING BLOCKS

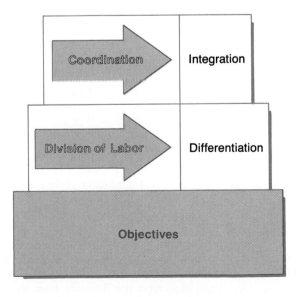

Organizational Objectives

Objectives, also referred to as goals or targets, are the specific ends an organization seeks to achieve. They should be clearly stated and communicated throughout the enterprise. Objectives provide a focal point for the activities of organizational members and shape decisions about the allocation of resources. Objectives can also be the source of conflict, however, when there are multiple objectives at the enterprise level, competition for limited resources, or differences in goal orientation, or when goal displacement exists.

Multiple objectives at the enterprise level

Organizations often pursue multiple objectives at the corporate level that appear to conflict with one another. Consider a large company whose goals are to make a profit, provide a high quality of work life for its employees, and to be a socially responsible citizen in the community. All of these goals are achievable, but the potential exists for them to interfere with one another. For instance, the plant manager would be faced with a complex decision if an employee informed him that the company had dumped untreated effluent into a nearby stream. The manager would know that local ordinances require the company to report the incident to city officials. This, in turn, might lead to a temporary shutdown of the plant while an investigation was conducted. As the manager decided what to do, he would probably wonder about the compatibility of the company's objectives concerning profitability, corporate citizenship, and treatment of employees. In addition to potentially creating confusion and inefficiencies, multiple objectives can lead to ethical dilemmas for managers. Such a situation was encountered at the Oak Ridge nuclear weapons facility and is described in the Ethical Dilemma on page 433.

Competition for limited resources

Conflict is likely to occur when subunits (e.g., departments or subdivisions) with different objectives must compete for limited resources. For example, dissension may occur when two hospital department heads both request state-of-the-art equipment upgrades when money exists to fund only one of the requests. Although departmental loyalties can bias individuals' perceptions of priorities, commonly held superordinate goals and group goal-setting meetings involving department heads and their superiors can prevent or help to resolve such competition.

Differences in goal orientation

Conflict can occur when various subunits have differing goal orientations. Members of a production department may be particularly concerned with product quality, while those in the sales force may be more interested in getting the product into the hands of waiting customers. Similarly, an industrial seller may lobby for a liberal credit policy in order to increase sales, while a company controller may oppose such a policy because she fears its impact on the firm's cash position. In both instances, the goal orientations of departments that should work closely with one another may be sufficiently different to create interdepartmental conflict.

Goal displacement

Goal displacement is the substitution of department, work group, or even individual goals for the objectives of the total enterprise. This condition can occur when an organization's official (or stated) objectives are different from those actually being

ETHICAL DILEMMA
A *Problem of*
Conflicting Objectives

The Oak Ridge nuclear weapons plant is run by the U.S. Department of Energy (D.O.E.). The D.O.E. has established stringent safety standards for such establishments to prevent potentially catastrophic mishaps from occurring. However, some older facilities, like Oak Ridge, may not conform to newly established standards and regulations.

Recently, D.O.E. was asked to investigate a report that a structural engineer was fired when he concluded that an earthquake could cause the walls of Oak Ridge to collapse. According to the engineer, pressure was then placed on other engineers to rewrite the report and to state that the walls of the plant could withstand the stress created by an earthquake. Safety modifications of the plant could cost several million dollars and would disrupt normal plant operations.

Questions

What conflicting objectives exist for managers and employees at the Oak Ridge facility?

What ethical dilemmas are created by this situation?

How should Oak Ridge's managers resolve similar dilemmas in the future?

SOURCE: Associated Press news release, 10 December 1989.

sought by individual members. Goal displacement is likely to take place when an organization's objectives are stated so vaguely that managers and other employees have difficulty responding directly to them. In such cases, **action goals** (goals established at the point of job performance) are likely to become the focus of attention for organizational members.[2]

The following example illustrates how differences in organizational units' objectives and goal displacement within those units can influence organizational behavior. MicroProc is a computer chip supplier with three product-related divisions, research and development, production, and sales. Each division operates as a stand-alone profit center (i.e., its profitability is evaluated separately from the profitability of the company as a whole).

Sales representatives submit their orders electronically; each order is evaluated by the production manager and placed into the queue according to its assigned priority. It is not unusual, however, for sales division personnel to phone production supervisors and ask that a special order be rushed or even "bumped" forward in the queue. These requests and other attempts to circumvent the scheduling system often create friction between the two divisions.

Sales personnel believe that by pressing for accelerated production schedules, they will be rewarded with future contracts from their customers. It is therefore not surprising that sales and customer service goals in the division sometimes displace corporate goals that attempt to balance the long- and short-term interests of customers and the company as a whole. Differences in stated and actual objectives should be resolved and resulting expectations clearly communicated if an organization expects its members to work toward a common purpose. Organizational effectiveness will be enhanced to the extent that organizational participants agree upon and pursue the same goals.

Division of Labor

Division of labor, also known as specialization, involves the subdivision of work into specialized operations. The purpose of division of labor is to increase the efficiency with which the total production process can be performed. For example, you may have found that preparing for final exams can be best accomplished if you organize and divide your time, effort, and resources between different classes rather than try to prepare for all your exams at once.

Division of labor is most often associated with the concept of *horizontal* job specialization (i.e., assigning an individual a small number of tasks of limited scope). Labor can also be divided *vertically* by separating a job's performance by workers from its management (i.e., scheduling, control over material flow, responsibility for insuring quality). Both horizontal and vertical division of labor are intended to create jobs that can be performed effectively and efficiently.

Although individual jobs can be divided into specific tasks, labor can also be divided at the organizational level. Division of work along organizational lines is referred to as **departmentalization** and usually involves grouping jobs according to either function, territory, product, customer, or process.

Functional departmentalization involves dividing work on the basis of the type of job performed. Most hospitals, for example, are organized by functional departments (surgery, laboratory, pharmacy, etc.). Your college or university business department is probably also organized along functional lines (accounting, finance, management, marketing, etc.). Retail distribution for Ford Motor Company is divided by *territory* on the basis of regions, districts, zones, and local dealerships, while the Honda organization consists of three major *product* divisions (automotive, motorcycles, and power products). An office supply company that markets products for commercial users through one division and retails to the general public through another division is departmentalized according to *customer*. *Process*-based departments are more likely to be found in manufacturing companies or in organizations where products or services pass through distinct steps or stages. Production at Reebok, for example, is organized around each step of the manufacturing process: raw materials receiving, tanning and dying, cutting and stamping, assembly and sewing, trimming, finishing, inspection, packaging, and shipping.

The company in Exhibit 13.2, Plastic Products, Inc., is organized differently by levels and areas. Labor is divided initially on the basis of function. Sales is departmentalized according to region and each region according to the type of customer served. Manufacturing is divided on the basis of process, while finance is organized according to function.

Division of labor enables an organization to operate more efficiently by grouping persons who have common interests and responsibilities (type of work, resource requirements, etc.). At the same time, however, workers may find themselves isolated physically and mentally from those in other departments. The result can be inadequate communication, and a tendency for the organization to operate as a group of separate *compartments* rather than as a unified whole. Therefore, once the benefits of division of labor are achieved, management attention must be focused on coordination of the enterprise as a whole.

Coordination

For the benefits of formal organization to be fully realized, the various products of divided labor units must be recombined. The second purpose of structure is to

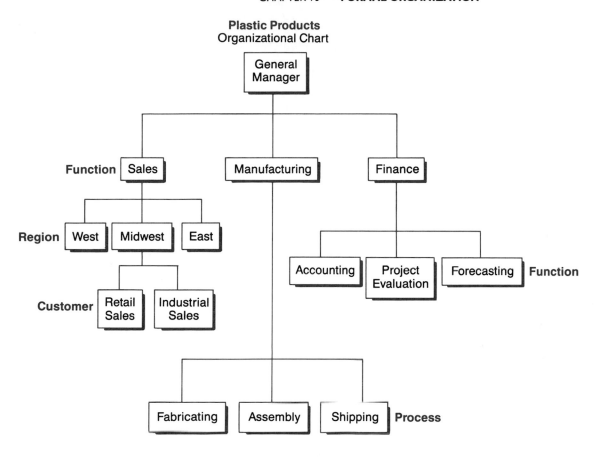

Plastic Products is organized by *function* at the division level; sales is organized by *region* and sales regions by *customer,* manufacturing by *process,* and finance by *function.*

EXHIBIT 13.2   DIFFERENT BASES FOR DIVISION OF LABOR AT PLASTIC PRODUCTS, INC.

coordinate the activities of organizational members and units. Coordination can be brought about in at least five different ways, including mutual adjustment, direct supervision, and standardization of work processes, work outputs, and worker skills.[3]

Mutual adjustment

Mutual adjustment is a process by which individuals coordinate their activities through one-to-one informal communication. This form of coordination is most likely to be found in small, simple organizations having limited division of labor. However, it may also be prevalent in organizations having highly complex structured relationships; workers may find that it is the most efficient way to achieve organizational goals. Two workers discussing how they can solve a problem concerning flow of goods from one work station to another is an example of mutual adjustment.

Direct supervision

Direct supervision occurs when one individual is responsible for directing the work of others (issuing instructions, monitoring behavior, evaluating performance, etc.).

An office manager overseeing and coordinating the activities of workers assembling multiple copies of a large report is an example of direct supervision.

Standardization of work processes

Standardization of work processes involves carefully defining the steps that must be used to perform a job. You have probably experienced work process standardization when learning how to use a new type of computer software (e.g., "Pull-down menus can be accessed by striking the ALT-M key combination; use spacebar to scroll menu items."). Work processes can also be standardized by technology designs which require that a prescribed sequence of activities be followed in order for equipment to be used.

Standardization of work outputs

When such things as product dimensions or grades or other performance criteria are specified, standardization of work outputs occurs.

Standardization of worker skills

When worker skills are standardized, individuals are given uniform training and job descriptions so that all individuals perform their jobs in the same way. This technique is used when neither standardization of inputs (or work process) nor standardization of outputs is possible. Worker skills are likely to be standardized in situations where training specifies or delimits the job-related activities of employees, as in the case of bookkeepers or machine operators.

As work becomes more complex, organizations tend to use these five coordinating mechanisms approximately in the order they are listed here. In other words, direct supervision replaces mutual adjustment, standardization of outputs replaces direct supervision, and so on. (Of course, more than one form of coordination may be used at a time.) In the *most* complex situations, however, organizations typically revert back to mutual adjustment (see Exhibit 13.3).

Differentiation and Integration

Division of labor and coordination affect the location of people and equipment and the formation of work groups. Perhaps even more important, however, they lead to the development of highly specialized ways of thinking and acting in each of an organization's various subsystems (e.g., divisions, departments, work teams). **Differentiation** is the development of these specialized patterns of thought and behavior within distinct organizational subunits. Differences that are likely to emerge between subunits include the extent to which the units (1) rely on formality; (2) show concern for work versus concern for people; and (3) value short-term versus long-term time perspectives. Subunits may also have different goal orientations.[4]

Earlier we looked at MicroProc. Each of the company's three divisions operates in a unique manner. For example, members of the production division are primarily concerned with long-term "bread and butter" contracts, and special orders are viewed as disruptions of normal activities. Important goals of the division are to control costs and meet deadlines. Sales representatives, as we saw, are less concerned with order and sometimes ask production supervisors to rush or even to bump special orders ahead in the queue. Research and development personnel approach their work in a slow and meticulous manner. In fact, salespersons often complain, "Time is critical in the industry, but it never seems to matter to the R & D group." Members

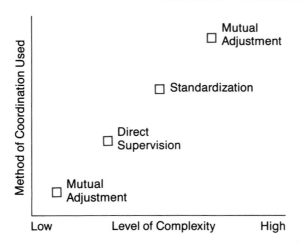

Changes in methods of coordination are required as
organizations become more complex.

EXHIBIT 13.3   METHODS OF COORDINATION

of the research group work closely with one another and go to great lengths to
maintain good personal relationships both inside and outside the laboratory. Exhibit
13.4 shows differences in orientation that exist between the three MicroProc divisions regarding formality, importance of work versus people, time perspective, and
goal orientation.

EXHIBIT 13.4   DIFFERENCES IN ORIENTATION

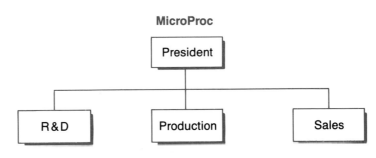

	R & D	Production	Sales
Formality	Informal, Friendly Atmosphere	Adherence to Work Rules	Flexibility
Importance of Work vs. People	Closely Knit Group Working Relationships Considered Important	Production More Important than Relationships	Strong Commitment to Achieving Goals Relationships Unimportant
Time Perspective	Very Long-Term	Long-term	Short-term
Goal Orientation	Product Development	Meeting Schedules Cost Control	Increasing Sales Providing Customer Service Timeliness

EXHIBIT 13.5   INTEGRATIVE DEVICES IN HIGH-PERFORMING ORGANIZATIONS

ENVIRONMENT	DYNAMIC[a]	STABLE[b]
Degree of Differentiation	Relatively High	Relatively Low
Integrative Devices	1. Integrative department	1. Direct managerial contact
	2. Permanent cross-functional teams	2. Managerial hierarchy
	3. Direct managerial contact	3. Paper system
	4. Managerial hierarchy	
	5. Paper system	

[a]Plastics Industry
[b]Containers Industry
Adapted from: Paul R. Lawrence and Jay W. Lorsch, *Organizational and Environment* (Boston: Division of Research, Graduate School of Business Administration, Harvard University) 138. Copyright 1967 by the President and Fellows of Harvard College.

Differentiation tends to fragment an organization and inhibit coordination. Certain structures and processes (e.g., hierarchy or integrative teams), therefore, must be used to reunify various subunits. The process of reunifying differentiated cognitive and behavioral patterns is known as **integration.** The more differentiated an organization, the greater its need for integration. Effective organizations tend to be highly integrated, although excessive integration can lead to ineffectiveness. Finally, there is a relationship between the effectiveness of integrative devices and the nature of a firm's environment (i.e., whether the environment is stable or dynamic.)[5] Exhibit 13.5 shows the integrative devices used by effective firms under different environmental conditions.

There is no one best way to integrate all organizations. Moreover, even though an organization can influence effective integration, historical conditions such as an earlier structure or other factors can also affect the cognitive and behavioral patterns of individual organizational units.[6]

ORGANIZATIONAL STRUCTURE: TRADITIONAL CONCEPTS

Organizational structure encompasses a number of different concepts. Structure defines the work to be done and the authority relationships of those responsible for accomplishing that work. In this section, we will explore a number of structural concepts beginning with the form of organization known as bureaucracy. Next, we will examine the impact of centralization and decentralization, span of management, and staff organization on traditional structures. We will conclude with a discussion of changes taking place in traditional organization structures as executives and managers prepare to meet the competitive challenges of the 1990s.

Bureaucracy

Max Weber,[7] a pioneer in the study of large, complex organizations, used the word **bureaucracy** to describe what he considered to be the ideal organizational form.

Needless to say, the term has come to mean something different to most of us today. Weber concluded that bureaucracies possessed certain characteristics which enabled them to operate efficiently, accomplish their goals, and meet the demands of their clients in a fair and equitable manner. These characteristics include hierarchy of authority, specialization, rules and regulations, and formalized impersonality. Taken together, they constitute a working definition of "bureaucracy."

Hierarchy of authority

As was indicated earlier, the distribution of authority is one of four distinct functions of organizational structure. Formal organizations normally have many separate levels. These different levels are typically identified by the titles of position holders (e.g., president, vice-presidents, division heads, department heads, and group leaders.) The legitimate power associated with such positions is known as **authority.** Authority represents only one form of power, and others such as the power derived from information and that associated with reward and punishment are discussed more fully in Chapter 11, "Power and Conflict." It is authority, however, that *formally* allows managers to require organizational members to perform certain work-related activities. In a bureaucracy, people at higher organizational levels have more authority than those below them. In the military, for example, generals have more authority than majors, majors have more authority than captains, and so on.

Specialization

Specialization, also know as division of labor, refers to the identification and delimitation of a position holder's duties and responsibilities. The purpose of specialization is to permit individuals performing various tasks and roles to attain a higher level of proficiency in their work than might be possible if they were required to do many different jobs. Specialization encourages promotion on the basis of ability rather than personal loyalty.

Rules and records

Above all else, bureaucracies are noted for their stability. An organization's ability to function over time is enhanced by a system of formal rules and records of past decisions. These rules and records are intended to answer most questions organizational members are likely to face. To assure equal treatment of clients and continuity over time, guidelines for making day-to-day decisions are found in books of regulations and files of past transactions.

Rules and records of past decisions (also known as *precedents*) serve two additional functions. First, they directly influence the way in which work is structured by indicating how, when, and where work is to be performed. Rules and precedents supplement, and in some cases, replace, direct supervision as a means of coordinating work. At Procter & Gamble, for example, rules and hierarchy are an important part of the corporate culture. Even executives must follow a strict set of rules about many company matters.[8] Second, rules and precedents impact organizational communication by reducing the need for informal communication activities.

Formalized impersonality

In theory, bureaucracies function efficiently due to their rational design. We have intentionally used the term *position holder* throughout our discussion of bureaucracy because it is to positions, not to persons, that specialized duties, responsibilities, and authority are assigned. Position holders' activities are identified by job descriptions rather than by the personal qualities that individuals bring to their positions. Such formalized impersonality is largely responsible for the label "bureaucrats" given to people who work in bureaucracies.

The rules and regulations discussed in the preceding section can contribute to or reinforce a bureaucracy's impersonality. The rules structuring behavior at Procter & Gamble, for example, led to the departure of one salesperson who complained, "My bosses told me I was using my personality too much in selling."[9]

The impact of bureaucracy

In our opening vignette, a member of the research team raised the question, "What kind of an organization is this, anyway?" The answer, of course, is a bureaucracy; and the bureaucratic regulations, red tape, and "endless channels" of this organization frustrated the group's efforts to obtain and implement their contract.

Bureaucratic organizations can affect organizational behavior both positively and negatively. Hierarchy and specialization, for example, help us to order work and clarify human relationships. Yet, specialization can also inhibit the interaction necessary to stimulate creativity, solve problems, and maintain healthy relationships. Exhibit 13.6 indicates how specialization may interfere with employee interaction. Rules and records insure that people are treated equitably and in the same manner. But is it always legitimate or beneficial that everyone be treated alike? Is some degree of individuality necessary in an organization?

Many benefits can be derived from bureaucracy, but managers must also weigh its associated costs and be prepared to modify or replace it with other arrangements when necessary. In the following sections, we will discuss modifications, such as decentralization and the addition of staff departments, that have changed the way in which traditional bureaucracies operate.

EXHIBIT 13.6

"At 4:15 we're all going berserk.
Pass it on."

Centralization and Decentralization

The term hierarchy of authority suggests that decisions are always made at the top of organizations and communicated to position holders at lower levels. The terms centralization and decentralization refer to the actual location of decision-making authority in the organization's hierarchy. **Centralization** means that decision-making power is concentrated at the top of an organization and is traditionally associated with bureaucracies. **Decentralization,** on the other hand, means that greater decision-making authority is given to persons at lower levels of the organization.

The extent to which an organization is decentralized can be measured using four standards: (1) the number of decisions made at lower levels of the hierarchy; (2) the importance of decisions made at lower levels; (3) the number of functions affected by decisions made at lower levels; and (4) the extent to which decisions made at lower levels are reviewed at upper levels.[10] An organization is therefore centralized if important decisions are made at higher levels or if decisions made by lower managers must be reviewed by their superiors before being implemented.

In large department store chains such as J.C. Penney, Sears, or Wal-Mart, store managers' decisions are generally restricted to hiring and managing personnel. Other functional decisions (type of merchandise to be carried, advertising, extension of credit, etc.) are made or controlled by managers at corporate headquarters.

By contrast, managers in a decentralized organization are given greater latitude in making important decisions and do not need to have all such decisions reviewed by superiors. Plant managers at the Firestone Tire & Rubber Company, for instance, are permitted to spend up to fifty thousand dollars to meet on-site needs such as rebuilding existing equipment, purchasing new equipment, or meeting environmental demands without obtaining specific authorization from company headquarters. Plant managers also have authority over staffing and production planning.

Centralization and decentralization are relative terms. An organization rarely concentrates all decision-making authority in either its upper- or lower-level managers. It is usually more accurate, therefore, to refer to a given organization as being *relatively* centralized or decentralized. Large United States corporations, for instance, have traditionally centralized their control functions (finance, planning, and policy making) and decentralized their operations (day-to-day production activities).[11]

Impact on behavior

The location of decision-making authority can affect managers' behavior patterns. Decentralization expands the breadth and significance of a lower manager's role by providing additional decision-making responsibilities and greater power as well as by altering interactions with superiors and subordinates. The manager's capabilities and self-esteem may grow as a result. Loss of authority resulting from recentralization, on the other hand, can damage a manager's senses of security and self-esteem. Ultimately, the impact of either centralization or decentralization on a manager's behavior depends on his personality, the support of other organizational members, and the training or preparation that the manager receives.

Neither centralization nor decentralization are dependent on the physical relationships of people or organizational units to one another. A manager can delegate authority to subordinates located outside her door as easily as to subordinates in organizational units thousands of miles away. However, one company, Kemper Corporation, underscored its desire to decentralize by purposely locating certain departments in separate, unconnected buildings. Referring to the impact of decentralization on one such unit located over thirty miles from the executive offices, Chairman Joseph Leuke observed that "a different corporate culture" exists in their work area. [12]

Decentralization and entrepreneurial spirit

Executives in a growing number of organizations are decentralizing authority and giving greater responsibility to middle- and lower-level managers in order to nurture and support corporate entrepreneurs. The term **entrepreneur** is generally reserved for those in the business world who independently develop new ideas and begin their own companies rather than those who attempt to innovate within an existing organization. The tight controls that typically exist in many centralized corporations often stifle innovation and initiative, two key entrepreneurial ingredients. Today, however, companies such as Firestone, 3M, Johnson & Johnson, and IBM are increasing decentralization in order to foster the entrepreneurial spirit within their organizations. Exhibit 13.7 lists ten "freedom factors" that facilitate "intrapreneurial" activity in an organization.

3M

The term *intrapreneur* describes those individuals who engage in entrepreneurial activities in their existing corporate jobs. An example of one successful intrapreneur is 3M's Art Fry.

Fry is the intrapreneur who invented and developed 3M's Post-it Notes. He came up with the idea as a way to keep slips of paper he used as page markers from falling out of his hymnal between church services. The slips had to be sticky on one side, but couldn't damage the hymnal pages when they were pulled off. Although some non-3Mers may have questioned his use of company resources to solve his problem (3M permits technical employees 15 percent of their time

EXHIBIT 13.7   TEN INTRAPRENEURIAL FREEDOM FACTORS

1. **Self-selection:** The organization allows intrapreneurs to appoint themselves rather than to appoint someone to implement an innovation.
2. **No handoffs:** Individuals are encouraged to see their idea through from beginning to end rather than to "hand it off" to someone else.
3. **The doer decides:** Innovators are permitted to pursue their ideas without clearing their actions with the hierarchy.
4. **Corporate slack:** Intrapreneurs are given discretionary resources.
5. **Ending the home-run philosophy:** Every idea doesn't have to be the greatest ever.
6. **Tolerance of mistakes and failure:** Taking risks is expected and encouraged; success often follows a few dead ends.
7. **Patient money:** Innovation takes time and doesn't fit neatly into organizational planning cycles.
8. **Freedom from turfiness:** New ideas often cross organizational boundaries; don't try to keep an idea within a department.
9. **Cross-functional teams:** Small teams with full responsibility for developing ideas should be permitted to form.
10. **Multiple options:** Intrapreneurs should be able to secure resources from wherever they can be located.

SOURCE: G. Pinchot III, *Intrapreneuring* (New York: Harper and Row, 1985), 198–199.

to work on their own ideas), Fry persisted until he created one of the most widely used commercial products today. Obstacles included finding the right adhesive, manufacturing personnel who told Fry it couldn't be done, and his initial inability to conceptualize the marketing opportunities and to convey his ideas to others. Nevertheless, Fry was given support and the freedom to pursue his idea by his immediate supervisor, Robert Molenda. Molenda can attest to Fry's perseverance. He once discovered Fry at a pilot plant working his fifth consecutive eight-hour shift. Fry even designed the equipment that was used to produce the pads, though that job was technically the responsibility of manufacturing engineers.[13]

3M, perhaps more than any other company, has been applauded for the entrepreneurial spirit it nurtures among its employees.[14] According to Allen Jacobson, chief executive officer of 3M, "We keep trying to reinvent ourselves."[15] Jacobson knows how important innovation and the entrepreneurial spirit are. He, like many others at 3M, is convinced that many employees are motivated not only by the immediate rewards they can achieve but also by the fact that they are in a position to create their own career opportunities.

Entrepreneurial activity at 3M is carried a step further than in many organizations in that cross-fertilization and integration of separate organizational units is strongly encouraged. Manufacturing completely unrelated products as 3M can lead to differentiation and a lack of cohesiveness. Therefore, Jacobson believes that the interchange of technology as well as ideas is critical to 3M's continued success. Other companies are following 3M's lead. John F. Akers, IBM chief executive officer, characterizes the decision to decentralize his company's operations as "perhaps as significant as any we've ever made." IBM has reorganized into five business lines whose general managers have worldwide product authority. IBM made the decision in order to make managers more entrepreneurial and more responsive to customers and to increase the sense of employee ownership of the company.

Span of Management

Many early management writers assumed that restricting the number of subordinates reporting to a manager would increase her ability to control subordinate behavior and therefore increase her effectiveness. Such an assumption, however, raises important questions. How many people can a manager coordinate? What effect do too many or too few subordinates have on the manager-subordinate relationship? These questions relate directly to the concept of span of management. **Span of management,** also known as span of control, refers to the number of subordinates (or activities) that one person can effectively manage.

Your professor, for example, may believe that a class of ten is an ideal size. He can spend more time with each student, have fewer papers to grade, and be more flexible in administering the class than if he has a larger enrollment. Similarly, a manager may feel that she is able to do a better job with three or four subordinates than with fifteen or twenty people reporting to her. A manager who effectively manages few subordinates or activities is said to have a *narrow span of management;* a manager who effectively manages a larger number of subordinates or activities is said to have a *wide span of management.*

The size of a manager's span of management depends on a number of factors including the manager's individual characteristics and leadership style, the persons being supervised, the location of those being supervised, and the type of work being performed. Some managers may be unable to coordinate large numbers of people or activities, while others may have little or no difficulty doing so in the same situation. Subordinates can also influence the span of control. Some may require more supervision than others. New trainees, for example, may desire to have a supervisor close at hand, while experienced workers or individuals who prefer to work independently may find that the close supervision often associated with narrow spans of management is oppressive and stifles their creativity.

Location of subordinates or activities is yet another important consideration. It is usually easier, and often more efficient, to have a wide span of management when workers are centrally located than when they are geographically dispersed. Finally, the type of work performed may also influence the management span. Many employees performing relatively simple tasks can be supervised by a single manager. More complex assignments, however, such as those performed by project engineers, may require much narrower spans of management.

Span of management directly affects the number of persons or activities to be coordinated (e.g., a wide span with fifty subordinates requires more coordination than a narrow span with six subordinates) and indirectly affects the number of levels in an organization. Thus, narrower spans tend to result in *tall* organizations having more levels, while wide spans result in *flat* organizations having fewer levels (see Exhibit 13.8).

EXHIBIT 13.8   TALL AND FLAT STRUCTURES

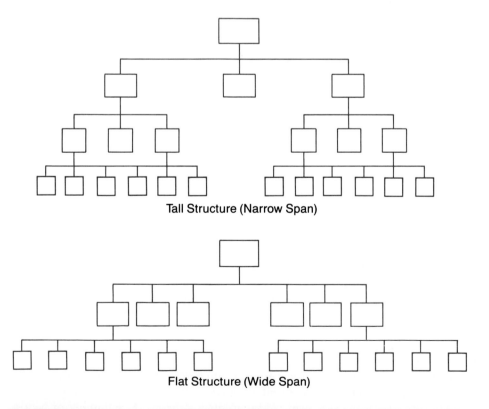

Tall Structure (Narrow Span)

Flat Structure (Wide Span)

Narrow spans of management result in tall structures, while wide spans reduce the number of organizational levels and result in flat structures.

Lower-level managers in a tall structure may feel isolated from the people and decisions made at the top. Their counterparts in flatter structures may feel more comfortable taking a problem "upstairs" because fewer levels of management exist between them and the top. Flat organizations also tend to place top management in closer contact with first-line personnel and customers.

Line and Staff Organization

The terms *line* and *staff* refer to two types of organizational positions. A position's relationship to organizational objectives and its accompanying authority determines whether it is a line or a staff position. Line managers, such as supervisors in manufacturing plants or sales managers in insurance companies, for instance, are directly accountable for accomplishing organizational objectives and have the authority to make decisions that influence the behavior of other organizational members. Staff personnel, such as records managers, market researchers, personnel managers, and information systems specialists, on the other hand, are responsible for supporting and facilitating the work of line managers by providing information, assistance, and advice.

Staff managers' authority is restricted to their own departments and cannot normally be exercised in the line organization. Only in limited instances (e.g., quality control) and functions (e.g., financial or legal) do staff managers exercise control over line operations. In actuality, however, staff personnel may have considerable implied or implicit authority in an organization's everyday life. Such authority may result from their location in the organization (often reporting directly to a key line manager) or from the special status their educations afford them. (Staff members, whose positions frequently require specialized knowledge, often have advanced degrees, licenses, and professional status.)

Line and staff organizations represent a fundamental departure from the traditional bureaucratic concept of authority. Reallocation of authority, whether real or perceived, resulting from the creation of staff positions can lead to both interpersonal and interdepartmental conflict. An incident in a state department of mental health illustrates this problem. The director, Gail McGhee, hired a staff assistant (see Exhibit 13.9) to gather information and prepare special reports required by various legislative committees. The assistant, Mark Langley, was given a small office adjoining McGhee's. He was efficient and quick to try to please the director. Langley sat close to McGhee during meetings and sometimes used the conference table in her office when she was out of town. Some of the facility managers were unhappy about the influence they believed Langley had with the Director. One manager commented, "McGhee tends to take whatever Langley says as gospel; I think she's forgotten that we know more about our own operations than he does."

The problem became even more acute when Langley sent all facility managers a letter requesting their presence at a Monday morning meeting and told them to prepare and bring with them certain statistics concerning their facility operations. One senior manager penned her reply on the bottom of Langley's memo and returned it to him. The reply read, "Gathering this material is not a high priority for me. As for the meeting, if it's important, please tell Director McGhee to let me know." The facility managers not only perceived Langley to have undue influence with the director, but also believed that he was exercising authority he did not have.

Line-staff conflict can also be either a function of differences in perspectives held by line and staff managers or a result of the unique output pressures placed upon each of them. For example, line managers tend to react directly to the demands of

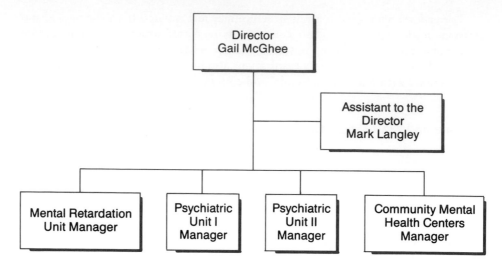

EXHIBIT 13.9   DEPARTMENT OF MENTAL HEALTH ORGANIZATIONAL CHART

the marketplace; staff managers are more apt to be concerned with what is professionally or technically correct. Recall that the research team described at the beginning of this chapter found the university's research office, a staff department, a source of red tape rather than of help. Other factors that may create line-staff friction include differences in educational backgrounds, differences in working conditions, and poorly defined roles (i.e., duties, responsibilities, and authority).

Recent Changes in Traditional Organizations

Although decisions about structure should be made consciously, many organizations have realized that they have grown randomly rather than by design. This discovery and concurrent pressures to reduce costs in the face of severe competition are leading many companies to restructure dramatically. Layers of line managers and many staff departments are being stripped away, leaving leaner, flatter organizations. DuPont has eliminated fifteen percent of its middle managers and Mobil seventeen percent, and General Electric's Medical Systems Group has stripped away thirty-five percent of its management group.[16]

Such changes have had important effects on those managers who have been dismissed, those who have been relocated, and those who as yet remain untouched.[17] The immediate impact of these structural changes is to alter the nature of individual managers' jobs. Those moving to new positions must learn new jobs and orient themselves to different ways of thinking about goals, values, and methods. Work loads are often increased for those who remain in their present positions. Many of those responsible for managing wider spans enjoy the new challenges they encounter, but others report feeling overworked and under greater stress. Some managers who are moved to higher levels in organizations take on more meaningful and exciting jobs. Others, however, find themselves back in the field selling or on the plant floor doing more "hands-on" work. The relocation of managers to both higher and lower levels has resulted in the transformation of some organizations' structures from the traditional pyramid into the "hourglass" structure shown in Exhibit 13.10.

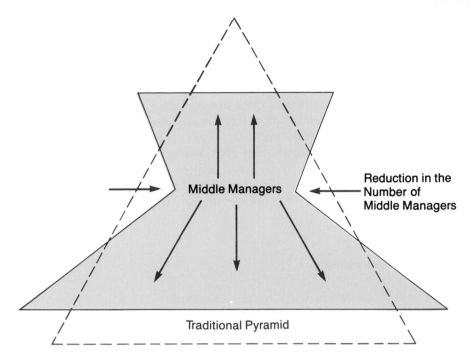

Reduction in the
Number of
Middle Managers

Middle Managers

Traditional Pyramid

Reduction in the number of middle managers and the reassignment of remaining middle managers may transform the traditional pyramid into an "hourglass" structure.

EXHIBIT 13.10   REDUCTION IN THE NUMBER OF MIDDLE MANAGERS

CONTEMPORARY ORGANIZATIONAL STRUCTURES

Decentralization of decision-making authority and the widespread use of staff departments has changed the face of traditional bureaucracies. Yet some authorities believe that no form of bureaucracy can survive the conditions facing organizations today. Bureaucracy, they conclude, fails to provide for human needs, hinders interpersonal relations, and cannot adapt to environments undergoing rapid change. While such concerns may be exaggerated, some structures having rigid and narrowly defined work roles are giving way to structures having more loosely defined jobs and more complex patterns of communication.

Earlier, we suggested that organizations can be departmentalized in a variety of ways. For example, many organizations are departmentalized around major *functional* activities such as production, marketing, and finance. Such a design strategy is intended to take advantage of a division of labor which groups tasks naturally around the type of work (of function) performed. This structure benefits by (1) grouping specialists; (2) clarifying career paths; and (3) increasing coordination and control.[18] However, internal coordination becomes increasingly difficult as an organization grows or as it adopts more complex business strategies. This is particularly true when a firm wishes to explore existing areas for growth or to move rapidly into new markets.

An alternative to the *functional* structure is the *product* structure, in which personnel are organized around a particular product or service to be delivered rather than around specialized functions. Larger companies often select product structures as a means of overcoming the coordination problems mentioned above. Functional capabilities are either provided to each product division by centralized staff departments or exist within each division. Centralized staff departments can provide product divisions with necessary support, but staff members of such departments usually lack line authority. Decentralization of functional activities, on the other hand, places specialists in the chain of command, but can also result in duplication of personnel throughout the organization.

Certain contemporary structures can help overcome some of these problems associated with functional and product organizations. These structures are more responsive to dynamic environments and to internal pressures from organizational members. We will now examine four such structures, *project, matrix, organic,* and *network* organizations.

Project Organization

Let us look at a situation in which a project organization might be appropriate. Ted Zachary was planning to diversify his electronics firm. The company had experienced considerable success in the home electronics market, but competition from abroad and declining sales were expected to reduce Ted's profit margins in the future. In response, Ted had recently hired two medical engineers to investigate the possibility of entering the rapidly growing field of biomedicine. At first, Ted was content to let the engineers brainstorm about how involvement in biomedicine might contribute to the firm's future. It was evident, however, that the engineers' lack of knowledge about basic business practices (i.e., manufacturing, marketing, and financing) was leading them to consider many impractical ideas.

The obvious answer, it seemed to Ted, was to form a committee composed of two engineers and representatives from each of the company's functional departments. Unfortunately, this plan encountered problems when put into action. Members of each department accused the others of not understanding the situation. At one point, the group agreed to go through the steps of developing an actual product. However, cooperation problems seemed to escalate; most meetings ended with committee members stating that they did not have the authority to commit their department to a decision or that they would have to get advice from "upstairs."

Forming a project group might have minimized some of the problems the committee encountered. A **project organization** is an organizational unit formed to accomplish a specific goal, such as the design or development of a product or service, or the production of a limited quantity of a product, or to perform a function for a limited time. These units, unlike traditional departments, are made up of members representing a number of functional or technical areas. They are concerned with highly specific tasks or goals and are usually disbanded upon completion of their intended task.

The necessary resources to accomplish a project are usually found in functional departments within the firm, although some resources may also be obtained from outside consultants or subcontractors. Authority for coordinating the efforts of all contributors resides with a single individual, the project manager (PM). The project manager is responsible for administrative matters, but authority to resolve technical matters remains with appropriate functional departments. Specialists under the PM's direction retain their association with colleagues and functional managers in their original departments. This dual authority structure, in which project group members are responsible to two or more superiors, is an important difference between traditional line-and-staff and project organizations.

Project structures vary widely in terms of the resources the PM controls. A project manager may be given little more than a desk and a promise of cooperation from other units (e.g., functional departments) in the organization (see Exhibit 13.11). In such cases, she must rely extensively on negotiating skills to secure necessary resources and accomplish project goals. In other instances, limited staff or even line support may be dedicated to the project, and some personnel may be physically relocated to work more closely together. The project manager may even be provided with all personnel needed to complete the project (aggregate project organization, see Exhibit 13.12).

Let us look at how a project organization might evolve and be used in a small college of business administration. The college is organized traditionally according to function (accounting, economics, finance, management, and marketing). The Dean wishes to increase the international orientation of the school but has neither the existing expertise nor the resources to do so in every department. His first step is to formally designate an international coordinator, whose responsibilities include identifying and reporting on curriculum and resource needs (simple project organization). The coordinator (project manager) works informally with faculty representatives from existing departments in order to accomplish the Dean's original goals. She has no authority over departmental representatives and relies, instead, on interpersonal skills to facilitate project activities.

Demonstrating further support for the internationalization effort, the Dean and the coordinator establish an International Business Group (IBG) consisting of faculty from each department (aggregate project organization); the international coordinator formally becomes the head of that group. The IBG is responsible for developing the college's international program, advancing international research, and teaching classes in various areas of international business (international marketing, international finance, etc.). All faculty members will continue to be members of their parent departments. They will rely on earlier training in their original disciplines and will continue to function as professors in those areas. All members of the IBG will report both to the IBG coordinator and to their functional department heads.

EXHIBIT 13.11   SIMPLE PROJECT ORGANIZATION

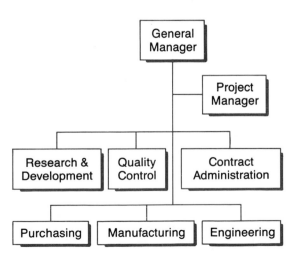

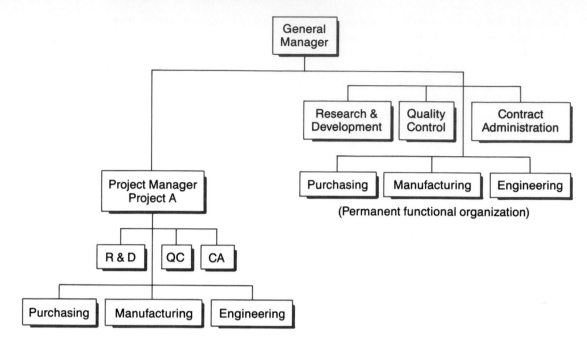

EXHIBIT 13.12   AGGREGATE PROJECT ORGANIZATION

When the Dean determines that the project group has met its original goals, he may make any of three decisions concerning its future: (1) The IBG may be disbanded, with group members returning to their respective departments; (2) the group may be designated an independent department comparable to those in the other functional areas; or (3) the group may function indefinitely as a project organization. Exhibit 13.13 shows how the college structure has evolved through the various project stages.

Project organization results in the decentralization of decision making to the project level. Even so, top management may find it easier to monitor and control projects because the concentration of authority for project-related tasks is placed in the hands of a single project manager.[19]

Project organizations have several advantages over traditional organizations. First, the structure decentralizes decision making and facilitates horizontal coordination. This, in turn, enables the organization to adapt more rapidly to environmental pressures.[20] Second, the interfunctional nature of the project organization provides an excellent opportunity for personnel from individual departments to broaden their exposure to a variety of activities that are normally assigned to other departments. Third, the relatively small size of project groups facilitates communication between individuals having different backgrounds and perspectives.

Although many benefits can be derived from project organizations, the structure can also create certain management problems. For example, the dependence of project managers on other departments or individuals over whom they have no direct authority may lead to confusion. Because of the dual lines of authority, conflicts may arise about goal priority (project versus functional).

Even the termination of a project can lead to problems for former project members. Project groups are generally created to address problems of particular importance to the organization. Therefore, group members are likely to receive privileges such as new equipment, access to restricted information, and more flexible budgets. Re-

Original College Structure

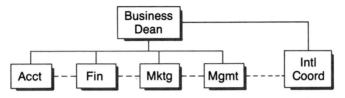

Step 1:
Project Manager

Step 2:
Fully Developed Project Group

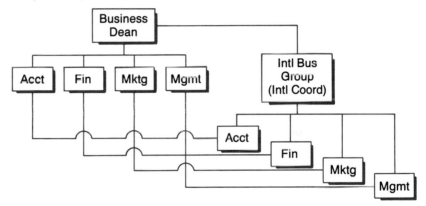

When an adequate level of international integration has been achieved for the faculty and curriculum, the project may be disbanded or an international department may be created.

EXHIBIT 13.13   USING A PROJECT STRUCTURE TO INTERNATIONALIZE A
SMALL COLLEGE OF BUSINESS

turning to original departments once the project group has disbanded can lead to frustration and impatience for the returning employees as well as for their old co-workers. Moreover, changes that have taken place in the functional department (e.g., personnel and programs) while employees were assigned to the project team can cause employees to feel "out of the mainstream" once they return.

Matrix Organization

A project structure enables an organization to increase coordination at the task level and to meet changes in a dynamic environment more efficiently. A matrix organization may be chosen by organizations that require similar coordination and flexibility throughout the enterprise.

A **matrix organization** exists when a functional structure is *overlaid* on a product structure creating a *matrix* of relationships (see Exhibit 13.14). Permanent functional departments are maintained; however, *all* operations are conducted through individual project organizations. Combinations such as product-territory, function-territory, or program-function may constitute the matrix dimensions.[21] Both functional and project managers have line authority in their respective areas of expertise, and middle managers report through both lines of authority. In effect, project groups exist *throughout* the organization.

In a stable matrix (permanent form), project units are responsible for long-term goals; such a structure is used at General Electric and IT&T. In a more flexible structure (shifting form), project goals are short-term and the structure changes once the project is completed. The shifting matrix is used by NASA.

Any of three conditions may call for adoption of a matrix structure. First, external pressures may require a structure in which two or more orientations (e.g., product and function) receive equal attention. In matrix organizations, neither project managers nor functional managers have sole authority for the end-product. Rather, authority is jointly exercised by both managers. For example, a human services organization may need to establish "state of the art" services in areas such as rehabilitation, social work, and psychological programs while keeping in touch with the needs of its various constituencies, including local governments and specific user groups. A psychologist and an agency administrator may therefore share authority to make important project-related decisions.

Second, large amounts of information from more than one source may need to be processed simultaneously. In our human services example, for instance, managers in the field need to be aware of both the organization's resource capabilities and different client groups' constantly changing demands for services. A matrix structure can help the organization cope with the magnitude and complexity of these infor-

EXHIBIT 13.14   MATRIX ORGANIZATION

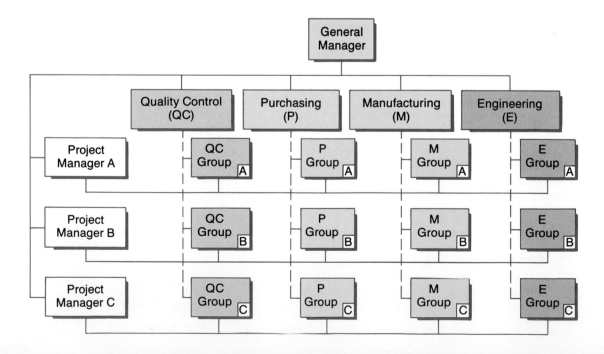

mation needs by creating an environment in which project managers and functional specialists work closely together and share responsibility for important decisions.

Third, in many organizations, pressure exists for shared resources. Shifting personnel from one project to another may be necessary if a limited number of specialists are available or if project demands are not sufficient to require the full-time services of a particular specialist.

Many organizations have attempted to implement matrix organization structures. NASA, TRW Systems Group, Liberty Mutual Insurance, and Pirelli, S.A. have all benefited from the matrix. Other organizations have not been so successful. Executives at Citibank found that the matrix led to confusion and excessive conflict between decision makers. And the Holland-based multinational, Philips Gloeilampenfabrieken, concluded that the matrix stifled entrepreneurship. Both companies discontinued use of the structure.[22]

Matrix-related problems

Failures like these demonstrate that managers should be aware of the disadvantages as well as the advantages of matrix organizations.[23] For example, managers of individual projects within a matrix organization must manage project resources (people, material, information, etc.) as well as project interfaces (relationships with other departments, outside contractors, and existing organizational systems). The number and complexity of demands on the manager and other group members can lead to higher levels of stress and conflict than in traditional line organizations.

Another frequent problem is that functional specialists often have insufficient input into project plans and so may not adequately understand the project or its significance. As a result, they often lack necessary commitment to it. Involving functional managers during planning and during early negotiation for functional resources are two ways to help alleviate this problem. Exhibit 13.15 outlines other problems and solutions associated with matrix organizations.

The matrix organization has been heralded by some management authorities as the organization of the future. As noted, however, it can be plagued by a variety of management and interpersonal problems, including power struggles, feeling of insecurity, and conflict. These difficulties can lead to high levels of stress as well as over-involvement in group and committee meetings, excessive overhead due to dual staffing of management positions, and unnecessary complexity.[24]

In one recent study, a matrix structure introduced in a major aircraft manufacturing firm had unanticipated consequences for the company. Originally, it had been expected that the matrix would improve the quality of communication in the organization, although greater volume of communication and increased role conflict were also anticipated. However, the matrix had little impact on the behavioral patterns of organizational members. Neither quantity of communication nor role conflict increased. Likewise, anticipated improvements in the quality of communication did not occur. The study's findings seem to show that the full impact of matrix organization will only be realized when the matrix has matured and behavioral changes accompanying the formal restructuring have taken place.[25]

Organizations that evolve toward a matrix structure appear to pass through an early matrix phase before actually obtaining full matrix stature.[26] During this phase, the organization acquires the structural appearance of the matrix but lacks the behavioral sophistication necessary to function smoothly. Support systems such as dual evaluation and reward systems, dual accounting and control systems, team building, and role reassessment are formalized. However, the transition from early matrix to mature matrix requires changes that are more behavioral than structural.

Processes and behaviors that are put in place under the "early matrix" form reach maturity in the true matrix structure. In essence, a true matrix is reached

EXHIBIT 13.15　MATRIX PROBLEMS AND MANAGEMENT ANSWERS

PROBLEM	SOLUTION
Tendencies toward anarchy due to dual lines of authority.	Explicitly define all relationships; don't rely too heavily on the "informal organization."
Power struggles due to dual command structure.	Educate managers and facilitate win–win conflict solution.
Groupitis: too much reliance on group decision making.	Identify when and where group decisions are important, as well as when they are not.
Excessive overhead due to excess management staffing.	Share human resources: assign individuals to more than one project or function when merited.
Navel gazing: overconcern with maintaining relationships within the matrix.	Diminish other problems to lessen the likelihood of internal conflict.
Decision strangulation: too much negotiation; not enough action.	Delegate authority; do not allow individual managers to impede the decision process.

Adapted from: Stanley M. Davis and Paul R. Lawrence, "Problems of Matrix Organizations," *Harvard Business Review*, Vol. 56 (May/June 1978): 131–142.

when "matrix behaviors" such as high flexibility and adaptability, intensive boundary transactions, resource sharing and multiple team memberships, and proactive rather than reactive management behavior become accepted ways of organizational life. Research findings support the position that an effective matrix structure depends on the presence of support systems that facilitate these behaviors.

The International Dimension on the facing page provides further evidence of the importance of matrix organizations to companies that pursue international strategies.

NCR CORPORATION

The matrix structure is normally used at the corporate level. However, Giuseppe Bassani, vice-president for stakeholder relations at NCR Corporation, decided that the matrix would be especially appropriate within his division. Bassani echoes CEO Charles E. Exley, Jr., when he says that NCR has always been stakeholder oriented, and the structure he has adopted reflects that orientation. The division is structured with stakeholder-oriented departments (employee relations, customer relations, supplier relations, community relations, government relations, and shareholder relations) on one axis and media and communications activities (public relations, audio-visual, editorial services, advertising and marketing communications, and information systems and services) on the other axis. According to Bassani, "The matrix structure facilitates the interaction needed for the development and interchange of ideas."[27]

Organic Organization

Contemporary organizational structures are characterized by their tendency to be more flexible than traditional structures. The most flexible of all such structures

INTERNATIONAL DIMENSION
Is *There a Matrix in Your International Future?*

Matrix organizations emerged during the 1970s and began to achieve a faddish popularity in corporations throughout North America by the early 1980s. Since then, however, the number of companies adopting the matrix has dropped and an increasing number of firms have turned away from the structure. Explanations are numerous, but most center on many organizations' inability to make the necessary transitions in ways of thinking and failure to create the support system necessary to insure the matrix's success.

Now, however, there are indications that the matrix may be the structure best adapted to the needs of tomorrow's large multinational companies (MNCs). Conflicting demands by executives for greater central control and by host countries for local decision-making authority may call for a form of global matrix organization. While the matrix has already become the structure of choice for some MNCs, David Cleland, an authority on matrix organizations, has concluded that managers in the parent hierarchy may experience a "culture shock" when required to share decision making with other, "in-country" managers.

Questions

Why might a matrix organization be more appropriate than a traditional line and staff structure for international operations?

How might the use of a matrix structure lead to problems in international operations?

SOURCE: J. R. Galbraith and R. K. Kazanjian, "Organizing to Implement Strategies of Diversity and Globalization: The Role of Matrix Designs," *Human Resource Management*, Vol. 25 (1986): 37–54; D. I. Cleland, "Matrix Management: A Kaleidoscope of Organizational Systems," *Management Review*, Vol. 70 (1981): 48–56.

is the organic organization. The **organic organization** is an adaptive, rapidly changing, temporary system organized around problems to be solved by groups of relative strangers representing diverse professional skills.[28] It can be viewed as a *structureless* structure. Such organizations are termed organic because they continually adapt themselves on the basis of needed functional inputs rather than stabilize along traditional bureaucratic lines of authority. Like project organizations, their lifespan is usually short; they are "temporary systems used to achieve a limited agenda."[29] The university research team described in this chapter's opening vignette is an example of an organic organization.

Consider the operation of Management Systems, Inc. (MSI), a small management consulting firm. Each member of the company possesses a particular area of expertise, such as accounting, data processing, marketing, finance, and human resources. Each person is actively involved in a number of outside projects and any member of the firm can be approached by potential clients. Jane Goodson, whose expertise is in the area of management information systems, was approached by a client interested in developing a career-tracking system for a multi-plant manufacturing firm. Jane believed that the consulting group could provide the system requested; however, she knew the project required other specialists with skills in the areas of human resources and long-range planning. The structure of the project-group organization was molded from the functional areas within MSI to fit the problem.

The organization's structure continued to change as the solution was found and implemented. Additional staff joined the group, including individuals with knowledge similar to current members' (e.g., another planner) and professionals who possessed unique skills required for the project (e.g., interviewers and programmers). On the other hand, as the need for certain types of knowledge and skills decreased, some organizational members left the group. In fact, the human resources specialist ultimately oversaw the implementation of the new system and was responsible for bringing closure to the consultant-client arrangement. Jane, who served as the original liaison with the client, had already left the group to work on a new project.

Organic organizations avoid sharp divisions of labor, unit differentiation, and highly formalized behaviors. Members act in an integrated manner, sharing both knowledge and resources. The ability and information possessed by organizational participants are the fabric from which new information is created and problem solutions are derived. However, the ability of the group to function effectively depends primarily on the interpersonal skills and mutual adjustment of group members.

Although it is difficult to envision a large enterprise being organized on an organic basis, smaller units such as research and development teams, planning departments, and internal consulting groups frequently operate in this manner. The idea of a highly flexible organization that is able to adapt rapidly to changing environmental demands remains an attractive one to large organizations and has given rise to the latest in the line of contemporary structures, the network organization.

Network Organization

Global and other international corporate strategies have created new demands on corporate structures. Legal and regulatory requirements of host governments concerning the establishment and local control of joint ventures and other consortia vary by industry and by country. The scale and complexity of such relationships present new management problems and require a highly flexible structure through which corporate-wide goals can be attained.

The network organization offers one answer to these problems. A **network organization** is a matrix that extends beyond traditional organizational boundaries.[30] The matrix links different companies to one another in temporary joint undertakings and other contractual relationships. These highly flexible "multi-company" companies have a number of unique characteristics. For example, network organizations lack a "senior tie-breaker" to resolve disputes between organizational units. Thus, certain matrix skills, such as negotiating and developing a proactive dual orientation (e.g., to product and country) are critical to the network organization. Another important aspect of the network organization is its willingness (and need) to expand and cut back in response to changing internal and external conditions. Network organizations, for example, are likely to go "outside" for expertise rather than to retain permanently all of the personnel necessary to solve future problems. Under such an arrangement, organizational design is no longer dependent on geographic or other physical arrangements. Information technology has largely altered organizational structures by facilitating information gathering, decision making, and communication in large, complex corporations.

Network organizations are not unique to international ventures. Similar situations face hospital managers whose administrative responsibilities are complicated by the need for coordination of independent physicians and laboratories. Likewise, general contractors, who rely on a wide range of subcontractors, also find themselves managing formal relationships over which they lack complete control.[31] Such arrangements present special challenges and further emphasized the importance for managers of using interpersonal skills effectively.

Contemporary Structures in Perspective

The contemporary structures we have examined in this section are distinctly different from traditional line and staff organizations. They are characterized to varying degrees by organizational instability and uncertainty, which bureaucratic organizations are designed to minimize. The structural ambiguity, relative power relationships, and confusion about communication and decision making that are often found in contemporary structures can become fertile ground for interpersonal differences. Solutions to such problems often lie in mutual adjustment and increased reliance on interpersonal skills and integrative devices rather than in direct supervision, standardization, and other types of formalized control.

Contemporary organizations present unique managerial problems. Nevertheless, the desire of and the need for organizations to provide enriched jobs and rapid, innovative responses to environmental change continue to lead an increasing number of organizations toward project, matrix, organic, and network structures.

FORMAL ORGANIZATION: CONCLUSIONS

Managers sometimes believe they are solely responsible for the behaviors of their subordinates. However, as we have seen throughout this book, many factors, such as individual characteristics and group pressures, may also influence behavior. Formal organizations themselves can also facilitate as well as impede organizational cooperation.

In an attempt to secure greater economies through division of labor, managers may unknowingly contribute to organizational conflict. Conflict can occur when individuals or departments form different perceptions concerning people and work, the importance of following rules, and even how they view the organization's purpose. Reintegrating these "specialized" groups is therefore also an important managerial activity.

Traditionally, managers have relied on bureaucratic solutions to organizational problems. Clear, descending lines of authority, specialization, rules, and impersonality are adopted to bring order to the enterprise. Overreliance on bureaucracy, however, can cause an organization to become sluggish and to fail to capitalize on the talents of its human resources. Such modifications as decentralization and the use of staff organizations have helped to overcome some of the problems of growing companies. However, recent changes brought on by rapidly changing technology and global competition have resulted in further restructuring of traditional organizations and the emergence of relatively new organizational forms such as project, matrix, organic, and most recently, network organizations. These new structures represent a dramatic departure from traditional structures and have substantially altered formal relationships for many managers.

Project, matrix, organic, and network structures can present unique problems. The potential for conflict, confusion, and personal stress is high in some cases. As a result, managers must increasingly rely on understanding and careful management of individual and organizational behavior. No one structure, either traditional or contemporary, is appropriate for every organization. Therefore, managers must carefully evaluate environmental demands and understand individual employees before selecting the *best* structure for a company or organizational unit.[32]

Remember, organizations exist to unify human activities so that goals can be efficiently attained. Managing complex organizational relationships requires an understanding of both formal organization and the impact of various structures on human behavior. It is the formal organization, its goals and its structure, that is the *context* in which organizational behavior takes place.

QUESTIONS FOR REVIEW AND DISCUSSION

1. What is meant by the terms *horizontal* and *vertical division of labor*? Give examples of each.
2. List and define five ways in which organizations coordinate work. Give an example of each.
3. What is the relationship between differentiation and integration in an organization?
4. What is likely to be the consequence when an organization's stated objectives and actual objectives are different?
5. To what do the terms *centralization* and *decentralization* refer? What are the managerial implications for each condition?
6. What is meant by the term *intrapreneur*? What dimensions do intrapreneurs add to a decentralized organization?
7. In what ways does a project organization differ from the more traditional line and staff organization?
8. What types of problems are likely to arise in a matrix organization? Why do some companies adopt a matrix structure despite the apparent hazards?
9. What have been the organizational and human impacts of the recent restructuring of many large organizations?
10. Is there a *best* structure? Explain your answer.

REFERENCES

1. J. R. Galbraith and D. A. Nathanson, *Strategy Implementation: The Role of Structure and Process* (St. Paul: West Publishing Company, 1978), 5; H. Mintzberg, *Structure in Fives* (Englewood Cliffs: Prentice-Hall, 1983), 2.
2. W. K. Warner and A. E. Havens, "Goal Displacement and the Intangibility of Organizational Goals," *Administrative Science Quarterly*, Vol. 12, No. 4 (March 1968): 539–555.
3. H. Mintzberg, *The Structuring of Organizations* (Englewod Cliffs, N.J.: Prentice-Hall, 1979), 3–8.
4. P. R. Lawrence and J. W. Lorsch, *Organization and Environment: Managing Differentiation and Integration* (Boston: Division of Research, Graduate School of Business Administration, Harvard University, 1967), 9–11.
5. P. R. Lawrence and J. W. Lorsch, "Differentiation and Integration," *Administrative Science Quarterly*, Vol. 12 (1967): 1–47.
6. R. H. Hall, "Review of Organization and Environment: Managing Differentiation and Integration," *Administrative Science Quarterly*, Vol. 13 (1968): 180–186.

7. M. Weber, *The Theory of Social and Economic Organizations*, trans. A. Henderson and Talcott Parsons (New York: Oxford University Press, 1947).
8. A. Swasy, "In a Fast-Paced World, Procter & Gamble Sets Its Store in Old Values," *Wall Street Journal*, 21 September 1989, 1, X.
9. Ibid.
10. E. Dale, "Planning and Developing the Company Organization Structure," *American Management Association Research Report*, Vol. 20 (1952): 118.
11. A. Chandler, *Strategy and Structure* (Cambridge, Mass.: The MIT Press, 1962), 13–14.
12. J. M. Laderman, "The Loose-Reins Approach Pays Off for Kemper," *Business Week*, 8 September 1986, 78, 79.
13. G. Pinchot III, *Intrapreneuring* (New York: Harper and Row, 1985), 198, 199; R. E. Levinson, "Why Decentralize?" *Management Review*, Vol. 10 (October 1985). 50–53; L. Baum, "Delegating Your Way to Job Survival," *Business Week*, 2 November 1987, 206.
14. Pinchot, 137–139.
15. "Inside Business," Cable News Network, 4 June 1989.
16. J. Byrne, "Caught in the Middle," *Business Week*, 12

September 1988, 80–85, 88; J. Main, "The Winning Organization," *Fortune*, 26 September 1988, 50–52, 56, 60.

17. Byrne, op. cit.; J. Spackey, "The Ripping of Mid-Managers," *Newsweek* 18 April 1988, 10.

18. J. H. Jackson and C. P. Morgan, *Organization Theory*, 2nd ed., (Englewood Cliffs, N.J.: Prentice-Hall, 1982), 125, 126.

19. H. F. Kolodny, "Evolution to a Matrix Organization," *Academy of Management Review*, Vol. 4, No. 4 (October 1979): 543–545.

20. Ibid.

21. Kolodny, "Managing in a Matrix," *Business Horizons*, Vol. 24, No. 2 (March/April 1981): 20.

22. Ibid., 18, 19. T. J. Peters, "Beyond the Matrix Organization," *Business Horizons*, Vol. 22, No. 5 (October 1979): 17.

23. W. C. Wall, Jr., "Integrated Management in Matrix Organization," *IEEE Transactions on Engineering Management*, Vol. EM31, No. 1 (February 1984): 30–36; W. Jerkovsky, "Functional Management in Matrix Organizations," *IEEE Transactions on Engineering Management*, Vol. EM30, No. 2 (May 1983): 89–97.

24. S. M. Davis and P. R. Lawrence, "Problems of Matrix Organizations," *Harvard Business Review*, Vol. 56 (May/June 1978): 131–142.

25. W. F. Joyce, "Matrix Organization: A Social Experiment," *Academy of Management Journal*, Vol. 29 (September 1986): 536–561.

26. Kolodny, "Evolution . . ." op. cit., 543–553.

27. J. H. Sheridan, "Building Alliances," *Industry Week*, 21 September 1987, 28.

28. W. G. Bennis, "Organizational Development and the Fate of Bureaucracy," *Industrial Management Review*, (Spring 1966); M. Liu et al., "Organizational Design for Technological Change," *Human Relations*, Vol 43, No. 1 (January 1990): 7–22.

29. Peters, op. cit., 20.

30. J. S. McClenahen, "Flexible Structures to Absorb the Shocks," *Industry Week* 18 April 1988, 41, 44; J. R. Galbraith and R. K. Kazanjian, "Organizing to Implement Strategies of Diversity and Globalization: The Role of Matrix Designs," *Human Resource Management*, Vol 25 (Spring 1986): 37–54; J. R. Galbraith and R. K. Kazanjian, *Strategy Implementation: Structure, Systems and Process* (St. Paul: West Publishing Co., 1986).

31. R. L. Drake, "Innovative Structures for Managing Change," *Planning Review*, Vol. 14 (November 1986): 18–22.

32. R. Duncan, "What Is the Right Organization Structure? Decision Tree Analysis Provides the Answer," *Organizational Dynamics*, Vol. 7, No. 3 (Winter 1979): 59–80.

CASE 13.1

Organizations in transition: from taller to flatter structures

DONALD D. WHITE   *University of Arkansas*
RAGHAV SINGH   *University of Arkansas*

In the early 1950s, many United States companies experienced significant growth as they entered a new peace-time economy. This growth was reflected in "tall" organizations having layer upon layer of man-

SOURCE: J. Spackey, "The Ripping of General Managers," *Newsweek*, 18 April 1988, 10; J. Byrne, "Caught in the Middle: Six Managers Speak Out on Corporate Life," *Business Week*, 12 September 1988, 80–88; J. H. Sheridan, "Sizing Up Corporate Staffs," *Industry Week*, 21 November 1988, 46–52.

agement personnel. By 1980, for example, AT&T had over one hundred levels of management and in the United States as a whole, managers made up over 10 percent of the industrial workforce.

Today, corporate structures and staffing are changing. Large companies are restructuring and downsizing. Yesterday's tall pyramids are being replaced by flatter structures with fewer layers and fewer people. Nowhere has the change been more apparent than in the elimination of vast numbers of middle management positions. By some estimates, over one million, or approximately one-third of all middle management jobs have been eliminated since 1980.

In most cases, the cutbacks have made companies more competitive. Corporate bureaucracies have been reduced and decision making has been sped up. However, many middle managers have felt the impact. Most obvious have been the increases in spans of control and responsibility for those who remain. At Ameritech, many middle managers are finding their jobs more challenging than before and like the increased power and responsibility that has resulted. But some Ameritech managers complain that downsizing has reduced their opportunities for advancement. This same concern is voiced by managers at many other companies, such as General Electric, General Motors, and Georgia-Pacific, that have gone through similar changes.

Flattening organization structures has also affected the careers of lower-level managers. Not only are promotion avenues reduced, but increased work loads and responsibilities have left their superiors with little time to devote to the professional development of new lower-level managers. At General Electric, managers' spans of control have increased from as few as four subordinates to as many as twenty. Increased supervisory burdens leave managers little time to mentor their subordinates, and developing personal relationships is all but impossible.

Restructuring at General Motors was intended to speed up decision making, but a number of remaining managers question its effectiveness. According to some, not enough layers of management were eliminated to make a significant difference. Moreover, several middle managers with many years of service and experience were forced into early retirement. While these retirements created openings for bright, young, lower-level managers, it also left them leaderless. One of the survivors summed up the current situation: "The effect of our reorganization was that the people who took early retirement were the most talented, most knowledgeable, most experienced. Essentially, those were the people who knew how to run the company. They've been replaced by young, bright talent, but there's nobody left to lead and develop them." As a result of new managers' inexperience, an increasing number of decisions have been made by committees or been pushed to higher levels in the organization.

Georgia-Pacific attempted to solve a similar leadership problem by bringing in a few experienced outsiders. However, the move generated resentment among remaining managers, who thought the outsiders didn't understand the company's problems and further reduced their own opportunities for advancement.

IBM has handled its restructuring both cautiously and constructively. The elimination of layers of middle management at IBM is part of a five-year restructuring program intended to achieve a net employment reduction of twenty thousand people. However, the program has not involved handing out a barrage of pink slips. Most reductions are carried out by transferring employees in staff positions to positions in operational areas as those positions become vacant. Those who do not wish to transfer to other positions are offered generous severance benefits.

The restructuring has created a new division, called IBM United States, which handles domestic marketing and worldwide product development. Almost five thousand employees from IBM's seven thousand-member headquarters staff have been transferred to IBM United States. The move is not just intended to achieve a workforce reduction, but is part of a larger decentralization effort. The reorganization is intended to speed up product development and reduce the time taken by products to reach the market. The accomplishment of these objectives will be facilitated by eliminating the need for decisions to be approved by a management committee at IBM's corporate headquarters.

Additionally, people are placed in positions where they can provide maximum utility to the organization. For example, about two thousand of the five thousand transferred to IBM United States were part of the corporate education staff. Having this group at corporate headquarters kept them away from the people they were supposed to train, and required extensive travel and communication links between them and other divisions. The education/training function is now located much closer to its "internal customers." The group can also be much more precise about its staffing needs and the kinds of courses that must be developed and taught.

As IBM's organization planning director, Steve Austin, puts it:

Fewer issues now come to Armonk (corporate headquarters) for review and approval. The decisions are made lower in the company. And a whole set of things flow out of that . . . including speed and efficiency. Fewer staff people are needed to 'stickhandle' matters through the review process. There is less preparation time, and fewer resources are chewed up. So I can take my best people and have them work on getting products out. . . .

While the thinning and flattening of many corporate structures has been perceived negatively by some middle managers, others admit that it has been necessary. Too many middle management jobs involve analyzing and disseminating information for top management and passing orders down the line. These functions became redundant in many companies as advanced information systems that do the same work better and faster came on line.

Downsizing can cause a company to be undermanaged. Nonetheless, the trend toward restructuring is likely to persist.

CASE 13.2   *The case of two masters*

The Adamson Aircraft Company has in the last decade expanded its product line to include the design, development, and production of missiles for the United States government. For this purpose, a missile division was established, and over five thousand personnel were gathered to staff this portion of the firm.

The traditional type of organization in aircraft manufacturing calls for functional specialization like that found in the automobile industry. Aircraft are made up of such items as engines, radios, wheels, and armament. The manufacture of component parts was standardized and the aircraft put together on an assembly line. It was quickly recognized that such a simplified approach would not meet future requirements, as the demand for greater capability and effectiveness increased and forced the designers to insist upon optimum performance in every part or component. Several components, each with an operational reliability of 99 percent, may have a combined reliability of only 51 percent. Even with the most judicious selection and usage of standard parts, a system could end up with a reliability approaching zero. To overcome this reliability drop, it became necessary to design the entire system as a single entity. Many of the parts that were formerly available off the shelf must now be tailored to meet the exacting demands of the total system. Thus, the "weapons system" concept was developed, which necessitated a change in organization and management.

For each weapons system project, a chief project engineer is appointed. He assembles the necessary design personnel for every phase of the project. In effect, he organizes and creates a small, temporary company for the purpose of executing a single weapons system. On his staff are representatives of such functional areas as propulsion, secondary power, structures, flight test, and "human factors." The human factors specialist, for example, normally reports to a human factors supervisor. In the human factors department are men with training in psychology, anthropology, physiology, and the like. They do research on human behavior and hope to provide the design engineers with the basic human parameters applicable to a specific problem.

James Johnson, an industrial psychologist, has been working with the missile division of Adamson for six months as a human factors specialist. His supervisor, George Slauson, also has a Ph.D. in psychology and has been with the firm for two years. Johnson is in a line relationship with Slauson, who conducts his annual review for pay purposes, and prepares an efficiency report on his work. Slauson is responsible for assembling and supervising a group of human factors experts to provide Adamson with the latest and most advanced information in the field of human behavior and its effect on product design.

Johnson has been assigned to a weapons system project, which is under the direction of Bernard Coolsen, a chief project engineer. In a committee meeting of project members, Coolsen stated, "I am thinking about a space vehicle of minimum weight capable of fourteen days' sustained activity, maneuverability, and rendezvous with other vehicles for maintenance and external exploration. How many men, how big a vehicle, and what instruments, supplies, and equipment will we need?" Johnson immediately set to work on his phase of the project. The data for the answer to this request were compiled and organized, and a rough draft of the human factors design criteria was prepared in triplicate. Johnson took the original to his supervisor, Slauson, for review, retaining the other two copies. Using one of the copies, he began to reedit and rewrite, working toward a smooth copy for presentation to Coolsen. A week later Johnson was called in by Slauson who said, "We can't put out stuff like this. First, it's too specific, and secondly, it's poorly organized." Slauson had rewritten the material extensively and had submitted a draft of it to his immediate superior, the design evaluation chief. In the meantime Coolsen had been calling Johnson for the material, insisting that he was holding up the entire project. Finally, taking a chance, Johnson took his original copy to Coolsen, and they sat down together and discussed the whole problem. An illustrator was called in, and in two days the whole vehicle was sketched up ready for design and specification write-up. The illustrator went to his board and began converting the sketches to drawings. Coolsen started to arrange for the writing of component and structural specifications, and Johnson went back to his desk to revise his human engineering specifications in the light of points brought out during the two-day team conference.

Three days later the design evaluation chief called Johnson into his office and said, "Has your supervisor seen this specification of yours?" Johnson replied that he had and that this was Slauson's revision of the original. The chief then asked for the original, and Johnson brought in the third original copy. Two days later the chief's secretary delivered to Johnson's desk a draft of his original specification as modified by Slauson as modified by the design evaluation chief. Johnson edited this for technical accuracy and prepared a ditto master. Slauson and the design evaluation chief read the master, initialed it, and asked for thirty copies to be run off. One copy was kept by Johnson, one by Slauson, one by the chief, five put into company routing, and the balance placed in file. Those in company routing went to the head of technical staff, head of advanced systems, and finally to the project engineer, Coolsen. Coolsen filed one copy in the project file and gave the other to Johnson. The latter dropped it in the nearest waste basket, inasmuch as several days previously, Coolsen had combined his, the illustrator's, and Johnson's material and submitted it to publications. Publications had run off six copies, one each for Coolsen, the illustrator, Johnson, the head of advanced systems, the U.S. Patent Office, and one for file. Also, by this time, the vehicle had been accepted by the company management as a disclosure for patent purposes. Johnson breathed a sigh of relief, since he thought that he had gotten away with serving two masters.

EXERCISE 13.1
DIVISION OF WORK

Time: one hour for exercise; thirty minutes to one hour for discussion.

1. Three students are selected from the class and seated in front of the class, side by side, facing the class.
2. The three students are production employees of an organization. Each has a set of cards, numbered from 0 to 9, which represent from 0 to 9 machines. The instructor is going to put a number on the board from 0 to 27. Each employee puts up any card she or he wishes, from 0 to 9, *simultaneously*, *without communicating* with the others. The total of the numbers of the three cards has

to equal the number put on the board by the instructor. Ten trials (a different number placed on the board each time) will be run, and the number of correct and incorrect responses will be recorded, a correct response being when the three numbers added together match the number on the board.

3. At the completion of the first trial, three other class members will be selected and will become the management team for the three original employees. It is their task to formulate a strategy for increasing the effectiveness of the production team. They must develop the strategy and communicate the strategy to the production team within ten minutes. This group of three employees and three managers is called Company 1.

4. At the same time the rest of the class is divided into companies consisting of three employees and three managers. The task of the newly formed companies is the same as Company 1. Any class members left over will be assigned to companies as observers.

5. After the ten-minute period, another ten trials are run. Scores are recorded for each company.

6. Complicating factors emerge with which each company has to cope. The instructor will communicate these complicating factors to the companies.

7. The managements of the companies have ten minutes to develop a strategy which deals with the new factors. Within the ten-minute period management must communicate their strategy to their employees.

8. Another ten trials are run. Scores are recorded for each company.

9. Five minutes are available for strategy modification and refinement.

10. Ten more trials are run. Scores are recorded.

11. Steps 9 and 10 are repeated two more times.

12. General class discussion of the experience using questions under "ANALYSIS" as guides.

ANALYSIS

1. Is it possible to draw an analogy between the simulation and the process of industrialization? Did the simulation proceed from complex problem solving to a highly rationalized work process?

2. What impact did the increasing division of work have? Did it improve productivity? Did it result in lower labor and equipment costs?

3. What was the impact of the utilization of the management team?

4. What was the nature of the communications between labor and management?

5. How did employees feel as the work became increasingly rationalized? Would you like to do this work for the rest of the day? For a week? For a year? As a career? Would you do it for $10,000 a year? For $20,000 a year? For $50,000 a year?

6. What kinds of behaviors were evident in the classroom? What patterns of behavior emerged? Can you identify the structural variables that "caused" the behaviors observed?

EXERCISE 13.2

ORGANIZING

The purpose of this exercise is to increase your awareness of the importance of structure in organization. In addition, the exercise focuses on the importance of management in organizing a venture.

THE PROBLEM

Select one of the following situations to organize. Then read the background material before answering the questions.

a. The registration process at your university or college.
b. A new hamburger fast-food franchise.
c. A Jetski rental in an ocean resort area.

Do steps 1 to 7, below, as homework. In preparing your answers, use your own experience, or think up logical answers to the questions.

BACKGROUND

Organization is a way of gaining some power against an unreliable environment. The environment provides the organization with inputs, which include raw materials, human resources, and financial resources. There is a service or product to produce which involves technology. The output is to be sold to a client, a group that must be nurtured. The complexities of the environment and the technology determine the complexity of the organization.

PLANNING YOUR ORGANIZATION

1. In a few sentences, write the mission or purpose of your organization.
2. From the mission statement you should be able to write down specific things that must be done in order to accomplish the mission.
3. From the list of specifics that must be accomplished, an organizational chart can be devised. Each position on the chart will perform a specific task or is responsible for a specific outcome.
4. Add duties to each job position on your organizational chart. This will form a job description.
5. How would you ensure that the people that you placed in these positions worked together?
6. What level of skill and abilities is required at each position and level in order to hire the right person for each position?
7. Make a list of the decisions that would have to be made while you planned and built the organization. Make a second list of those decisions you would have to make just after your organization began operating.

IN CLASS

1. Form into groups up to three members that organized the same project, and share your answers to the questions.
2. Come to agreement on the way to organize utilizing everyone's responses.
3. Present the group's approach to the class.

CHAPTER **14**

 # WORK DESIGN

LEARNING OBJECTIVES

1. To recognize the importance of work design in modern organizations.
2. To understand significant historical developments in work design.
3. To become familiar with contemporary approaches to work design.
4. To understand the significance of quality of work life (QWL) for both employees and organizations.

CHAPTER OUTLINE

The Importance of Work Design

Early Approaches to Work Design
   Scientific Management
   Job Enlargement
   Job Rotation

Contemporary Approaches to Work Design
   Job Enrichment
   Job Characteristics
   Sociotechnical Design

Quality of Work Life
   Concern About the Quality of Work Life
   Applying the Quality of Work Life Concept in Modern
      Organizations

Work Design: Conclusions

Questions for Review and Discussion

References

Cases: 14.1 Teamwork at General Motors:
            Progress and Problems
      14.2 The Workplace Revolution

Exercises: 14.1 Productivity/Quality Task Force Project
              14.2 Improving Organizational Effectiveness

KEY TERMS

Work design	**Feedback**
Scientific management	**Motivating potential score**
Job enlargement	**Growth-need strength**
Job rotation	**Vertical job loading**
Horizontal job loading	**Sociotechnical design**
Job enrichment	**Quality of work life**
Critical psychological states	**Cross-training**
Skill variety	**Innovative reward systems**
Task identity	**Flexitime**
Task significance	**4/40 work week**
Autonomy	

M arcella Bradley typed another series of numbers and then stared blankly at the monitor of her computer. "Only thirty more minutes till break time," she mumbled as she glanced at her watch while preparing to enter another series of numbers. "At least then," she thought, "I can get away from this boring job for a few minutes."

Marcella had worked as a data entry operator at Nunco, Inc., for two years. She had no complaints about the working conditions in the office or the pay. In fact, Marcella earned relatively good money and received excellent health and vacation benefits. She also got along well with her co-workers and had several close friends at Nunco. What made the job difficult was the monotony of performing the same basic tasks over and over again—scan, type, check, enter; scan, type, check, enter. When Marcella first started at Nunco, the newness of the job and the surroundings had been a challenge. Now, however, the only challenge was surviving the eight-hour shift day after day. Marcella was a conscientious worker, but she frequently daydreamed while performing her job and sometimes made mistakes that seriously affected the quality of her work. She also skipped work or called in sick occasionally just to get away from the boredom. Marcella often found herself wondering, "Is this what I'm going to do for the rest of my life?"

Marcella's situation highlights the important relationship between a person and her job. Work is a vital source of individual motivation, satisfaction, and fulfillment; it can also be the cause of frustration, discouragement, and alienation. In recent years, managers and behavioral scientists have devoted increased attention to designing work to meet people's needs and abilities. Our purpose in this chapter is to examine the process of work design and the impact it can have on both individuals and organizations.

THE IMPORTANCE OF WORK DESIGN

Most jobs are comprised of tasks and activities defined primarily by an organization. **Work design** is thus the formal and informal specification of an employee's task-related activities, including both structural and interpersonal aspects of the job, with considerations for the needs and requirements of both the organization and the worker.[1] Understanding work design is important to a manager for several reasons.

First, the type of work an individual performs affects many aspects of his life. Since people spend a substantial proportion of their adult lives working, a person's job is a central role in life. Who we are and what we become as individuals are determined in large measure by what we do at work (e.g., "I am a manager," or "I am a physician"). Furthermore, the nature and characteristics of work significantly affect individual motivation, job and life satisfaction, and organizational commitment and can also influence mental and physical health.

Second, a job is the interface or link between an individual and an organization. Through the systematic and coordinated execution of work, individuals contribute to the achievement of organizational goals. Routine, boring, and/or stressful work can have a negative impact on an individual's job performance and lead to such organizational problems as decreased productivity, absenteeism, grievances, turnover, and sabotage. Consequently, work design is important as a means of minimizing these dysfunctional effects.

Third, an increased concern with improving productivity and quality, and the technological innovations associated with this concern, are significantly affecting the design of work in modern organizations. Robotics, computer aided design/computer aided manufacturing (CAD/CAM) systems, just-in-time (JIT) inventory management, and streamlined, simplified work processes are today common in many businesses and manufacturing firms. These changes will continue to accelerate as the United States and Canada attempt to remain competitive in the international marketplace.

Finally, changes in today's labor force are drawing attention to the importance of work design. The increased educational levels and expectations of most workers are expanding the gap between what people want in their jobs and what they actually experience. Workers today are concerned not only with wages and benefits, but also with an overall quality of work life, including responsible, meaningful work and participation in the making of decisions directly affecting them. In much the same way that the dominant managerial philosophy and assumptions are being questioned today, so are the traditional approaches to work design being challenged. Many employees in contemporary organizations are not willing to endure the fragmented and highly specialized jobs characteristic of work in so many United States industries.

EARLY APPROACHES TO WORK DESIGN

We can better understand the modern perspectives on work design if we know the significant historical developments in the field. Interest in work design can be linked most directly to the Adam Smith classic, *The Wealth of Nations*, published in 1776, and to its discussion of the concept of division of labor. However, not until the late 1800s and early 1900s were management techniques for applying this concept in industrial organizations developed and widely implemented (e.g., Henry Ford's assembly line). Three early approaches to work design were particularly important: scientific management, job rotation, and job enlargement.

Scientific Management

The first systematic attempt to identify principles for designing work to fit the abilities of individuals can be traced to the work of Frederick W. Taylor (see Chapter 1). Taylor basically conceived of **scientific management** as a cooperative effort by management and workers to ascertain the one best way of performing a job, to select workers most capable of doing the job, and to provide incentive pay for people selected to work in the prescribed manner.[2]

Taylor's proposals were considered revolutionary at the time because his efforts marked the first attempt to apply scientific principles to management problems. Through scientific experimentation, he determined the exact procedures for executing particular tasks, the amount of work employees could be expected to perform, and the proper tools and implements necessary for a worker to perform a job with maximum efficiency. Jobs designed according to the principles of scientific management were characterized by a high degree of specialization and standardization. This approach emphasized efficient employee task-performance and management responsibility for planning, organizing, and controlling work.

Taylor described one early application of scientific management in the coal yards of Bethlehem Steel Company as "developing the science of shoveling. You . . . give each workman each day a job to which he is well suited and provide him with just that implement which will enable him to do his biggest day's work."[3] Taylor experimented to determine the optimum shovel load that would lead to maximum productivity without overworking the employee. He also tested shovels of various sizes and shapes in an effort to discover the right tool for the job. After approximately four months of experimentation, he concluded that a twenty-one-pound load was optimal, regardless of the material being shoveled.

Bethlehem Steel accepted this figure and improved work planning and measurement by adding more staff. The best workers were selected on the basis of performance and given the correct tools to perform the task most efficiently (eight to ten different types of shovels were required for different types of coal). The application of these principles, including the expense of new equipment and additional personnel, reduced the cost of handling a ton of coal from approximately eight cents to about four cents, a savings of about $78,000 a year. The workers also increased their wages by approximately 60 percent over what they had been earning.

Frank and Lillian Gilbreth, close associates of Taylor, applied the principles of scientific management to a wide range of jobs and revolutionized the nature of work in many occupations. (The scientific management of their family life is described in the book *Cheaper by the Dozen*.) The Gilbreths specialized in the study of motion and sought to eliminate wasted movements and simplify work patterns by assigning different functions to different employees consistent with their abilities. Time and motion studies, as practiced today in many industries, began in the general approach and specific methods developed by Taylor and the Gilbreths.

The principles of scientific management have had a profound and lasting impact on the nature of work in the industrialized nations of the world. Many of today's manufacturing, service, and related jobs that achieve efficiency through simplification, standardization, and repetition of work processes have their roots in scientific management. Although this approach to work design has done much to improve efficiency and productivity, it is not without problems. Standardized and repetitive tasks can be a major cause of boredom, dissatisfaction, and decreased organizational commitment. The contemporary approaches to work design discussed later in this chapter specifically focus on overcoming the disadvantages of jobs designed according to principles of scientific management.

Job Enlargement

The scientific management approach to work design produced job procedures that were highly specialized, simple, repetitive, and usually carried out at one work position or station. **Job enlargement** emerged in the late 1940s and 1950s and was one of the first attempts by management to reduce the boredom and dissatisfaction caused by high levels of job specialization and standardization.

Job enlargement basically refers to increasing the number and variety of tasks an employee performs. This approach to work design is also called horizontal job loading. For example, a worker on an automobile assembly line might usually install only the radio. This job can be enlarged by having the employee also install the steering wheel and portions of the dashboard. The rationale for this work design strategy is simple—

enlarged jobs give an employee greater task and skill variety and thus an increased interest in the work being performed.

The earliest reported uses of job enlargement were at IBM, Detroit Edison Company, AT&T, and Maytag. Job enlargement was generally credited with improving worker satisfaction, decreasing production costs, and increasing quality. However, no empirical evidence was provided to support these claims.

Although job enlargement reduces the specialization and monotony of many tasks, employees frequently resisted it. Many workers saw job enlargement as a tactic for getting them to perform more work for the same cost. Labor leaders also argued that this approach eliminated jobs by reducing the total number of workers necessary to manufacture a product. Other critics suggested that job enlargement did not really change an employee's task variety but added more of the same boring and routine tasks to the work. Although limited in terms of its application and effectiveness, job enlargement was the first important step toward increased employee task variety and responsibility in work design.

Job Rotation

Job rotation is another work design strategy that managers implemented in many industries. This strategy involves moving workers from one job to another without changing the job's basic operations or nature. For example, a worker can learn the tasks to be performed at three different work stations (e.g., assembling, inspecting, and packaging) and then be assigned to these work stations on a rotating basis (e.g., daily or weekly). Similarly, employees in a secretarial pool can rotate the tasks of typing, filing, and copying. The logic of job rotation is similar to that of job enlargement— it increases individual motivation and satisfaction by giving an employee an opportunity to use a wider range of skills and abilities in performing a task.

Job rotation is basically a short-term strategy for overcoming the boredom and dissatisfaction caused by high levels of job specialization. Because it did not change the nature of work itself, job rotation consistently failed to improve employee satisfaction or productivity over time. Even when this approach to work design was used, specialized tasks remained specialized and routine jobs stayed routine. Thus, both job enlargement and job rotation produced disappointing long-term results because neither approach significantly altered the tasks an employee actually performed.

CONTEMPORARY APPROACHES TO WORK DESIGN

During the 1950s, 1960s, and 1970s, new approaches to and techniques of work design were developed and tested. (Exhibit 14.1 traces the historical development of work design.) These innovations have had a significant impact on work design in contemporary organizations and today remain the focus of considerable theoretical and research interest. Three of the most influential contemporary approaches to work design are job enrichment, job characteristics, and sociotechnical design.

Job Enrichment

One of the most influential theories of work design to date is the Two Factor Theory of Frederick Herzberg.[4] As we explained in Chapter 5, this theory suggests

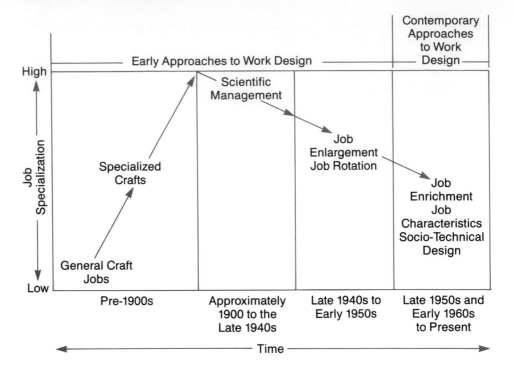

EXHIBIT 14.1   HISTORICAL DEVELOPMENT OF WORK DESIGN

Adapted from: A. C. Filley. R. House, and S. Kerr, *Managerial Process and Organizational Behavior* (Glenview, Ill.: Scott, Foresman and Co., 1976), 33. Reprinted by permission.

that the primary determinants of an employee's satisfaction and motivation are factors intrinsic to the work itself. These factors, called **motivators,** include recognition, achievement, responsibility, advancement, and personal growth. Dissatisfaction, on the other hand, is caused by factors extrinsic to the work a person performs. **Hygiene factors,** as Herzberg calls the extrinsic factors, include company policies, working conditions, compensation plans, and supervisory practices. The Two Factor Theory suggests that (1) hygiene factors prevent dissatisfaction but do not contribute to an employee's motivation, and (2) motivators are related to an individual's work motivation. Thus, a job will positively influence an employee's motivation to the extent that motivators are designed into the work. According to this theory, changes focusing primarily on hygiene factors do not affect employee motivation.

The Two Factor Theory has been applied in business and other types of organizations in the form of job enrichment programs. **Job enrichment,** also referred to as vertical job loading, gives employees greater responsibility for planning, organizing, controlling, and evaluating their own work. Rather than giving an employee more of the same kinds of tasks to perform (i.e., job rotation and job enlargement), a job is enriched by designing motivators into the work itself. For example, employees can be provided with minibudgets that make them directly responsible for costs or can be given the authority to schedule their own work within the requirements of certain task deadlines. Job enrichment is thus a more comprehensive approach to work design than is job rotation or enlargement. Job enrichment increases an employee's task variety and also changes the nature of the work to provide opportunities for new learning, direct feedback on performance, self-control over job methods and schedules, direct access to communication sources, and individual accountability for results.

The flexibility and employee control emphasized by job enrichment are key characteristics of many Japanese manufacturing firms. It is not surprising, for example, to walk onto a Sanyo production floor and see a panel of controls and notification lights at each work station that permits an operator to request assistance from a supervisor, to tell other employees on the line to pick up the pace, or actually to shut down the production line until a problem can be corrected. Such responsibility and control are common features of enriched jobs in Japanese plants and are becoming more common in the United States.

Kanban inventory control is another system that increases worker control over the job and work environment. The Kanban system places responsibility for replenishing inventory with each worker on the assembly line. Rather than being fed a continuous flow of parts and materials with which to work, employees are responsible for notifying inventory suppliers when parts are running low. This procedure allows employees to have greater control over their own work rather than to be pressured by the speed of a moving assembly line. In addition, the number of quality control inspectors, located at the end of an assembly line in most other systems, may be cut because workers continuously check the quality of their own work as well as the quality of material passed from previous work stations.

Research indicates that "even in the most appropriate context, 10 to 15 percent of those exposed to job enrichment do not respond positively, and that in other contexts the total effect may be nil."[5] The potential benefits of job enrichment thus can be moderated by such situational factors as the characteristics of the job, the organizational level, or the employees' personal needs and values.

The Two Factor Theory was instrumental in focusing attention on the nature of work itself as a source of motivation. Although Herzberg's work has prompted a great deal of controversy and criticism, it has been and continues to be an important contemporary approach to work design.

Job Characteristics

During the latter half of the 1970s, the **job characteristics model** (JCM) of work design received widespread attention from both researchers and practitioners.[6] The JCM builds on the work of Herzberg and other theorists and attempts to explain how work design affects employee attitudes and behavior. Five core job dimensions influence three critical psychological states that subsequently affect a number of important personal and work outcomes (see Exhibit 14.2). According to the model, the relationships among job dimensions, psychological states, and outcomes are moderated by an employee's growth-need strength. Each of this model's basic components is discussed briefly below.

Psychological states

The JCM suggests that three psychological states affect an employee's satisfaction and work motivation: experienced meaningfulness of the work, experienced responsibility for work outcomes, and knowledge of results. The model postulates that "internal rewards are obtained by an individual when he *learns* (knowledge of results) that he *personally* (experienced responsibility) has performed well on a task that he *cares about* (experienced meaningfulness)."[7] The more employees experience these three psychological states, the greater the likelihood they will feel good about themselves when performing a task well. For example, John James, the personnel director at B&W Enterprises, believes an employee's first few weeks on the job are crucial for

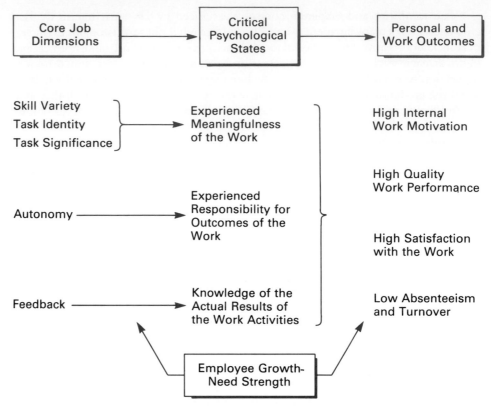

EXHIBIT 14.2   THE JOB CHARACTERISTICS MODEL

SOURCE: J. R. Hackman and J. L. Suttle, eds., *Improving Life at Work* (Santa Monica: Goodyear, 1977), 129. Reprinted by permission.

both the individual and organization. Consequently, he has always been concerned about the quality of the orientation program for new employees. After soliciting input from various department managers, he spent many hours revising the program. The modified program was presented on two different occasions, and the feedback from both management and the new employees was positive and supportive of the improvements. As he read the evaluations from the latest program, he felt a sense of pride and satisfaction in his accomplishments at work.

Intrinsic rewards such as those experienced by John are reinforcing and serve as incentives for continued efforts to perform well. When an employee does not perform well, he does not experience this reinforcement. As a result, the employee may try harder in the future to regain the intrinsic rewards good performance brings. The result is a continuous cycle of positive work motivation powered by intrinsic rewards.

Care job dimensions

According to the model, the three psychological states are activated by five core job dimensions:

1. **Skill variety:** the degree to which a job requires a variety of activities involving the use of a number of different skills and talents.
2. **Task identity:** the degree to which the job requires completing a whole and identifiable piece of work; that is, doing a job from beginning to end with a visible outcome.

3. **Task significance:** the degree to which the job has a substantial impact on the lives or work of other people, whether in the immediate organization or in the external environment.
4. **Autonomy:** the degree to which the job provides substantial freedom, independence, and discretion to the individual in scheduling the work and determining the procedures to be used in carrying it out.
5. **Feedback:** the degree to which carrying out the job's required work activities results in the individual's obtaining direct and clear information about the effectiveness of his or her performance.

The job characteristics of skill variety, task identity, and task significance influence the psychological state of experienced meaningfulness of work. Autonomy affects experienced responsibility for work outcomes, and feedback influences knowledge of results. The overall potential of a job to produce intrinsic work motivation is reflected in a summary index created by combining the scores on the five job dimensions. Job dimensions are measured using the Job Diagnostic Survey (JDS).[8] Scores obtained from the JDS on the five core job dimensions are combined as follows to produce the **motivating potential score** (MPS) of a particular job:

$$\text{Motivating Potential Score} = \left[\frac{\text{Skill variety} + \text{Task identity} + \text{Task significance}}{3} \right] \times \text{Autonomy} \times \text{Feedback}$$

Jobs with a low MPS are likely targets for job redesign efforts. A job high in motivating potential must be high on at least one of the three dimensions that lead to experienced meaningfulness and also high on autonomy and feedback. A near zero score on either autonomy or feedback will reduce the overall MPS of a job to near zero. Thus, all three psychological states must be present for a job to have the maximum motivational potential.

Employee growth-need strength

Hackman and Oldham introduced employee **growth-need strength** (GNS) as a variable that moderates employee responses to the work environment. Growth-need strength refers to a collection of higher-order needs for learning, accomplishment, and challenge. GNS is believed to be most significant at two points in the model: (1) at the interface between the objective job dimensions and the psychological states, and (2) at the interface between the psychological states and the outcome variables.

The first interface suggests that high growth-need individuals are more likely or better able to experience the psychological states when their job is enriched than are low growth-need employees. In other words, high growth-need individuals will be more responsive to changes in task identity, task significance, skill variety, autonomy, and feedback. The second interface means that individuals with high growth-need strength will react more positively to the presence of the psychological states than will low growth-need employees. Thus, employees may perform tasks with the same or similar characteristics but will have diverse reactions because of individual differences in growth-need strength.

Outcome variables

The model includes several personal and work-related outcomes resulting from the core job dimensions and critical psychological states. To the extent that employees experience the three critical psychological states, they should exhibit high levels of internal work motivation, quality performance, and job satisfaction. In addition, low levels of absenteeism and turnover should also occur. It is important to note that although these particular outcomes are not the only ones influenced by employee responses to job characteristics, they are some of the most important.

Using the job characteristics model to redesign work

Specific action principles have been developed for applying the job characteristics model in work redesign efforts.[9] These principles give a manager a systematic method of changing the work an employee or employees perform.

The first principle suggests that, as much as possible, tasks should be divided into natural units of work. For example, an employee working in a typing pool may be assigned all reports and letters for a particular manager or department. Instead of typing only one section of a report or a certain number of pages, the typist can prepare the entire document and see the project through to completion. **Forming natural work units** thus increases an employee's responsibility for and ownership of the work and improves the likelihood that the employee will perceive the work as important and meaningful.

The second principle, **combining tasks,** is based on the assumption that specialized and fractionalized jobs can be combined to create new and more complete modules of work. In the Medfield, Massachusetts, plant of Corning Glass Works, for example, the job of assembling laboratory hot plates was redesigned by combining a number of highly specialized tasks.[10] After the change, each hot plate was assembled, inspected, and shipped by one operator. Combining tasks in this way increases task identity and allows the employee to use a wider variety of skills.

Workers frequently have little or no contact with the ultimate user of their product or service. This lack of contact often makes it difficult for employees to generate commitment and motivation to do a job well. By **establishing client relationships** between workers and their clients, a job can be improved in three specific ways. First, feedback increases because the employee can communicate directly with the ultimate user. Second, skill variety may increase because the employee must develop the social and interpersonal skills necessary to interact effectively with the client. Finally, autonomy increases to the extent that employees are given responsibility for managing their relationship with the client.

At Lechmere, Inc., a twenty-seven-store retail chain owned by Dayton Hudson, employees are trained to perform a variety of tasks. Forklift operators in the warehouse, for example, are also encouraged to work as and learn the skills of cashiers and salespersons. Working periodically in these jobs helps to establish relationships between the forklift operators and the ultimate recipients (clients) or their service, the store employees and Lechmere customers. The operators can observe and experience firsthand the employee and consumer problems that arise because of delayed, damaged, or improperly handled merchandise. As described above, this contact with clients increases feedback to the forklift operators and requires greater skill variety.

The fourth principle, **vertical loading,** attempts to close the gap between the doing and controlling aspects of work. When a job is loaded vertically, responsibilities and powers formerly reserved for management (e.g., selecting work methods, establishing work schedules) are assigned to employees as a part of their job. This principle focuses on increasing autonomy.

The fifth action principle, **opening feedback channels,** seeks to give employees direct, job-provided feedback. Most employees receive feedback about their job performance from a supervisor or manager. Frequently, however, such feedback is not well timed and can be threatening to an employee. Job-provided feedback is more immediate and private and increases a worker's feelings of personal control over the work. For example, a computer-based quality control screen is one method of providing workers with direct feedback about their performance.

TRAVELERS INSURANCE

The job characteristics model was the basis for a work redesign program in a keypunching operation of the Travelers Insurance Companies.[11] Ninety-eight keypunchers and verifiers, seven assignment clerks, and one supervisor were employed in the department. Most of the jobs were fragmented, highly specialized, and provided workers with little autonomy, skill variety, or feedback. The assignment clerks usually received jobs from user departments and, after checking the incoming work for obvious errors, placed acceptable work into batches which could be completed in approximately one hour. When batches were assigned to keypunchers, the keypunchers were told to punch only what they saw and to make *no* corrections. All keypunching work was rechecked and verified, a task which resembled keypunching and required almost as much time. Errors detected in verification were given to various keypunch operators to be corrected.

Before the intervention, absenteeism was higher than average, and schedules and due dates were frequently missed. The supervisor spent a considerable amount of time responding to employee complaints about their jobs. Diagnosis using the Job Diagnostic Survey indicated that the keypunching and verifying jobs had extremely low motivating potential scores. Skill variety was low because operators used only a single skill (keypunching or verifying). Task identity and significance were also low. Workers had no freedom to schedule work, solve problems, or correct obvious errors (low autonomy). In addition, feedback about results was low since operators rarely received information about the quality of their work.

The following steps were taken to redesign the work of the keypunchers and verifyers:

1. **Natural work units.** Rather than receiving batches on a random basis, each operator was assigned continuing responsibility for certain accounts.
2. **Task combination.** Some planning and controlling functions were combined with the task of keypunching or verifying.
3. **Client relationships.** Each operator was given several channels of direct contact with clients. The operators inspected their incoming materials for correctness and resolved errors and discrepancies with the user departments directly.
4. **Feedback.** Operators were provided with direct feedback about their work from clients and from the computer department. This included a weekly record of errors and productivity.
5. **Vertical loading.** Operators could now correct obvious data errors and set their own schedules as long as they met department schedules. Some competent operators were given the option of not verifying their work and of making program changes.

As a result of the work redesign program, the quantity of work increased 39.6 percent. Poorly performing operators declined from 11.1 percent to 5.5 percent. Absenteeism declined 24.1 percent, and employee satisfaction improved significantly. The number of operators in the department was reduced from ninety-eight to sixty, primarily through attrition, transfers, and promotions. Overall, these improvements enabled (1) the operators to work with fewer external controls, and (2) the supervisors to spend their time supporting the work redesign program.

The five guidelines for implementing work redesign shown in Exhibit 14.3 are straightforward and may lead you to believe that work redesign is a relatively easy process. However, such a conclusion would be a serious error. Redesigning work is a complex and complicated process made even more difficult by many organizational constraints. An organization's technology, for example, can inhibit the effectiveness of work redesign by limiting the number of ways a job can be changed. An organization's personnel and control systems can also inhibit the implementation of work redesign programs by restricting who can perform certain jobs or imposing rigid performance evaluation procedures. Inadequate diagnosis, union and/or middle management resistance, and cost can also negatively affect implementation of a job redesign program. A successful work redesign program thus requires a manager or management to deal simultaneously with the nature of a particular task and the surrounding organizational subsystems.

The results of work design using the job characteristics approach

The job characteristics model and the job diagnostic survey can be used to determine if a job is low in motivating potential and to identify specific job aspects that may need to be redesigned. Results from a large number of work redesign programs using the job characteristics model generally indicate that employees whose jobs are high on the core job dimensions are more satisfied and motivated than employees whose

EXHIBIT 14.3   ACTION PRINCIPLES FOR APPLYING THE JOB CHARACTERISTICS MODEL OF WORK DESIGN

Adapted from: J. R. Hackman, "Work Design," in J. R. Hackman and J. L. Suttle, eds., *Improving Life at Work* (Santa Monica, Calif.: Goodyear, 1977), 136.

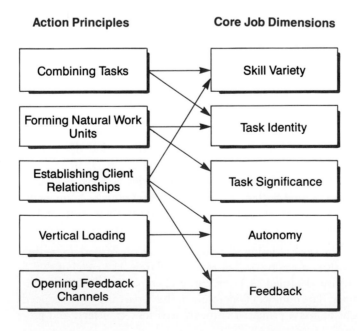

jobs are low on the dimensions.[12] The core dimensions were also found to be related to absenteeism and performance, although the relationship to performance was not strong. In addition, responses for people with high growth-need strength were more positive than individuals with low GNS. Recent reviews of the job characteristics model have emphasized several weaknesses, including inadequate empirical testing of the model and failure to account for the influence of organizational contexts on employee responses to tasks.[13] While there is support in the research literature for the basic job characteristics model, it would be inappropriate to conclude that the model provides a correct and complete picture of the motivational effects of job characteristics.[14]

The job characteristics approach to work design presented by Hackman and Oldham is not the final answer. It does, however, provide a useful framework for understanding the relationships between an employee and the characteristics of the job the employee performs.

Sociotechnical Design

The **sociotechnical** approach to work design focuses simultaneously on the social and technological systems of an organization. In contrast to work design strategies that emphasize designing individual jobs to meet employee needs, the sociotechnical model suggests designing and implementing work to optimize the fit between the social and psychological needs of people and the technical aspects of work.

The sociotechnical approach assumes that the basic unit of work design is the group. Consequently, applying the sociotechnical model has most often been accomplished by using autonomous work groups or teams (see Chapter 9, "Putting Groups to Work"). Many organizational tasks can be accomplished more effectively by a group or team than by an individual. Under such a work arrangement, groups are usually given considerable autonomy in planning and assigning tasks among group members. In addition, pay and other rewards are often based on group rather than individual performance.

The sociotechnical approach to work design, developed in Europe more than thirty years ago, has gained widespread acceptance and been widely implemented. Sociotechnical principles were used in designing new production plants for Alcoa, Volvo, Shell, Sherwin-Williams, Procter & Gamble, General Foods, and General Motors. Two of the best known sociotechnical experiments are described briefly below.

VOLVO[15]

In the early 1970s, Volvo constructed a new car assembly plant in Kalmar, Sweden. Managerial, technical, and social innovations were incorporated into the plant's design to meet the needs of employees. The factory was designed to assemble sixty thousand automobiles annually, using teams of fifteen to twenty workers for each major task. One group, for example, assembles electrical systems; another group assembles brakes or suspension systems. Each group has its own work area and is given considerable autonomy. The team totally controls assigning work among group members and the pace of its work. Each team contracts with management to produce a certain number of finished products (e.g., doors, brake systems, electrical systems) per day. The work teams conduct their own inspections, and a computer-based quality control screen flashes the results directly back to the work stations on a television screen.

The Kalmar plant cost approximately 10 percent more to build than a conventional automobile assembly facility and can produce only about one-third as many automobiles as a typical United States plant. However, the product quality is higher, and absenteeism and turnover are lower than for other plants in the same geographic area.[16]

Volvo has continued to experiment with new approaches to work design. The International Dimension on page 481 describes several innovative work processes at Volvo's newest automobile production facility in Uddevalla.

GENERAL FOODS[17]

An innovative sociotechnical system was built into a General Foods pet food plant that opened in 1971. The plant was designed to use work teams of seven to fourteen members, and steps were taken to reduce the traditional status symbols found in most production plants (e.g., a common parking lot for managers and employees, a common entrance to the plant, and similar decor in the offices and locker rooms). The usual distinctions between technical specialists and workers were reduced because many support activities (e.g., quality control, custodial work, and personnel tasks) were assigned to each operating team. Teams were given control over almost all activities to which they were assigned. The plant also used the following innovations:

All employees were given a single job classification. Pay raises were based on an individual's ability to learn new skills or master new jobs. Workers were paid for what they were capable of doing instead of what they actually did.

Jobs were enlarged and enriched to increase task variety, feedback, and autonomy. The most routine and boring tasks were eliminated.

Detailed information about plant operations was made available to the work teams.

Teams were given responsibility for governing their own actions. Each team determined policies and procedures as it saw fit and counseled team members who failed to meet team standards.

Compared to plants using a traditional production system, the initial results of this sociotechnical experiment were favorable. Sabotage, absenteeism, and turnover declined, quality rejects were reduced by 92 percent, and employee morale increased. Productivity increased, but this result was due in part to the new technology used in the plant. Evaluations of the General Foods experiment conducted several years after the initial assessment, however, revealed serious problems in maintaining the sociotechnical innovations.[18] These difficulties were not caused by the work design techniques themselves but by (1) the incompatibility of the plant's work group system with General Foods' overall organizational structure, and (2) the turnover and relocation of key managers who were highly supportive of the experiment.

Two important conclusions emerged from these sociotechnical experiments.[19] First, groups appear to be a reasonably effective means of organizing work in some organizations. Even though there are technological constraints to what an organi-

INTERNATIONAL DIMENSION
Volvo's New Plant in Uddevalla:
Eliminating the Assembly Line?

In 1987, Roger Holtback, president of Volvo Car Corporation, conducted an important experiment. He exchanged his usual business suit for coveralls and assembled a car all by himself at a new Volvo plant in Uddevalla, Sweden. Holtback managed to drive the finished Volvo 740 off the assembly line, although it was by no means free of defects. "It started nicely, but it would not have been delivered to a customer," Holtbeck said.

The results of Holtbeck's experiment reinforced Volvo's radical decision to mass-produce the midline 740 at Uddevalla without using assembly lines. In full production since 1989, the plant employs teams of seven to ten hourly workers. Each team works in one area and assembles four cars per shift. Since members are trained to handle all assembly jobs, they work an average of three hours before repeating the same task. Uddevalla thus avoids classic problems of boredom, inattention, poor quality, and high absenteeism associated with work cycles of only one or two minutes on conventional assembly lines.

Volvo has long been recognized as a leader in innovative work design. The Kalmar plant, opened in 1974, grouped employees into teams of fifteen to twenty that also operated without a moving assembly line. The Uddevalla plant, however, goes much further than Kalmar. It is divided into six assembly areas, each having eight teams. The teams largely manage themselves and handle scheduling, quality control, hiring, and other duties normally performed by supervisors. There are no first-line supervisors and only two tiers of managers. Each team has a spokesperson/ombudsman who reports to one of six plant managers, each of whom report in turn to Leif Karlberg, president of the entire complex.

The innovations at Uddevalla have attracted worldwide attention. Throngs of reporters, many from Japan, recently attended an open house for visitors. The concept has also generated interest in the United States, where the United Auto Workers and carmakers are searching for an assembly system that can compete in terms of productivity and quality with Japanese plants while making employees' work less repetitive and mundane.

Questions
What aspect of Swedish culture may affect the success of the work design system in Uddevalla?
Can a similar work system be effective in the United States? Japan? Germany?

SOURCES: Paul Bernstein, "The Learning Curve at Volvo," *Columbia Journal of World Business*, Vol. 23, No. 4 (Winter 1988): 87–95; Jonathan Kapstein, "Volvo's Radical New Plant: The Death of the Assembly Line?" *Business Week*, 28 August 1989, 92–93; Stephen Kindel, "Check Your Brakes," *Financial World*, Vol. 158, No. 22 (1989): 32–34.

zation can do, the Volvo example suggests that work can be redesigned and improved even in such capital-intensive industries as automobile manufacturing. Second, the work-group approach must be integrated carefully into the total organizational system to maintain the change over time and to be effective. An organization must focus not only on designing tasks for groups but also on establishing a fit between the work-design strategy and the organizational structure and culture.

SHENANDOAH LIFE

Shenandoah Life Insurance Co. welcomed the world of high technology in the early 1980s by installing a $2 million system to computerize processing and claims operations at its headquarters. [20] However, the results were disappointing. Using the new system, it took twenty-seven working days and handling by thirty-two clerks in three departments to process a typical application for a policy conversion.

Shenandoah's problem stemmed from its rigid organizational structure, not from defects in technology. Only by radically reorganizing its work system did it reap the benefits of automation. The company grouped the clerks in "semiautonomous" teams of five to seven members. Each team learned to perform all the functions that were once spread over three departments. As a result, typical case-handling time dropped to two days, and service complaints were practically eliminated. By 1986, Shenandoah was processing 50 percent more applications and queries with 10 percent fewer employees than it had in 1980.

The productivity gains at Shenandoah Life and other companies are part of a powerful synergism taking root in the United States—the appropriate matching of people with automation. American managers are learning what the Japanese discovered years ago: The solution to fading competitive ability, sluggish productivity growth, and poor quality cannot be found in technology alone. To realize the full potential of automation, companies are integrating workers and technology in sociotechnical systems that revolutionize the way work is organized and managed. This is an immensely important trend, one that is producing a new model of job design and work relations that will shape the workplace well into the twenty-first century.

QUALITY OF WORK LIFE

In recent years, increasing attention has been given to the overall quality of work life an individual experiences in an organization. As traditional assumptions about managing are challenged and as the technological and human aspects of work change, organizations are devoting more resources and energy to developing work environments that are excellent for both people and production. **Quality of work life** (QWL) describes this broader concern for the total work environment.

Concern About the Quality of Work Life

During the last fifteen to twenty years, social and economic forces have converged to bring about important work innovations. The composition of the work force changed dramatically during this period; women entered the labor force in unprecendented numbers, the proportion of older workers declined, the ethnic composition became more diverse, and the average level of education increased. In addition, the rate of productivity declined in the United States, and European and Japanese manufacturers emerged as strong competitors in markets previously dominated by American companies. Quality of work life had its beginnings during this period.

It [quality of work life] has evolved in a period of both rising inflation and deepening recession, when the problems and uncertainties facing American business are all but overwhelming and the capital needed to support any new venture is especially scarce. The concern seems, furthermore, to be part of a significant change in the management philosophy—a change that is being expressed in permanent alterations of corporate structures and policies. The improvement of life at work seems to be a direct response by many organizations to problems of rising unemployment and falling productivity, and it is bringing about changes that are likely to persist long after the current popularity and novelty of the topic have subsided. [21]

The areas of concern and activity encompassed by quality of work life are broad and diverse in nature. Consequently, the term has acquired many different meanings. [22] To some managers and employees, quality of work life refers to industrial democracy, increased worker participation in decision making, or achieving the ultimate goals of the human-relations approach to management. To others, the term suggests various strategies and techniques for increasing productivity through human resources rather than capital or technology. Unions and worker representatives often view changes in the quality of work life as leading to healthier working conditions or as a means of achieving equitable distribution of the work organization's income and resources. Some labor leaders, on the other hand, view quality of work life improvements as methods of obtaining greater productivity from workers without paying higher wages. Finally, some managers and employees interpret the quality of work life concept as closely related to, if not as another term for, such concepts as job satisfaction, organizational commitment, or humanistic organizations.

Perhaps the most comprehensive and well-known definition of QWL suggests eight major criteria that characterize a high quality of work life. [23] Each criterion is described briefly below.

1. *Adequate and fair compensation.* Pay should meet socially determined standards of sufficiency and bear an appropriate relationship to pay received for other work.
2. *Safe and healthy environment.* Employees should not be exposed to physical conditions or work arrangements that are unduly hazardous or unhealthy. Furthermore, future standards may be imposed to increase personal comfort at work by minimizing odors, noise, or visual annoyances.
3. *Immediate opportunity to use and develop human capacities.* Work has tended to be fragmented, deskilled, and tightly controlled. To facilitate the development of human capacities, work should possess the following qualities: autonomy, skill variety, information and feedback about the total work process, whole tasks, and involvement in both planning and implementing.
4. *Future opportunity for continued growth and security.* Work should provide opportunities for continued learning and development, organizational or career advancement, and employment and income security.
5. *Social integration in the work organization.* The nature of personal relationships in an organization is an important dimension of the quality of work life. For an individual to have a satisfying identity and experience self-esteem, work should have the following attributes: freedom from prejudice, supportive primary groups, a sense of community in the work organization, interpersonal openness, and upward mobility.

6. *Constitutionalism in the work organization.* A high quality of work life is characterized by adherence to the following institutional principles in the work organization: the right to personal privacy, the right of free speech, the right to equitable treatment in all matters, procedures for due process, and access to appeals.
7. *Work and the total life space.* The relationship of work to the total life space is best expressed as balance. Work should be balanced so that work schedules, career demands, and travel requirements do not take up leisure and family time on a regular basis. Balance also refers to advancement and promotion opportunities that do not require frequent geographical moves.
8. *The social relevance of work life.* The work organization should be socially responsible in its products, waste disposal, employment practices, marketing strategies and techniques, participation in political campaigns, and so on. Organizations that are not socially responsible can cause employees to depreciate the values of their own work and careers.

As we indicated earlier, quality of work life encompasses a wide range of concerns and activities. The relationships among these eight criteria are complex and sometimes appear to be contradictory. For example, the extensive rules governing job security and job rights often inhibit efforts to make work more challenging. A high level of employee involvement may make a balance between work and family/leisure pursuits difficult to achieve. These issues and dilemmas are and will continue to be of great interest to managers and scholars as they attempt to improve the quality of work life in modern organizations.

Applying the Quality of Work Life Concept in Modern Organizations

The concept of quality of work life is a useful tool for thinking about people, work, and organizations. When applied in an organization, QWL programs can involve a number of different activities such as participative problem solving and decision making, employee selection, personnel policies, training, work design, reward systems, and work environment improvements.[24] Features and characteristics common to many QWL, or "high involvement," programs are described below.

Participative problem solving and decision making

Achieving greater employee involvement in problem solving and decision making at various organizational levels is a focus of many QWL efforts. Methods used to expand employee involvement include quality circles, cooperative labor-management committees or teams, autonomous work groups, and project or matrix organizations. These techniques and methods can be used to increase employee knowledge about and participation in a wide range of organizational decisions and issues.

Employee selection

Instead of using the personnel department to screen, test, and select job applicants, high involvement organizations may use a process designed to help applicants make valid decisions about whether they can fit into potential positions. Rank and file employees may be involved directly in making selection decisions. In such plants, group interviews may be held with the manager and candidates' potential co-workers; work-team members assume the major responsibility for selecting new team members.

Potential employees are questioned about their job skills, experience, and attitudes toward participation, and their interpersonal skills are observed to determine whether they will perform effectively under this management approach. Emphasis is placed upon acquainting candidates with the details of the jobs they may fill and the nature of the managerial style that will be used. This direct exchange of expectations enables team members and job candidates to assess realistically the fit between a particular person and an available position and thereby to enhance the likelihood of a mutually satisfying working relationship.

Egalitarian perquisites

Rank and status differences are minimized in many QWL programs. For example, rather than providing separate areas for managers to eat and spend their nonwork hours, facilities are designed so that everyone uses the same dining area, restrooms, recreational facilities, entrances, and parking areas. Special parking spaces, dining rooms, and other "perks" are conspicuous by their absence in organizations having QWL programs. Companies such as Apple, Intel, Rolm, Honda, Nissan, Union Carbide, and DEC have taken steps such as these to remove rank and status symbols.

The traditional dress code, in which people at different levels of management wear different clothes, is also abandoned in many high involvement organizations. In Honda's United States plants, for example, all employees wear a Honda uniform. In other high involvement plants, no one wears ties or uses other symbols of power such as large desks, receptionists, plush carpet, or large offices.

Personnel policies

Most high involvement plants place a high value on employment stability. Consequently, an initial commitment to all regular employees is made. This commitment, based on the assumption that layoffs have negative effects on productivity and job satisfaction, typically stipulates that every reasonabale effort will be made to avoid involuntary terminations. Due to economic realities, organizations typically stop short of adopting "no layoff" policies. The expectation is created, however, that layoffs will occur only as a last resort.

This policy has been implemented in a number of ways. For example, temporary employees can be used in times of high business volume. Regular employees can also do maintenance work or even make-work jobs during slow periods. In some instances where a forced reduction has seemed inevitable, employees have elected to shut down the plant for a limited period to avoid terminating a few individuals.

High involvement organizations also usually solicit employee input during the formulating and implementing of personnel policies related to hours of work, flextime, benefits, and discipline. For example, employees in the TRW plant in Lawrence, Kansas, are asked to staff all three shifts on whatever basis they decide. They are, of course, expected to meet production demands.

Organizational structure

A key feature of high involvement organizations is their structural hierarchy. In such organizations, the plant manager or operating officer is located only a few levels above the production workers. Frequently, the role of foreman has either been eliminated completely or made directly accountable to the plant manager. Intermediate levels of the hierarchy, such as general foreman or superintendent, are frequently eliminated.

Several work teams usually report to a single supervisor and the teams are considered self-managed (see the "Self-Managed Work Groups" section in Chapter 9). In most cases, an elected team leader is responsible for communicating with the rest of the organization. This person undertakes the time-consuming task of lateral integration with other functional and line departments.

In large corporations, high involvement management almost inevitably means a decentralized organization that is structured around businesses. It does not mean large, highly specialized corporate staffs organized around such functions as manufacturing, finance, sales, legal affairs, and marketing. TRW, 3M, and Honeywell are examples of companies organized around businesses that, as a result, are better positioned for high involvement management.

3M

3M Corporation is a large organization whose structure allows it to act small. 3M has forty-two divisions, each organized around a particular product or service. Each division typically got its start in the following way. A 3M employee (or employees) who had an idea for a new product formed an action team. The team leader recruited full-time members from technical areas, manufacturing, marketing, sales, and sometimes finance. The team worked together to design the product and formulate the production and marketing strategies. The team then manufactured, used, and developed line extensions of the new product. Members of the team were promoted and received raises as the new product (business) continued to grow. When sales for the new product reached $5 million, the product's originator became a project manager. At the $20 million sales level, the originator became a department manager. An originator of a new business usually becomes a division manager when sales reach the $75 million level.

Any 3M employee can potentially develop a new product or business into a division of the company. The results of this business-focused organizational structure are high levels of innovation and involvement by employees.

Training

QWL programs place a heavy emphasis upon training, career planning, and the personal growth and development of employees. This emphasis is supported by extensive on-site training programs and encouragement for individuals to take off-the-job training. Off-site training is often financially supported by the organization.

One specific type of training used in many organizations today is **cross-training.** Cross-training simply means that an employee (or group of employees) is trained to perform several related jobs. For example, a particular task may involve 20 percent welding and 80 percent pipefitting. A cross-trained employee has mastered both the welding and pipefitting skills necessary to perform the job.

Many manufacturers have found that teams of cross-trained workers can make a significant contribution to the improvement of product quality. Members of such groups can detect flaws in each other's work, apply problem-solving techniques more effectively, and fill in for each other as needed on various work assignments. At General Motors' Detroit gear and axle plant, for example, a team of thirty cross-trained workers building parts for rear-wheel-drive suspension systems cut warranty costs related to the suspensions by 400 percent in just two years.[25]

The increased skill variety which results from cross-training can also have a positive influence on job satisfaction and the overall quality of work life experienced by the employee. Kathleen Horan, a customer service representative at Lechmere, Inc., studied on her own time to learn how to sell home health products, work the cash register, and fill in at the switchboard. She also learned how to sell in the sporting goods, housewares, and photo departments. "I feel like I'm in charge of my own destiny," she reported.[26]

Open information system

In high involvement organizations, financial information is widely shared among all employees and used for goal setting. This willingness to disclose financial data, when combined with economic education, creates a working environment in which employees can understand how well the organization is doing. Workers can experience the satisfaction of being part of a larger team and can relate their efforts to the performance of the total organization.

In the DEC Enfield, Connecticut, plant, for example, a toll-free telephone number on the shop floors allows customers to call directly the team that built their product. This aspect of the information system provides feedback to employees about the quality of their product and shows just how serious top management is about high quality performance.

Work design

As discussed earlier in this chapter, work design involves structuring or rearranging tasks to meet employee needs and technological requirements. To achieve this objective, individual jobs are enlarged, enriched, or totally redesigned in many QWL projects. The sociotechnical approach can also be used to achieve the best possible fit between the technological aspects of work and the psychological needs of people.

Innovative reward systems

An important aspect of many QWL projects is developing reward systems that contribute to a participative, high performance work environment. One example of such a reward system is the **all-salaried work force;** management and nonmanagement employees working under such a program do not punch time clocks, do not lose pay if they are late to work, and have well-developed leave programs.

Many plants with ongoing QWL programs have established **skill-based job evaluation systems** for employees. Instead of a traditional job evaluation program, in which jobs are scored according to their characteristics to determine a common pay rate for equivalent jobs, the skills of each individual are assessed independently. All employees begin at the same salary and receive increased compensation as they learn new skills. When this pay system is combined with job rotation, people doing relatively low-level jobs may be highly paid because they are capable of performing a large number of other, more skilled tasks.

At Motorola, for example, responsibility for detecting product defects was shifted from inspectors at the end of the assembly line to individual production workers. Then, because workers who understand the entire production process are the most adept at defect diagnosis, the company overhauled its compensation system to reward those who learned a variety of job skills. This innovative compensation system helped to reduce the defect rate by 77 percent between 1985 and 1989, from 1,000 per million parts to 233.

An attempt is also made in many QWL programs to link pay to performance. Some organizations, for example, have introduced a merit component into the skill-based pay system. Other organizations have implemented plant-wide profit sharing plans in which profits generated by productivity beyond an established standard are distributed equitably among employees. Steelcase, Inc., a producer of office furniture, provides profit- and productivity-based bonuses averaging 60 percent of base pay. In addition, the firm contributes 15 percent of total compensation to a deferred profit-sharing plan. Bonuses are based on individual and team performance; they also include quarterly and annual profit distribution.

Work environment improvements

These activities frequently focus on improving the physical conditions and aesthetics of the work area (the lighting, ventilation, climate control, or interior design). The attractiveness of the work environment can also be enhanced with innovative work schedules such as flexitime (employees select, within certain guidelines, work hours and schedules that best meet their individual needs) and the 4/40 work week (forty hours of work are performed in four ten-hour days).

In summary

QWL efforts are designed and implemented to achieve two basic objectives: (1) to increase organizational effectiveness and productivity, and (2) to develop human resources. These objectives are broad and comprehensive in nature. Achieving such encompassing goals frequently requires changing the work-related philosophy, attitudes, and practices of both managers and workers. It is thus important to remember that QWL improvements are not the result of a single program or a series of techniques. A high quality of work life is created through sustained, cooperative, and usually lengthy efforts to solve production-, people-, and technology-related problems in an organization. Such QWL efforts usually require using a variety of work-innovation techniques and approaches. Exhibit 14.4 summarizes the characteristics of QWL/high involvement work settings.

Quality of work life interventions have been implemented in such organizations as General Motors, Sherwin-Williams, AT&T, Xerox, Lincoln National Life, Texas Instruments, IBM, and Procter & Gamble. The QWL movement has struck a responsive chord in many areas of the industrialized world and is expanding into organizations of all types.

WORK DESIGN: CONCLUSIONS

Contemporary managers must be knowledgeable about work design for several reasons. First, jobs are the links or interfaces between individuals and organizations; employees contribute to achieving organizational goals through the coordinated performance of work. Work design is thus an important determinant of organizational effectiveness. Second, a person's work is an important source of self-identity, motivation, and satisfaction. Consequently, the type of work an individual performs affects many aspects of his or her life. Finally, today's highly educated and mobile labor force has expectations about what work can and should be that differ from those of previous generations. In a world of rapidly changing technology and social expectations, a manager must be aware of the impact work design can have on both employee and organizational performance.

The nature and types of work people perform in organizations have changed dramatically since the industrial revolution. The advent of the assembly line, Taylor's principles of scientific management, and an emphasis on efficiency brought a high degree of specialization and standardization to many jobs. Early innovations in work

EXHIBIT 14.4 CHARACTERISTICS OF A HIGH INVOLVEMENT WORK SETTING

ORGANIZATIONAL STRUCTURE
Flat, lean, mini-enterprise-oriented, team-based, participative structure.

JOB DESIGN
Individually enriched or self-managed teams.

INFORMATION SYSTEM
Open, inclusive, tied to jobs, decentralized, participatively set goals and standards.

CAREER SYSTEM
Tracks and counseling available, open job posting.

SELECTION
Realistic job preview, team-based, potential and process skill oriented.

TRAINING
Heavy commitment, peer training, economic education, interpersonal skills.

REWARD SYSTEM
Open, skill-based, gainsharing or ownership, flexible benefits, all-salaried, egalitarian perquisites.

PERSONNEL POLICIES
Stability of employment, participatively established through representative group.

PHYSICAL LAYOUT
Egalitarian, safe and pleasant, congruent with organizational structure.

design such as job rotation and job enlargement attempted to reduce the repetitive nature of work through horizontal job loading—increasing the number of different tasks an employee performs. These initial work innovations produced disappointing results, however, because they did not alter the nature of the tasks an employee performed.

Contemporary approaches to work design such as job enrichment and the job characteristics theory emphasize the importance of allowing employees to assume greater responsibility for planning, organizing, controlling, and evaluating their own work. These approaches stress vertical job loading as a means of designing jobs to meet employees' needs. By designing or redesigning jobs to include greater responsibility, autonomy, task significance, feedback, and recognition, a worker's attitudes and outcomes can be affected positively. The sociotechnical approach focuses simultaneously on an organization's social and technological systems. In contrast to work design strategies that focus on designing individual jobs, the sociotechnical approach suggests that work should be configured to optimize the fit between the social and psychological needs of people and the technical aspects of work.

During the late 1960s and 1970s, increased attention was given to the overall quality of work life (QWL) individuals experienced in organizations. Organizations are devoting more resources and energy to developing total work environments ex-

ETHICAL DILEMMA
How Much Can You "Bug" Employees?

True or False:

1. I am very strongly attracted to members of my own sex.
2. I believe in the second coming of Christ.
3. I have no difficulty starting or holding my urine.

Most people would not readily volunteer the answers to these questions. However, applicants for security guard positions at Minneapolis-based Target stores must answer these and 701 similar questions. A recent job applicant passed the test and accepted employment with the firm. After the exam, the applicant said he felt embarrassed and humiliated by having to disclose his innermost beliefs and feelings. He subsequently accused Target of illegal prying in a class action suit filed in late 1989.

The dispute over workplace privacy highlights one of the hottest employment issues of the 1990s. Today, new technology is leading to more frequent and foolproof opportunities for spying. Video display terminals (VDTs), for example, allow employers to track number of tasks completed, amount of time spent on tasks, time between tasks, and time away from the terminal for each of their employees. Employers are bugging and tapping workers, monitoring them at their computers, and even using special chairs to measure body movements. Organizations use this information to monitor employee work performance and to investigate and prevent theft, drug abuse, and other forms of dysfunctional behavior.

General Electric reports that it uses tiny, fish-eye lenses installed behind pinholes in walls and ceilings to watch employees suspected of crimes. DuPont uses hidden, long-distance cameras to monitor its loading docks around the clock. At Delta and other airlines, computers track which employees write the most reservations. And Management Recruiters, Inc., headquartered in Chicago, evaluates computerized schedules to see which recruiters interview the most job candidates.

Some forms of electronic monitoring can be used as legitimate tools for supervision. Care must be exercised, however, that such tools do not violate individuals' basic rights of privacy. The debate concerning this sensitive issue will undoubtedly continue to intensify during the 1990s.

Questions

Is it ethical for organizations to use these new technologies to collect information about employees?

Do employees have a right to know that such information is being collected?

SOURCES: Gary T. Marx and Sanford Sherizen, "Monitoring on the Job: How to Protect Privacy as Well as Property," *Technology Review*, Vol. 89, No. 8 (November-December 1986): 63–72; Don Nichols, "Monitoring Employees: When Measurement Goes Too Far," *Incentive Marketing*, Vol. 161, No. 12 (December 1987): 27–30, 92–93; Mark McLaughlin, "An Attempt to Tether the Electronic Workplace," *New England Business*, Vol. 11, No. 10 (October 1989): 13–16; Jeffrey Rothfeder and Michele Galen, "Is Your Boss Spying on You?" *Business Week*, 15 January 1990, 74–75.

cellent for both people and production. QWL and high involvement programs can affect organizational policies and practices in areas such as employee selection, personnel, training, work design, reward systems, and the work environment. The QWL movement is a reflection of changing assumptions about management in the United States and other industrialized countries and is expanding into organizations of all types.

QUESTIONS FOR REVIEW AND DISCUSSION

1. What is work design?
2. What are the main characteristics of the scientific management approach to work design?
3. Explain the difference between horizontal and vertical job loading.
4. What contribution has Herzberg made to the field of work design?
5. Describe the four basic components of the job characteristics model.
6. What steps or guidelines can a manager follow when using the job characteristics model to redesign work?

7. What are some potential problems with work redesign? What can managers do to overcome such problems?
8. What conclusions or lessons for management emerged from the sociotechnical experiments at the Volvo and General Foods plants?
9. Why has concern about the overall quality of work life increased during the last fifteen to twenty years?
10. How is the quality of work life concept applied in modern organizations?

REFERENCES

1. R. W. Griffin, *Task Design: An Integrative Approach* (Glenview, Ill.: Scott, Foresman and Company, 1982), 4.
2. Frederick W. Taylor, *The Principles of Scientific Management* (New York: Harper and Row, 1911).
3. Ibid., 57.
4. Frederick Herzberg, B. Mausner, and B. Snyderman, *The Motivation to Work* (New York: Wiley, 1959).
5. J. B. Miner, *Theories of Organizational Behavior* (Hinsdale, Ill.: The Dryden Press, 1980), 104.
6. J. R. Hackman and G. R. Oldham, "Motivation through the Design of Work: Test of a Theory," *Organizational Behavior and Human Performance*, Vol. 16 (August 1976): 250–279.
7. Hackman, "Work Design," in Hackman and J. L. Suttle, eds., *Improving Life at Work* (Santa Monica, Calif.: Goodyear, 1977), 129.
8. Hackman and Oldham, *Work Redesign* (Reading, Mass.: Addison-Wesley, 1980), 275–315.
9. Hackman, Oldham, R. Janson, and K. Purdy, "A New Strategy for Job Enrichment," *California Management Review*, Vol. 17 (Summer 1975): 57–71.
10. E. Huse and M. Beer, "Eclectic Approach to Organizational Development," *Harvard Business Review*, Vol. 49 (September-October 1971): 49, 103–112.
11. Hackman, Oldham, Janson, and Purdy, op. cit., 57–71.
12. Hackman and Oldham, *Work Redesign.*
13. K. H. Roberts and W. Glick, "The Job Characteristics Approach to Task Design: A Critical Review," *Journal of Applied Psychology*, Vol. 66 (April 1981): 193–217; Glick, G. D. Jenkins, Jr., and N. Gupta, "Method Versus Substance: How Strong Are Underlying Relationships Between Job Characteristics and Attitudinal Outcomes?" *Academy of Management Journal*, Vol. 29,

No. 3. (1986): 441–464; R. W. Griffin, "Toward an Integrated Theory of Task Design," in L. L. Cummings and B. W. Staw, eds. *Research in Organizational Behavior* (Greenwich, Conn.: JAI Press, 1987), 79–120; Y. Fried and G. R. Ferris, "The Validity of the Job Characteristics Model: A Review and Meta-Analysis," *Personnel Psychology*, Vol. 40 (1987): 287–322.
14. Hackman and Oldham, *Work Redesign*, 97.
15. P. G. Gyllenhammar, *People at Work* (Reading, Mass.: Addison-Wesley, 1977).
16. R. J. Aldag and A. P. Brief, *Task Design and Employee Motivation* (Glenview, Ill.: Scott, Foresman and Company, 1979), 134.
17. R. E. Walton, "The Plant That Runs on Individual Initiative," *Management Review* (July 1972): 20–25.
18. D. A. Whitsett and L. Yorks, "Looking Back at Topeka: General Foods and the Quality of Work Life Experiment," *California Management Review*, Vol. 25 (Summer 1983): 93–109.
19. R. W. Griffin, *Task Design*, 198.
20. "Management Discovers the Human Side of Automation," *Business Week*, 29 September 1986, 70–71; John B. Myers, "Making Organizations Adaptive to Change: Eliminating Bureaucracy at Shenandoah Life," *National Productivity Review*, Vol. 4, No. 2 (1985): 131–138; Lee W. Frederiksen, "A Case for Cross-Training," *Training*, Vol. 23, No. 2 (February 1986): 37–43; "Case History: Benefits of Cross-Training, " *Small Business Report*, Vol. 11, No. 5 (May 1986): 98–99.
21. Suttle, "Improving Life at Work—Problems and Prospects," in Hackman and Suttle, op. cit., 6.
22. Ibid., 3.
23. Walton, "Quality of Work Life: What Is It?" *Sloan Management Review* (Fall 1973): 11–21.
24. Edward E. Lawler III, *High Involvement Management*

(San Francisco: Jossey-Bass Publishers, 1986), 194–215; Brian Meskal, "Quality of Life in the Factory: How Far Have We Come? *Industry Week*, 16 January 1989, 12–16.

25. Norm Alster, "What Flexible Workers Can Do," *Fortune*, 13 February 1989, 62–66.
26. Ibid., 64.

CASE 14.1

Teamwork at General Motors: progress and problems

DONALD D. WHITE   *University of Arkansas*
RAGHAV SINGH   *University of Arkansas*

In the late nineteenth and early twentieth century, industrial engineers led by such men and women as Frederick Taylor, Henry Gantt, and Frank and Lillian Gilbreth focused the business world's attention on improving worker productivity. The principles that Taylor and his lieutenants espoused involved breaking work down into simple, specialized tasks, each performed by narrowly trained workers. This "production system," coupled with piece-rate wages, emphasized the importance of individual productivity.

To be sure, the system was efficient, and significant gains in output were widely recorded. There were, however, noticeable side effects. Highly specialized jobs designed to be simple and repetitive were also monotonous and numbing. Workers, who performed their tasks mechanically as though they were robots, quickly lost interest in what they were doing and who they were doing it for. Thus, the gains achieved on carefully engineered jobs have often been offset by shoddy workmanship, absenteeism, and turnover. Today, these work systems are more likely to be associated with low quality and decreasing productivity than

with the high levels of efficiency for which they were originally designed.

In a bid to improve both quality and productivity, the auto industry has attempted to introduce work teams into its factories. Although European manufacturers, especially those in Scandanavia, have used work teams for over two decades, it has been intense competition from Japanese auto makers that has prompted American manufacturers to experiment with team-based production. Teams consist of multi-skilled workers who are given far greater job-related freedom than in the past. Working together, teams like those at New United Motor Manufacturing, Inc. (NUMMI, a GM-Toyota joint venture at Fremont, California) work with little management supervision under a revolutionary manufacturing system.

The Fremont facility has already seen spectacular gains in productivity. The plant was able to cut its work force in half while meeting all production schedules. Now General Motors is attempting to introduce work teams throughout many of its other facilities.

At NUMMI, job classifications have been cut to three; production workers are in one category and skilled-trade workers in the other two. (In some automotive plants, over one hundred such classifications may exist). Workers are then divided into small teams (usually of five members), each having a leader who is a union member. Team members are trained to perform all the jobs assigned to their unit so that they can help out as the need arises. General Motors believes that this kind of cross-training is the key to successful work teams. Employees are able to rotate

SOURCE: "Detroit vs. the UAW: At Odds over Teamwork," *Business Week*, 24 August 1987, 54–55; "Is Teamwork a Management Plot? Mostly Not," *Business Week*, 20 February 1989, 70; "Three Plants, Three Futures," *Technology Review*, January 1989, 38–45; Clair Brown and Michael Reich, "When Does Union-Management Cooperation Work? A Look at NUMMI and GM-Van Nuys," *California Management Review*, Vol. 31, No. 4 (1989): 26–44; Lee Branst and Agnes Dubberly, "Labor-Management Participation: The NUMMI Experience," *Quality Progress*, Vol. 21, No. 4 (April 1988): 30–34; Daniel Forbes, "The Lessons of NUMMI," *Business Month*, (June 1987): No. 6 Vol. 29, 34–37; Bryan H. Berry, "What Makes the NUMMI Plant Different," *Iron Age*, 5 September 1986, 27–34.

tasks among themselves and reorganize work as needed. In addition, management has greater flexibility in the use of workers, since individual employees are no longer tied to specific jobs. Consequently, qualifications count more than seniority.

In some cases, team members at Fremont have been given even greater authority. Group members schedule work and assign tasks to individual employees. When special problems arise, members of the team meet to solve the problems and address other issues that might influence the group's activities in the future. Although some work teams have even been given the authority to evaluate individual performance and recommend increases, GM executives decided that Fremont work teams would concern themselves only with day-to-day work activities.

The work-team concept was originally pioneered by Volvo, and is based on the idea that employees may be able to administer a work place more efficiently than can management. Workers can also address product-related matters. For example, a work team that came up with a better way to install a windshield was allowed to implement the idea itself.

A majority of workers prefer the new system. One worker summed up their feelings: "We like being treated with respect, working in a clean and efficient environment, and having our advice and opinions actively solicited."

While the advantages of having work teams are obvious, GM has encountered stiff resistance from the UAW. Although some UAW leaders believe that teams make work fulfilling and save jobs by making the companies more competitive, others see it as a threat to existing jobs. They fear that increased efficiency

and cuts in supervisory jobs may ultimately lead to the elimination of union jobs as well. Some union members point out that the introduction of teams reduces job classifications, thereby giving management more control over moving workers from job to job. The teamwork concept is therefore seen by some as part of a management plot to cut union power in the workplace. The People's Caucus, an opposition group within one local union, complains that there is constant pressure to work harder and faster, not just smarter. They argue that close cooperation between unions and management makes the two indistinguishable and doesn't permit the union to provide strong representation for its members. At the same time, Caucus members are careful to emphasize that they support NUMMI and the team concept and only want to make the system more humane and democratic.

Unions have not been the only stumbling blocks faced by General Motors in its attempt to introduce teams. Major cultural changes have also been required. Supervisors may find it difficult to shift from the traditional top-down approach to a democratic management style. As one foreman concluded, "We need to start discussing and suggesting rather than issuing orders."

Nevertheless, it appears to be only a matter of time before a large-scale introduction of work teams to the auto industry takes place. Self-managing work groups have gained ground in other industries, and their advantages are increasingly clear. The question of flexible, more autonomous work teams throughout the American auto industry appears to be one of when and how rather than if.

CASE 14.2   *The workplace revolution*

ALECIA SWASY   *The Wall Street Journal*
CAROL HYMOWITZ   *The Wall Street Journal*

At Swift Textiles, Inc., David Owen used to lug around a thirty-pound tool belt so he could manually repair broken looms. Today he's shed his heavy belt

for a hand-sized terminal that can diagnose one hundred different problems on new computer-driven equipment.

CUNA Mutual Insurance Group's Barbara Schutz once spent her entire workday typing stacks of claims checks. Now she talks with customers and decides how claims will be settled—a responsibility once given only to managers.

Call it the workplace revolution.

Computer technology and automation have taken the sweat and tedium out of many jobs, from coal mining to clerical work. Yet work has become far more complex and mentally demanding. No longer can workers count on performing one task day in and day out. Now they must handle a variety of skills, make snap decisions and adapt to unpredictable changes.

In manufacturing, assembly-line methods are being replaced by flexible, "customized" production, which requires mastering an ever-multiplying line of products. In service industries, too, employees are being called upon to think differently and operate in new ways. Bank tellers, for example, must not only demonstrate facility with computers but also be marketers rather than just numbers crunchers and clerks.

The new jobs involve wrenching adjustments for both managers and workers. Managers who must delegate more decision making feel threatened about relinquishing their power. Among workers, problem solving, analytical skills and teamwork are in high demand—and short supply.

"People who've never been asked for an opinion suddenly have to make decisions—and they're scared," says Sue Berryman, director of the Institute on Education and the Economy at Columbia University's Teachers College in New York. "If you've been programmed to be fairly passive and supervised, it's a real change in the rules to be told to take responsibility."

The Hudson Institute, in a study for the Department of Labor called Workforce 2000, confirms the growing complexity of most jobs. By the year 2000, it says, below-average skills will be good enough for only 27 percent of jobs created between 1985 and then, compared with 40 percent of the jobs existing in the mid-1980s. And 41 percent of the new jobs will require average or better skill levels, up from 24 percent, the study says.

LOOMING CHANGES

Nowhere is the upheaval more apparent than in the textile industry, which for generations relied on low-skilled, low-paid labor to make fabric. Now mechanical looms have been replaced by microprocessing equipment. Those who operate and repair the new equipment must read complex manuals and conceptualize how the machines run—the sort of abstract thinking they weren't taught in school.

"Everything used to be mechanical, and if it didn't work you got a bigger hammer," says Dennis Walsh, director of training at Swift Textiles, a Columbus, Georgia, unit of Dominion Textile, Inc. "But those days are over."

When Swift installed Japanese-made computerized looms last August, it found that many of its workers simply couldn't function. Jobs that once were done by hand—such as splicing thread together when it broke—have now been automated. But some of Swift's workers couldn't read or do simple arithmetic nearly well enough to operate the equipment. For those who've survived the technological transition, the work is less physically taxing. Helga Campbell, a nineteen-year Swift veteran, works in the beaming room, operating a machine that winds thread on giant spools in preparation for weaving. In the past, she had to manually brake the machine with a wooden hand paddle. Now she can use an electric foot pedal.

"The thread doesn't break as often, and this machine runs better," she says. Paid by the yard, she can wind 100,000 yards of thread a day, three times the amount she used to do. (She's now paid less per yard but still earns more than she used to.)

But there's also more pressure. The looms are faster, and instead of turning out one kind of denim material, Swift now makes thirty different varieties of the cloth. In addition, the computerized equipment is often difficult to understand.

One recent winter day, Mr. Owen, the loom repairman, spent hours trying to fix a machine that had stopped twenty-seven times between 7 A.M. and noon. He couldn't see the problem, the way he might have on a mechanical loom with its visible levers and dials; the only visible part on the new computerized machine is an electronic circuit board. So Mr. Owen kept fiddling with his terminal, punching in various number combinations to try to diagnose the problem.

The technology will probably become increasingly more sophisticated in the future. And that will result in automated equipment that's easier to operate. But it will also mean that more things can go wrong that are harder to remedy—creating the need for more highly skilled technicians. "We're scared to death of the next ten years—of the technology and what we'll do with our employees," concedes Donald W. Sawtelle, Jr., Swift's director of human resources.

Corning, Inc. faces an equally daunting challenge at its Blacksburg, Virginia, ceramics-substrates plant. The facility is a glass plant that was renovated in 1988 to make auto pollution-control parts, and Corning screened seventy-five hundred applicants for one hundred jobs—selecting the most educated and versatile employees. Still, the plant's emphasis on teamwork and decision making is a stark contrast to workers' previous jobs.

There are no time clocks here and no foremen. In fact, the plant employs just eight managers and twenty technicians. Everyone else has one of two job titles—operating associate or maintenance worker. (At Corning's other ceramics-substrates plant, in Erwin, New York, there are forty-eight job classifications.)

ROTATING JOBS

With few layers, the plant is organized around just five key jobs, which everyone must eventually learn. Employees spend one-fifth of their time in training. And each time they master a new skill, they receive as twenty-five-dollar-a-week raise.

Ultimately, "I want people rotating jobs on a daily basis," says Robert Hoover, the plant manager who worries about encroaching foreign competition. He makes sure workers worry, too, posting notices on the bulletin board about a Japanese competitor that is launching a ceramics plant in North Carolina.

By insisting that workers rotate jobs, he figures they'll have more job security. "Here everybody shares in the good, the bad and the ugly," he notes. "Most production workers at most factories are tuned out. We've got to tap the brains of everyone."

Linda Young stands at a work station with five team members, inspecting finished ceramic substrates that will be part of a car's catalytic converter. The twenty-four-year-old former cashier weighs and studies a batch that will be shipped to Hyundai Motor Co. in South Korea. She has final say over whether a piece will be shipped or thrown away, although the computer screen at her station offers guidelines on what's acceptable.

While this inspection job requires steadfast precision, Ms. Young is also training for other jobs at the plant. "The variety here makes you want to come to work," she says.

But there are also new stresses. The old assembly-line approach, in which each employee worked alone doing one job, has been replaced by Japanese-style teams. Everyone is assigned to a team of about six workers, who together set goals and schedules, and even assign each other jobs. And although that method is proving efficient, it's also the source of numerous conflicts.

"People problems are the issue," says Sherrie Hadrich, a twenty-nine-year-old kiln operator. For in-

stance, some teams have felt pulled down by one lazy member. "If there's conflict," she says, "we're expected to resolve it" instead of turning to a supervisor. "If someone isn't feeling well or pulling their weight, we can't let it go on or it'll just be a bigger problem," she adds, noting how it's difficult to confront a co-worker. (A new training course focuses on how to get along with teammates.)

But teams at Corning and elsewhere are spotting problems once overlooked by managers. At Ford Motor Co.'s Romeo, Michigan, engine plant, a team of electricians concluded that many of the machine switches were defective. They went directly to the plant manager with the problem, who in turn called in the supplier.

Ultimately, the electricians' ideas led to a major change. "We redesigned switches in every single Ford engine plant and achieved huge savings in quality and downtime," says Ernest J. Savoie, Ford's director of employee development.

Those suggestions are crucial as Ford speeds up its model changes. "A decade ago we launched a new car every five to six years, but now it's every two to three years and soon it'll be even faster," says Mr. Savoie.

MANAGER'S RESISTANCE

Not all managers, however, embrace innovation from their subordinates. Even at Ford, which is enlisting all employees in problem solving, "our biggest difficulty has been getting managers to be less controlling," says Mr. Savoie. "There has to be a hell of a lot more delegation."

Eastman Kodak Co. is bumping up against the same problem. Besieged by intense foreign competition, the Rochester, New York, photographic giant is demanding that workers devise ways to improve quality and productivity. But some managers resist worker participation.

"Theoretically, managers know they need an educated work force who can think for themselves—but for years they've discouraged that and even organized jobs so they didn't need it," says Thomas Bailey, a researcher at Columbia University's Conservation of Human Resources. "Most managers are a long way from abandoning traditional, hierarchical organizations."

At Kodak's apparatus division, which makes parts for such Kodak products as printers, copiers, and film processors, workers now track their own quality and suggest changes in product design and the manufac-

EXHIBIT 14.5 A NEED FOR GREATER SKILLS

Occupations of the future will require higher skill levels, based on the Labor Department's breakdown of the skills needed by workers to perform a wide range of jobs. In 1984, for instance, 6 percent of jobs required workers with the two highest skill levels; for jobs to be created between 1984 and 2000, that figure will rise to 13 percent.

SKILL LEVEL	DEFINING SKILL LEVELS		SKILL LEVEL NEEDED		
	Language Skill Level	Math Skill Level	Occupation	Language	Math
6	Reads literature, book and play reviews, scientific and technical journals, financial reports, and legal documents. Writes novels, plays, editorials, speeches, critiques.	Advanced calculus, modern algebra, and statistics.	Biochemist	6	6
			Computer-applications engineer	6	6
			Mathematician	6	6
			Cardiologist	6	5
			Social psychologist	6	5
			Lawyer	6	4
			Tax attorney	6	4
5	Same as level 6, but less advanced.	Knows calculus and statistics; econometrics.	Newspaper editor	6	3
			Accountant	5	5
			Personnel manager	5	5
4	Reads novels, poems, newspapers, manuals, thesauri, and encyclopedias. Prepares business letters, summaries, and reports. Participates in panel discussions and debates. Speaks extemporaneously on a variety of subjects.	Is able to deal with fairly complex algebra and geometry, including linear and quadratic equations, logarithmic functions, and deductive axiomatic geometry.	Corporate president	5	5
			Weather forecaster	5	5
			Secondary school teacher	5	4
			Disk jockey	5	3
			Elementary school teacher	5	3
			Financial analyst	4	5
			Corporate vice-president	4	5
			Computer-sales representative	4	4
			Management trainee	4	4
3	Reads a variety of novels, magazines and encyclopedias, as well as safety rules and equipment instructions. Writes reports and essays with proper format and punctuation. Speaks well before an audience.	Understands basic geometry and algebra. Calculates discount, interest, profit and loss, markup, and commissions.	Insurance-sales agent	3	4
			Retail-store manager	3	4
			Cement mason	3	3
			Manager of dairy farm	3	3
			Poultry farmer	3	3
			Tile setter	3	3
			Travel agent	3	3
			Directory assistance operator	3	2
			Janitor	3	2
			Short-order cook	3	2
2	Recognizes meaning of 5,000–6,000 words. Reads at a rate of 190–215 words per minute. Reads adventure stories and comic books, as well as instructions for assembling model cars. Writes compound and complex sentences, with proper end punctuation and using adjectives and adverbs.	Adds, subtracts, multiplies, and divides all units of measure. Computes ratio, rate, and percent. Draws and interprets bar graphs.	Assembly-line worker (appliances)	2	2
			Toll collector	2	2
			Laundry worker	1	1
1	Recognizes meaning of 2,500 (two- or three-syllable) words. Reads at rate of 95–120 words per minute. Writes and speaks simple sentences.	Adds and subtracts two-digit numbers. Does simple calculations with money and with basic units of volume, length, and weight.			

Source: The Labor Department

EDUCATION
- ■ New Jobs (created 1985–200)
- ■ Existing Jobs (1985)

4 years of college or more
- 30%
- 22

1–3 years of college
- 22
- 20

4 years of high school
- 35
- 40

3 years of high school or less
- 14
- 18

Median years of school
- 13.5 years
- 12.8

Source: The Hudson Institute

turing process. "We used to want them to work harder and faster and perspire a great deal," says Frank Zaffino, the division's vice-president and general manager. "Now we ask for recommendations. And workers are overlapping with engineers and financial people."

Some professionals and managers, however, can't adjust to the overlap. "Some of them got to where they are by being like Prussian soldiers, but today we need a whole different management style," says Mr. Zaffino. He cut his management team by thirty percent, he says, keeping only "the communicators and listeners."

Still, he believes Kodak should have begun encouraging worker participation at least "five years ago. There still aren't enough of us who feel [the need to change] in our hearts and minds."

TELLING CHANGES

Regardless of resistance, work itself continues to change dramatically. Consider a bank teller's job. At Barnett Banks, Inc. in Jacksonville, Florida, tellers once spent their days processing deposits and cashing checks. The work was tedious—and predictable. What mattered most was making sure that the cash drawer was balanced at the end of the day.

But today, being a teller "isn't stuffy order-taking," says Jacqueline Roush Franco, an assistant vice-president at Barnett's Ponte Vedra Beach branch. Many numbers-crunching jobs have been automated or transferred to one central location. Thus, tellers and branch managers no longer have to balance their cash drawers or try to trace bad checks.

What they must do is sell a range of products, from credit cards to retirement accounts. Lynn Boston, head teller at the Ponte Vedra Beach branch, used to spend three hours a day on paper work but now gets that done in forty-five minutes. She spends far more time "making sure the Visa applications are out and asking customers if they have an [automated-teller-machine] card." She hands out happy-face cards to tellers who remember to say "thank you" to customers; those who don't get a card reading "You blew it."

Barnett also offers video training to employees, before and after banking hours, on how to "cross-sell" products. "Some people are turned off by the term 'sales' and think of the Fuller Brush man, but we can no longer afford to sit back and wait for customers to come through the door," says Catherine Cosby, director of employment and compliance at Barnett Banks.

At CUNA Mutual, based in Madison, Wisconsin, claims analysts also spend less time with paper and more time with people. They talk directly with customers and try to settle claims as quickly as possible. "You've got to know the contracts and also put yourself in the customers' shoes," says Ms. Schutz.

These negotiations were once handled only by middle managers. "It's definitely more interesting" than clerical work, says Ms. Schutz, "and you get to see the results of your work."

EXERCISE 14.1
PRODUCTIVITY/QUALITY TASK FORCE PROJECT

BACKGROUND INFORMATION

The largest division of the Davis Corporation is located in central California. Eight thousand employees work in the division, and sales for the last fiscal year were approximately $800,000,000. The division has been growing at a rate of around 15 percent per year compounded, and the long-range plan projects continued growth at that rate. For the past three years, the gross margin, as a percent of sales, has been about 7 percent and ROIC (Return on Invested Capital) has averaged 10 percent. The division is a direct supplier to the Air Force on several large, long-term defense contracts. In addition, the division is a supplier of subsystems and components to several major defense contractors and to other divisions of the Davis Corporation.

Over the past eighteen months, several customers have complained bitterly about product quality. The division was directed by corporate executives to improve both the margin to sales and ROIC by 1.0 percent per year over the next five years and to take steps to improve the quality record and reputation. Following a thorough analysis of the division's technologies, marketing opportunities, competition, human resources, and existing programs, the management team established the following goals:

In the next five years, each major function is to achieve a minimum of 15 percent improvement in overall costs in then-year dollars.

In the next twenty-four months, each major function is to achieve a minimum of 25 percent improvement in overall quality in product and/or service.

Also, it was decided that no more than 1.5 percent of the employees would be laid off in any twelve-month period unless caused by an unforseen program cancellation.

Of the 8,300 employees in the division, 2,000 are in engineering, 350 in logistics, 200 in contracts and pricing, 50 in program management, 100 in marketing, 3,500 in manufacturing, 500 in materiel, 300 in quality assurance, 300 in facilities, 300 in finance, 200 in human resources, 100 in management information systems, and 400 in administrative services.

The following productivity task forces have been organized: (1) engineering and logistics management, (2) marketing, contract administration, pricing and program management, (3) manufacturing, materiel, quality assurance, and facilities, and (4) finance, human resources, and administrative services.

Your task force is scheduled to give a presentation to Bernard Wilkins, president of the division. Each member is to share in the presentation.

DIRECTIONS

1. Have all participants read the background information.
2. Divide the class into task forces.
3. Each task force will prepare a presentation based on the following assignments:
   a. Develop a comprehensive plan to accomplish the goals established for overall cost and quality.
   b. Describe your employee involvement strategy or strategies, if any, and how they would be introduced to those employees and managers who would be affected most directly.
   c. Describe the changes, if any, in work and organizational design strategies that you feel are necessary to improve productivity and quality.
   d. Describe changes, if any, in the pay/reward system you would make on a short-term and long-term basis to support your plan.

EXERCISE 14.2

IMPROVING ORGANIZATIONAL EFFECTIVENESS

BACKGROUND INFORMATION

You have been working as a consultant to a small machinery manufacturer in the midwestern United States. This organization custom designs and builds machines for a variety of manufacturing applications. The workers are represented by a union, and you have been working with a joint union-management committee in analyzing the organization. The president of the company and the president of the union are both on the committee, as are influential representatives of the key groups in the organization.

The organizational diagnosis has revealed the following information:

1. Lower levels of management have never had any management training, but most have been on the job for a considerable amount of time.
2. The union leaders are mostly younger workers.
3. The more senior workers are highly skilled. They object to management interference, which keeps them from doing their work, and they complain that they frequently get misinformation from engineering, which causes a significant amount of rework.
4. Older and younger employees alike complain about the quality of the company's training programs. Formal training programs do not exist (for either the workers in the plant or the engineers who design the machines), and no one puts any energy into maintaining or running the apprenticeship programs.
5. Most lower-level employees and many of the foremen feel that important decisions about work are made by top management without adequate lower-level input. Top management feels that lower-level employees resist taking responsibility for making decisions.
6. Rapidly changing control technologies, made possible because of recent innovations in computer chips, are causing significant changes in machinery design and manufacturing procedures that have been stable for years.
7. Pay levels and fringe benefits are adequate, and people generally feel the company is a good place to work.
8. Neither the union leadership nor the management perceived any major problems in the union-management relationship.

DIRECTIONS

1. This exercise can be accomplished by individuals or groups.
2. Participants should outline the specific changes, if any, they would recommend and the strategies they would use to implement those changes.

CHAPTER 15

ORGANIZATIONAL CHANGE AND DEVELOPMENT

LEARNING OBJECTIVES

1. To appreciate the pervasiveness and importance of change in modern organizations.
2. To become familiar with Lewin's force field model.
3. To identify factors that cause resistance to change.
4. To recognize the conditions associated with successful organizational change.
5. To understand the role of organizational development (OD) in modern organizations.

CHAPTER OUTLINE

The Nature of Change in Modern Organizations
    A Model of Change: Force Field Analysis

Resistance to Change
    Sources of Resistance
    Overcoming Resistance to Change

Organizational Development: The Theory and Technology of Change
    A Definition of Organizational Development
    Change Agent
    Intervention Strategies and Technologies
    Do OD Interventions Really Work?

Organizational Change and Development: Conclusions

Questions for Review and Discussion

References

Cases: 15.1 A Time for Change
         15.2 The Shipping Department

Exercises: 15.1 Diagnosis, Change, and Implementation
           15.2 Using Force Field Analysis as a Diagnostic Tool

KEY TERMS

Unplanned change	**Intervention**
Planned change	**Management by objectives**
Force field analysis	**Survey feedback**
Driving forces	**Job enrichment**
Restraining forces	**Team building**
Unfreezing	**Process consultation**
Refreezing	**Grid organizational development**
Resistance to change	**Sensitivity training**
Organizational development	**Sociotechnical design**
Change agent	**Institutionalization of change**

M ilicent started her car, backed out of her parking space, and began the thirty-minute drive to her home. She usually used commuting time to evaluate the day's work activities and to plan for the next day. Today, however, she felt a real sense of pressure and frustration. She was just glad to be going home on a Friday night. Things at work had been particularly hectic, and she was having a hard time identifying and establishing specific priorities for the coming week.

"Things change so fast around this place it's hard to know what to expect," Milicent thought to herself as she slowed to a stop for a red light. She had worked in retail businesses for almost seven years, and she had recently accepted a job as a department manager at Value Center, a large discount retail store. "Missy," as she preferred to be called, enjoyed the challenge of her work, her co-workers, and the opportunities for advancement that Value Center offered. She was having a difficult time, though, adapting to the rapid pace of change in discount retailing. "Last month the big push was for control of personnel costs; this month the top priority is our in-stock position on "hot" items; who knows what it will be next month? Just when I get things in place and set up to accomplish one goal, everything changes. Priorities seem to shift on a daily basis, and the effectiveness of my planning really suffers. I feel kind of foolish every time I go to the employees and explain another new, urgent priority."

Missy looked to her left and began accelerating onto the freeway. As she moved into the flow of traffic she wondered to herself, "Surely things will settle down in the months ahead, won't they?"

Missy's experience at Value Center emphasizes an important fact of life in contemporary organizations: coping with change is a constant challenge for managers. Pressures for change in organizations of all types will continue to increase in the future because of rapidly changing markets, technologies, personnel, administrative requirements, and products.

To appreciate the pace of change in our modern world, try to imagine the events and changes that an eighty-five-year-old person has witnessed in his or her lifetime:

The development of the technology of flying—from the Wright brothers' first flight at Kitty Hawk to modern jet aircraft, men on the moon, and the space shuttle.
The emergence of new social roles and opportunities for women, blacks, and other minorities—from housewives and unskilled laborers to business executives, governors, and astronauts.
The development of varied modes of ground-transportation—from trains and horse-drawn carriages to automobiles, monorails, and rapid-transit systems.
The growth of the telecommunications industry—from the telegraph to telephones and teleconferencing via satellite.

Significant advances have also been made in such other fields as medicine, education, agriculture, and architecture. Indeed, an eighty-five-year-old person has seen many changes.

Technological advancements, social movements, and political reforms continue to spur immense and widespread change. Just as the vacuum tube and transistor ushered in respectively the first and second ages of electronics earlier in this century, so today the computer chip has again revolutionized the electronics industry and the lifestyles of all who use electronic products. The recent political reforms in Eastern Europe have brought significant social and economic changes into the lives of millions of people. Such technological and political changes have a direct impact on the functioning of organizations and on the people who work with and in those organizations.

One technological source of potentially revolutionary change in the 1990s is superconductivity. Scientists have long known that certain metals conduct electricity with no resistance when they are cooled to absolute zero (minus 459 degrees Fahrenheit); however, that temperature is too cold to allow superconductivity to be of much practical use in industrial, transportation, scientific, or electronic applications. Now, in a series of important advances, scientists have raised the superconductivity threshold to practical levels. The possibilities this technology introduces are stunning. They include superconducting motors that efficiently power electric cars and ships without emitting pollution, superfast trains that travel at speeds of up to three hundred miles per hour on magnetic fields, more powerful computers that pack one hundred or more times as much information-crunching capacity as today's computers, and a revolution in the way electricity is generated, transmitted, and stored.

Because of these recent advances in superconductivity research, innovations and products once only dreamed of are suddenly coming within reach. Consider the ways this technology and other influences may affect your organizational life and work during the next ten or twenty years. Imagine, if you can, how different your organizational life may be just five years from now. As you contemplate these possibilities, it should be apparent that coping with an ever-accelerating pace of change will be a major challenge in the 1990s.

THE NATURE OF CHANGE IN MODERN ORGANIZATIONS

Change occurs in a system whenever the elements of that system (inputs, processes, outputs) are altered or replaced. Two primary types of change take place in organizations: unplanned and planned. **Unplanned changes** are those that happen spontaneously, at random, and without advance notice. An ill co-worker, for example, may force an unplanned change in a manager's daily work schedule. The late arrival of a committee member may cause a last-minute change in the agenda and scheduling of an important meeting. Such unanticipated changes require immediate action to minimize any potential negative consequences and to maximize possible benefits.

Planned change is a deliberate attempt to alter the status quo. In an organizational setting, planned change is an "effort with a stated goal on the part of a change agent to create a modification in the structure and process of a social system such that it requires members of that system to relearn how they perform their roles."[1] The specific goals underlying planned-change efforts in organizations might include increased productivity, improved product quality, reduced costs, and increased job satisfaction.

Change and the challenges it presents are particularly evident in large, complex organizations because of (1) the large number of elements and components in a system, and (2) the nature of the environments in which such organizations exist. External conditions such as foreign competition, government regulation, shortages or surpluses of raw materials, and variable demand for goods and services significantly influence an organization and can render today's successful policies ineffective in just weeks or months. Just as individuals must learn to keep pace with change, so organizations must monitor and adapt to a rapidly changing environment.

Change is a pervasive aspect of modern organizational life for five basic reasons:[2]

1. *The knowledge explosion.* The rate at which new knowledge is developed has accelerated tremendously in recent decades. For example, 90 percent of all the scientists who have ever lived are reportedly still living.
2. *Rapid product obsolescence.* As new knowledge is acquired, old knowledge and products quickly become obsolete. Personal computer models and parts, for example, are often out-of-date within months of their introduction into the marketplace.
3. *The changing composition of the labor force.* The labor force is younger, increasingly urbanized, and more highly educated. In addition, women now account for more than 50 percent of the total work force. Today's labor force also comprises fewer blue-collar and more service employees. These trends have significantly affected social customs and mores and the nature of work in modern organizations.
4. *Growing concern over personal and social issues.* Today's younger, mobile, and educated work force is devoting increased attention to the problems of society and the world. The baby boomers are bringing the social and political concerns of the 1960s and 1970s to business organizations of the 1990s.
5. *Increasing internationalization of business.* Organizations today compete in world markets. General Motors, for example, vies for sales not only in the United States with Ford and Chrysler but also with manufacturers from abroad, including Nissan, Audi, Volvo, and Mercedes-Benz. Foreign markets are also of vital importance to United States producers of goods and services. More and more, domestic markets are being replaced by the intricacies of the world marketplace. (The International Dimension on page 505 highlights a planned change in the European Common Market that will occur in 1992.)

These factors help to explain why change is an important challenge for all organizations and will continue to increase in both pace and complexity.

A Model of Change: Force Field Analysis

Force field analysis, a model developed by Kurt Lewin,[3] is a useful tool for visualizing the concept of change. Lewin argued that any existing condition or level of performance in an organization is an equilibrium locked between two sets of opposing forces—driving and restraining. **Driving forces** promote and facilitate change to a desired condition or level of performance; **restraining forces** impede and hinder such change. Organization A, for example, currently has an 18 percent annual rate of turnover among nonsalaried employees. The level of turnover management desires is 5 percent. According to the force field model (see Exhibit 15.1), the current

INTERNATIONAL DIMENSION
European Community
1992

Change has a special meaning for European Community nations today. The EC consists of twelve European countries and represents over 320 million people united by economic agreements. In the near future, six other European nations, representing an additional thirty-two million people, may become EC members or associate members. Changes eminent in the European economy include (1) increased freedom of movement of goods, services, and money between countries; (2) application of a uniform European standard of trade; (3) uniformity of taxes; and (4) freedom of movement of labor and expertise. In addition, improved rail systems, a network of roads, and competitive air services will facilitate movement between major European industrial centers, making them no more than twenty-four hours distant from each other. Having from 320 to 360 million customers, the 1992 European Community (EC) will be a key market for investors and exporters.

For United States companies, the battle for market share in Europe will be a decisive test of organizational strength and adaptability. In the past, United States companies have competed against a fragmented Europe. However, unification will create a $600 billion consumers goods market in Europe unhindered by trade barriers among member nations. French companies will be able to do business in Germany, Great Britain, Italy, and a dozen other nations as easily as a Seattle-based United States company does business in Cincinnati or Toledo.

How are United States companies preparing for these major changes? The biggest and the best of the United States multinationals began in 1988 to shore up their European operations with a modest investment of about $2.4 billion; this figure rose to a budgeted $19.7 billion for 1989, and $40 billion for 1990.

Some United States firms are so well-established in Europe that competition with European firms is not threatening. Coke and Kellogg are classic continental name brands, Ford and General Motors vie for the top spots in automobile markets, and IBM and Digital Equipment dominate their European markets. Nevertheless, these and other United States companies are modifying their products, altering organizational structures, and looking for European acquisitions and joint ventures in order to solidify their market positions.

Major shifts in consumer demand and competition will result from the unification. Definitions of markets and consumers will change as well. A United States division in France, for example, will no longer compete against a French company in France for French customers; it will compete against French, German, British, Italian, Dutch, Austrian, Belgian, and Spanish companies for customers in those and other countries. And while United States companies are fighting for market share in Europe, European companies will move into the United States market with comparable strength.

Questions

What problems and barriers will inhibit the success of United States firms in the European Community of 1992?

What steps do you think United States firms must take in order to compete successfully in the European Community of 1992?

SOURCES: Richard A. Melcher and Gregory L. Miles, "Will the New Europe Cut U.S. Giants Down to Size," *Business Week*, 12 December 1988, 54–58; Sami M. Abbasi and Kenneth W. Hollman, "Making the Most of EC '92: Background, Issues, and Strategies," *Review of Business*, Vol. 11, No. 3 (1989): 7–14; Carla Hills, "EC 1992: Opportunity and Challenge," *Business Forum*, Vol. 14, No. 4 (1989): 25–27; George Weimer, "EC 92: Economic Integration in Europe," *Automation*, Vol. 37, No. 2 (February 1990): 18–24.

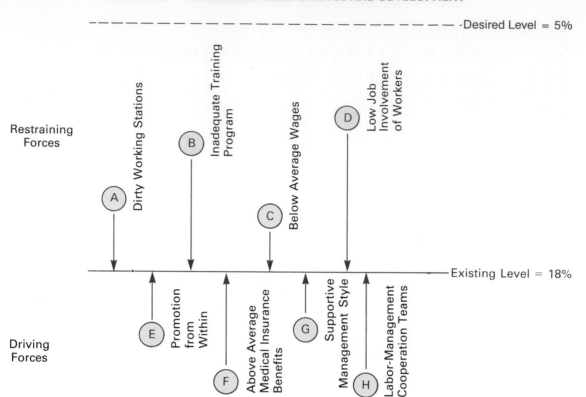

EXHIBIT 15.1   FORCE FIELD ANALYSIS: ORGANIZATION A'S TURNOVER PROBLEM

turnover rate of 18 percent is the balance point among a multitude of forces working both to promote and impede achieving the desired level.

Given the forces outlined in the model, change can be brought about in three basic ways:

1. By increasing the driving forces.
2. By decreasing the restraining forces.
3. By both increasing the driving forces and decreasing the restraining forces.

In Organization A, for example, removing restraining force B (by improving the quality of the training program) will permit a gradual change in the direction of the desired level. Removing restraining force B while simultaneously increasing driving force H (by resolving organizational problems through labor-management cooperation teams) will facilitate an even more rapid change to the desired level. It is important to note that increasing the driving forces without decreasing the restraining forces can result in greater tension and resistance in the organization. Thus, decreasing the forces against change is usually preferable to applying greater pressure toward change.

Lewin further describes change as a process comprising three basic phases: (1) unfreezing, (2) moving to the desired level, and (3) refreezing (Exhibit 15.2).

Unfreezing involves recognizing the need for change. Rarely, if ever, is a work procedure or behavior pattern intentionally altered in an organization without good reason. Change occurs because a gap or disparity between the current level and

EXHIBIT 15.2   THE PROCESS OF CHANGE

desired level of performance is identified and is large enough to hurt. In other words, the status quo is disturbed when the organization recognizes that the distance between where we are (the existing level) and where we want to be (the desired level) must be reduced. Such awareness literally unfreezes the system from established behaviors, attitudes, and policies and prepares it for adaptation and innovation.

Many United States companies experienced the unfreezing phase of the change process during the 1970s and 1980s. As a result of fierce competition and market share erosion, major companies such as Kodak, Xerox, IBM, and Ford recognized that the status quo was no longer adequate to remain competitive in the international marketplace. Changes and improvements in products, production processes, services, and management were needed to regain consumer acceptance and loyalty.

Having recognized the need for change, an organization then attempts to **move to a desired level.** This phase of the change process is action-oriented and includes the following six steps:

1. Identifying the various driving and restraining forces.
2. Assessing the relative strength of each force.
3. Deciding which forces can realistically be changed.
4. Formulating a strategy to increase the driving forces and reduce the restraining forces.
5. Implementing the strategy.
6. Evaluating the outcome.

Xerox, for example, after losing nearly one-half of its market share, focused on improving product quality and service through an ambitious program of "leadership through quality." The very culture of the company was changed to reflect the emphasis on quality. Xerox executives worked to (1) instill quality as the basic business principle in the company, and (2) ensure that quality improvement became the job of every Xerox employee. Extensive training was provided to all employees and compensation systems were altered to reinforce quality. This strategy enabled Xerox to regain much of its lost market share and to become a leader in the movement among United States corporations for improved quality.

The final phase of the process, **refreezing,** stabilizes the change at the new, desired level through the use of extrinsic and intrinsic rewards, new training programs, organizational restructuring, policy changes, and other support mechanisms. Many organizational changes fail because insufficient attention is given to this critical phase of the change process. Indeed, sustained effort is essential for any successful, long-term change.

Let us look at an example of how a change situation can be analyzed using this model. Gil is taking several difficult classes this semester, and his performance is below what he considers to be an acceptable (or desired) level. He has not been able to meet the demands of the courses, and he recognizes the need to improve his study habits (unfreezing). To improve, he decides to (1) find a suitable place to study where he can avoid such distractions as television and casual conversations; (2) set aside specific periods of time to study for particular classes; and (3) take more complete notes in class (changing). To reinforce these new behaviors, Gil decides to reward himself with a treat after each successfully completed study session (e.g., a favorite television program, a candy bar, or a trip to the gym) (refreezing). Gil will also be reinforced positively as he associates his improved test and quiz performance with the altered behavior patterns.

Our discussion of freezing, moving to a desired level, and refreezing may give you the impression that change is a relatively easy process—just recognize the need for change and make the necessary adjustments. In practice, nothing could be further from the truth. Change, in general, and organizational change, specifically, requires considerable effort, resources, and persistence. For example, Organization A's management may formulate a change strategy, implement it, and reduce turnover by 4 percent over a four-month period. However, a sizeable gap will still exist between the current and desired levels of performance. Another strategy must be formulated, implemented, and evaluated—and perhaps another—until the gap or hurt is eventually reduced. Such a process of change, evaluation, and more change, may take months or even years before satisfactory results are achieved.

CAMPBELL SOUP

The Campbell Soup Company provides an example of how change must be implemented, evaluated, and constantly monitored in order to achieve a desired level of performance.[4] There is probably no more durable emblem of American mass marketing than the Campbell soup can. The familiar red-and-white label is a widely recognized symbol of standardization, volume production, and national brand identity. For most of this century, it has stood for a line of products made the same way and sold the same way all across the country.

Changes are occurring at Campbell, however. As markets become more splintered and technologically sophisticated, Campbell is customizing its products and marketing efforts to the local characteristics of various United States regions. In Texas and California, where many people like "hot" food, Campbell now makes its nacho cheese soup spicier than in other parts of the country. In New York, a local sales manager used part of her new local ad budget to arrange a football-related radio promotion for Campbell's Swanson frozen dinners. In Nevada's Sierra mountains, Campbell is treating skiers at Ski Incline to hot samples of its soup of the day.

These are the first indications of a significant change at Campbell that could eventually redefine mass marketing in the United States. Instead of developing a single set of products and marketing programs to win over American consumers, Campbell has formulated a new approach. It is tailoring its products, advertising, promotion, and sales efforts to fit different regions of the country—and even individual neighborhoods within a city.

This strategy has required changes in corporate philosophy and structure; product and sales managers have also had to assume a greater role in the decision-making process at Campbell's. Advertising budgets and campaigns are no longer determined exclusively at corporate headquarters. Rather, managers closest to and most familiar with specific target markets must make key advertising decisions. Many managers at Campbell's have responded positively to the increased responsibility and authority; others have been reluctant to accept change and the accountability associated with increased decision-making power.

Campbell's moves so far have been preliminary and experimental, but other consumer-goods companies are watching closely. The company is continuing to evaluate and monitor the new approach to assess its effectiveness in achieving greater sales and market share.

RESISTANCE TO CHANGE

Organizational changes such as those described at Xerox and Campbell Soup are frequently resisted by managers and employees. As Lewin suggested, individual and organizational behavior patterns are often frozen firmly in place and may require an unfreezing process before change can occur. But why would anyone oppose changes if they are designed to improve an organization's efficiency or effectiveness?

Sources of Resistance

One source of resistance is **uncertainty.**[5] Generally, both individuals and organizations seek to avoid uncertainty. Change, however, increases uncertainty because the known is traded for the unknown. Adapting to the unknown usually requires a process of relearning—developing and testing new behavior patterns, attitudes, interpersonal relationships, and work procedures. Associated with the relearning process is the possibility of embarrassment, failure, and discouragement. Change thus requires an individual, group, or organization to cope with the uncertainty and the potential difficulties of doing things in new ways.

Change can also be perceived as **a threat to vested interests** and can arouse defensive behavior intended to maintain the status quo. For example, organizational members usually invest a considerable amount of time and energy learning the ropes of their jobs. Resistance to change occurs because employees find it difficult to give up the confidence and security of established work procedures, acquired through long hours of diligent effort, for the awkwardness of a new routine. People lose their investments in the status quo if the time and energy devoted to mastering a specific job or a particular set of work skills are lost as a result of change.

Inertia, the tendency to want to do things in an accustomed manner, is another source of resistance to change. By their nature, most organizations are designed to promote stability. Selection processes, training programs, and reward systems within organizations are used to ensure that tasks are performed reliably and predictably. Much effort and many resources are invested in influencing people to perform in prescribed ways. Consequently, it is often difficult to overcome the resistance created by the forces intended to promote stability.

Resistance to change can also stem from a variety of other sources, including:

> Misunderstandings about the purpose and scope of a proposed change.
> Low tolerance for change.
> The belief that a change will reduce status and power.
> Insufficient explanation about or employee participation in designing
> and implementing a change.
> Lack of trust between management and employees.
> The belief that a change will alter an individual's or a group's
> autonomy.
> Differing assessments about the impact of a change.

Given the potential sources of resistance, it should not be surprising that organizational change is difficult to achieve. However, forces working to maintain the status quo, although formidable, can be overcome.

Overcoming Resistance to Change

Researchers have investigated various strategies and techniques for overcoming resistance to change. Two classic studies are particularly helpful in understanding how resistance can be managed.

In a study designed and conducted by Kurt Lewin,[6] the effectiveness of a group-decision method was compared to a lecture as a means of reducing resistance to change. A sample of homemakers was asked to use organ meats (e.g., hearts, lungs, brains, kidneys) instead of the more traditional cuts. Participants received information about the favorable economic and nutritional benefits of these meats through either a lecture or a group discussion conducted by an experienced leader. The researchers were careful to present the same information to all participants. Data collected several weeks later indicated that only 3 percent of the homemakers who received the information through the lecture actually used the organ meats. In contrast, 32 percent of the women exposed to the group-decision method changed to the new variety of meats. Involvement and group pressure, Lewin concluded, significantly reduced the women's resistance to changing their established food habits.

In another classic study, conducted in a textile factory, Lester Coch and John French[7] studied methods for overcoming resistance to changes in work procedures. These researchers specifically compared three ways of bringing about change: (1) management alone formulating new work procedures and subsequently announcing them to employees; (2) employees participating in designing new work procedures through elected representatives; and (3) all employees fully participating in designing new work methods. Productivity measurements taken after implementing the new work procedures indicated that in the first group, output actually dropped from a previously established standard of sixty units per hour to forty-eight. In comparison, the participation-by-representation group produced sixty-eight units per hour, and the total-participation group averaged seventy-three units per hour. From these findings, Coch and French concluded that people are more likely to accept and support changes they have had a say in planning and implementing.

Given these findings, what can managers do to overcome resistance to change? The first step a manager should take is to *secure the commitment* of individuals, groups, and departments directly affected by the change. Without ongoing and widespread support, a change effort within an organization is unlikely to succeed. Second, a manager should *involve employees in the change effort* as a method of fostering commitment. Individuals actively involved in planning and implementing an organizational change are in a better position to understand the need for change and are, therefore, less likely to resist it. Third, a manager should *provide accurate and timely information* to employees about proposed or anticipated changes. Such information can dispel the uncertainty and misunderstanding frequently associated with changes in policy, procedures, or personnel. Finally, the manager should *reinforce desired new behaviors*. Appropriate reinforcement can help shape new behavior patterns and provides an example through which other employees may learn vicariously (see Chapter 4, "Learning, Reinforcement, and Behavior Analysis").

Research has identified six additional factors that help reduce opposition and promote successful change:[8]

1. A strongly felt need, tension, or hurt that motivates people to change.
2. Adequate resources to bring about change.
3. A highly esteemed sponsor and promoter of the change.
4. A plan of action that moves from general proposals to specific plans and goals.

5. A plan of action that increases the self-esteem of the people involved in the change.

6. A change plan that results in new social relationships or the reformulation of old relationships around new behaviors and attitudes.

Thus, resistance to change can be minimized through effective planning and considering these six factors. The following examples illustrate both ineffective and effective attempts to overcome resistance to change.

Eric had known for some time that changes in the personnel evaluation system would be implemented. During the last three years, both management and employees had voiced dissatisfaction with the evaluation criteria and procedures. He had been asked to devise a system that would be fair and acceptable to the various departments. During the last two months, Eric had considered the parts of the system he personally found objectionable. He had progressed through the ranks of the company and knew that his opinions were similar to those of his employees. Based on his experience and observations, he formulated a plan for changing the evaluation system and received approval from division headquarters to move ahead. Eric was proud of the new system. Year-end reviews were scheduled to begin early next week, and he was sure his subordinates would be pleased to learn of the new system when they met with him to receive their annual ratings.

Evelyn had never been timid about change; she viewed it as an opportunity for improvement. Recently, she noticed that customer traffic in her specialty shop had declined. At the same time, she observed that certain standard procedures for marking and arranging merchandise were not being performed as she expected. In addition, the number and frequency of back room conversations among sales clerks were increasing. She believed the decrease in customer traffic was directly linked to these undesirable employee behaviors. Evelyn decided to hold a meeting of all employees after working hours. She assembled the sales figures for the last two months and planned to report on the recent decline in sales. She hoped to appeal to the clerks' sense of pride in the shop and to ask them for suggestions to improve the situation. "If I'm lucky," she thought, "we'll come out of this meeting with a few practical suggestions for getting things back on track."

What do you think of Eric's and Evelyn's approaches to introducing change? Should either of them expect to encounter resistance to change? Evaluate each approach using the concepts and information you have read thus far in the chapter.

IBM

At the corporate level, the chief executive officer of IBM, John F. Akers, believed he could improve the performance of the world's largest computer company by turning decision-making authority over to managers far removed from IBM's Armonk, New York, headquarters. Akers and IBM's directors felt decentralization would make IBM more responsive to customers and quicker to develop new products and services.

Akers characterized the change as perhaps the most significant ever made by the giant computer company. The plan, introduced and implemented in 1988, reorganized IBM into five lines of business and gave general managers worldwide authority for various groups of products, from personal computers to giant mainframes. The general managers were given not only authority but personal responsibility for achieving results. The basic challenge, Akers believed, was to make managers more entrepreneurial and responsive to customers.

> Do you think there was resistance to some or all of the changes undertaken by Akers? What steps could be taken or guidelines followed in order to deal with such resistance?

ORGANIZATIONAL DEVELOPMENT: THE THEORY AND TECHNOLOGY OF CHANGE

By now, you have developed a better understanding of what change is, why organizational change is so complicated, and how resistance to change can be minimized. You may still be wondering, however, *how* change is actually carried out in an organization. Are there tools a manager can use to facilitate change? How does a manager plan an effective change strategy? The answers to these and other questions are found in the field of organizational development.

A Definition of Organizational Development

Organizational development (OD) is defined as a system-wide process of data collection, diagnosis, action planning, intervention, and evaluation aimed at (1) enhancing congruence among organizational structure, process, strategy, people, and culture; (2) developing new and creative organizational solutions; and (3) developing the organization's self-renewing capacity.[9] Typically, organizational development occurs through collaboration of organizational members and change agents, using behavioral science theory, research, and technology. OD, then, is an attempt to use the concepts and methodologies of applied behavioral science (psychology, sociology, anthropology, and social psychology) to help organizations develop and maintain their health. Management development focuses primarily on the growth of individual managers; OD, as the name implies, is concerned with the growth and development of the entire organization.

The pervasive societal and technological changes occurring in our modern world dictate that organizations continuously reassess where they are, where they are going, and how they are going to get there. Managing such organizational transitions requires that managers (1) consciously address the need for change; (2) develop explicit processes and procedures for establishing performance criteria and priorities for improvement; (3) collect data about the organization; (4) promote systematic and timely feedback; and (5) devise and implement appropriate incentives for participants in the change process. These activities constitute the heart of organizational development.

EXHIBIT 15.3   THE CHANGE AGENT IN CONTEMPORARY ORGANIZATIONS

The change agent links theory and application in contemporary organizations.

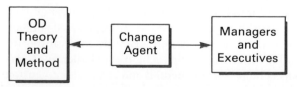

Change Agent

An important person in planning and implementing an organizational development strategy is the OD consultant, or **change agent.** An effective change agent is well versed in behavioral science theories and methods and uses this knowledge to help managers solve their own problems. The basic role of a change agent is to (1) help the organization diagnose itself, and (2) assist organizational members in learning processes and techniques for actually bringing about planned change.

Whether a permanent member of the organization (internal change agent) or an outsider invited from a university or consulting firm (external change agent), the job of the change agent remains the same. The consultant does not make changes or suggest solutions. Instead, he or she first facilitates diagnosis and problem solving by collecting data to assess the organization's current status. Data are often collected through the use of tests, questionnaires, observation, and interviews. Definitions of these methods and brief outlines of the advantages and disadvantages of each appear in Exhibit 15.4.

EXHIBIT 15.4 DATA COLLECTION METHODS

METHOD	DEFINITION	ADVANTAGES	DISADVANTAGES
Interview	A meeting or conversation during which an interviewer poses questions to an interviewee and records the responses.	Immediate feedback and the opportunity to probe and clarify ambiguous questions or answers; complete and detailed responses; flexibility; adaptability.	Time and expense (interviews frequently are lengthy and require trained personnel), the interviewer is the measurement instrument and may introduce personal bias.
Questionnaire	A written set of questions to which a person is asked to respond.	Relatively low-cost method for reaching large samples; uniform stimulus for all respondents.	Low response rate; lengthy response time (e.g., when administered through the mail); lack of immediate feedback—incomplete or unclear responses cannot be clarified; questionnaire design requires time and expertise; respondents must be literate.
Tests	A collection of questions, problems, and/or critical incidents used to measure some attribute, property, or behavior (e.g., achievement, aptitude, stress, assertiveness).	Standardized tests permit comparison with established norms.	Test design construction, and validation are time consuming and require specialized expertise; questionable validity (e.g., does an IQ test actually measure intelligence or language skills?).
Observation of Behavior	A process of watching and recording the behavior of individuals.	Behavior is observed *as* it occurs; observation may yield information respondents are unwilling to provide themselves.	The observer is the measurement device and may introduce personal bias; presence of an observer may alter or influence an individual's behavior; training observers is costly; time-consuming.

Using data collected through these methods, the change agent then helps organization members as they find answers to such questions as:

Where are we now? Where do we want to go?
What weaknesses inhibit achieving important organizational goals?
What can be done to overcome these weaknesses?
What strengths do we have?
How can we use these strengths even more effectively?

As the change agent helps participants probe more deeply into the organization's current status, data are generated that enhance understanding of the system and its problems. This understanding and subsequent analysis provide the basis for a specific intervention designed to alter the status quo.

Again, the change agent does not personally perform the diagnosis or execute the change. Rather, he or she guides the diagnostic process and leads the client toward self-renewal.

Intervention Strategies and Technologies

An **intervention strategy** is a planned effort to bring about individual, group, or organizational change through specific procedures or techniques. Specific technologies for change vary in terms of both their approach and the depth of the resulting intervention. An intervention technique should be designed for or adapted to the particular problem at hand. It must also be carefully evaluated in terms of the degree of emotional impact it will have on organizational members.

Exhibit 15.5 describes the relative cost, personal risks, and relevant systems affected by specific types of interventions. The shallowest penetration takes place in an intervention involving an analysis of the operations and related managerial activities in the technological system. Such an intervention would usually result in machine-type changes designed to increase efficiency. A more deeply felt intervention might involve changes in the administrative system or organizational structure. The deepest emotional penetration would be achieved by using such techniques as sensitivity training and intrapersonal analysis.

The monetary and emotional costs of an intervention increase with the depth of the intervention. Two basic rules should be used to choose the appropriate depth

EXHIBIT 15.5   DEPTH OF VARIOUS INTERVENTIONS

Techniques	Depth	Cost	Risk	Relevant System
Operations analysis	Shallow	Low	Low	Formal or required
Structural changes				
Management by objectives				
Survey feedback				
Job enrichment				Group or emergent
Team building				
Process consultation				
Grid				
Sensitivity training				
Transactional analysis	Deep	High	High	Individual or
Intrapersonal analysis				personal

of an intervention: (1) intervene at a level no deeper than necessary to produce enduring solutions to the problem at hand; and (2) intervene at a level commensurate with the client's energy and resources to commit to problem solving and change.[10]

OD focuses on applying appropriate intervention techniques to specific organizational problems. Such a matching process requires skillful diagnosis of the organization's resources, culture, and commitment. In addition, questions about the intended scope of the change (single task unit or organization-wide) must be addressed. A specific intervention, then, is determined by the requirements of a particular problem and the situation in which it exists.

Efforts to bring about organizational change usually focus on one or more of the following targets: people, tasks, technology, or structure. To provide a better understanding of the OD technologies used to effect such changes, we will briefly describe several specific intervention techniques. Please keep in mind, however, that each technique is considerably more complex than presented in these brief descriptions.

Management by objectives[11]

Management by objectives (MBO) is a technique designed to (1) increase the precision of the planning process at the organizational level, and (2) decrease the discrepancy between organizational and employee goals. MBO encourages systematic performance improvement and provides a basis for employee appraisal through a process of shared goal-setting and evaluation.

An MBO program is usually initiated by upper-level management's developing long-range organizational goals. These goals are then transmitted down the levels of the hierarchy in a cascading manner through superior-subordinate meetings. Such meetings are designed to integrate superior-subordinate perceptions of goals and to pinpoint subordinate contributions to organizational goals at each level of the enterprise. Objectives for each manager are negotiated and written down so future performance can be measured against them. Goal-setting meetings facilitate upward communication by allowing subordinates to share personal goals with their immediate supervisors. In addition, the process permits subordinates to influence the goals formulated at other levels of the hierarchy. An appraisal of employee goal-related performance takes place at the end of the specified time period. This evaluation provides information for compensation and promotion decisions and establishes a basis for goal-setting for the next operational cycle. Exhibit 15.6 shows the MBO cycle.

TENNECO

Tenneco, a large, multi-industry company, employs about eighty-two thousand people, of which approximately fifteen thousand are managers and professionals. The company's goal-setting program, similar to MBO, is referred to as the performance planning and evaluation (PP&E) system. It is used by Tenneco's professional and managerial staff.[12]

The idea for PP&E originated in the office of the president. Top management strongly believed that goal setting should include both hard performance measures and employee development; they were also committed to the fact that the basis for continuing development of an employee is ongoing dialogue between a manager and that employee.

A key feature of Tenneco's approach to implementing PP&E in such a large, diversified corporation is that it provides each divisional company with minimum

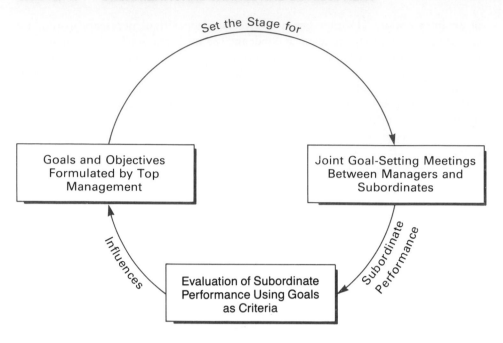

EXHIBIT 15.6   THE MBO CYCLE

standards for using the program while allowing flexibility in integration of the program with each company's policies, operating practices, and systems. The ongoing operation of PP&E follows a number of distinct steps. First, the manager and employee engage in performance planning. They define key job responsibilities, set specific objectives, and assign relative priorities to the goals. The agreed-upon plans are recorded and reviewed periodically by the boss and subordinate to assess progress, to develop methods for improvement, and to make necessary changes. Second, the employee's actual performance is measured against the planned goal after one year. The supervisor completes a tentative evaluation, and the subordinate reviews it to assure consistency and fairness. The two then discuss the assessment, placing their major focus on developing the employee. They discuss the employee's strengths, weaknesses, and opportunities for improvement. Third, the supervisor completes an employee-assessment report that includes information about the performance planning and evaluation. The report is reviewed by the supervisor's boss and maintained within each division and at corporate headquarters for purposes of identifying people with potential for advancement.

An important point to emphasize about Tenneco's program is the separation between employee development and salary review. The progress reviews and evaluation/development sessions are conducted at different times from meetings determining salary increases. This separation helps to assure that employee development will not take a back seat to concerns about compensation.

Survey feedback[13]

Survey feedback is one of the most popular and widely used intervention techniques in the field of organizational development. It involves two basic activities: (1) collecting data about the organization through the use of surveys or questionnaires, and (2) conducting feedback meetings or workshops in which the data are presented to organizational members.

Using standardized questionnaires, data are collected from organizational members about individual attitudes, organizational climate, and the general health of the enterprise. The questionnaires are distributed to all organizational or work unit members, completed, and returned to the change agent for tallying and analysis. These data are then fed back to top management and other participating groups down through the hierarchy. During the final step of the process, organizational leaders conduct group meetings with the change agent's help in which the questionnaire results are discussed, problems are identified, and corrective strategies are developed.

The primary changes brought about by survey feedback appear to be in the attitudes and perceptions of participants. The empirical literature contains little evidence to suggest that survey feedback alone leads to changes in individual behavior or organizational performance. However, survey feedback does function as an effective bridge between organizational diagnosis and the implementation of active problem-solving methods.

Job enrichment[14]

The purpose of **job enrichment** is to increase individual satisfaction and motivation by giving employees more responsibility for planning, directing, and controlling their own work. This intervention technique focuses on changes in the nature of work itself rather than on the environment in which a job is performed (see Chapter 14, "Work Design"). Jobs are enriched through vertical loading—a process of increasing authority and responsibility for decision making in the job itself. For example, workers in many manufacturing firms perform highly specialized and narrowly defined tasks. Such jobs can be enriched by providing workers the opportunity to participate in solving work-related problems and actually granting them the authority to stop the assembly line if problems arise during the production process. Corrective steps can then be quickly taken to ensure a reliable and high-quality product. Job enrichment not only increases authority and responsibility but can also positively affect a worker's sense of achievement and opportunities for personal growth and development.

Team building[15]

Team building is an OD intervention designed to improve the task performance of and relationships among work-group members or others seeking to achieve a common goal. Team building is used to accomplish the following major purposes: (1) to set goals and priorities; (2) to analyze or allocate how work is performed according to team members' roles and responsibilities; (3) to examine how the team is working—its processes such as decision making, communication, and leadership; and (4) to examine relationships among group members.

Data are collected from group members and used to identify problems of role ambiguity, interpersonal or group conflict, cohesiveness, and participation. Workshops are then held in which the change agent focuses on the processes necessary to enhance group communication, conflict resolution, and problem solving. Team building is usually conducted with individual work units or task groups; the approach can also be applied throughout an organization. Team building sessions can last from a half day to several days depending on the needs of the group(s). If sensitive issues or confrontations are anticipated, a trained expert should conduct the meeting rather than a group member.

EBASCO

Andrew O. Manzini, vice-president for human resources for Ebasco Services, Inc., observed an array of operating problems as his company attempted to implement a matrix organization structure. Manzini set out to minimize the negative impact of these problems on Ebasco; his approach was to use organizational development techniques throughout the matrix organization. Multiple pressures on middle-level managers had created interpersonal conflicts between functional specialists and project managers. Manzini focused his attention on defusing the emotional aspects of these conflicts in order to pave the way to resolution of underlying issues.

Of the wide variety of OD techniques used at Ebasco, two techniques were particularly effective. First, OD facilitators conducted numerous team-building interventions to either head off anticipated problems or resolve those conflicts that had already arisen. Second, OD staff members were brought in to facilitate meetings and assist in resolving conflicts. This approach did much to foster smooth relationships among "suspicious colleagues with different priorities."[16]

Process consultation[17]

Process consultation is designed to help a client become aware of and able to operate on process events (e.g., procedures for problem solving, methods of communicating information) occurring in an organization. Process consultants do not act as experts. Their role is to observe activities in the organization and to feed information back to the client. The process consultant attempts to help the client understand how organizational processes operate so the client, rather than the consultant, can solve problems and improve those processes.

The process consultant most frequently uses four approaches. **Agenda-setting interviews** are low-key, question-and-answer periods in which the consultant attempts to heighten the management team's sensitivity to its own internal processes. Participants in such meetings often engage in experiential exercises and role playing and read relevant theoretical articles. **Data feedback** is another technique often used by process consultants. Data on operating processes are provided to managers for use in diagnosing and improving those processes. **Coaching** or **counseling** often follows data feedback and provides a means whereby organizational members receive specific insights and recommendations from a consultant on the "how-to" of change. For example, a manager may learn through data feedback that she lacks certain decision-making skills. A change agent can provide individual instruction and assistance through coaching or counseling as the manager experiments with new behaviors (e.g., methods of facilitating participative decision-making) and plans actions to overcome the deficiencies.

A process intervention is considered a success when managers can diagnose and solve process problems themselves without assistance from a consultant. Disengagement of the consultant from the organization takes place when both client and consultant agree that an acceptable level of problem-solving skill has been obtained.

Grid organizational development[18]

Grid organizational development, an extension of the managerial grid concept (see Chapter 12, "Effective Leader Behavior"), is usually carried out on an organization-wide basis. Grid OD is a highly formalized, step-by-step process that takes a one-best-way-to-organize approach. The major objective of this intervention is for managers throughout an organization to adopt an ideal management style (9,9—high concern for people and for production). Initially, individual management styles are evaluated and compared to the 9,9 style. Meetings are then conducted in which managers formulate individual strategies for improving their present behavior to become more like the ideal style. Group sessions emphasizing teamwork and the need to overcome win-lose norms between organizational units are also held. Barriers preventing the organization from achieving the ideal style are identified, and specific action plans are created to achieve maximum effectiveness and efficiency throughout the organization. A grid OD intervention is accomplished in a series of seven stages and can take from three to five years to complete. Exhibit 15.7 describes the seven stages of grid organizational development.

Sensitivity training[19]

The purpose of **sensitivity training** sessions, or T-groups, is to increase an individual's awareness of interpersonal behaviors and defense mechanisms. This technique provides an opportunity to clarify personal values and goals and to reflect about how one interacts with others. Sensitivity training is a powerful learning laboratory in which individuals can gain insight into the meanings and consequences of their own and others' behaviors and into the dynamics and processes of group behavior.

Sensitivity training sessions usually involve five to ten individuals and a group facilitator. No formal agenda is provided; instead, individual personalities and group interactions, processes, and relationships become the focus of discussion. The facilitator is not a teacher. Rather, he or she promotes a supportive atmosphere encouraging individual growth through openness and genuineness. At the same time, the facilitator observes the rate of disclosure and self-awareness to help ease participants through high-risk situations that, if not handled properly, might result in serious psychological damage. Sensitivity training is an intervention technique of considerable depth and risk (see Exhibit 15.4) and requires careful use under the direction of a skilled facilitator.

T-groups usually meet away from the job site and address issues not directly related to job performance. As a result, questions have been raised about the long-

**EXHIBIT 15.7   THE SEVEN PHASES OF GRID ORGANIZATIONAL
                 DEVELOPMENT**

Preparation Phase	Training key managers who will be instructors in the organizational development process.
Phase 1: The Managerial Grid	Trained managers conduct grid seminars for all managers in the organization.
Phase 2: Teamwork Development	Skills facilitating teamwork and coordination within individual teams are emphasized.
Phase 3: Intergroup Development	Strategies for reducing win-lose conflict between groups are emphasized to move toward an ideal model of intergroup relationships.
Phase 4: Developing an Ideal Strategic Organization Model	The emphasis is on strategic planning and developing a model that would describe the organization if it were truly excellent.
Phase 5: Implementing the Ideal Strategic Model	Restructuring the organization to meet the requirements of the ideal model.
Phase 6: Systematic Critique	Evaluating the previous phases to assess what progress has been made, what barriers still exist, and what opportunities for further development are available.

range impact of personal changes brought about through sensitivity training and the extent to which such changes are related to individual and organizational performance. The popularity of sensitivity training has decreased in recent years, although some consulting firms and institutes still consider it a viable method for bringing about change.

Sociotechnical design[20]

In all organizations, a relationship exists between the technical system (task and process design) and the human system (individual and group behavior patterns). In most instances, however, a technology is developed first (including equipment and work flow) and people are then trained to fit the technology. The assembly line is a classic example of how an organization's social system must fit the existing technical system. Even though the educational level of the work force has increased significantly since the development of this technology, today's workers are still required to perform the same kinds of narrow, specialized, and routine tasks designed for their assembly-line predecessors.

Sociotechnical design focuses simultaneously on the social and technical systems and is based on the belief that both systems must operate jointly to produce a desired outcome. The basic objective of sociotechnical design is to optimize the relationship between the social and technical systems to increase both productivity and quality of work life. As mentioned in Chapter 14, "Work Design," many organizations, including General Foods, TRW, Proctor & Gamble, Rockwell, and Sherwin-Williams, have used sociotechnical design.

NUMMI

General Motors and Toyota, two of the world's largest automobile companies, have undertaken a joint venture named the New United Motor Manufacturing, Inc. (NUMMI). The two auto giants combined forces to produce Chevrolet Novas in Fremont, California, using a type of sociotechnical design and less automation than the average United States car plant. Workers are organized into work teams with unprecedented control over their jobs, and the quality of the cars they produce outranks the best from GM's most highly automated factories.

As a result of the NUMMI experience, GM is expanding its use of labor management techniques learned from the Japanese. In Lansing, Michigan, for example, factory workers are divided into small teams that define their own jobs and monitor the quality of their output. The groups even conduct their own daily quality audits, a chore that was once relegated to a separate group of inspectors. They also have "stop-line" cords that allow them to shut down the line if they encounter a problem.

These actions have allowed the plant to eliminate 37 percent of its audit jobs since 1985, and it has driven the cost of making a car down by 21 percent. Such moves have also boosted the quality of the plant's cars, including the Pontiac Grand Am and Buick Somerset, nearly 46 percent since 1985.[21]

In summary

Exhibit 15.8 briefly describes a number of other OD intervention techniques. Remember, the basic purpose of any intervention strategy or technique is to promote

EXHIBIT 15.8   OD INTERVENTIONS CLASSIFIED BY TARGET GROUP

TARGET GROUP	TYPES OF INTERVENTIONS
Interventions designed to improve the effectiveness of individuals	Life- and career-planning activities. Role analysis technique. Coaching and counseling. T-group (sensitivity training). Education and training to increase skills, knowledge in the areas of technical task needs, relationship skills, process skills, decision making, problem solving, planning, goal-setting skills. Grid OD phase 1. Some forms of job enrichment. Gestalt OD. Transactional analysis.
Interventions designed to improve the effectiveness of dyads/triads	Process consultation. Third-party peacemaking. Grid OD phases 1, 2. Gestalt OD. Transactional analysis.
Interventions designed to improve the effectiveness of teams and groups	Team building—Task directed. 　　　　　　—Process directed. Family T-group. Survey feedback. Process consultation. Role analysis technique. "Start-up" team-building activities. Education in decision making, problem solving, planning, goal setting in group settings. Some forms of job enrichment and MBO. Sociotechnical systems and Quality of Work Life programs. Quality circles.
Interventions designed to improve the effectiveness of intergroup relations	Intergroup activities—Process directed. 　　　　　　　　　—Task directed. Organizational mirroring (three or more groups). Structural interventions. Process consultation. Third-party peacemaking at group level. Grid OD phase 3. Survey feedback.
Interventions designed to improve the effectiveness of the total organization	Technostructural activities such as collateral organizations and sociotechnical systems. Confrontation meetings. Strategic planning/strategic management activities. Grid OD phases 4, 5, 6. Survey feedback. Interventions based on Lawrence and Lorsch's contingency theory. Interventions based on Likert's Systems 1–4. Physical settings.

SOURCE: Wendell L. French/Cecil H. Bell, Jr., *Organization Development: Behavioral Science Interventions for Organization Improvement*, © 1984, pp. 131. Reprinted by permission of Prentice-Hall, Inc., Englewood Cliffs, New Jersey.

organizational health and self-renewal by (1) helping an individual or organization collect valid information; (2) using that information to make informed decisions and formulate change strategies; and (3) implementing such decisions with commitment.[22] The use of a particular intervention technique must therefore be based on careful diagnosis and planning if these desired outcomes are to be achieved.

Do OD Interventions Really Work?

Implementing any of the previously described OD techniques requires considerable amounts of time, resources, and commitment. Managers and executives frequently ask if the tremendous investment is worth it—do OD interventions really work? To answer this question, several studies have been conducted assessing the effectiveness of OD methods in bringing about organizational change.

In one study, researchers analyzed 160 different studies reporting the results of OD interventions.[23] From these studies, thirty-five were selected that used rigorous scientific standards to evaluate an intervention's effectiveness. Although the methods and procedures used in the various studies differed, each study focused on two basic aspects of an organization's performance: (1) outcome variables such as profits, productivity, and absenteeism, and (2) process variables such as communication, openness, motivation, and decision making. The thirty-five studies were analyzed to determine if OD techniques brought about substantial changes in outcome and/or process variables.

Outcome variables were measured in twenty-two of the studies; analysis indicated that in 51 percent of the cases, substantial positive changes occurred. Forty-six percent of the process variables showed positive changes. The analysis also provided fairly strong evidence for the effectiveness of many major OD techniques such as team building, survey feedback, and grid organizational development.

In one of the most extensive reviews of the OD literature to date, the reports of 574 OD interventions occurring between 1945 and the mid-1980s were investigated.[24] Researchers made a "global estimate of efficacy" by examining each case and assigning it to one of four evaluative categories: (1) highly positive and intended effects; (2) definite balance of positive and intended effects; (3) no appreciable effects; and (4) negative effects. More than 80 percent of the cases showed either highly positive or a definite balance of positive outcomes. On the other hand, only 8 percent of the cases reported negative effects. In summary, then, research results suggest that many OD interventions do work and have produced positive effects in a wide range of organizational settings.

It is important to remember, however, that not all interventions are successful. The literature also reports many instances of intervention failure caused by such factors as insufficient managerial support, unclear objectives for the change effort, inadequate resources, and union resistance. Evidence also suggests that management frequently does not sustain OD interventions over time. Recent evaluation of a number of OD interventions several years after they were executed indicates that many changes that appeared to be successful and permanent when first reported have regressed or disappeared.[25] Thus, some interventions may successfully meet short-term needs but do not necessarily stimulate a long-term, continuous process of organizational renewal.

As the research evidence suggests, sustaining change over time (refreezing or institutionalizing) is perhaps the most difficult aspect of the change process. Five factors make the institutionalization of change difficult:[26]

1. Transfer of managers. Managers who participate in getting an OD intervention started are often transferred to other units within the company. When they leave, their collective learning about OD and the mechanisms created to sustain the change are lost.
2. Time pressures. Other demands compete with organizational development efforts for the managers' attention (e.g., short-term pressures for profitability and a continual stream of new crises).
3. Linking requirements. The systems nature of organizations requires a considerable amount of linking, communicating, and coordinating to facilitate organizational change.
4. Management defensiveness. Like most people, managers can be defensive about their behavior and ideas and have difficulty seeing them as barriers to change and renewal. Consequently, feedback mechanisms initiated by a change agent tend to disappear as subordinates find that confronting management does not pay off.
5. Power differences. Even if management wants feedback and is not defensive, the power differences in contemporary organizations prevent people from being completely open in their upward communication.

Because of these and other problems, sustaining an organizational change is a complicated and time-consuming task. Such steps as altering the reward system, carefully socializing new personnel, and developing employee commitment may be necessary to bring about permanent change. In addition, an intervention should be systematically evaluated to insure that its goals and objectives are being achieved. Only by taking such steps can organizational changes be successfully implemented and sustained.

ORGANIZATIONAL CHANGE AND DEVELOPMENT: CONCLUSIONS

Advances in technology, the internationalization of business, trends in the composition of the labor force, and many other factors provide a dynamic environment for modern organizations. The ever-accelerating pace of change is one of the greatest challenges facing contemporary managers and organizations. A manager must understand what change is, how it occurs, and the factors associated with successful change in order to cope effectively with this important challenge.

Lewin's force field model is a useful tool for understanding the process of planned change. Any situation can be analyzed in terms of driving and restraining forces, and the stages of unfreezing, moving to a desired level, and refreezing. Force field analysis is particularly helpful in assessing an individual's, group's, or organization's current level of performance, desired level of performance, and the factors inhibiting and promoting achievement of desired outcomes. The model also provides helpful guidelines for managers formulating change strategies (reduce restraining forces, increase driving forces, or some combination of both).

Organizational changes are often resisted because of uncertainty, threats to vested interests, lack of trust, misunderstandings, and so on. These sources of resistance can be managed, however, through effective participation, a specific action plan, and sufficient resources for a proposed change.

ETHICAL DILEMMA
Who's Responsible for Day-Care?

Changes in demographics are having a significant effect on the workplace of the 1990s. For example, approximately 57 percent of the mothers of United States preschoolers work outside the home. However, according to a recent Harris poll, more than half of all parents of young children are unhappy with the quality of the child care they are buying. With many parents facing an impasse, child care has become and will continue to be a key issue for both employees and employers in the 1990s.

Some organizations are taking steps to address this need. For example, AT&T recently signed a contract with its employees to provide an array of child-care benefits; approximately two hundred corporations and six hundred hospitals have established day-care centers on their premises; and New York's Neighborhood Child Care Initiatives Project, funded by the American Express Foundation, has recruited four hundred women to be family day-care providers. Other companies offer services such as child-care referral, maternity or parental leaves of absence, flexible work schedules, care-assistance plans for dependents, and reimbursement accounts.

Efforts such as these are still the exception in most business organizations. With growing numbers of single parents and dual-career couples and the increasing participation of women in the labor force, the need for quality, affordable day care will continue to expand.

Questions

Do corporations and business firms have an ethical or moral responsibility to provide day-care assistance for their employees?

What are the advantages and disadvantages of offering such a benefit?

SOURCES: Susan B. Garland, "America's Child-Care Crisis: The First Tiny Steps Toward Solutions," *Business Week*, 10 July 1989, 64–68; Harriet B. Presser, "Can We Make Time For Children: The Economy, Work Schedules, and Child Care," *Demography*, Vol. 26, No. 4 (November 1989): 523–543; Lisa R. Cole, "Child Care and Business," *Business and Economic Review*, Vol. 35, No. 2 (1989): 4–9.

OD attempts to improve organizational effectiveness by using planned diagnosis and intervention. Rather than addressing itself to individual growth, as in management development, organizational development focuses on the goals, processes, and resources of the total organization. The basic purpose of OD, then, is organizational renewal through the use of behavioral science concepts and methods.

The change agent plays an important role in creating an atmosphere in the organization conducive to data collection and feedback. A careful diagnosis of the system is conducted with the assistance of the client organization. Appropriate interventions are then selected to bring about desired changes based on the change agent's assessment of the organization and the client's readiness to respond. Intervention techniques range from very shallow—such as operations analysis—to very deep—such as sensitivity training and intrapersonal analysis. Between these extremes lie a variety of approaches for facilitating organizational change. Only through the cooperation of the change agent and key organizational members can a successful OD intervention be planned and executed.

QUESTIONS FOR REVIEW AND DISCUSSION

1. Why is change such a pervasive aspect of modern organizational life?
2. Explain how force field analysis can be used as a diagnostic tool.
3. What are some common sources of resistance to change? What can a manager do to overcome these sources of resistance?
4. Why should managers be familiar with the theory and technology of organizational change?
5. What is organizational development? What is the role of organizational development in modern organizations?
6. Discuss the role of a change agent.
7. What is the basic purpose of an intervention strategy or technique?
8. Do organizational development interventions really work?
9. What factors inhibit the institutionalization of change?
10. What can a manager do to sustain organizational changes over time?

REFERENCES

1. G. Zaltman and R. Duncan, *Strategies for Planned Change* (New York: Wiley, 1977), 10.
2. T. G. Cummings and E. F. Huse, *Organization Development and Change*, 4th ed. (St. Paul: West Publishing Co., 1989); Ronald D. Elliott, "The Challenge of Managing Change," *Personnel Journal*, March 1990, 40–49.
3. Kurt Lewin, *Field Theory in Social Science* (New York: Harper and Row, 1951).
4. Christine Dugas et al., "Marketing's New Look," *Business Week*, 26 January 1987, 64–69; Dillard B. Tinsley, "New Niche Strategy May Rule Marketing by January 1, 2037," *Marketing News*, Vol. 21, No. 15 (17 July 1989): 6–7; Larry Carpenter, "How to Market to Regions," *American Demographics*, Vol. 9, No. 11 (November 1987): 44–45.
5. R. M. Cyert and J. G. March, *A Behavioral Theory of the Firm* (Englewood Cliffs, N.J.: Prentice-Hall, 1963); D. A. Nadler, "The Effective Management of Organizational Change," in J. W. Lorsch, ed., *Handbook of Organizational Behavior* (Englewood Cliffs, N.J.: Prentice-Hall, 1987).
6. Lewin, "Forces Behind Food Habits and Methods of Change," *Bulletin of the National Research Council*, Vol. 108 (1943): 35–65.
7. Lester Coch and John R. P. French, Jr., "Overcoming Resistance to Change," *Human Relations*, Vol. 1 (November 1948): 512–532.
8. G. Dalton, P. Lawrence, and L. Greiner, *Organizational Change and Development* (Homewood, Ill.: Irwin-Dorsey, 1970).
9. M. Beer, *Organization Change and Development: A Systems View* (Santa Monica, Calif.: Goodyear Publishing Co., 1980).
10. R. Harrison, "Choosing the Depth of an Organizational Intervention," *Journal of Applied Behavioral Sciences*, Vol. 6 (April/May/June 1970): 183–184.

11. W. L. French and R. W. Hollmann, "Management by Objectives: The Team Approach," *California Management Review*, Vol. 17 (Spring 1973): 13–22; J. P. Muczyk and B. C. Reimann, "MBO as a Complement to Effective Leadership," *Academy of Management Executive*, Vol. III, No. 2 (1989): 131–138.
12. Cummings and Huse, op. cit., 330–331.
13. D. R. Nadler, *Feedback and Organization Development* (Reading, Mass.: Addison-Wesley, 1977).
14. R. M. Steers and L. W. Porter, *Motivation and Work Behavior*, 3rd ed. (New York: McGraw-Hill, 1983).
15. W. G. Dyer, *Team Building: Issues and Alternatives* (Reading, Mass.: Addison-Wesley, 1977).
16. Thom O'Connor, "How Ebasco Makes the Matrix Method Work," *Business Week*, 15 June 1981, 128–131.
17. E. Schein, *Process Consultation: Its Role in Organization Development* (Reading, Mass.: Addison-Wesley, 1969).
18. R. Blake and J. Mouton, *Building a Dynamic Corporation Through Grid Organizational Development* (Reading, Mass.: Addison-Wesley, 1969).
19. R. Golembiewski and A. Blumber, *Sensitivity Training and the Laboratory Approach* (Itasca, Ill.: F. E. Peacock, 1970).
20. W. L. French, C. H. Bell, Jr., and R. A. Zawacki, *Organization Development: Theory, Practice, and Research*, rev. ed. (Plano, Texas: Business Publications, 1983).
21. William J. Hampton and Zachary Schiller, "Why Image Counts," *Business Week*, 8 June 1987, 138–140; Clair Brown and Michael Reich, "When Does Union-Management Cooperation Work? A Look at NUMMI and GM-Van Nuys," *California Management Review*, Vol. 31, No. 4 (1989): 26–44; Lee Branst and Agnes Dubberly, "Labor-Management Participation: The NUMMI Experience," *Quality Progress*, Vol. 21, No. 4 (April 1988): 30–34; Daniel Forbes, "The Lessons of NUMMI," *Business Month*, June 1987, 34–37; Bryan

H. Berry, "What Makes the NUMMI Plant Different?" *Iron Age*, 5 September 1986, 27–34.

22. C. Argyris, *Intervention Theory and Method: A Behavioral Science View* (Reading, Mass., Addison-Wesley, 1973).

23. J. I. Porras and P. O. Berg, "The Impact of Organization Development," *The Academy of Management Review*, Vol. 3 (July 1978): 249–266.

24. Golembiewski, C. W. Proehl, and D. Sink, "Estimating the Success of OD Applications," *Training and Development Journal*, Vol. 36 (April 1982): 86–95.

25. R. E. Walton, "The Topeka Story: Part II," *The Wharton Magazine*, Vol. 4 (Winter 1978): 36–41; J. M. Nicholas and M. Katz, "Research Methods and Reporting Practices in Organization Development: A Review and Some Guidelines," *Academy of Management Review*, Vol. 10, No. 4 (1985): 736–749.

26. Beer, *Organization Change*, 255; Beer "Revitalizing Organizations: Change Processes and Emergent Model," *Academy of Management Executive*, Vol. 1, No. 1 (1987): 51–55.

CASE 15.1   A *time for change*

DONALD D. WHITE   *University of Arkansas*
H. WILLIAM VROMAN   *Tennessee Technological University*
WAYNE T. MEEKS   *University of Georgia*

The maintenance sector of a United States Air Force wing has the responsibility for keeping the wing's aircraft in a state of operational readiness. Maintenance is an autonomous organizational unit under the direction of the deputy commander of maintenance. The appropriate specialists were dispatched from the central maintenance shop at Harley Air Force Base whenever it was determined that maintenance was required on a squadron's aircraft. Upon completion of the job, the men returned to the shop.

Flying squadrons at Harley were sometimes required to deploy their aircraft to overseas bases. In these instances, certain key maintenance specialists and crew chiefs were temporarily assigned to the squadron. These men accompanied the squadron on its mission and were responsible for providing normal service to the aircraft. Typically, then, Maintenance had to bring together various specialists and decide who would accompany a squadron each time an overseas deployment occurred. The procedure was time consuming and often created friction among the various specialists in the maintenance department. In some cases the specialists would vie with one another for "plush" assignments or try to use their seniority to stay away from certain squadrons.

AN INFORMAL REORGANIZATION

Both the flying crews and maintenance specialists were aware of the personnel problems that often accompanied overseas deployments. The subject was the major topic of conversation in the squadrons and maintenance shop as well. Finally, a decision was made jointly by the squadron commanders and ranking officers in the maintenance shop to request that a change be made in assignment procedures. A meeting was scheduled with the deputy commander of maintenance to discuss their ideas.

At the meeting, Major Henry Owens, a squadron commander, presented the group's thoughts on the assignment of maintenance specialists:

The aircraft at Harley are permanently assigned to each squadron. Therefore, it seems logical that a complete team of maintenance specialists and crew chiefs also be assigned or attached to each squadron. A squadron could automatically take along its own maintenance personnel if it was deployed. While the aircraft are at Harley, this same maintenance unit can be responsible for repairs and servicing.

The deputy commander was in agreement with the position taken by the officers. He liked the idea of the reorganization but believed that a formal reorganization would be rejected further up the chain of command. He suggested, instead, that an informal reorganization similar to that proposed take place. The officers agreed. In addition, they decided that the effects of the experimental change should be evaluated approximately six months after the new assignments were made.

Within thirty days of the meeting, most maintenance personnel at Harley were assigned to individual aircraft on this informal basis. The new reorganization worked smoothly. Besides simplifying the assignment of personnel, the relationship between maintenance specialists and the air crews themselves improved. There was pride and competition between the maintenance sections of each squadron and records were kept to see which squadron had the least number of late take-offs or cancelled missions because of maintenance problems. Aircraft commanders reported that their equipment was cleaner and in better shape than before the reorganization. In addition, mission effectiveness ratings improved and complaints pertaining to deployments were practically eliminated.

A PERSONNEL SHORTAGE

However, before a formal assessment of the change could take place, problems began to plague the squadrons. A demand for qualified maintenance personnel to fill overseas assignments began to take its toll at Harley AFB. The ranks of the maintenance group were depleted as an increasing number of men were sent to other bases to fill vacancies. The personnel losses at Harley were not unexpected. However, replacements were not immediately available. As a result of these personnel shortages, squadrons found themselves having to "borrow" specialists from each other. Conflicts began to arise as to who would be sent, when they would be released, and how soon they must be returned to their informally assigned "home" squadrons. In addition, many of the specialists felt that they were being overworked and that they did not have adequate time to maintain their own squadron's aircraft.

Requests by Maintenance were put in for additional personnel. However, it soon became obvious that replacements could not be expected in the near future. After some discussion of the problem in the maintenance group, the decision was made to return all maintenance personnel to a central dispatching area. Thus, maintenance specialists were placed back under the direct control of the maintenance group. The informal reorganization was terminated, and once again the group resembled its original formal structure.

THE LATE TAKE-OFF

Captain Phil Rogers arrived at the base and immediately drove to Base Operations. There, he began preparing the flight plan for his day's mission. Captain Rogers was scheduled to fly an aero-medical evacuation flight with three severely burned patients to Brooks Medical Center in Texas. He considered his medi-vac duties to be an important responsibility and took his job quite seriously. Suddenly, he heard his name being paged over the loudspeaker system.

He picked up the phone and recognized the voice of Glenn Kennedy, his flight engineer.

Msgt. Kennedy: Captain Rogers, I don't think we will be able to get off when we are supposed to.

Capt. Rogers: What's the problem? Is the aircraft out of commission?

Msgt. Kennedy: I don't know yet, sir. The crewchief was supposed to be here two hours before me to open the aircraft and perform his "Dash-Six Inspection." He hasn't made it in yet, and I can't perform my own preflight inspection until he gets here and does his job. I did get the aircraft opened and there are several write-ups that haven't been taken care of. The aircraft isn't very clean either.

Capt. Rogers: Have you called Maintenance for assistance?

Msgt. Kennedy: Yes, sir, but they haven't been able to do much so far.

Capt. Rogers: O.K. Go back to the aircraft and wait there. I'll try to get some help.

(Phil Rogers placed a call to Maintenance Control).

Capt. Rogers: Sergeant Vinson, this is Captain Rogers. Are you aware of the fact that I have a critical mission, and the aircraft hasn't shown up yet?

Tsgt. Vinson: Yes, sir, we are trying to find Sergeant Andrews now. But he either isn't home or isn't answering his phone.

Capt. Rogers: Is this the Sergeant Andrews who was the crewchief on Aircraft 7885 in the 40th Squadron?

Tsgt. Vinson: Yes, sir, it is.

Capt. Rogers: That's strange. He was my crewchief for six weeks in South America and was one of the best I've ever seen. He took pride in the cleanliness of his airplane and always bragged that he'd never had a late take-off or mission aborted because of maintenance.

Tsgt. Vinson: I know, sir. I've heard some good reports on him, but frankly, his performance here lately has been less than desirable. We've had complaints about the condition of his aircraft several times. He had two late take-offs last week. Once he was late with his preflight, and the other time a write-up wasn't corrected when it should have been. He doesn't seem to care anymore.

Capt. Rogers: Andrews isn't alone in this matter. I've noticed that we've been having a helluva problem with morale, supposed sickness, quality of work, and so on around the flight line.

Tsgt. Vinson: I know what you mean, Captain. It seems that a lot of these guys just don't give a damn anymore. Frankly, I'm afraid that we might be losing some good men. I've heard Sergeant Andrews and Sergeant Janson talking about getting an early out. Both of those guys are top-notch; it just doesn't figure.

Capt. Rogers: No, and it doesn't do much for encouraging re-ups among the troops either. Well, I can't worry about that, now. I've got to have a crewchief out there soon. We have to get off as soon as possible. Try to find one from another aircraft.

Tsgt. Vinson: Yes, sir. We'll try our best, but it's getting more and more difficult to find these guys and get them to pre-flight someone else's aircraft.

DEPLOYMENT

Later that week Captain Rogers was in the hanger checking out his aircraft. The 38th had received orders for deployment to Germany. Captain Rogers had been attempting to determine what, if any, maintenance would be needed to make the long trip. As he was preparing to leave, he was approached by Sergeant John Ryan, a hydraulic specialist who was at one time attached to the 38th squadron of maintenance.

Capt. Rogers: Hello, Sergeant Ryan, I haven't seen you since you came down to Lima that time to fix the hydraulic leak in the #3 engine. How has life been treating you?

Sgt. Ryan: Well, not too bad, sir, but it could be better. That's what I want to talk to you about. I know you're getting ready for a rotation, and I wondered if you could possibly help get a couple of changes made?

Capt. Rogers: Well, I don't know. I'll do what I can, but you know that now we don't really have any say-so or control over who goes on rotation with us from Maintenance.

Sgt. Ryan: Yes, sir, I realize that. But I thought maybe you might talk to them or get your commander to talk to them. They don't seem to hear us, or else they just don't care.

Capt. Rogers: What seems to be the problem?

Sgt. Ryan   Well, we have two hydraulic specialists now—myself and Sergeant Joyce. You guys are my old squadron and the 36th is Sergeant Joyce's old squadron. The 36th is going to Germany in three months to replace you, I suppose. I had counted on going with you guys since I know most of you and also the aircraft. But now they say I can't go, and Joyce is going. Then I'll have to go with the 36th. I don't know any of those guys and Joyce doesn't know any of your guys, but they said that didn't matter. Somebody set it up, and the commander's office said that it would be too much trouble to change it. We talked to our supervisor, but he said to forget it. Joyce and I have to spend two or three months overseas away from our families, and it makes the tour a lot easier to take if you know the people you're with. On top of everything, Sergeant Joyce is having some family problems and really needs to be here to try to straighten them out. We even went in together and explained this. I volunteered to go in his place. They still wouldn't change us. There is no logical reason I can see why it would matter to them which one of us went. You would think they would try to keep us happy with our work since there are only two of us when we're supposed to have four hydraulic specialists.

Capt. Rogers: Sergeant, I wish I could give you more encouragement, but you know how these things are handled now. I'll talk to the colonel and explain your problems to him since he has a little more pull than I do. I'll tell him you're a good hydraulics man. He probably remembers how you rescued me in Lima without any spare parts. Maybe he'll call your commander and make a personal request for you to be sent with us. As I said, officially, we have to take whoever Maintenance gives us, but I'll see what we can do.

Sgt. Ryan: I really appreciate it, sir. Boy, things have really changed! When I was in the 38th, at least I could count on someone listening to my problems and trying to help out. No one seems to care anymore.

CASE 15.2   *The shipping department*

H. WILLIAM VROMAN   *Towson State University*
DONALD D. WHITE   *University of Arkansas*

Workers crowded around Chuck Wilcox to welcome him back to the shipping department. Chuck was returning to his old position as department supervisor after a brief period in another location in the plant. Laura Roland spoke up, "Damn it, it's good to have you back, Chuck. I still think someone tried to pull a fast one on us. But they should know better than to try to put one over us in the shipping department. We didn't mind it when that efficiency fellow came in here and made a few changes. But Gaylord was just a little too much. We just stuck together and let the plant manager know we wanted you back."

Laura Roland had been referring to a series of incidents that had taken place in the shipping department during the last few months. Chuck Wilcox was well-liked by the people in his department. Many of them were intensely loyal to him. He was respected as a supervisor and liked as a friend. Chuck was liberal with his people as long as they got their work done. He recognized that most of the workers in the department were close friends. Many of them lived around one another and traveled to and from work together. As a result, he permitted them to talk freely with one another while on the job as long as their conversations did not interfere with accomplishing a day's work. Turnover in the department was low and morale and output were high in spite of low pay and obsolete equipment. Chuck had been supervisor of the department for six years and over that time he and the people who worked for him had come to understand and accept one another.

THE REORGANIZATION

Approximately six months earlier, the shipping department had been reorganized. Many new people were hired, and much of the obsolete equipment was replaced with new and better equipment. The reorganization itself was supervised by a trouble-shooter from the home office. Mary Johnson was given the authority to make certain decisions regarding new

methods, procedures, and the reassignment of jobs. Although she reorganized many of the working stations, she left the work groups themselves intact. At first, there was much concern about the reorganization. However, the workers showed confidence in Johnson and believed that her actions were in their best interest.

When she first arrived in the department, Johnson approached the workers in a friendly manner and sought their advice. She worked with Chuck Wilcox and often credited the success of various stages of the changeover to Wilcox and his people. Most workers liked the new ways of doing things and attempted to make the new system work. Within two weeks after the changeover had been completed, production surged from 4,000 units to 6,000 units a day. After five weeks, production leveled off at 7,000 units per day. Morale in the department seemed to be at an all-time high, especially since the men had all received small pay increases.

The new workers who had been hired were, with few exceptions, accepted by the original work group. Satisfaction with the increased output was high, and it was generally conceded that they all had more pride in their work after the reorganization than before the changes had been instituted. This situation was to change dramatically within the next few weeks.

THE "ADMINISTRATIVE" ASSISTANT

R. D. Gaylord rambled through the plant without being noticed by most of the workers. Since the reorganization a few months ago, a new face on the work floor was not much of a surprise to anyone. He stopped and talked to a few of the workers and at one point was drawn into a discussion that took place during the morning break. Everyone in the group talked freely, never imagining that Gaylord was not "one of them." Later in the day, when Chuck Wilcox returned from a staff meeting, he was approached by one of the workers and questioned about Gaylord.

Chuck was somewhat taken aback by the question since he was not familiar with the man in question. After the worker left his office, Chuck phoned the plant manager's office to ask about the new man. The manager was out and his secretary explained that he would not be back until later that afternoon: "He's having lunch with his new administrative assistant, R. D. Gaylord."

The following day, Chuck received a memo from the plant manager's office. The memo directed that a notice be placed on the department bulletin board informing the men that there would be no more talking while on the job. In justification for the decision, it was explained that "the elimination of extraneous conversation was necessary to maintain and ultimately further increase the new production levels." The memo was signed, R. D. Gaylord, Administrative Assistant. Again, Chuck picked up the phone and called the plant manager's office. This time he was able to get through to the manager and ask for an explanation concerning the memo and the newly hired administrative assistant. At once, the plant manager apologized for the fact that Chuck did not know of the new appointment. He explained that Gaylord had been sent by the home office in a surprise move in order to follow up on the reorganization changes that had taken place during the previous few months. The plant manager told Chuck that he had been sent a memo regarding Gaylord two days before but that evidently it had gone astray in the company mailing system. Chuck accepted the explanation of the plant manager and decided to wait and see what further actions, if any, Gaylord might take.

Neither Chuck nor the workers had to wait long. By the end of the week, another note had been received by Chuck and signs had been posted throughout his department prohibiting smoking while on the job. The workers resented the "No Smoking" signs, and one of the signs was mutilated. Shortly thereafter, Gaylord approached Chuck Wilcox on the parking lot and told him he wanted the person responsible for destroying the sign in his office by Monday morning. He added that he had already talked to a couple of the workers and had told them that they had better comply with the directive if they wished to keep their jobs in the company.

When Chuck arrived at work on Monday morning, he interrupted what sounded like a dull roar coming from the dressing rooms. He stepped inside to see what was going on, and the workers immediately began to complain about Gaylord's personally telling them what to do. One man stated, "I might not mind hearing things like that from you (referring to Chuck Wilcox), but what the hell is he doing here in the plant, anyway?" The situation was aggravated further when Gaylord and the plant manager showed up in the department just after lunch. Nothing was said about the incident with the "No Smoking" sign. However, the plant manager informed Chuck that Gaylord would be remaining in the shipping department on a more permanent basis for some time to come. In addition, he told Chuck that Gaylord represented him (the plant manager) and that Chuck and his men "should do whatever Gaylord says."

Gaylord lived up to the men's expectations of him. He personally began to direct the operations of the department. He told the workers that the production figures for the department looked good, but that he knew "they could be much better." Since the workers were not used to such close supervision, they began resisting his instructions. Individual workloads mysteriously increased, production records were not complete or were inaccurate, and certain "nonsense work" began to complicate the controlling efforts of Chuck Wilcox. Soon Chuck himself was siding with the workers and complaining about Gaylord.

He claimed that Gaylord was inconsistent with his decisions and would sometimes deny even having had the conversation at a later date. Chuck had little recourse against Gaylord and felt that any complaints he had lodged with the plant manager had fallen on a deaf ear. On one occasion, Chuck even "sabotaged" Gaylord although he felt bad about it afterward. A call had come in from the plant manager for Gaylord. Chuck answered the phone and told the plant manager that Gaylord "was not around" and that "if this day was like most others, I probably will have a tough time finding him around the plant." Actually, Chuck was not lying to the plant manager, since Gaylord sometimes observed the working of the loading dock and other areas in the department by inconspicuously standing away from the activity that he was watching. On the other hand, Chuck knew that Gaylord was never far from the workers on the job.

Ironically, Gaylord himself was not aware of the level of animosity that had built up against him. Only in one instance had a subordinate openly confronted him in the shop. At that time, Chuck stepped in and told the woman to go back to work. Chuck later stated that he believed the woman would have struck Gaylord had he not stepped in.

The straw that broke the camel's back occurred during the week before Christmas. Gaylord advised Chuck that production for the week was far below the department's average output figures. Chuck explained that most of the men were probably thinking about

Christmas and that the holiday atmosphere sometimes had a way of disrupting normal activities in the plant. Gaylord was unswayed by Chuck's appeal. He told Chuck that he had decided that the workers would have to work the full day on Christmas Eve and would not be permitted to take off early as had originally been planned. He concluded, "If they wanted to get a few hours off on Christmas Eve, they should have thought about it during the week. We simply have to have this production out."

Word of the decision spread rapidly throughout the department. Without warning, the workers suddenly encircled Gaylord as he was walking through the department. Some of them yelled and shook their fists. Although cooler heads eventually prevailed and there was no violence, a great deal had been said and there could be no mistake in Gaylord's mind about the attitude of the workers toward him. He finally agreed to let them off early on Christmas Eve as had originally been planned. However, some of the men failed to show up at all when the day arrived. Gaylord was convinced that it was unhealthy to have both he and Chuck in the same department. He explained to the plant manager that he was not sure whether Chuck Wilcox had influenced the men against him; but he did believe that it would be better for all concerned if Chuck were transferred out of the department. Chuck was transferred to another department within the plant. A replacement could not be recruited immediately. Therefore, two of the men were given joint supervision of the department. Gaylord hoped that an internal promotion in the department would encourage the workers to improve their output. However, many of the men regarded the move as a ploy. As far as they were concerned, Gaylord was 'still calling the shots!'

The two new supervisors were inept at handling their new situation since they had had no previous supervisory training. In addition, some of the workers regarded them as "traitors." Production dropped from the high level of earlier months to a level lower than that which had been achieved before the original reorganization took place a few months earlier.

Eventually, a vice-president from the home office personally intervened and reinstated Chuck in his old position. Gaylord seemed to realize that he had been wrong in the way he had handled many of the situations in the department. He began to spend more time in the office and less time in the shop, and the notes and the speeches to the men soon disappeared. Unfortunately, much of the uneasiness and bitterness that surrounded the events of the past few months remained in the department. The most prominent sign of these ill feelings revolved around the issue of pay. In Chuck's absence, Gaylord had hired a totally inexperienced man and offered him a wage higher than that being paid to some of the more experienced workers in the department. Word about the new employee's wage spread quickly through the department. To date, a number of the workers in the department have filed a grievance demanding wage adjustments.

EXERCISE 15.1

DIAGNOSIS, CHANGE, AND IMPLEMENTATION

INTRODUCTION

The object of this simulation is to illustrate the phases of diagnosis, development of a change strategy, and implementation of change in an organizational setting where absenteeism and turnover is a problem. As you get involved with each of these concepts and wrestle with the critical questions, the complexities and multiple relationships will become evident.

There is no "right" way to solve the problem. There are many ways to deal with it. Some ways will have more merit than others. Look carefully at the facts of the case and use your empathetic skills to understand some of the unwritten feelings, views, and attitudes of the participants.

NARROW RIVERS

Narrow Rivers is a private continuing education center/health spa with 350 apartments, a constant population of 535 who stay from 3 days to several months, and a staff of nearly 200 full- and part-time employees. A part-time staff of 40, 2 full-time supervisors, and 2 cooks run the facility for the manager-trainees who attend. Part-timers work 4 hours daily and range in age from 18 to 60.

The employees work in three shifts during the day. Starting times for the help are 6:00 A.M., 10:00 A.M. and 4:00 P.M. One of the cooks starts at 6 A.M. and the second quits at 8:00 P.M. The supervisors are expected to oversee the entire project and fill in where necessary.

Narrow Rivers draws its part-time employees from the surrounding rural area. Seventy percent of the group are women. Most are homemakers. The males are an assortment of old and young people partially supported by other jobs. The initial racial composition of the group was 70 percent white, 12 percent black, and 18 percent Hispanic.

THE PROBLEM

Martin Traynor, the director, has hired you to be a change agent with the organization. There are many sources of irritation at Narrow Rivers due, Traynor believes, to its recent opening just a year ago. There seems to be some client understanding of the "opening" problems, but none for food service difficulties. The clients have no patience for the slip-ups in the kitchen/dining area. They harangue, criticize, send food back, and visit the cook and director frequently. The situation has gotten so bad that the attitudes toward other services in the community are being affected. Educational efforts are hampered; maids and gardeners are being hassled. On some days 20 percent of the part-time help are missing. There have been five new cooks hired during the year. All who left found other employment without difficulty.

The food service has been subcontracted to TRISTAR. Narrow Rivers had agreed to a two-year contract with a clause for review after one year. Martin is presently in the process of reviewing that subcontract in light of the difficulties. His attitude is that there is obviously some problem and that TRISTAR has been as diligent as he has in trying to find a solution. Wages and benefits seem to be in line with the surrounding wage rates, and the people hired do not seem to be "the" problem. Troubles are now intensifying as Narrow Rivers and TRISTAR have to go further away to acquire their labor force. Over the year, the racial composition of the employees has changed from that stated earlier to 50 percent white, 30 percent black, and 20 percent Hispanic.

ASSIGNMENT

1. Prior to coming to class, your job is to establish an orderly approach for dealing with the problem. Separate your analysis into three sections: diagnosis, change strategy, and implementation. Detail your analysis and provide the rationale for your choice. Use the intervention of Process Analysis to start with. Develop a notebook just as though you were actually a change agent at Narrow Rivers. In developing the notebook entries, use your imagination about incidents you confronted and how you responded to them.
2. Form groups of three to five students in class and take turns presenting your analysis. This is done without critical comment. Clarifying questions are appropriate. (30 minutes)

3. Develop a common view of the intervention, change strategy and implementation within your group. Analyze the pros and cons of each plan, determining feasibility, and potential resistance. (40 minutes)

4. Prepare a two-part role play. First, assign one member of your group to be Martin Traynor. The remaining two will be on the consultant team. Prepare in reasonable detail a dialogue between the characters. Martin Traynor *is* dubious about the process and your findings. The remaining member(s) of your group should observe the proceedings and be prepared to discuss the consultants' activities and techniques when the role play is completed.

EXERCISE 15.2
USING FORCE FIELD ANALYSIS AS A DIAGNOSTIC TOOL

The purpose of this exercise is to give participants experience in using force field analysis as a diagnostic tool.

DIRECTIONS

1. Divide the class into groups of three or four.
2. Each group should select a subject or topic that is currently the focus of a change effort. The subject should be one about which all group members have some knowledge or in which they have some interest (e.g., school busing as a method of achieving integration, university policies or procedures, school prayer, adoption of the metric system in the United States). Your instructor will provide assistance in selecting timely and relevant topics.
3. Using the force field model described in the chapter, analyze the situation. You should use the following four steps as guidelines:
   Step 1. Identify the various driving and restraining forces.
   Step 2. Assess the relative strength of each force.
   Step 3. Decide which forces can realistically be changed.
   Step 4. Formulate a strategy to increase the driving forces and reduce the restraining forces.
   Actually draw the force field as you proceed with the analysis. (Use Exhibit 15.1 in this chapter as a model.)
4. Outline several strategies that can be used to bring about change.
5. The instructor will call on several groups to present their analyses and strategies to the class.

DISCUSSION QUESTIONS

1. Can force field analysis be used to make changes in your personal life?
2. Why is it important to assess the relative strength of each driving and restraining force?
3. What methods and techniques can you use to identify the driving and restraining forces?
4. What are the advantages of concentrating on restraining forces when formulating a change strategy?

CHAPTER 16

STRESS IN ORGANIZATIONS

LEARNING OBJECTIVES

1. To understand the nature of stress.
2. To learn about the factors that create stress.
3. To understand how stress affects a person's work.
4. To learn how stress can be controlled.

CHAPTER OUTLINE

Understanding the Nature of Stress
    The Elements of Stress
    The Physiology of Stress

Sources of Work-Related Stress
    Role Conflict
    Role Ambiguity
    Overload and Underload
    Responsibility
    Career Development
    High-Stress Situations in Today's Workplace
    Work-Related Stress in Perspective

Effectively Managing Stress
    Individual Responses to Stress
    Organizational Responses to Stress

Stress in Organizations: Conclusions

Questions for Review and Discussion

References

Cases: 16.1 Happiness Is Success!?
           16.2 Decision at Sea

Exercises: 16.1 Behavior Activity Profile
               16.2 Are You Stress-Prone at Work?

KEY TERMS

Stressors	**Role conflict**
Context	**Role ambiguity**
Vulnerability	**Overload**
Type A	**Underload**
Type B	**Burnout**
General Adaptation Syndrome	**Personal stress audit**
Alarm	**Biofeedback**
Adaptation	**Organizational stress audit**
Exhaustion	**Ombudsman**
Inverted U	**Wellness programs**

Barbara was the founder and president of a small advertising agency. She had personally hired each member of the firm and prided herself on knowing everyone both professionally and personally. Barbara had suspected that Larry, one of her most creative employees, was having problems. The personnel report on her desk confirmed it. Larry had used more sick leave during the last six months than during his first six years on the job.

It was a little less than a year ago that Barbara first noticed a change in Larry. He had never been "easy going," but a number of things were different about the way he had begun to behave. Larry seemed to be smoking more than usual, and he complained about not being able to sleep at night. In one meeting, he became angry when two of the company's clients could not agree on whether they liked the advertising campaign that Larry had proposed. He later apologized and explained, "I'm sorry; I've had a lot on my mind lately."

A few weeks later, a similar flare-up took place in a weekly staff meeting. This time, Larry stormed out of the room. He later returned and sat silently, although he appeared to be quite nervous. When the others left, Barbara asked if there was anything that she could do. At first, Larry appeared irritated by the question. However, his defensiveness soon gave way to a rambling explanation of his problems with co-workers and working conditions. "I've explained it all to my wife, but she really doesn't understand," he said. "All she can say is 'don't worry' and 'it will get better.' "

Now, Larry's problems had entered another phase—absenteeism. He had explained to Barbara that he was having medical problems, including severe allergic reactions and higher than normal blood pressure. He even brought a letter from his physician, although the letter stated that no cause for his symptoms had yet been determined.

Barbara didn't know what to make of it all, but she was sure about one thing. Larry's problems were getting worse, and something had to be done or he would lose his job permanently. Discussing the situation with a fellow executive, she observed, "Larry's job is no different from those of a lot of other people around here. Others can cope with the pressure. I hope he can too, or we'll have to find someone else who can. I wonder if there is anything that we can do to help?"

How is Larry's situation different from that of other employees in the firm? Is it the job? Is it Larry himself? Or are other factors responsible for his behavior? In fact, any or all of these explanations may account for Larry's symptoms and for what we today refer to as stress.

Stress is not a new phenomenon. Only recently, however, has it been recognized and treated as anything more than a mild psychological disorder. For years, stress was accepted as an unfortunate but relatively normal part of life with which some individuals were better able to cope than others. Employees who blamed poor or unusual performance on stress might be viewed as either "weak" or simply unable to do the job.

Stress is viewed quite differently today. It is now recognized by the medical community as an illness, and stress-related health care claims account for over 15 percent of all worker's compensation occupational disease claims. Stress costs business and other organizations over $150 billion a year. Claimants are on average younger than those filing other types of claims (thirty-eight years old compared to forty-one years old for other claims), and women account for nearly half of all stress-related claims (compared to 24 percent for all other claims).[1] These figures indicate that stress in general, and job-related stress in particular, have become serious concerns for organizations and those who manage them.

In this chapter, we will examine stress from both an individual and an organizational perspective. First, we will look at aspects of stress (e.g., stressors, context, and vulnerability) and their personal and organizational consequences. Next, we will explore more specifically sources of work-related stress. Finally, we will discuss ways that both organizations and individuals can respond to and effectively manage stress. Exhibit 16.1 shows the relationship of factors that contribute to stress, specific stress consequences, and some of the individual and organizational responses to those consequences.

UNDERSTANDING THE NATURE OF STRESS

Stress has been defined differently by various authorities. Some view stress as a behavioral outcome. To them, any deviation from normal psychological or physiological functioning caused by an external stimulus may be viewed as stress.[2] Others see stress more simply, as an internal, psychological feeling of discomfort. For the purpose of this book, we have taken a broader view of the concept of stress.

EXHIBIT 16.1   A GENERAL MODEL OF STRESS

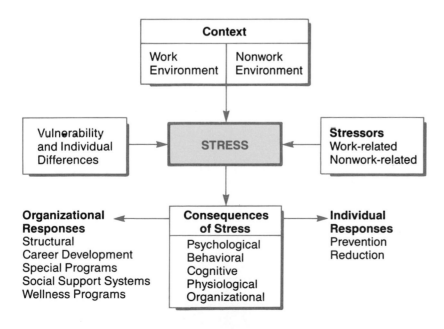

The Elements of Stress

Stress is not caused by a single factor. Rather, it is the result of a complex interaction of specific stressors, the context or situation in which a stressor occurs, and the individual's personal vulnerability to stress.[3] Exhibit 16.2 shows these three factors' relationship to one another and suggests that stress occurs in the area where the three overlap. Let us examine each factor separately.

Stressors

Stressors are external stimuli that initiate stress. Stressors may include physical surroundings such as a messy desk, long lines, a ringing telephone, or other people (e.g., a demanding boss, a poorly performing subordinate, an overbearing co-worker, etc.). Marlene Maranda, a secretary in a packaged-goods company, described an incident in which she was run off the road by another automobile.[4] At first she panicked, but then recognized her boss. His comment to her: "Take a letter." Computer or supervisory monitoring of clerical employees and receptionists to keep track of productivity or the length of time employees spend on breaks are also examples of stressors. Stressors may also include mental demands such as an impending deadline or an upcoming meeting. Maybe you have experienced a nervous stomach or sweaty palms just *thinking* about making a speech or presenting a report in class. Although perception of a stressor is normally related to stress outcomes,[5] in some cases you may not be consciously aware that the stressor exists. In one study, healthcare executives experienced a higher incidence of stress-related disorders associated with unknown stressors than with known stressors.[6]

Context

Context refers to the immediate environment in which a person finds him- or herself. The same stressor may be perceived differently depending upon the context or

EXHIBIT 16.2   RELATIONSHIPS BETWEEN STRESSORS, CONTEXT, AND VULNERABILITY

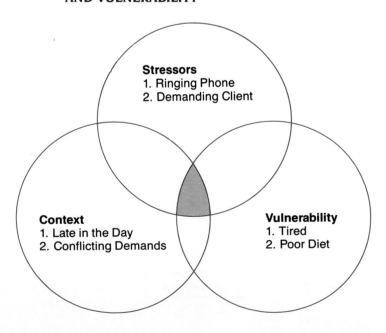

circumstance in which it occurs. For instance, you may have to make a major decision during a meeting with the boss. The stressor is the decision, while the context is the time constraint and the presence of your immediate superior. The same decision in another context (e.g., while you are alone in your office) might not be nearly as stressful.

Vulnerability

Vulnerability is the extent to which a person is unable to resist a stressor in a given situation. Although we all experience stress, some of us are more susceptible to its negative effects than are others. Some individuals have learned to live with stressful events and stressful environments better than others have. In the example at the beginning of this chapter, Barbara observed that Larry's job was similar to those of others in the organization, but that he was less able to handle the pressure.

Vulnerability to stress can be reduced through both psychological and physical preparation. Examples of psychological preparation include focusing on the positive rather than the negative aspects of an upcoming event and rehearsing or practicing a behavior (e.g., giving a speech or shooting a free throw) until it becomes second nature. Physical factors that influence vulnerability to stress include rest, diet, and exercise.

Type A versus Type B personalities

As we indicated, vulnerability is to some extent a function of controllable factors (diet, rest, etc.). There is considerable evidence, however, that individual personality differences may affect resistance to stress. Two cardiologists at San Francisco's Mt. Zion Hospital and Medical Center made a surprising discovery while examining the medical records of middle-aged and young patients. Comparing cardiac and noncardiac patients, they found that fewer than 50 percent of cardiac disorders were related to traditional high-risk factors such as cholesterol level and smoking. Instead, most heart attack victims possessed an identifiable pattern of *behavioral characteristics.*

This pattern, labeled **Type A,** is characterized by (1) Explosive, accelerated speech; (2) A heightened pace of living; (3) Impatience; (4) Concentration on more than one activity at a time; (5) Competitiveness; (6) Aggressiveness and hostility.[7]

Type B individuals, on the other hand, tend to possess characteristics opposite of their Type A counterparts'. Type B persons are less likely to be aggressive, hostile, impatient, or to use explosive or accelerated speech patterns. More importantly, extreme Type Bs suffered three time fewer heart attacks than comparable Type As.

Recent studies have begun to alter our understanding of the relationship of Type A and Type B patterns to disease. For example, some Type A individuals may actually need the stress of their work. Japanese accountant, Takechi Uehara, sometimes spends the weekend in bed with severe back pains and looks forward to Monday morning, when he can get back to work. This "holiday syndrome," as it is known in Japan, exists for some managers who find that relaxing "just isn't relaxing!"[8] Researchers at Harvard University have also found that certain types of Type As, known as charismatics, may even be healthier than mellower Type Bs. Charismatics are driven and emotional, but they "laugh, move a lot and seem to be genuinely confident people."[9] Much more research is necessary to determine which Type As are at greatest risk.

The impact of Type A behavior on individuals and those with whom they live and work can be significant. Understanding Type A symptoms may help a manager identify those employees and co-workers who are more prone to stress than others.

In addition, it may provide an "early warning system" for stress-related illness in your own life.

The Physiology of Stress

According to one noted authority, a complex series of physiological changes occurs when the body responds to stress.[10] Changes may include increased flow of adrenaline and blood to muscles, higher blood pressure, faster heartbeat, rapid breathing, and altered digestive and urinary functions. (Eighteen separate chemical changes can be detected in the blood alone.) These changes are in turn reflected in a number of easily recognized symptoms and other consequences ranging from boredom and poor performance to life-threatening disease.

For example, a Maryland fire fighter, Eric Proctor, was so traumatized by the death of a mother and her seven-year-old daughter in an automobile accident that he was unable to eat or sleep and suffered from periodic crying spells. Ed Edmondson, a forty-one-year-old bus driver in Los Angeles, experienced similar symptoms after a man committed suicide by throwing himself in front of Edmondson's bus. In both cases, the "post-traumatic syndrome" and its related physical and psychological effects were alleviated only after extensive counseling.[11] A list of some of the known consequences of stress is shown in Exhibit 16.3.

Stress is not, as some have claimed, "the American Disease." Serious stress reactions have been observed around the world. The International Dimension on page 541, for example, demonstrates the severity of executives' and managers' stress-related illnesses in Japan.

The body's response to stress is known as the **general adaptation syndrome** (GAS) and occurs in three identifiable stages: (1) alarm, (2) adaptation, and (3) exhaustion. In the *alarm* stage, stressors are perceived and their threat is communicated through the nervous system to the brain. Initially, the body's resistance to the stressor is lowered. Once alerted, however, the body begins to adapt to the threat.

This *adaptation* takes the form of immediate chemical changes in the body. These changes occur both immediately at the point at which the stressor impacts a person (*local* adaptation, as when, for example, blood rushes to the point of a wound) and

EXHIBIT 16.3   CONSEQUENCES OF STRESS

Psychological Effects	Anxiety, aggression, boredom, depression, fatigue, guilt, general irritability, nervousness, loneliness.
Behavioral Effects	Accident proneness, drug and alcohol use, emotional outbursts, excessive eating or loss of appetite, nervous laughter, ticks, trembling, grinding teeth.
Cognitive Effects	Inability to concentrate or make decisions, forgetfulness, mental blocks, overly sensitive to criticism.
Physiological Effects	Increased heart rate and blood pressure, muscle contraction leading to lower-back pain and tightness in neck and shoulders, chest pain, numbness and tingling in extremities, headaches, low-grade fevers.
Organizatonal Effects	Absenteeism, low productivity, poor labor-management relations, job dissatisfaction, lowered organizational commitment.

INTERNATIONAL DIMENSION
The High Price of Success in Japan

The world is learning what physicians have known for some time: Stress is a killer! This has become particularly evident in Japan in recent years. In the first half of 1987 alone, twelve chief executives from such companies as Epson, Seiko, Kawasaki Steel, and All Nippon Airways died suddenly as a result of stress-related illnesses. According to one Tokyo psychiatrist, the Japanese are obsessed with perfection and this may lead to particularly high stress during difficult economic times. For example, he found that the incidence of heart attacks among Japanese managers was nearly four times higher during the oil crisis than at other times.

Other factors also take their tolls. Dr. Yasuo Matsuki claims that long days (many Japanese work twelve hours a day, six days a week), late-night parties, and rich foods also contribute to Japanese managers' inability to deal adequately with stress. Alcoholism, emotional breakdowns, and suicide are increasing throughout the Japanese business community. But the latest rash of executive deaths has focused renewed attention on stress in Japanese business.

Questions
Do you believe that certain cultures may either increase or decrease the risk of stress-related illness?

How may high stress levels in Japan affect non-Japanese people who conduct business with Japanese companies?

SOURCE: J.M. Horowitz and Y. Ishikawa, "A Puzzling Toll at the Top," *Time*, 3 August 1987, 46.

---

generally over a longer period of time (*general* adaptation). If the stressor is perceived to be dangerous, adaptation may take the form of "fight or flight"; that is, body and mind will work together to determine whether a person will stay and face the situation or leave and avoid it.

When an elevated level of response must be maintained for a long period, increased levels of adrenaline secreted into the blood cause the body to become "drained" by the stressor, producing the stage known as *exhaustion*. The general adaptation syndrome is depicted in Exhibit 16.4.

Let us look at the case of JoAnn Brooks. JoAnn instructed her secretary not to take any calls while she completed a report. She knew the report was already a day late, and if she couldn't find the error in her figures immediately, Don Edwards, her new boss, would have to leave for his meeting without it. JoAnn had spent most of the night at the office. A pot of coffee, some cold pizza, and concern about how Don would react to her first special assignment were about all that was keeping her going.

Suddenly, the door opened and she saw Don Edwards out of the corner of her eye. "How are you coming on that report, Mrs. Brooks?" she heard. JoAnn never noticed his smile. Before either one knew what had happened a half a cup of coffee had found its way onto the report, and JoAnn had begun to tremble convulsively. Edwards did what he could to calm her down, but JoAnn was unable to continue working on the report. She apologized for not having the work completed and left the office a few minutes later. When she arrived at home, JoAnn sat down to reflect on the stress and strain she had experienced over the past few days. At half past ten the following morning, she awoke to find herself still sitting in her living room.

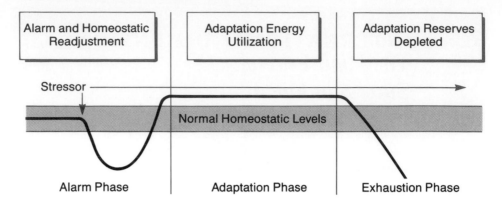

The level of resources available to meet stress are represented by the curve. These resources remain at normal homeostatic levels in the absence of a stressor.

EXHIBIT 16.4   GENERAL ADAPTATION SYNDROME

What factors contributed to the stress JoAnn experienced? Were you able to identify the three stages of the general adaptation syndrome in this example?

The general adaptation syndrome is activated in *all* stressful situations. Stress is normally associated with negative events (e.g., taking a dreaded test, facing a reprimand). This type of stress is known as distress. However, stress (and the associated GAS) also occurs in situations that we may view as positive. This second form of stress is known as eustress. You are likely to experience many of the same symptoms (rapid breathing, higher blood pressure, etc.) when celebrating a victory or laughing at a joke as when you are waiting to see the dentist or to meet an important client.

Stress can help as well as hinder performance. In one study of three hundred managerial and professional employees, researchers found stress enhanced performance up to a point, although performance suffered when stress became excessive.[12] The diagram in Exhibit 16.5 is known to stress researchers as the **Inverted U.** The

EXHIBIT 16.5   STRESS: THE INVERTED U CURVE

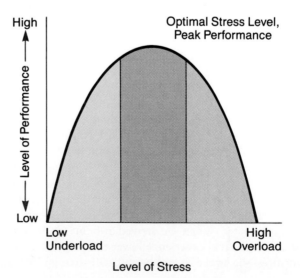

Inverted U suggests that an *optimal* level of stress is necessary for peak performance. Too little stress can lead to lack of motivation or interest, while too much stress can result in an aversion to tasks at hand, inability to concentrate, or wasted nervous energy.

SOURCES OF WORK-RELATED STRESS

Earlier, we suggested that stress was initiated by the occurrence or recognition of an external threat. Such threats can take many forms. Some are physical (e.g., a sudden noise, a bright light, or the appearance of a particular person), while others are cognitive (e.g., feeling anxious about an upcoming event). We will examine five work-related stressors and discuss them as they relate to both work and nonwork settings. These five stressors are role conflict, role ambiguity, work overload and underload, responsibility, and career development[13] (See Exhibit 16.6).

Role Conflict

A *role* is a set of behaviors normally associated with a particular organizational or other societal position. A manager's role may include making certain decisions, communicating those decisions to others, and maintaining production records. In addition to his organizational activities, the manager may have roles as a spouse, parent, or community leader.

Role conflict is the result of incompatible role demands. In some cases, the behaviors required in a single role may conflict with one another. For example, a manager may be required to discipline as well as to be supportive of subordinates. A person may also find herself occupying two or more conflicting roles. A newly appointed department head may be told that her job is to represent the interests of her subordinates but not to forget that she is now a member of the management team. Similarly, a job which requires a substantial amount of out-of-town travel (job-related role) may create considerable pressure for a parent whose scheduled trips conflict with attending a child's school play (parent-related role).

In some cases, the potential for role conflict is clearly evident. We can anticipate that a wife and mother or husband and father who is expected to travel in her or his new position as an account representative will experience some role conflict. In other

EXHIBIT 16.6   SOURCES AND EFFECTS OF WORK-RELATED STRESS

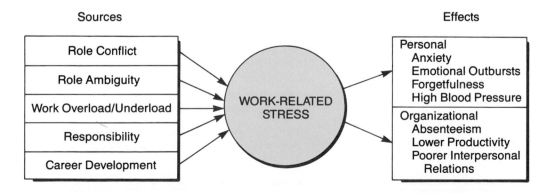

cases, role conflict may be more subjective. For instance, individuals' personal values, needs, or goals may significantly influence the role conflicts they experience. The level of stress experienced by traveling salespeople no doubt depends upon their personal values and the expectations that they place on their jobs and home lives. In one study of marketing managers, researchers found that high self-esteem lessened the role stress they experienced.[14]

Four separate types of role conflict are described in Exhibit 16.7. Can you identify specific instances in which you have experienced one or more of these stressful role conflicts either at work or elsewhere?

Role conflict and accompanying stress can be felt by organizations, their individual members, and in some cases, other important people in members' lives. The ethical dilemma below raises important questions concerning organizations' and individuals' responsibilities to prevent or minimize such conflict whenever and wherever possible.

Role Ambiguity

Role ambiguity is a lack of clarity about the task or job a person is expected to perform. Few, if any, jobs are without some ambiguity. However, some jobs are more

---

ETHICAL DILEMMA
Job Versus Family:
A Conflict of Roles?

Corporations often place heavy demands on their executives and managers. Sometimes those demands take the form of time or effort; other times they require certain qualities such as intensity and single-mindedness that can indirectly take their toll on families. All too often, executives find out that the qualities and commitments that have secured them high marks as corporate leaders can also lead them to rate low marks as parents.

A survey of AT&T executives and managers found their single greatest cause of stress was their children. Although children of business leaders are likely to live in "the best" neighborhoods and drive high-priced cars, they are also *expected* to perform well in school and gain acceptance by a top college or university. Unfortunately, the seventy-hour work week and business-related social activities of many top managers, and added household responsibilities created by the increasing

number of working spouses, severely limits the time managers have available to provide needed social and moral support to their children. Whether doing too little as parents or overcompensating and doing too much, top managers have found that their jobs can produce more (and less) for their families than they had anticipated.

Questions
What, if any, responsibilities do employing organizations have to help executives, managers, or other employees balance their work and home lives as they progress along career paths?

Why is it important for executives or managers to balance their responsibilities to their organizations with those to their families?

SOURCE: B. O'Reilly, "Why Grade 'A' Execs Get an 'F' as Parents," *Fortune*, 1 January 1990, 36–46.

likely to result in role ambiguity than others. For example, a newly hired salesclerk may be placed on the salesfloor with little instruction. Similarly, someone promoted to her first supervisory position may not understand what it is that a supervisor actually does.

Role ambiguity becomes particularly distressing when it takes place over a prolonged period of time. In such cases, it has been found to be related to job dissatisfaction, tension, and even physical ill health. Some individuals are better able to tolerate role ambiguity than others. Nevertheless, most people need some idea of what their jobs entail and what expectations have been placed upon them.

Overload and Underload

Earlier, we concluded that individuals are likely to perform better when they experience an *optimum* amount of stress. As you will see by referring back to Exhibit 16.5, overload is that area to the right of the optimum point of the curve. In **overload,** quantitative or qualitative demands placed on a person are more than he or she can manage. As we do from role ambiguity, virtually all of us suffer at one time or another from work overload. The condition of chronic overload has, however, been linked to organizational consequences such as higher accident rates and poorer interpersonal relations, and to individual consequences such as coronary heart disease.

Overload may be quantitative or qualitative. Quantitative overload occurs when an individual feels that there is "too much to do and not enough time in which to do it." You have probably suffered from quantitative overload if you have ever failed to keep up with classroom assignments and then had your instructor suddenly announce an exam for the following day.

Qualitative overload, on the other hand, occurs when a person feels that she is unable to do what is required or that performance standards have been set too high. In other words, the job is too hard. You may have taken a class or received an assignment that you simply found to be too difficult. "I'll never get this!" is one symptomatic response to qualitative overload. Although more research has been done on quantitative than qualitative overload, a recent study of 121 undergraduate

EXHIBIT I6.7   TYPES AND EXAMPLES OF ROLE STRESS

ROLE CONFLICT	CREATED WHEN	EXAMPLE
Intra-sender	Message received contains inherent contradictions.	Order is late; supervisor tells worker, "work faster but avoid errors."
Person-role	Person's required actions conflict with his/her personal values.	Co-worker is asked by employee to clock-in on time for him, although employee will be late to work.
Inter-sender	Conflicting directions are received from two or more sources.	Secretary receives requests for immediate completion of work from two separate managers at the same time.
Inter-role	Person experiences conflicting demands related to two or more roles.	Boss wants subordinate to work late at office; subordinate has family obligation.

students found that qualitative overloads were generally more stressful for the subjects than quantitative overloads. [15]

Underload is the opposite of overload, but it can be equally as stressful. Not having enough stimulation or enough to do may lead to feelings of frustration, boredom, depression, and even moments of panic. Underloaded workers sometimes feel trapped by their jobs and are likely to look for on-the-job diversions. One worker on an automobile assembly line, for example, described the way in which he spent his "spare" time on the job. "I have four or five seconds between operations, so I read paperback books during the 'break.' " Such diversions may cause workers to ignore the few job requirements they have or may result in carelessness that in turn leads to mistakes and even injury.

Responsibility

Although some management authorities believe that people react favorably to responsibility, [16] increased responsibility may also be accompanied by higher levels of stress. Moreover, responsibility for people has been found to be more stressful than responsibility for "things." [17] Stress related to people-responsibility is linked to the need for individuals to make unpleasant interpersonal decisions (performance reviews, disciplinary actions, correction of errors, etc.), and may also be related to role conflict and role ambiguity. In addition, personal accountability for the actions of others can produce stress for managers whose own work loads force them to delegate duties to others but who have (or choose to take) little direct control over how those duties are performed. [18]

Career Development

An individual's perception of his career status and career progress can cause **career development**-related stress. Such stress may result from (1) psychological reactions to one's career situation; (2) differences that may exist between one's perceived career status and career expectations; [19] or (3) critical transitions along the career development path. Career development may thus affect stress when a person lacks job security, fears obsolescence or retirement, or questions her career choice. In addition, stress may occur when an individual compares her rate of promotion to an internally conceived standard or to the actual progress of those with whom she works. In this case, stress would be likely to occur if the person senses that she is "falling behind."

Finally, certain career stages coupled with periods of adult development (see the discussion of adult development in Chapter 2) are stressful for many individuals. These "transitional periods" are characterized by examinations of one's past and present and may lead to significant changes in future personal and job-related decisions. Both the Age Thirty Transition and the Mid-Life Transition can be particularly volatile life stages. The linkage of career stages to life stages is discussed further in Chapter 17, "Careers and Career Development."

High-Stress Situations in Today's Workplace

The work-related stressors discussed above can occur in any organizational environment and are manifest in a variety of specific situations. We will now briefly discuss three such situations that are receiving increasing attention in contemporary work settings. They include corporate realignments, work-family conflicts, and burnout.

Corporate realignments

The past decade has seen a rash of corporate realignments in the form of mergers, divestitures, and downsizing. Whether changes are government induced like those at AT&T, unfriendly maneuvers like the Tyson Food takeover of Holly Farms, or planned restructurings to improve cost competitiveness or to hold off corporate raiders, all realignments have a significant impact on the stress levels of executives, managers, and other company employees.

Stress in such cases results from the loss of personal control over and anxiety about one's future,[20] longer hours and increased demands related to broader spans of control, and increased responsibility.[21] Managers have also reported that persons not directly affected by these changes often feel the stress of not knowing, "if I will be next."[22]

Consultants who have worked with companies involved in major realignments have recommended that communication regarding changes be improved and that managers and other persons affected be given an opportunity to vent their emotions.[23] In one study of merger impacts, executives reported that stress and conflict continued long after mergers had taken place and that problems encountered were similar to those experienced in marriage and family settings.[24] Executives' reactions were likened to childrens' reactions to a parent's second marriage and involved five common themes (see Exhibit 16.8).

SAFEWAY

Leveraged buyouts (LBOs) like that at Safeways Stores, Inc., have been profitable for some and exacted a heavy toll from others. While CEO Peter Magowan and other Safeway executives quadrupled their cash investment as a result of the Safeway LBO, over 63,000 Safeway managers and workers lost their jobs. Those who were rehired were given lower wages or forced into part-time work. More than a year after they were laid off, nearly 60 percent had still not found full-time employment.

The Safeway LBO is credited with raising corporate productivity and profits. However, it also had a stressful impact on many families and individuals. Ron Seaboldt spent seventeen years with Safeway; he, his wife Kay, a human resources supervisor, and their daughter were all let go on the same day. Kay Seaboldt reports a wide range of impacts on employees, ranging from bankruptcies and the loss of homes to illnesses and worse. Pressures brought about by James White's

EXHIBIT 16.8   TYPICAL EXECUTIVE REACTIONS TO MERGERS

- Anxiety and Uncertainty
- Helplessness and Rejection
- Divided Loyalties
- Withdrawal and Avoidance
- Conflicts Over New Values

LBO-related job loss caused the thirty-year Safeway trucker to commit suicide one year to the day after he was let go. A systems analyst, Patricia Vasquez, was found the morning after her layoff dead of a heart attack, and the wife of another employee was hospitalized for high blood pressure and died within weeks.

Safeway officials do not accept responsibility for these incidents but have expressed concern over them. Said one laid-off engineer who was refused a letter of reference for fear he would use it to sue the company, "I am ashamed. I am like an old thrown-out mop." Although some employees who remain with Safeway are doing well, the morale of others has suffered and many fear that they will be among the next to be let go.[25]

Work-family conflicts

The relationship between responsibilities to work and responsibilities to family have long been a source of stress. Recently, however, work-family conflicts resulting from role conflict have been exacerbated by an increasing number of dual-career couples in the work force. The placement of more women in management and other positions of higher responsibility and many male managers' desire to spend more time with their families have also increased work-family conflicts.

Evidence continues to build suggesting that such stress affects job satisfaction specifically and life satisfaction generally for both men and women.[26] Results from a recent study of middle-aged adults in dual-career families indicated that organizations need to help employees more clearly define the boundaries between work and home and that these boundaries must be more flexible.[27]

Both men and women experience work-family stress, although sex stereotypes and traditional expectations concerning women and work add to the stress that affect women. Furthermore, women often lack the immediate social support of co-workers because, in many situations, most of their co-workers are men, many of whom have difficulty identifying with women's unique work-family experiences.[28]

Special programs for those who experience work-family conflict and programs intended for those who manage such persons can help lessen stress-related impacts on both individuals and organizations.[29]

Burnout

Burnout is a subtle and progressive syndrome related to job stress. Those who suffer from burnout often become lethargic and lose interest in their work. As one executive put it, "I'm tired, and frankly I just don't care anymore. I'm just worn out."[30] Classic symptoms of burnout include physical, mental, and emotional exhaustion.[31] Anyone is subject to burnout. But individuals who are most likely to suffer from burnout tend to

▶ experience high levels of stress on the job;
▶ be idealistic and/or high achievers; and
▶ seek unattainable goals.[32]

Other factors can also contribute to burnout. The results of one study of corporate managers indicated that frustrated expectations about their jobs contributed to burnout. Managers were first asked to list the expectations they had when coming to their jobs. Next, they were asked to list the most stressful aspects of those jobs. Responses indicated that an inability to fulfill their initial hopes and expectations was particularly stressful.[33]

EXHIBIT 16.9   MANAGEMENT BEHAVIORS THAT CAN INFLUENCE EMPLOYEE STRESS

STRESS-INDUCING BEHAVIORS

1. Piling excessive work on employees with little or no direction as to priorities.
2. Holding frequent, lengthy meetings and then criticizing employees for not spending enough time at their desks.
3. Setting goals that are too high.
4. Putting employees on the spot, especially in front of others.
5. Constantly moving employees from one project to another, thereby creating a "juggling" syndrome.

STRESS REDUCING BEHAVIORS

1. Emphathize! Try to understand employees' perceptions of work and of you from their points of view.
2. Keep crises to a minimum.
3. Improve your communication skills; be clear and ask for feedback.
4. Be quick to praise and otherwise reinforce good work.
5. When a correction or reprimand is necessary, be calm and do it in private.
6. Leave room for discussion. Employees who feel powerless over their own work environments are likely to experience a higher level of stress.

SOURCE: S. Nelton, "Getting Over Giving Ulcers," *Nation's Business*, Vol. 74 (September 1986) 42.

Finally, supervisory style appears to be an important cause of burnout. A survey of part-time M.B.A. students found a direct relationship between initiating structure (task-oriented style) and burnout, and an inverse relationship between consideration (person-oriented style) and burnout.[34] The relationship between supervisory style and burnout may be moderated by individual characteristics.[35] Nevertheless, attention to style and other external factors (immediate work group, nature of work, etc.) merits additional attention from researchers and managers alike. Exhibit 16.9 lists specific management behaviors that can induce and reduce subordinate stress.

Burnout might be more understandable, and even acceptable, if it occurred toward the end of people's productive years. Unfortunately, however, it is a problem increasingly faced by people in midcareer. A job that demands much of a person emotionally or physically is likely to cause midcareer burnout. Exhibit 16.10 identifies ten such jobs. These jobs often require the impossible, demanding that employees control the uncontrollable or never make wrong decisions.

Work-Related Stress in Perspective

As you can see, there are a number of conditions that may cause work-related stress affecting both individual and organizational health. Although preventing the occurrence of these conditions entirely is neither possible nor desirable, managers must be aware of their potential effects in order to minimize their negative impact in the work setting. In the following section, we will examine individual and organizational responses to stress.

EXHIBIT 16.10   TEN JOBS THAT CAUSE BURNOUT

• Air Traffic Controller	• Stock Trader
• Nurse or Doctor	• Social Worker
• Teacher	• Truck Driver
• Psychologist	• Insurance Executive
• Garment Industry Buyer	• Lawyer

SOURCE: J. Batten, "10 Jobs That Cause Burnout," *Careers*, December 1985, 41–43.

EFFECTIVELY MANAGING STRESS

Our discussion and the research on which it is based suggest that stress is a necessary and unavoidable part of organizational life. Yet inappropriate levels of stress can have serious negative consequences for individuals and organizations alike. In this section, we will briefly examine steps that individuals and organizations can take to manage job-related stress more effectively and discuss some specific guidelines that managers can follow to lessen stress-related disruptions for their employees.

Individual Responses to Stress

As a manager, you will be required to address the job-related stress of employees and other persons with whom you work. Thus, your knowledge of organizational relationships and resources is important. At the same time, you yourself are also subject to job-related stress. In this section, we will explore individual responses to stress that can be adopted by you and by others in your organization.

Personal stress audit

Individuals must assess their own vulnerability to stress. This can be accomplished through a **personal stress audit.** A personal stress audit (PSA) involves a complete examination of one's physical condition, lifestyle, and personal history.

A physical examination giving special attention to heart, lungs, body weight, and blood chemistry analysis may show early signs of stress-related disease and is likely to influence any specific stress-management program that is subsequently adopted. An objective assessment of one's present lifestyle can provide additional insight into important stress factors such as rest, exercise patterns, and diet. It is also helpful to evaluate the impact of personal and work-related events that may have contributed to a build up of stress over a period of time. The Behavior Activity Profile found at the end of this chapter (see Exercise 16.1) will help you determine the stress-related impact of certain of your life events and of your work setting.

After a personal stress audit is completed, appropriate techniques for effectively managing stress at the individual level can be identified. Individual stress management techniques fall into two broad categories, (1) preventive techniques, and (2) stress reduction techniques. Preventive techniques are those that can be employed before stress symptoms emerge, thereby reducing the likelihood or severity of stress symptoms. Reduction techniques are employed after stress is detected and are intended to reduce or eliminate stress.

Preventive techniques

Preventive techniques include those approaches designed to prevent stress before it occurs or otherwise lessen the impact of potentially stressful situations. Such techniques may focus on either stressors, the context of the stress (the situation), or a person's vulnerability to stress.

Two commonly used preventive techniques include physically removing oneself from a source of stress and eliminating the stressor itself. For example, reading the daily mail away from the telephone or asking the budding musician in the house to play the trumpet in the other room removes potential stressors (telephone interruptions and loud noise), and should reduce the incidence of stress. In each of these situations, conscious and selective behavior toward stressors is employed to reduce stress.

Karen Ivory, a TV producer who worked her way up from stations in St. Louis and Philadelphia to WCBS-TV in New York, found her new job to be too debilitating. Ultimately, she left her high-tension job for a lower-profile one in public relations at a small Pennsylvania college in order to alleviate her stress. Whether it means leaving a job as Ivory did or simply getting away from the office and unwinding by reading and doing aerobics as Alameda, California, real estate broker and workaholic Susan Silver does, avoiding stressors can be a successful strategy for coping with stress.[36]

Managing the context of work may also lessen stressful situations. Managers often find that they can do certain kinds of work in one environment better than in another. For example, a district sales manager may be better able to make difficult personnel decisions when he is traveling from one store to another than while he is on a store's premises. Managing one's work context may also involve altering the immediate work environment. Managers and other office workers usually personalize their desks and offices with pictures and other mementos, while workers in United States manufacturing plants may hang calendars or bring personal radios onto the work floor. Assembly-line workers in Sanyo's Shiga appliance manufacturing facility personalize their work stations with their own uniquely designed flower arrangements. Such personalization enables individuals to create more familiar and comfortable working environments.

Earlier, we stated that managing diet, exercise, and rest can all affect the stress experienced by an individual. A complete, integrated personal fitness program addressing each of these areas can help to prevent stress symptoms and can lessen the severity of unavoidable stress consequences.

Certain steps like those suggested above can help to prevent stress or minimize the negative impact of stressful situations. In the following section we will look at specific techniques for reducing existing stress.

Stress reduction techniques

No matter how hard we try to prevent counterproductive stress, we are unlikely to entirely eliminate it from our lives. Although stress is to be expected, prolonged exposure to stressful situations may lead to serious psychological and physiological problems. The cumulative effect of stress can be mitigated by the use of certain stress reduction techniques.* Three such techniques are (1) biofeedback, (2) relaxation response, and (3) exercise.

Biofeedback.   **Biofeedback** is the process of monitoring one's own vital signs (e.g., pulse rate, breathing, temperature) and then using this information as a basis for the

---

*Stress reduction techniques may also reduce the likelihood of subsequent stress by lowering an individual's vulnerability to stressors or stressful situations.

self-regulation of selected bodily activities.[37] Individuals who practice biofeedback as a stress-management technique monitor those processes that increase or are otherwise altered by stress and practice relaxation techniques to bring monitored indicators back within acceptable tolerance limits. For example, you may gauge your own pulse rate periodically while involved in a aerobic activity and take steps to maintain your heartbeat at a desired level.

Biofeedback technique has been aided by the development of a broad range of biofeedback instruments. These instruments permit an individual to measure accurately and display (visually or audibly) a variety of physical and mental processes. Among the wide range of equipment available are feedback thermometers that can be attached to fingers or other parts of the body, machines that measure alpha waves emitted by the brain, and dermographs, which measure galvanic skin response (the skin's ability to conduct electricity, which is related directly to activities of the central nervous system).

Biofeedback has attracted considerable attention in recent years. Although the accuracy and reliability of some biofeedback equipment are suspect, the biofeedback concept itself has proven to be effective in reducing migraine and tension headaches, lowering blood pressure, and reducing stomach acid, which can lead to ulcers.[38] Although it is difficult to measure precisely the organizational benefits of biofeedback, Equitable Life Assurance Society has reported that the cost of administering its own broadly based program was more than recovered by increases in gained time and productivity (three dollars recovered for each dollar spent).[39]

Relaxation Response.   Relaxation response (RER) can be practiced regularly without special training or equipment and has proven to be a highly effective means for reducing stress symptoms. Relaxation response involves the following steps:

1. Sit in a comfortable position wearing comfortable clothing (you may want to loosen your collar or belt).
2. Relax muscles, starting with feet and moving up to face (this can be done by first tensing and then relaxing various muscle groups).
3. Inhale, mentally "following" air through your nose and into lungs.
4. Exhale silently through your mouth; you may breathe a one-syllable word.
5. Disregard distractions; remain passive.
6. Repeat process for ten to twenty minutes.

Relaxation response can be practiced in almost any setting, and variations of the technique can be used to alleviate specific stress symptoms. For example, persons suffering from headache or back or other pain are encouraged to "inhale directly through the pain." Of course, this is not physiologically possible. However, an individual can create the mental image of such a phenomenon and may experience a decrease in the specific symptom.

Exercise.   Experts in the area of human physiology have long argued that a carefully planned, ongoing exercise program can reduce vulnerability to stress and actually dissipate existing stress. Research conducted on men and women of all age groups consistently supports this contention.

Exercise, within prescribed limits, has been found to reduce physical signs of stress (e.g., high resting heart rate and muscle tension) as well as anxiety, depression, and hostility. However, unlike many other approaches to stress management, "there is a potential element of risk involved with exercise."[40] Persons who choose to initiate a vigorous exercise program should first check with a physician to insure that it can be undertaken safely.

Organizational Responses to Stress

Organizations have given considerable emphasis in recent years to reducing stress in the work setting. Although the popular press has given greater attention to individual stress management strategies, organizational stress management programs may ultimately have the greatest impact on both organizations and individuals. In this section, we will explore a variety of organizational approaches to stress management.

Organizational stress audit

The first step in any attempt to reduce nonproductive stress in an organization should be to conduct an **organizational stress audit** (OAS). Information gathered through questionnaires, interviews, and even a review of organizational documents (e.g., organization charts and manuals) can be used to identify areas of stress that exist presently or potentially in the work environment. A stress audit should examine existing conditions such as work design, organizational climate and leadership styles, and structural characteristics (e.g., degree of centralization/decentralization, authority-responsibility relationships, spans of management, communication channels).[41] In addition, the audit should identify existing programs that already contribute to stress management (e.g., employment counselors and psychiatric services).

Organizational audits do not contribute directly to stress reduction. However, they provide information upon which future strategies for managing stress at the organizational level can be based.

Structural interventions

Structural interventions include organization and job redesign and improved job placement activities. A considerable proportion of stress in organizations occurs in individuals' immediate work environments. Factors most often contributing to such distress include a lack of autonomy,[42] being responsible to more than one superior, ambiguity about job requirements, and poor communication.[43] These conditions can be addressed directly by redesigning and clarifying responsibilities and organizational relationships.

Specifically job-related interventions include job rotation and job enlargement. These techniques are intended to reduce the stress of menial or repetitive work activities by rotating job holders through a series of task assignments (job rotation) and by increasing the number of task assignments performed by a person at a single work station (job enlargement). These interventions have met with mixed success. A third job-design approach, job enrichment, attempts to alter the fundamental nature of work by making the job more psychologically rewarding. Job rotation, job enlargement, and job enrichment are all discussed in greater detail in Chapter 14, "Work Design."

Efforts to alter organizations and jobs may also take into consideration those persons who will occupy specific positions. Selection and placement may be governed by broad patterns of characteristics (skill levels, tolerance of ambiguity, cognitive complexity, etc.) required in certain jobs. In some cases, job definitions and organizational relationships may intentionally be left flexible in order to accommodate the needs of individual position holders.

Career development programs

A significant amount of organizational stress is related to career expectations and career progress. Organizations that consciously manage career development (see Chapter 17, "Careers and Career Development") can help balance individuals' career aspirations with organizational opportunities. Effective career development programs can reduce stress by facilitating an improved job-person fit and by helping individuals manage their rate of career growth in order to minimize both underload and burnout. In addition, career development programs can address the changing pressures on work life imposed in the broader context of adult development.

Stress management and related programs

Organizations cannot manage stress directly because stress is an *individual* phenomenon. Nevertheless, organizational resources can be used to increase employee awareness of stress and to help individuals develop personal strategies for minimizing its adverse effects. Stress management seminars can be provided to help employees understand the nature and impact of stress, and workshops covering such topics as relaxation and time management can be offered to teach specific techniques for preventing and coping with stressful situations. Programs can even be designed to meet special needs of groups such as women,[44] managers,[45] or individuals who are having difficulty sorting out work and family responsibilities.[46]

Social support systems

Research findings suggest that unhealthy consequences of stress can be reduced through social support. Social support refers to relationships individuals have with one another both on and off the job. Supportive relationships can be provided by supervisors. Managers, for example, who have effective interpersonal skills can help prevent or reduce employee distress.[47]

Co-workers can also play an important role in reducing stress symptoms, and providing opportunities for positive working relationships among peers can reduce stress symptoms for some individuals by lessening role conflict and role ambiguity[48] and by providing general ego support. A study of nearly eight hundred social workers found that those who received social support experienced less stress in their jobs. In addition, workers who perceived higher levels of available social support were more likely to use that support.[49] These findings suggest not only that social support is a valuable means for reducing stress, but also that individuals should be made aware of the support systems that are available to them.

Social support systems also can be *designed* into the formal organization. Employment counselors located in personnel departments or other human resource groups can mitigate job-related stress with improved orientation and career planning and counseling, and by helping supervisors recognize situations requiring their own intervention.[50] Some companies even employ full-time psychologists or make similar services available to employees as part of their overall benefits packages.

Ombudsmen may also help provide support to managers and other employees and to reduce tensions experienced in the work environment. An **ombudsman** is an individual whose role in the organization is to listen to employee concerns and to help resolve problems by mediating between aggrieved parties. Ombudsmen, unlike line managers, are free to move throughout the organization, cut red tape, and facilitate the resolution of problems outside traditional lines of authority.[51]

Although group support systems often emerge naturally due to employees' physical proximity (i.e., their work locations, common eating or dressing facilities, etc.), company sponsored recreation activities such as softball and bowling teams, picnics, and weekend retreats can also provide opportunities for social support. Of course, not all social support takes place on the job. Most people also receive support from family, friends, and social organizations away from the job.

Employers cannot manage external social support systems directly. However, company requirements (overnight travel, overtime, and shiftwork) can indirectly influence the support provided by these external sources by curtailing the amount of time employees have to experience such support. It should be noted that external support systems may not always effectively reduce work-related stress. For example, talking about work-related problems with spouses was found to be not nearly as effective as discussing such problems with co-workers, because spouses had difficulty understanding and relating to problems experienced on the job.[52] Nevertheless, awareness and accommodation of external sources of social support may contribute to the effective management of work-related stress.

Wellness programs

Wellness programs are fully integrated health programs designed to promote and maintain physical as well as psychological good health.[53] Medical research indicates that psychological and physiological stress are systemically related to one another. Prolonged emotional or psychological distress may manifest itself in either physiological or psychological symptoms. Similarly, physical health problems experienced over a long period of time may result in anxiety, depression, or other forms of psychological distress.

There is no limit to the number or type of possible wellness program components. Common to many wellness programs are (1) pre-entry physical and mental assessment (a wellness examination), and (2) modules covering weight control, nutrition, exercise, and general fitness. Employees are encouraged to participate in company-related group exercise programs such as walking, jogging, biking, or aerobic dancing during their lunch breaks or before or after work. "Stop smoking" clinics and sessions that teach self-examination for various types of disease symptoms may also be included. Employees often receive incentive awards such as gift certificates, T-shirts, and even days off with pay for their participation and successful progress toward various health-related goals.

Wellness programs can affect the work setting directly when they are linked to company safety programs. They can also affect the personal lives of employees through the implementation of an employee assistance program (EAP). EAPs meet special health needs of individuals experiencing drug, alcohol, or other medical problems requiring professional attention. Assistance is generally provided by private contractors (physicians, psychologists, etc.) unless such professionals are employed full-time by the company.

Although it is difficult to evaluate completely the impact of wellness programs, organizations have reported significant increases in attendance, satisfaction, and productivity, as well as the medically measured improved general health of program participants. These conditions, have in turn led to decreased employee health-care costs and fewer workers' compensation losses. Exhibit 16.11 shows reductions in health and accident costs at the United Methodist Publishing House after a wellness program known as "TryUMPH for Health" was initiated.[54] UMPH health-care costs decreased 10.2 percent in the program's first year, while comparable costs rose 9.1 percent nationally for the same period.

**EXHIBIT 16.11   IMPACT OF THE TryUMPH FOR HEALTH WELLNESS
PROGRAM***

Total Employee		
Health Care Costs	1984 ▬▬▬▬▬▬▬▬▬▬▬▬▬▬▬▬▬	$826,871
	1985 ▬▬▬▬▬▬▬▬▬▬▬▬ $742,884	
	1986 Not Available	
Workers Compensation		
Losses	1984 ▬▬▬▬▬▬▬▬▬▬▬▬▬▬▬▬▬	$82,000
	1985 ▬▬▬▬▬▬▬▬▬▬▬ $29,000	
	1986 $1,000	
Lost Work Days	1984 284	
	1985 169	
	1986 6	
	1984—Preprogram	
	1985—Inaugural Year	
	1986—Second Year	

*The TryUMPH wellness program involved early detection, preventive treatment and safety
programs, as well as more traditional elements such as weight control, exercise, etc.
SOURCE: D. Patterson, "Can A Company Evaluate the Cost/Benefits of Its Wellness Efforts?" *Risk
Management*, Vol. 33, No. 11 (November 1986): 30–36.

Over 90 percent of the five hundred largest companies in the United States,
including AT&T, Johnson & Johnson, and Cullinet Software, today have some form
of wellness program. [55]

STRESS IN ORGANIZATIONS: CONCLUSIONS

Only a few years ago, someone claiming to be under too much stress would probably
not have received much sympathy. Today, however, a deeper understanding of the
psychological and physiological implications of stress has led to greater concern about
its impact.

The price of prolonged periods of intense stress is high. Impaired decision making
abilities and interpersonal relationships, time lost from work due to mental and
emotional illnesses, dependencies on alcohol or drugs, and life-threatening diseases
are all too common consequences of stress in the workplace. Persons whose occupations and careers accelerate or intensify stress cycles may pay a high price for
success unless preventive measures designed to manage organizational and personal
stress are adopted.

Today, the factors contributing to stress—specific stressors, individual vulnerability, and the context (or situation) in which the stress occurs—and the process
through which our bodies adjust to stress (general adaptation syndrome), are well
understood. However, many managers still fail to recognize the serious personal and
organizational implications of high-stress environments.

Companies can play an important role in the management of stress. In addition
to educating managers and other workers about stress awareness and stress management, such important factors as job and organizational design, career management,
and a supportive work environment can significantly reduce counterproductive stress
in organizations.

Stress is an individual phenomenon. Ultimately, therefore, stress management
depends on the actions of each person. Our unique responses to stress require that

each person becomes aware of specific stressors that are likely to initiate the stress cycle and the situations in which those stressors are most apt to lead to distress. In addition, each of us must be sensitive to his or her personal lifestyle (rest, diet, exercise), recognize the relationship of that lifestyle to personal stress, and understand how to manage that lifestyle sensibly. Of course, awareness and understanding must be accompanied by a willingness to take actions that will contribute to an optimal level of stress.

Keep in mind that stress is not the product of work alone. Stressors outside the workplace (family discord, financial pressures, illness, etc.) can create stress symptoms. Similarly, stressors that occur off the job may lead to job-related stress symptoms or exacerbate those symptoms which already exist. Managers must therefore be sensitive to off-the-job as well as on-the-job pressures to which they and their employees are subjected.[56] Only through such sensitivity and a willingness to take necessary steps to reduce stress can stress in the workplace be managed effectively.

QUESTIONS FOR REVIEW AND DISCUSSION

1. Briefly describe the relationship among stressors, context, and vulnerability to stress.
2. Describe a stress related situation using the components of the General Adaptation Syndrome.
3. What is a Type A personality and how is this personality type related to stress?
4. Name the six major consequences of stress and discuss how each impacts our daily lives.
5. What is meant by the term *optimal stress level?*
6. Name and briefly discuss the sources of work-related stress. How may such stress sources be minimized or eliminated?

7. Briefly describe the four types of role conflict and provide an example of each in a work setting.
8. How does the impact of stress overload differ from that of stress underload?
9. Describe what is meant by the term *personal stress audit.* What stress-related components should be evaluated in such an audit?
10. Name and briefly discuss organizational responses to stress in the work place.

REFERENCES

1. D. DeCarlo, "Don't Let Stress Claims Broadside You," *Business and Health,* Vol. 7 (January 1989): 43–45; D. Fasel and S. W. Schaef, "The High Cost of Workaholism," *Business and Health,* Vol. 7 (January 1989): 38–42; D. DiBlase, "Workplace Stress Cuts Costs: Experts," *Business Insurance,* 28 April 1986, 53; C. M. Cain, "Job Stress Cases Mounting: Experts," *Business Insurance,* 2 March 1987, 1,28; D. Gilbride, "Emotional Trauma at Work: The Occupational Disease of Our Times."
2. J. E. Newman and T. A. Beehr, "Personal and Organizational Strategies for Handling Job Stress: A Review of Research and Opinion," *Personnel Psychology,* Vol. 32 (1979): 2–43.
3. A. A. McLean, *Work Stress* (Reading, Mass.: Addison-Wesley, 1979), 37–88.
4. A. Miller, "Stress on the Job," *Newsweek,* 25 April

1988, 40–45.
5. P. E. Spector, D. J. Dwyer, and S. M. Jex, "Relation of Job Stressors to Affective, Health, and Performance Outcomes: A Comparison of Multiple Data Sources," *Journal of Applied Psychology,* Vol. 73 (February 1988): 11–19.
6. D. White and B. Wisdom, "Stress and the Hospital Administrator: Sources and Solutions," *Hospital & Health Services Administration,* Vol. 30 (September/October 1985): 112–119.
7. M. Friedman and R. H. Rosenman, *Type A Behavior and Your Heart* (New York: Alfred A. Knopf, 1974); K. A. Matthews, "Psychological Perspectives on the Type A Behavior Pattern," *Psychological Bulletin,* Vol. 92 (1982): 292–323.
8. L. Helm and C. Gaffney, "The High Price Japanese Pay for Success," *Business Week,* 7 April 1986, 52–54.

9. Ibid.

10. Hans Selye, *The Stress of Life* (New York: McGraw-Hill, 1956). Selye, director of experimental medicine and surgery at the University of Montreal, has authored 28 books and over 1400 articles on stress.

11. Miller, op. cit.

12. S. A. Joure, J. S. Leon, D. B. Simpson, C. H. Holley, and R. L. Frye, "Stress: The Pressure Cooker of Work," *Personnel Administrator*, Vol. 34 (March 1989): 92–95.

13. J. M. Ivancevich and M. T. Matteson, *Stress and Work: A Managerial Perspective* (Glenview, Ill.: Scott, Foresman and Company, 1980); D. F. Parker and T. A. DeCotiis, "Organizational Determinants of Job Stress," *Organizational Behavior and Human Performance*, Vol. 32 (1983): 160–177.

14. R. D. Howell, D. N. Bellenger, and J. B. Wilcox, "Self-Esteem, Role Stress, and Job Satisfaction Among Marketing Managers," *Journal of Business Research*, Vol. 15, No. 1 (February 1987): 71–84.

15. J. B. Shaw and J. A. Weekley, "The Effects of Objective Work-Load Variations on Psychological Stress and Post-Work-Load Performance," *Journal of Management*, Vol. 11 (Spring 1985): 87–98.

16. D. McGregor, *The Human Side of Enterprise* (New York: McGraw-Hill, 1960); Frederick Herzberg, *Work and the Nature of Man* (New York: Thomas Y. Crowell Co., 1966).

17. C. L. Cooper and J. Marshall, "An Audit of Managerial (Di)stress," *Journal of Enterprise Management*, Vol. 1:185–187; for additional information on responsibility, stress, and the blue-collar worker, see R. Martin and T. D. Wall, "Attention Demand and Cost Responsibility as Stressors in Shopfloor Jobs," *Academy of Management Journal*, Vol. 32 (March 1989): 69–86.

18. Ivancevich and Matteson, op. cit., 114–115.

19. Cooper and Marshall, op. cit., 190.

20. S. J. Ashford, "Individual Strategies for Coping with Stress During Organizational Transitions," *Journal of Applied Behavioral Science*, Vol. 24 (1988): 19–36.

21. R. Zemke, "Putting the Squeeze on Middle Managers," *Training*, Vol. 25 (December 1988): 41–46; J. S. McClenahen, "Managing People in the '90s," *Industry Week*, 20 March 1989, 30–38.

22. J. A. Byrne, "Caught in the Middle," *Business Week*, 12 September 1988, 80–85, 88.

23. M. L. Marks, "How to Treat the Merger Syndrome," *Journal of Management Consulting*, Vol. 4 (1988): 42–51.

24. R. M. Fulmer and R. Gilkey, "Blending Corporate Families: Management and Organization Development in a Postmerger Environment," *Academy of Management Executive*, Vol. 2 (November 1988): 275–283.

25. S. C. Faludi, "Safeway LBO Yields Vast Profits But Exacts a Heavy Human Toll," *Wall Street Journal*, 16 May 1990, A1, A10–A11.

26. A. G. Bedeian, B. G. Burke, and R. G. Moffett, "The Experience of Burnout and Work/Non-Work Success in Male and Female Engineers," *Human Resource Management*, Vol. 27 (Summer 1988): 163–179.

27. D. T. Hall and J. Richter, "Balancing Work Life and Home Life: What Can Organizations Do to Help?" *Academy of Management Executive*, Vol. 2 (August 1988): 213–233.

28. L. H. Chusmir and V. Franks, "Stress and the Woman Manager," *Training and Development Journal*, Vol. 42 (October 1988): 66–70; A. F. Buono and J. B. Kamm, "Marginality and the Organizational Socialization of Female Managers," *Human Relations*, Vol. 36 (December 1983): 308–329.

29. J. Foster, "Balancing Work and the Family: Divided Loyalties or Constructive Partnership?" *Personnel Management*, Vol. 20 (September 1988): 38–41.

30. J. Batten, "10 Jobs That Cause Burnout," *Careers*, December 1985, 41–43.

31. Stanley J. Modic, "Surviving Burnout: The Malady of Outrage," *Industry Week*, 20 February 1989, 29–36; D. P. Rogers, "Helping Employees Cope with Burnout," *Business*, Vol. 69 (October-December 1984): 615–622.

32. O. Niehouse, *Controlling Burnout: A Leadership Guide for Managers*, 81–82.

33. A. Pines and E. Aronson, "Why Managers Burn Out," *Sales and Marketing Management*, Vol. 141 (February 1989): 34–38.

34. J. Seltzer and R. E. Numerof, "Supervisory Leadership and Subordinate Burnout," *Academy of Management Journal*, Vol. 31 (June 1988): 439–446.

35. R. T. Golembiewski, R. F. Munzenrider, and J. G. Stevenson, *Stress in Organizations: Toward a Phase Model of Burnout* (New York: Praeger Publishers, 1986).

36. Miller, op. cit.

37. T. O'Sullivan, "Stress and Biofeedback," *Canadian Manager*, Vol. 13 (July 1988): 16–17.

38. Ivancevich and Matteson, op. cit., 219–220; McLean, op. cit., 117–119.

39. *Controlling Stress: A Manager's Manual* (Waterford, Mass.: Bureau of Business Practices, 1980), 33–34.

40. Ivancevich and Matteson, op. cit., 220–221.

41. Parker and DeCotiis, op. cit.

42. K. Hall and L. K. Savery, "Probing Opinions: Tight Rein, More Stress," *Harvard Business Review*, Vol. 64, No. 1 (January-February 1986): 160–167.

43. L. R. Smeltzer, "The Relationship of Communication to Work Stress," *The Journal of Business Communication*, Vol. 24, No. 2 (Spring 1987): 47–58.

44. N. Nykodym, J. L. Simonetti, J. C. Christen, and J. D. Kasper, "Stress and the Working Woman," *Business*, January-March 1987, 8–12; D. L. Nelson and J. C. Quick, "Professional Women: Are Distress and Disease Inevitable?" *Academy of Management Review*,

Vol. 10, No. 2 (April 1985): 206–218; L. H. Chusmir and V. Franks, op. cit.

45. D. Duckworth, "Managing Without Stress," *Personnel Management* Vol. 18 (April 1986): 40–43.

46. Foster, op. cit.

47. Seltzer and Numeroff, op. cit.

48. J. Schaubroeck, J. L. Cotton, and K. R. Jennings, "Antecedents and Consequences of Role Stress: A Covariance Structure Analysis," *Journal of Organizational Behavior*, Vol. 10 (January 1989): 35–58.

49. S. Jayaratne, D. Himle, and W. A. Chess, "Dealing with Work Stress and Strain: Is the Perception of Support More Important than Its Use?" *Journal of Applied Behavioral Science*, Vol. 24 (1988): 191–202.

50. I. A. Miner and N. Nykodym, "Designing Stress Management Systems," *Journal of Systems Management*, August 1987, 16–20.

51. J. T. Ziegenfuss, Jr., "Corporate Ombudsmen," *Personnel Journal*, Vol. 68 (March 1989): 76–79.

52. P. A. Rechnitzer and D. A. Cunningham, "Coping with Job Tension-Effective and Ineffective Methods,"

Public Personnel Management, September-October 1975, 317–326.

53. Patricia Braus, "A Workout for the Bottom Line," *American Demographics*, October 1989, 34–37; R. P. Sloan and J. P. Allegrante, "Corporate Health Is More Than A Robust Balance Sheet," *Training and Development Journal*, December 1985, 57–59; "Health Plans Stress Choice, Wellness, and Concern," *Employee Benefit Plan Review*, Vol. 41 (March 1987): 10–12.

54. D. Patterson, "Can a Company Evaluate the Cost/Benefits of its Wellness Efforts?" *Risk Management*, Vol. 33, No. 11 (November 1986): 30–36.

55. J. Levine, "Preventive Medicine," Vol. 12 (December 1988): 68–73.

56. J. H. Greenhaus and N. J. Beutell, "Sources of Conflict Between Work and Family Roles," *Academy of Management Review*, Vol. 10, No. 1 (January 1985): 76–88; S. E. Jackson, S. Zedeck, and E. Summers, "Family Life Disruptions: Effects of Job-Induced Structural and Emotional Interference," *Academy of Management Journal*, Vol. 28, No. 3 (September 1985): 57–586.

CASE 16.1   *Happiness is success!?*

DONALD D. WHITE   *University of Arkansas*

Roseland Florist opened for business sixteen years ago as a one-room, privately owned business specializing in occasion floral arrangements. The shop was opened by Mrs. Ann Conrad because, "I wanted to have something to keep me occupied and bring in a few extra dollars." Palos, the town in which the shop was located, had a population of 25,000. However, it, and many of the towns in the area, were growing rapidly. Two larger florists were already operating in Palos when Roseland opened.

At first, Ann had only one employee, Ellen Holland. Ellen was a neighbor and long-time friend of Ann. Ellen was also interested in "occupying her time" while her children were at school. Although business was slow at first, their friends in the community constituted a large enough patronage to allow

the women to maintain an adequate level of business. Soon, Roseland's reputation for quality service and low prices began to expand its list of customers. By the end of the first year of operation, Ann had added a combination secretary-bookkeeper and another part-time floral arranger.

"UP" THE LADDER OF SUCCESS

One day, a close friend of Ann's mentioned that he had just heard about a new hospital which was to be built close to an existing medical center. Ann immediately saw the opportunity for which she had been waiting. That night, she sat down with her husband, Paul, and talked over the potential for opening a new shop closer to the hospital site. "Is this what you want?" asked Paul. Ann thought for a moment and then replied, "I've always wanted to see the shop be successful. And I think that this is the way to do it." The two discussed the matter further, and Ann decided at least to look into the matter.

Ann spent the next week talking with the various merchants and a banker about her plan. She told them that her work force had climbed to as high as fifteen persons on holidays and special occasions and that she needed more room for the people to work. In addition, she explained, "I think this may be the opportunity that every business person wants . . . a chance to grow and be successful. You know, I've never really had an experience in business before, and neither Paul nor I graduated from high school. So you see, we really do need some advice about this move." The advice Ann received was mixed. But when she heard later that week that a shop in the medical center would soon be vacant, she made the decision to move Roseland Florist.

Roseland's success continued for several years. Sales grew and profits became larger, but Roseland was plagued by one continuous problem. The turnover among the shop's employees was high. Three to four months were required to train flower arrangers adequately. And employees often left within five to six months after they were hired. Some took positions in other florist shops while others sought other types of employment. Since Ann had built the reputation of Roseland on the high quality of its work, she was faced with a serious problem. The volume of business was increasing rapidly; however, the lack of trained personnel had caused the quality of work to fall off badly.

NEW PROBLEMS

A climax was reached when Ellen, Ann's first employee, quit her job at Roseland and took employment with a rival florist. Ellen explained her reasons for leaving to a fellow employee.

> This used to be a pleasant atmosphere to work in, but Ann has changed. All she cares about now is money. Roseland is her whole life. She is so involved in making money that she forgets that people have to work with her. It's making me a nervous wreck; I just couldn't take it any

longer. And frankly, Paul is just as bad. We have been friends and neighbors for years. But he hangs around the shop, gets in the way, criticizes your work, and well, just sticks his nose in where it doesn't belong.

The profit margin at Roseland has not been good for the last two years. Ann explains her money problems in the following way:

> Costs have really gone up over the years. It's harder to get certain types of flowers and wholesale prices are much higher. In fact, transportation costs for my shipment of flowers have gone up as much as 600 percent in the last five years. This energy crisis has hurt us too. You know, artificial flowers are made of plastic and they are in short supply. Plus, it costs more to operate by delivery truck. I have tried to raise my prices as little as possible and they are lower than my competitors, so I try to increase my volume. It used to be that I would turn down some funeral pieces and cut off orders early on special occasions because I could not handle them all, but since my profits are lower I take as much as I can get.

Recently, Roseland workers have been complaining about having to remain on the job after regular working hours in order to get all orders out. One employee confided in a friend,

> The thing that bothers me is that either Mr. or Mrs. Conrad always seem to be watching you to be sure you don't waste anything. Even if we drop a small piece of wire that we use to make arrangements, they tell us to pick it up and use it. Mr. Conrad is like a watchdog. One of Mrs. Conrad's favorite practices is, when we do flowers for a wedding, she waits until after the ceremony and tries to get the flowers and candles so that she can use them again.

Before leaving Roseland Florist, Ellen and Ann talked about Ellen's reasons for leaving. After listening to what Ellen had to say, Ann replied, "Hard work is the secret to success, and since I opened this business, I have worked hard seven days a week with only a couple of vacations. That is the only way that I know how to run the business."

CASE 16.2   *Decision at sea*

H. WILLIAM VROMAN
KENT MITCHELL

PART A: THE NEW ASSIGNMENT

A new assignment in any organization generally brings with it pleasures as well as problems. These costs and benefits may be amplified when the organizational members are confined to definite unyielding physical boundaries. Such was the case when a young Navy ensign just out of training school was assigned aboard the USS *Duarte*. His experiences are recorded in this case.

First Impressions

It seemed like only yesterday that I had graduated from college and entered the navy's Officer Candidate School. Upon completing my officers' training, I was sent to Navy Supply Corps School (NSCS) where I was subjected to a six-month barrage of navy business administration indoctrination. The program had been designed to provide future supply officers with the tools necessary to perform a management job afloat. The training itself was excellent. However, once afloat, I realized that I would have to constantly practice what I had learned or be doomed to failure no matter how bright a politician I might be.

I was met at the processing office by LTJG Collins. It was Lieutenant Collins whom I would be replacing aboard the USS *Duarte*. Collins told me that he would take me directly to the ship and let me "look her over." When we arrived at the dock, I was overwhelmed by the *Duarte's* size. Although I had seen a picture of the ship, I had no idea that it was so large (almost the length of two football fields). The USS *Duarte* was a new attack cargo ship with 30 officers, a 320-man crew, and 300 Marine Corps troops. By civilian standards she easily could have provided enough electricity for 2,000 homes, enough food to feed 650 men for 90 days, and enough items in stock (26,000) to fill a large department store. The ship had fully air conditioned living spaces, a recreation room,

library, bakery, soda fountain, laundry, dry cleaning plant, hospital, barber shop, post office, and a ship's store with sales of $40,000 a quarter. In short, the *Duarte* was a floating small town. The supply officer's responsibilities aboard a ship like this would be very time consuming.

Officers aboard the *Duarte* were not rank conscious as a general rule, but, rather, were job conscious. All officers, except the skipper, ate and socialized in the same wardroom and were generally close and open in communications about day-to-day management. On the other hand, the formally structured chain of command was noticeably present when the ship was loading cargo/troops or was at General Quarters (wartime cruising, all battle stations manned).

I learned that the supply department had two officer billets (assignments): the Supply Officer, Lieutenant Roberts, and the Assistant Supply/Disbursing Officer, who would be me. The department consisted of sixty men. As their division officer, I had by far the largest division on the ship, with the average division size being twenty men per officer. This responsibility alone would later command me respect from my peers.

After a cup of coffee and some small talk, LTJG Collins said it was time to go meet the executive officer (XO). We knocked on his cabin and heard the customary reply to come in. The office we entered was impressive. It had two couches, a large executive desk, and dark blue wall-to-wall carpeting. LTJG Collins entered the office first. As he greeted the XO, he suddenly appeared to become very nervous. I then noticed, much to my shock, that as I was being introduced, Collins's hands were shaking like dry leaves in a breeze. I spoke to the XO a few minutes describing my background, the trip over, and so on. He seemed easygoing enough, though he obviously demanded a fair day's work. During the whole conversation, I worried about Collins's "shakes." The same thing happened later in the captain's cabin when we went to meet him, I was worried about Collins, but decided to keep the observation to myself. After all, he was leaving the ship in a few days and surely recognized his own problem.

Lieutenant Roberts, the supply officer, had been off the ship when I arrived. However, he came out of his office just as we were completing our rounds. He seemed to be an easygoing person. I was relieved to see that my immediate superior for the next year would not be too hard-nosed. We talked briefly. However, I again noticed Collins's nervousness, so I suggested I get settled in. Lieutenant Roberts agreed, and Collins and I proceeded to my quarters. I did not see Lieutenant Roberts again until we sailed.

No one ever bothered to tell me exactly what my job would or would not entail. Most NSCS graduates had a pretty good idea of their responsibilities before leaving the school. On the other hand, I did expect Lieutenant Roberts to take the initiative at some time and discuss his procedures, problems, and philosophy with me. I approached him about these matters a number of times while I served under him, but he never did provide me with much information.

My functional replacement of LTJG Collins went about as well as could be expected. I reviewed all of the accounts, took possession of about $200,000, and assumed the title of Disbursing Officer. The records of many of the accounts were in poor condition although no gross negligence could necessarily be proved. The enlisted disbursing clerk who was to work under me was a "short-timer" (would soon be leaving the navy), and I would be without help for about six weeks. All of my training at NSCS was based on the fact that I would have two disbursing clerks maintaining the accounts at all times. However, it appeared that this would not be the case.

The training programs at OCS and NSCS were excellent, but the curricula were basically technical. The managerial training we received was more extensive than that which I had encountered in college, but it still seemed overly cut and dried. I soon learned that management decision making was a completely different game. My most important managerial attributes, it seemed, would be flexibility and common sense.

After I was aboard ship a few days, I was approached by Chief Resor, the senior chief petty officer aboard the ship. Chief Resor quietly asked if we could have a few words alone. We went out on deck and leaned against the starboard rail and began talking. The chief was well-educated and alert. He was small in stature but very impressive in know-how. He had served as an aide to two admirals and was serving out his final cruise before retirement. Chief Resor was thought of highly by enlisted men and officers alike. I listened carefully as the chief spoke:

> I hope that I don't sound out of place, Lieutenant, but I think it would be best for both of us if you understood some of the facts aboard this ship. You probably already found Lieutenant Roberts to be a pleasant person. But a pleasant person isn't necessarily going to do the best job aboard ship. I've served under many supply officers in my day, and he certainly is among the worst. The supply department here on the *Duarte* is inefficient. The men's morale is probably lower than in any other department aboard. Frankly, no one from the CO down to the enlisted men has much respect for Lieutenant Roberts. One of the most serious problems we have is that Roberts doesn't carry his weight well in department head meetings. As a result, Roberts always seems to bend the rules to try to do something just the way another officer wants it done. On more than one occasion, I have had to sit him down and explain why we couldn't do a job the way he had told us to. Then, he spends the better part of the day trying to backtrack to everyone involved and get out of his commitment.

I could hardly believe what the chief had just said. Perhaps I just didn't want to believe it! I told the chief that I appreciated his concern and would do what I could to hold up my end of the department. I did suggest, however, that nothing more be said about Lieutenant Roberts.

It wasn't long before I noticed certain symptoms of what Resor had described to me. It seems that Lieutenant Roberts lack of functional ability often resulted in a power vacuum that was automatically filled by other officers from outside the supply department. Thus, the leadership was there; but decisions were seldom made in the interest of the supply department and its men.

That evening I went to my quarters and sat down to think about the things that the chief had said. I recognized that Roberts was not in good standing with the other officers on the ship. This, together with his failure to take on the responsibilities of his billet, undoubtedly were responsible—at least in part—for LTJG Collins' poor job as disbursing officer. I thought about my own future on the ship as well as what my performance might mean in terms of subsequent assignments. I was troubled by the implications of my thoughts. Having completed the book *Caine Mutiny* only a few months before, my imagination began to run wild. I began to question what actions I might be forced to take in the months ahead.

The next morning, I awoke with a clearer head. I wondered if the chief had exaggerated his story. Had he had a run-in with Lieutenant Roberts? Was he trying to use me to shake up the department or was he seriously concerned about what had been taking place? I decided to keep a cool head about the matter and wait until I saw everyone in action while the USS *Duarte* was at sea.

PART B: A TIME FOR ACTION

The training I received was thorough in most respects although I soon found that there is no substitute for experience. Performing duties aboard ship is different than performing them in a classroom. Even the physical aspects of the job were different. It was easy to become slightly nauseated and get a headache from it. These symptoms were a mild form of sea sickness. Under such conditions, it was hard to sit still at a desk and run a calculator, and the conditions had to be overcome in order to function. Other adversities presented more formidable problems, however.

We arrived in the Philippines, and we bid farewell to LTJG Collins. I admired Collins in that he openly admitted he had not done a good job, and that perhaps it was partially his fault morale was low in the department. As he left the ship, I couldn't help but wonder what was in store for me.

As I learned my billet and observed those around me, I began to see just what could and could not be taught in the navy schools. In particular, I quickly realized that the functions I was called upon to perform were broader in scope than I had been led to believe. More often than not, it seemed that Lieutenant Roberts could not be found when requests for information came down from the executive officer. I attempted to provide the necessary reports but found myself thinking, "This isn't my job." After a while, it seemed to me that neither the XO nor the department heads even sought out Roberts. Instead, they came directly to me. I made it a point to always inform him when a request was made of me, but he didn't show any concern. Usually, he politely thanked me for helping out and nothing else was said.

Lieutenant Roberts's behavior seemed strange to me. He was not at all what I had expected in a superior. If he asked me to do something, he was very polite about it; in fact, he was too polite. He was kind to everybody and anybody. In my opinion, this trait was a fine personal attribute, but his gentleness coupled with his lack of confidence and lack of professional know-how caused many problems. It seemed as though the junior enlisted men, who knew better, would take advantage of him and use him to get around the orders of their chiefs. It was not too long before the chiefs began to look my way for support and policy decisions. The department heads began to look my way also. I wasn't prepared for this kind of attention, and it often made me feel uncomfortable.

Lieutenant Roberts and I received the same training, and I knew that things weren't supposed to work this way. It finally started getting to me, and I decided to ask Lieutenant Roberts what the deal was. After being aboard the ship only a short time, I possessed more power—if that's the term—at least informally, than he did. When we talked about it, he told me that he knew he had "screwed-up" a lot of things. He said that the skipper, XO, and department heads were stacked against him. The supply corps had a great deal of *esprit de corps*, and I didn't want to scuttle my boss. My conscience really bothered me on that subject. I personally hoped that carrying him would keep us both out of hot water. We each knew the situation, and perhaps it would work itself out. Nevertheless, I felt as though I were sitting on a time bomb.

After a while, I started putting together a mental dossier on Lieutenant Roberts. He was held back a month at OCS. He was at the bottom of his class at NSCS. He had completed two back-to-back disbursing officer assignments (both were shore duty) before coming to the *Duarte* as Supply Officer. He had been "passed over" twice for promotion to LCDR. (If passed over a third time, he would be released from the navy.) He constantly said, "The Captain wants us to . . ." He never once audited my work. He constantly referred to the chief for help. He disappeared often. He often did work that should have been performed by his subordinates. He associated too closely with the junior enlisted men. He was not respected by the chiefs aboard ship. As an individual, he was easygoing and hard to dislike.

I felt sorry for him when I realized that Lieutenant Roberts was weak in his billet. He wanted to stay in the navy badly, but he failed to recognize his over-all responsibilities. It was a fact that many chiefs and first class petty officers "carried" their bosses professionally when it came to running the shop. A superior does not have to know all of the intricacies and technical details of jobs performed below him. However, any superior should have a good idea of the functions, relationships, job responsibilities, and the capabilities of his men. Chief Edwards was perfectly willing to go beyond his call to assist Lieutenant Roberts. I was too. Evidently LTJG Collins had not been able to do so. I wondered how long I would be this willing.

After being at sea about six weeks, things began to get on my nerves. Lieutenant Roberts's actions were hurting the men (although he didn't seem to realize it). The supply department was not well represented topside in the skipper's cabin. The skipper was a tough man, and he was under a lot of fire. The *Duarte* was a "deep draft vessel," an assignment that all navy captains had to fill before promotion to "Admiral." Naturally, the name of the game was to make the skipper look good in the eyes of other commands. It was rumored that the navy supply systems command did not think well of USS *Duarte*. Too many mistakes had cost her more than one efficiency rating. Supply decisions simply weren't being made by the supply department. For all practical purposes, the department had become a pawn of other officers on the ship.

Finally, I decided that some action would have to be taken if I were to salvage the department and my own rating. No one made decisions concerning the supply division or disbursing unless I okayed them. I often consulted my senior petty officers on matters which I felt unsure of. My goal was to provide strength at the top where it belonged. Lieutenant Roberts had been harassed by his fellow officers in the past and I had sometimes felt the impact of their criticism. Now, I had decided that much destructive criticism must be stopped. On two occasions I told officers, flatly, that I disagreed with their assessment of our operations or procedures. Where necessary, I pointed out our SOP's and their justifications and respectfully submitted that they should and must be followed. At the same time, I recognized the need for greater cooperation with other departments but on an even basis. Although I, on occasion, was asked for my opinion of Lieutenant Roberts, I declined comment. However, pressure on me to give my observations on the lieutenant increased as I dealt more directly with officers of his rank or higher.

One morning I was called to the XO's office to explain some budgetary calculations. As usual, I was being asked to explain work that was not mine. Normally, I explained what I could and researched the rest—quickly. The XO had never before discussed with me his feelings about Lieutenant Roberts. As a matter of fact, I was being asked to perform so much, and so often, that I actually started wondering whether people realized that the shoes I was having to fill were not my own. When asked one question that I was having difficulty answering, I jokingly remarked, "You do know this isn't my responsibility!?" The XO stood up and walked across the room. Never looking directly at me, he proceeded, "Alas, Mr. Disbursing Officer, the chips are on the table!"

EXERCISE 16.1
BEHAVIOR ACTIVITY PROFILE

Each of us displays certain kinds of behaviors, thought patterns, or personal characteristics. For each of the twenty-one sets of descriptions below, circle the number which you feel best describes where you are between each pair. The best answer for each set of descriptions is the response that most nearly describes the way you feel, behave, or think. Answer these in terms of your regular or typical behavior, thoughts, or characteristics.

1. I'm always on time for appointments.   7 6 5 4 3 2 1   I'm never quite on time.

SOURCE: *Executive Survival Manual*, Dennis P. Slevin, 1985, Innodyne, Inc.

2. When someone is talking to me, chances are I'll anticipate what they are going to say, by nodding, interrupting or finishing sentences for them.   7 6 5 4 3 2 1   listen quietly without showing any impatience.

3. I frequently try to do several things at once.   7 6 5 4 3 2 1   tend to take things one at a time.

4. When it comes to waiting in line (at banks, theaters, etc.) I really get impatient and frustrated.   7 6 5 4 3 2 1   it simply doesn't bother me.

5. I always feel rushed.   7 6 5 4 3 2 1   I never feel rushed.

6. When it comes to my temper I find it hard to control at times.   7 6 5 4 3 2 1   I just don't seem to have one.

7. I tend to do most things like eating, walking, and talking rapidly.   7 6 5 4 3 2 1   slowly.

TOTAL SCORE THIS SECTION _____ = S

8. Quite honestly, the things I enjoy most are job-related activities.   7 6 5 4 3 2 1   leisure-time activities.

9. At the end of a typical work day, I usually feel like I needed to get more done than I did.   7 6 5 4 3 2 1   I accomplished everything I needed to.

10. Someone who knows me very well would say that I would rather work than play.   7 6 5 4 3 2 1   rather play than work.

11. When it comes to getting ahead at work nothing is more important.   7 6 5 4 3 2 1   many things are more important.

12. My primary source of satisfaction comes from my job.   7 6 5 4 3 2 1   I regularly find satisfaction in non-job pursuits, such as hobbies, friends, and family.

13. Most of my friends and social acquaintances are people I know from work.   7 6 5 4 3 2 1   not connected with my work.

14. I'd rather stay at work than take a vacation.   7 6 5 4 3 2 1   Nothing at work is important enough to interfere with my vacation.

TOTAL SCORE THIS SECTION _____ = J

15. People who know me well would describe me as
    hard-driving and competitive.   7 6 5 4 3 2 1   relaxed and easygoing.

16. In general, my behavior is governed by
    a desire for recognition and achievement.   7 6 5 4 3 2 1   what I want to do—not by trying to satisfy others.

17. In trying to complete a project or solve a problem I tend to
    wear myself out before I'll give up on it.   7 6 5 4 3 2 1   take a break or quit if I'm feeling fatigued.

18. When I play a game (tennis, cards, etc.) my enjoyment comes from
    winning.   7 6 5 4 3 2 1   the social interaction.

19. I like to associate with people who are
    dedicated to getting ahead.   7 6 5 4 3 2 1   easygoing and take life as it comes.

20. I'm not happy unless I'm always doing something.   7 6 5 4 3 2 1   Frequently "doing nothing" can be quite enjoyable.

21. What I enjoy doing most are competitive activities.   7 6 5 4 3 2 1   noncompetitive pursuits.

TOTAL SCORE THIS SECTION _____ = H

Impatience (S)	Job Involvement (J)	Hard-Driving and Competitive (H)	Total Score (A) = S + J + H

The Behavior Activity Profile attempts to assess the three Type A coronary-prone behavior patterns, as well as to provide a total score. The three a priori types of Type A coronary-prone behavior patterns are shown below.

Items	Behavior Pattern		Characteristics
1–7	Impatience	(S)	Anxious to interrupt. Fails to listen attentively. Frustrated by waiting (e.g., in line, for others to complete a job).
8–14	Job Involvement	(J)	Focal point of attention is the job. Lives for the job. Relishes being on the job. Immersed by job activities.

15–21	Hard-driving/ Competitive	(H)	Hardworking, highly competitive. Competitive in most aspects of life, sports, work, etc. Racing against the clock.
1–21	Total Score	(A)	Total of S + J + H represents your global Type A behavior.

Score ranges for total score are:

Score	Behavior Type
122 and above	Hard-Core Type A
99–121	Moderate Type A
90–98	Low Type A
80–89	Type X
70–79	Low Type B
50–69	Moderate Type B
49 and below	Hard-Core Type B

Percentile Scores

Now you can compare your score to a sample of over 1,200 respondents.

Percentile Score		
% of Individuals Scoring Lower	Males	Females
99%	140	132
95%	135	126
90%	130	120
85%	124	112
80%	118	106
75%	113	101
70%	108	95
65%	102	90
60%	97	85
55%	92	80
50%	87	74
45%	81	69
40%	75	63
35%	70	58
30%	63	53
25%	58	48
20%	51	42
15%	45	36
10%	38	31
5%	29	26
1%	21	21

EXERCISE 16.2

ARE YOU STRESS-PRONE AT WORK?

Selecting a job as well as a career requires you to look closely at yourself both physically and psychologically. A major concern should be the level of stress at which you can best function. The following questionnaire may be helpful to you in determining how you react to stress on the job.

INSTRUCTIONS

1. Complete the questionnaire.
2. Score the questionnaire using the scale below.
3. In a small group, discuss the significance of your score and the score of others.
4. What do you believe your score means in terms of job selection? Be specific.
5. How can you operationalize your findings?

Rate yourself the way you usually react in each work situation listed below.

5–always   4–frequently   3–sometimes   2–seldom   1–never

Score

1. Do you try to do as much as possible in the least amount of time?   _____

2. Are you impatient with delays, interruptions?   _____

3. Do you have to win at games to enjoy yourself?   _____

4. Are you unlikely to ask for help with a problem?   _____

5. Do you constantly strive to better your position or achievements?   _____

6. Do you constantly seek the respect and admiration of others?   _____

7. Are you overly critical of the way others do their work?   _____

8. Do you have the habit of often looking at your watch?   _____

9. Do you spread yourself too thin in terms of time?   _____

10. Do you have the habit of doing more than one thing at a time?   _____

11. Do you ever get angry and irritable?   _____

12. Do you have a tendency to talk quickly or hasten conversation?   _____

13. Do you consider yourself hard-driving?   _____

14. Do your friends or relatives consider you hard-driving?   _____

15. Do you have a tendency to get involved in multiple projects?   _____

16. Do you have a lot of deadlines in your work?   _____

17. Do you feel vaguely guilty if you relax or go out of the office at
lunchtime?   _____

18. Do you take on too many responsibilities?   _____

TOTAL

If your score is 18–30, you probably work best in nonstressful, noncompetitive situations, like to set your own pace, and like to work at one task at a time. Interruptions drive you crazy. Stress is likely to hinder your performance rather than enhance it. If your score is 31–60, you can handle a bit of stress and probably enjoy it as long as it doesn't occur more than 20 percent of your working time. If your score is 61–90, look out! The people who work with you had better look out, too. You need constant pressure to perform. You probably grind your teeth!

CHAPTER **17**

CAREERS AND CAREER DEVELOPMENT

LEARNING OBJECTIVES

1. To understand the relationship of career planning to life planning.
2. To recognize the special career problems faced by women and dual-career couples.
3. To learn about organizational approaches to career development.
4. To become aware of the manager's role in career planning and development.

CHAPTER OUTLINE

Managing Career Development
   Career as Part of a Life System
   Self-Assessment
   Managing Your Career over Time
   Career Anchors

Special Considerations in Career Development
   Women and Career Development
   Dual-Career Couples
   Specialized Organizational Responses

Organizational Approaches to Career Development
   Which Way to the Top?
   Organizationally Developed Career Paths

Careers and Career Development: Conclusion

Questions for Review and Discussion

References

Cases: 17.1 Latino Glass, S.A. (Latino, South America)
   17.2 Predicting the Future

Exercises: 17.1 Life and Career Planning
   17.2 Your Perception of Career Advancement
   Practices

KEY TERMS

Career	**Disengagement**
Career development	**Career anchor**
Life system	**Dual-career couple**
Career stages	**Specialized career path**
Exploration	**Circular career path**
Trial	**Multiple career ladders**
Establishment	**Career fast track**
Growth	**Mommy track**
Maintenance	**Slow burn plan**
Career plateaus	**Career path clusters**
Stagnation	**Direction counseling**

Patrick Riley had seen these patterns too many times before—men and women showing signs of restlessness and disinterest in their work. He had heard all the jokes about midlife crisis and knew that he, too, had been guilty of blaming the problems of some managers and executives on middle age. Unfortunately, jokes and complaints did little to correct the poor performance evaluations he had before him. As he looked at the reports on Bob Tabor and Sharon Young, he questioned whether the company could do anything to protect itself or these individuals from what seemed to be unnecessary pain and expense.

Bob Tabor had been with the company for eighteen years, joining it shortly after graduating from college and getting married. Now, his children were leaving home and his wife had decided to return to school. Sharon Young, on the other hand, had spent nine years as a design engineer at the firm and had been married for about six years. At thirty-two, she was unsure about her future. Although she and her husband had decided to put off having children, she was beginning to feel increasing pressure to start a family.

Patrick confided to a colleague, "Both Bob and Sharon are going through some difficult times right now, and to tell you the truth, it could cost us over $100,000 if we have to replace the two of them. Surely, we can come up with a program to help people plan their lives and their careers better than this!"

Managers must often deal with situations similar to those Bob and Sharon face. These situations often represent a delicate balance between one's personal development as an adult and personal development along a career path. In this chapter, we will look at what is meant by the term career. We will also look at why career development plays such an important role for each of us individually and for the organizations for which we work.

MANAGING CAREER DEVELOPMENT

Just as organizations develop goals and strategies to meet future demands, so, too, must managers and employees plan their work lives. Such planning contributes to the conscious development of an individual's career path. Your career path reflects your work experience over time and helps you map out your future in the work world.

Career refers to the individually perceived sequence of attitudes and behaviors associated with work-related experiences over the span of a person's life.[1] One's career is not determined by a single job decision about work (e.g., "I'm going to be an accountant."). It is the sum of a series of decisions made throughout a lifetime. A career is typically characterized by a high degree of commitment and tends to have a continuous developmental character.

An individual's career is largely a personal matter concerned with attaining the material, social, and psychological goals the individual believes are important. At the same time, a person's career should be of concern to the organization for which she or he works. Although companies often provide the training and support necessary to accomplish a job, it is equally important to address each individual's career goals and plans. One recent study of 383 Israeli managers indicated that career management was a joint responsibility; the organization's active involvement enhanced career attitudes and identity for individuals and was also beneficial to the organization.[2]

Career development is a conscious effort to contribute to a person's selection of a career area and to enable that person to grow and become more involved in that area. Career development is intended to place the individual in a position to make important career choices rather than allow career movement to drift aimlessly. In addition, career development provides the foundation on which specific training and development decisions can later be made. Ultimately, the goal of career development is to promote a healthy adjustment to career choices, thereby contributing to feelings of self-esteem and competence.

Career as Part of a Life System

Even though job and career decisions are of particular importance to organizations, they are only one part of each individual's overall life system. The **life system** is made up of the important subsystems that constitute a person's personal and social existence (see Exhibit 17.1). As such, it includes the job and career subsystem, family and social subsystem, and self subsystem as well as other aspects of one's lifestyle that the individual believes are important.[3]

Job and career subsystem

The job and career subsystem consists of the organization for which one works, the job and the tasks it entails, the work relationships accompanying the job, and job-related rewards (extrinsic and intrinsic). These, of course, are the central issues in career planning. However, it is important to note that job and career are part of the larger life system. Although they may represent the aspects of career planning that usually receive the most attention, they cannot be addressed adequately without considering the other subsystems and the overriding life system itself.

Self subsystem

The self subsystem refers to the individual's psychological and physiological well-being. In Western society, work is generally viewed as a means to an end. Therefore, career decisions should logically consider the impact of work on all aspects of our lives, including our health. Similarly, our present health can also affect our decision to enter a particular occupation or career path.

In certain Eastern societies, work is viewed as central to a person's existence and an end in itself. In his treatise on "Buddhist economics," E.F. Shumacher concluded:

> If a man has no chance of obtaining work he is in a desperate position,
> not simply because he lacks an income but because he lacks this nour-
> ishing and enlivening factor of . . . work which nothing can replace.[4]

These perspectives on the relationship of work and personal health underwrite the importance of the self subsystem to all of life and to career planning.

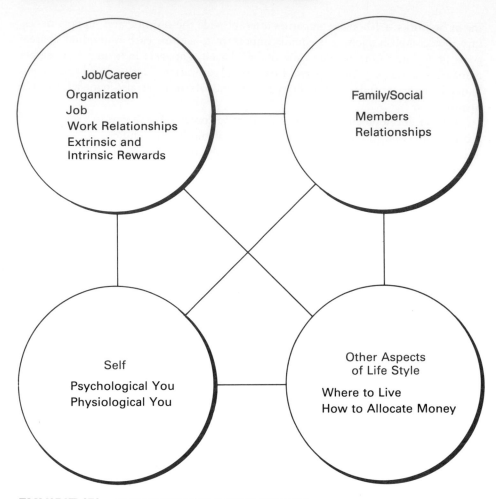

EXHIBIT 17.1   PLANNING FOR A LIFE SYSTEM

Family and social subsystems

Family and friends play major parts in most of our lives. Consequently, many personal decisions are made with these people in mind. Work decisions, for example, affect how, when and where we will spend our time. This work time, of course, is usually traded off against time spent in relationships away from the job. In addition, our job or career may alter where and under what conditions family and other relationships take place. Since most human beings have some need for affiliation and feel strong ties to their families, family and social subsystems are a vital part of the overall life system.

Other aspects of life style

In addition to these subsystems, every individual should consider the life-style he or she desires or is comfortable with. Such considerations no doubt depend on the experiences each of us has had as well as our aspirations for the future. Where we live, our socioeconomic status, and how we wish to allocate our financial resources are examples of life-style considerations that ultimately influence our choice of a career.

Integrating the life system

In Chapter 1, we defined a system as "a group of interrelated and interdependent elements viewed as a single entity." The elements of the life system described here fulfill that definition. Each element is an essential part of every individual's existence and should be considered when planning for the future. Moreover, planning relative to the job and career subsystem is relevant only to the extent that the individual considers the overall (life) system and each of its other parts. In the following section, we briefly look at the role of self-assessment as a first step in the process of career development.

Self-Assessment

Any attempt to develop a career plan should focus on your personal values, interests, and aspirations. A systematic approach to self-assessment and career development should identify the relatively stable themes or characteristics you possess.[5] This can be accomplished using a number of paper-and-pencil tests, including those assessing values, attitudes, and personality characteristics (e.g., Edwards Personal Preference Schedule, Wechsler Adult Intelligence Scale, Harvard Speed Alphas, and Miller Analogies). Other instruments, such as interest and aptitude tests and a daily diary, can provide additional insight into work-related likes and dislikes.

A variety of tools should be used to assess various aspects of your life. For example, the mental and emotional strains of specific work situations are important considerations when you select a job or evaluate a possible career. Your self-assessment tool kit should therefore include tools that assess job-related stress (see Exercise 16.1) and provide an overall stress profile (see Exercise 16.2 for an example of such a tool).

Once sufficient information has been collected, it must be analyzed and interpreted to identify individual themes and career-related implications. Taking a close look at yourself can be intellectually and emotionally demanding, as you may already have discovered in this course. Furthermore, professional assistance may be required to interpret the information you have compiled.

Career-planning materials are available in a variety of forms and many are offered commercially. Some, like *What Color is Your Parachute?* by Richard Bolles (Ten Speed Press), are straightforward and conventional; others, like *The Lotus and the Pool* by Hilda Lee Dail (Shambhala Publications, Inc.), take a unique approach to looking at your future. Other career planning books that can be acquired at most local book stores include

▶ *Go Hire Yourself an Employer* by Richard Irish (Doubleday).
▶ *Where Do I Go from Here with My Life?* by John Crystal and Richard Bolles (Ten Speed Press).
▶ *Career Map* by Neil Yeager (Wiley).
▶ *How to Create a Picture of Your Ideal Job or Next Career* by Richard Bolles (Ten Speed Press).

Two books that may be particularly helpful to business students are

▶ *Choosing a Career in Business* by Stephen A. Stumpf and Celeste K. Rodgers (Simon and Schuster).
▶ *Business Careers* by Robert H. Luke (Houghton Mifflin Co.).

The Educational Testing Service has also developed a "high-tech" approach to career planning known as SIGI. There is a good chance that SIGI, an interactive career-planning computer program, is available on your campus. Exhibit 17.2 explains SIGI more completely.

Managing Your Career Over Time

Career development and planning are ongoing activities. Both self-assessment and analysis of career options should be repeated many times throughout one's life. In a world of rapidly changing job opportunities, an individual cannot afford to become locked into a dead-end career or to ignore new opportunities. Similarly, each of us changes individually and socially over time. As we adopt new values, seek new goals, and form new relationships, our changing interests and aptitudes open career doors not yet explored. In fact, do not be surprised if you change the direction of your career several times in your lifetime.

Relating career changes to life changes

Research on careers indicates that most people pass through distinct **career stages.**[6] These stages (exploration, trial, establishment, growth, maintenance and stagnation, and disengagement) create a frame of reference through which work-related and other organizational events are interpreted.[7] We have seen that adults (beginning at about age seventeen) also pass through certain periods of personal development (see Levinson's adult development model in Chapter 2). An examination of career stages and a review of adult development reveals an important relationship between life and career stages. Exhibit 17.3 shows the relationship of career stages (in blue) to corresponding life stages (in red).

Exploration.   The **exploration** stage of career development roughly parallels the periods of adult development known as Early Adult Transition and Getting Into the Adult World. This stage is characterized by identifying career possibilities through education, part-time work, and, in some cases, early job selection. Exploration usually occurs during the late teens and up through the midtwenties.

Trial.   The **trial** stage results in an initial selection of a career area and closely parallels the Getting Into the Adult World period. Decisions about work tend to be central and usually reflect an individual's first serious encounter with a career-related

EXHIBIT 17.2   "WELCOME TO SIGI"

The computer-based SIGI (System of Interactive Guidance and Information) allows an individual to interface directly with a computer and to participate in a "dialogue" with the programmed career counselor. SIGI permits the user to establish priorities in ten work-related values (high income, prestige, independence, helping others, security, variety, leadership, interest field, leisure time, and career preparation) and compares the information with data gathered on over 220 occupations. Those using SIGI also take a battery of tests, the results of which influence the occupational suggestions that SIGI will ultimately provide.

At the present time, SIGI is available at over 250 college and university campuses at no charge to users. Have you met SIGI yet? Perhaps it would be a good way for you to begin investigating a career that you will one day find rewarding.

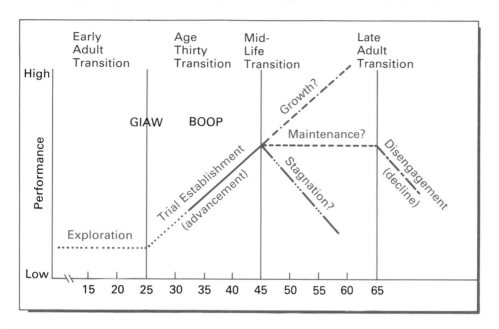

EXHIBIT 17.3   CAREER STAGES AND ADULT DEVELOPMENT

job. Although these decisions are important, young adults do not typically feel pressured by age or by a lack of options, as can occur later in life.

The transition from trial to the next career stage, establishment, is likely to be interrupted by the Age Thirty Transition. This transition revolves around family, social, and career considerations. For many people, it may be the first serious *reexamination* of career decisions made during their early twenties. Since these earlier decisions were made when reliable information and experience were probably negligible, the transition is likely to produce new insights about occupational and personal preferences.

Career women are likely to experience many of the same frustrations as their male counterparts during this transition, although their decisions may be further complicated by anxieties about marriage and childbearing. Women who have not yet entered the job market are inclined to become more active and independent, evaluating (or reevaluating) career opportunities as they seek to establish their own identities. Factors such as the feeling of being overshadowed by a husband or his career and concerns about traditional role expectations can also produce anxiety. The pattern of career-related decisions for women who establish a career during their late twenties or early thirties may be similar to those of younger men during the Getting Into the Adult World Period.

MARIA MONET, OGDEN CORPORATION

Some individuals go through more than one trial stage and choose to alter their career course for more than one reason. Such is the case of Maria Monet, currently president and chief operating officer of financial services for Ogden Corporation in New York City. Monet graduated with a degree in law from Boston University and spent seven years with the New York firm of Shearman & Sterling. Deciding that it would be difficult to penetrate the "boys' club" in any law firm, she left and entered the field of corporate finance. This second career led Monet to become an investment banker with Wall Street-based Lehman Brothers. Once again, it appeared to Monet that advancing to the level of managing director might not be worth the time and energy it required. After only a year and a half with Lehman Brothers, therefore, Monet accepted an offer to work as a financial manager with Ogden Corporation. Monet found that Ogden was a company in which hard work and long hours would give her the opportunity to do more than simply make a six-figure salary. Today, she is a high-ranking corporate executive responsible for building and managing sports and entertainment facilities throughout the United States. This is precisely the kind of opportunity and responsibility that Maria Monet sought as she explored various careers.[8]

Establishment.   A significant investment in the job takes place during the **establishment** (or advancement) period. Considerable time is spent developing a level of competence that will lead to personal satisfaction with a chosen line of work. Establishment occurs at about the same time as the development period known as Becoming One's Own Person. An individual may spend long hours on the job and make major personal commitments to work, such as accomplishing certain goals or significantly improving job performance. He or she may also feel constrained by people in authority or others who have considerable influence. Feelings that superiors control too much and delegate too little are common.

The coaching and modeling of mentors (see "Development Through Mentoring," page 598 may be acknowledged. However, establishment is usually characterized by the feeling that, "I need to make it on my own." Thus, as the desire to become one's own person increases, the reliance on mentors and others decreases.[9]

Growth, Maintenance, and Stagnation.   The Midlife Transition can have a major impact on a person's life and career. Individuals ask important questions about personal as well as career choices. They often want more out of their work and personal lives but question their ability to obtain it in their present situation. This inner conflict may be further aggravated by the perception that competition from younger, better-educated employees has made personal recognition and reward more difficult to achieve. Decisions made at this time can either reinforce or significantly alter earlier career decisions and will lead to career growth, maintenance, or stagnation.

Growth typically reflects a decision to reinvest in previous choices, thereby improving performance in one's present job or a decision to move forward along a known career path. Individual reassessment and the need for personal development are particularly important during a growth stage.

Maintenance reflects a leveling off in career development. It may accompany an individual's acceptance of an earlier career choice or satisfaction with his or her present position or level of performance. Some individuals who reach such **career plateaus** may simply no longer be interested in career growth, and therefore do not experience severe dissatisfaction with their situation.

On the other hand, career plateaus may be the result of organizational, rather than individual, choices.[10] Focusing on high-potential employees while neglecting others or allowing an employee's age to influence promotion decisions, for example, may lead to negative consequences for individuals and organizations alike. Studies indicate that plateaued managers, for example, are more often absent from work, suffer more health problems, and have lower confidence in their marketability.[11]

Stagnation is best characterized as a begrudging acceptance of one's lot in life and a lack of desire to do more than ride it out. People who stagnate in their careers may feel a sense of frustration or despair about their work. They have reached a point in their jobs at which they feel they have no future, but there seems to be nothing they can do about it. Individuals who experience stagnation during this period are likely to be dissatisfied with their work and with their organization.

Disengagement.   The final career stage, **disengagement,** is sometimes referred to as withdrawal or decline. Disengagement involves a period of anticipating (or planning for) retirement. In some cases, the older worker may become apprehensive about the future. He or she may be concerned about physical limitations relative to job performance, status in the organization, and future financial security. Disengagement can thus be a particularly stressful time in a person's life.

Of course, some individuals welcome retirement. While still on the job, they may offer assistance to others by passing on what they have learned through the years, or they may simply attempt to reorient themselves to a life-style not related to the job. To them, disengagement is an opportunity to leave behind work-related frustrations and devote time to travel, hobbies, or other leisure activities. Other people retire from one career only to begin another career in a new or related field or to become involved in volunteer work. One group, the Association of Retired Executives (ARE) recruits retired managers and executives to assist small private businesses, minority enterprises, and government organizations in need of special managerial assistance.

Disengagement can be either a positive or a negative experience. Both task-related and socio-emotional needs can be affected by gradual withdrawal from the work organization, and a successful transition requires individuals to readjust their understanding of themselves and their new environments.

Summary.   Effectively managing your career over time requires that you understand the normal stages of both career and adult development. These theories continue to be studied and refined by researchers. In addition, their relevance to organizational behavior has become increasingly clear. In a study of 675 salespersons, for example, researchers found that career issues, work-related attitudes, and career-related behaviors were significantly related to an individual's career stage. Moreover, different attitudes and behaviors predicted sales performance within each stage.[12] Understanding such patterns will permit you to anticipate career-related attitudes and behaviors and take the appropriate managerial actions.

Managing life transitions

Career development is an ongoing process for individuals and organizations alike. Of particular significance, however, are the times in a person's life or career at which transitions are made from one stage to another. As we have seen, such transitions are more likely to occur at certain times. For example, transitions during the late twenties and early thirties, the early forties, and the early to midsixties can place considerable strain on individuals. Personal problems that result can in turn impact directly on organizational productivity.

Organizations can respond to these strains by helping employees understand career transitions and providing the technical and psychological support necessary to make them successfully. Although organizations cannot exercise complete control over personal or career development, it is logical that easing career-related traumas during transitions will contribute to employees' mental health and the organization's fiscal soundness. This, in fact, is already the case at Lockheed Aircraft, where such efforts have contributed to the successful retirement transition of many company employees.[13] Other programs designed to improve managers' sensitivity to their employees or intended to provide direct assistance through counseling can also benefit selected individuals.

Career Anchors

Passing through distinct stages of adult development may result in significant changes in patterns, including disruptions in our jobs and careers. But do the fundamental underpinnings of our careers change, or, for that matter, do such underpinnings even exist?

Researchers at the Massachusetts Institute of Technology Sloan School of Management addressed these questions by studying the career patterns of a select number of university graduates.[14] Their findings suggested that each individual's career appeared to be characterized by a central theme, known as a **career anchor.** Career anchors give continuity to a career and have three components:

1. Self-perceived talents and abilities (derived from successful experiences in a variety of work settings).
2. Self-perceived motives and needs (recognized through self-diagnosis in job situations and feedback from others).
3. Self-perceived attitudes and values (based on the individual's active interface with norms and values in numerous work settings).[15]

Over time, these self-perceptions stabilize and come together to form the career anchor. Career anchors guide, constrain, stabilize, and integrate each individual's career. In addition, they help a person organize experience, identify an area in which a long-run contribution is apt to be made, define the nature of the work setting in which one wishes to function, and establish or influence the criteria by which the success of one's career can be evaluated.

Five career anchors

Early studies identified five distinct career anchors. They included technical/functional competence, managerial competence, security, autonomy, and creativity (see Exhibit 17.4). The first two anchors, technical/functional competence and managerial competence, were most common among those studied. The other three anchors, however, also were found to exist for a significant number of individuals. These five career anchors have continued to emerge in subsequent studies, although there is evidence that other anchors, such as basic identity (title, uniform, trappings of office, etc.), service to others (the desire to help others), power, influence, control, and variety, may also exist.[16]

Significance of the career anchor concept

The existence of career anchors is significant in that individuals may actually gravitate to certain types of careers or careers with certain dimensions. Thus, experimenting by changing your career dramatically might lead to confusion or dissatisfaction. Whether anchors are related to the stability of certain personality characteristics (as might be suggested by our knowledge of personality) or are the function of learned behaviors and comfort zones (see Chapter 4), individuals and organizations alike should examine career anchors when career plans are developed.

Your career anchor may not be clear until you have had adequate work experience and have faced a number of career choices. On the other hand, examining one's own likes and dislikes in light of the work experiences of others may provide special insights into career choices. Speaking with and carefully observing mentors or others whose own careers are of interest to you, relating your personal interests to career opportunities, or even reading about the lives of individuals who have chosen different careers may help you learn more about your own "emerging" career anchors.

EXHIBIT 17.4   FIVE CAREER ANCHORS

Technical/Functional Competence	Career organized around area or type of work (selling, accounting, engineering, etc.). Status measured according to the achieving of an expert status.
Managerial Competence	Career organized around a combination of factors including: 1. Ability to identify, analyze, and solve problems under conditions of uncertainty. 2. Ability to influence, lead, or manipulate people toward achieving organizational goals. 3. Capacity to act decisively in crises, bear responsibility, and exercise authority.
Security	Career organized around doing what is required to maintain job security, reasonable income, and a stable future.
Creativity	Career organized around the need to build or create something entirely on one's own.
Autonomy	Career organized around the desire to be free of organizational constraints to pursue personal interests, aspirations, and goals.

(Biographies of business and nonbusiness leaders are often featured in *Business Week, Careers, Inc., Forbes, Fortune,* and *The Wall Street Journal.*)

For example, you may have an interest in music, electronics, or some specific athletic activity. You can investigate career-related opportunities in such areas by learning from those who are directly involved (e.g., musicians, engineers, or athletes) or those who have focused on specific business activities such as arts management, the production or sale of electronic equipment, or the running of a sporting goods store. Finding out more about the actual experiences of others in their work and what needs and values particular careers seem to satisfy may help you identify and better understand your own career anchors.

Your knowledge of career anchors should help you make more informed career choices whether you are making decisions about your own career or decisions that will influence the career development of others.

SPECIAL CONSIDERATIONS IN CAREER DEVELOPMENT

Throughout this chapter, we have examined career development issues as they affect both men and women. However, special consideration should be given to the problems faced by women and to those encountered by dual-career couples.

Women and Career Development

Life stages and career stages have been largely established using data from male experiences and thus tend to be biased. Today, however, an increasing number of women are pursuing careers and competing on an equal basis with men. Many of these women follow career stages similar to those outlined in Exhibit 17.3, but some do not. The pattern women follow is often related to childbearing decisions.[17] A decision to have a child in her early twenties may result in a woman's starting her career later in life, obtaining her work experience at a later age, and consequently not receiving the same consideration for promotion as similar-aged males. The decision is complicated by traditional cultural expectations concerning women and childbearing and the changing role of women in the work world over the past two decades.

A second major childbearing decision occurs during the early to midthirties. Pressures at this point are related to a "last chance" syndrome and the belief that the probability of having healthy children decreases after age thirty. Although medical evidence substantiates that greater risks do exist, recent studies report that four times more women in the thirty to thirty-nine age group had first babies in 1986 than in 1970 and that they had fewer underweight babies than women in other categories. Researchers attributed the births of these generally healthier babies to the fact that women in this age group obtain earlier prenatal care than mothers in younger age groups.[18] Although few women may go as far as the career woman in Exhibit 17.5, women must often go to considerable lengths to juggle childraising and jobs.

Early childbearing gives some women a "late start" along a career path. Traditionally held views of women as secondary rather than primary breadwinners may also delay their acquisition of necessary education or location in areas where certain types of job opportunities exist.

Today, more women are embarking on career paths during their early twenties and are therefore making career decisions at a younger age. The trend is altering the timing and evolution of career-development stages for women and has not been without trauma. Recent studies indicate that an increasing number of women who initially opted for career rather than a family have either "dropped out" of corporate life to start families or have found new careers in which they can devote time more flexibly to their work and families.[19]

Women have made significant strides in many sectors of the work force. Today, there are twenty-four times more women attorneys and judges and twenty-three times more engineers than in 1960. Nevertheless, the price of a career for many women is high. Only 35 percent of women executives over forty are mothers, while 90 percent

EXHIBIT 17.5

SOURCE: *The New Yorker*, May 22, 1989, p. 89. Drawing by Rini; © 1989 The New Yorker Magazine, Inc.

of their male counterparts are fathers.[20] Elizabeth Mehren, a feature writer for the *Los Angeles Times,* expressed the frustration that many women have experienced: "We believed the rhetoric. We could control our biological destiny. For a lot of us the clock ran out, and we discovered we couldn't control infertility."[21] This problem is complex and continues to plague women and young married couples who struggle with career-family issues.

Other pressures felt by many career women must also be addressed. Carolyn Lo Galbo Goodfriend is a thirty-nine-year-old mother of five who manages over $300 million worth of accounts for Kraft General Foods. Goodfriend observed, "We were promised that we could do it all and we would be as successful as men. But the trade-offs and sacrifices a woman has to make are far greater than a man's." Goodfriend represents a growing number of *second shift* women who have attempted to meet the income-producing demands of a working wife and/or mother as well as the expectations that families and society have placed on them in the home (the "second shift").[22] Although such problems are of growing concern to women and the organizations for which they work, answers may be found by addressing a broader question concerning the roles of both *men and women* in work and at home. This will be addressed in the following section on dual-career couples.

Another dilemma faced by women is the "glass ceiling" that seems to exist between them and top-level positions in their organizations.[23] Although more women are finding themselves in management positions, the executive office still remains an elusive goal. Women managers report that they are told to be patient, but breaking through the barrier can be difficult. Only two of *Forbes's* 800 most powerful executives in corporate America were women, and only one, Katherine Graham, chairman of the Washington Post Co., was listed among the top twenty-five executives. (The other woman in the top 800 was Elizabeth C. Ortenberg of Liz Claiborne.)[24]

According to one recent study, a "narrow band" of acceptable behavior often frustrates women managers on their road to the top. Researchers found that it may not be enough for women executives to be successful; they may have to be successful in the "right" way! Some of the contradictory expectations women executives face include:

▶ Take risks, but be consistently outstanding.
▶ Be tough, but don't be macho.
▶ Be ambitious, but don't expect equal treatment.
▶ Take responsibility, but follow the advice of others.[25]

CAROLE ST. MARK, PITNEY BOWES, INC., AND MARGE SCHOTT, CINCINNATI REDS BASEBALL TEAM

Carole St. Mark, president of the business supplies and services group at Pitney Bowes, Inc., of Stamford, Connecticut, has discovered the value of being a competent woman executive. Though only forty-eight, St. Mark has held positions at General Foods, St. Regis Paper Company, and General Electric, as well as at Pitney Bowes. Today, her four divisions (each headed by a male president) contribute approximately 20 percent of Pitney's $2.9 billion income. Pitney Bowes appears to be a good company when it comes to giving women opportunities in the executive suite. There are three women on the board of directors and three of eleven officers are either women or members of minority groups. St. Mark acknowledges that it is difficult for women to reach the top in organizational life: "We won't see women running many large publicly held companies for a while. We don't have the breadth of experience in operations." Still, St. Mark believes that "a woman in a position of power . . . can still generate enough shock value to catch a friendly opponent off guard."[26]

One woman who has made it to the top on her own terms is Marge Schott, owner of the Cincinnati Reds baseball team. Schott has been successful at a variety of business ventures including manufacturing, automobile sales, and baseball. She has used her straightforward, no-nonsense style to win the respect of both her employees and her competitors. In a sport dominated by a "good old boys" network, she has won more baseball games than most other major league owners and has done so with a flair that is all her own. According to Schott, "I definitely think that women can do anything if they put their mind down to it."[27]

For nearly two decades, employers in Canada, the United States, and Europe have enacted laws, adjusted work rules, and struggled with deeply held attitudes about the role of women in society in order to ease women's way into the work force. Even so, as the number of females in management and professional positions has increased, social transitions have often been difficult. A similar but even more difficult struggle is being waged by women in Asia, where societal norms and cultural expectations have severely restricted the role of women. The International Dimension on page 585 addresses the challenges faced by both women and employing organizations in Japan as women attempt to secure more meaningful positions in the workforce.

Finally, it is possible that the recent opening of Eastern Europe and the Soviet Union, where women have been integrated into professional jobs in engineering, medicine, and other fields, may provide additional insights into factors affecting both the success and failure of support systems for working women.

Dual-Career Couples

Traditionally, the model family has consisted of husband as breadwinner and wife as homemaker. Dual-career couples are becoming increasingly common, however. In some cases, husbands and wives both work out of economic necessity. In others, women desire to join the work world to fulfill important psychological needs for opportunities to achieve growth and other forms of personal satisfaction. (Both reasons can simultaneously influence the decision.) Despite the potential benefits of both individuals enjoying careers, the problems of managing dual-career relationships can be a serious source of stress.

The term **dual-career couple** implies that both husband and wife have separate careers and therefore separate and distinct work roles. A two-person career, on the other hand, refers to an arrangement in which both persons share the same career. People involved in two-person careers are likely to have similar goals and work with one another directly to achieve them. Our focus here is on the dual-career couple, some of the problems such couples face, and how they can manage those problems successfully.

Types of two-career families

Not all couples approach managing two careers in the same way. Five general types of dual-career couples have been identified. Each has different degrees of commitment to career and home life and is likely to experience different types of conflict. The

INTERNATIONAL DIMENSION
Japan Discovers Woman Power

It's not hard to find women working in Japan, but don't expect to see them in the professional or management ranks. Japanese women have traditionally taken jobs as clerks, secretaries, or factory workers; but economic necessity and changing aspirations among young Japanese females have begun to change the face of Japan's work force.

The number of women in Japanese management positions alone grew 50 percent between 1982 and 1987, and companies such as Fujitsu, Nissan, NEC, and IBM Japan have had particular success placing young women in professional and management jobs. Still, there are many obstacles that must be overcome. Some companies do not feel that women are a "good investment" for positions that have traditionally been filled by men who made lifetime commitments. Women must also overcome strong male prejudices as well as their own long-held views of their role in Japanese society.

Inroads have been made, and a number of success stories can be cited in everything from investments to automotive design and politics, but for some women, the journey may still be difficult. Noriko Nakamura, president of the Japan Association for Female Executives, gives this advice to young women; "First, stick it out for ten years, no matter how routine your work is, because women must prove their loyalty. Second, when asked to serve tea, do it brilliantly, to show you can do anything."

Questions

A non-Japanese may have trouble accepting Nakamura's advice. What is your reaction? How do you think young Japanese women may react?

What factors do you believe will accelerate Japanese women into the work force?

What do you believe the opportunities are for American women to play an important role in or with Japanese firms?

SOURCE: S. Solo, "Japan Discovers Woman Power," *Fortune*, 19 June 1989, 153–158; E. Shinotsuka, "Japanese Women's Limited Job Choices," *Economic Eye*, Spring 1989, 27–30.

---

five types include accommodators, adversaries, allies, acrobats, and transition couples.

Accommodators.   Accommodators are couples with differing levels of commitment to career and home. One partner usually has a high level of career involvement and a low level of involvement in the home; the other partner has a low level of career involvement and a high level of involvement in the home. Each person thus accommodates the other. Although this type of dual-career couple is most like the traditional husband and wife, it is possible that traditional roles can be switched, with the female devoting most of her time to her career and the male being concerned with home and family matters. The level of stress accommodators experience is relatively low as long as the division of labor between career and family commitments is clearly understood and fulfilled by one spouse or the other.

Adversaries.   In some cases, both husband and wife are highly committed to their careers and have little involvement in the home or family. These adversaries think their careers come first and are thus likely to dispute who is responsible for home and family activities. The basic support systems, such as cooking, housekeeping, and childraising, must still be provided. Unfortunately, however, both persons expect such support from their spouse, while neither wants the responsibility.

Allies.   Allies, the third type of dual-career couples, perceive career and family considerations in the same manner. Both may place considerable emphasis on either their career or their home or family life. Unlike adversaries, neither party expects the other to cover the area of lesser importance. The husband and wife may jointly share such responsibilities as maintaining the home or may minimize the importance of those roles in their relationship. Conflict over secondary roles usually does not arise for allies since neither party places much importance on their accomplishment. For example, both parties may agree to eat out rather than requiring one or the other to prepare meals regularly. Stress, when it does occur in the relationship, may be tied to an overinvolvement in their respective careers, with not enough time spent in the husband-wife role.

Acrobats.   In some cases, two high-energy partners may be fully involved in both career and domestic roles. These acrobats are gratified through their career as well as their home lives. Conflict between the two parties is minimized since both actively engage in both roles. On the other hand, stress can occur as each partner tries to find the necessary time and maintain the necessary energy to continue the juggling act. Each party tries to perform all roles effectively, but one or both may find the demands of such a life to be too great.

Couples in transition

Dual-career couples may experience transitions from one type of dual-career relationship to another. Acrobats may become adversaries; accommodators may become allies. As these transitions take place, the stresses of career and home roles are likely to change, resulting in new or different demands on the relationship. The patterns described here suggest the variety of problems that two-career couples can face. Although no formula exists for effectively managing two careers, researchers have found that certain ingredients can increase the likelihood of dual-career effectiveness and lessen the possibilities of stress.

Researchers have drawn the following conclusions about two-career families:

1. Two careers are likely to be more compatible if one partner ranks career first and the other ranks family first (accommodators) or if both rank family first (allies) than if both partners give their respective careers top priority.
2. Two careers are more likely to be more compatible if both partners are in similar fields.
3. Two careers are more likely to be more compatible if there are no children.
4. Two careers are more likely to be compatible if they are in different stages. (Being in the same career stage may lead to competition between marriage partners especially during exploration and establishment. Similarly, if both parties are heavily committed to "advancement" or "becoming one's own person," concentration on one's self may be compounded if both parties neglect their mates.)
5. The more freedom and flexibility partners have, the better able they are to adjust career demands with family needs and the less likely they will be to experience conflict.
6. Two careers are more likely to be compatible if the partners are mutually supportive, skilled in problem solving, and committed to each other's career.[28]

Managing dual-career relationships

A study of British couples found four important factors in successful dual-career relationships: mutual commitment, flexibility, coping mechanisms, and energy and time management.[29]

Mutual Commitment.   Mutual commitment to both careers was seen as an important contributor to effective dual-career couples. Mutual commitment results in both parties' identifying with both careers. Although neither party necessarily desires to pursue the other's career, both individuals actively support one another's work-related efforts and show pride in the other's accomplishments.

Flexibility.   Flexibility includes personal as well as job flexibility. A personally flexible individual adapts his or her plans and activities to the spouse's needs. For example, a husband might be willing to join his wife at an important business-related social event or stay at home with the children while she attends such a meeting, even though he would prefer to stay late at the office.

Job flexibility can be equally important. Careers that structure the use of time or dictate that a job holder locate in a particular geographic area can severely constrain a person's ability to be flexible where the other party is concerned. A spouse who spends considerable time in business travel, for example, may not be available to lend support or to accommodate the partner in other ways. The greater each partner's personal and job flexibility, the less the likelihood that conflicts will arise about independent or shared time.

Coping Mechanisms.   A third factor important to successful career couples is the development of coping mechanisms. Coping mechanisms are means of minimizing or compensating for the stresses placed on dual-career couples. Such coping mechanisms include role redefinition (restructuring roles), personal reorientation (changing attitudes about various roles), and reactive role behavior (accepting role demands and finding ways to meet rather than question or challenge them).[30]

A couple can choose to minimize the stress of their dual-career relationship in a number of ways. The husband can offer to share such duties as cooking or child-raising that women in traditional households usually perform. Similarly, both partners must be flexible and willing to consider the specific career needs of one another, including such important issues as geographic location, work schedules, and travel. In all cases, both husband and wife must directly address the problems they are likely to encounter and approach decisions with an open mind and positive attitude.

Energy and Time Management.   A final factor influencing successful management of dual careers is energy and time management. Simply stated, dual-career couples must commit energy and time to help make their potentially conflicting relationship work. This requires them to insure that adequate quantity and quality of each (time and energy) exist to insure a successful dual-career relationship.

Planning and talking about effectively managing dual careers is one thing; doing something about it is another. Dual-career couples must approach their relationships with open eyes and open minds. A high degree of social and psychological maturity is required to meet the special demands dual-career couples face. Gaining such maturity is especially vital for men who continue to view working wives as individuals who hold "second" jobs.

Traditionally, women have followed their husbands when career moves required them to do so. Today, however, dual-career couples are carefully reevaluating "who will follow whom." Russ Rinol, for example, gave up his position as vice-president of human resources for Playboy in Chicago to move to Los Angeles where his wife, Karen, became vice-president for nursing services at a large hospital. Another pattern that has emerged is that of commuter marriages, in which husbands and wives live in separate locations. About 700,000 couples in the United States now maintain commuter marriages.[31]

In some cases, husbands and wives find that working together in a business venture at home allows them to avoid some of the hassles associated with conventional jobs. Peter and Suzann Matthews, for example, no longer commute long distances to work. Today, the couple operates a commodity investment service out of their home. Although such a venture would have seemed unlikely only a few years ago, computers, telephone modems, and fax machines now enable Peter and Suzann to keep in touch with clients and information sources around the world without having to conduct business from a crowded, high-rent office.

Home work can be particularly beneficial to those starting their own businesses. In a recent survey, 37 percent of female entrepreneurs and 33 percent of male entrepreneurs found working at home to be better than opening a business in another location. The average home worker is thirty-nine years old and part of a dual-career couple. Just over half of all home-based workers are women and most have a number of years of job experience before they set out on their own. Practical solutions to both business and domestic problems are often given for working out of the home. Ann Ensley runs her business out of her home because, "I like the low overhead, the convenience, and the ease of child rearing."[33] Peter Matthews has his own reasons: "I can get work done much faster at home . . . I have all the advantages of being an executive without having to dress up for it."

Perhaps most basic to the dual-career relationship is a mutually agreeable definition of what constitutes success or effectiveness. No single criterion of career-related growth or personal happiness exists for all individuals, all couples, or all careers. Still, each couple should agree on such personal measures before embarking on a dual-career path.

Specialized Organizational Responses

Addressing the special problems women and dual-career couples encounter can increase organizational flexibility and lead to a more efficient use of human resources. Accommodating the needs of individuals with these special career and family considerations can open the door to a personnel source most organizations do not yet effectively tap.

The following are suggestions for developing company strategies to meet the challenges of managing dual-career couples:

1. Conduct audits of company hiring and other personnel policies to recognize (and ultimately eliminate) obstacles to dual-career couples.
2. Adopt special recruiting techniques such as seeking husband/wife teams.
3. Provide specialized counseling and orientation for dual-career couple recruits.
4. Examine and revise (where necessary) career development and transfer policies.
5. Provide special assistance for couples to help them manage two careers.[34]

ORGANIZATIONAL APPROACHES TO CAREER DEVELOPMENT

In this chapter, we have emphasized the importance of career development to the individual. All of us should look carefully at who we are, where we are, and what we would like to achieve in our lifetimes. This process can be significantly enhanced by using the techniques and perspectives discussed.

As a manager, you also should be concerned with the careers of other organizational members. Creating programs or other activities that focus on career development can contribute to job satisfaction and improved attitudes. People who feel good about their chosen career path are apt to be more satisfied with work and develop more positive attitudes toward co-workers and the organization itself. In addition, career development activities initiated by an organization can influence individual and organizational performance by providing the employee with increased job-related knowledge and skill. Thus, organizations such as AT&T, Exxon, McCormack and Dodge, and BDM that invest heavily in career development activities facilitate the career progression of individual employees while helping insure that their own future personnel needs are met.[35]

The importance of the organization's role in career planning was underscored by a recent study of 266 working adults.[36] Effective matching of individual and organizational career plans was found to be the primary determinant of employee satisfaction and of decisions to remain with the present employer. The researchers concluded that such organizational efforts, rather than individual involvement in a career management program, were the critical element in effectively matching career plans. Finally, a successful match was more likely to occur if both the organization and its employees were able to develop flexible career plans and if steps were taken to avoid mismatches rather than to react to them after they occurred.

Which Way to the Top?

Not every employee desires to move to the top. As many companies have discovered, career aspirations differ depending on each individual's needs, values, goals, and experiences. On the other hand, vertical mobility in an organization is usually encouraged and is sought by most employees. Thus, an important question to many individuals and organizations concerns the route an employee should take as he or she progresses vertically in the organizational hierarchy.

Specialized paths

In the United States and other Western societies, individual managers have traditionally trained for and ultimately moved to the job immediately above them in the chain of command. Such highly **specialized career paths** provide in-depth training and experience in a single functional area and contribute to the level of functional expertise an employee brings to the job. Vertical growth is sometimes slow since the number of positions available at higher levels in most organizations (which are bureaucratic pyramids) are fewer than those at lower levels in the hierarchy.

The specialization gained through a direct route to the top can be viewed as an asset in some organizations. However, some people perceive such paths as too narrow and as leading to a form of departmental tunnel vision. In other words, managers who are developed along vertical lines may see the organization and its problems only from the perspective of that department or division. For example, no matter how far up the line someone in the marketing area progresses, he or she is likely to see the firm's problems as marketing problems. In the same way, an employee who has moved through various levels in the controller's office may be unable to see managers' problems in other divisions as anything other than financial control in nature. Vertical career paths are illustrated in Exhibit 17.6.

Circular paths

United States firms have sometimes used a form of job rotation (moving an employee horizontally from one job to another) to broaden the perspectives of their managers. Such job rotation gives managers an opportunity to see the organization from different departmental points of view. Unfortunately, job rotation is often confined to the first few months of a management training program. Furthermore, the short time spent in each area, together with the relatively low-level perspective gained, rarely provides sufficient insight into the true nature of all units' problems.

Japanese organizations have for many years approached career development through circular rather than vertical career paths. Vertical movement in Japanese firms is often slow, with promotion from one level to another taking anywhere from three to seven years. During this period, managers are exposed to the organization's operations in various functional areas throughout the firm. Progress along a career path is nonspecialized, resulting in each manager's gaining a broader, more systemic perspective on the company's operation. This circular movement continues throughout various levels of the promotion process in an upwardly spiraling fashion (see Exhibit 17.7).

Nonspecialized or **circular career paths** increase work-force flexibility, promote interpersonal and interdepartmental cooperation, nurture the goals of the total firm rather than those of individual subunits, and produce high-quality general managers.[37] Circular career paths in Japanese companies discourage mobility between competing firms. It is not clear, however, that this would be the case in United States

EXHIBIT 17.6   SPECIALIZED VERTICAL CAREER PATHS

Promotions within specialized career paths are to the next highest position in the chain of command (e.g., 1 to 2 to 3).

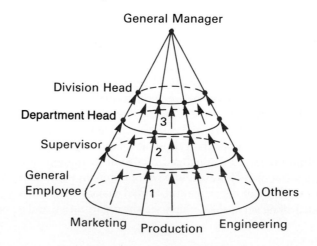

Promotions within nonspecialized career paths may be lateral (1,2,4,5), diagonal (3,6), or vertical (7), and probably will be mixed.

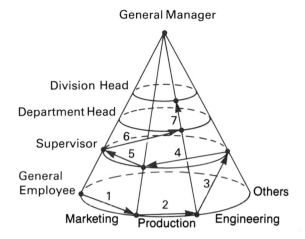

EXHIBIT 17.7   NONSPECIALIZED CAREER PATHS

or other Western companies where interorganization mobility has traditionally been greater than in Japan.

An increasing number of firms in the United States and Canada have experimented with nonspecialized career paths. According to one authority, managers whose career development involves a circular path "retain their enthusiasm, their effectiveness, and their satisfaction" even before they begin to move vertically in the hierarchy.[38]

It is not easy for people or organizations to break with established patterns. Convincing an upper-level manager who has risen on a specialized path that subordinates may require greater breadth may be difficult. Similarly, an accountant or computer specialist may not immediately see the value or wisdom of leaving an area of expertise to develop skills in an area that is foreign to his or her technical training or personal interests. Yet, experiences of Japanese and some United States firms suggest that circular career paths can benefit both employees and organizations.

External moves: an individual alternative

Not all career progression necessarily takes place within a single organization. Some individuals believe that growth along a career path may best be achieved if they leave a present employer and find opportunities with another organization.

MARIA MONET: REVISITED

Earlier, we looked at the case of Maria Monet, president and chief operating officer of financial services for the New York City-based Ogden Corporation. Monet chose external moves as the path to her own career advancement. She sought to find an organization that would allow her to rise into top management and a position that would permit her to exercise authority and judgment. Her external moves included moving from the practice of law with a prestigious New

York firm to becoming an investment banker on Wall Street and finally to her present position as a corporate executive with Ogden. Needless to say, both talent and opportunity must converge if external moves are to be successful.[39]

External moves may increase personal risks (loss of seniority and other accumulated benefits, separation from an existing support group, etc.). Such moves, however, may accelerate career advancement, provide opportunities not made available by the previous employer, and expose an individual to new work-related philosophies and methods. Furthermore, leaving an organization does not preclude a later return and may even make a job candidate more attractive to his or her former employer. The Scrambler-Stabilizer Scale in Exhibit 17.8 may help you evaluate the possible value of external moves to your own career.

Organizationally Developed Career Paths

Some organizations have concentrated on formalizing career paths and career preparation. In some cases, one or more career ladders chart the path along which an employee may progress. Each step on the ladder represents a different position in a sequence of career moves. Although such moves are usually thought of as vertical, as we have seen they can also entail horizontal or diagonal shifts in the organization.

EXHIBIT 17.8   SCRAMBLER-STABILIZER SCALE

Circle the number from 1 to 5 that best describes your reaction to the two items on either end of each continuum.

I will always welcome any geographic move that enhances my career.	5 4 3 2 1	I would turn down any job opportunity that involves moving.
Zigzagging from one firm to another would be intriguing to me.	5 4 3 2 1	I hate the process of adjusting to new work environments.
My career is first; my personal life-style is second.	5 4 3 2 1	My personal life-style is first; my career is second.
Getting to the top through zigzagging is more of a challenge.	5 4 3 2 1	Getting to the top in one organization is more of a challenge.
I am willing to take risks even though I may lose my job.	5 4 3 2 1	I will not take any risk that puts my job in jeopardy.
My ultimate loyalty is only to myself and my career.	5 4 3 2 1	I am 100-percent loyal to my organization.
I do not intend to follow traditional rules in order to get to the top.	5 4 3 2 1	I intend to follow traditional rules to the fullest extent.
I enjoy the job-seeking process, especially interviews.	5 4 3 2 1	I hate the job-seeking process, especially interviews.
I am willing to spend the extra energy to have a plan B ready and waiting.	5 4 3 2 1	I do not bother with a plan B. I devote my energy to my firm and my job.
It would not bother me in the least if I lost my job tomorrow.	5 4 3 2 1	I would be devasted if I lost my job tomorrow.

TOTAL SCORE _____

If you rated yourself 25 or higher, you should give the zigzagging pattern (scrambling) careful consideration. If you rated yourself under 25, the straight-line pattern appears to be a better choice for you.

Multiple career ladders

The use of **multiple career ladders** gives both organizations and employees more latitude in planning career development. BDM Corporation, for example, uses three distinct career ladders—technical, management, and administrative.[40] Two additional paths also exist—technical with leadership option and administrative with leadership option. These additional ladders let individuals become involved in management without giving up their technical or administrative interests and experiment rather than commit too early to the management ladder (see Exhibit 17.9).

At the heart of the BDM system is the recognition that individuals have unique career aspirations and that multiple ladders permit each employee to choose a career path that best fits his or her work-related goals. All employees can advance in the organization while maintaining their respective areas of expertise, and the stigma is reduced for those choosing not to progress along a career path that may ultimately lead to upper management.

Each step of each ladder is considered a career advancement and is rewarded with an increase in pay.

Comp. Level (*)	Technical Ladder	Technical with Leadership Option				Management Ladder	Administrative with Leadership Option				Administrative Ladder	Comp. Level (*)
		Leader	Associate Manager	Manager	Director		Director	Manager	Associate Manager	Leader		
Office of the President, Chief Executive Officer (35); Chief Financial and Administrative Officer (35)												
32						Corporate Executive						32
31	Senior Principal A					General Management Executive						31
30	Senior Principal B					Senior Executive					Senior Principal A	30
29	Senior Principal C				●	Executive					Senior Principal B	29
28	Principal Staff Member			●	●	Senior Associate Executive	●				Senior Principal C	28
27	Senior Staff Member		●	●			●	●			Principal Staff Member	27
26	Staff Member	●	●	●		Associate Executive		●	●		Senior Staff Member	26
25	Staff Member A	●	●	●				●	●	●	Staff Member	25
24	Associate Staff Member	●	●			Junior Associate Executive			●	●	Chief Associate Staff Member	24
23	Associate Staff Member A	●	●						●	●	Associate Staff Member	23
22	Assistant Staff Member	●								●	Chief Assistant Staff Member	22
21	Assistant Staff Member A									●	Assistant Staff Member	21
20	Non-Exempt Positions										Non-Exempt Positions	20
19					Progression within Career Ladders:							19
18					Horizontal							18
17					Diagonal							17
16					Vertical							16
15												15
14					*Compensation Level: this differs in some							14
13					cases from the employee's position level							13
12					(e.g., "Staff Member A" on the Technical							12
11					Ladder carries a position level of 26A).							11

EXHIBIT 17.9   CAREER LADDERS AT BDM CORPORATION

SOURCE: Reprinted by permission of the publisher, from "How to Operate a Successful Career Development Program," by John P. Riceman, *Management Review*, May 1982, p.23, © 1982 AMACOM, a division of American Management Associations, New York. All rights reserved.

Using multiple career ladders has increased BDM's flexibility as well as its ability to meet staffing demands in technical, administrative, and management areas. In addition, the system has shown employees that they have many career options and that, within certain constraints, the corporation can and will attempt to accommodate each individual's career goals.

Targeting career development

A carefully designed, flexible system can facilitate career development. By targeting jobs, career paths, and specific training needs, organizations can clarify job progression for employees and provide alternatives for employers.[41] These and other suggestions for improving career development programs are discussed below.

Identify Logical Paths to Target Jobs.   Establishing alternative, logical paths to target jobs contributes to both flexible and innovative approaches to career development. For example, an employee in the main bank who wishes to advance to the next highest level can do so by choosing one of a number of different paths. He can (1) train specifically for the job, hoping to move directly into the supervisor's position when it becomes available; (2) transfer to another unit within the main bank to obtain a different perspective on bank operations; or (3) take a comparable position in a smaller branch office to gain further insight into the integrative nature of bank functions.

Identify Fast Tracks to Target Jobs.   Career **fast tracks** can benefit people whose abilities and skills permit rapid movement toward a particular target job. Such tracks can also help organizations accomplish affirmative action goals by expediting the promotion of women and minorities. A fast-track plan for new managers may call for those identified as "fast trackers" to be sent to assessment centers and placed in accelerated training programs. The remaining managers would continue in traditional career tracks. Under this plan, high-potential managers should reach middle management in a much shorter period of time than those who follow normal career tracks. The plan minimizes undue pressure on first-year employees and allows each manager to progress at an appropriate pace.[42]

Although careful evaluation of career progress is important for all individuals, it is probably even more critical for those on fast tracks. Problems that have been associated with fast tracks include:

1. too much focus on short-term results;
2. insufficient time to adequately experience important company roles;
3. increased likelihood of employee burnout;
4. early career plateaus when opportunities to move vertically in the management hierarchy do not exist;
5. lack of opportunity for employees to have adequate input in their own career decisions; and
6. neglect of employees *not* on the fast track.[43]

Slow Down Career Path Progression.   Objections to fast tracks have lead to other advancement alternatives. Under a **slow burn plan,**[44] *all* individuals move more slowly along their career paths. This approach is similar to that taken by many Japanese companies, where individuals often spend five to seven years in a single position. A slow burn plan gives individuals more time to assimilate their preparation at each career stage, encourages cooperation rather than competition, and is intended to reduce anxiety about advancement. In addition, individuals are less likely to be discouraged when opportunities for promotion are not available and may develop a longer-range perspective on their careers.

Women who wish to slow down their careers in order to have children have caused numerous businesses and professional organizations to experiment with a specially designed "mommy track." The **mommy track** is a career path that permits women to work shorter, more flexible hours (for example, forty as opposed to seventy hours a week) with the understanding that they probably will not progress beyond middle management or move as far professionally as others not on the mommy track who enter the organization at the same time. Such a track is designed specifically for those women who wish to combine career and motherhood with less stress than is often felt by the traditional career-family mother.[45]

Nevertheless, slowing down career tracks for women can create problems. Peers and managers may consider women choosing mommy tracks to be less-than-full organizational members. In addition, such women may discover that they have missed important opportunities or that significant changes in their field have placed them at a disadvantage if and when they decide to reenter the organizational "mainstream." Although availability of the mommy track to some women may lessen career-family stress, the decision to embark on such a path may itself be stress-producing.

A case can be made for both fast track and slow burn career development systems and experimentation with both continues to provide useful information to individuals and organizations alike. Ultimately, the decision to adopt one or both systems will be influenced by a company's business and employment philosophy, economic and other environmental conditions, and the individuals recruited.

Identify Lateral Moves.   Organizations that are not growing rapidly and so are forced to slow down vertical career progression must continue to challenge employees and satisfy their desires for personal or professional growth. This can be accomplished through the use of lateral moves. Lateral career moves can provide training in skills that may not have been acquired earlier and encourage a more holistic view of the company's operations. Although increases in compensation are normally associated with promotions, lateral moves can also be rewarded with lump-sum payments or permanent increments similar to those used in pay-for-knowledge compensation systems.[46]

Lateral moves can also be used when an employee's performance in his or her present job is unsatisfactory. Some situations may even call for a return to a previously held position. Although downward moves are often viewed negatively, when properly handled they can actually reduce, rather than increase, employee anxiety about poor performance. The Peter Principle described in Exhibit 17.10 is concerned with the broader organizational consequences of failing to address poor performance.

Identify Career Path Clusters.   **Career path clusters** are groups of jobs toward which a single career path might lead. By identifying job clusters rather than focusing on a single target job, individuals and organizations are given greater latitude in accepting or assigning positions. Aiming at a single target job may be unrealistic given the number of aspirants and the limited number of positions. Clusters increase the number of potential career choices available to employees and encourage the efficient use of training and development resources by logically grouping training and development activities for more than one job.

Identify Career Development Moves from a Given Job.   Most development activities are directed toward target jobs, but it is also possible to give employees infor-

EXHIBIT 17.10   THE PETER PRINCIPLE

Laurence F. Peter is a scientist and writer who has devoted considerable time to studying incompetence. As he looked at organization after organization, he observed an almost universal phenomenon—occupational incompetence! His analysis of hundreds of cases of this occupational incompetence led him to formulate the following principle:

In a hierarchy, every employee tends to rise to his or her level of incompetence!

What Peter observed was this. Individuals are usually promoted to a higher level in an organization because they have done an exceptional (or at least acceptable) job in their former position. When a person's performance is no longer exceptional and he or she is considered only moderately competent or even incompetent, promotions cease, and the employee is left in the present position. Unfortunately, concludes Peter, it is likely that the employee will remain there indefinitely.

1. What impact would the Peter Principle have on an organization if it were carried to its logical conclusion?
2. Is the Peter Principle a reality in many organizations? What do you think?
3. How can a carefully designed career development program help an organization avoid the Peter Principle trap?

SOURCE: Laurence F. Peter *The Peter Principle* (New York: William Morrow & Company, 1969).

mation on paths leading *from* present jobs. Designating target jobs may delimit career opportunities for an employee and can cause tunnel vision in his or her present job. Identifying paths leading from a position gives the employee greater latitude as she or he develops unique career-related interests. For example, when Karen completes her assignment on the product planning task force, a number of career options are available to her. She can return to the engineering group to which she was originally assigned, move to a first-line supervisory position in the manufacturing department, or join a newly created quality assurance team. Her decision will no doubt be based on her career aspirations and her work-related experiences to date.

Identify Training Needs for Future Jobs.   Identifying a target job alone will not enable an individual to obtain that job. The individual must also understand the specific training needs associated with the job. Being aware of these training needs will allow management to plan related educational programs and provide the necessary resources when and where they are required. In addition, individual employees will benefit from knowing the timing and nature of training before them. It may be particularly helpful for persons in a given position in the organization to outline the types of training and development from which they believe others will benefit. This information can then be maintained in a central career development office.

Identify Personnel Pools for Open Jobs.   Personnel information systems (PIS) can contribute significantly to any career development program. Such systems provide a centralized source of information to use to identify who among existing personnel aspire to certain positions as well as those who are prepared to move further along a career path. Having such information available enhances the decision-making process of the people responsible for career development activities. Computerized systems can enable human resource specialists to identify specific training and development needs for each organizational member and to match those needs with position requirements throughout the organization.

Information from a PIS should be shared with line managers to give them an accurate human resource picture. In addition, such information sharing will discourage the stockpiling of talent in a single unit or area in the organization.

Of course, not all career moves are either planned or even desirable. As we saw in the chapters on formal organization and stress, the restructuring of much of corporate America has disrupted the career plans and personal lives of many middle managers. Some of the ethical questions facing upper-level managers responsible for planning and implementing such major structural changes are reflected in the Ethical Dilemma below.

Implement Direction Counseling.   **Direction counseling** involves "a combination of diagnostic interviews that focus on specific performance problems and subsequent counseling sessions concerned with how to improve an individual's job and his or her job performance."[47] The technique can be used to provide specific guidance for employees who have plateaued in their careers or who are being considered for further advancement. In some cases, due to the special assessment skills needed and the fact that the employee may be more open with someone not directly involved in the company, an external consultant may conduct the interviews.

Recommendations that emerge from direction counseling should ideally provide a series of steps or activities aimed at improving employee performance, reassigning the employee to a different job or superior, or enrolling the employee in a training or counseling program. Of course, separation from the company may also be a viable outcome.[48]

ETHICAL DILEMMA
Changing the Old Order

Middle managers in corporate America are becoming an endangered species. Increasing numbers of jobs in middle management are being eliminated as companies restructure and downsize to become more efficient and competitive. This restructuring has increased the pressure on remaining middle managers as their spans of management have grown.

When Georgia-Pacific Corp. restructured, a large number of its middle managers were asked to take early retirement. Those who remained were passed over for promotion and new positions were staffed by people hired from outside the organization. New hirees were usually younger and better educated, but they were unfamiliar with the workings of the company and sometimes found it difficult to get their work done.

Middle managers in companies throughout the United States are feeling isolated and unwanted. They complain that their top management has created an atmosphere of uncertainty. Many managers believe that companies may also be endangering their own futures, since there are few managers left who can take up the reins of leadership. Management experts raise another important question: Will the new and increased pressures placed on middle-level managers by restructuring dissuade others from taking up these jobs in the future?

Questions
Should the effects of downsizing and restructuring on individuals be a major concern to organizations? Explain.

What steps could organizations take to minimize the emotional impact of restructuring on middle managers who leave as well as those who stay?

SOURCE: J.A. Byrne et al., "Caught in the Middle: Six Managers Speak Out on Corporate Life," *Business Week*, 12 September 1988, 80–88; J. Spackey, "The Ripping of General Managers," *Newsweek*, 18 April 1988, 10; J.H. Sheridan, "Sizing Up Corporate Staffs," *Industry Week*, 21 November 1988, 46–52.

Development through mentoring

No matter what career path an individual takes, career development can be enhanced through the mentoring process. A **mentor** is "a person who advises, counsels or helps younger individuals in the organization."[49] Mentors are typically individuals whose successful experiences in an organization cause them to be good teachers and role models for newer, younger organization members. The mentoring relationship is often established either when a senior employee takes a new employee "under his or her wing" or when the newer employee seeks out the senior employee. Organizations may also, however, choose to formalize the mentoring process. Under such circumstances, new employees are assigned to experienced individuals whose role it is to coach and guide the employee. In addition, the mentor may "open doors," protect the employee from others when mistakes are made, support the employee with praise and compliments, and champion him or her among other influential managers in the organization.

Although mentors are usually senior personnel, mentoring activities can also be performed by peers. Peers can perform informational, colleagial, and other special roles that can support individual development during successive career stages.[50]

Organizations may have to deal with special issues surrounding mentoring relationships. For example, women often have a more difficult time than men establishing relationships with mentors. This is due to a number of factors including the small number of women in upper-level positions who can serve as mentors, norms limiting cross-gender relationships, sex stereotypes that limit the interest in developing women for upper-level positions, and the lack of access by women to important information networks. A failure to provide adequate mentoring for women is detrimental both to women employees and to the organizations within which they work. To the extent that mentoring does influence performance positively, women without mentors are at a distinct disadvantage in the organization. This can in turn adversely affect organizational performance and may even raise legal questions relative to sex discrimination.[51]

Finally, companies must be prepared to end or redefine mentoring relationships. The mentoring process goes through distinct phases, known as initiation, cultivation, and separation, over a period of four to five years.[52] A final phase, redefinition, takes place when the relationships established during earlier years take on a new form in which the intense bond between the two parties is replaced by a new pattern of interaction. This pattern is usually characterized by (1) the senior manager's continued interest in the younger person, and (2) the younger manager's appreciation of the mentor even though the modeling process itself no longer continues.

Of course, redefinition can result in anxiety for both parties. Young managers may temporarily feel abandoned, while senior managers may feel threatened by their "new competitor." New mentoring relationships may occur at different career stages since it is unlikely that having a single mentor throughout one's career would be either practical or productive. The phases of the mentoring process may therefore be repeated more than once during career development.

CAREERS AND CAREER DEVELOPMENT: CONCLUSIONS

Choosing a job and choosing a career are two different decisions. Many jobs are chosen without considering the impact such a choice may have on one's overall career. As we pointed out, both your job and your career will have a significant impact on other areas of your life (e.g., health, family and other social groups, and life-style). Consequently, career planning should be considered an essential part of life planning.

Although many people who are drawn into the job market make their initial decisions without much thought about later personal and career implications, careful career planning, beginning with a thorough self-assessment, can result in both personal and job-related satisfaction. Special consideration must be given to career development for certain individuals. For example, both men and women may face career-versus-family choices. However, choices such as these are more likely to alter the timing of career opportunities for women and to affect the developmental patterns they will experience throughout adulthood. Of course, maintaining a family and a career simultaneously also represents a potential choice. Dual-career couples are growing in number as a new generation of young adults with new values enters the job market. Such couples encounter unique tradeoffs as they attempt to negotiate a more complex life-style successfully.

You yourself may soon face (or perhaps have already faced) the complex decisions and problems encountered by members of dual-career families. On the other hand, even if you do not experience these problems personally, you are likely to work with and/or manage people who do.

Managers, as the primary decision makers in organizations, must take a fresh look at the special concerns of women and dual-career couples and develop ways to minimize the impact of those concerns on the organization. This may mean reexamining established company policies affecting persons in these special categories (vacations, work scheduling, antinepotism, etc.) or providing unique types of assistance (e.g., child day care or dual-career counseling) to facilitate employing such individuals successfully.

Management decisions to encourage hiring and retaining women and dual-career couples go beyond legal considerations alone. Such decisions make available an important segment of the work force that many employers have overlooked up until now. These decisions, along with those to promote and facilitate career development in general, represent a smart approach to human resource management.

Not every employee, of course, seeks to rise to the top of the organization. Top management should understand each employee's intentions and accurately assess career opportunities available in the organization. Providing career alternatives, as done through the multiple career ladders used at BCM Corporation, can accommodate unique career aspirations of each organizational member. Identifying career anchors early in a person's career also facilitates the tailoring of individual programs by providing further insight into links between job requirements and individual needs.

A well-designed and administered career development program can benefit all parties regardless of long-range career opportunities in an organization. At Exxon Corporation, nearly all the board members and a majority of the corporation's top executives have been developed within the company. The company, however, has also gained a reputation as a major training ground for top-level executives throughout the petroleum industry. As one Exxon executive confided, "We get the best they [the employees] have to offer while they are with us, and they know that opportunities await them either in Exxon or elsewhere in the industry; everybody is happy."

Company involvement in career development need not stop upon termination of an employee. Involuntary job loss resulting from shifting labor patterns and other economic factors may result in employees at any organizational level losing their jobs or having opportunities in particular career fields severely curtailed. In addition to the associated economic problems such employees face, the psychological success cycle that people experience in their careers is also broken by involuntary job loss.

Properly managed, involuntary job loss can lead to a positive career growth experience. A transition to a new job or career path can provide new opportunities for psychological success and a chance to gain from experiences of the past. Company programs intended to create career-growth opportunities from involuntary job loss include severance benefits intended to minimize economic burdens, outplacement programs designed to assess the personal and new training needs of terminated employees, retraining programs, and outplacement counseling.[53]

Who benefits from career development? The answer is everyone—you, the organization for which you work, and ultimately the customers you serve. Effective career management can enhance your productivity and job satisfaction, and, in a larger sense, your life satisfaction. It can influence an organization's performance, growth, and long-term survival and should therefore be an integral part of any human resource system. Knowing how to facilitate effective career development is an important responsibility that you will assume when you become a manager.

QUESTIONS FOR REVIEW AND DISCUSSION

1. What is meant by the term *career?*
2. What are the four elements of the life system and what are their relationships to one another?
3. What are the five career stages and how is each significant?
4. How do these career stages and Levinson's periods of adult development relate to one another?
5. What are career anchors and what factors influence them?
6. Name and describe five major career anchors. Why are career anchors significant to (a) individuals, (b) organizations?
7. How and why might managers choose to accommodate women or dual-career couples in their companies?
8. What steps may dual-career couples take to improve their personal and organizational lives? How can each of these actions contribute to a successful relationship?
9. Contrast specialized career paths with circular paths. Describe the advantages and disadvantages of each.
10. Name and describe five ways in which organizations may influence an employee's career path.

REFERENCES

1. D. T. Hall, *Careers in Organizations* (Pacific Palisades, Calif.: Goodyear Publishing, 1976), 4.
2. A. Pazy, "Joint Responsibility: The Relationship Between Organizational and Career Management and the Effectiveness of Careers," *Group and Organizational Studies,* Vol. 13 (September 1988): 311–331.
3. J. P. Kotter, V. A. Faux, and C. C. McArthur, *Self-Assessment and Career Development* (Englewood Cliffs, N.J.: Prentice-Hall, 1978).
4. E. F. Schumacher, *Small Is Beautiful* (New York: Harper and Row, 1973), 53.
5. Kotter et al., op. cit.
6. Hall, op. cit.

7. L. A. Isabella, "The Effect of Career Stage on the Meaning of Key Organizational Events," *Journal of Organizational Behavior,* Vol. 9 (Oct 1988): 345–358.
8. M. Billard, "Women on the Verge," *Business Month,* April 1990, 36–37.
9. D. J. Levinson, M. D. Darrow, E. B. Klein, M. H. Levinson, and B. McKee, "Periods in the Adult Development of Men: Ages 18–45," *The Counselling Psychologist,* 26 (January 1976): 22–23.
10. J. P. Near, "A Discriminant Analysis of Plateaued versus Nonplateaued Managers," *Journal of Vocational Behavior,* Vol. 26 (1985): 177.
11. D. C. Feldman and A. B. Barton, "Career Plateaus in

the Salesforce: Understanding and Removing Blockages to Employee Growth," *Journal of Personal Selling and Sales Management,* Vol. 8 (November 1988): 23–32.

12. J. W. Slocum, Jr., W. L. Cron, R. H. Hansen, and S. Rawlings, "Business Strategy and the Management of Plateaued Employees," *Academy of Management Journal,* Vol. 28 (March 85): 133–154.

13. W. R. Davidson and K. R. Kunze, "Psychological, Social, and Economic Meanings of Work in Modern Society: Their Effects on Workers Facing Retirement," in W. C. Sze, ed., *Human Life Cycles* (New York: Lason Aronson, 1965), 691–700.

14. E. H. Schein, "How 'Career Anchors' Hold Executives to Their Career Paths," *Personnel,* Vol. 52 (May-June, 1975): 11–24.

15. E. H. Schein, *Career Dynamics: Matching Individual and Organizational Needs* (Reading, Mass.: Addison-Wesley, 1978), 125.

16. Ibid., 128–172.

17. G. Sheehy, *Passages* (New York: Dutton Press, 1976).

18. "Older Women Having Children," Associated Press News Release, 7 July 1989.

19. A. T. Taylor III, "Why Women Are Bailing Out," *Fortune,* 18 August 1986, 16–25; E. Ehrlich, "The Mommy Track: Juggling Kids and Careers in Corporate America Takes a Controversial Turn," *Business Week,* 20 March 1989, 126–134; C. Coulson-Thomas, "Reconciling. Work and Home, Career and Family," *Equal Opportunities International,* Vol. 7 (1988): 19–20.

20. C. Wallis, "Onward Women," *Time,* 4 December 1989, 80–89.

21. Ibid.

22. Ibid.

23. Center for Creative Leadership Staff, et.al., *Breaking the Glass Ceiling: Can Women Reach the Top of America's Largest Corporations?"* (Reading: Addison-Wesley, 1987); for an excellent presentation of issues and conditions facing women internationally, see N. J. Adler and D. N. Izrael, *Women in Management Worldwide* (Armonk, N.Y.: M. E. Sharpe, 1988).

24. "The Pay: Ranking the 800 Top Executives," *Forbes,* 28 May 1990, 266–317.

25. A. M. Morrison, R. P. White, E. Van Volson, "The Narrow Band," *Issues and Observations,* Spring 1987, 1–7.

26. Billard, op. cit.

27. "Pinnacle," Cable News Network, 15 October 1988.

28. F. S. Hall and D. T. Hall, *The Two-Career Couple* (Reading, Mass.: Addison-Wesley, 1969), 51–53.

29. Rhona Rapoport and Robert Rapoport, "The Dual Career Family," *Human Relations,* Vol. 22 (1969): 3–30; S. Morgan, "How Working Parents Cope: Issues and Strategies for Family Management," in V. J. Ramsey, ed., *Preparing Professional Women for the Future* (Ann Arbor, Mich.: Division of Research, University of Michigan, 1985).

30. N. Gupta and D. Jenkins, "Dual-Career Couples:

Stress, Stressors, Strains, and Strategies," in T. A. Beehr and R. S. Bhagat, eds., *Human Stress and Cognition in Organizations* (New York: Wiley Interscience, 1985).

31. A. Tonfexis, et al., "Dual Careers, Doleful Dilemmas," *Time,* 16 November 1987, 90–91.

32. D. C. Bacon, "Look Who's Working at Home," *Nation's Business,* October 1989, 19–31.

33. J. H. Tannenbaum, "Both Sexes Are Drawn to Working at Home," *Wall Street Journal,* 24 May 1990, B1.

34. Gupta and Jenkins, op. cit.; Beehr and Bhagat, op. cit.

35. L. M. Carulli, C. L. Noroian, and C. Levine, "Employee-Driven Career Development," *Personnel Administrator,* Vol. 34 (March 1989); 66–70; S. A. Laser, "Career Development in a Changing Environment," *Journal of Managerial Psychology,* Vol. 3 (1988): 23–25; J. P. Riceman, "How to Operate a Successful Career Program," *Management Review,* Vol. 71 (May 1982): 21–24.

36. C. S. Granrose and J. D. Portwood, "Matching Individual Career Plans and Organizational Career Management," *Academy of Management Journal,* Vol. 30 (December 1987): 699–720.

37. S. P. Sethi, N. Namiki, and C. L. Swanson, *The False Promise of the Japanese Miracle* (Boston: Pitman Publishing, 1984), 45–46; W. J. Kuchta, "Options in Career Paths," *Personnel Journal,* Vol. 67 (December 1988): 28–32.

38. W. Ouchi, *Theory Z* (Reading, Mass.: Addison-Wesley, 1981): 121, 29–37, 121–123.

39. Billard, op. cit.

40. Riceman, op. cit.

41. H. A. Wellbank, D. T. Hall, M. A. Morgan, and W. C. Hammer, "Planning Job Progression for Effective Career Development and Human Resource Management," *Personnel,* Vol. 55, No. 2 (March-April 1978): 54–64; M. A. Von Glinow, M. J. Driver, K. Brousseau, and J. B. Prince, "The Design of a Career Oriented Human Resource System," *Academy of Management Review,* Vol. 8 (January, 1983): 23–32.

42. M. London and S. A. Stumpf, *Managing Careers* (Reading, Mass.: Addison-Wesley, 1982), 125–129.

43. P. H. Thompson, K. L. Kirkham, and J. Dixon, "Warning: The Fast Track May Be Hazardous to Organizational Health," *Organizational Dynamics,* Vol. 13 (Spring 1985): 21–33.

44. L. Bailyn, "The Slow Burn Way to the Top: Some Thoughts on the Early Years of Organization Careers," in C. B. Derr, ed., *Work, Family, and Career* (New York: Praeger, 1980), 94–106; R. E. Gerevas, "Keeping Good Managers Happy on a Slower Track," *Business Month,* May 1989, 79.

45. F. N. Schwartz, "Management Women and the New Facts of Life," *Harvard Business Review,* Vol. 67 (January-February 1989), 65–76.

46. B. Kaye and K. McKee, "New Compensation Strategies

for New Career Patterns," *Personnel Administrator*, Vol. 31 (March 1986): 61–68; G. D. Jenkins, Jr., and N. Gupta, "The Payoffs of Paying for Knowledge," *National Productivity Review*, Vol. 4, No. 1 (Spring 1985): 121–130.

47. W. L. Polsky and L. D. Foxman, "Career Counselor," *Personnel Journal*, July 1986: 24.
48. C. R. Leana and J. M. Ivancevich, "Involuntary Job Loss: Institutional Interventions and a Research Agenda," *Academy of Management Journal*, Vol. 12 (April 1987): 301–312.
49. D. C. Feldman, *Managing Careers in Organizations* (Glenview, Ill.: Scott, Foresman and Company, 1988).

50. K. E. Kram and L. A. Isabella, "Alternatives to Mentoring: The Role of Peer Relationships in Career Development," *Academy of Management Journal*, Vol. 28 (March 1985): 110–132.
51. R. A. Noe, "Women and Mentoring: A Review and Research Agenda," *Academy of Management Review*, Vol. 13 (January 1988): 65.
52. Kram, "Phases of the Mentor Relationship," *Academy of Management Journal*, Vol. 26 (December 1983): 608–625.
53. J. C. Latack and J. B. Dozier, "After the Ax Falls: Job Loss as a Career Transition," *Academy of Management Review*, Vol. 11 (April 1986): 380–381.

CASE 17.1   *Latino Glass, S.A. (Latino, South America)*

DONALD D. WHITE   *University of Arkansas*

Production superintendent Angel Ramos was obviously upset. Angel had been with Latino since the company began its operations in his country twelve years ago. He had worked hard during these years and had been recognized for his efforts with numerous promotions. However, he had counted heavily on replacing Roy Webster as plant manager at Latino Glass when he heard that Webster was being promoted to president. Now, he waited outside Webster's office having just learned that an "outsider" was being brought in as the new plant manager of the company. He was unaware that Webster himself was concerned about Angel's predicament and that he was discussing it with the company controller at that very moment.

BACKGROUND

Latino Glass was founded as a joint venture in Latino, South America. The parent United States company, Stateside Glass Company, produced a wide variety of glass products for both domestic and foreign markets. Latino Glass, unlike most glass plants, produced two products rather than specializing in a single product. Therefore, managers could acquire experience in two product areas simultaneously. The Latino operation was considered by ambitious middle-level managers in Stateside Glass as a good opportunity to gain valuable managerial experience. In addition to the two-product experience, the Latino operation was thought to provide decision-making opportunities that comparable level managers in Stateside did not have. On the other hand, it was generally believed that many of the decisions made by Latino managers were reviewed by corporate level managers at the home office of Stateside Glass.

Latino's primary product was black-and-white television picture tubes. Competition in the area had been limited for some time as a result of a government decree prohibiting the importation of picture tubes into the country. However, one Japanese firm did build and operate a similar plant in Latino. The Japanese firm had gained about 20 percent of the total market. In addition, recent trade agreements among several Latin American countries allowed a Mexican producer of picture tubes to market its product in Latino. To date, Latino has not been hurt seriously by the Mexican competition, and sales outside the country are on the increase.

Approximately one year ago, the company decided to expand its present production and add a line of picture tubes for color television. However, a government declaration made shortly after the decision caused the parent company to hold up any action on the addition of the new line. The original plan had called for Stateside Glass to form a second joint venture company in Latino for the express purpose of producing the color television picture tubes. However, the government declaration stated that all new enterprises begun in Latino must have at least 51 percent Latino ownership. A final decision as to whether or not the company's plans will be nullified by the declaration has not yet been made by the Latino government.

ROY WEBSTER'S OBSERVATIONS

When Angel Ramos found out by way of the grapevine that we were bringing in Joe Kent to be plant manager, he was quite upset, even somewhat emotional. Indirectly, he threatened to quit. Ramos is a good man and has performed well as production superintendent for three years. He's only thirty-two years old.

When I was plant manager, I never had any trouble with him—we always got along pretty well though he tends to be a little impulsive. I guess when I moved up to president from plant manager, he assumed he would replace me as plant manager. While I was never free to tell him, he was my choice for the job even though I knew he would have had some problems because of his lack of experience in the areas reporting to him—plant accounting and industrial relations, especially. I guess Paula Moore (vice-president for Latin American Operations, Stateside) felt Ramos's lack of experience would create too many problems. That's on our agenda of topics to be discussed on my next trip to the states. It is the policy of Stateside Glass to promote nationals as rapidly as they are capable of assuming greater responsibility—and we follow it. Of the 250 people employed by Latino Glass, there are only 3 Americans—the project manager who is coordinating the introduction of the lab products line in terms of production and sales, the plant manager, and myself, the president. Besides, we can't do much without government permission and the industry department likes to see Latinos in high company positions—it improves our image with the government. But, Joe Kent was assigned the job by Moore and that's the way it will have to stay.

There is another aspect of the Ramos problem that must be considered. The heads of the department reporting to the plant manager are used to having an American over them. When the time comes to move

a Latino person into the job of plant manager, we might have problems with the Latino people who report to him. It's all right if an American is the plant manager, but as soon as a Latino native is in that job each of the other Latino people will feel that he should have had the job. I'm not sure they're ready to accept another Latino guy as their boss. When Joe Kent's time is up here and he returns to Stateside Glass, in about three years, I think Angel Ramos will be ready for the plant manager's job. I can't promise him anything because I'll be leaving Latino Glass about that time myself. But I wouldn't be surprised if he were the next plant manager.

Latino Glass has progressed nicely in the past five years. We've had some problems, but I think we're really sailing now. Joe Kent worries me a little. His confidential file indicates he has a short temper, lets everybody know it when things don't go right—or so his file indicates. He spent the first four weeks after being assigned here in an intensive Spanish course—he's actually been on the job less than two weeks. I've noticed that he never uses his Spanish. I guess he's afraid or embarrassed to make mistakes. Our home office personnel committee reviewed the records of the top production superintendents in the Stateside plants, and Joe, evidently, came out as the strongest prospect. Before coming to Latino, he was production superintendent in a color television tube plant. He has been with Stateside Glass for fifteen years—almost all of them in line positions in production. Two years ago he was offered a promotion to plant manager in an overseas operation, in Asia to be exact, but he turned it down. Some people feel that if he had turned down a second promotion, namely plant manager here in Latino, he'd never be offered another chance. I don't think Stateside really operates like that—but Joe might think so. I just hope that he and Angel Ramos get the job done and don't crash head on. If those two don't work together, they will make us all look bad.

I've suggested to Joe, subtly of course, that he use the work objectives program that I started when I was plant manager. It worked for me, it should work for him if I can just get him to try it. I don't know when I'll get around to starting it with the people who report to me. The work objective program, some call it "management by results," consisted of my sitting down with each of my subordinates individually and discussing what goals they should strive to reach in the forthcoming six-week period. Then we get together as a group, my subordinates and I, and each subordinate would tell the others what he was going to achieve in the coming period. We discussed each person's objectives as a group because sometimes they can help each other achieve their objectives. I like to see them set objectives that are a little higher than what is likely they can achieve—something to shoot at, so to speak. As I said, though, I haven't had time

since I've been president to start it with my immediate subordinates. I wish Joe Kent would continue the work objectives program in his area. It could help him do a better job; but if he and Ramos don't get along and don't support each other, we're all going to look bad.

CASE 17.2   *Predicting the future*

RICHARD M. HODGETTS   *Florida International University*

Jed Barket and Bill Thomas, both members of the board of directors of ABC Manufacturing, were discussing a major dilemma—that of deciding which of three men under consideration should be offered the company's presidency. The former president, Will Ziebuld, had been doing an excellent job when he suddenly collapsed at his desk. Suffering an apparent heart attack, Ziebuld was rushed to a nearby hospital. After extensive tests, Ziebuld was told he would have to go easy from then on. Following this advice, he tendered his resignation as president.

This turn of events left the company's top management stunned. However, the board decided to fill the vacancy as quickly as possible. After screening all possible candidates, the board narrowed its list to three men, two outsiders and one insider. The first two individuals were both presidents of competitive firms, but each indicated that he would be willing to change jobs if given the offer. The third man was the company's executive vice-president and the individual Will Ziebuld had been grooming for his job for the past two years.

The board of directors was charged with choosing the new president. However, Jed and Bill were the most senior members and the five other members generally agreed with their recommendations. As a result, the two men were asked to evaluate the three candidates, arrive at a consensus, and present their findings to the board.

The best method of choosing the new president was not clear to either Jed or Bill. Nevertheless, Jed believed strongly that human behavior was predictable from past history.

"You know," he told Bill, "a systematic analysis of an individual can give you a behavioral profile of that person. On the basis of this information, you can predict quite a bit about their behavior. All we really have to do is obtain such a profile of the three men under consideration." Bill, however, was not so sure: "I just don't think you can do it that easily. Give me an illustration."

"I'll do better than that. Let me get you a clipping from a past issue of *Time* and I'll show you how this idea of a behavioral profile is used." Jed left the office and returned a few minutes later. He opened the magazine to the "law" section and handed it to Bill. The story to which he was referring related to some of the latest techniques used by defense attorneys in choosing jurors. In recent years a system has arisen for screening these jurors. It essentially entails bringing in a special team of individuals skilled in psychology and sociology to work with the defense attorneys. The team identifies those most likely to vote for 'acquittal' or 'not guilty.'

In arriving at a decision of whether or not to oppose the sitting of a particular juror, the group divides its operation into three parts: a) making a sociological profile of the community in which the trial will be held; b) a scrutiny in court of potential jurors; and c) a field investigation of their backgrounds. To indicate how successful this approach has been, *Time* reported that the team helped pick thirty-four of thirty-six jurors who voted for acquittal.

Bill: Are you suggesting that we merely obtain this type of profile of each candidate?

Jed: No, that would be too simple; it would only provide us with a brief sketch of the individual. We might be able to determine how he would vote on a given issue. However, that is too limited in scope. We need to obtain behavioral information that will give us an overall profile of the person.

Bill: How would you suggest we get such information?

Jed: Well, I think we ought to hire some qualified people to gather data on the early, formative years of each candidate.

Bill: Why?

Jed: Because by the time a person is eighteen years old, his options are limited. He's either capable of being a company president or he isn't. The basic behaviors have already been developed.

Bill: That sounds like a way-out idea to me.

Jed: Look, I'll give you an illustration. Is there anyone you went through grade school with whom you can remember?

Bill: Sure, there was a boy named Larry Mc-Cracken. He was the smartest kid in the class. Of course, we moved away after seventh grade so I don't know what ever happened to Larry. However, his father was the mayor, so my guess is that the family had roots there and may still be living in the same city.

Jed: What do you think Larry is doing today?

Bill: Well, if he's not the mayor there, I'd say he's either a successful businessman or a college professor—maybe in mathematics or accounting.

Jed: Why do you say that?

Bill: Because he was both analytical and good at math.

Jed: Okay, let's take a wild shot and call your old home city and find out what he's doing today.

Bill: Heck, nobody will remember him. Besides, whom do I call?

Jed: Is there any school teacher you had who, if he or she were still alive, would be living there?

Bill: Probably Miss Anna Dunworthy. She was unmarried in those days and the school was her whole life.

Jed: Okay, call the information operator, see if Miss Dunworthy still lives there. If she does, ask her about Larry; maybe she remembers.

Bill placed the call and, to his surprise, learned that there was indeed an Anna Dunworthy living in the city. Furthermore, upon talking to her he learned that Miss Dunworthy not only remembered him but was able to tell him about Larry—he was the president

of the largest bank in the metropolitan area. In fact, at the last annual high school get-together, she and Larry had spent over an hour talking abut old times. They wondered what had ever happened to Bill. By the time Bill hung up the telephone, he was amazed.

Bill: I can't believe it. He not only still lives in the town but he's in a profession similar to the one I guessed.

Jed: Sure, it's like I told you. Tell me something about the person's early years and I'll project his future.

Bill: Okay, but you've got to admit that we had awful skimpy data to go on.

Jed: Oh, sure, but we could get a lot more information on the candidates for the presidency of the firm. We could have a complete check made on each one.

Bill agreed that the suggestion was a good one and upon hearing it, the board of directors also agreed. An investigative agency was then hired to obtain the requisite background information. Ten days later the data was in the hands of the two men.

The report revealed that one of the outside candidates, Roger Kenan, was a star pupil in grammar and high school. In addition, he was active in baseball and basketball and was elected president of his high school class. Neighbors and friends remembered him as an easygoing boy who never seemed to get in any trouble. He was fairly well liked although he did not seem to have any close friends. Meanwhile, his grammar school teachers remembered him as industrious and likable. The second outside candidate, William Rheem, was apparently something of a cut-up in both grammar and high school. School reports indicated that he was twice reprimanded for fighting during recess. Nevertheless, he was well remembered by his teachers because of his success in midget, junior varsity, and varsity football. Bill was apparently a superb quarterback. Neither his grammar school nor his high school ever lost a game while he was there. In fact, he was still affectionately known by his old English teacher as "Touchdown" Bill Rheem, because of a ninety-one-yard winning touchdown he ran from scrimmage in the last minute of the state finals. Old neighbors and friends called him a "likable roughneck." One of his friends said, "We figured he'd either do very well for himself or wind up in jail. There's no in-between with Bill."

The third candidate, Martin McChorder, was the inside man Will Ziebuld had been grooming for the presidency. The investigators learned that Martin's parents had been killed when he was a child and Martin had been raised by an elder aunt. Around his neighborhood, Martin was regarded as shy and introverted, a marked change from his behavior in the firm where he was outgoing and gregarious. Martin had also been quite sickly as a child and missed quite a few days of school. In the sixth grade he was almost left back because he had been absent so often. While he engaged in no contact sports, he was active in the band, glee club, chess club, and was president of the high school's debating team. One of his old school friends said he was "outstanding in intellectual or noncompetitive endeavors."

Jed was still a bit skeptical. However, he knew he and Bill must sit down and make their decision.

EXERCISE 17.1
LIFE AND CAREER PLANNING

This exercise will help you look at your personal life as well as your career plans. In a sense, you are already in motion along a career path. Your past and present have contributed to your future choices, although they will not necessarily govern them. As you complete your life and career planning exercise, keep in mind your goals and the opportunities that lie ahead.

INSTRUCTIONS

1. Form groups of three persons each.
2. Think carefully about the issues raised by each of the directions below. Then complete that part of the exercise.
3. (a) Outside of class, write a brief statement concerning the goals you had when you graduated from high school. Then list five adjectives that describe your present progress toward those goals. In class, state your goals to group members and discuss along with them the meaning and significance of your list of adjectives.

   (b) What career goals would you like to achieve five years after you graduate or leave school? Ten years? Twenty years? List five adjectives that best reflect your

EXHIBIT 17.11   YOUR CAREER PATH

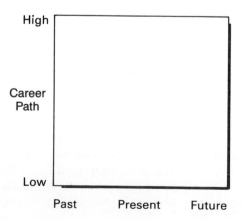

career goals. Discuss with group members why the list of adjectives are significant.

(c) Complete the graph (Exhibit 17.11) by drawing a line that depicts your past, present, and future career path. Share your graph with the other members of the group. Explain the meaning of the slopes and levels of your career line.

(d) Develop a written "contract' with yourself describing what you expect to receive (career goals) and what you are willing to give (education, training, work experience, time commitment, and the like) in order to achieve those goals. This document represents your personal commitment to your career plan.

EXERCISE 17.2
YOUR PERCEPTION OF CAREER ADVANCEMENT PRACTICES

DAVID E. BLEVINS   *University of Mississippi*

Aspiring executives who value advancement highly may engage in different career enhancement practices from those less motivated to move up in the organization. However, even those who value advancement equally may differ in career enhancement practices for many reasons. For example, they may have different beliefs and values regarding what is or is not ethical and/or moral.

ACTIVITY

Complete the Career Advancement Questionnaire on the following page.

Evaluate each of the questionnaire statements in terms of how well you think they describe the traits/values/attitudes of people climbing the career advancement ladder. There are no right or wrong answers. But you must commit yourself to a response in order to gain the most from the exercise.

Meet in groups of four to six persons and discuss similarities and differences in your individual responses. Your group should then discuss the questions listed below. (Your professor has aggregate response data from students at other universities as well as response data from managers in Fortune 500 companies. Responses from both groups will be provided to your group.)

QUESTIONS

1. Do your responses differ appreciably from those of your classmates? From those of other students at other universities? From those of actual managers?
2. Why might differences in opinions occur?
3. Are the opinions of Fortune 500 managers more accurate than yours? Why or why not?

4. Would you have responded differently if you were asked what *should* be the frequency of each practice (rather than what is your perception of the actual frequency of each practice)?

5. Would you have responded differently if you were describing your own actual or intended practices for climbing the ladder?

CAREER ADVANCEMENT QUESTIONNAIRE

Please evaluate the following statements in terms of how well you think they describe the traits exhibited by those people climbing the career advancement ladder in a *Fortune* 500 firm.

	Almost Always	Frequently	Occasionally	Infrequently	Almost Never
1. To progress, one has to develop the philosophy that winning is everything.	5	4	3	2	1
2. The career pressures of advancing leave one with an overdeveloped head and an underdeveloped heart.	5	4	3	2	1
3. One can succeed even if one's work is not the most important thing in one's life.	5	4	3	2	1
4. Even though one might say and believe that something like "customer satisfaction" is the primary goal of the organization, one has to develop an attitude that making money is the single most important objective.	5	4	3	2	1
5. One just about has to "sell one's soul" to the organization to get ahead.	5	4	3	2	1
6. To progress, one will occasionally have to indulge in "dirty tactics." (For example, taking credit for work done by someone else or insinuating that someone else did not do something they were supposed to do.)	5	4	3	2	1
7. To advance, the corporation has to come first, even before one's family.	5	4	3	2	1
8. One cannot progress without "stepping on a few people."	5	4	3	2	1
9. All personal values have to be set aside in order for one to advance.	5	4	3	2	1
10. To advance, one has to develop the philosophy that what does not relate to winning and career advancement, including one's family, does not really matter.	5	4	3	2	1
11. To climb the ladder, one must not only be prepared to aggressively move past those who stand in the way, but may find it necessary to "clear the path."	5	4	3	2	1

INTEGRATIVE CASES

I. *Bruised Apple*
II. *A Simple Problem of Communication?*
III. *The Skil Circular Saws Plant*
IV. *Davis Regional Medical Center*
V. *Electro-Tec, Inc.*

INTEGRATIVE CASE I

Bruised apple

G. PASCAL ZACHARY   *The Wall Street Journal*

In his autobiography *Odyssey,* Apple Computer chief executive John Sculley relates how he regretfully ousted founder Steve Jobs and then turned the company around in spectacular fashion.

Mr. Sculley's latest odyssey, over the past three months, has been a bit different. He has just forced one of his two top officers to resign. The other is on the verge of leaving. Once-heady growth is slowed by tactical and strategic mistakes, necessitating cost-cutting and layoffs. Competitors are gaining ground with new machines that rival the ease-of-use of Apple's mainstay Macintosh.

Now Mr. Sculley, until recently lionized by employees as Apple's savior, has become a lightning rod for disaffection in the ranks.

All this puts the 50-year-old executive in a tough spot. "As far as the events of the last few months go, there's an element of rude awakening," says Albert A. Eisenstat, a senior vice president. "Apple was getting an attitude: We know how to walk on water. That has been hammered."

Compared with many older computer makers, whose mainframe and minicomputer businesses are being chewed up by ever-more-powerful PCs, Apple's prospects still seem healthy. Apple has $900 million in cash, carries virtually no long-term debt, and, according to one survey, had a 53 percent gain in revenue from its Macintosh computers in December. Analysts expect growth of nearly 10 percent in revenue and net income in fiscal 1990, even though sales rose only 6 percent and earnings fell 11 percent in the first quarter ended December 29.

A SOBER PICTURE

Yet Sculley himself is painting a sober picture. He is warning that Apple's annual growth may dwindle to 10 percent to 15 percent during the 1990s. Questions are being raised about whether Apple's go-go growth

over the past four years might have owed more to industrywide forces than to Sculley. As he himself concedes, "Sales growth solves a lot of problems."

Apple's image as a growth company means much to stockholders, largely determining the price-earnings multiple that the market puts on the stock. From 1987 to 1989, the stock's multiple fell from about twenty-five times per-share earnings to about ten—less than the average for Standard & Poor's 400-company index. Apple's shares have plunged 30 percent since October, and ended at $34.25 in over-the-counter trading on February 14, 1990, near the low of the past several years.

In jeopardy as well is Apple's image as a kind of New Age organization where employees change the world. Many employees are confused by Apple's repeated reorganizations, doubtful about its future direction, and angered, amid the talk of layoffs, by huge payments to either hire or get rid of top executives.

MUCH CONFUSION

"Apple still hires bright young people, but instead of getting fired up, they go through one or two reorganizations and get disoriented," says Ellen Nold, a Palo Alto, California, consultant who worked at Apple for five years.

Nold puts part of the blame for the disaffection on Sculley's "very guarded" personal style. "When you have a leader who really isn't present in many ways," she asserts, "you have a problem with people not knowing where they stand. That's an issue for John's top managers, and it filters down to the lowest part of the organization."

Such malaise may complicate Sculley's campaign to instill a new sense of discipline. In recent weeks, hundreds of Apple workers have exchanged a letter accusing Apple of dividing itself between haves and have-nots. Written by Kirk Loevner, a middle manager, the letter criticizes Apple for rewarding executives who fail and cites a spate of special deals handed out by Sculley last year. The deals include a $2.1 million severance package for a sales vice-president and a $1.5 million cash signing bonus and a severance package worth as much as $2.4 million for a new chief financial officer.

In contrast, ordinary managers and employees don't even have a retirement plan. At a recent meeting about a possible plan, a human-resources staffer dismissed the idea with the comment that "we don't expect people to last that long," because the pace at Apple "burns out" many white-collar workers. Asked about the incident, Kevin J. Sullivan, Apple's human-resources chief, says someone who worries about a retirement plan probably isn't an Apple type of person.

Sculley himself earned $2.3 million last year, and has stoked the resentment through a lavish life style. He is currently trying to sell, for $4.8 million, one of his three homes in Silicon Valley and, for a reported $1.25 million, one of his two vacation homes in Maine. For eighteen months, about a dozen workers have been constructing a Sculley-designed four-building residential compound.

Sculley has also built three elaborate barns, mainly for his wife's dozen horses, and plans "some more." The barns are so well-appointed "I'd like to be a horse in one of them myself," comments Ann Griffiths, his real-estate broker.

Executive perks add to employee discontent. Last month, Sculley trumpeted his decision to save money by no longer providing roughly one hundred senior executives with cars, usually Mercedes-Benzes and Jaguars. However, employees are just learning that Apple couldn't simply take the cars away because the executives got them under contract. The executives will receive in compensation as much as $50,000 each.

Even some Apple executives think the company should slam on the brakes. When Bernard Gifford, a former university dean, became Apple's director of education sales a year ago, he moved up from a 1984 Toyota to a company-supplied Jaguar. "Maybe it's time," he says, "to get rid of some of the perks that irritate people."

A MORE CAREFUL APPROACH

Sculley admits that big bonuses for top managers "clearly bother a lot of people at Apple" and pledges to be "very careful" about similar packages in the future. He also pleads guilty to reorganizing some parts of Apple too often. "I don't feel very good about that," he says.

Doubts about Sculley's management surfaced late last year, when Apple reported slowing sales of its lowest-priced Macintosh computers and the collapse of its older Apple II line. Some industry observers declared the end of Apple's four-year boom, in which yearly sales grew from $1.9 billion to $5.3 billion. Others disagreed, saying Apple can rebound by slashing costs and prices on some machines and by introducing more new products.

"It's a very delicate balance," says John Rollwagen, the chairman of Cray Research and an Apple director. "The problem for Apple is that its freedom becomes constrained to some extent by all the successes of the past. You want to preserve the Mac base, the Apple II base, yet at the same time you want to be innovative."

It was Mr. Sculley's ability to rescue the brilliant but flawed Macintosh that made him famous in the first place. The original Macintosh, conceived by Mr. Jobs, was an underpowered, dead-end machine when Jobs left Apple in September 1985. Then, Jean-Louis Gassee, picked by Sculley to head product development, made it easier to enhance the computer with various add-ons and increased its power. The so-called opening-up of the Macintosh was Mr. Gassee's main goal for several years; business people and not just computer enthusiasts began to buy it.

CORPORATE SALES SOUGHT

But in the past two years, Sculley has directed Apple's efforts almost exclusively at developing powerful machines for large companies, and he has virtually ignored products aimed at the small-business, education and individual users who remain the company's mainstay customers. Sales to big companies have increased, but critics say Apple's growth in the corporate market is limited because, unlike International Business Machines Corp. and Hewlett-Packard Co., it doesn't offer minicomputers and mainframes.

Mr. Sculley also has allowed differences among his senior executives to stall work on a much-anticipated lower-cost Macintosh, which would sell for under fifteen hundred dollars and give buyers a choice of either a color or black-and-white monitor. A year ago, three of Sculley's division heads agreed on the design, but Allan Z. Loren, who last month departed as head of Apple USA, dissented. Apple is hard at work on the machine again, but may not have it out in time for this year's Christmas season.

Meanwhile, Apple is churning out pricier computers. Next month, it probably will introduce its fastest yet, a ten-thousand-dollar machine for engineers and designers.

The failure to move more quickly on a low-priced machine has pushed down Apple's overall unit share of the PC market to 18.4 percent from 23.7 percent,

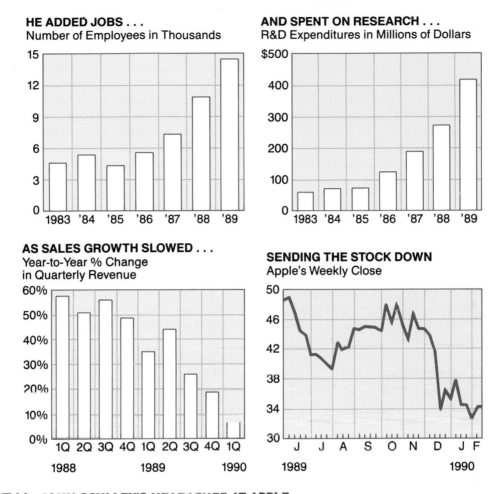

HE ADDED JOBS . . .
Number of Employees in Thousands

AND SPENT ON RESEARCH . . .
R&D Expenditures in Millions of Dollars

AS SALES GROWTH SLOWED . . .
Year-to-Year % Change
in Quarterly Revenue

SENDING THE STOCK DOWN
Apple's Weekly Close

EXHIBIT I.I   JOHN SCULLEY'S HEADACHES AT APPLE

according to Audits & Surveys Inc., a market-research firm. Last fall, customers shunned Apple's least-expensive Macintosh, the Plus, because it can't easily be upgraded to use future Apple software that will require more memory and faster processing. Sales of the Plus declined even after Apple slashed its price, which last fall slid below a thousand dollars in stores.

An even more serious challenge comes from IBM and compatible PC makers such as Compaq. A new software package, to be released this month by Microsoft, will give these PCs many of the easy-to-use commands and powerful graphics that have made the Macintosh so popular. That hurts Apple because makers of IBM-compatibles offer speedier machines and more features, such as color monitors or sturdier printers, for 10 percent to 25 percent less money.

As the markets shift, Sculley tends to meet the changing conditions by shuffling his executives. "John believes in borderline anarchy," says William Campbell, who heads Apple's software subsidiary. "He

believes a good company should constantly be stretching. Just when you think you want to put your feet up and say, 'There, we've done it,' he comes in and provokes change."

Although Sculley's nimble management helped him steer Apple through past crises, he lately may have provoked too much change. Last year, he added thousands of workers in anticipation of future growth. But in January, he said Apple would cut costs; although he won't provide details, he is expected to trim the work force of fourteen thousand by as many as eight hundred people in the first three months of this year.

Sculley also evidently botched his last major reorganization, in August 1988. Last month he obtained the resignation of Mr. Loren and demoted Mr. Gassee—the men who had emerged in 1988 as his two top operating executives.

Sculley's choice of Loren to head the United States division in 1988 is widely viewed by insiders as a disaster. Loren, a former chief of Cigna Corp.'s information unit, joined Apple in 1987 to improve its internal use of computers, but he quickly convinced Sculley that Apple could double its annual revenue by turning the Macintosh into the PC for big business. Although Loren increased Apple's sales to Fortune 500 companies, he directed lackluster marketing campaigns and cut efforts aimed at smaller customers. His seeming indifference to education demoralized staffers in that market. Sculley now says he saddled Loren with too many duties and probably should have given someone else the job of overseeing education sales—a third of Apple's domestic revenue.

Loren disputes the notion that his efforts were unsuccessful and says he resigned because he was tired of the hectic place at Apple. And his problems were compounded by the fact that Gassee controlled Apple's product-marketing group, which plays a critical role in defining the features of a new product. Last September, Loren created his own fifty-member product-marketing group. The two groups now coexist.

The problems in the United States division are so messy that Sculley is having difficulty replacing Loren. People close to Apple say Campbell has declined an offer to return to his old post. Campbell won't comment. Also saying no were Charles Boesenberg, who also once held the job and now works for a competitor, and Delbert Yocam, who quit as head of Apple's Pacific division last year.

For now, Michael H. Spindler, whom Sculley last month appointed to a new position of chief operating officer, will direct the division. Spindler, a native of West Germany, formerly headed Apple's European operations, where sales surged 40 percent in the fiscal year ended September 30, 1989.

GASSEE POPULAR

The sudden change in the status of Gassee, who is expected to resign soon but probably will stay at Apple through the summer, poses another challenge. Until recently, Gassee won effusive praise from Sculley. "Gassee represented Apple at its best—slightly irreverent, at times arrogant, but always incredibly insightful and smart," Sculley wrote in *Odyssey.* Last November, he awarded Gassee the highest bonus he could.

Now, Sculley says it was a mistake to put so much of the company's operations—research and development, manufacturing and product marketing—in Gassee's hands. Gassee declines to comment. However, the break with Gassee, who is immensely popular

among Apple's engineers, is apt to be seen by some employees as proof that Sculley is unpredictable. Last Friday, about 150 employees picketed the company's headquarters, carrying signs backing Gassee; although the protest was mild, even light-hearted, one sign— "JLG 4 CEO"—seemed to call for Sculley's ouster.

Sculley's job, however, is hardly in jeopardy. Board members say his frequent management changes are justified by Apple's rapid growth in recent years. "John has done an excellent job of balancing some of these strong personalities he's attracted here," says Eisenstat, the senior vice-president and a director.

And in recent months, Sculley has begun bearing down on Apple's problems. He canceled overseas trips, including a January visit to the Soviet Union, and withdrew from speaking engagements. Nevertheless, he intends to leave day-to-day operations to Spindler. "I'm a builder—I don't like minding the store," Sculley says. That's a bit ironic: Jobs hired him in 1983 to do just that.

SEEKING FASTER INTRODUCTIONS

Sculley wants to shorten the time it takes to produce a new computer from eighteen months to as little as twelve months. He also may be more willing than was Gassee to fight Apple's "not invented here" mentality, which encourages engineers to design products readily available from outside suppliers. One example of how Apple could benefit: Rather than trying to manufacture a lightweight portable computer, Apple might marry its Macintosh software with Japanese hardware. Now, Apple is losing out on a huge market because its own portable, introduced last year, is cumbersome.

The portable's lackluster start is a sore reminder that Sculley's Apple, unlike Jobs's, doesn't have a reputation for technological innovation. But Sculley plans to wade into new-product development in the hope of pulling off a technological coup rivaling the Macintosh, Jobs's most enduring legacy to Apple. If Sculley could launch a new computer that would complement Macintosh sales while leading Apple into the next century, he would finally put to rest talk that he's heavily indebted to Jobs for his success at Apple.

That's a big if. Sculley isn't an engineer. He came to Apple with a reputation as a successful marketeer at PepsiCo. Nonetheless, he appears eager to galvanize Apple's researchers to get the job done.

"I'm convinced that under John's leadership, we'll produce an innovation on par with the Macintosh" by the mid-1990s, says Lawrence G. Tesler, the vice-president of advanced technology.

INTEGRATIVE CASE II

A simple problem of communication?

H. WILLIAM VROMAN   *Towson State University*
DONALD D. WHITE   *University of Arkansas*

Chicago Chemicals is one of the three largest producers of chemicals in the United States. Due to the size of the organization and nationwide scope of its activities, Chicago Chemicals relies on a regional system for recruiting future personnel. Each regional office is responsible for locating, screening, and hiring all persons to be employed in that area. Depending on the part of the country, this may include engineers, production staff, and marketing personnel, in addition to persons employed in other supporting departments. The North Central Regional Office is responsible for recruiting in Wisconsin, Illinois, Michigan, Indiana, Ohio, and Pennsylvania. In addition to the North Central main office, there are seven smaller district recruiting offices that in turn employ sixty-seven full-time recruiters.

There are thirty-five persons currently working in the regional office under the management of Richard Thompkins. The office itself is composed of four departments: Administration and Personnel; Scheduling; Advertising and Publicity; and Recruiting Operations (see Exhibit II.1).

DEPARTMENTAL RESPONSIBILITIES

Director of the Administration and Personnel department is Mary Charles. The department is responsible for coordinating activities at the regional office, designing and printing all recruiting materials, and developing specific programs for all recruiting activities in the region. In addition, the department maintains a reporting and control system and initiates security checks on potential employees when necessary. The department is also responsible for selecting and training all recruiters and for assigning them to individual offices.

The Advertising and Publicity department, under Terrence Reddin, directs the advertising and publicity

program for the regional office in support of its recruiting function. Members of the department provide guidance and assist recruiters on special projects. Reddin has initiated a high school education information program and a widely based public relations program in the region. These two programs are not directly related to activities of the individual recruitment offices. An internal information program for the region has been initiated by the department.

The Scheduling department is a small but powerful unit under the direction of Ben Holdridge. Holdridge's department prepares, maintains, and monitors all contracts and contract agreements for office space, vehicle rental and maintenance, and other forms of transportation. The time frames for all recruitment trips must be cleared through the Scheduling department. In addition, the Scheduling department provides staff assistance to the regional director and to each recruitment office supervisor.

Work in the Scheduling department is often exacting and requires a considerable amount of detailed paperwork. Staff members find it necessary to be thorough and deliberate when completing assigned tasks. An expansion at the Chicago office which took place one year ago drained off many of the department's "older hands." Therefore, existing members of the department average a little over two years' experience in their jobs (see Exhibit II.2.) The department received a rating of "excellent" in the last regional office evaluation. Some of the group norms are: strive for accuracy; pay attention to detail; do the job right the first time.

Recruiting Operations, under Harold Johnson, is responsible for a wide range of activities. Principally, it directs the development of plans and programs pertaining directly to personnel selection. The department establishes policies and carries out plans from the Chicago office to achieve personnel procurement objectives. Johnson's staff formulates and initi-

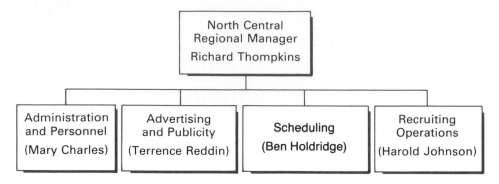

EXHIBIT II.I   ORGANIZATION CHART, CHICAGO CHEMICALS' NORTH CENTRAL REGION

ates recruitment programs and policies for the region. Evaluation of the performance of individual recruiters is handled by the department, and certain personnel programs, such as a recent incentive awards program and a safety program, were initiated there. It is not unusual for Johnson or individual department members to recommend additions, changes, or new programs to other departments or to Thompkins himself.

No serious problems have ever arisen between Recruiting Operations and the other departments. However, some members of other departments have complained of interference from Operations. For example, all divisions are required to make staff assistance visits into the field. Recruiting Operations often exhausts its travel money before the end of the quarter. The department claimed that there were numerous unanticipated changes in requirements. On the other hand, many persons outside the department suggested the difficulty was the result of poor planning. Additional travel funds were eventually obtained from Chicago, and the matter was dropped.

A final function of the department is to analyze district operations and investigate "slow employment areas" or unduly large numbers of unsuccessful placements. Reports concerning these investigations are forwarded directly to the regional manager.

The members of the department averaged more than eleven years' experience and each had served in the field for up to three years as a recruiter (see Exhibit II.2). In fact, their appointment to the Recruiting Operations department was based on "outstanding performance" as a recruiter. Department members take pride in their appointments. They are a cohesive group and often socialize off the job. Norms of the operations group include: keep the recruiters in the field well informed; delays hamper accomplishment.

PERSONNEL PROBLEMS AT HOME

In recent months, word of conflict between the Recruiting Operations and Scheduling departments filtered up to Thompkins. Symptoms of conflict were numerous and varied. For example, he noted that members of each department seemed to avoid having conversations with one another whether on or off the job. On more than one occasion, he had observed a group of employees from one of the two departments quickly disperse when members of the other department entered into the discussion. Moreover, activities of the two departments have been marked by a noticeable lack of communication. On three separate occasions during the last six months, directives from the operations department to local recruiters in the field have instructed those recruiters to move out of old facilities and into new ones before the Scheduling department had finished the paperwork on the move. On another occasion, field offices were instructed by the Operations department to have additional telephone lines installed in their offices before approval had been received from Scheduling. Scheduling had an extremely difficult time justifying them after the fact, since expenditures of this nature were closely scrutinized by the Chicago office.

Richard Thompkins decided that steps must be taken to discover the underlying cause of the interdepartmental difficulties. After talking with members of each of the two departments on an informal basis, he began to make some notes to himself about the conversations. His findings are summarized as follows:

1. No one really wants to talk about the other department; most do not complain readily.

EXHIBIT II.2 DEPARTMENT MEMBERS (RECRUITING OPERATIONS AND SCHEDULING)

POSITION	NAME	AGE	YEARS' EXPERIENCE ON THE JOB
Recruiting Operations Department			
Manager	Harold Johnson	52	18
Staff	Gerald Thomas	34	8
Staff	James Lawson	38	7
Staff	Betty Jennings	36	3
Staff	Richard Horn	44	14
Staff	Joe Sutton	46	11
Staff	Gene Maddox	46	14
Staff	Gordon Edwards	49	14
Staff	Tom Campbell	36	7
Scheduling Department			
Manager	Ben Holdridge	48	9
Staff	Gary Ford	22	New employee
Staff	John McGee	34	4
Staff	Robert Webb	35	3
Staff	Barbara Peterson	24	2
Staff	Jan Owens	21	New employee

2. Members of each department believe that they are doing their job, but they claim that the other department hinders their work.

3. Attitudes of Scheduling and Personnel about the Operations department is best summed up in comment of Scheduling supervisor: "Those guys just seem to me to be pushy and self-centered. They're too much rah-rah and go-go-go. Who do they think they are, anyway?"

4. Operations department members describe the Scheduling department as "slow as hell;" "They never want to cooperate with us;" "We really care about this recruiting operation, but those guys just don't seem to understand the importance of getting to these people (potential employees) the fastest with the most!"

5. A comment from Harold Johnson: "My people know the importance of their jobs and I think they have real company loyalty. To tell you the truth, I can't say the same for the fellows in some of the other departments."

After reading over the list a couple of times, Thompkins leaned back in his chair and smiled knowingly. Later that day he called the two department heads into his office. He began his discussion by saying, "Ben, Harold, I think we have a bit of a communication problem here. It's as simple as that."

INTEGRATIVE CASE III

The Skil circular saws plant

JOHN T. TODD   *The University of Arkansas*

PART A

Bob Tegarden was named operations manager of the Skil circular saws plant in November 1984. Now, only a few months later, he was faced with several critical problems. Although he believed that one should never look back once a decision was made, he had to admit to himself some doubt about his decision to take this job. More importantly, he had to find a way to improve the plant operations.

The New Plant Manager

Tegarden had previously been employed by General Electric Corporation (GE) for twenty-eight years. Eighteen of those years had been in the large, unionized GE Consumer Products plant complex at Louisville. He had completed his bachelor's degree in business administration at the University of Louisville during that time and had gradually progressed upward in the manufacturing organization. A transfer to a new motors division plant near Nashville, Tennessee, was soon followed, in 1981, by a promotion to plant manager there. That plant employed six hundred nonunion employees.

Although he liked being plant manager, he was bothered by the plant's bare-bone budgets and limited discretion, which were by-products of GE's "cash cow" strategy for the plant's products. Therefore, in spite of the additional retirement benefits he would gain by staying on with GE, he was interested when the then-president of Skil Corporation called him with an offer to become operations manager at Skil's circular saws plant; this position was actually that of plant manager.

Even though the salary and size of plant represented no major advance, the situation appeared to be an attractive opportunity in other ways. He looked forward to managing the technically advanced plant. He was particularly impressed with the growth potential of the plant's product and Skil's aggressive strategy for accomplishing that potential. Also, the plant was located in an attractive rural resort area near Heber Springs, Arkansas, a small town seventy miles from Little Rock.

The Plant History

The new plant had commenced operations in 1979. At the time, Skil Corporation was a family-controlled, publicly traded company having headquarters in Chicago. The Heber Springs plant was designed to manufacture chain saws.

Shortly after the plant opened, Emerson Electric Co. acquired Skil Corporation. Since an Emerson subsidiary already produced another brand of chain saws, it was decided to cease production of Skil chain saws. The Heber Springs plant was then converted to production of Skil circular saws; these saws' fabrication and assembly had previously been done in various smaller Skil plants in the Chicago area. At Heber Springs, nearly all of the saws' components could be fabricated as well as assembled.

Changes in Competitive Strategy

In 1981, Emerson decided that some major changes were needed if Skil was to maintain its strong competitive position in circular saws, its most important product area. Skil was the second largest producer of small power tools in the United Sates market, trailing Black & Decker. In the worldwide market, Skil had the third largest market share. Although the industry had historically been stable, it showed signs of increasingly stiff competition. For example, a Japanese newcomer, Makita, had been gaining a significant market share in recent years. Emerson believed that future success in the circular saw market would depend upon significant improvements in both cost and quality of the Skil saws.

As part of its new strategy, Emerson also decided to consolidate circular saw production at the Heber Springs plant over the next three years (1981–1984). In order to expand the plant's production capacity and efficiency and to improve product quality, a major equipment/process modernization plan was developed. Robotics, electronic quality-control equipment, and high-technology work stations were to replace many of the manual, repetitive operations which had characterized the plant since its opening. The responsibility for the planning of the change and the acquisition of the equipment was assigned to the Advanced Manufacturing Engineering Division of Skil Corporation, located in the Chicago headquarters. The overall modernization plan was divided into sixteen major projects with a total cost exceeding $15 million, including engineering and vendor tooling.

Another important change undertaken at the same time was redesign of the circular saws. The primary reason for this change was to provide a more functional product. Additional design changes were made in order to standardize the components of the various saw models. Previously, each saw model was largely independent of the other. The new designs called for a high degree of interchangeability of parts. This allowed greater efficiency and quality in the production process, particularly given the new automated equipment.

The Plant's Management and Employees

The previous operations manager of the plant, who had started the plant in 1979, was transferred to a corporate staff position in the fall of 1984 but still maintained his home and an office at Heber Springs. Many of the managers, supervisors, and technicians had transferred from the Chicago plants as those plants were closed down.

The management of the plant was based on traditional principles, including centralized decision making and close supervision. The various functional department heads reported to the operations manager. Corporate staff was involved on a frequent basis in identifying and solving problems. Much of the plant managers' time was spent in dealing with the corporate staff. Communication between the managers and other employees was largely impersonal and one-way downward—giving directions and exercising control. The operations manager and the corporate staff relied heavily upon detailed budgets and various production reports as control tools.

The plant was planned for approximately 450 employees. During 1983 and 1984, the employment level had increased to 570 employees as the production was transferred from Chicago. The last 120 employees had been hired as "temporary" employees, with the understanding that they would not be retained when the automation equipment was received. Most employees had limited technical skills when they were hired, but they had shown a willingness to learn and to meet production standards. They had consistently demonstrated a strong work ethic. Most lived in the local rural area within a radius of approximately twenty-five miles. Approximately 60 per cent of the plant employees were female.

Management Problems

When Tegarden arrived in November 1984, he found a chaotic situation. The new equipment started to arrive the same week. No one at the plant had been involved in its acquisition, so the installation was delayed until the headquarters staff arrived. That staff was going through a transition itself and was not able to offer as much assistance as originally planned. Several pilot assemblies on the new equipment for the newly designed products were initiated with very little success. Inventory for the new products was arriving faster than it could be used. Storage of inventory took up nearly half the floor space of the plant; due to the crowded conditions, materials and parts were even stored in the aisles. Meanwhile, in order to keep up with sales, the plant was still attempting to produce the old saws—often with inadequate inventory because

purchasing of materials for those products had been phased out.

Although a commitment had been made to the employees (except the "temporaries") to keep them on after the automation, training for operation of the new equipment had not been completed. Because of the extended employment time of the temporaries (some for over a year), many had forgotten that they did not have a permanent job. Their continued employment also created severe budget overages.

To further compound the new manager's problems, the corporate staff had administered an employee-attitude survey which showed employee morale to be even lower than the previous year, which was already unsatisfactory. Employees expressed a low level of confidence in management in the surveys. Turnover had tripled in the past three years, to 2.1 percent per month.

Product quality was also a major concern. Warranty returns and scrap cost were excessive. Rework costs represented 12 percent of total direct costs, an unacceptable level. Tegarden realized that a major improvement in product quality and production efficiency was necessary for success of the plant. He also believed that the turnaround would be even more difficult to bring about because of the close direction and control exercised by the corporate staff.

PART B

Leadership

Tegarden quickly realized the low morale of the employees. Although some training had been provided in order to prepare them for the new equipment, they were still very concerned about whether they could handle the revamped production requirements. The corporate staff had been in charge of the acquisition of the equipment, and no one at the plant really knew what to expect. In addition, the plant was overcrowded with temporary employees and extra inventory.

Tegarden, in his first meeting with his staff, told them that he was not a technical expert but that he was confident that they, as a team could manage the transition ahead. He described his managerial style to them as "letting everybody do their own thing" within the teamwork parameter and that he would be there to help in any way possible. This style was quickly recognized by the staff as a departure from the previous manager's style, which was one more oriented to close supervision, technical expertise, and centralized decision making.

The staff meeting was immediately followed with a meeting of all plant employees where Tegarden quietly and impressively introduced himself and talked about his background of working himself up through the manufacturing ranks. He emphasized his dedication to an improvement of the plant for everyone's benefit and asked them for their cooperation in meeting the challenges ahead. Although initially somewhat skeptical of his intentions and abilities to accomplish the plant turnaround, the employees were impressed by the new manager's sincerity and openness.

Tegarden's actions quickly backed up his words. He delegated authority and encouraged participation of everyone affected by the various problems and decisions. He was extremely accessible, spending considerable time in consultation with others on the plant floor and in their offices. His friendly and helpful demeanor emphasized his open-door policy, both literally and symbolically. He always took time to discuss with employees their personal concerns and interests. At the same time, he never missed an opportunity to promote the importance of improved product quality, new cost-saving ideas, and plantwide teamwork. He publicly recognized special plant achievements, such as production of the millionth saw of the particular model during a year, with celebration parties and mementos (coffee mugs, t-shirts, etc.) for all employees. He also expanded the annual picnic for employees and their families; in 1988, employees planned and implemented the picnic with a twenty-thousand-dollar budget.

Decentralization

Within a year of Tegarden's arrival, there was a significant change of management at Skil headquarters. A new president and three new vice-presidents replaced the existing officials; one of the positions was the vice-president of manufacturing, to whom Tegarden reported. Although initially unsettling, the change quickly created a new opportunity for the plant. Previously, the division staff in Chicago had closely controlled the plant decisions and operations; the new management team decided to eliminate the close involvement of the divisional staff.

In effect, this change meant a decentralization to the plant of many decisions and activities previously reserved at the division level. For example, more of the capital budget formulation was now done at the plant. One of the plant staff, when asked about the impact of the decentralization, said, "They showed that they had confidence in us by letting us run this plant. They began to let us plan and control our own destiny." At the time, given the magnitude of the problems facing the plant, the new independence was not viewed entirely as an unmixed blessing.

Open Communication

As described above, Tegarden from the beginning signaled greater openness of communication. In addition to the informal daily contacts with employees on the shop floor and in the lunchroom, he has regularly participated in three scheduled meetings:

1. Daily half-hour meetings with his staff for open discussion of plant operating results, problems, and plans.
2. Two informal "roundtables" monthly with employees who have birthdays that month. Tegarden usually makes some opening comments about plant accomplishments and plans, then opens up the meeting for questions and answers while a birthday cake is served. If an answer is not available to a question, one is always provided within four working days. A transcript of all questions and answers is posted on bulletin boards for everyone to see. Transcripts of recent meetings reflected a wide range of topics. For example, employee ideas were advanced for new products, plant recreational facilities, new distribution outlets, modification of product design, and improved working conditions.
3. A quarterly meeting of all employees to keep them informed of progress toward goals, using ten measures such as quality and cost savings (the same measures that are reported to the Skil president). The business outlook for the plant is also presented, along with information on new plant programs. For example, at a recent meeting, Tegarden made a presentation about the objectives and techniques of Statistical Process Control (SPC); this was done primarily in order to inform those who had not yet received SPC training.

The emphasis on open communication extends throughout the plant. In addition to daily informal contacts with his or her employees, each foreman meets with the whole group of employees in the conference room one hour monthly to discuss items of particular interest and importance to that group. The transcript of the questions and answers from each meeting is reviewed by the plant manager as another means of identifying problems and ideas, as well as another way of understanding what is on the employee's minds. Topics typically range from safety, housekeeping, quality, and scheduling to future equipment acquisitions and training programs, Recent foremen comments in the transcripts include the following:

> "This plant is a showcase for SKIL and with the increased sales and staff, keeping it clean and orderly is a task that requires the cooperation and determination of each individual here. THANKS for a job well done!!!"

> "Since January there have been twenty-six recordable accidents in this plant. . . . Accidents do unfortunately occur but let's keep on our toes and try to prevent these accidents through safe job practices before one of us becomes the next accident victim."

> "We are making the best circular saws in the world. This is because everyone is doing such a good job."

It was noted that the emphasis on open communication also now comes down from the corporate level. The Skil president visits the plant quarterly for a business review with the plant staff. He also talks to all employees in an open meeting in December each year. Other Skil staff also visit the plant as needed for assistance; their approach is described by the plant staff as being supportive, rather than directive.

Training Programs

The company made a major commitment to training and education of employees. This was done initially as a means of preparing the employees for the new technology. Only half of the employees had high school diplomas, so the plant developed and supported basic courses such as math, blueprint reading, computers, and tool measurement. More advanced training was provided for those operating and maintaining the automated equipment. Practically every employee's

skills were upgraded through one or more courses or training visits to vendor's plants.

Throughout the transition, the guiding philosophy was to "grow our own" rather than going outside to hire new employees with the required expertise. This was reflected in the policy that no permanent employees would be put out of work by the automation. The company estimated that over $500,000 were spent on employee training and education during the initial automation installation. That commitment was continued as new technology and processes have been added. For example, employees are now being trained on company time in SPC at an estimated cost of $180,000 for this year. (The plant manager was in the first SPC training group, spending sixty hours in the program.) Cross-training of employees, which enables them to perform more than one job, has also been initiated on a limited basis; this allows more flexibility in responding to production and maintenance needs while at the same time upgrading employee skills.

In addition to technical training, supervisory training has become a priority. A week-long training session sponsored by Emerson emphasizes communication skills for all new foremen. The plant manager provides ideas and information covering topics such as product distributors, quality, and safety for foremen to use in their monthly meetings. He also meets quarterly with the foremen as a group away from the plant in order to provide coaching and other assistance.

Evaluation and Rewards System

Plant hourly employees' pay is based on each job's labor grade; within the grade, there is a progression of steps available from entry rate to one for fulfilling the job requirements, and then to two premium steps for superior performance. The range within each labor grade is approximately 20 percent. Hourly employees are evaluated annually by their supervisors on the basis of work quantity, work quality, reliability and attitude. That evaluation determines the progress of the employees through the steps within each job's labor grade. In addition to the corresponding pay increases for those advancing a step, all hourly employees receive an increase about once a year for a general percentage increase of the pay structure which is authorized by the corporation.

The plant has followed a policy of filling job openings with current employees who wish to move to a higher labor grade. Selection for job openings up to group leader is based on past performance, qualifications to meet minimum job requirements, and length of service. The length of service prevails if the other factors are similar for the applicants.

Supervisors are evaluated annually on a broader range of factors than those applied to the hourly employees. Part of the evaluation is based on the degree of success in meeting departmental goals that are mutually established between the supervisor and his or her superior at the beginning of each year for such factors as productivity, product quality, maintenance of area, and absenteeism. Other evaluation factors include communication, innovation, reliability, and planning, delegation, cooperation, cost consciousness, and training of personnel. Specific objectives for the next period are established at the same time the evaluation takes place. Salary increases are based on the performance evaluations. An outstanding performer would likely get approximately twice the average, a poor performer might get no increase. The average percent of increase for all exempt employees at the plant is determined by the corporation; that was 4 percent last year.

An employee suggestion system has produced significant results. a total of 845 suggestions have been submitted in the past five years, of which 268 were implemented. Suggestion awards are paid to the person(s) responsible at the rate of 10 percent of the annual savings. For non-savings ideas, such as safety improvement, $25 is awarded. Examples of recent suggestions include the following:

1. Modification of a sanding fixture in the die cast department. Annual savings estimated at $37,172.
2. Changing cutting procedure on screw machine. $10,994 annual savings estimated.
3. A team of four hourly employees came in voluntarily on Saturdays and solved the problems to make four workstations on a new line operable. The problems had previously defied extensive "expert" attention. Estimated first-year savings over $30,000.

Recipients of awards receive not only cash but also extensive recognition from the management staff as well as credit on performance reviews.

Supervisors and other salaried employees who share a related interest in, or responsibility for, certain broad work areas form Operations Improvement Teams. The teams' stated objective is to "assist management in achieving plant goals by analyzing operations, recommending improvements, and implementing change." The primary focus is on cost savings, and each team has a savings goal for the year; the total for all teams for 1989 is over $1.5 million. Although a sizable portion of the anticipated savings can be specifically identified with new equipment and technology, the goals still represent a significant challenge for team innovations. Team performance as well as individual performance within the team become part of the employees' performance review. All staff members are assigned to a team, including Tegarden.

The use of the multi-discipline teams just described reflects not only the plant's emphasis on innovation but also the emphasis on cooperation of the various functional specialties within the plant. The teamwork concept is also emphasized in the departmental measures of productivity, which are based strictly on out-the-door production. This means that it is in everybody's interest to help each other break a bottleneck when necessary. For example, if one department is running behind, employees may be "loaned" to that department from other departments until it is caught up.

One other noteworthy aspect of the evaluation system is the reaction to failures. This reaction was described by an employee as follows: "At one time, a failure meant unemployment. Local and corporate management has now given us room to fail. So, now we reach, rather than take a safe, conservative approach."

Delegation of Authority

Along with increased information and training, production employees were also given more authority for getting their job done. Each employee is now responsible for the quality of the product when it leaves his or her workstation. A new non-synchronous assembly line technology allows any employee to delay forwarding a saw until he or she is satisfied with its quality. When the employees started controlling their pace on the assembly line, their productivity immediately increased by 10 percent—and quality improved, too.

As part of a move toward self-inspection, traditional inspectors were removed from the production process. The finished tools were still sampled by a small group of "auditors," but the primary responsibility for quality now resides with the production employees. The SPC training for the employees further reflects this self-inspection philosophy, allowing still more authority to be delegated to the employees for quick response to quality problems.

Results

The Heber Springs plant has shown significant improvement since 1984 on several dimensions. Production volume has increased by 30 percent with 30 percent fewer production employees. Plant management estimates that one-half of the productivity improvement can be directly attributed to automation; the remainder is attributed to better quality and processes which have been developed from the cooperative efforts and training of the employees and plant staff.

Quality improvements have received the most attention. Warranty returns and end-of-line rejects have each decreased by 75 to 80 percent. Scrap cost per saw has been reduced by two-thirds. In 1984, rework costs represented 12 percent of total direct costs; in 1988, it was 1 percent. All of these statistics represent drastic improvements in the quality of the products produced by the plant. That has been cited by management as the primary reason for increased market share the past two years, especially in the professional end of the market.

Another significant improvement has been a reduction of inventory from 5.5 million to 1.25 million. The just-in-time system has been implemented with great success, thereby reducing investment and also providing space in the plant for more machines.

Monthly employee turnover has been reduced from 2.1 percent to 1.3 percent. Based on an analysis of employee opinion surveys conducted at the Heber Springs plant by the corporate personnel department, that department concluded that the 1987 survey scores had "improved significantly" since the prior survey, conducted in 1985. Improved scores were cited at all levels of the plant. Following are scores from the hourly workers on selected items (five-point scale, with three being average and five being the most positive):

Question (abbreviated)	1985	1987
Pride in plant	3.60	3.76
Management of plant	2.70	3.25
Management interest in employees	2.80	3.09
We believe management	2.80	3.17
Quality of plant's work	—	3.65
Efforts for cost effectiveness	—	3.61
Understand need for changes	—	4.08
Direct supervisor does good job	3.70	3.44
Supervisor listens to suggestions	2.60	3.37
Overall job satisfaction	3.30	3.45
Communication from management	2.80	3.29
Job training received for job	2.60	3.26
Treated as an individual	3.10	3.31

The improved climate of the plant, as expressed by the employees on the 1987 survey, offers further support for the transformation which seems to have started in 1985. Personal leadership, improved communication, job training, encouragement of suggestions, and greater confidence in management have all been important factors in creating the improved climate.

The Outlook for the Future

In spite of the plant's recent success, Tegarden realizes that the plant cannot rest on its laurels. Along with the continuing Japanese competition, the industry leader, Black & Decker Corp., is now aggressively rebounding from an extended downturn in its business. It is likely that the circular saw business will be increasingly competitive.

His overall view of Skil's competitive strategy was expressed as follows: "Quality is the spearhead; productivity, cost reductions, and customer satisfaction will follow." He also predicted that an increasingly important competitive factor will be flexibility—the ability to respond quickly to sudden changes in customer needs. This poses an additional challenge for the plant: to make these quick adjustments while at the same time maintaining operating efficiency and quality.

Tegarden expects continuing process improvements from new equipment and technology; for example, further automation and additional implementation of SPC is expected to improve quality and costs in the next year. Looking ahead, however, he believes that further sustained improvement in product quality, manufacturing cost, and customer responsiveness will be partially dependent upon a broader approach. With this mind, he is considering development of a formal strategic plan for management of the Heber Springs plant. He is particularly interested in what the stra-tegic plan should include as well as in other ideas which could further increase the effectiveness of the plant.

INTEGRATIVE CASE IV

Davis regional medical center

DONALD D. WHITE   *University of Arkansas*

Davis Regional Medical Center is an acute care, general hospital located in Charlesville, a community of 35,000 in the southwestern United States. The organization was founded as a thirty-five-bed facility known as Davis County Hospital. The hospital grew to a capacity of fifty-five beds after its first three years of operation. Economic growth in the region along with a rapid influx of people resulted in additional expansions, and in eighteen years the hospital had reached its present capacity of 166 beds.

The population in the region has grown steadily over the last fifteen years (approximately a 53 percent increase). However, the hospital size has remained unchanged. Approximately five hundred people are employed at Davis. The medical staff consists of seventy-five doctors and dentists. A substantial ma-jority of the medical staff are specialists. Therefore, the hospital offers a wide range of medical services. Current estimates are that the hospital serves ten thousand inpatients and approximately sixteen thou-sand outpatients each year.

REGIONAL MEDICAL CENTER

Three years ago, the hospital's board of directors concluded that it was necessary to undertake a major expansion of the hospital's physical plant if it were to continue to serve residents adequately in and around the Charlesville area. Hospital managers and board members had received many complaints about over-crowded conditions in the hospital. Beds for patients were often found in the halls and waiting rooms, considerable delays were experienced by new patients

registering at the hospital due to the lack of available space, and many offices and hallways had become storage places for inventory materials and equipment. At one point, State Health Department officials informed hospital administrators that if equipment and cartons of supplies were not removed from various hallways, the hospital would not be licensed for the coming year and therefore could not be accredited by the Joint Commission (a national accrediting agency).

The situation had become critical by the time the final decision was made on the expansion. It was decided that a major building effort costing $12 million would be undertaken. The number of beds in the medical facility were to be increased from 166 to 248, and a number of existing services were to be expanded in the new facility. Shortly after the expansion decision was made, the board also changed the name of the hospital from Davis County Hospital to Davis Regional Medical Center. The purpose of this name change was to reflect more accurately the services available and the population served by the growing medical complex. A fund-raising drive in Charlesville managed to provide a base of $1 million with which to begin the expansion. However, a feasibility study completed during the drive suggested that the hospital's perfor-mance (based on past figures) could not financially support the total planned expansion. Therefore, a revised plan was decided on.

ADMINISTRATIVE AND ORGANIZATIONAL BACKGROUND

Davis Regional Medical Center, like similar county hospitals in the state, is governed by a seven-member board of directors. State law provided that the board be appointed by the local county judge. As with any political system, appointments are based on a combination of individual qualifications and the political postures of board members. Historically, the board had not provided strong leadership to the hospital. However, recent appointments, together with strong leadership from a new board chairman, had greatly increased the activity and contribution of the board to the operation of the hospital.

The administrator of any county hospital is placed in a unique position of having to respond to political pressures and medical needs of the people whom he or she serves. In addition, such administrators are often found between pressures created by their medical staffs, employees, and the public. The toll these pressures create is sometimes quite high. Such was the case at Davis Regional Medical Center. Within a ten-year period, the hospital had four separate administrators. Three of those administrators and the one acting administrator have served in the position during the last five years (see Exhibit IV.1).

Reasons for the turnovers were numerous. One administrator, Frederick Harold, was asked to resign after the hospital lost more than $250,000 in a period of two years. His replacement, Glenda Easton, was charged with the responsibility of putting the hospital back in the black. Within one year, Easton had done so. However, during the end of her term as administrator, her decisions affecting patients and employees

alike became more and more autocratic and seemingly unrealistic. For example, she once forced an orderly to enter the room of a critically ill patient to collect a dollar-a-day charge for TV service. She had instructed the employee to collect one dollar from each patient each day the patient was in the room. Acts such as these received considerable attention throughout the community. Later, it was discovered that Easton had leukemia, and she retired from her position as administrator. (A number of her later decisions were attributed, in part, by those around her to her illness.) Her replacement was Robert Winston, who had served as assistant administrator under his predecessor for two years.

Winston served as administrator of the hospital for three years until he was asked to resign. Persons who worked with the hospital during his tenure as administrator (outside consultants and hospital managers), described him as unimaginative and unwilling to put in the necessary work to develop and maintain a strong medical facility. In his final months as administrator, he was on the hospital premises from four to six hours a day. Although reasons for his requested resignation were never made public, personal problems that were believed to interfere with the fulfillment of his administrative responsibilities were cited by the board.

Due to the suddenness with which Winston had been asked to tender his resignation, the board had not yet begun its search for a new administrator. In

EXHIBIT IV.I   PAST ADMINISTRATION AT DRMC

ADMINISTRATOR	YEARS EMPLOYED	REASON FOR TERMINATION
G.B.	4	Under pressure to resign (personal)
B.C.	2	A series of problems both financial and political, asked to resign
H.M. (R.N.)	7	Considered to be a good administrator; resigned under positive circumstances; she may have felt the job was becoming too big for her
F.H.	5	Hospital showed a $250,000 loss; was asked to resign
G.E.	4	Illness; under mild pressure to resign
R.W.	3	Was asked to resign
C.B.	I	Currently the DRMC Administrator

the interim period of five months, Donald Dale, who served as assistant administrator under Winston, was named as acting administrator. He was closely assisted by Larry Engels, the director of personnel. The two men worked closely as a team, making day-to-day operating decisions.

Dale and Engels were aware of acute employee morale and motivation problems within the medical center. They attributed these problems to the lack of leadership under which the hospital had been operating and employee concerns about what the new administrator would be like. Both had recently attended a seminar for hospital administrators in which the importance of employee attitudes and participation had been a major subject. In particular, they had been impressed by the discussion and illustration of a management by objectives (MBO) system designed for health care organizations. They were convinced that such a system would help create greater esprit de corps at Davis Regional Medical Center and improve the exchange of ideas and information among department heads within the hospital. Furthermore, the director of personnel believed that supervisory and department head training programs would have to be conducted in order to prepare management personnel throughout the organization for the hoped for MBO-type system.

In July, the director of personnel contacted Dr. John Connors, university professor and management consultant. Earlier that year, Connors had presented the administrative seminar Engels and Dale attended. They arranged to meet together and to discuss the present situation at Davis Regional Medical Center. During the next month, the two administrators and Connors met on numerous occasions and discussed the problems and needs of the hospital.

Both Dale and Engels were emphatic about wanting to develop a more employee-oriented administration. For example, they created a nonsupervisory employee council that met once a month to discuss with the two men problems and conditions throughout the hospital. The intended purpose of this council was to provide a means by which Dale and Engels could enhance two-way communication between the hospital administration and the employees at Davis. Each department elected one person to represent them in the council. Initially, most of the communication was from the top down. However, shortly after the council had been created, a core of employees rose to take leadership of the group. They elected a spokesperson and requested that they be permitted to meet once a

month without either Dale or Engels present. Thereafter, the employee representatives met twice monthly, once with the administrators and once without them.

Dale and Engels also shared the view that some form of management training should be developed and conducted for department heads and hospital supervisors, whom they saw as the key to hospital effectiveness. There was some hesitancy on the part of Connors and Dale to initiate such a program before the selection of a new administrator. Both men believed it might be unfair to saddle a new administrator with a program he or she might not favor. The director of personnel, however, felt strongly that the program should be initiated "as soon as possible."

Such a program subsequently was designed by Connors and agreed on by the three men. Shortly thereafter, Dale was informed that a new administrator had been selected by the Board of Directors. The new administrator was scheduled to take over his post at DRMC in approximately four weeks. Dale told Connors that his discussions with the new administrator, Arnold Benson, led him to believe that Benson would be favorable to a management development program. However, both men decided to wait until a formal meeting could be held with Benson before proceeding with the actual program.

A NEW LEADER FOR THE "TROOPS"

Arnold Benson came to Davis Hospital from a multi-facility complex in St. Louis, Missouri. He had been selected out of seventy applicants for the position of administrator at Davis County Hospital. Benson was a young man, thirty-three years of age. He held bachelor's and master's degrees in business administration and had considerable experience working in hospital organizations. In his words, "My objective was to become a professional hospital administrator. I realized that since I did not yet have a master's degree in hospital administration I would have to go with a 'back door approach' by working my way up the ranks.

Thus, Benson's first position in a hospital was that of director of purchasing and personnel in a 118-bed facility. He next took the position of assistant administrator in a 156-bed Catholic hospital. In a period of two years, he rose from assistant administrator to associate administrator and finally to that of administrator of the hospital. Finally he became administrator of a 144-bed and a 134-bed multi-hospital complex in St. Louis, Missouri. He remained in the hospital for four years "gaining exposure, experience and expertise." Before his hospital experiences, Benson had worked for a year and a half on a General Motors assembly line while going to college. He had also spent four years in the Marine Corps, having enlisted when he was seventeen years old.

A few months before, Arnold Benson had begun looking for a new position as a hospital administrator. He believed he had learned a great deal in his present job; however, he was anxious to relocate in a smaller community. The St. Louis Hospital of which he was administrator was located in a drug-plagued, low-income area. His hospital had been a prime target for numerous union drives (none of which were successful) and he had overseen a major expansion of the hospital facilities. He wanted to relocate in a community of less than 50,000 population somewhere in the southwestern United States. His salary requirements were rather stringent due to his experience in administration. Therefore, he was very pleased when he was selected as the new administrator at Davis Regional.

Benson was a tall, athletic-looking man whose mild manners and easy-going Texas drawl tended to hide his down-to-business approach to administration. Soon after arriving, he realized he would be facing many problems inside and outside the hospital in the next few months. He knew the most pressing of these was the hospital expansion. Moreover, it was clear to him that the first concern of certain members of the board of directors was the hospital's financial position.

Financial concerns plagued Benson from the moment he arrived at Davis Regional Medical Center. During his first weeks on the job, the building program finances consumed almost 50 percent of his time. In addition, two particular decisions, both of which would have a direct impact on hospital employees, had to be made.

The first decision concerned a 10-percent across-the-board pay increase that was due to all hospital employees in January. Benson had not been told of this promised increase until he had been at the hospital for some time. Immediately upon learning of the proposed increase, he sat down and calculated its impact on his budget. The total cost of the medical center appeared to be well in excess of $200,000. Feeling the need to hold the line on expenses, Mr. Benson decided not to put through the wage increase. In his words, "When I 'came aboard,' the board charged me with the financial responsibility of the medical center. If the troops were to get their pay

increase in January, it would throw the entire budget out of kilter. I have only been here three weeks, and quite frankly the budget didn't get the attention it deserved." After making his decision, Benson dictated a memo announcing that while employees at Davis could expect to receive up to a 6 percent increase for the new year, the 10-percent across-the-board increase would not be given. Mr. Benson also stressed that the total financial posture of the hospital would have to be reevaluated. The memo was posted on the employee bulletin board.

Soon after the memo was posted, a rumor circulated throughout the hospital that the board of directors was about to purchase a new automobile for Benson. Pictures of Cadillacs and Mark IV Continentals were placed on the bulletin board on an almost daily basis. His memo concerning denial of the pay increase was slashed with a knife and various comments were written on it. (The hospital-owned automobile which Benson actually used was a Ford Galaxy driven by the previous administrator.)

Recognizing the discontent over his decision, Benson met with members of the employee advisory council to discuss the pay question. Several members of the group quoted statistics showing that on the average blue-collar workers throughout the United States were being paid more than were most hospital employees. Benson replied that he thought it was unfair to quote blue-collar statistics and that he believed the most that a hospital employee at the medical center could look forward to would be to live comfortably. He then asked the members of the advisory council if they would work harder if they received a 10 percent increase. According to Benson, "When all responded negatively, I told them point blank that it appeared that it would be foolish to reward people ten more cents per hour with no increase in productivity." He did go on to tell those present that he would do his best to see to it that they received some pay increases (up to 6 percent based on merit) as soon as the necessary funds became available. In addition, he told them that he hoped to put in effect a new wage and salary administration program in the near future.

The employee council also voiced complaints about other conditions at Davis hospital. Over a period of the next few weeks, Benson saw to it that many of the problems were dealt with to the group's satisfaction. However, when the last "demand" was met he announced that he believed there was no longer a need for the advisory group. A question was raised by one employee about whether the group would be permitted to re-form if subsequent problems arose. Benson replied that it would not be permitted to do so.

Benson was confronted by a second important decision not long after the incident involving the pay increase memo. The hospital had been able to obtain the money necessary for expansion through tax exempt revenue bonds. However, the building program itself did not include much-needed parking lots. Arnold Benson, therefore, found it necessary to take his request for an additional $1.3 million to the local banking community. Although the bankers agreed to underwrite the project, the feasibility study on which their decision was based indicated that the parking lots would have to be income-generating entities in their own right. Before this time, all parking in hospital lots was provided without charge to the medical staff, employees, and visitors. Now, however, it was clear to Benson that *all* parties would in the future be required to pay a parking fee.

Although he expected resistance on the issue from the doctors, he was more concerned about the reactions of general employees to the decision. The fact that he had been confronted by this second decision so shortly after his refusal to grant the across-the-board pay increase further aggravated his situation. As far as Benson was concerned, the decision had been made. However, he and Connors agreed that its announcement should be temporarily postponed.

MANAGEMENT DEVELOPMENT

In early January, department heads from throughout the hospital began meeting with Connors as part of an overall management development program. (See Exhibit IV.2 for information on program participants.) Those participating met in a series of seven two-hour

EXHIBIT IV.2   MANAGERIAL PERSONNEL ON PAYROLL WHEN BENSON WAS HIRED

EMPLOYEE	DEPARTMENT	TENURE WITH DRMC YEARS EMPLOYED	YEARS AS DEPARTMENT HEAD
J.C.	Physical Therapy	25	21
D.T.	Nuclear Medicine	18	6
D.D.	Assistant Administrator	11½	11½
B.G.	Housekeeping	9	2
G.H.	Radiology	8½	8½
K.F.	Nursing	7	2½
L.H.	Dietary	7	7
L.E.	Personnel	5	4
J.H.	EMS	5	1
P.G.	Purchasing	4	1
L.C.	Child Care	4	3
T.M.	Pharmacy	4	2
E.B.	Laboratory	7	2½
D.B.	Medical Records	2½	2½
J.G.	Maintenance	2½	2½
L.P.	Respiratory Therapy	2	2
E.I.	Social Service	1	1
M.R.	Volunteers	1	1
M.K.	Comptroller	1	1

Explanation:
1. Two new departments, EKG and EEG, were added shortly after Benson's arrival. Previously, their functions and personnel were under Nuclear Medicine.
2. Of those department heads listed, the following persons left DRMC within six months after Benson's arrival. K.F. (resignation requested); L.H. (resigned following demotion); L.E. (resignation requested); P.G. (resigned, but was to have been replced); E.B. (resigned to take promotion elsewhere); L.P. (resigned to take a similar position elsewhere; was dissatisfied at DRMC).

sessions. The total program took place over a period of approximately one month. (A similar program was conducted for supervisors during the following month.)

According to Dale, the purpose of the management programs was twofold. He believed it was necessary to provide those hospital employees in management positions with some form of supervisory training. He also felt the program would be a good way to single out the department heads and supervisors for special attention.

The sessions were recommended to the department heads and supervisors by Benson; however, participation remained voluntary. All but two department heads attended the series of sessions. (Although Benson and Dale requested that they be permitted to attend the classes, it was agreed that their presence might inhibit the participation of department heads. Both men were provided with copies of all materials distributed, but neither attended the formal sessions.)

The content of the programs included such traditional subjects as the elements and techniques of supervision. However, emphasis was also placed on achieving improved interpersonal relations among department heads and improving the exchange of information between the departments themselves (see Exhibit IV.3).

One event that took place during the sessions dramatized that a certain amount of distrust and lack of cooperation existed among many department heads throughout the hospital. During one early session, the participants were asked to complete evaluation forms to be used in connection with an exercise known as the Johari Window. The purposes of the exercise were to help the managers see themselves more clearly as others saw them and to help others in the group in a similar manner by providing them with "image feedback" information. The theory behind the exercise together with its purposes were explained to those present. Each manager was asked to write the name of every department head (including himself or herself) and to list at least one asset and one liability of that person. Connors requested that the completed forms be returned to him at the beginning of the next session. The name of the individual providing the feedback information was not to be placed on the sheet itself. Connors explained that he would facilitate the exchange of feedback at the next session by reading the name of a participant followed by the assets and liabilities as they were identified by peers.

As planned, Connors began the next session by asking that all feedback sheets be passed in to him. Much to his surprise, only about half of the sheets were returned and most of them were insufficiently completed. After a short pause, he asked those present to explain why they had failed to complete the assignment. Following a brief discussion, it was evident that the department heads had decided in another

EXHIBIT IV.3   OUTLINE OF SUPERVISORY DEVELOPMENTAL PROGRAM, DAVIS REGIONAL MEDICAL CENTER

SESSION[1]	ASSIGNMENTS
1 Introductory comments and an icebreaker supervisory functions: Models and the environment preparing for our sessions	Case study
2 The hospital organization. Authority, power, and informal relationships	Case study ch. 15[2]
3 Understanding ourselves and others	Case study
4 Leading and motivating employees	Case study, film ch. 1, 2
5 Improving interpersonal and interdepartmental communications	Ch. 4, nominal grouping exercise, role play
6 Setting goals and making decisions	Case study, role play, ch. 6, 9
7 Evaluating and handling employee conflicts	Ch. 11, 12, case study, role play

[1]Sessions—(1 hour and 50 minutes; last 15–20 minutes spent answering questions and dealing with problems on an individual basis.)

[2]Chapters were taken from a hospital supervisory management book selected for the program by Connors

meeting that they would not complete the feedback sheet. Reasons for not wanting to complete the assignment ranged from claims that the participants did not know one another well enough (before the management program many of the department heads did not know one another by name, although a get-acquainted exercise was used in the first session) to fear that the information assembled on each individual would in some way be used against him or her. One woman openly expressed concern that other department heads at the meeting might misuse the information. Another head privately suggested that some of those in attendance thought that Connors himself might take the information to the administrator. The discussion that followed the failure to hand in the assignment had a cathartic effect on the group. For the first time, many of those in attendance opened up and talked about the lack of communication and trust that existed among the department heads and between the department heads and the administrator.

Connors ended the session by again explaining that the purpose of the exercise was to "improve our understandings of ourselves as well as of those with whom we associate throughout the hospital." After another brief discussion, it was agreed by all that the feedback sheets would be completed and returned at the following session. At that next session, the exercise was completed smoothly. Many managers commented afterwards that they believed the exercise had been beneficial and had helped open up the group. One department head did comment, however, "To tell you the truth, I think our refusal to complete the feedback sheets helped to break the ice between us. You know, it it the first time we really ever got together and agreed on something."

Subsequent sessions of the department head development program produced many positive comments and favorable evaluations of the overall program. Upon completion of the program, each participant received a certificate signed by Benson and Connors.

FOLLOWUP

A few days after the department heads' program was completed, Benson asked Connors to meet with him. He began their conference by stating that he was pleased with what he had heard about the sessions and was anxious to insure that the momentum that had been created would not be lost. He asked Connors what he thought of bringing all of the department heads together for a weekend retreat at a resort area

not far from Charlesville. Connors was pleased with Benson's suggestion. He told the administrator that he had seriously considered recommending such a retreat, but was hesitant to do so because of the financial situation at the hospital. Benson replied that the money for the retreat could be found since he anticipated that the outcome of the retreat would have a positive impact on the operation of the facility.

The following week, Benson told department heads at their weekly meeting on January 31 that the retreat had been scheduled for the weekend of February 14 and 15. He went on to explain that the department heads would gather on Friday morning at the hospital and would drive directly to the resort. All expenses would be paid by the medical center. He told them that he hoped that the meeting would permit a free exchange of ideas.

During the week before the scheduled retreat, Connors received an invitation from Benson to meet with the department heads in their meeting on Thursday. Connors agreed to do so as long as neither Benson nor Dale would be present at the meeting.

The meeting itself brought quite a surprise. It was immediately evident to Connors that the mood of the department heads was not what he had expected. As he walked into the room he heard the men and women present voicing numerous complaints to one another. When they saw Connors the group immediately quieted down. It was not clear to him whether they had been told he would be attending the meeting. Therefore, he explained his presence and told them that he was interested in how things had been going during the two or three weeks since their last session. Much to his surprise, the grumbling began immediately. Some complaints were minor. However, one complaint in particular took Connors by surprise. That complaint focused on the upcoming retreat. A few department heads stated that they did not know whether they would go to the resort with the rest of the group. One newly married woman stated that it was Valentine's Day and her husband did not want her to leave. Two other heads said they had previous plans to attend a Valentine's Day dance at the Country Club that Friday evening. As discussion continued, it became apparent that the department heads had been told rather than consulted about the retreat. Some expressed displeasure with being forced into going to the retreat and using part of their weekend without first being asked their opinion.

Connors listened carefully and explained to the managers that he himself believed that the retreat was a good idea. He told them about how he had planned on suggesting such an activity to the administrator, but how Benson had come up with the idea on his own. Moreover, he told them that he believed that they should give Benson "a chance" during the weekend to see what might come out of the retreat. There were a few supportive comments made by one or two department heads and the meeting broke up.

Connors left the meeting disturbed. He had not expected to find this level of dissatisfaction among the department heads. As he walked toward the entrance of the hospital, he asked himself whether he should try to provide any further assistance to Benson before the group left for the retreat the next morning. He decided to stop in and see the administrator before leaving the hospital.

INTEGRATIVE CASE V

Electro-Tec, Inc.

ROBERT E. COX   *University of Arkansas*

The day had been productive, as had many others during Kristin Turner's short tenure at Electro-Tec. Kristin had begun work at Electro-Tec as the company's first vice-president of human resources only two months ago, but she had learned and accomplished much in that short period. As the late afternoon winter sun began to set outside her window, Kristin reflected on what she had found at Electro-Tec and the issues that still had to be addressed.

Kristin's first in-depth discussion with Bill Cunningham, chairman and CEO, was still fresh in her mind. "Things are not as they should be at Electro-Tec," was his opening comment. He continued, "It's not like the early days when everyone was on fire to get the job done. People are not nearly as enthused or committed anymore, and it shows. I think we are starting to have some people problems, and I don't know why. We may have been a little late in getting focused on our human resource issues, but that's the reason you're here Ms. Turner, and I want you to start getting the organization back on track."

Cunningham continued, "Our job at Electro-Tec is to produce high-quality, specialized integrated circuits for our industry customers. All our efforts must be directed to that end. If our quality goes down, or if we fail to meet our delivery promises, we won't be in business very long. Lately, I'm worried about our performance in both areas.

"We have some specific business targets for the next three years. We want to double our sales each year, increase the quality index by 5 percent each year, and improve our on-time delivery performance by 10 percent each year. To accomplish all that, our employees have to do a lot better than they are doing right now. In fact, we will all have to do better; not to mention having to add new people to the organization to meet higher production requirements."

Cunningham looked Kristin straight in the eye, "You must understand, we have grown very quickly, and we do not have the mechanics in place to ensure orderly future growth. Your job is to tell us what we should be doing with our people in order to meet our goals. Technology will carry us only so far. If we do not have a capable, committed team at Electro-Tec, we are going to be, at best, an average organization. And that's one thing I won't settle for."

As a result of her discussion with Bill Cunningham, Kristin clearly understood her charge and knew that she had his solid backing.

COMPANY BACKGROUND

Electro-Tec was a modern-day success story, growing in five years from a handful of engineers and technicians into an organzation of almost five hundred employees. Electro-Tec was located on a hundred-acre campus-like site in a high-tech industrial park in a Columbia, Maryland, suburb. The facility was just about midway between Baltimore and Washington, D.C.

Electro-Tec supplied electronics manufacturers with custom-designed, high-quality integrated circuits (ICs) for unique product applications. Production runs usually averaged two to three weeks, with several products being made at the same time. Most production activities were carried out in clean rooms, while design and computer support work was done in conventional office and computer areas. Research work was done in both the laboratory and office. The administrative and executive offices were located in a separate building, adjacent to the engineering and manufacturing facility.

The first few steps in developing a formal organization structure at Electro-Tec had been taken last year when five divisions were formed. Those divisions included Research, Manufacturing, Marketing and Sales, Administration, and Human Resources. Each was headed by a vice-president who reported directly to Cunningham. Previously, work had been organized around projects, with a small administrative staff supporting all engineering and manufacturing work.

Fortunately, qualified individuals were available from within Electro-Tec to fill the newly created vice president positions, except in the area of Human Resources (HR). Consequently, all of the new divisions got off to a flying start, with the noted exception of HR. It had taken Cunningham nearly ten months to locate and hire Kristin Turner and then bring her on board. At first, the press of day-to-day business kept Cunningham from filling the HR position. Finally, he had called on an executive search firm to assist him. A number of candidates had been screened, and Kristin Turner had been selected.

HUMAN RESOURCE FUNCTIONS

Prior to Kristin's arrival, the personnel functions and activities had been handled by the line organizations. For example, the accounting department was responsible for getting all new employees signed onto the payroll, including arranging their deductions, saving bonds, insurance, etc. The accounting department also handled all the paper work for employee status changes, department transfers and other related matters. Each division was responsible for its own help-wanted advertising, did its own interviewing, and made its own hiring decisions. In the early days, Cunningham had done the hiring, but as the company grew, he had had to delegate the job to others.

Salary offers and merit promotional increases were determined by the respective divisions, but were reviewed by a committee consisting of Cunningham and the vice presidents. Each vice president was expected to keep "book" on his own employees, and, if he or she felt that a particular salary action was appropriate, the executive committee normally went along with the recommendation. The committee usually met once or twice each month but more often if necessary. Bill Cunningham had expressed confidence in the system of salary administration (all of Electro-Tec's employees were on salary, and there was no bargaining unit). He once asked, "Who knows more about what a person's worth is than his boss (the vice presidents)?"

There had been a sporadic effort on the part of a few divisions when first formed to develop written job descriptions for their employees. But the press of the work at hand had caused this effort to dwindle away. Only generic titles were used to describe positions (e.g., accountant, technician, engineers, etc.) and there were no written descriptions of duties or responsibilities.

PERFORMANCE AND REWARD

Cunningham had decided early on that if Electro-Tec was to succeed, the people in the organization would have to be above-average performers. He would also have to recognize and reward that performance. He had therefore initiated a performance appraisal program which identified three levels of performance:

▶ Above average, 3 points
▶ Average, 2 points
▶ Below average, 1 point

These ratings were coupled with the following performance characteristics:

▶ Quality of work
▶ Quantity of work
▶ Cooperation
▶ Attitude
▶ Initiative
▶ Attendance

Each characteristic was scored on the three-point scale. An employee who was rated above average in all six characteristics would score eighteen points. A person who scored below average in all characteristics would total six points. a review of the company's records indicated that, on average, Electro-Tec employees were rated 15.635 points.

The appraisal system had been in use for over three years. Some supervisors and managers complained about the paper work, but, all-in-all, the program was pretty well-accepted. The appraisal form, which was pre-printed and one page long, required only that the appropriate block be checked. Appraisals were done once a year, and feedback was to be given to all who were evaluated. Most supervisors, however, were uncomfortable in such sessions and many avoided them entirely.

One of Kristin's early actions had been to centralize all employee records into an Employee Information System under her direct control. This had been an interesting undertaking. She had received a variety of records, notes, forms, reports, letters, and other assorted materials from supervisors and department heads, each of whom had his or her own view of what was important. In pulling all this material together, she had individually met with all of the company's supervisors, as well as with employees from every department. This gave her an opportunity to get to know a lot about the people at Electro-Tec, how they viewed the company, and their roles in it. Through her many discussions, she heard comments such as "It's not like the early days. I'm not recognized for my contributions," and "I don't think he really knows what or how I'm doing."

Some workers had expressed concern about not understanding how their salaries were determined. Others wondered about what their future held at Electro-Tec. The comment of one particular engineer stuck in her mind: "Where do I go from here? In fact, where is Electro-Tec going?"

Other more specific concerns were also raised. Some wondered why job openings were not publicized throughout the company. Others asked about the insurance programs, and vacation and sick-leave policies, long-term disability, and the Employee Stock Ownership Plan. The questions seemed endless.

Kristin felt that she was beginning to understand the views and needs of the rank and file, and she had begun a continuing dialogue with vice presidents in the other divisions. In her early discussions with the other vice presidents, she sensed some differences in their perceptions about how she and the Human Resource Division should best operate and support the rest of the organization. However, comments such as "When I need your help, I'll yell," and "I think we can work together, but we're used to doing things for ourselves around here" made her aware that her job would not be an easy one.

"Bill," she had said to Cunningham on the phone, "when you get back in here from L.A., I'm ready to sit down with you and the rest of the executive committee and outline what I have in mind for Electro-Tec. We're at a point where we need to start moving, and we all need to agree on where we're headed."

"Great," Cunningham replied. "Let's do it. Set up a meeting for Monday morning with all the vice presidents. I want to hear your analysis and any proposals you have.

"I'd like to see these changes put in place right away!"

MANAGER'S DICTIONARY

Achievement Need (n ach)—The desire to do something better or more efficiently than it was done before.

Action Goals—Goals established at the point of job performance.

Actor-Observer Effect—A common attribution error in which we tend to explain other people's behavior as internally caused and our own behavior as externally caused.

Adaptation—The second stage of the body's response to stress. In this stage, chemical changes occur at the point at which a stressor is impacting a person (e.g., blood rushing to the point of a wound).

Adjourning—The final stage of group development, during which members begin to separate themselves from the group.

Administrative Model—A descriptive model of decision making which suggests that a person's ability to process information is limited. The model posits that: (1) decision makers do not search out all possible alternatives but rather choose the first acceptable solution; (2) the search for alternatives is guided primarily by past experiences or rules of thumb (heuristics); and (3) decision makers satisfice rather than maximize.

Administrative Era—A period in the development of managerial philosophy characterized by a concern for finding the best way to do a job and manage a company.

Affiliation Need (n aff)—A person's need for friendly relationships, group acceptance, and being liked by others.

Age Thirty Transition—The period in Levinson's Theory of Adult Development (approximately ages twenty-eight to thirty-two) in which initial occupational and family decisions are reevaluated.

Alarm—The first stage in the body's response to stress when the body is alerted to the presence of stressors in the environment. Initially this results in lowered resistance to the stressor.

Anchoring and adjustment—A heuristic which uses a natural starting point (anchor) as a first approximation to judgment and subsequently adjusts it to accommodate the implications of additional information.

Arbitrator—A third party who acts as a judge. The arbitrator collects relevant information, analyzes the alternatives, and presents a binding settlement to the parties.

Attitudes—Mental "states of readiness" to respond to specific objects or persons in a particular way; predispositions to act.

Attribution Process—The process of reasoning backward from the observation of an event or behavior to a judgment about its cause.

Authoritarianism—The degree to which an individual believes that lines of power and status should be clearly delineated.

Authority—The ability to bring about changes in the behavior and attitudes of others with their knowledge or consent; the legitimate power associated with positions in an organization.

Autonomy—The degree to which the job provides substantial freedom, independence, and discretion to the individual in scheduling the work and determining the procedures to be used in carrying it out.

Availability—A heuristic that suggests that the ease with which events can be remembered or imagined is an important factor in making judgments about frequency.

Bargaining—A process whereby two or more parties attempt to settle what each will give and take, or perform and receive, in a transaction between them. Bargaining involves the presentation of demands or proposals by one party, and the evaluation of these by the other party, followed by counterproposals and concessions.

Baseline—The initial measurement of a performance-related behavior.

Becoming One's Own Person—The second phase of the "Settling Down" period in Levinson's Theory of Adult Development (approximately late thirties), characterized by the desire to obtain some life- or work-related goal without the aid of others.

Beliefs—Ideas held to be true about specific objects or persons; accepted pieces of information.

Benevolents—Individuals who think more in terms of giving than receiving.

Biofeedback—The process of monitoring one's own vital signs (e.g., pulse rate, breathing). A part of stress management for self-regulation of selected bodily activities.

Bounded Rationality—A concept which suggests that a person's cognitive ability to process information is limited. Therefore, even if complete information were available to a decision maker, cognitive limitations would impede completely rational decision making.

Brainstorming—A technique designed to bring greater creativity into the group problem-solving process by taking advantage of the positive effects of synergy and by removing factors which inhibit the group process.

Bridges—Individuals who perform a linking and connecting function between two or more groups; unlike liaisons, bridges are actual group members who communicate with members of other groups.

Bureaucracy—An organizational form or type having the following characteristics: hierarchy of authority, specialization, rules and regulations, and formalized impersonality.

Burnout—A subtle and progressive syndrome related to job stress that causes people to become lethargic and to lose interest in their work.

Career Fast Track—Special career tracks designed to allow rapid advancement and promotion in the organization to those individuals demonstrating unusually high potential.

Career—The individually perceived sequence of attitudes and behaviors associated with work-related experiences over the span of a person's life.

Career Stages—The distinct stages of career transitions and development which parallel the adult stages identified by Levinson. These include exploration; trial; establishment; growth, maintenance, stagnation; and disengagement.

Career Development—A conscious effort to contribute to a person's selection of a career and to enable that person to grow and become more involved in chosen career areas.

Career Anchors—Underlying career patterns and tendencies which give continuity to one's career.

Career Path Clusters—Groups of jobs toward which a single career path may lead.

Centralization—The relative concentration of decision-making power at the top of an organization. Centralization is normally associated with traditional bureaucracies.

Change Agent—An individual whose role in the organizational development strategy is to (1) help the organization diagnose itself, and (2) assist the organizational members in learning processes and techniques for actually bringing about planned change.

Change and Acquisition—The final phase of the socialization process during which an individual adapts to group expectations and works through conflicts experienced during the encounter stage.

Channel—The pathway or avenue through which a message is conveyed from a sender to a receiver.

Circular Career Paths—Career paths that provide nonspecialized training, resulting in a broader, more systemic perspective of the organization.

Classical Learning Theory—The theory that learned behavior represents a response to a specific stimulus. This theory is basically concerned with reflexive responses rather than with responses consciously controlled by the individual.

Closed System—Self-contained systems that are not dependent on the environment as a source of inputs or as a receiver of outputs.

Closure—A principle for organizing stimuli in which the individual fills in the gaps or missing information, thereby organizing stimuli into whole figures.

Co-opting—A strategy which seeks to increase or acquire power by absorbing people or groups, whose support is needed, into positions of limited influence. Co-opting is used to eliminate threats and opposition to an individual's base of power.

Coalescing—The process of forming coalitions in order to increase power through greater control of resources.

Cohesiveness—The degree to which group members desire to remain in the group. Three factors are likely to contribute to cohesiveness: (1) attraction to individual members in the group; (2) the instrumental value of the group; and (3) risk taking that occurs in the group.

Commitment-Oriented Philosophy of Management—An approach in which jobs are designed to be broad in scope and include responsibility for planning and implementation.

Committee Management—Placing responsibility and authority in the hands of committee members.

Communication—The process of sending and receiving messages.

Communication Audit—A systematic appraisal of communication effectiveness within an organization which provides a means of analyzing and improving the flow of messages.

Conciliator—A third party who intervenes when parties have stopped all bargaining. The conciliator seeks to establish or repair the channels of communication by breaking deadlocks and steering discussions away from highly sensitive issues until the parties are ready to handle them.

Conflict—The interaction of interdependent people or groups who perceive incompatible goals and interference from each other in achieving those goals.

Conflict Episode—A step in the conflict process which consists of four primary phases: (1) frustration, (2) conceptualization, (3) behavior, and (4) outcome. Each episode sets the stage for future conflict episodes.

Consequence Management—The process by which an individual initiates control over the consequences of his/her behavior.

Consideration—The extent to which a leader provides psychological support and displays concern for the needs of group members. Consideration is one of the dimensions of effective leader behavior identified in the Ohio State studies.

Context—The immediate environment in which a person finds himself or herself.

Contingency Theory—A leadership theory which posits that a leader can only be effective if her or his natural style is appropriately matched with a given set of situational variables.

Contingency Factors—Factors or conditions which affect the determination of which leadership style is appropriate.

Continuous Schedule—A reinforcement schedule in which a behavior is reinforced every time it occurs.

Control-Oriented Philosophy of Management—An approach to managing which emphasizes order, control, and efficiency within an organization.

Creativity—The ability to generate ideas that are both new and useful.

Critical Psychological States—Three psychological states that affect an employee's satisfaction and work motivation, including (1) experienced meaningfulness of the work; (2) experienced responsibility for work outcomes; and (3) knowledge of results. The more employees experience these three psychological states, the greater the likelihood that they will feed good about themselves when performing tasks well.

Cross-training—Training an employee or group of employees to perform several related jobs.

Decentralization—The allocation of decision-making authority to individuals at lower levels of an organization.

Decision Making—The process of selecting among available alternatives. Decision making is part of the problem-solving process and requires skill in evaluating, judging, critiquing, and choosing.

Decoding—The process by which the receiver of a message interprets symbols and assigns meaning.

Delegation—The assignment of specific duties or responsibilities to an individual lower in the hierarchy.

Delphi Technique—A technique that utilizes multiple rounds of questionnaires to arrive at a consensus decision. Unlike other problem-solving/decision-making techniques, the Delphi technique does not require group members to meet together in a common location.

Departmentalization—The division of work along organizational lines.

Developmental Stages (Group)—The steps a group progresses through as it develops and evolves, analogous to the stages of personality development in individuals. The most frequently cited stages are forming, storming, norming, performing, and separating.

Developmental Stages (Individual)—Specific periods during which personality development is hypothesized to occur. Many different models of developmental stages have been identified including those advocated by Freud, Erikson, and Levinson.

Differentiation—Development of highly specialized patterns of thought and behavior within distinct subunits of an organization.

Direction Counseling—A combination of diagnostic interviews and counseling sessions that are concerned with improving an individual's job and performance.

Distortion—The changing or altering of a message as it passes through a network. Distortion acts as a barrier to effective organizational communication.

Division of Labor—The division of work into operations which are narrow in scope in order to increase the efficiency with which each operation can be performed.

Doing the Right Things—A strategy for obtaining power based on engaging in activities that are highly visible, extraordinary, and related to the accomplishment of organizational goals.

Downward Communication—Messages transmitted from superiors to subordinates.

Driving Forces—Forces existing within an organization which promote and facilitate change.

Dual-Career Couples—Couples in which both the wife and husband have separate careers and, therefore, separate and distinct work roles.

Effort—The amount of energy expended to accomplish a task.

Emergent Leader—A leader who is informally selected by group members. Emergent leaders tend to be (1) socially compatible with group members; (2) prominent in the eyes of group members; and (3) perceived by others in the group to be able to help the group attain its objectives.

Encoding—The process by which the sender of a message translates a thought or idea into symbols.

Encounter—The identification of the differences between an individual's premembership beliefs and conditions that actually exist within the group.

Entitleds—Individuals who assume they deserve more than their referents.

Entrepreneur—A person who independently develops new ideas and begins his or her own company.

Equifinality—The process by which open systems can achieve their purposes using diverse sets of inputs and different arrangements of systems components.

Equity Theory—A process theory of motivation which is based on three variables: (1) an individual's perceived inputs; (2) an individual's perceived outcomes or rewards; and (3) an individual's inputs and outcomes relative to the inputs and outcomes of others. According to equity theory, motivation is the result of a desire to reduce perceived inequities between the perceived input/outcome ratio of the individual and the perceived input/outcome ratio of a referent other.

ERG Theory—A need-based theory of motivation developed around three need categories: existence needs, relatedness needs, and growth needs (ERG). The theory suggests that if higher-level needs are not satisfied, a person's desire to satisfy lower-level needs will increase. In addition, the theory suggests that certain needs (relatedness and growth) may become more, not less, important as they are satisfied.

Espoused Theory—The system of ideas an individual advocates or supports but may not actually follow.

Ethics—The set standards and code of conduct that define what is right, wrong, and just in human actions.

Exhaustion—The final stage in the body's response to stress. This is the result of increased levels of adrenaline being secreted into the blood due to an elevated level of response being maintained for a long period of time.

Expectancies—Assessments of the probabilities associated with the relationship between (1) behaviors and outcomes, and (2) situational cues and behavior.

Expectancy Theory—A process theory of motivation which concentrates on the relationships between (1) effort and performance, and (2) performance and reward. The five fundamental elements of the model are effort, expectancy, performance, instrumentality, and outcome. The theory views motivation as a function of both the value of a desired outcome and the probability that effort will lead to the desired reward.

Expectancy—The probability that a given level of effort will yield a particular level of performance.

External Locus of Control—The belief that outside forces (e.g., fate, luck, chance) are the principal determinants of one's behavior.

Extinction—Withholding a positive consequence which has already been associated with a behavior in order to decrease the frequency of a behavior.

Extrinsic Motivation—Motivation caused by incidents or stimuli that occur externally to an individual.

False Consensus Bias—An attribution error in which we tend to believe that the attitudes we hold are appropriate for a particular situation and thus must be widely shared by others.

Feedback—A receiver's response to a sender's message.

Feedback Receptiveness—The willingness to receive feedback from others.

Feedback Responsiveness—The willingness to give feedback to others.

Figure/Ground—A principle for organizing stimuli in which the most salient stimulus becomes the focal point (figure) and the less salient stimulus takes the position of background.

Fixed Schedules—Reinforcement of a behavior on a regular, nonvarying basis. Fixed schedules facilitate rapid learning of new behaviors but can also result in rapid extinction.

Flexitime—A work schedule system in which employees select, within certain guidelines, work hours and schedules that best meet their individual needs.

Follower Readiness—A follower's job-related ability and psychological willingness to perform.

Force Field Analysis—A model of change which proposes that any existing level of performance within an organization is an equilibrium locked between two sets of opposing forces: (1) driving forces, and (2) restraining forces.

Formal Organization—The activities of a group of individuals who are pursuing a common goal through formalized structures and processes.

Forming—The initial period of group development in which members attempt to orient themselves both to the task and to each other.

4/40 Work Week—A work schedule system in which forty hours of work are performed in four ten-hour days (contrasting with the traditional five eight-hour day schedule).

Frame of Reference—The subjective and biased point of view from which an individual perceives the surrounding environment.

Frequency Counts—A measurement of the number of times a behavior occurs.

Functional and Dysfunctional Consequences of Conflict—Conflict is an inevitable aspect of behavior in organizations and can produce both positive and negative consequences. The task of the manager is not to avoid or eliminate conflict, but rather to manage it in such a way that its positive aspects (e.g., innovation, change, search for new ideas) can be realized and the negative aspects (e.g., distrust, fear, resentment) can be reduced.

Gatekeepers—Individuals who, by virtue of their positions within the network, can screen, filter, or control the flow of messages and information.

General Adaptation Syndrome—The body's response to stress.

Getting Into the Adult World—A period of exploration in Levinson's Theory of Adult Development occurring from the early to the late twenties in which a person encounters critical events such as searching for an occupation, searching for a mate, and deciding whether to raise a family.

Goal Displacement—The substitution of department, work group, or individual goals, for the objectives of the total enterprise.

Goal Setting Theory—A theory of motivation which suggests that consciously set goals will influence individual performance. Performance is mediated by goal specificity, goal difficulty, goal acceptance, feedback, expected or unexpected evaluation, and other factors.

Goal Difficulty—The concept that difficult goals will lead to higher levels of performance.

Goal Specificity—The concept that the more specific the goal is the greater the likelihood of its being achieved.

Great Man Theory—One of the earliest theories of leadership which suggested that great leaders are born, not made. Great leaders were believed to possess certain qualities that made them successful leaders.

Grid Organizational Development—A seven-stage program which is an extension of the Managerial Grid. The major objective of this intervention is the adoption of an ideal management style (9,9) by managers throughout the organization.

Group—Two or more individuals who communicate (verbally and/or non-verbally), and who function interdependently in the pursuit of some common goal or mutual interest(s).

Group Norms—Informal rules of behavior for group members.

Group Polarization—The tendency for group decisions to become more extreme than those that would be made by the group's individual members. The initial positions of the group members are exaggerated through group discussion. The risky shift and the cautious shift are examples of group polarization.

Groupthink—A deterioration of mental efficiency, reality testing, and moral judgment which results from pressure within a group for conformity and cohesiveness.

Growth Need Strength—A collection of higher-order needs for learning, accomplishments, and challenge which moderate employee responses to the work environment.

Halo Effect—The tendency to let one characteristic or trait of an individual influence the evaluation of that individual's other characteristics.

Horizontal Communication—The sending and receiving of messages between people at the same level of the organizational hierarchy.

Horizontal Job Loading—(also job enlargement) Increasing the number of different tasks an employee performs.

Human Relations—A period in the development of managerial philosophy during which managers became more concerned about the importance of paying attention to the needs of their workers.

Hygienes—Characteristics of the work environment (e.g., pay, working conditions, relations with others, technical supervision) hypothesized by Herzberg to affect dissatisfaction but not to contribute directly to employee motivation. They are also known as dissatisfiers.

Implicit Personality Trait—A relatively stable collection of associations among human traits. To the extent that the personal theory is incomplete or inaccurate, it contributes to distortion and misunderstanding.

Implicit Favorites—A barrier to effective decision making in which the decision maker selects a favorite alternative early in the decision-making process. Subsequent alternatives are distorted perceptually to insure that the implicit favorite is eventually selected.

Individual Bases of Power—Six interrelated types or bases of power have been identified: (1) reward power, (2) coercive power, (3) legitimate power, (4) referent power, (5) expert power, and (6) information power.

Individuality—The unique characteristics which distinguish one person from another.

Industrial Revolution—An era representing widespread mechanization of work and the growth of large, centralized centers of output known as factories.

Influence—The process of affecting or altering the behavior and/or attitudes of others.

Initiating Structure—The extent to which a leader is likely to define and structure a job for subordinates. Initiating structure is one of the dimensions of effective leader behavior identified in the Ohio State studies.

Innovative Reward Systems—Modern reward systems that contribute to a participative, high-performance work environment (e.g. an all-salaried work force, skill-based job evaluation, and various types of gainsharing plans).

Inputs—According to equity theory, inputs are an individual's perceived contribution to an organization.

Institutionalization of Change—Refreezing the organizational development changes so that they are sustained over time and become "permanent."

Intrinsic Motivation—Motivation that results from a need or other stimulus that occurs within an individual.

Instrumentality—The probability that a given level of performance will lead to a desired outcome.

Integration—The process of tying together and reunifying differentiated cognitive and behavioral patterns within an organization.

Interacting Group—The traditional idea of a group in which group leaders and dominant individuals tend to consume a disproportionate amount of time. As a result, some people in the group rarely contribute to the group process and the nature of the group interaction inhibits the group's effectiveness.

Intergroup Competition—A phenomenon in which competition occurs between groups. Competing groups tend to view one another as "the enemy," tend to distort the views of their own group members positively, and tend to distort the views of the competing group's members negatively.

Intermittent Schedule—A reinforcement schedule in which reinforcers occur after selected, but not all, behaviors.

Internal Locus of Control—The belief that the control of personal behavior rests primarily within oneself.

Interorganizational Groups—Groups with members representing more than one organizational unit.

Interval Schedule—Reinforcing a behavior in relation to time. For example, reinforcing an employee every hour on the hour.

Intervention—A planned effort to bring about individual, group, or organizational change through specific procedures or techniques.

Intrapreneur—A person who engages in entrepreneurial activities (is innovative and develops new ideas) on his or her existing job without leaving the company for which he or she works.

Inverted U—Graphic representation of stress versus performance. The curve suggests that an optimal level of stress is necessary for peak performance.

Isolates—Individuals who have very few or no communication contacts with the rest of the organization.

Job Enlargement—(also known as horizontal job loading) Increasing the number of different tasks an employee performs.

Job Enrichment—The vertical loading of jobs in order to increase individual satisfaction and motivation by providing employees with more responsibility for the planning, directing, and controlling of their own work.

Job Rotation—A work design strategy involving the movement of workers from one job to another without changing the jobs' basic operations or nature.

Knowing the Right People—A strategy for obtaining power based on cultivating relationships with key individuals.

Law of Effect—The proposition that, of several responses made to the same situation, those accompanied or closely followed by satisfaction will be more likely to recur, and those accompanied or closely followed by discomfort will be less likely to recur.

Learning—Any relatively permanent change in behavior that occurs as the result of reinforced experiences or practices.

Levinson's Theory of Adult Development—A model which focuses on personality change and adult development. The theory suggests that adults pass through intermittent periods of stability and transition.

Liaisons—Individuals who interpersonally connect two or more groups or departments within an organization. The liaison is usually not a member of either group, but serves to join or link the groups communicatively.

Life System—The system composed of the important subsystems which constitute a person's personal and social existence (i.e., the job and career subsystem, the self subsystem, the family and social subsystems, and the other aspects of life-style subsystem).

Listening—The active process of receiving and interpreting aural stimuli.

Management by Objectives—An OD intervention technique used to (1) increase the precision of the planning process at the organizational level, and (2) decrease the discrepancy between organizational and employee goals.

Managerial Grid—A leadership model developed by Robert Blake and Jane Mouton which identified five primary leadership styles through the use of a grid. The model suggests that there is one best leadership style (the "9,9" team manager), and is used to help leaders adopt this style.

Maslow's Need Hierarchy—Five basic needs (physiological needs, safety [security], belongingness and love, esteem, and self-actualization) identified by Abraham Maslow, who believed they motivated behavior. Maslow contended that the needs were arranged in a distinct order of importance and that the appearance of one need usually rested upon the prior satisfaction of other more prepotent needs.

Matrix Organization—An organizational structure which simultaneously (1) maintains permanent functional departments, and (2) conducts all production-related activity through individual project organizations. The matrix organization can be conceptualized as the overlaying of a project structure on a functional structure.

Maximizing—The act of developing a complete set of possible courses of action, specifying all possible outcomes resulting from any of these actions, and judging the actions according to appropriate criteria.

Media—The mechanisms that are used to transmit messages.

Mediator—A third party who intervenes by offering original alternatives and encourages the parties to adopt a particular solution. The recommendation is nonbinding.

Mid-Life Transition—The period in Levinson's Theory of Adult Development (early forties) in which individuals seriously question and reexamine the central issues of their lives. A desire to eliminate the current life structure often leads to irrational actions. Behaviors common to those in this period of development include divorce, quitting one's job, and leaving one's family.

Modeling—Learning a new behavior by observing the behaviors and consequences of others as well as by direct personal experience.

Mommy Track—A career path that permits women to work shorter, more flexible hours, and thus to combine career and motherhood.

Motivating Potential Score—The overall potential of a job to produce intrinsic work motivation. MPS is based on scores from the Job Diagnostic Survey (JDS):

$$MPS = \left[\frac{\text{Skill Variety} + \text{Task Identity} + \text{Task Sign}}{3} \right] \times \text{Autonomy} \times \text{Feedback}$$

Motivation—Those psychological processes that cause arousal, direction, and persistence of voluntary actions that are goal-directed.

Motivators—Those factors, also known as satisfiers, identified by Herzberg as contributing to motivation on the job; they include achievement, recognition, meaningful work, growth, responsibility, and advancement.

Multiple Career Paths—Providing more than one "ladder" for individuals to "climb" in the organization. The multiple paths give greater opportunity/flexibility to individuals planning their career development, and allow individuals to pursue individual career goals.

Negative Reinforcement—Withholding an aversive consequence (stimulus) in order to increase the frequency of a behavior.

Negative Bias—A common attribution error in which we tend to be disproportionately influenced by the negative information we have about a person.

Networks—Pathways through which the flow of messages and information is guided. Five common networks that exist in organizations include the authority network, the information network, the task expertise network, the friendship network, and the status network.

Noise—Anything that interferes with or disrupts the accurate transmission and reception of messages.

Nominal Group Technique (NGT)—A technique developed to ensure that all members of the group participate in the problem-solving/decision-making process. Each member of the group presents his or her ideas which are recorded and subsequently voted on and ranked on the basis of numerical weighting to select the best alternative.

Nonprogrammed Decisions—Decisions which are new and unique and for which established guidelines and procedures do not exist.

Nonverbal Messages—Messages which transcend written or spoken symbols (e.g., eye behavior, gestures, tone of voice).

Norming—The stage of group development during which a feeling of oneness begins to emerge in the group.

Objectives—The specific ends that an organization seeks to achieve.

Ombudsman—An individual whose role in the organization is to listen to employee concerns and to help resolve concerns by mediating between aggrieved parties.

Open System—System that exchanges information and energy (interact) with its environment.

Operant Learning Theory—The theory that behaviors (responses) are associated with given situations and occur in order to bring about some form of reinforcement or reward. Thus, the behavior operates on the environment.

Organic Organization—A fluid, continuously changing organizational structure in which individuals, positions, and structure adapt to the immediate needs of the organization; can be thought of as a "structureless" structure.

Organizational Politics—Those activities and behaviors through which power is acquired, developed, and used in organizations to obtain what one wants. Politics is power in action.

Organizational Development—An attempt to use the concepts and methodologies of applied behavioral science to aid organizations in developing and maintaining their health.

Organizational Stress Audit—The process of gathering information on an organization to identify areas of stress that presently or potentially exist in the work environment.

Organizational Structure—The system of formal relationships through which an organization is managed.

Organizational Behavior Modification—An approach to behavior change based on an analysis of overt causes and/or consequences of behavior. OB Mod consists of a series of steps which are designed to increase the frequency of performance-related behaviors.

Organizational Behavior—The study of human behavior in organizations.

Managerial Philosophy—Patterned ways of thinking and acting with respect to the managing of human resources that are transmitted from generation to generation.

Outcomes—According to equity theory, outcomes are the perceived rewards received by an individual.

Overconfidence—The tendency to be more confident in one's own ability to assess probabilities and make judgement than is justified by actual performance.

Overload—A condition that creates stress due to quantitative or qualitative demands being placed on a person in excess of what he or she can manage.

Overload—A barrier to effective organizational communication that occurs when an individual receives more messages than she or he has the capacity or ability to handle.

Participative Decision Making—Joint decision making that occurs between a supervisor and a subordinate, within a single group, or among many groups of subordinates.

Path-Goal Theory—A leadership theory which is closely linked to the expectancy theory of motivation. According to Path-Goal Theory, the leader's job is to affect subordinate performance by providing desirable rewards for successful performance and clarifying the subordinate's paths to these rewards or goals.

Perception—The psychological process of selecting, organizing, and interpreting stimuli from the environment.

Perceptual Differences—No two individuals select, organize, and interpret stimuli from the environment in the same way. Therefore, no two people have the same frame of reference, and it is impossible for one person to exactly recreate in another person's mind her or his original perception.

Performance—A level of output-related behavior.

Performing—The stage of group development during which meaningful activity directly related to the group's goals actually takes place.

Personal Stress Audit—Assessment of one's vulnerability to stress. This involves a complete examination of one's physical condition, life-style, and personal history.

Personality—A distinctive set of characteristics that tend to remain the same across similar situations and which are relatively stable over time.

Planned Change—A deliberate attempt to alter the status quo.

Positive Reinforcement—Adding a positive consequence (stimulus) in order to increase the frequency of a behavior.

Power Need (n pow)—A concern for obtaining and maintaining control over others.

Power—The ability or capacity to influence people or things, usually obtained through the control of important resources.

Previous Commitments—A barrier to effective decision making in which a previous commitment to an idea or position is allowed to bias the decision-making process. Thus, decision makers may commit additional resources to a previously selected alternative (even though it may be failing) in order to justify the initial decision.

Primacy Effect—A perceptual effect in which the initial cues and information about another person or object have the greatest influence in shaping an overall impression.

Primary Group—A small group which is characterized by intimate face-to-face associations between members. Primary groups exert a great deal of influence on the day-to-day activities of their members.

Problem Solving—A systematic process which is characterized by the activities of searching, inventing, reacting, and creating, with the major objective being the identification of acceptable alternatives. Problem solving includes the decision-making process.

Process Consultation—An OD intervention technique in which a consultant observes activities within an organization and then feeds back the information to the client in an attempt to help the client understand how organizational processes operate. This is so that the client, rather than the consultant, can solve the problems and improve those processes.

Programmed Decisions—Decisions that are made repeatedly according to established principles and policies that are applicable to all similar situations.

Project Group—A formal but temporary group to which members are assigned (e.g., a committee, a special project, an R&D team, an internal consultant group, a medical team). Project group members will return to their "normal" work activities or go on to another temporary project group after the project has been completed.

Project Organization—An organizational structure in which an organizational unit is formed to accomplish a specific goal (e.g., designing a new product).

Projection—The tendency for people to see in others traits or characteristics they themselves possess.

Protestant Work Ethic—A social doctrine which promoted a strong desire for job-related achievement and a belief in the value of hard work.

Proximity—A principle for organizing stimuli based on the tendency to group together stimuli which are located close together.

Punishment—Providing a negative consequence (stimulus) to a behavior in order to decrease the frequency of that behavior.

Quality of Work Life (QWL)—A broad concern for the total work environment. QWL involves devoting more organizational resources and time to developing work environments that are excellent for both people and production.

Quality Circle Facilitator—A key member of the quality circle program who coordinates the overall circle program, trains circle leaders, and assists in the training of individual circle members.

Quality Groups—Small groups of employees who do similar work and who voluntarily meet on a regular basis to identify, analyze, and solve problems in their own work area.

Ratio Schedule—Reinforcing a behavior in relation to the number of times that the behavior occurs. For example, reinforcing an employee for each unit she or he produces.

Rational-Economic Model—A prescriptive decision-making model which posits that decision makers are economically rational, seek to maximize their outcomes, evaluate all possible alternatives, and select the single best alternative. The model also assumes that decision makers have perfect information about all available alternatives as well as the consequences of the alternatives.

Realistic Job Preview—The process of giving those who are considering joining a group a realistic impression of the roles, conditions, and relationships that are likely to be found in the group.

Recency Effect—A perceptual effect in which the last or most recent cues and information about another person or object exerts the greatest influence on an overall impression.

Refreezing—The final stage in the change process during which the changes are stabilized and institutionalized.

Reinforcement Theory—An approach to motivation that uses rewards and punishments in order to bring about a repeat of, or an increase in, learned behaviors.

Reinforcement Schedule—The systematic pattern by which reinforcers are administered.

Representativeness—A heuristic that reflects the tendency to make decisions based on the belief that object A belongs to class B.

Resemblance—A principle for organizing stimuli whereby stimuli (objects or individuals) of similar appearance are grouped together.

Resistance to Change—The tendency for components of a system to oppose change, often making change difficult to achieve.

Restraining Forces—Forces existing within an organization which impede and hinder change.

Reward—A valued outcome desired by an individual.

Risk-Taking Propensity—An individual's predisposition to take risks.

Role—The set of expectations which group members share concerning the behavior of the occupant of a given position within the group.

Role Ambiguity—Lack of clarity about the task or job a person is expected to perform.

Role Conflict—The result of incompatible role demands on an individual.

Satisficing—The act of choosing an alternative which is satisfactory rather than ideal.

Scientific Management—An approach to work design that emphasized greater efficiency gained through the systematic analysis and design of work.

Scientific Management—A cooperative effort by management and workers to ascertain the one best way of performing a job, to select workers most capable of doing the job, and to provide incentive pay for people selected to work in the prescribed manner.

Secondary Group—Groups that are larger and less intimate than primary groups. Secondary groups tend to have little *direct* influence on group behavior.

Selective Perception—The process by which a person systematically screens out or focuses upon particular cues and information.

Self-Assessment—Helps an individual develop a career plan by having her or him focus on personal values, interests, and aspirations.

Self-Managed Work Groups—Autonomous work teams which function in a manner relatively independent from direct supervision of managers.

Self-Serving Bias—A common attribution error in which we perceive internal causes for our "successes" and external causes for our "failures."

Sensation—The physiological process by which we take in stimuli from and interface with the environment.

Sensitivity Training—An OD intervention designed to increase an individual's awareness of his or her interpersonal behaviors and defense mechanisms.

Shaping—Learning a complex behavior by reinforcement of successive approximations of that behavior.

Situational Leadership Theory—A leadership model which states that the effectiveness of leader behaviors is situational. There is no one "best" leadership style for all situations and a manager should choose the style which best fits the follower's psychological and task "readiness."

Skill Variety—The degree to which a job requires a variety of different activities involving the use of a number of different skills and talents.

Slow Burn Plan—The opposite of a fast track. Individuals on a SBP move slowly along their career paths and are expected to be more cooperative than competitive.

Social Cognitive Theory—The learning theory that considers the importance of human cognition in learning and suggests that individuals can learn vicariously as well as through direct experience. The SCT model consists of three basic elements: individual cognitive processes, behaviors, and the environment.

Social Darwinism—A doctrine that views those individuals who rise to the top of the social and economic ladder as superior.

Socialization—The process by which individuals "learn the ropes" and are incorporated into groups and larger organizations.

Socio-concept—A term used to describe a group's self-concept. The socio-concept represents a conscious self-awareness on the part of group members of the purpose, structure, and process of the group and of its relationship with its environment.

Sociotechnical Design—An approach to work design which focuses simultaneously on the social and technological systems of an organization. This model suggests designing and implementing work to optimize the fit between the social and psychological needs of people and the technical aspects of work. The basic unit of work design in the sociotechnical model is the group.

Specialized Career Paths—Career paths which provide in-depth training and experience in a single functional area (e.g., marketing).

Steering Committee—A committee made up of representatives from all levels of the organization that oversees the overall quality circle program in the organization.

Stereotyping—Creating a mental picture of a group or category of people, objects, or things.

Stimulus Management—The process of increasing or decreasing antecedent cues which are responsible for certain behaviors.

Storming—The state of group development during which members are likely to vie with one another for group as well as task roles.

Strategic Contingencies Theory—A framework for understanding the process through which organizational departments or subunits (rather than individuals) acquire, develop, and exercise power within organizations. The theory posits that those organizational subunits or departments which are best able to cope with critical problems affecting the mission of the organization will acquire power.

Stressors—External stimuli that initiate stress.

Substitutes for Leadership—Conditions (which exist in many organizations) that may aid, inhibit, or override a leader's influence.

Superordinate Goals—Goals that are more important to each party involved than their own independent goals. Superordinate goals are an addition to group goals and do not replace the other goals the group has or the incompatibility of those goals.

Survey Feedback—An OD intervention technique which involves (1) collecting data about the organization through the use of surveys or questionnaires, and (2) conducting feedback meetings or workshops in which the data are presented to organizational members.

Synectics—An approach to group problem solving and decision making that makes use of analogies and metaphors to allow the problem to be viewed in a unique and foreign context.

Synergy—A quality of systems whereby inputs combine in unique ways to create something more than the sum of the inputs alone.

Syntality—A term used to describe the "personality" of a group.

System—A collection of interdependent and interrelated parts that function as a single entity.

Task Group—A group which is brought together for the purpose of transforming some inputs (raw materials, ideas, objects) into an identifiable output (a physical product, a decision, a report). Task groups are also known as functional groups. Their members typically interact with one another on a day-to-day basis and take the form of departments or ongoing work teams.

Task Significance—The degree to which the job has a substantial impact on the lives or work of other people, whether in the immediate organization or in the external environment.

Task Identity—The degree to which the job requires completing a whole and identifiable piece of work; that is, doing a job from beginning to end with a visible outcome.

Team Building—An OD intervention designed to improve the task performance of and relationships among work group members or others seeking to achieve a common goal.

Theory in Use—The system of ideas which actually governs an individual's behavior.

Theory X—A management style based on the belief that most employees work primarily for wages and are motivated by little else.

Theory Y—A management style based on the belief that employees are motivated by more than just money. Theory Y places emphasis on concepts generated by the human relations movement.

Third Party Intervention—The use of a neutral third party to help reduce conflict resulting from a "stalemate" situation. The intervention of an objective third party can help reduce the tension by promoting increased openness, trust, and understanding of opposing positions.

Timeliness—The extent to which accurate and complete messages reach the receiver at the proper time.

Trait Theory—A theory of leadership which attempted to identify specific traits and characteristics that successful leaders held in common.

Transactional Leaders—Leaders who bring about desired actions from followers by using certain behaviors, rewards, or incentives.

Transformational Leaders—Leaders who inspire others to reach beyond themselves and to do more than originally thought possible by raising their commitment to a shared vision of the future.

Tunnel Vision—A barrier to effective decision making in which individual biases and past experiences cause the decision maker to restrict the search for an acceptable solution to a very narrow range of alternatives.

Type A—A personality type. Individuals having Type A personalities tend to be aggressive, hostile, impatient, and given to using explosive or accelerated speech patterns.

Type B—The opposite of Type A. Individuals with Type B personalities are less likely to be aggressive, hostile, or impatient.

Underload—The opposite of overload (see above). A lack of stimulation that creates stress for an individual.

Unfreezing—The first phase in the change process during which the need for change is recognized.

Unplanned Change—Changes that happen spontaneously, at random, and/or without advance notice.

Upward Communication—Messages transmitted from a subordinate to a boss.

Values—A concept of the desirable; an internalized criterion or standard of evaluation that a person possesses.

Verbal Messages—Messages exchanged through the use of written or spoken symbols.

Vertical Job loading—An approach to work design that increases an employee's task variety and changes the nature of the work to provide opportunities for new learning, direct feedback on performance, self-control over job methods and schedules, direct access to communication sources, and individual accountability for results.

Vicarious Motivation—Motivation that is caused by seeing others rewarded or punished, thereby arousing expectations that an individual will experience similar outcomes for comparable performance.

Vulnerability—The inability or ability to resist a stressor in a given situation.

Wellness Program—A fully integrated health program designed to promote and maintain physical as well as psychological good health.

Work Design—The formal and informal specification of an employee's task-related activities, including both structural and interpersonal aspects of the job, with considerations for the needs and requirements of both the organization and the worker.

NAME INDEX

Abbas, Sami M., 505
Acton, Lord, 347
Adams, F. T., 193
Adams, J. S., 193
Aday, Don, 299
Adler, N. J., 601
Adler, T., 91
Adorno, T. W., 58, 261
Agarwala-Rogers, R., 332
Ajzen, I., 58
Akers, John F., 443, 511, 512
Aldag, R. J., 225, 491
Alderfer, Clayton P., 148, 160, 162
Alexander the Great, 386
Allegrante, J. P., 559
Allen, R. W., 371
Allford, Suzanne, 119, 122
Alliger, G. M., 418
Allport, Gordon W., 34, 57
Alster, Norm, 492
Amabile, Teresa M., 226
Ambrose, M. L., 193
Anderson, D. C., 193
Anderson, J. A., 371
Andrep, G. V., 133
Anger, W. K., 133
Anonyuo, C., 419
Argyris, C., 20, 526
Aronson, E., 255, 261, 558
Ashford, S. J., 193, 558
Athos, Anthony G., 20
Austin, Nancy K., 19
Avolio, B. J., 419
Axley, Stephen R., 332

Bacon, D. C., 601
Baer, George F., 4
Bailyn, L., 601
Baker, P. M., 192
Bandura, Albert, 105, 133, 146, 162, 193
Barnard, Chester, 245, 261, 332
Barnes, L. B., 162
Baron, Robert A., 210
Barry, David, 223, 224
Barsky, N., 59
Barton, A. B., 600
Bass, B. M., 419
Bassani, Guiseppe, 454
Batten, J., 550, 558
Baum, Joe, 110, 116
Baum, L., 458
Baumler, J. V., 193
Beals, Vaughn, L., Jr., 240, 260
Beatty, M. J., 58
Bebb, M., 419
Beck, John C., 81
Beck, Martha N., 81
Bedeian, A. G., 558
Bednar, David A., 57, 133, 298, 327
Beehr, T. A., 557, 601
Beer, M., 491, 525, 526
Bell, Cecil H., Jr., 521, 525
Bell, Mylle, 392
Bellenger, D. N., 558
Belt, Brian, 228

Bennis, W. G., 371, 459
Berg, P. O., 526
Berkowitz, L., 226
Bernstein, Aaron, 193, 298, 372
Bernstein, Paul, 481
Berry, Bryan, H., 492, 525-526
Beutell, N. J., 559
Bhagat, R. S., 601
Billard, M., 418, 600
Birnbaum, D., 261
Blake, Robert, 391, 418, 525
Blanchard, Kenneth H., 400, 419
Blevins, David E., 607
Block, P., 371
Blumber, A., 525
Bodenhause, Galen V., 90
Bolles, Richard, 575
Bonjean, C. M., 192
Borgide, E., 91
Bower, J. L., 421
Boyatzis, R., 162
Bradley, K., 298
Bradley, Omar, 391
Braham, Jim, 162
Branst, Lee, 492, 525
Braus, Patricia, 559
Brekke, N., 91
Brief, A. P., 491
Brigham, J. C., 90
Brightman, Harvey J., 91
Brim, O. G., Jr., 58
Brousseau, K., 601
Brown, B. R., 372
Brown, Clair, 492, 525
Brown, Gary, 177
Brown, Paul B., 90
Bruner, J. S., 91
Buono, A. F., 558
Burke, B. G., 558
Burke, W. W., 371
Burlingham, B., 58, 193, 261
Burnham, David H., 162
Burns, J. M., 419
Byrne, J. A., 57, 458, 459, 558, 597

Cain, C. M., 557
Calpin, J. P., 193
Carlson, B. M., 133
Carlzon, Jan, 219
Carpenter, Larry, 525
Carroll, Lewis, 314
Carroll, S., 162
Cartwright, D., 371
Carulli, L. M., 601
Carver, C. S., 91
Cassidy, T., 133
Catlin, G. E. G., 371
Cattell, R. B., 34, 57, 261
Cavanaugh, M. J., 57
Chah, D., 193
Chandler, A., 458
Chapman, Elwood N., 592
Charsley, W. F., 162
Chase, Stuart, 314, 332
Chemers, M. M., 418
Cherrington, D. J., 57
Chess, W. A., 559
Chhokar, J. S., 133

Childs, D. William, 11
Christen, J. C., 558
Churchill, Winston, 386
Chusmir, L. H., 558, 559
Cleland, David, 455
Clurman, C., 162
Cobb, George, 136
Coch, Lester, 243, 261, 510, 525
Cochran, D. S., 298
Cohen, Ben, 154
Cole, Lisa R., 524
Collins, J. A., 133
Conger, Jay A., 371, 419
Coons, A. E., 418
Cooper, C. L., 558
Corder, J., 192
Costa, P.T., Jr., 58
Costello, T. W., 90
Cotton, John L., 226, 222, 559
Coulson-Thomas, C., 601
Cox, Robert E., 20, 631
Cramer, Aubrey, 301
Creighton, Mandell, 347
Cron, W. L., 601
Crouch, A., 419
Crowell, C. R., 193
Crystal, John, 575
Cummings, L. L., 91, 193, 225, 226, 312, 332, 371, 491
Cummings, T. G., 525
Cunningham, D. A., 559
Cusella, Louis P., 332
Cyert, R. M., 525

Daft, Richard L., 312, 332
Dail, Hilda Lee, 575
Dale, E., 458
Dalton, G., 525
Daniel, T. L., 133
Darrow, M. D., 600
Darwin, Charles, 4
Datan, N., 58
Davidson, W. R., 601
Davis, B., 133
Davis, K., 333
Davis, S. M., 459
Day, D. V., 58
Dean, J. W., 298
Dearborn, D. C., 91
Deaux, Kay, 91
DeCarlo, D., 557
Deci, E. L., 133
DeCotiis, T. A., 558
DeGeorge, G., 421
DeGregario, E., 91
Delbecq, A. L., 279, 298
Deming, W. Edwards, 283
Derr, C. B., 601
DeVader, C. L., 418
Devanna, M. A., 298, 419
DeVos, Richard, 189
DiBlase, D., 557
Dickson, W. J., 260
Dierks, W., 133
Dixon, J., 601
Dobrzynski, J. H., 412
Doman, M., 193
Dorfman, P. W., 419

Dornstein, M., 193
Douglas, A., 372
Dozier, J. B., 602
Drake, R. L., 459
Driver, M. J., 601
Drucker, Peter, 225
Dubberly, Agnes, 492, 525
Duckworth, D., 559
Dugan, K. W., 419
Dugas, Christine, 525
Dumaine, Brian, 298
Duncan, R., 459, 525
Dunnette, M. D., 57, 58, 371
Dwyer, D. J., 557
Dyer, W. G., 525

Earley, P. C., 193
Eason, H., 35
Ebert, R. J., 58
Eddy, George, 333
Edelstein, B., 193
Edmondson, Ed, 540
Ehrlich, E., 601
Elliot, S., 59
Elliott, Ronald D., 525
Ensley, Ann, 588
Erez, M., 193
Erikson, Erik, 49, 58
Esser, J. K., 133
Evans, M. G., 193
Evert, Chris, 350
Exley, Charles E., Jr., 454

Falkenberg, Loren, 90
Faludi, S. C., 558
Farace, Richard V., 330, 333
Farrell, Christopher, 226
Farrell, M. P., 58
Fasel, D., 557
Faux, V. A., 600
Feldman, D. C., 254, 261, 600, 602
Feldman, J. J., 333
Fenn, D., 58
Ferris, G. R., 491
Ferris, S. R., 332
Festinger, L., 193
Fiedler, Fred E., 395, 418
Filley, A. C., 472
Fischhoff, Baruch, 225
Fishbein, M., 58
Fisher, Dalmar, 330
Flippo, Edwin B., 461
Flower, Joe, 226
Fomon, Robert, 356
Forbes, Daniel, 492, 525
Ford, Henry, 469
Fortune, Bill D., 228
Foster, J., 558
Foust, Dean, 57
Fowler, Richard, 294
Fox, D. K., 133
Fox, Michael J., 350
Fox, William F., 298
Foxman, L. D., 602
Franks, V., 558, 559
Fredericksen, Lee W., 133, 491
French, J. R. P., Jr., 243, 261, 371, 510, 525

French, Wendell L., 521, 525
Freud, Sigmund, 34, 49, 57
Fried, Y., 491
Friederich, O., 58, 59
Friedman, M., 557
Froggatt, Kirk L., 222, 226
Frost, J., 371
Fry, Art, 442–443
Frye, R. L., 558
Fulmer, R. M., 558

Gaffney, C., 557
Galbraith, J. R., 458, 459
Galen, M., 57, 490
Garland, Susan B., 524
Gates, William, 111, 410
Gay, D. E. R., 648
Georgopolous, B. S., 419
Gerevas, R. E., 601
Gershenfeld, M. K., 261
Gersick, C. J. G., 261
Ghandi, Mahatma, 386, 410
Gibb, Jack R., 332
Gibson, R., 393
Gilbreth, Frank, 470
Gilbreth, Lillian, 470
Gilbride, D., 557
Gilkey, R., 558
Gillis, R., 91
Ginter, P. G., 133
Girard, Keith F., 418, 420
Gladstein, D., 261
Glick, W., 491
Goddard, R. W., 58
Goethals, G. R., 91
Gofer, B., 298
Goldhaber, Gerald, 330, 333
Goldsmith, R. E., 225
Goldstein, A. P., 133
Golembiewski, R. T., 525, 526,
    558
Goodfriend, Carolyn L. G., 583
Goodheim, L., 419
Goodman, P. S., 261
Gorbachev, Mikhail, 291
Gordon, W. J. J., 280, 281, 298
Gore, G. J., 298
Gore, William, 392
Gowan, J. C., 225
Graham, John, 367
Graham, Katherine, 583
Graham, William, 216
Granrose, C. S., 601
Grant, C., 189
Green, S. G., 416, 419
Greenberg, B. S., 333
Greenberg, J., 193
Greenberger, D. B., 419
Greene, C. N., 19
Greenfield, Jerry, 154
Greenhaus, J. H., 559
Greenwood, J. W., Jr., 57
Greenwood, J. W., III, 57
Greiner, L., 525
Gren, S. G., 91
Griffin, R. W., 298, 491
Grimes, A. J., 371
Grush, J. E., 192
Guetzkow, H., 333
Gupta, N., 193, 491, 601, 602
Gustafson, D. H., 279, 298
Guzzo, R., 162
Gyllenhammar, P. G., 491

Hackel, Lori, 30
Hackman, J. R., 261, 298, 474,
    475, 478, 491

Hahhar, L., 418
Hall, D. T., 558, 600, 601
Hall, F. S., 601
Hall, K., 558
Hall, R. H., 458
Hammer, W. C., 601
Hamner, W. C., 193
Hampton, William J., 525
Hansen, R. H., 601
Hanson, L. R., 91
Hare, A. P., 260
Harris, H., 19
Harrison, R., 525
Harrison, S., 193
Hart, Johnny, 145
Hartman, K., 261
Hatfield, J. D., 193
Havens, A. E., 458
Hawken, Paul, 333
Hazleton, V., 58
Habden, J. E., 261
Heider, F., 91
Helm, Leslie, 372, 557
Heneman, R. L., 419
Hepburn, C., 91
Herman, C. P., 133
Herold, D. M., 261
Hersey, Paul, 400, 419
Herzberg, Frederick, 19, 148, 152,
    160, 162, 471, 472, 491, 558
Hickson, D. J., 371
Higgins, E. T., 133
Hill, S., 298
Hills, Carla, 505
Himle, D., 559
Hinings, C., 371
Hinton, B., 372
Hitler, Adolph, 386
Hodgetts, Richard M., 604
Hoerr, John, 226, 298
Hofstede, G., 41, 57, 393
Holley, C. H., 558
Hollman, Kenneth W., 505
Hollmann, R. W., 525
Holtback, Roger, 481
Homans, G. C., 193
Hopkins, B. L., 133
Hopper, Robert, 317
Horan, Kathleen, 487
Horn, J. C., 298
Horowitz, J. M., 541
House, R. J., 371, 419, 472
Howard, G. S., 193
Howell, P., 419
Howell, R. D., 558
Hubbard, Charles W., 60
Huberman, S., 261
Huey, John, 420
Hugel, Charles E., 412
Hughes, F., 58
Hurst, M. W., 57
Huse, E. F., 491, 525
Huseman, R. C., 193
Hyatt, J., 194
Hymowitz, Carol, 493

Ignatius, A., 183
Imberman, W., 298
Inman, B., 412
Ireland, D., 298
Irish, Richard, 575
Isabella, L. A., 600, 602
Ishikawa, Y., 541
Ivancevich, J. M., 558, 602
Iverson, Kenneth, 122
Ivey, M., 421
Ivory, Karen, 551

Izrael, D. N., 601

Jablin, Frederic M., 332
Jackson, J. H., 459
Jackson, Jesse, 156
Jackson, S. E., 559
Jacobs, R., 91
Jacobson, Allen, 443
Jacobson, M. B., 91
Jago, A., 419
Jamal, M., 57
Janis, I. L., 226
Janson, R., 491
Jayaratne, S., 559
Jenkins, D., 601
Jenkins, G. D., Jr., 193, 491, 602
Jennings, Kenneth R., 222, 226,
    559
Jensen, M. A. C., 261
Jerkovsky, W., 459
Jenson, T. D., 57
Jermier, J. M., 414, 419
Jewell, L. N., 261
Jex, S. M., 557
Joan of Arc, 386
Jobs, Steve, 37, 157, 158
Johnson, F. Ross, 411, 412
Johnson, H. E., 58
Johnson, Lyndon, 579
Jones, E., 91
Jones, G. R., 261
Jones, M. R., 162
Jones, N. W., 419
Jordan, Michael, 350
Joure, S. A., 558
Joyce, W. F., 459
Juran, Joseph M., 283

Kagan, J., 58
Kahle, L., 57
Kahn, R. L., 332, 371, 418
Kahneman, Daniel, 225
Kamm, J. B., 558
Kanfer, F. H., 133
Kanouse, D. E., 91
Kanter, Rosabeth M., 19, 346, 371
Kanungo, R. N., 371, 419
Kaplan, J., 158
Kaplan, R. R., 162
Kapstein, Jonathan, 481
Karlberg, Leif, 481
Kasper, J. D., 558
Kast, F. E., 20
Katz, D., 332, 371, 418
Katz, M., 526
Kaye, B., 601
Kazanjian, R. K., 459
Kelleher, Herb, 413
Kelley, H. H., 91
Kelley, R. E., 419
Kellogg, Calvin, 372, 419
Kelly, J., 371
Kennedy, John F., 216, 324
Kerbs, Ken, 57
Kerr, S., 261, 414, 418, 419, 472
Kiechel, W., III, 419
Kim, J. S., 193
Kimmel, Ellen, 91
Kindel, Stephen, 481
King, Martin Luther, Jr., 410
Kirkham, K. L., 601
Kirkpatrick, David, 226
Klein, E. B., 600
Kluckhohn, Clyde K., 57
Knapp, M. L., 332
Knouse, D. E., 91
Koch, S., 57

Kochetkov, Gennady B., 291
Kohn, M. L., 58
Kolb, D. A., 162
Kolodny, H. F., 261, 459
Korn, Lester B., 13
Kotter, J. P., 600
Kovach, J. L., 39, 57
Kozlowski, S. W. J., 91
Kram, D. E., 602
Kreitner, R., 133, 194
Kuchta, W. J., 601
Kuhnert, K. W., 418
Kulik, C. T., 193
Kunda, Z., 133
Kunze, K. R., 601

Labich, K., 419, 421
Laday, Kerney, 239
Laderman, J. M., 458
Lamm, H., 226
LaMothe, William E., 393
Land, Edwin, 410
Laser, S. A., 601
Latack, J. C., 602
Latham, D. R., 298
Latham, G. P., 193
Lawler, Edward E., III, 192, 261,
    298, 491
Lawler, G. E., 298
Lawrence, Paul R., 438, 458, 459,
    525
Leach, R., 162
Leana, C. R., 602
Lee, C., 371
Lengel, Robert H., 312, 332
Lengnick-Hall, Mark L., 222, 226
Leon, J. S., 558
Leuke, Joseph, 442
Level, Dale A., 337
Levine, C., 601
Levine, D., 91
Levine, J., 559
Levinson, Daniel J., 49, 50, 58,
    600
Levinson, M. H., 600
Levinson, R. E., 458
Levy, R. B., 261
Lewicki, Roy J., 372
Lewin, Kurt, 57, 418, 504, 506,
    510, 523, 525
Lewis, D. V., 58
Lewis, Laurie L., 91
Lewis, P., 418
Lichtenstein, Sarah C., 225
Lindzey, Gardner, 91, 193
Lippitt, R., 418
Litterer, Joseph A., 372
Liu, M., 459
Livingston, J. A., 14
Locke, Edwin A., 57, 193, 226
Locksley, A., 91
London, M., 601
Lord, R. G., 418
Lorenzo, Frank, 151, 391
Lorsch, Jay W., 438, 458, 525
Louis, M. R., 261
Lovejoy, Lorie, 177
Lovejoy, Matthew, 177
Lovrich, N., 153
Luke, Robert H., 575
Lustgarten, N., 193
Luthans, F., 133, 194

Maccoby, N., 418
MacDonald, D., 333
Madison, D. L., 371
Magnet, Myron, 57

Magowan, Peter, 547
Mahoney, G. M., 419
Mahoney, M. J., 133
Mahoney, Richard, 391
Maier, N. R. F., 298
Malik, S. D., 261
Mandel, M., 193
Mans, Gary T., 490
Manz, C. C., 133
Manzini, Andrew O., 518
March, J., 333, 525
Marino, K. E., 58
Markham, Scott, 337
Markham, W. T., 192
Marks, M. L., 298, 558
Marr, J. N., 133
Marshall, J., 558
Martin, J. E., 193
Martin, R., 558
Marx, R. D., 133
Maslow, Abraham, 148, 149, 150,
   151, 158, 159, 162
Matherly, T. A., 225
Matsuki, Yasuo, 541
Matteson, M. T., 558
Matthews, K. A., 557
Matthews, Peter, 588
Matthews, Suzann, 588
Mausner, B., 491
Mayes, B., 371
Mazzuca, L., 57
McArthur, C. C., 600
McClelland, David C., 155, 162
McClenahen, J. S., 459, 558
McDowell, J., 58, 59
McGrath, J. E., 258, 261
McGregor, Douglas M., 5, 19, 558
McIlroy, J. C., 419
McKee, B., 600
McKee, J. P., 91
McKee, K., 601
McLaughlin, Mark, 490
McLean, A. A., 557
McNamara, Robert S., 579
McNanny, K. A., 133
McNeil, A., 419
McRae, R. R., 58
Means, B. L., 133
Meeks, Wayne T., 526
Meese, J. L., 91
Mehrabian, A., 332
Mehren, Elizabeth, 583
Melcher, Richard A., 505
Meskal, Brian, 492
Meyers, D. G., 226
Miles, E. W., 193
Miles, Gregory L., 505
Miles, R. E., 20
Milken, Michael, 30, 32
Miller, A., 557
Miller, J. G., 333
Miller, Katherine I., 226
Miller, L. E., 192
Miller, L. W., 133
Mills, T. M., 261
Miner, F. C., Jr., 298
Miner, I. A., 559
Miner, J. B., 193, 491
Mintzberg, Henry, 203, 225, 332,
   371, 458
Mischel, Walter, 57
Mishne, Patricia P., 226
Mitchell, Kent, 561
Mitchell, R. T., 91
Mitchell, Russell, 226
Mitchell, T. R., 58, 416, 419
Mitchell, T. E., 161

Mitchell, V. F., 57
Modic, Stanley J., 558
Moffett, R. G., 558
Mohrman, S. A., 298
Molenda, Robert, 443
Monet, Maria, 577–578, 591–592
Monge, Peter R., 226
Monsner, B., 162
Moon, Steven G., 134
Moore, T., 39
Morgan, C. P., 459
Morgan, David, 220
Morgan, J. P., 30
Morgan, James, 32, 411
Morgan, M. A., 601
Morgan, S., 601
Morita, Akio, 332
Morris, B., 412
Morrison, A. M., 601
Morriss, Curtis, 223
Morse, N. C., 418
Moss, H. A., 58
Mouton, Jane S., 391, 418, 525
Mowday, R., 91
Muchinsky, P., 57
Muczyk, J. P., 525
Mulloy, Lawrence, 216
Munzenrider, R. F., 558
Murchison, C., 57
Murry, Henry A., 57
Myers, John B., 491

Nadler, D. A., 525
Nadler, D. R., 525
Nakamura, Noriko, 585
Namiki, C. L., 226
Namiki, N., 601
Nanus, B., 371
Napier, R. W., 261
Nathanson, D. A., 458
Near, J. P., 600
Neff, Robert, 91
Nelson, D. L., 558
Nelton, S., 549
Neugarten, B. L., 58
Neuliep, J. W., 58
Newman, J. E., 557
Newman, Ruth G., 333
Nicholas, J. M., 526
Nichols, Don, 490
Nichols, Ralph G., 332
Niehouse, O., 558
Nielsen, Richard P., 20
Niland, Powell, 20
Nimmo, D., 57
Nisbett, R. E., 91
Noe, R. A., 602
Noroian, C. L., 601
Noujaim, K., 162
Nulty, P., 418, 421
Numerof, R. E., 558
Nykodym, N., 558, 559

O'Boyle, Thomas F., 333
O'Connor, Thom, 525
Oldham, G. R., 193, 475, 479,
   491
Olmstead, M., 261
O'Lone, Richard, 372
Olsen, Roger, 182
O'Reilly, Brian, 57, 544
O'Reilly, C. A., 333
Organ, D. W., 57
Ortenberg, Elizabeth C., 583
Osborn, Alex F., 278, 298
O'Sullivan, T., 558
Ouchi, William, 20, 601

Pacanowsky, M., 371
Palmore, E., 57
Park, C., 153
Parker, D. F., 558
Parson, J. E., 91
Parsons, T., 57
Pascale, Richard T., 20
Pasztor, A., 294
Patrick, C., 225
Patterson, D., 556, 559
Patton, George S., 391
Pavlov, Ivan P., 105, 133
Payne, S. K., 58
Pazy, A., 600
Peake, Philip K., 57
Peck, R., 58
Pennings, J., 371
Penrar, K., 193
Perot, Ross, 48, 391
Perrow, C., 19
Peter, Laurence, 596
Peters, Thomas J., 19, 108, 133,
   226, 459
Peterson, M. M., 193
Pfeffer, J., 20, 418
Pfeiffer, John, 367
Pinchot, G., III, 442, 458
Pines, A., 558
Polsky, W. L., 602
Porras, J. I., 526
Porter, Lyman W., 57, 333, 371,
   525
Portwood, J. D., 601
Posner, B. G., 193
Power, D. J., 225
Presser, Harriet B., 524
Prince, G. M., 298
Prince, J. B., 601
Prising, Jan, 13
Proctor, Eric, 540
Proehl, C. W., 526
Purcy, K., 491
Putman, Linda L., 332

Quick, J. C., 558

Ramsey, V. J., 601
Rapoport, Rhona, 601
Rapoport, Robert, 601
Raven, B. H., 371
Rawlings, S., 601
Reber, R. A., 120, 133
Rechnitzer, P. A., 559
Redding, W. Charles, 327, 332
Redmon, W. K., 193
Reed, John, 391
Reich, Michael, 492, 525
Reich, R. B., 19
Reichers, A. E., 261
Reimann, B. C., 525
Reimer, E., 418
Reinke, B. J., 58
Reitz, H. J., 57, 261, 372
Renwick, P. A., 371
Riceman, John P., 594, 601
Richter, J., 558
Rinol, Russ, 588
Ritchie, J. Bonner, 81
Rizzo, A., 162
Roberts, Karlene H., 332–333, 491
Roddick, Anita, 45, 251, 252
Rodeheaver, D., 58
Rodgers, Celeste K., 575
Rodgers, Thurman, 37
Roethlisberger, F. J., 260
Rogers, C. R., 57, 332
Rogers, D. P., 558

Rogers, E. M., 332
Rogers, Michael, 57
Rokeach, Milton, 40, 57, 69,
   261
Rollinson, H., 193
Rose, R., 57
Rosen, Corey, 226
Rosenberg, S. D., 58
Rosenfeld, Anne, 58
Rosenman, R. H., 557
Rosenzweig, J. E., 20
Ross, J., 225
Ross, M., 133
Rothfeder, Jeffrey, 490
Rotter, J. B., 58
Rubin, J. Z., 372
Rubin, Z., 58
Russell, J., 57
Ryan, R. M., 133

Saegert, Jerry, 333
Saporito, B., 412
Sarnoff, I., 58
Sashkin, M., 419
Savery, L. K., 558
Saxe, John G., 75
Schaef, S. W., 557
Schaubroeck, J., 559
Schein, E. H., 298, 601
Schein, E., 525
Schiller, Zachary, 525
Schine, Eric, 57
Schmidt, Mike, 14
Schneck, R., 371
Schon, D. A., 20
Schooler, C., 58
Schott, Marge, 584
Schroeder, Horst, 392, 393
Schumacher, E. F., 600
Schutz, W. C., 261
Schwartz, F. N., 601
Schwartz, S. H., 133
Schwartz, T., 59
Schweiger, D. M., 226
Scib, G. G., 421
Scott, W. E., Jr., 57
Sculley, John, 57, 158
Seaboldt, Kay, 547
Seaboldt, Ron, 547
Sedgwick, John, 57, 419
Seelye, H. N., 298
Seltzer, J., 558
Selye, Hans, 558
Sethi, S. P., 226, 601
Shalley, C. E., 193
Shao, Maria, 372
Shaw, J. B., 558
Sheatsley, P. B., 333
Sheehy, G., 601
Sheeran, L. R., 58
Shefif, M., 372
Shephard, C. R., 260
Sheridan, J. H., 459, 597
Sherizen, Sanford, 490
Sherriffs, A. C., 91
Shlepentokh, Vladimir, 291
Shopler, J. H., 293, 298
Shumacher, E. F., 573
Sills, E. A., 57
Silver, Susan, 551
Silverman, S. B., 58
Simmons, John, 58
Simon, Herbert, 91, 208, 225
Simonetti, J. L., 558
Simpson, D. B., 558
Sims, Henry P., 133, 298
Sinai, L., 57

Singh, Raghav, 59, 420, 421, 459, 492
Sink, D., 526
Skinner, B. F., 133
Skulley, John, 35, 36, 37, 55
Sloan, Alfred, P., 410
Sloan, R. P., 559
Slocum, J. W., Jr., 601
Slovic, Paul, 225
Smeltzer, L. R., 558
Smith, Adam, 3, 19, 161, 469
Smith, Alan, 144
Smith, B., 419
Smith, E. T., 226
Smith, K. K., 162
Smith, Roger, 55, 58
Snyder, M., 133
Snyderman, B., 162
Soden, D.L., 153
Soelberg, P. O., 225
Solo, S., 585
Solomon, Charlene M., 226
Solomons, Helen, 36, 57
Somers, M. J., 261
Spackey, J., 459, 597
Spector, P. E., 557
Srivastva, S., 371
St. Mark, Carole, 583–584
Stack, John P., "Jack," 177, 398
Stark, Elizabeth, 58
Staw, B. W., 491
Staw, B., 91, 226, 312, 332
Staw, Barry M., 225, 371
Stayer, Ralph, 355
Steers, R. M., 57, 525
Stepina, L. P., 193
Stevenson, J. G., 558
Stewart, Thomas A., 371
Stogdill, R. M., 386, 418
Stokes, J. P., 261
Stryker, P., 418
Stumpf, Stephen A., 261, 575, 601
Summers, E., 559
Susman, E. J., 58

Suttle, J. L., 298, 474, 478, 491
Sutton, R. I., 261
Swanson, C. L., 226, 601
Swasy, Alecia, 458, 493
Sween, J. A., 298
Syderman, B., 491
Sze, W. C., 58, 601

Tagiuri, R., 91
Tannenbaum, A. S., 371
Tannenbaum, J. H., 601
Taplin, P. T., 193
Taylor, A. T., III, 601
Taylor, Alex, 226
Taylor, Frederick W., 4–5, 19, 469, 470, 488, 491
Taylor, G., 39
Taylor, R., 58
Tedeschi, J. T., 371
Thelen, H. A., 332
Thomas, Kenneth, 361, 371
Thompson, K., 133
Thompson, P. H., 601
Thorensen, C. E., 133
Thorndike, E. L., 133
Tichy, N. M., 298, 419
Tinsley, Dillard B., 525
Todd, John T., 618
Tonfexis, A., 601
Tossi, H. L., 162
Treece, James B., 226
Tregginger, D. J., 225
Triandis, H. C., 57
Trump, Donald J., 48, 59
Tsui, Fannie, 81
Tuckman, Bruce W., 246, 261
Tully, Shawn, 13
Turriff, Lowell, 37
Tversky, Amos, 225

Ulrich, D. O., 419
Umstot, Denis, D., 207
Unikel, Jeff, 30

Valins, S., 91
Van Andel, Jan, 189
Van de Ven, A. H., 279, 298
Van Volson, E., 601
Vasquez, Patricia, 548
Vecchio, R. P., 419
Vittoria, Joseph V., 221
Vollrath, David A., 222, 226
Von Glinow, M. A., 601
Vroman, H. William, 164, 262, 526, 529, 561, 615
Vroom, V., 192, 419

Waldman, D. A., 419
Wall, T. D., 558
Wall, W. C., Jr., 459
Wallin, J. A., 120, 133
Wallis, C., 601
Walsh, James P., 91
Walton, R. E., 491, 526
Walton, Sam, 48, 319, 320, 410, 411
Wanous, J. P., 261
Warner, W. K., 458
Wartzman, R., 294
Waterman, Robert H., 19
Watson, John B., 105, 133
Weber, Max, 438, 458
Webster, E. C., 91
Weekley, J. A., 558
Weick, K. E., 20
Weimer, George, 505
Weinberg, M. W., 421
Weiner, B., 91
Weinig, Sheldon, 74
Weiss, S., 133
Welch, Jack, 363
Wellbank, H. A., 601
Welles, C., 59
White, Donald D., 22, 57, 59, 60, 95, 133, 134, 136, 162, 164, 226, 262, 298, 299, 375, 393, 419, 420, 421, 459, 492, 526, 529, 557, 559, 602, 615, 624

White, James, 547–548
White, R. P., 418, 601
White, Rene, 313
White, S. E., 58
Whitsett, D. A., 491
Whittaker, Larwood L. W., 91
Whyte, Glen, 226
Wiener, M., 332
Weisman, W., 332
Wilcox, J. B., 558
Wilkinson, Sophie, 226
Williams, A. M., 110
Williams, R. M., 57
Williams, Richard "Rick," 156, 157, 162, 186, 187
Wilmot, W., 371
Wisdom, B., 557
Wisdom, Barry L., 194
Wood, Kimba M., 30
Wood, R., 91
Woods, W., 39
Woodworth, W., 226
Wozniak, Steve, 158
Wright, R. G., 298
Wyer, Robert S., J., 90

Yates, Peter, 226
Yeager, Neil, 575
Yorks, L., 491

Zachary, G. Pascal, 611
Zalkind, S. S., 90
Zaltman, G., 525
Zander, A. F., 162
Zanna, M. P., 133
Zawacki, R. A., 525
Zedeck, S., 559
Zeller, W., 298
Zemke, R., 558
Zetlin, M., 58
Ziegenfuss, J. T., Jr., 559
Zimmerer, T., 39
Zimmerman, M., 256

SUBJECT INDEX

A. E. Staley (Co.), 276
Achievement, need for (n ach), 155–157, 161
Acquired immune deficiency syndrome (AIDS), 223
Actor-observer effect, 87
Adjourning, 246, 247–248
Adjustment, 210
Administrative era, of managerial philosophy, 5–6
Administrative decision-making model, 208–211
Adult development:
  Erikson's theory of, 49
  Levinson's theory of, 49–54
  permanency of, 55
  of women, 54–55
Advertising, ethics in, 84
Affective component, of attitudes, 42
Affiliation, need for (n aff), 155, 157, 161
AFL-CIO, 352
Agenda-setting interviews, 518
Alagasco, 154
Alcoa, 479
All Nippon Airways, 541
Allstate Insurance Co., 321
American Airlines, 182
American Express Foundation, 524
Amway Corp., ethics of, 189
Anchor, 210
Andersen Corp., 176
Andy Frain Services, 53
Apple Computer, 35, 36, 37, 39, 55, 157, 158, 245, 485
Applied learning theory, 118–131
Applied Materials, Inc., 32, 411
Arbitrator, 369
Art of Japanese Management, The (Pascale and Athos), 10
Association of Retired Executives (ARE), 579
AT&T, 39, 244, 471, 488, 524, 544, 547, 556, 589
Attitudes:
  beliefs and, 45
  defined, 42
  job satisfaction and, 42–44
Attribution:
  influences on leadership, 415–416
  theory of behavior, 84–86
Audi, 504
Audit:
  communication, 329, 330
  organizational stress, 553
  personal stress, 550
Authoritarianism, 47
Authority, 347
  hierarchy of, 439
Authority network, 322–323
Availability heuristic, 209
Avis, employee ownership at, 221
AZT, 223–224

Bank of America, 186
Baseline, 121
Bay of Pigs, 216
BDM Corp., 589, 593, 599
Behavior. See also Organizational behavior (OB)
  attitudes and, 42–44, 45
  attribution theory of, 84–86
  authoritarianism and, 47

beliefs and, 44–45
cognitive complexity and, 47
conflict, 362
impact of centralization/decentralization on, 441–442
locus of control and, 46
modeling and shaping of, 127–129
modification of, 112–118
personality and, 34–35, 36, 37, 47–48
reinforcement and, 187–188
risk-taking propensity and, 47
type A versus type B personality and, 539–540
values and, 39–42
Behavioral intention, of attitudes, 42
Behavioral leadership theories, 388–392
Behavioral self-management, 129–131
Beliefs, 44–45
Believe (DeVos and Van Andel), 189
BellSouth Corp., 392
Ben & Jerry's Homemade, Inc., 154
Benevolents, 181
Berlitz, 313
Bethlehem Steel Co., 470
Beverly Enterprises, 280
Bias:
  false consensus, 89
  negative, 89
  self-serving, 88
Biofeedback, 551–552
Black & Decker, creativity at, 214
Body Shop International, The, 45, 251–252
Boeing, 294, 365
Boise Cascade, variable pay incentives at, 123
Bounded rationality, 208–209
Brainstorming, 278
Brazil, negotiating in, 367
Bridge, 325, 326
Brooks Co., 14
"Buddhist economics," 573
"Buddy system," 251
Bureau of Standards, U.S., 314
Bureaucracy, 438–440
Burnout, 548–549, 550
Burroughs Wellcome Co., 223–224
Business Careers (Luke), 575
Business Week, 581

CAMECO, Inc., 119, 120
Campbell Soup Co., 110, 508–509
Canada, 12, 155, 283, 285, 290, 469, 584, 591
Canon, 2
Career, 572–573
  multiple ladders for, 593
  stages of, 576
Career anchor, 580–581
Career development, 546
  defined, 573
  dual-career couples and, 584–588
  management of, 572–581
  organizational approaches to, 589–598
  targeting, 593–597
  women and, 581–584
Career Map (Yeager), 575
Career path(s):
  circular, 590–591
  clusters of, 595
  organizational, 592–598
  specialized, 589–590

Career plateaus, 578
Careers, 581
Caterpillar, 292
  team-based management in, 155
Centrality, 354–355
Centralization, 441–443
Change:
  acquisition and, 250
  force field analysis and, 504–509
  organizational, 512–523
  planned, 503–504
  reasons for, 504
  resistance to, 509–512
  unplanned, 503
Change agent, 513–514
Channel, communication, 309, 311
Charisma, 409–410
Charlotte Observer, 39
Chase Manhattan Bank, 119
Cheaper By the Dozen (Gilbreth), 470
Chesapeake Corp., 355
Chevron, 311
China, People's Republic of, 221, 312, 313
  conducting business in, 81
  factory towns in, 183
Choosing a Career in Business (Stumpf and Rodgers), 575
Chrysler Corp., 2, 177, 217, 290, 504
  representative participation at, 221
Cincinnati Reds, 584
Citibank, 453
Citicorp, 12, 391
Clark Equipment Corp., 292
Classical learning theory, 105–106, 107, 109–110
Client relationships, 476
Clique, The, 294
Closed systems, 18
Closure, 76–77
Coaching, 518
Coalescing, 351
Coca-Cola Co., 505
Coercive power, 349
Cognitive complexity, 47
Cognitive component, of attitudes, 42
Cohesiveness, group, 257
Colgate (Co.), 355
Colt Industries, 598
Combining tasks, 476
Commitment-based management, 9
Committee management, 276
Common enemy, 368
Communication:
  barriers to, 311–316
  defined, 308
  elements of, 308–310
  facilitating, 316–321
  media of, 311
  networks for, 321–326
  organizational, 321–329
  verbal and nonverbal, 310–311
Communication audit, 329, 330
Compass Computer, 39
Competition, intergroup, 293–296
Conciliator, 369
Conflict:
  consequences of, 363–364
  defined, 359

651

Conflict (*Continued*)
  management of, 364–370
  as process, 359–363
Consequence management, 130
Consideration, 389
Constructive conflict, 363
Consultative participation (CP), 220, 222
Content theories of motivation, 147–158, 191
  application of, 158–159
Context, 538–539
Contingency factors, 397
Contingency leadership theory, 392–396, 405, 408
Continuous reinforcement, 117
Control-oriented management, 8
Co-opting, 352
Corning Glass Works, 476
Counseling, 518
  direction, 597
"Cradle to grave" system, 183
Creativity, steps involved in, 213–214
Cross-training, 486–487
CTI (Co.), 555
Cullinet Software, 556
Cypress Semiconductor Corp., 37

Daimler-Benz AG, 177
Dare to Dream, 156–157, 186–187
Data feedback, 518
Day care, 524
Dayton-Hudson, 476
Decision making:
  barriers to, 211–214
  defined, 203
  group, 214–217, 276–283
  individual, 214–217
  managers and, 203–207
  models of, 207–211
  participation in, 217–224
  problem solving versus, 206
Decode, 309
Delegation, 218
Delphi technique, 281–283
Delta Airlines, 490
Department of Energy, U.S., 433
Department of Labor, U.S., 487
Department of the Treasury, U.S., 354
Departmentalization, 434
Desire for group success (dgs), 156
Detroit Edison Co., 471
Differentiation, 436
Digital Equipment Co. (DEC), 485, 487, 505
  team-based management at, 155
Disengagement, 579
Dispositional attribution, 85
Distortion, 326–327, 328–329
Distributive negotiation, 366
Division of labor, 3, 434, 435, 439
Dow Corning, creativity at, 214
Downsizing, ethics of, 597
Downward communication, 323
Drexel Burnham Lambert, 30
Drexel Firestone, 30
Driving forces, 504, 506
Du Pont Co., 277, 446, 490
Dual-career couples, 584–588

E. F. Hutton, 356–357
Eastern Airlines, 151
Eastman Kodak, 2–3, 245, 507
Ebasco Services, Inc., 518
Educational Testing Service, 576
Edwards personal preference schedule, 575
Effectiveness, group, 252–259
Effort, 172–173, 175, 176
Electrolux, 13
Emory Air Freight, 119

Employee:
  assistance program (EAP), 555
  input-outcome ratio of, 178–180
  ownership (EO), 221, 222
  stock ownership plans (ESOPs), 221, 398
Empowerment, 355, 357–359
Encode, 308
Encounter, 250
Entitleds, 181
Entrepreneur, 442
Epic Healthcare, 221
Epson, 541
Equifinality, 18
Equity sensitives, 181
Equity sensitivity, 180–181
Equity motivation theory (ET), 178–183
ERG theory, 148, 150–152, 158, 161, 191
Espoused theory, 7
Esprit de Corps (Co.), 320
Establishment, 578
Ethics:
  of accounts payable practices, 331
  in advertising, 84
  of conflicting objectives, 433
  of day care provision, 524
  of downsizing and restructuring, 597
  of drug pricing practices, 223–224
  of group performance, 239
  of internal versus external policies, 189
  of interorganizational groups, 294
  of job and family conflicts, 544
  of leveraged buyouts, 412
  organizational behavior and, 12–13
  of personality tests, 39
  power and, 158, 356–357
  of reinforcement, 122
  of sports endorsements, 14
  of workplace privacy, 490
European Economic Community, 282, 505
Executive search firms, 13
Expectancy, 173
Expectancy motivation theory, 172–178, 182–183
Expert power, 349–350
Exploration, 576
Extinction, 113–114
Extrinsic motivation, 145, 146
Exxon Corp., 347, 589, 599
  use of personality tests by, 39

Facilitator, 284
Factory towns, in China, 183
False consensus bias, 89
Famous Amos Cookie Shop, 156
Fast track, 593–594
Federal Aviation Administration, 402
Feedback, 18, 185, 309, 319–321, 476–477
  data, 518
  receptiveness to, 319
  responsiveness to, 319
  survey, 516–517
Figure/ground relationships, 76
Firestone Tire and Rubber Co., 2, 119, 186, 441, 442
Fisher Price Toys, 176, 281
"5-15 report," 320
Fixed interval counts, 121
Fixed schedule, 118
Follower readiness, 400–401
Food and Drug Administration, 223
Forbes, 581
Force field analysis, 504–509
Ford Motor Co., 2, 358, 402, 434, 504, 507, 579
  employee involvement (EI) program of, 217–218
Formal communication network, 323–324
Forming, 246

Fortune Magazine, 2, 356, 581
France, 505
Frequency counts, 121
Friendship network, 323
Frustration-regression phenomenon, 150–151
Fuji, 2
Fujitsu, 585
Functional organizational structure, 447

Gatekeeper, 325, 326
General Accounting Office, 405
General adaptation syndrome, 540–543
General Alum & Chemical Corp., 53
General Electric Co., 39, 119, 327, 363, 392, 446, 452, 490, 583
  creativity at, 214
General Foods, 479, 520, 583
  work design at, 480
General Motors Corp., 2, 55, 144, 177, 290, 405, 410, 479, 488, 504, 505
  joint venture with Toyota by, 10–11, 124, 125, 520
  positive leadership program of, 118
  variable pay incentives at, 123
Georgia-Pacific Corp., 597
Giant Foods, 182
Gillette Co., 280
Glasnost, 291
Go Hire Yourself an Employer (Irish), 575
Goal, superordinate, 368
Goal displacement, 432–433
Goal-setting motivation theory, 183–187, 191
Gold Star, 153
Grady Memorial Hospital, 223
Grapevine, 324
Great Britain, 505
Great man leadership theory, 386, 387–388
Grid, managerial, 390–391, 399, 518
Grid organizational development, 518–519
Group(s):
  competition among, 293–296
  decision making in, 214–217, 276–283
  defined, 240–243
  effectiveness of, 252–259
  ethics involved with, 239
  expanding role of, 283–293
  interacting, 277
  interorganizational, 291–293, 294
  in Japan, 256
  nominal technique for, 278–280
  quality, 283–289
  self-management work, 289–291, 486
  socialization into, 249–252
  stages of development for, 245–249
  types of, 243–245
Group norms, 254–256
Group polarization, 216
Groupthink, 215–216
Growth, 578
Growth-need strength (GNS), 475, 479
Guanxi, 81
Gulf Corp., 311
Gulf Refining & Marketing, 350

Hai, 312
Halo effect, 80, 82
Harley-Davidson, 240
Harvard Speed Alphas, 575
Harwood Manufacturing, 242, 255
Hawthorne Electrical Plant, 6, 238
Hawthorne Studies, 6, 43, 238
"Headhunters." *See* Executive search firms
Heinz USA, 355, 357–358
Hertz, 405
Heuristics, 209
Hewlett-Packard, creativity at, 214
Hitachi, 256

Holly Farms, 547
Honda, 434, 485
Honeywell, 486
Horizontal communication, 324
House Committee on Science, Space, and
    Technology, 216
*How to Create a Picture of Your Ideal Job or Next
    Career* (Bolles), 575
Hughes Aircraft, 182
Human relations, managerial philosophy and, 5,
    6–7
Human resources, importance of, 2
Humana Heart Institute International, 438
Hyatt Hotel International, 476
Hygiene factors, 152, 472
Hyundai, 153

IBM, 245, 442, 443, 471, 488, 505, 507,
    511–512
    industrial espionage against, 256
    value system of, 41
IBM Japan, 585
Implicit favorite, 212
Implicit personality theory, 82
In Search of Excellence (Peters and Waterman), 2,
    108
Inc., 581
Individuality, 31, *See also* Personality
    attitudes and, 42–44
    beliefs and, 44–45
    group effectiveness and, 253
    managerial decisions and, 55–56
    mental ability and, 38
    physical ability and, 38
    values and, 39–42
Individualized consideration, 410
Industrial Revolution, managerial philosophy
    and, 3–4
Industry Week, 189
Inertia, 509
Influence, 347
Informal communication network, 324–325
Informal groups, 245
Informal participation (IP), 220, 222
Information network, 323
Information power, 350
Initiating structure, 389
Input-outcome ratio, 178–180
Inputs, organizational, 17
Institute for Research on Intercultural
    Cooperation, 41
Instrumental value, 41
Instrumentality, 173
Integration, 437
Integrative negotiation, 368
Intel (Co.), 485
Intellectual stimulation, 410
Interacting groups, 277
Intergroup competition, 293–296
Intermittent reinforcement, 118
International Brotherhood of Teamsters, 352
Internationalization of business:
    cross-cultural communication and, 312–313
    cultural differences and, 35, 81, 393
    cultural similarities and, 153
    European Community and, 505
    joint ventures and, 10–11, 124, 125, 520
    managers for, 13
    matrix organization and, 455
    negotiation techniques and, 366–367
    organizational behavior and, 11–12
Interorganizational groups, 291–293, 294
Interval schedule, 116
Intervention strategy, 514–515
Intrapreneur, 442
Intrinsic motivation, 145, 146
Inverted U curve, 542–543

Iowa leadership studies, 388, 391
Iskra (Co.), 291
Isolate, 325–326
Israel, 179
    goal-setting practices in, 185
IT&T, 452
Italy, 505
Ivo Lola (Co.), 291

J. C. Penney, 221, 349, 441
Japan, 9, 34, 155
    career paths in, 590–591, 594–595
    cultural differences between U.S. and, 35
    decision-making process in, 217
    investment opportunities in, 74
    management style of, 10–11
    negotiating in, 367
    perceptions of U.S. in, 87–88
    quality circles in, 283
    role of groups in, 256
    telephone conversations in, 312–313
    women in, 584
    work-related stress in, 541
Japan Association for Female Executives, 585
Japanese Union of Scientists and Engineers
    (JUSE), 283
Job characteristics work design model (JCM),
    473–479
Job Diagnostic Survey (JDS), 475, 477
Job enlargement, 470–471
Job enrichment, 471–473, 517
Job evaluation, skill-based, 487
Job performance, job satisfaction and, 42–43
Job rotation, 471
Job satisfaction, 42–44
    motivation and, 176–178
Johnson & Johnson, 442, 556
    creativity at, 214
Johnsonville Foods, 355, 357

Kaiser Permanente Medical Care Program, 182
Kanban inventory control system, 473
Kawasaki Steel, 541
Kellogg Co., 392, 393, 505
Kemper Corp., 441
Kimberly-Clark, 281
Kodak. *See* Eastman Kodak
Kohlberg Kravis Roberts, 412
Komatsu (Co.), 292
Konica, 2
Korea, Republic of, 9, 34, 241–242
    negotiating in, 367
    motivation in, 153
Kraft General Foods, 583

Labor. *See also* Employee
    division of, 3, 434, 435, 439
    unions. *See* Unions
Language:
    cross-cultural communication and, 312, 313,
        314, 315
    meaning and, 314
Law of effect, Thorndike's, 110, 111–112
Leader, emergent, 253
Leadership:
    attribution influences on, 415–416
    behavioral theories of, 388–392
    contingency theory of, 392–396, 405, 408
    great man theory of, 386, 387–388
    group effectiveness and, 253–254
    path-goal theory of, 396–398, 405, 408
    situational theories of (general), 392–407
    situational theory of (SLT), 398–402, 405,
        408
    styles of, 389, 390–391, 393, 394–397,
        399–400, 402–405, 408
    substitutes for, 414–415

trait theories of, 386–388
transactional, 407, 409
transformational, 407–413
Learning:
    applied, 118–131
    conditions for, 110–111
    defined, 105
    principles of, 110–112
    programmed, 118
    theories of, 104–110
Least preferred co-worker scale (LPC), 393, 394,
    396
Lechmere, Inc., 476, 487
Legitimate power, 349
Lehman Brothers, 578
Leveraged buyouts (LBOs), 547
    ethics of, 412
Levinson's theory of adult development, 49–55
Liaison, 325, 326
Liberty Mutual Insurance, 453
Life structure, 50–51
Life system, 573–575
Lincoln Electric, 176
Lincoln National Life, 488
Line and staff organization, 445–446
List of values (LOV), 40, 42
Listening, skill of, 316–318
Liz Claiborne, 583
Lockheed Aircraft, 56, 283, 579
Lockheed Missiles and Space Co., 283
Locus of control, 46
Los Angeles Times, 583
Lotus (Co.), 281
Lotus and the Pool, The (Dail), 575
Louis Harris and Associates, 87
Lovejoy Medical, Ltd., 177
LTV Steel Co., 290

Maintenance, 578
Malaysia, 313
Management:
    commitment-based, 9
    control-oriented, 8
    espoused theory of, 7
    scientific, 469–470
    span of, 443–445
    theory-in-use of, 7
Management by objectives (MBO), 186, 515–516
Management Recruiters, Inc., 490
Manager:
    decision making by, 203–207
    internationalization of business and, 13
    project, 448–449
    role of, 4
Managerial grid, 390–391, 399, 518
Managerial philosophy:
    current, 8–12
    history of, 3–8
Maslow's hierarchy of needs, 148–150, 158, 161,
    191
Materials Research Corp., 74
Matrix organization, 451–454, 455
Maximize, 207
Maytag, 471
McCormack and Dodge, 589
McDonald's Corp., 53, 156
McDonnell Aircraft Co., 288
Meaning transfer assumption, 309
Mediator, 369
Mental ability, 38
Mentor(ing), 598
Mercedes-Benz, 504
Merck (Co.), creativity at, 214
Mexico, 12, 367
Michigan leadership studies, 388–389, 390
Microsoft, 410
Miller Analogies, 575

Milliken (Co.), 363–364
Milwaukee Urban League, 156
Mitsubishi Electric, 256
Mobil Oil Co., 446
Modeling behavior, 127–128, 251
Mokusatsu, 314
"Mommy track," 595
Monsanto, 391
Morale, job satisfaction versus, 42
Morton-Thiokol, 216
Moshi moshi, 312
Motivating potential score (MPS), 475
Motivation:
 content theories of, 147–159
 defined, 144–145
 extrinsic, 145, 146
 goal-setting theory of, 183–187
 intrinsic, 145, 146
 process theories of, 172–183
 reinforcement theory of, 187–190
 vicarious, 145, 146–147
Motivator-hygiene theory. *See* Two factor
  motivation theory
Motivators, 152, 472
Motorola, 2, 487
Myers-Briggs Type Indicator (MBTI), 39

National Aeronautics and Space Administration
  (NASA), 216, 245, 452, 453
National Baseball League, 14
National Council on Compensation Insurance,
  553
National Football League Players Association, 255
National Institutes of Health, 223
Natural work units, 476
Naval Medical Research Institute, 246
Navistar, 177
NCR Corp., 454
NEC, 585
Need theories. *See* Content theories
Needs, Maslow's hierarchy of, 148–150, 158, 161
Negative bias, 89
Negative reinforcement, 112–113, 114
Negotiation, 364–368
Network, communication, 321–326
Network organization, 456–457
Networking, 351
New United Motor Manufacturing, Inc.
  (NUMMI), 10–11, 124, 125, 520
New York Stock Exchange, 223
Nike, Inc., 14
Nikon, 2
Nissan, 485, 504, 585
Noise, 314–315
Nominal group technique (NGT), 278–280
Nonprogrammed decision, 203
Nonverbal communication, 310–311
Nordstrom Department Stores, 8–9
Normative leadership model, 402–407, 408
Norming, 246, 247
Norms, group, 254–256
Northrup Corp., group performance at, 241
NUCOR, variable pay incentives at, 122–123
NUMMI. *See* New United Motor
  Manufacturing, Inc.

Oak Ridge nuclear weapons plant, 432, 433
Objectives, 432
Ogden Corp., 577–578, 591–592
Ohio State leadership studies, 389–390, 391,
  398, 399
Ombudsman, 554
Open systems, 18
Operant learning theory, 105, 106–107, 109–110
Operation Push, 156
Opinion Research Corp., 326
Organic organization, 454, 456

Organization:
 contemporary structure of, 447–457
 formal, 432–438
 responses to stress in, 553–556
 traditional structure of, 438–447
Organizational behavior (OB):
 defined, 2, 14–16
 ethics and, 12–13
 internationalization of business and, 11–12
 multidisciplinary contributions to, 14–15
 sources of information about, 205
 systems theory and, 17–18
 units of analysis in, 14
Organizational behavior modification (OB Mod),
  119–127
Organizational development (OD):
 change and, 512–523
 defined, 512
 effectiveness of, 522–523
 grid, 518–519
Organizational politics, 352–355
Organizational stress audit (OAS), 553
Outputs, organizational, 17
Overload, 328–329, 545

Pacific Gas and Electric, 186
Panzhihua Iron and Steel Co., 183
"Parable of the Blind Men and the Elephant,
  The," 75
Participative decision making, 218
 consultative (CP), 220, 222
 employee ownership (EO), 221, 222
 Ford's Employee Involvement (EI), 217–218, 219
 informal (IP), 220, 222
 representative (RP), 221, 222
 short-term (STP), 220, 222
 in work decisions (PWD), 219–220, 222
Passion for Excellence, A (Peters and Austin), 2
Patagonia Sportswear, Inc., 154, 320
Path-goal leadership theory, 396–398, 405, 408
Paul Revere Insurance Group, 283, 288
Pay for knowledge (PFK) program, 177–178
PepsiCo, 35, 158
Perceived probability, 173–174
Perception:
 activities of, 74–79
 defined, 73
 influences on, 79–83
 selective, 82–83
Perestroika, 291
Performance, 172–173, 175, 176
 goals and, 184–185
 in group development, 246, 247
 planning and evaluation system (PP&E),
  515–516
Personal stress audit (PSA), 550
Personality. *See also* Individuality
 adult development of, 48–55
 behavior and, 34–35, 36, 37, 47–48
 changes in, 48–55
 defined, 31–32
 ethics of tests for, 39
 influences on, 32–34
 psychological characteristics of, 46–47
 theory of implicit, 82
 type A versus type B, 539–540
 using concept of, 35–37
Personnel information systems (PIS), 596
Peter Principle, 595, 596
Philadelphia Phillies, 14
Philips Gloeilampenfabrieken, 453
Physical ability, 38
Pirelli, S. A., 453
Pitney Bowes, Inc., 583
Pittston Coal Co., 360
Playboy, 588
Plum Creek, 220

Polaroid, 221, 328, 410
Politics, organizational, 352–355
Positive reinforcement, 112, 114
Postal Service, U.S., team-based management
  in, 155
Power:
 acquisition of, 351–352
 defined, 347
 determinants of, 348
 distribution of, 355–359
 individual bases of, 348–351
 need for (n pow), 157–158, 161
 organizational politics and, 352–355
Power moment, 352
Premack reward, 188
Previous commitment, 212
Price Waterhouse, 386, 588
Primacy effect, 83
Primary groups, 243–244
Problem solving:
 decision making versus, 206
 dimensions of, 277–278
 process for, 204–207
Process consultation, 518
Process theories of motivation, 172–183, 191
Procter & Gamble, 221, 277, 439, 440, 479,
  488, 520
Product organizational structure, 447–448
Programmed desision, 203
Project groups, 244–245
Projection, 82
Protestant work ethic, managerial philosophy
  and, 4
Proximity, 77
Psychoanalytic theory, 34
Punishment, 113, 114, 188–189

Quality circles, (QC), 220, 256, 283–289
 at Harley-Davidson, 240
Quality of work life (QWL), 482–488

Rating measure, 122
Ratio schedule, 116
Rational-economic decision-making model,
  207–208, 210
Realistic job preview (RJP), 251
Recency effect, 83
Referent power, 350
Refreezing, 507
Reinforcement:
 context of, 114–116
 ethics of, 122
 extinction and, 113–114
 extrinsic versus intrinsic, 115–116
 negative, 112–113, 114
 positive, 112, 114
 punishment and, 113, 114
 scheduling of, 116–118
 theory of, 187–190, 191
Relaxation response (RER), 552
Renewal Factor, The (Waterman), 2
Representative participation (RP), 221, 222
Representativeness heuristic, 209
Resemblance, 77–78
Restraining forces, 504, 506
Restructuring, ethics of, 597
Retirement, 579
Reward, 172–173, 175–176
 premack, 188
Reward power, 348–349
Reward system, innovative, 487–488
Ringisei, 217
Risk-taking propensity, 47
RJR Nabisco, 411, 412
Rockwell, 520
Role, 253
Role ambiguity, 544–545

Role conflict, 543–544
Rolm (Co.), 485
Rubbermaid, creativity at, 214

Safeway Stores, Inc., 547, 554
Sanyo, 551
Sara Lee, 355
Satisfice, 209
Scandinavian Airline Systems (SAS), 219
Scanlon plan, 220
Scientific management, 4–5, 469–470
Scrambler-Stabilizer Scale, 592
Sears, 441
Second shift, 583
Secondary groups, 244
Securities and Exchange Commission, 30
Seiko, 541
Selective perception, 82–83
Self-management:
    behavioral, 129–131
    work groups, 289–291, 486
Self-serving bias, 88
Self theories, 35
Sensation, 73
Sensitivity training, 519–520
7-Eleven Stores, 517
Shaping behavior, 128–129
Shearman & Sterling, 577
Shearson Lehman Brothers, 356
Shearson Lehman Hutton, 412
Shell Oil, 350–351, 479
Shenandoah Life Insurance Co., 482
Sherwin-Williams, 479, 488, 520
Short-term participation (STP), 220, 222
SIGI, 576
Singapore, 313
Situational attribution, 85
Situational leadership theories (general), 392–407
Situational leadership theory (SLT), 398–402,
    405, 408
Skippy (Co.), 290
Slow burn plan, 594–595
Social cognitive learning theory (SCT), 105,
    107–110
Social Darwinism, 4, 386
Social Foundations of Thought: A Social Cognitive
    Theory (Bandura), 105n
Socialization:
    defined, 249
    managing process of, 250–252
    phases of, 249–250
Sociotechnical work design, 479–482, 520
Sony Corp., 74
South Community Hospital, 126
Southland Corp., 517
Southwest Airlines, 413
Soviet Union. See USSR
Span of management, 443–445
Specialization. See Division of labor
Sponsor, 251
Springfield Remanufacturing Corp., 177, 398
St. Regis Paper Co., 583
Stagnation, 578–579
"Star Wars," 294
Status network, 323
Steelcase, Inc., 79, 487
Steering committee, 284
Stereotyping, 79–80
Stimulus management, 129–130
Storming, 246
Strategic contingencies theory, 354–355
Stress:
    consequences of, 540
    elements of, 537–540
    managing, 550–556
    organizational audit for, 553
    personal audit for, 550

physiology of, 540–543
    work-related, 543–550
Stressors, 538
Substitutability, 354–355
Subsystems, 17
Superordinate goal, 368
Suprasystem, 17–18
Survey feedback, 516–517
Sweden, 12
Swissair, 471
Synectics, 280–281
Synergy, 18, 239–240
Syntality, 245
System of Interactive Guidance and Information
    (SIGI), 576
Systems & Computer Technology Corp., 36
Systems theory, organizational behavior and, 17–18

T-groups, 519–520
Taiwan, 9, 12, 34
Target Stores, 490
Task, group, 257–259
Task groups, 244
Task-expertise network, 323
Team building, 517
Tenneco, 515–516
Terminal value, 40–41
Texaco, 221
Texas Air, 151, 391
Texas Instruments, 488
Theory:
    defined, 16
    espoused, 7
Theory-in use, 7
Theory X, 6, 7
Theory Y, 6, 7
Theory Z (Ouchi), 10
Thorndike's law of effect, 110, 111–112
3M Corp., 39, 442–443, 486, 504
    creativity at, 214
Thriving on Chaos (Peters), 2
Thriving on Excellence (Peters), 108
Through the Looking Glass (Carroll), 314
Throughput process, 17
Time and motion studies, 470
Time (magazine), 12
Time-sample counts, 121–122
Timeliness, 328–329
Tomei, Inc., 81
Toyota Motor Corp., joint venture with General
    Motors by, 10–11, 124, 125, 520
Trait theories:
    of leadership, 386–388
    of personality, 34–35
Transactional leader, 407, 409
Transformational leadership, 407–413
Travelers Insurance Co., 477
Trial, 576–577
TRW Systems Group, 453, 485, 486, 520
Tunnel vision, 211
Two factor motivation theory, 148, 152–154,
    161, 191, 471–472
Type A personality, 539–540
Type B personality, 539
Tyson Food, 547

U. S. Steel, 441
U. S. West, 221
Uncertainty, 354–355, 509
Underload, 546
Unfreezing, 506–507
Union Carbide, 485
Unions:
    AFL-CIO, 352
    International Brotherhood of Teamsters, 352
    United Auto Workers, 209, 217, 368
    United Mine Workers, 360

United Auto Workers (UAW), 209, 217, 368
United Methodist Publishing House, 555–556
United Mine Workers, 360
Upward communication, 324
USSR, 13, 291, 365
    representative participation in, 221
    women in, 584
USX, 441

Valence, 173
Value system, 41
Values, 39–42
    list of (LOV), 40, 42
Values survey module (VSM), 41, 42
Valuing, 411
Verbal communication, 310–311
Vertical job loading, 476
Vicarious motivation, 145, 146–147
Vietnam, 242
Visioning, 410–411
Volvo Car Corp., 12, 290, 292, 479, 504
    work design at, 479–480, 481
Vulnerability, 538, 539

W. L. Gore and Associates, 358, 392
Wage(s):
    compression of, 182
    equity of, 178–183
    two-tiered system of, 182
Wal-Mart Stores, Inc., 122, 280, 319, 357, 410,
    411, 441
    positive centered leadership program of, 118,
        119, 122
Wall Street Journal, The, 581
Walt Disney World, 108–109
Washington Post Co., 583
Watergate, 216
WCBS-TV, 551
Wealth of Nations, The (Smith), 3, 469
Wechsler Adult Intelligence Scale, 575
Wellcome PLC, 223
Wellcome Trust, 223
Wellness programs, 555–556
West Germany, 9, 177, 393, 505
    representative participation in, 221
Western Electric, 238
Westinghouse, 2
Westray Capital Corp., 221
What Color Is Your Parachute (Bolles), 575
When Giants Learn to Dance (Kanter), 2
Where Do I Go From Here With My Life? (Crystal
    and Bolles), 575
Williams Partnership, The, 156
Women:
    adult development of, 54–55
    career development of, 581–584
    in Japan, 584
    stereotyping of, 80
Work design:
    contemporary, 471–482
    early, 469–471
    importance of, 468–469
Work force, all-salaried, 487
Work life, quality of. See Quality of work life
Worker, role of, 4
World Bank, 579
World War II, 9
    group performance during, 241
    Japan after, 312
    leadership styles during, 391

Xerox Corp., 288, 402, 488, 507, 509
    group performance at, 239, 241

Yugoslavia, 290, 291

Zeitgeist leadership theory, 386, 387–388